# SECRET AFFAIRS

## OTHER BOOKS BY IRWIN F. GELLMAN

*Roosevelt and Batista: Good Neighbor Diplomacy in Cuba, 1933–1945* (1973)

*Good Neighbor Diplomacy: United States Policies in Latin America, 1933–1945* (1979)

# SECRET AFFAIRS

Franklin Roosevelt, Cordell Hull, and Sumner Welles

## IRWIN F. GELLMAN

The Johns Hopkins University Press
Baltimore and London

This book has been brought to publication with the generous assistance of the
Chester Kerr Publication Fund.

The Johns Hopkins University Press
2715 North Charles Street
Baltimore, Maryland 21218-4319
The Johns Hopkins Press Ltd., London

ISBN 0-8018-5083-5

Library of Congress Cataloging-in-Publication Data will be found at the end of this book.
A catalog record for this book is available from the British Library.

To Susan, Scott, and Charles

*my hope and your mother's for a brighter tomorrow*

# CONTENTS

*Illustrations follow page 172.*

# PREFACE

CONSIDER FOR A MOMENT the possibility of nominating a candidate for the American presidency who would be paralyzed from the waist down. Have him win the general election in the midst of a terrible economic depression and embark upon a program of landmark legislation to ease the devastation. Allow him to break with the two-term presidential tradition and win four national elections. Finally, let him remain in the Oval Office while disease gradually constricts his heart and arteries until just before the end of World War II, when a cerebral hemorrhage ends his life and turns him into an instant martyr.

Add to this scenario the crippled president selecting an elderly yet well-respected politician, a man without any experience in foreign affairs, as secretary of state. Have him contract tuberculosis at a time when it was still stigmatized by the label the White Plague. Grant him the longest tenure of any American secretary of state. Make this man so insecure that he writes "READ AND DESTROY" at the end of sensitive correspondence, but retains carbon copies for his own files. Under these extraordinary circumstances, have him agree to take a secondary role to the president in shaping foreign policy.

Add one last player to the mix. Have him be a professional diplomat who rises from assistant secretary of state to serve as under secretary of state, and for protracted periods, acting secretary of state. Give him an air of intellectual aloofness and pomposity. Make him deeply troubled with his masculinity: have him marry three times, but have him also turn to homosexual unions with black railroad porters, shoeshine boys, and taxicab drivers.

Surely such an implausible triumvirate could not conceivably direct U.S. foreign policy for over a decade. But, in stark reality, they did. Franklin Roosevelt was president; Cordell Hull was secretary of state; and Sumner Welles was under secretary of state. This trio established the nation's main diplomatic guidelines while simultaneously struggling to maintain their emotional stability. Roosevelt's physical disabilities forced him to rely on others throughout his waking hours. His widely publicized romantic interlude with his wife's social secretary nearly destroyed their marriage. His refusal to acknowledge his gradually worsening heart condition guaranteed governmental discontinuity after his death.

Hull, too, faced seemingly insurmountable barriers. He took control of the State Department without any training in foreign affairs. He hid his wife's Jewish heritage for fear that it would cause controversy and keep him from the presidential nomination he so passionately desired. He was incredibly sensitive to any adverse criticism. Bothered by rotting teeth, he wore uncomfortable false wooden dentures, and a diabetic condition further weakened his resistance. Yet these medical problems were insignificant compared with the diagnosis of tuberculosis that was rendered shortly before he entered the cabinet; only those closest to him knew that he had contracted this dread disease.

Welles confronted his own unique problems. Lauded as the U.S. specialist on Latin America, he began his career under Roosevelt with a dismal failure in Cuba. After that disappointing experience, he became the technician who made the term "good neighbor" synonymous with inter-American solidarity. As a reward, he won promotion to the post of under secretary, in which he helped shape most of the country's major wartime foreign policies. Yet despite his accomplishments, Welles came to personify controversy. Those who knew him either admired or detested him, and with good reason, for he viewed issues as black or white, right or wrong. This rigid attitude extended to his formal, reserved exterior; he was invariably impeccably dressed, carefully groomed, and perfectly spoken. But when he became intoxicated, his formal mask dropped, and he would proposition blacks. As long as his drunken and homosexual escapades went undetected, Welles functioned admirably, but once his enemies learned of his sexual proclivities, his downfall was assured.

The three men concurred on most of the momentous diplomatic decisions of their era, and yet the events that molded the characters of each were a mystery to the others. They could not cope with their secret affairs and subordinate their private demons for the benefit of the nation that they were sworn to serve. That tragic weakness ultimately destroyed much of what they had hoped to leave as their legacy. Roosevelt, even though he knew that his health was failing, never explained his major foreign policy objectives to Vice-President Harry Truman or anyone else. Although Hull was bedridden at the end of his tenure, he never groomed a successor. Welles kept his foreign assignations as classified as his sexual orientation.

Although Roosevelt, Hull, and Welles allowed few into their private thoughts, they relied heavily on the women in their lives. Franklin's mother Sara dominated many of her son's actions; his wife Eleanor assumed the role of White House spokeswoman. Frances Hull and Mathilde Welles became their husbands' most trusted confidantes and loyal supporters.

Their husbands selectively depended on male associates at different times to carry out their wishes. Louis Howe and Harry Hopkins sat the closest to the Oval Office, while advisers like Henry Morgenthau, Jr., James Farley, and Harold Ickes gladly carried out presidential directives. Secretary Hull had his own followers, in what became known as the "croquet clique." Welles often sought the advice of subordinates like Laurence Duggan and Adolf Berle. Outside government circles, each chose sympathetic newspapermen to project their viewpoints. Drew Pearson shamelessly distorted his column in order to promote Welles; Hull relied on Arthur Krock; and the president used and abused a variety of reporters to launch trial balloons.

My exploration of the myriad personal relationships and foreign policies of this period has been a journey of more than two decades. Had I known where this enterprise was going to take me, I probably would have never attempted to set down what you are about to read. I initially set out to write a biography of Welles, but I quickly realized that Hull had played such an integral role that he, too, needed careful scrutiny. Of course, Roosevelt sat at the top of the pyramid. As I examined this trio, it became clear that their associations with scores of others had to be included as well. Forgotten figures like R. Walton Moore and Edward Stettinius, Jr., demanded attention, as did William Bullitt and Drew Pearson. As a result of these complex interactions, I have interconnected portions of the biographies of Roosevelt, Hull, and Welles, along with those of Moore, Bullitt, Pearson, and others as they entered and exited the stage.

Novelists have no trouble constructing their make-believe schemes because plot and character development may be conveniently intertwined as the need arises. They dream up heroes and villains, weave complex plots, and spice them with lurid sexual liaisons and heinous murders. Nonfiction writers do not have this freedom; instead, they have a duty to examine the evidence and tell the story as best they can within its confines. I have extended the traditional boundaries of nonfiction writing by linking multiple biographies with accounts of American diplomatic events, for this was the only acceptable device that I could find to tell the most fascinating and tragic story of the New Deal years. I hope, for the sake of you the reader, that I have succeeded.

# DRAMATIS PERSONAE

**Dean Acheson**—assistant secretary of state, 1941–1945

**William Bankhead**—speaker of the House of Representatives, 1936–1940

**Adolf Berle**—assistant secretary of state, 1938–1944, and member of the Brain Trust

**Francis Biddle**—attorney general of the United States, 1941–1945

**Robert Bingham**—owner of the Louisville *Courier-Journal* and ambassador to Great Britain, 1933–1937

**Claude Bowers**—ambassador to Chile, 1939–1952, and ambassador to Spain, 1933–1939

**Ralph Owen Brewster**—Republican senator from Maine, 1941–1952

**William Bullitt**—ambassador to France, 1936–1940, and ambassador to the Soviet Union, 1933–1936

**Louise Bryant**—William Bullitt's second wife

**James Byrnes**—secretary of state, 1945–1947, and presidential adviser, 1942–1945, who was dubbed "assistant president"

**Wilbur Carr**—minister to Czechoslavia, 1937–1939, and assistant secretary of state, 1933–1937

**William Castle**—under secretary of state during the Hoover administration, 1931–1933

**Leo Crowley**—foreign economic adviser, 1943–1945, previously alien property custodian, 1942–1943, and Federal Deposit Insurance Corporation chairman, 1934–1945

**Josephus Daniels**—ambassador to Mexico, 1933–1941

**Joseph Davies**—ambassador to Belgium, 1938–1940, and ambassador to the Soviet Union, 1936–1938

**Norman Davis**—diplomatic adviser to the Roosevelt administration, 1933–1944, and under secretary of state during the Wilson administration, 1920–1921

**William Dodd**—American ambassador to Germany, 1933–1938

**Laurence Duggan**—diplomatic ally of Sumner Welles, specializing in Latin American affairs, 1930–1944

**James Dunn**—assistant secretary of state, 1944–1945, and close adviser to Cordell Hull, 1933–1944

**James Farley**—postmaster general, 1933–1940, and chairman of the Democratic National Committee, 1932–1940

**Herbert Feis**—economic adviser to the State Department, 1931–1943

**Felix Frankfurter**—associate justice of the Supreme Court, 1939–1965, professor at Harvard Law School, and presidential adviser

**John Nance Garner**—vice-president of the United States, 1933–1941

**Joseph Green**—diplomat specializing in arms sales, 1935–1941

**Averell Harriman**—ambassador to the Soviet Union, 1943–1945

**Herbert Hoover**—president of the United States, 1929–1933

**J. Edgar Hoover**—director of the Federal Bureau of Investigation, 1924–1972

**Harry Hopkins**—presidential adviser, 1941–1945, and secretary of commerce, 1938–1940

Stanley Hornbeck—diplomatic adviser on far eastern affairs, 1928–1944

Edward House—President Wilson's most trusted adviser, 1914–1919; consulted with Democrats until his death in 1938

Louis Howe—closest political adviser to Franklin Roosevelt, 1912–1936

Cordell Hull—secretary of state, 1933–1944

Harold Ickes—secretary of the interior, 1933–1946

Samuel Inman—American scholar specializing in Latin America

Hiram Johnson—Republican senator from California, 1917–1945

Robert Kelley—chief of the Eastern European division of the State Department, 1933–1937

Frank Kellogg—secretary of state, 1925–1929

Joseph Kennedy—ambassador to Great Britain, 1937–1940

Frank Knox—secretary of the navy, 1940–1944

Arthur Krock—Washington bureau chief for the *New York Times*

Marguerite "Missy" LeHand—Roosevet's private secretary, 1920–1944

Breckinridge Long—assistant secretary of state, 1939–1944, and ambassador to Italy, 1933–1936

Ross McIntire—admiral and private physician to Franklin Roosevelt, 1933–1945

Lucy Mercer—private secretary to Eleanor Roosevelt, 1914–1918; later Lucy Mercer Rutherford

George Messersmith—ambassador to Mexico, 1942–1946, ambassador to Cuba, 1940–1942, and assistant secretary of state, 1937–1940

George Milton—Tennessee journalist and a special assistant to the secretary of state, 1937–1938

J. Pierrepont Moffat—professional diplomat who served under Roosevelt, 1933–1943

Raymond Moley—assistant secretary of state, 1933, and member of the Brain Trust

R. Walton Moore—counselor to the State Department, 1937–1941, and assistant secretary of state, 1933–1937

Henry Morgenthau, Jr.—secretary of the treasury, 1934–1945

Carmel Offie—William Bullitt's most trusted foreign service adviser, 1934–1943

Leo Pasvolsky—special assistant to the secretary of state, 1936–1946

Eleanor "Cissy" Patterson—owner of the Washington *Herald* and mother of Felicia Gizychi, wife of Drew Pearson

Endicott Peabody—founder and headmaster of the Groton School and an Episcopal minister

Drew Pearson—influential reporter who created the "Washington Merry-Go-Round" column

George Peek—foreign trade adviser, 1933–1934

Frances Perkins—secretary of labor, 1933–1945

Matthew Perry—private physician to Cordell Hull, 1932–1944

William Phillips—ambassador to Italy, 1936–1941, and under secretary of state, 1933–1936

Key Pittman—chairman of the Senate Foreign Relations Committee, 1933–1940

Nelson Rockefeller—assistant secretary of state, 1944–1945, and coordinator of inter-American affairs, 1940–1944

Eleanor Roosevelt—wife of Franklin Delano Roosevelt

Franklin Delano Roosevelt—president of the United States, 1933–1945

James Roosevelt—father of Franklin Roosevelt

Sara Delano Roosevelt—mother of Franklin Roosevelt

Theodore Roosevelt—president of the United States, 1900–1908, cousin of Franklin, and uncle of Eleanor

Samuel Rosenman—special counsel to the president, 1943–1945, and speech writer

G. Howland Shaw—assistant secretary of state, 1941–1944, and chief of the foreign service personnel division, 1937–1941

Alfred Smith—defeated Democratic candidate for president in 1928 and governor of New York, 1919–1928

Edward Stettinius, Jr.—secretary of state, 1944–1945, and under secretary of state, 1943–1944

Henry Stimson—secretary of war, 1940–1945, and secretary of state during the Hoover administration, 1929–1933

Arthur Sweetser—American advocate for an international peace organization

Mathilde Townsend—second wife of Sumner Welles

Harry S Truman—president of the United States, 1945–1952, and vice-president of the United States, 1945

Frank Walker—postmaster general, 1940–1945

Henry Wallace—vice-president of the United States, 1941–1945, and secretary of agriculture, 1933–1941

Edwin "Pa" Watson—army officer and secretary to the president, 1933–1945

Benjamin Sumner Welles—under secretary of state, 1937–1943, assistant secretary of state, 1933–1937, and ambassador to Cuba, 1933

Francis White—critic of Sumner Welles, minister to Czechoslovakia, 1933–1934, and assistant secretary of state, 1927–1933

Rosetta Frances Witz Whitney—wife of Cordell Hull

Woodrow Wilson—president of the United States, 1913–1921

Stephen Wise—powerful American Zionist rabbi

# SECRET AFFAIRS

# CHAPTER 1

# THE CHIEF SETS THE TONE

B Y THE AUTUMN OF 1943, President Franklin Delano Roosevelt sensed that the Allies had seized the military initiative from the Axis Powers. Allied forces had already recaptured North Africa and landed on Italian soil, and plans were now being laid for the Normandy invasion. The Russians had stopped the Nazi onslaught just outside of Moscow, and the Red Army was driving the once-invincible Wehrmacht from Soviet soil. The disaster at Pearl Harbor had begun to fade from the minds of Americans, replaced by pride in the victories at Guam, Midway, and Guadalcanal. Finally, the tremendous losses to American shipping in the Atlantic Ocean from silent U-boat attacks had been dramatically reduced.

These military successes, holding out as they did the hope of an ultimate Allied triumph, heartened the president, but they mitigated only marginally the worst personal humiliation he had suffered in his decade as chief executive. In the closing days of September, his friend and loyal supporter since the advent of the New Deal, fellow New Yorker Sumner Welles, had been forced to leave his post as under secretary of state in disgrace. Welles's resignation came just as Roosevelt needed his seem-ingly inexhaustible energy and perceptive counsel most urgently. Equally troubling was Welles's realization that Roosevelt had known that it was Secretary of State Cordell Hull, a man held in great esteem by the vast majority of Americans, who had engineered Welles's downfall, not be-cause of policy differences or poor performance, but rather as the denouement of a personal vendetta.

The underlying issue was one of power, sometimes real and some-times imagined—a contest between Hull and Welles over which of them was to run the State Department. Even though Hull was by then so physically incapacitated that he could not take charge of the department on a day-to-day basis, he could not admit to himself that Welles not only commanded the diplomatic bureaucracy but also functioned efficiently, with White House guidance, as America's global technician. Hull refused to accept that fact because he genuinely hated Welles. In October 1942 he seized upon a Federal Bureau of Investigation inquiry completed in early January 1941, documenting the fact that Welles had made homo-sexual advances to several Negro railroad porters, as the deadly weapon to drive Welles out of office.

For a brief moment in wartime Washington, the removal of Welles made the front page. But the tragedy slipped to the inside columns as soon as news of the shifting Allied battlefronts captured the public's attention. Thereafter Welles became one of many wartime casualties, mourned but then forgotten by all except a few loyalists.

Shortly after Welles's precipitous resignation, in a heated exchange with former ambassador William Bullitt in which Roosevelt lashed out at the diplomat for allegedly abetting Hull, the depth of the president's feeling was palpable: "You cannot speak that way about Welles to me. So far as Welles is concerned, he is an exceptionally able, honest, straight-forward, high-minded public servant. He would never stoop to malice. And I want to say to you, that when you and Welles meet St. Peter, Sumner will probably go to heaven, but you will go to hell. So far as I am concerned, that is where you can go now."[1] Yet, his anger notwithstanding, Roosevelt had only himself to blame for much of the debacle. As chief executive, it was he who set the professional and personal standard for his administration.

If anyone was a creature of his environment, it was Franklin Roosevelt. Born and reared in the fading light of America's Gilded Age, he had seen his personality shaped long before he reached the White House. For the future president, the lessons learned from his upstate New York upbringing would always be at the core of his being.

Springwood was the name that James Roosevelt, a wealthy entrepreneur, chose for the large and comfortable home that he purchased for his first wife in Hyde Park, New York, shortly after the Civil War. The thickly wooded estate projected a mood of serenity and security. Shortly after James became a widower, in 1875, he courted and married Sara Delano, and in the autumn of 1880 she moved into the spacious seventeen-room estate. They enjoyed these rustic surroundings and their status as members of the aristocratic landed gentry. The only thing they lacked within this idyllic setting was a child of their own.[2]

James and Sara filled this void when their sole offspring, Franklin, was born in 1882. James was already past fifty when he became a father for the second time. His position in New York's social elite was secure, yet he differed from many of his relatives in belonging to the Democratic party. Sara also came from a patrician background, but unlike her husband, an only child, she was one of eleven children. Married relatively late (at the age of twenty-five), she devoted herself almost exclusively to her husband, and, after a difficult labor, divided her time between James and her young son.[3]

Franklin grew up in Hyde Park surrounded by a tranquil environment of open spaces and woods, with the Hudson River flowing past his comfortable home. His parents' marriage was a happy one, and he experienced the domestic stability about which many can only dream. As the scion of a Social Register family, he had private tutors to direct his early secular education and the Episcopal Church to provide him with a firm moral grounding. For recreation, he became an accomplished sailor;

yet he also found quiet pleasure in stamp collecting. As would be expected for a child of his standing, his parents took him on frequent holidays to Europe, especially to England and Germany—two nations that were to figure prominently in his adult life.

His formal education began in 1896, when he entered the Groton School, a prestigious Massachusetts boarding school. Its founder, Endicott Peabody—an Episcopal minister commonly referred to as "the Rector"—still ruled as headmaster. Franklin adapted to the school's exacting routine and grew to respect Peabody, whose virility and athleticism seemed to embody Groton's ideals and its patrons' aspirations. The affluent Americans who sent their sons to Groton expected a strong religious orientation in an academic setting. Peabody gladly provided that environment and inculcated in his young charges a sense of noblesse oblige. Children of the upper class, he held, had to recognize their sacred obligation to aid the needy. His students revered him for this idealism, and when they married it was often Peabody who was asked to officiate at the ceremony. When they had children, it was their old schoolmaster who christened their sons, as if his mere presence would ensure the transmission of an unbroken and unquestioned moral standard down through the generations.

As part of their training, Groton students conformed to strict guidelines that were intended to emphasize group identification rather than individualism. They lived in six-by-nine-foot bare wood dormitory rooms, in which the only pictures allowed were those of their families. The boys adhered to a Spartan routine. They took cold showers at 7:00 A.M.; breakfast was served half an hour later; chapel was compulsory at 8:15, seven days a week. Classes lasted until noon, and dinner was followed by sessions of Greek and Latin, algebra, English literature, and French. American history, of course, was excluded because it was not considered part of a classical education. Sports filled the rest of the afternoon. At supper, a stiff collar, black tie, and patent leather shoes were required. After supper the boys returned to the chapel for evening prayers, and then retired to their dormitories to prepare for the next day's activities. Yet even within this regimen, the privileged boys of Groton did not make their beds, wait on tables, or polish their shoes.

They were given twenty-five cents spending money and five cents for the Sunday collection plate. Peabody molded his charges to share a common set of values. The youngsters under his supervision were made to accept what his clients—their parents—considered the essential foundation for later life: completion of an academic program for college entrance, adherence to Episcopal beliefs, and the social contract that with wealth went responsibility.

Franklin was slightly older than many of his peers. He was also highly motivated and finished his four years at the academy in the upper fourth of his class. His extracurricular success came on the debating team, for he did not excel in the most popular sport, football. Like most of his classmates, Roosevelt headed to Harvard University upon graduation in 1899. His father died during his freshman year. The event had two immediate consequences for him: he lost his father's guidance, and Sara turned most of her energies toward her son. In contrast to his academic success at boarding school, Franklin's attention at college focused primarily on activities outside the classroom, for he found that his peers gauged his worth not so much by his grades but by his campus reputation. While receiving gentleman's C's, he tried to measure up to this social pressure but only emerged as a campus leader in his senior year, when he became editor of the *Harvard Crimson*. Despite this achievement, however, he could not duplicate his cousin Theodore Roosevelt's record of being tapped for Phi Beta Kappa and selected to Porcellian, the top social club. Franklin did not win either honor, never earned a varsity H in sports, and was not chosen as one of the three senior marshals who led the class in the commencement procession.

After graduating from college, he attended Columbia University Law School until he passed the New York bar examination in 1907. After joining the prominent Wall Street firm of Carter, Ledyard, and Milburn, who represented such business giants as Standard Oil and American Tobacco, he announced to his colleagues that his legal career was just a starting point. Profoundly impressed by his cousin's presidency, young Franklin told his peers that he also expected to make 1600 Pennsylvania Avenue his residence.[4]

During this formative period, and much to his mother's chagrin, on St. Patrick's Day in 1905 he married Eleanor Roosevelt, a distant cousin, who was extremely insecure. Tall and dark haired, Eleanor considered herself ugly. Orphaned at the age of ten, she had been raised by a stern grandmother, along with a neurotic aunt and an alcoholic uncle. Despite this unhappy setting, she grew up with a deeply rooted social conscience that led her to support assistance in many forms to those in need. She also desperately wanted to become a wife and mother, and that, too, was precisely what Franklin expected. As anticipated, their family quickly mushroomed to include five children.[5]

By the time he married Eleanor, Franklin had developed certain character traits. He was quite spoiled and accustomed to being the center of attention; he had many acquaintances but few close friends. He had become a practicing attorney, even though he never had to earn a living in this or any other profession. His mother would always make certain that her son and grandchildren were comfortable, and since Sara controlled her son's finances, she took it upon herself to interfere regularly in his family life, much to Eleanor's consternation.

Franklin did not seem bothered by his wife's complaints, preferring to focus his attention on the advancement of his career. In fact, he quickly tired of the legal profession and soon entered local politics. In 1910 he won a seat in the New York State Senate by cleverly associating the Roosevelt name with Teddy's popularity and profiting from a local split within the Republican party. As a freshman Democratic senator from the Twenty-Sixth Senatorial District, he was soon initiated into Democratic party politics, learning about the power of the Tammany Hall machine in New York City and the consequences for those who opposed it. He energetically associated himself with the progressive movement and its attempts to pass legislative measures calling for such reforms as child-labor limitations, direct senatorial elections, and agricultural improvements.

By speaking out for these causes, Roosevelt the novice politician had an opportunity to identify with a national as well as a state constituency. When Woodrow Wilson triumphed as governor of New Jersey on a progressive platform, Franklin became an early supporter of his legislative reforms: once Wilson decided to run for the presidency, Roosevelt enthusiastically applauded this decision and offered to campaign for the governor. Wilson's stunning victory in 1912 moved Roosevelt a step closer to the White House. As a loyal Democrat and supporter of the president-elect, he asked for and received the position of assistant secretary of the navy, the same post that his cousin Teddy had once held.

Franklin left state politics for the federal government in the spring of 1913. As his principal assistant, he selected Louis Howe, a frail, ugly little forty-one-year-old man with chronic heart and asthma problems. They had met in 1910, when Roosevelt ran for the state senate, and two years later it was Howe who had directed Franklin's successful reelection bid. Trained as a journalist, Howe was also a shrewd political adviser. Most essentially, he and Roosevelt formed a close personal bond based on trust. Only with this most unlikely ally could Franklin let down his guard completely; Howe's reward was that, for the remainder of his life, he would hold the confidence of the future president.[6]

Roosevelt and Howe kept abreast of the wishes of their New York constituents because they formed Franklin's political base. In order to remain influential at the state level, the assistant secretary tried to direct federal patronage to his home district; although his recommendations were not always heeded, he came to recognize the importance of this powerful political weapon that national figures wielded. Roosevelt also interacted with powerful figures in other branches of the federal bureaucracy, for the department of the navy shared the same building with the departments of state and war. His decisions had far-reaching effects, and he preferred to confer with others in leadership roles. He also learned how to push for proposals within his own agency, in congressional committees, and with other cabinet officials. As an assistant secretary, he not only welcomed authority but also tried to broaden his powers, for with added responsibilities came more authority and the expanded role that Roosevelt coveted.[7]

The Wilson administration also served as an apprenticeship for Roosevelt through which he could gain managerial skills within the federal bureaucracy; he earned valuable national exposure by becoming a vocal proponent of rapid naval expansion to meet the challenge of a possible world war. He handled labor disputes and pressed for greater efficiency in the naval yards.

He also witnessed firsthand how German submarine warfare propelled the United States into the global conflict of World War I, and he expressed his own fervent brand of nationalism while warning his listeners of possible German penetration into the Americas, a theme upon which he would expand in speaking out against the Nazi menace in the late 1930s. In fact, Roosevelt developed such a profound distaste for Prussian militarism that he sometimes fabricated events to illustrate his point. For example, he claimed that during his teenage years he, his mother, and one of her friends were on a train bound for Berlin. They were sitting in a railroad compartment when a Prussian officer joined them and closed a nearby window. Sara's companion complained about a headache and asked that the window be reopened. Franklin complied, but the Prussian shut it again. This scene was repeated twice, and on the third attempt Franklin physically restrained the officer from touching the window. After the train reached its destination, he was arrested and taken to jail. Sara went to the United States embassy and had him released, but not before he had spent several hours incarcerated. Although this story was apocryphal, it showed the lengths to which Roosevelt would go to make his point. If lying served his purposes, the future president would not hesitate to do so.[8]

Yet such tall tales were immaterial compared to the severe test of his personal morality that almost destroyed his marriage. The handsome, youthful subcabinet member relished his official and social activities, whereas Eleanor, far more the introvert, was primarily a housewife caring for her growing youngsters. To assist with the obligations of an assistant secretary's spouse, in 1917 Eleanor hired Lucy Mercer—a young, tall, attractive woman from a well-respected Catholic family in Maryland—as her private secretary. In the intimate household setting, Franklin and Lucy became romantically involved. In the fall of 1918, Eleanor discovered their affair, and Lucy was summarily dismissed. Divorce temporarily threatened Eleanor and Franklin's marriage, but this option was soon discarded. The Roosevelts would remain together to raise their children, and to prevent Franklin's driving political ambition from being thwarted by public scandal. To reach the White House, he would have to create at least the illusion of marital bliss. As for

Eleanor, she never forgot the pain that this incident caused her, and she never forgave Franklin for his transgression.

With Lucy gone and the Wilson administration coming to an end, Roosevelt renewed his efforts to reach the White House in 1920 by following Teddy's example and accepting his party's vice-presidential nomination. He spoke out passionately in favor of the League of Nations, but the country, tired of world war and Wilsonian idealism, decisively rejected the Democratic ticket. Roosevelt found himself off the government payroll for the first time in almost a decade. Yet even in defeat he had matured politically, for he had had the opportunity to travel nationwide, meet with party leaders, and cement friendships that would serve him well in later years.

Roosevelt's loss at the polls did not affect his political future nearly so much as a crippling attack of poliomyelitis in 1921. He dealt with the affliction in several ways. At first, he had complete confidence that he would eventually walk again. Both he and his mother repressed their emotions about his paralysis, preferring simply not to address the topic. Refusing to acknowledge the reality of his permanent disability, he initially dismissed all thought of it. To remain in a positive frame of mind, he insisted on good cheer at all times from his staff, and he closely supervised immediate events to demonstrate that he was always in control. Eventually he recognized that he would in fact never recover the use of his legs and that he would need assistance for the rest of his life with everything from dressing to bathing. Able to remain erect for only short periods of time with the aid of crutches and ten-pound steel leg braces, he stood only on ceremonial occasions; otherwise, he spent his time in a specially designed wheelchair. He learned to endure great pain and to understand the power of patience, and he came to rely on others' eyewitness accounts and insights in formulating responses to a world that was now largely beyond at least his physical reach.

Franklin and Eleanor lived a partnership with little warmth or comfort; theirs had become a merger rather than a marriage. She became an additional set of eyes and ears and also substituted for Roosevelt in his speaking engagements. In addition to Eleanor, Howe, his closest political adviser and confidante, remained close to Roosevelt and continued to promote him, even in his bleakest days. He emerged as Roosevelt's chief strategist, never doubting that his client would eventually enter the White House.

To treat the pain of his paralysis, one of Roosevelt's greatest pleasures was taking polio treatments at a resort near the town of Warm Springs, Georgia. He went there for the first time in 1924 to sunbathe and swim in the mineral water pool. Each morning, he exercised in the pool, and after lunch he rested or went for a drive in a custom-built car with special hand controls. Two years later he bought the estate as an investment for $200,000. It was never a financial success, but its economic viability was not his main concern. He found relief there; he was at ease in this setting. An added benefit was that Eleanor disliked Warm Springs, so she seldom accompanied him. If he wished to be alone or to invite companions of whom Eleanor disapproved, Franklin could travel to Georgia, confident that his wife would be absent.

Polio dramatically altered his life-style. He was alone and yet could never be by himself. The painful and debilitating disease and his limited recovery from it did not alter his basic beliefs, but instead added another dimension to his personality. Realizing that the stigma attached to polio victims could damage his chances to resume his political career, he hid his disability from the public. Many of his constituents did not even realize that Roosevelt was the nation's most celebrated polio victim. Of the 125,000 still photographs (25,000 of the president) in the Franklin D. Roosevelt Library, just two show him in a wheelchair: in one facing the camera and in the other with his back to the camera. No newsreels recorded his impairment; no cartoons or caricatures depicted him as a paraplegic. His constituents seldom perceived him as disabled, which was precisely the illusion he sought to convey.[9]

Although his paralysis permanently impeded Roosevelt's mobility and temporarily postponed his political ambitions, he never distanced himself from the Democratic party. In fact he attended the 1924 national convention at Madison Square Garden in New York to nominate his friend and political ally Governor Alfred Smith of New York for the presidency. Smith lost his bid for the nomination in the longest and most disastrous Democratic national convention ever. However, four years later he led the ticket, and Roosevelt campaigned for him in what was to be a losing run for the presidency. Yet to help his candidate even further,

Roosevelt agreed to run for governor of New York, and he was victorious by the narrowest of margins.

After the Depression struck, Governor Roosevelt spent the largest part of his time on such local issues as farming, the provision of cheap electric power, and judicial reform. His achievements as the chief executive of the nation's most populous state and his driving personal ambition propelled him into the race for the presidency in 1932. Winning the nomination virtually assured him victory in November. Republican President Herbert Hoover, who had taken credit for America's post–World War I prosperity, now had to offer solutions to the worst depression in American history. As the incumbent hopelessly groped for answers to incredibly complex questions, his challenger, riding a wave of anti-Hooverism, needed only to offer vague promises of economic solutions to achieve a brighter tomorrow. Roosevelt had only to guard against any obvious misstep as he watched his opponent self-destruct.[10]

Roosevelt entered the White House triumphant in March 1933, bringing with him beliefs that were to stay with him throughout his long presidential tenure. First and foremost, he was an elitist whose upbringing was decidedly more urban than rural. He appeared most comfortable with his own social class, preferring to face the East coast and Europe rather than the heartland of America. He was the consummate politician who refused to become doctrinaire, an approach that led him to experiment willingly with various New Deal alternatives. His magnetic personality mesmerized the vast majority of his supporters who listened to him in person or on radio. What others took to be inconsistency on his part never bothered him, as long as his ultimate objective was attained. This flexibility troubled many of his associates, who worried about compromising their own principles, but their feelings did not deter Roosevelt. Instead, he relied upon his charming personality to win virtually everyone over to his way of thinking.[11]

Roosevelt developed a leadership style in which he acted at his own discretion and chose to address those topics, large or small, that appealed to him; but seldom did he commit his thoughts to paper. Nevertheless his was the last word, and to prevent him from changing a decision once it was reached, those who understood the presidential style developed a practice that guaranteed closure. Subordinates drew up a memorandum and Roosevelt initialed it: "FDR, OK." That ended discussion.

Such informal guidelines for the formulation of policy did not trouble Roosevelt. His imperative was control over everyone around him. Raised in a secure environment in which he had held center stage, he sought to continue to occupy such a position throughout his later public as well as private life. Indeed part of his reason for creating friction within government circles was to guarantee control. If an issue needed resolution, competing subordinates had to plead their cases to the ultimate arbitrator. Roosevelt welcomed this competition; in fact, he thrived on it.

Roosevelt quickly settled into the daily routine that would last throughout most of his years in the White House. He awoke early in the morning yet remained in bed, and at 8:30 A.M. habitually ate a hearty breakfast of grapefruit, coffee, cereal, and eggs. While eating, he skimmed major newspapers from New York City, Washington, D.C., Chicago, and Baltimore and reviewed his schedule with aides as his valet dressed him. He had great difficulty getting up and sitting down, but once erect, he managed to walk with the support of the steel braces on his legs and with a cane for balance and support.

At approximately 10:00 A.M. a manservant brought in his armless wheelchair, helped him get into it, and took him to the private elevator on the second floor of the White House for the short ride down to the Oval Office on the first floor. Roosevelt worked steadily throughout the rest of the morning, occasionally taking out a cigarette, placing it in a long holder, and puffing away while signing official documents and correspondence, consulting with advisers, and receiving visitors. His staff tried to limit interviews to fifteen minutes, but these often lasted longer at Roosevelt's whim. He would readily put his guests at ease, and by the time their meeting ended most left satisfied that their concerns would be addressed. Here was a chief executive who truly enjoyed company.

At lunch Roosevelt ate with aides or guests and then returned to his desk and resumed the hectic schedule of reading, answering mail, and attending more meetings until 5:00 P.M. Twice a week for fifteen to thirty minutes he held off-the-record press conferences with reporters from newspaper and radio services who gathered around his desk. After finishing his daily agenda, he sometimes swam in the enclosed heated White House pool and afterward enjoyed an alcohol rub. Roosevelt's work day ended with a review of his activities with his advisers and the making of plans for the following day. The "children's hour"—the name given to the time when his close associates, family, and staff gathered to review the day's events—began at 7:15 P.M. A social drinker who gained enormous satisfaction from mixing cocktails for his guests, Roosevelt sipped his own glass slowly and seldom had more than two drinks before dinner, all the while urging his concoctions on his company. The entire assemblage sat down to eat at 8:00. Afterwards, the president would converse with his company until he was tired and then retire to bed, usually by 10:00 or 11:00 P.M.

On Fridays the cabinet met in a long room at the White House whose tall windows looked out on the rose garden to the right of the south portico. Roosevelt chaired the meeting from the head of the table and would customarily open with his own statement about the issues he considered most pressing. The secretary of state sat to his right and the secretary of the treasury on his left; the remaining members sat alternately on either side down the length of the table in the order of the creation of their posts.

For relaxation, besides swimming, Roosevelt played penny ante as a social activity, bluffing excessively and losing more than winning. He was far more interested in his stamp collection, having been a philatelist since boyhood, and he tried to add to his huge holdings almost daily. He also enjoyed crossword puzzles and solitaire and liked to watch current movie releases in the company of friends. Although he made some effort to keep up with literature and popular songs, he was not widely read, nor did he appreciate classical music or fine art. Though raised a good Episcopalian, he was not a religious man and seldom turned to the church for direction in his daily life.

He traveled constantly by car, train, ship, or airplane and seemed reinvigorated by the slightest change of scenery. At Warm Springs, the mineral baths eased the pain of his polio. At Hyde Park, the secure setting comforted him and reminded him of his roots. As opportunities arose, he traveled on American warships to rest, sunbathe, fish, and assemble his thoughts.[12]

Franklin's wife and his domineering mother, however, had a significant impact on his family life. Sara sought to maintain her matriarchical standing by retaining control of a great deal of the family's wealth. Eleanor ran the household as best she could while serving him as an adviser. Although he wrote her "Dearest Babs" letters on his travels, they were not affectionate. Indeed, their marriage continued to be an accommodation in which each had loosely delineated tasks and obligations to the other. Any passion in their union had long since vanished. In fact, Eleanor and Franklin slept in separate bedrooms—a legacy of his infidelity. Yet the public never knew about this aspect of their private lives.[13]

Despite this lack of affection, Franklin coveted his patriarchical role and maintained a loving relationship with his five children. Over the years they brought him both pain and joy. Their divorces and the failed business ventures that traded on the president's popularity proved embarrassing, but Roosevelt seemed to accept these personal disappointments as part of his public charge.

His schedule revolved around politics, and he relished it. He thrived on the continual personal interaction that his office required. He was very patient with most of those in his orbit, but a mean streak occasionally surfaced; for example, he would deliberately appoint individuals to work together who hated each other. This cruelty sometimes caused bitter animosity among his subordinates, and when personal confrontations resulted, Roosevelt refused to intervene to settle the disputes. He preferred that the appointees become frustrated and then disillusioned, and finally resign in disgust. Such private antagonisms came to affect not only lesser officials but also cabinet members during his long tenure.

An apocryphal story reflects the lengths to which the president would go to avoid abrasive personal disputes, and the occasionally embarrassing consequences of his evasiveness. Roosevelt was sitting at his desk in the Oval Office working while Eleanor sat nearby knitting. A cabinet officer burst in and demanded that a bridge be built in Kentucky to reduce that state's unemployment. Roosevelt accepted the reasoning and told the official, "By George, you're absolutely right!" The official left, his victory in hand. Five minutes later another cabinet member rushed in and asserted that the bridge would hurt the local economy and therefore must not be constructed. The president looked puzzled for a moment and then declared, "By George, you're absolutely right!" His second visitor departed, assured that he had prevailed. Finally Eleanor, still in the room, broke her silence: "I am confused. The first man asked to build the bridge; the second did not want it. You told each that he could have his way. Maybe you should think about the proposal a little more before they come back to see you." Roosevelt turned to his wife and loudly trumpeted, "Eleanor, by George, you're absolutely right!"

Roosevelt had won the presidency by promising to solve the staggering problems brought on by the Depression. During his campaign, he had refrained from making any major foreign policy statement, preferring to avoid looking abroad in the face of the crushing economic upheaval at home. Thus, when he delivered his inaugural address, he concentrated on strategies for domestic recovery, with only vague allusions to world affairs.[14]

This apparent oversight did not mean that the president was disinterested; in fact, he made no secret of his intention to be an activist president in foreign affairs. J. Pierrepont Moffat, a career diplomat, captured the significance of this intent early in the New Deal: "Of course President Roosevelt is being his own Secretary of State in the best T.R. and Wilson tradition. It has its advantages, but it makes everybody jumpy, as to what the President has said to foreign representatives." Moffat later added another observation about the strengths and weaknesses of the president's style: "It gives a distinct finality and I think a degree of consistency to our policy that will bear fruit. On the other hand, it is extremely difficult to know what has gone before and this doubt of knowing the background extends even in high circles."[15]

Moffat's words emphasized the serious dilemma that was to confront the diplomatic corps for the next twelve years: Roosevelt made policy decisions, yet often did not share them with those who were most affected. The president recognized this fact, but he was not concerned. His self-confidence, bordering on arrogance, led him to dismiss normal organizational procedures. This neglect resulted in confusion among his own foreign policy experts, for the White House would make commitments to other governments without informing the State Department. To demonstrate his executive authority, Roosevelt refused to dictate memoranda summarizing his talks with foreign statesmen, leaving the department without a record of those discussions. This conscious refusal to provide the foreign service with presidential direction and policy goals continued throughout his years in office. Operating in this unorthodox manner, the president became the final arbiter. This crooked chain of authority caused unending confusion, but it accomplished the desired end—at least for the man at its origin.

Roosevelt took great pride in his knowledge of specific diplomatic issues and was acknowledged as one of the Democratic party's leading authorities on foreign relations. In 1928, for example, he wrote a widely read article, "Our Foreign Policy: A Democratic View," which was a partisan attack on Republican positions. In it he demanded an end to intervention in Latin America, the settlement of World War I debts, and naval disarmament. These pronouncements reflected the ideas of many prominent Democrats as a blueprint for the party but did not necessarily provide a clear picture of Roosevelt's global vision.[16]

Indeed, the president never followed a consistent set of principles in his conduct of international affairs. He had not carefully studied the subject in school, nor had he developed a scholarly interest in it in subsequent years. His views had been nurtured since childhood. Pivotal among them was a European orientation that remained with him throughout his years in the presidency. He grew to admire the British and the French, and these feelings were reinforced during World War I and throughout the years of Republican rule. After Roosevelt had won the presidency, he met with Hoover's secretary of state, Henry Stimson, early in 1933 and approved of the Hoover administration's initiatives for improved Anglo-French relations and European disarmament proposals. To achieve those ends, the new president held private discussions with the French and British, while excluding his own advisers. When his efforts failed, he unilaterally issued an unsuccessful appeal to world leaders for the elimination of offensive weaponry.

Conversely, Roosevelt grew to loathe German militarism. His election to the presidency closely paralleled the ascension of Adolf Hitler as chancellor of the Third Reich. The American chief executive ultimately came to despise everything the Nazis represented, especially their renewed efforts at rearmament and the brutality that they unleashed upon their opponents. Almost from the very start of the New Deal, Roosevelt spoke out forcefully against the German government's persecution of its Jewish population. The president drew attention to this emerging reign of terror in its infancy because it offended the sense of decency and fair play that had been preached to him and those of his social class since his days at Groton. Those who misread his sympathies as philo-Semitism were wrong. He deplored the brutality that Hitler heaped upon a vulnerable minority, nothing more.

Although his primary focus remained on European matters, Roosevelt also came to emphasize inter-American cooperation. Initially, he supported his cousin's role in the taking of the Panama Canal and military intervention in Latin America. During his years in the Navy Department Franklin exerted his own brand of imperialism by calling for United States occupations in several Latin American nations. He even boasted that he had written Haiti's constitution, a false claim that would later return to haunt him when adversaries used it to depict him as an imperialist. During his years in office he gradually modified some of his basic assumptions, such as his unequivocal support for armed intervention and the shouldering of the "white man's burden" during the 1920s. Indeed, he eventually favored ending the marine occupations of Cuba, Haiti, and the Dominican Republic since these brought loud cries of American intervention. After he won the presidency, he stressed a "good neighbor" approach. The term soon struck a responsive chord and became synonymous with hemispheric solidarity. Voters applauded and embraced regional exclusivity, believing that the United States had an unquestioned obligation to Fortress America.

As for East Asia, the president had little background or interest in the region, and he had never actually visited it. Like many Americans, he idealized closer contacts with China. In fact, he endorsed Stimson's plans for halting Japanese expansion on mainland China through multilateral consultation with many nations; but this push toward international cooperation never gained a following.[17]

His love for sailing and years as assistant secretary of the navy added another dimension. His early advocacy of a large fleet was a direct result of his comprehension of the geopolitical significance of sea power and his aggressive designs to expand the overseas role of the United States. During the 1920s he abandoned his call for a big navy as he saw the need for American forces to be stationed abroad diminish. Yet, despite these reduced military expectations, Roosevelt closely associated military preparedness with effective diplomatic action; few presidents have ever had a better grasp of the interplay of these imperatives than Franklin Roosevelt.

Finally, he believed in collective security, and he gave his unqualified support to Wilson's brand of internationalism, as expressed through his grand design for the League of Nations. During the 1920 presidential campaign, Roosevelt ardently preached this gospel and suffered the consequences of public rejection at the polls. To win the presidency twelve years later, he was forced to repudiate his earlier position endorsing U.S. entrance into the League, but he never totally abandoned the concept of global cooperation. As president, he cautiously advocated it as a means of bringing about a more peaceful world, but whenever opponents openly challenged him on this emotional issue, he retreated. He vividly remembered the humiliation of losing the 1920 election and had no intention of repeating the experience.

Roosevelt alone set the tone for his presidency. Self-assurance, strong management skills, political acumen, and an activist temperament were just a few of the qualities of the man who had set himself the task of leading the nation out of depression through an ethos of cooperation and sacrifice. He motivated like no president before him ever had, summoning up the best of his managerial, political, and personal qualities to advance his cause. Others gladly followed his lead, and he successfully moved his domestic programs forward.

Diplomatic affairs were another matter. Roosevelt came to the presidency with a frame of reference for deciding foreign policy issues that few before him had possessed. Always an elitist, he truly believed that he could resolve any problem by himself. Although his self-assurance helped him in making many decisions, it also brought to the fore his inherent weaknesses. He was not a team player and he greatly exaggerated the extent of his knowledge; he was secretive, and sometimes insensitive and inconsiderate. He set out to play a dominant role without fully trusting the foreign service, and he acted unilaterally to illustrate his distrust. He had his own private agenda, which he seldom shared with anyone. Yet these impediments to the development of clear and consistent foreign policies had not yet crystallized at the beginning of the New Deal, as the country's prayers were centered on economic revival, not diplomatic advances.

# CHAPTER 2

# ENTER HULL

NOT ONLY DID THE PRESIDENT handpick every major political diplomatic appointee at the start of the New Deal, he also spent a considerable amount of time deciding who should go where. Roosevelt clearly expected his nominees to understand that they owed their allegiance to the White House. Josephus Daniels, the president's former boss at the Navy Department during the Wilson administration, was named ambassador to Mexico; Breckinridge Long, a generous campaign contributor from Missouri, went to Rome; Claude Bowers, a prominent Midwestern newspaperman and historian, received the Spanish assignment; and Robert Bingham, a powerful newspaper publisher from Louisville, went to the Court of St. James's.[1]

These selections might also have been a slap at professional diplomats, against whom the president had a deeply rooted prejudice arising from his experiences in Wilson's administration. This resentment was to endure throughout the New Deal, as he continued to harbor suspicions about the motives of the white Anglo-Saxon males who made up the tightly knit foreign service fraternity. Many hailed from the East and had grown up with wealth, attended Ivy League schools, and entered the government to take their place as enlightened leaders in the service of their country. Built into the world view of the majority was adamant opposition to the communist menace and an unquestioning acceptance of their forebears' antipathy toward Jews, as a sly and untrustworthy race.[2]

Although Roosevelt's diplomatic appointments, like those of previous administrations, largely fell under the heading of political patronage, the selection process for a new secretary of state customarily turned to an influential member of the political party in power, preferably one with extensive experience in foreign relations. However, since Roosevelt had already demonstrated his clear intention to formulate much of American foreign policy by himself, he needed someone whom Democrats would applaud but with whom at the same time he could feel comfortable— someone who would be willing to fill the most senior cabinet post, only to be obedient to the whims of the chief executive.

After briefly considering several candidates who fit the traditional mold, Roosevelt surprised many by offering the job in early January 1933 to Senator Cordell Hull, a Tennessee Democrat who had virtually no qualifications in international affairs. Standing about six feet tall, lean of frame, and with white hair and dark eyes, Hull looked ideally suited for the post. Physical appearance, however, had had little to do with the decision; Roosevelt had made his choice owing primarily to party considerations. Hull had been a loyal Democrat, who had served in both houses of Congress and had actively promoted Roosevelt's presidential bid. By the middle of February, Hull had accepted the offer, and his appointment not only proclaimed the importance of the South in the New Deal coalition but also served to recognize the integral role of Democratic regulars in their party's victorious return to the White House. No longer could the eastern Ivy League–Wall Street clique lay unquestioned claim to the top portfolio at the State Department.[3]

Roosevelt had other compelling reasons for naming Hull. Louis Howe, for instance, favored him because he reflected the domestic concerns of most American voters. Outgoing Under Secretary of State William Castle wrote: "Although he [Hull] knows nothing about foreign affairs, he is a tremendously fine man and has never believed in the spoils system."[4] Despite such faint praise, Hull's admirers saw their man as the leader of the Democratic wing that would fight to lower trade barriers and preserve the party's power. Felix Frankfurter, a trusted Roosevelt adviser, professor at Harvard Law School, and future Supreme Court justice, welcomed the choice. Hull was perfect for the job: the secretary would be a figurehead, while the president, Frankfurter surmised, would provide the creative leadership in international relations.[5]

The chairman of the Democratic National Committee and incoming postmaster general, James Farley, assumed that Hull's selection was based both on his prominence in the party and on Roosevelt's confidence in his abilities. Farley described Hull as "very determined in his opinions," "a bit domineering," and one who gets "along well with other men," and "never gets excited." Yet these early mixed impressions had turned to accolades by the end of the first term; Farley, in fact, became one of Hull's staunchest admirers.[6]

Before Secretary Henry Stimson left the State Department, he met with his successor and painted a much bleaker portrait. After his initial meeting with Hull on February 25, 1933, Stimson observed in his diary, "He is a tall gentlemanly man, with a pleasant Southern quiet manner, rather slow. . . . On the whole I got a rather discouraging impression of his vitality and vigor." This opinion had grown more ominous by the next day, when Hull confirmed that "Roosevelt had told him that he intended to be his own Secretary of State, and Hull had apparently knuckled under to it."[7]

Hiram Johnson, the progressive senior Republican senator from California, was equally critical. During a conversation with the newly elected president in late January, Johnson told Roosevelt that his key cabinet appointment would be the secretary of state, who should be a man free from the Wall Street connections that had controlled the State Department since 1920. The president replied that he recognized the problem and was considering just such an individual, one who also had the advantage of having "an American outlook."

Shortly after the announcement of Hull's selection, Johnson and other senators expressed their surprise. Carter Glass, Democratic senator from Virginia, who had known Hull for many years while they served in Congress, knew that he was interested in tariff matters, but felt that he was unable to express his opinions with clarity. Whereas the press generally praised the president's choice, Johnson found him "a pleasant, kindly didposed [*sic*] individual, utterly colorless, wholly without position in the body at all. . . . To describe Hull as a tower of strength in the Senate, whose removal seriously affects the Senate, has been the subject of a good deal of laughter and joking the last couple of weeks. He is a nice man, and . . . may develop into a great man. He has not thus far in his sixty years displayed any elements which would lead one to believe in this development."[8]

Hull was probably unconcerned aboot such negative observations among his detractors, for he had gone from being one of many senators to serving as the highest-ranking cabinet member in the federal government. He also believed that he spoke as the voice of the Democratic rank and file, and he looked upon his appointment as a possible bridge between the regular party members and the White House. His three immediate Republican predecessors shared a common bond: all were lawyers. Hull had attained neither their legal stature nor their wealth, but he had joined their exclusive diplomatic fraternity.

Born on October 2, 1871, Hull grew up in the foothills of the Cumberland Mountains in central Tennessee, about halfway between Nashville and Knoxville. It was on this rolling farmland that his father William had settled. One man who knew him claimed that William came from "cool, hard headed, highly respected and self reliant stock." He "was a man very small and slight in stature, but nobody that I ever heard of questioned his ability to taking care of himself on any occasion." This opinion possibly arose from William's experiences during the Civil War, during which, depending on the account, he was either a Confederate soldier or at least a Confederate sympathizer. Toward the end of the fighting, as one story goes, three Yankees beat him, shot off the upper part of his nose, shot out one eye, threw him over a low bluff near the Cumberland River, and left him for dead. William recovered and went after his assailants. He tracked down only one, whom he promptly challenged and killed.[9]

Two years after the fighting had ended, William married. He and his wife, Elizabeth, reared five boys in a tiny wooden building with two windows and a door facing the road. Elizabeth taught them to read and write so that they could appreciate the Bible and the services at the local

Baptist church. William worked first at farming then in the logging industry; the family later moved to Carthage, where they ran a general store with a post office. William proved to be an excellent provider, and the family eventually moved into a spacious two-story frame house with a porch and driveway. The Hulls remained there and prospered.

Cord, as young Hull was nicknamed, benefited from his father's good fortune. At fifteen, he attended normal school, and after graduation he went to Cumberland Law School for ten months in 1891 and was admitted to the bar the following year at the age of twenty. He energetically practiced law until 1903, when he accepted an appointment as a circuit judge; from that time forward, friends nicknamed him "Judge." Even though he spent his days earning a living in the legal profession, politics consumed the rest of his time. He joined the Democratic Party, gave his first partisan speech at seventeen, served as chairman of the Democratic county executive committee two years later, and was elected to the state legislature at twenty-two. A tour of duty in Cuba as an army captain at the end of the Spanish-American War temporarily interrupted his political career.[10]

After the war Hull returned to politics, winning election to the United States House of Representatives in 1906. The vast majority of his constituents were native Tennesseeans associated with farming. At the time of his election, the primary means of funding the U.S. Treasury was through taxes on imported goods. Hull soon became an expert on this form of taxation, for he considered the tariff an unfair burden on his constituents. He believed that high protective duties, the program that most Republicans championed, unfairly benefited the wealthy. To redress this imbalance he proposed to replace the protective tariff with the graduated income tax. Although many legislators supported a constitutional amendment as the means for bringing about the reform, Hull opposed that approach because of the lengthy and difficult process of passage. Instead he favored a congressional act. In the end, his goal was achieved even if his approach was rejected, and income tax legislation became the Sixteenth Amendment.

During most of his years in Congress, Hull sat with the minority and spoke out for his principles without achieving appreciable results. His oratorical style was terse, and to bolster his arguments he would often rely on legal precedents. He tended to proceed cautiously after digesting enormous amounts of information; this careful, deliberate style remained with him for the rest of his career. His training in the law, coupled with his extreme innate cautiousness, led Hull to look for compromise and consensus.[11]

After Wilson won the presidency in 1912, Hull successfully supported lowering tariff rates. The lost revenue would, of course, come from the new legislation, the income tax that he had sponsored. He also favored organized labor, child-labor legislation, and the eight-hour day. However, he was ambivalent toward women's suffrage; in 1916 he voted affirmatively on this legislation but later opposed the Nineteenth Amendment. He followed the same inconsistent pattern on immigration matters. Sometimes he voted to eliminate quotas; at other times he sided with those who advocated restriction. During these debates, he never expressed any religious or racial bigotry against foreigners, nor did he make any anti-Semitic references.[12]

During this period of political maturation, Hull devoted almost all of his energies to congressional pursuits. Indeed, some thought that he had immersed himself so deeply in politics that he had no personal life. One of Hull's House colleagues, John Nance Garner, a Democrat from Texas, predicted that his friend's "chances of getting married were very remote."[13] Yet Hull shattered this prophesy after he met Rosetta "Rose" Frances Witz Whitney, a tall brunette with large dark brown eyes from Staunton, Virginia, a town about 150 miles southwest of Washington, D.C. Frances was born on September 8, 1874. Her father, Isaac Witz, was descended from Austrian Jews; after settling in Staunton he became a well-respected banker and industrialist and served in the Confederate Army. Her mother, Frances Heller, came from a socially prominent family with strong Presbyterian and Episcopalian attachments, and as a child Frances regularly attended the Emanuel Episcopal Church.[14]

Frances was educated in Staunton schools and graduated from Augusta Female Seminary in the class of 1892, but remained there for two additional years to take classes in music, drawing, and oil painting. Later she would recall her stay with fondness. Frances remembered the driving force behind the seminary, Mary Baldwin, as kind, noble, and loving, a woman who set high academic goals on the beautiful, distinctive campus that would later bear her name.[15]

After graduation, Frances moved to Washington, D.C., and married a Mr. Whitney, who often traveled to East Asia on business. It was on one such trip that he vanished mysteriously. After he was declared legally dead, Frances settled his estate and resumed her life as a single woman. Her bearing was erect, her dress conservative, and her demeanor dignified. She met Cordell Hull on a trip to Washington, D.C. They managed their courtship with discretion and opted for a secret wedding, on November 24, 1917. Because of his hectic congressional schedule, there was no time for a honeymoon. Indeed, everything in their lives was subordinated to Hull's career. Frances became more than his domestic partner; she did everything possible to advance his career. Husband and wife developed a political partnership that grew stronger with Hull's increasing stature. The fact that they never had any children allowed them to pursue their single-minded political agenda. Frances, for example, managed campaign headquarters, met voters, and helped to establish the Women's National Democratic Club in the early 1920s. They also regularly attended St. Margaret Episcopal Church on Connecticut Avenue in the capital. Although Frances had been raised in that faith, Cordell had converted from the Baptist Church, recognizing that if he aspired to national office, he would have to switch to the more socially preferable denomination.[16]

Hull supported Wilson's measures leading up to the United States' declaration of war against the Central Powers and tied them in with his own economic beliefs. Barriers to the free flow of commerce fostered war, he believed, and if nations would lower tariffs, peace would prevail. He called for an international trade congress to abolish commercial rivalry and promote trade. Although the administration rejected his proposal, Hull doggedly (and futilely) pressed for a congressional resolution on the matter. After the war, in 1920, he concentrated on winning reelection but gave the League of Nations minimal support, even though the state Democratic party and most Tennessee newspapers favored Wilson's vision. Nationally, this issue was crucial to the Democrats, but Hull nevertheless lost his seat. His allegation that the Republicans out-

spent him was an exaggeration. Voters simply believed that the Democrats had been in power too long, and the people were looking for a
change. The Republican victor, Wynne Clouse, was delighted by his
upset. The loser was stunned.

For the first time in fourteen years, Hull was in search of a job. He
snatched at an offer to become the Democratic National Committee
chairman and was soon concentrating on paying off the party's debt and
forming victory clubs in various states. Wherever he went, he still
stressed lower tariffs and traditional Democratic values. As for the
League of Nations, he ignored it, believing that this emotional issue had
ultimately harmed his party.

Although he did a creditable job as party chairman, the post was
only a temporary one for him. As early as January 1921, he had resolved
to recapture his congressional seat. As he prepared for the next campaign, he and Frances traveled together throughout his district, spending
more time there than Cordell had in many years. He rebuilt his campaign
organization and reminded Democratic women that they had to get out
the vote. Frances' quiet charm won her husband votes. He sought to
create in his constituents the perception that he possessed integrity and
sound judgment. He relied heavily on those positive perceptions, for his
campaigning was uninspired. Stiffness and reserve came much more
naturally to him, and he had never felt comfortable in the presence of
large audiences. To overcome these negative images when meeting an
individual, he would frequently thrust a cigar into one hand and shake
the other as a device for expressing cordiality.

Hull obviously was not charismatic, and as a result his campaigning
was dull. As for his public speaking skills, his slow and ponderous
delivery gave his speeches the tone of a poorly prepared lawyer's argument. His orations also had an unintended—and no doubt unappreci-
ated—comical side. He had a high, lean, rasping voice, and his dental
plates gave him a slight lisp that turned *r*s into *w*s. After his cherished
reciprocal trade agreements programs finally became law, he spoke of
"'weciprocal twade agweements pwogwams.'"[17]

His father lived to witness his son's victory in 1922 and died shortly
afterwards, leaving an estate with a value estimated at between
$200,000 and $300,000. Cordell managed several of the family's prop-

erties, some as far away as Florida. By 1924, he owned six farms himself and was a partner in other ventures. Despite this prosperity, the Hulls lived modestly in a small seven-room apartment at the Carlton Hotel near the White House.

Hull remained national chairman through the presidential convention of 1924, at which he sat through the long, arduous selection of John Davis as his party's nominee and the equally intense platform squabbles. A slim majority eked out a narrow victory over the Ku Klux Klan in its quest to stir up bigotry; the Democrats repudiated Wilson's dream of the League; and the party avoided a violent struggle over prohibition by censuring the Republicans for failing to enforce the Eighteenth Amendment. The divisive 1924 convention caused Hull such great physical and mental anguish that he may have suffered a breakdown in late June. Yet he recovered and left the Democratic party organization far stronger than when he had been appointed. Instead of the $186,000 deficit he had inherited, he left a surplus of $21,000. He had devoted all of his energies to the party, but now he needed to concentrate on his congressional duties.

After attaining national standing as party chair, Hull began to make halting political overtures to Franklin Roosevelt. The congressman had already appointed Eleanor in 1924 to head a platform committee formed to present the viewpoints of women at the Democratic convention. Two years later, he attended several meetings chaired by Roosevelt that gathered powerful Democratic politicians together in order to forge a wider Democratic consensus. Initially Hull did not think that Roosevelt should fill that leadership role. In fact, by the end of 1926, Hull had formed his own group of influential Democratic leaders and included Roosevelt in the group only reluctantly because of his close association with Alfred Smith, who appeared to be the party's likely nominee in the 1928 presidential campaign.[18]

By 1927 Hull had established a wide political base, and he seriously considered challenging Smith for the nomination. His state legislature had already placed its vote behind him when he agreed to a possible draft. With this encouragement, "Hull for President" committees were established in Tennessee as well as other Southern states. Hull hoped that the party might turn to him if Smith lost his bid, but that wish never became a reality. No Southern Democrat had ever received the party's nomination in its almost seventy-year history. Smith won on the first ballot, whereupon Roosevelt pushed Hull's vice-presidential candidacy on the basis of his voting record, his congressional experience, and the regional balance he would bring to the national ticket. Yet this too was not to be, and Hull chose another option. With his increased prestige and the onus of the Depression on the Republican candidate, he ran for and won a Senate seat in 1930.

Hull was looking forward to the next presidential campaign and spoke frequently to Roosevelt during the latter's stops in Washington on his way to Warm Springs. Hull's initial lack of enthusiasm for Roosevelt's candidacy in the summer of 1931 disturbed Louis Howe. The senator was, as always, cautious, but in February 1932, deciding that Roosevelt had the best chance of winning the White House, Hull came out strongly for the New York governor. That winter, when the "stop Roosevelt" drive reached its peak, the governor sought Hull's advice for winning the nomination and even considered him as a potential running mate. Hull lobbied his Senate colleagues to endorse his candidate and worked energetically at the national convention for Roosevelt's victory.[19]

By the time of his appointment to the cabinet, he had positioned himself near the ideological center of his party; he served as a moderator who could bring antagonists together in a spirit of cooperation. His sympathies lay with farmers and small businessmen, and, more broadly, he favored a philosophy of individualism whereby each citizen had to rely on his own efforts to improve his lot. If the free exercise of those liberties was in any way hampered, the government had the right to restore them. He supported low tariffs and the income tax because he believed that those measures restored balance for the public good. A degree of centralization of power was proper, but individual rights were sacred.

His colleagues' views of him were divided. Most congressmen, noting his tireless lobbying on behalf of the bills that interested him, respected his work ethic. No hint of scandal touched him, and there was no suggestion of dereliction or misconduct in office in his quest for national stature. Curiously, except where his particular interests were concerned, he refused to take a stand. During his long congressional tenure, he did not sponsor a single major piece of legislation that bore his name. This unwillingness to commit himself on controversial issues may have troubled some of his colleagues, who viewed it as a character flaw—as a way to avoid making tough decisions. That criticism haunted Hull. As always, he moved with extreme caution, sometimes to a fault. Some of his fellow members of Congress attacked him as a shallow individual who would never make a lasting imprint.[20]

His private life mirrored his public image. He made a fine personal impression with his old-fashioned Southern chivalry and his slow drawl, was strongly religious, and regularly attended church services with his wife. He possessed a rigid sense of morality, was a devoted husband, preferred old friends to suave dilettantes, and had an abiding distaste for social engagements. When given the choice, after a day's work on Capitol Hill, he preferred to spend a quiet evening at home, occasionally enjoying a very mild rye highball.[21]

Though ambitious, he never forgot his political obligations as a loyal Democrat. Comfortable in that role, he had strong ideas of what was right and wrong and sought to fit events and people into that world view. His new task as secretary of state was no exception. He was a provincial being with strong likes and dislikes, a nineteenth-century man who had stepped into the twentieth century without realizing that change was inevitable. His life was marked by a perennial search for order in all things, a quest that was of course ultimately futile. Nevertheless, many Americans related closely to this type of public figure—so much so that Hull was generally acknowledged to be the most popular member of the administration after Roosevelt.

Hull kept everything from the public that could remotely damage his image in their eyes, and this control especially applied to questions about his health. As a young man, he had been a passenger on a train that had stalled in a tunnel, and he had almost suffocated. Thereafter, he dreaded the thought of confinement. His claustrophobia remained a life-long impairment, so much so that he even avoided flying. Hull had smoked a great deal early in his career, but he gave up the habit after the removal of his tonsils. A more serious problem, but one that he kept under control, was a mild case of diabetes.[22]

In the summer of 1932, Hull retained Dr. Matthew Perry of Washington, D.C., as his personal physician. Perry confirmed his patient's diabetic condition and, during his examination, also found tubercular lesions in both lungs. Hull—fearful of the stigma attached to the disease, then known as the white plague—resolved to hide the findings. The possibility of his dying from consumption might have made him unacceptable for national office. By the time he entered the cabinet, over 100,000 hospital beds had been set aside for the victims of this dread illness; one-quarter of all patients died in sanatoriums, and of those released, one-half died within five years.[23]

Roosevelt—who had devoted considerable energy to concealing his own health problems—chose to focus on Hull's attributes and overlook his weaknesses. Indeed the president probably never knew about his appointee's tuberculosis. Even though the two men bonded as political allies, they were not personal friends, and never would be. They respected each other's political acumen, and such a meeting of the minds was essential, in the president's view, for a secretary of state. In the final analysis, Hull was, above all else, a survivor—one who thoroughly understood the pitfalls of his profession. He refused to become entangled with controversial causes and was not likely to make diplomatic blunders. If possible, at the start of the New Deal Hull was more politically circumspect than his boss.

Hull visited the State Department for the first time just two days before taking office. Even then, characteristically, he did not participate in any detailed briefings, preferring that the Democrats first officially take over the apparatus of government. After the inauguration, he took command of the imposing State, War and Navy Building, which was situated next to the White House and which, by 1933, in fact housed only the State Department. Completed in 1888, the building, with its many porticoes and pillars, suggested the baroque palaces of Austria and Germany. Outside a battery of antiquated cannon stood guard. The building squatted on more than five acres of grounds, lawns, and terraces. Five aboveground stories rose behind its granite walls. Within sprawled ten acres of floor area and almost two miles of corridors, which were twelve feet wide and paved with alternating one-foot squares of black slate and white marble. The spiral stairways featured steps of gray granite. Each one of the 553 rooms was entered through large two-inch-thick wooden latticed swinging doors, which suggested nothing so much as the entrance to a western saloon.

Despite its massive size and grandeur, the State Department still retained the intimate atmosphere of a private club—one whose members knew each others' pedigrees. There were no guards or outward signs of security. Charlie, the lone elderly doorman, moonlighted as a waiter at several Washington mansions. In between carrying coded documents, Negro messengers studied law in the corridors and even saw clients and offered legal opinions there.[24]

When the new appointee entered his second-story office, he looked out across the Mall toward the Washington Monument from a large mahogany desk in the center of the room. He had two phones, one connecting him to his staff and the other to the White House. The office was furnished with chairs for visitors, a large fireplace, and portraits of presidents Abraham Lincoln, Ulysses Grant, and Benjamin Harrison on the walls.[25]

Hull quickly established the daily routine that he would follow throughout his first term in office. Arriving at work by 9:00 A.M., he invariably faced a busy schedule. He expected his associates to bring unanswered questions to his attention at the Monday morning staff meeting, at which they reviewed current events and sought to formulate appropriate responses. When particularly complex issues required his attention, the secretary invited specialists to provide background information or voice expert opinions.

Early in his tenure he formed the habit of meeting on Sunday morning with his chief advisers for several hours. Although no one took notes, these sessions served to designate priorities for the coming week. Hull left for home at noon, while his staff sought solutions to the issues raised during the morning.

His sole source of exercise was croquet; he played the game several times a week in the late afternoon, if the weather permitted, at Henry Stimson's magnificent estate near Rock Creek Park in the northwest section of the city. The secretary found the sport challenging and usually played with members of his immediate staff. Critics later sarcastically labeled this group the "croquet clique."[26]

As he had done since his early days as a Tennessee lawyer, Hull read a tremendous amount of material and weighed it repeatedly. He acted slowly, sometimes refusing to make any decision at all, for he dreaded the possibility of being wrong. In matters of little consequence this unwillingness to proceed was immaterial; however, on questions of major significance, Hull's inability to make decisions could worsen already explosive situations.[27]

The secretary was uncomfortable in the vanguard and worked best behind the scenes. He had spent his life trying to avoid controversy and had become influential by rising above petty political bickering. Hull had always won respect for his objectivity and his calm demeanor in public. He preferred to maintain his composure, believing that open displays of emotion hardened positions and made compromise more difficult. Protracted public debate, he felt, settled very little and sometimes resulted in enduring hatreds.

The public never saw Hull's crude side. As a child, he had learned to cuss profusely, and his was probably the foulest mouth in the cabinet. Moffat recalled one explosion, during which the secretary's Southern manners vanished completely: "It was refreshing to watch oath after oath pour out of his rather saintlike countenance and then to have him smile and say, 'It's not more than once every six months that I use language like that!'"[28]

Even though he had become a national figure, Hull was incredibly insecure. Some thought that his sense of inferiority arose from his rural upbringing, his relatively poor education compared to that of his Ivy League subordinates, and his limited reading. Nothing satisfied him more than receiving favorable press headlines; nothing humiliated him more than public criticism.[29]

Smarting from speculation in the press that he was fading to secondary status within the government, Hull confronted Moffat on October 23, 1933, to ask if the media were deliberately attacking him or if some correspondents were merely voicing their independent judgment. Moffat averred that this bias was "scarcely worth worrying over as the Hearst press was largely discounted in the public eye anyway." Moffat later observed in his diary: "Apparently the Secretary honeycombs the papers and is far more sensitive to personal press attack than I had anticipated."[30]

If Hull had initially presumed that he would have the opportunity to select deserving Democrats for positions in the foreign service, he was soon rudely awakened. Overnight, his expectations for political plums disappeared in the face of Roosevelt's firm hold on the reins of patronage, but he still was "literally swamped with office seekers." Lobbyists angered him so much that he sometimes referred to them as "whores." He was not temperamentally suited to make personnel decisions, and professional diplomats played upon that reluctance by convincing him to save as many career officers as possible. That approach suited the secretary, who practically abdicated his responsibility for making diplomatic appointments. He preferred to have others do the hiring, firing, and transferring, and as a result not one major State Department official owed allegiance to the secretary of state at the start of his tenure.[31]

The secretary was never suited to the management of his department's large bureaucracy, but the president solved that problem with the appointment of William Phillips as the new under secretary of state. According to Hull, Phillips "possessed splendid capacity and character and was loyal to friends and to principles. In whatever position he served he was unusually efficient."[32] These qualities were evident throughout Phillips's life and career. When his appointment was announced, professional diplomats applauded it. Tall, lean, and possessed of a high forehead, a long nose, and carefully parted hair, Phillips was faultlessly tailored; with his polished Bostonian accent, he was the model career foreign service officer, striving for a well-trained diplomatic corps against those who wished to use the State Department for political patronage.

His roots were deeply buried in the nineteenth century. He had been born into a famous New England Social Register family on May 30, 1878. His father died when he was seven, leaving his mother to supervise his formative years. He attended private schools in Boston until the age of eighteen and then entered Harvard, three years before Roosevelt. After graduation, Phillips continued there in law school for two and a half years without obtaining his degree.

Instead, he chose to serve as private secretary to Joseph Choate, U.S. ambassador to Great Britain. After completing that assignment, he was transferred to Peking in the winter of 1905 as the second secretary of the embassy; two years later he returned to Washington as an East Asian specialist. He enjoyed his post in the capital and became a member of Teddy Roosevelt's "tennis cabinet". In 1908 he married Caroline Astor Drayton, who came from a similar aristocratic background, and they had five children. During his years at the department, he gained valuable administrative experience in Latin American affairs. He briefly left the foreign service to work at Harvard as an administrator in 1912, but this job lasted only until President Wilson offered him a special assignment in Mexico, then in the midst of revolutionary upheaval. When he finished this task, the president selected him for other positions.

Phillips and Franklin Roosevelt became acquainted during the Wilson presidency because their offices in the State, War and Navy Building were only a few rooms apart. They enjoyed each other's company because they came from similar backgrounds; in addition their wives were friends, moving in the same elite social circles in New York. After Warren Harding assumed the presidency, Phillips, a staunch Republican, continued to hold a succession of influential posts: minister to Holland, under secretary of state, and ambassador to Belgium. He was also the first U.S. minister to Canada. He resigned from government service in 1930, partly to protest his party's high tariff policies and partly because he and his wife wanted to raise their children in the comfort of Boston society.

Phillips had not expected to serve in a Democratic administration. He had enjoyed Roosevelt's companionship during the war years, but he had never dreamed that his friend would become president. Even though Phillips had some reservations about Roosevelt's ability to serve as chief executive, he had nevertheless made a substantial campaign contribution.[33] Shortly before the inauguration, the president-elect called him from Albany to offer him the under-secretaryship. Roosevelt would not accept no for an answer: "I have a great deal of respect for the man and his ability, and I believe that he performs the duties of his position in a most commendable way."[34]

Phillips fit neatly into Hull's order, for the two shared the desire to reduce trade barriers. Phillips also focused his diplomatic skills, honed during his years in the diplomatic corps, on European matters. The under secretary also knew how to weave his way through the bureaucratic maze that so baffled Hull. Phillips, in addition, enjoyed social engagements and so relieved Hull of the unpleasant chore of representing the department at numerous offical functions. Most important, Phillips made Hull feel at ease. He was an ally—someone to be trusted.

Despite his claims to be an expert in financial and economic matters, Hull had no federal managerial experience and little experience in resolving fiscal problems. If he were going to appoint deserving Democrats, he would have to enlarge his department's budget, but he showed no interest in the vital function of creating and managing budgets.

It was to Wilbur Carr, who was celebrating his fortieth anniversary in the diplomatic bureaucracy in 1933, that that complicated task fell. The son of a poor Ohio farmer, Carr passed his civil service exam in 1892, whereupon the State Department hired him as a clerk. From that humble beginning, he had advanced to the position of director of the Consular Service in 1909. In that capacity he personally evaluated each consul's performance. If a consul passed his exacting test, he was rewarded with promotions; if not, he was demoted. Although he worked energetically, some disapproved of the extent of his authority, for he did not serve abroad in a diplomatic post until 1916. After returning from his overseas assignment, he resumed his administrative duties, and in 1924, having made himself seem indispensable, he was promoted to assistant secretary of state. With his neat and conservative dress, bald head, a graying mustache, and large piercing eyes seen through thick glasses, Carr exemplified the professional diplomat. A staunch Republican, Carr, like Phillips, worried about Roosevelt's election because he too questioned his leadership abilities. During World War I they had had offices on the same corridor, and even though Roosevelt thought that Carr had done his job well during the Wilson years, the now–assistant secretary remained skeptical about Roosevelt well into his first term because of the president's haphazard administrative practices.[35]

Carr's first loyalty was always to the State Department. There had been cutbacks in the federal payroll, and this fiscal austerity had forced many to leave the foreign service. Carr fought to obtain appropriations, but when he asked Hull to testify before the congressional committees charged with making allocations to the department, the secretary refused. Even after economic conditions had improved, Hull showed no interest in restoring budget cuts. It was left to others to lead that fight.

Thus the State Department budget in 1932 was $18 million; a year later it had plunged by $4.5 million; by 1936, it had only reached $16 million. With a 15 percent cut in salary for all government employees and deep reductions in overseas allowances, those who could afford to remain were never threatened. But the first promotions and new appointments did not come until 1935, and even then the diplomatic corps still appealed to a small, select, and largely affluent group.

Most State Department employees held onto their jobs by carrying increased workloads, but the staff in the field was severely affected by the inadequate funding. Not only did many of those posted abroad leave the diplomatic corps, but those who remained suffered a real loss in wages of between 35 and 55 percent owing to the depreciated dollar and the reduction in allowances. All that remained were 730 civil service employees and another 73 outside merit employment. Indeed, at the start of the New Deal the foreign service, already a relatively small bureaucracy, was shrinking even more under the pressure of retirements and budget cuts.[36]

Although two of Carr's priorities were obtaining increased staffing and a larger budget, he also handled immigration matters. In this area he fought against increasing immigration quotas to the United States. Carr believed that in order to become a respected member of the diplomatic club he would first have to become a fervent restrictionist. He had helped draft the immigration policy of the 1920s, which generally reflected the exclusionary practices of its time. After the Depression struck, the Hoover administration promulgated new visa requirements under which potential citizens had to pass a test that sought to establish that they were not "likely to become public charges" (the so-called LPC test). The murkiness of the concept of LPC was never dispelled, nor was the rule enforced consistently, but Carr insisted that it generally be interpreted to the applicant's disadvantage. Once European Jews started to apply in large numbers, he opposed their admission because of his exclusionary beliefs and his anti-Semitism. (In August 1924, for example, he had confided to his diary that Detroit was full of "dust, smoke, dirt, Jews.") Wealthy Jews who dressed appropriately were barely passable, but admission of poorer ones (whom he called "kikes") was unthinkable.[37]

With the advent of the New Deal, Secretary of Labor Frances Perkins directed her department's Bureau of Immigration to help German Jews qualify for visas on humanitarian grounds, but the State Department objected because of the opposition voiced by labor unions. As long as American consuls would not relax LPC rules for visas, Perkins was stymied. In addition, Carr had a powerful backer in William Phillips, for he shared Carr's opinions about Jews and made similar anti-Semitic references to them. His diary contained numerous derogatory entries, such as the notations that Atlantic City was "infested with Jews" and that on weekends "slightly clothed Jews and Jewesses" flocked to the beach.[38]

Hull seldom became involved in immigration matters since he as a rule avoided controversial subjects; besides, he spent a considerable portion of 1933 outside the country. His first foreign assignment was attendance at the London Economic Conference. The Hoover administration had originally planned this international gathering in the hope that it would help alleviate the worldwide depression. At first, Roosevelt warmly endorsed the idea, but as the opening of the conference drew closer, his enthusiasm and interest dampened. He had talked with the British about preferential trade relations, with the French concerning currency stabilization, and with other nations regarding a moratorium on World War I debt payments owed to the United States. Yet, since Roosevelt did not take any definitive stand on any of these topics or discuss them with Hull, American foreign economic policy remained largely undefined and world leaders were confused.

Roosevelt further impaired Hull's effectiveness by his selection of an ill-informed delegation that departed on May 31 without a clear purpose. To compound problems, the president decided to take his first vacation, sailing off the coast of New England with friends and family, during the conference. How could the secretary of state confer with his chief executive over complicated international economic issues when the president's first priority was relaxation?[39]

Hull hoped to offer his program for lowering tariff barriers as the American contribution to the meeting, but Roosevelt crushed that plan on June 7 by telegraphing the secretary at sea that the White House would not ask Congress for trade legislation that year. Hull recalled this bleak moment: "I left for London with the highest of hopes, but arrived with empty hands."[40]

The meeting opened in the midst of worldwide economic chaos. Each nation voiced its government's solution for recovery, but with so many competing and divergent opinions, the participants found no common ground for agreement. Frustration rose. The deadlock had to be broken, but no delegate could offer a solution. One day after the conference convened, a member of the American staff wired the president about Hull's inability to cope: "The Secretary was in a condition which can only be described as 'complete collapse' and had written his immediate resignation to be telegraphed to you. I have rarely seen a man more broken up, and his condition was reflected in that of Mrs. Hull, who literally wept all night. I did what I could to soothe the Secretary and told him that I was going to cable you on my own responsibility."[41]

This bleak situation was further complicated when Raymond Moley, identified as the principal architect of Roosevelt's Brain Trust, decided to become involved in the proceedings. Moley had met Roosevelt during his governorship and later assisted in the presidential campaign. After Roosevelt triumphed, he appointed Moley an assistant secretary of state to serve at the pleasure of the White House. Moley at first minimized the value of the London meeting while searching for domestic answers to the Depression's problems—a nationalistic viewpoint that contradicted the State Department's quest for international solutions as well as Hull's own fervent passion for lowering trade barriers. Since the secretary regarded Moley as an interloper encroaching on the power of a cabinet officer, and, in any case one who had chosen to involve himself in a hopeless situation, the State Department as a whole came to resent his presence.

Nevertheless, Moley believed in his ability to present positive recommendations to the conference. He met with Roosevelt, and even though the president did not agree to any specific proposals, Moley announced his immediate departure for London. The trip created a sensation. He left the president on June 21, and during his seven-day voyage the delegates could do little but wait and speculate about his forthcoming proposals. Much of their heightened optimism could be traced to Moley himself, for he had helped create the false impression that he was carrying special White House instructions. Few realized that their hopes were unfounded. For the time being Moley held center stage, as the world awaited his pronouncements.

While Moley rushed to Europe, Roosevelt continued his sailing holiday off the New England coast. Yet his absence did not alter his stipulation that no one, including the members of his Brain Trust, could take independent action. That privilege was reserved for the president alone, and by the end of June, he was publicly repudiating the solutions being advanced for the issues discussed at the meeting. At a late June news conference he told reporters of his opposition to nonpayment of war debts, tariff reductions, and currency stabilization. His thinking was almost completely in the negative, objecting to everything on the conference's agenda.

Moley, not realizing the degree of presidential antipathy for the gathering, arrived to a spectacular reception; he dominated discussions while Hull was pushed aside. Hull was certain that his subordinate had planned to humiliate him, and Moley attempted to comfort the secretary, but without success. Despite this ill will, Moley negotiated a nebulous currency stabilization agreement that did not in fact bind the United States to any concrete action. Rather than accept even this vague declaration, Roosevelt repudiated any multilateral action in his "bombshell message" of July 3. When this declaration reached London, the European delegates' anger boiled over. To be sure, the gathering had never had a chance to achieve constructive results, but now the Europeans could vent their frustration by condemning the president for the meeting's collapse. Roosevelt, unaware of the hostile reception accorded his message, had undermined both his personal and America's national prestige.

Furious at Roosevelt's action, European leaders sought to end the meeting and brand him as the cause of its failure. But Hull, for the first time exerting his authority and calling upon the political acumen that had served him so well back home, took charge. He sent Moley home and kept the delegates in session for three more weeks to cool the antagonism directed against the United States. The secretary returned in August and met with Roosevelt at Hyde Park. The president—who by that time had come to realize that his actions had been presumptuous and that Hull had saved him from great embarrassment—warmly praised Hull for his efforts at London.

Although the likelihood of producing positive results at London had been remote from the outset, Roosevelt had destroyed any slight chance of success the meeting might have had. He had initially helped to create false illusions with his early private talks with European leaders, had sent an inferior delegation without any direction, and had rejected Moley's harmless stabilization declaration in order to avoid any blunders that could be laid at the steps of the White House. His unwillingness to ask for tariff legislation rendered Hull's initiative useless, but the White House did not perceive this. Instead, Howe felt that the secretary himself was the cause of the failure because he had gone to the conference without any plan except for lowering trade barriers.

Hull, in turn—blind to his own inadequate understanding of international economic conditions—bitterly blamed the White House for the fiasco. While at the conference, Hull accused the president of sabotaging the conference and sarcastically admitted to an acquaintance, "I am a dumb fellow, but despite my dumbness the same idea has occured [*sic*] to me."[42]

Since neither the president nor the secretary had openly attacked one another, Moley was left as the most vulnerable scapegoat. He left London dejected, but before departing he unwisely used diplomatic codes to cable Roosevelt and criticize most of the members of the delegation. With the failure of these talks, Moley had clearly outlived his usefulness, and he soon fell from presidential grace. Although he was to play some additional minor roles after returning from Europe, Moley saw his ready access to the White House slowly erode. He correctly recognized that this development signaled the end of his influence, and he quietly left government service in September 1933 to pursue a publishing career in New York.[43]

Hull welcomed Moley's resignation. The secretary's supporters in Washington had obtained Moley's unflattering comments about the delegation to show Hull, who replied with his own outlandish accusations: "You can never begin to imagine the difficulties and disadvantages that faced me at every step almost, after leaving our shores." The secretary had "discovered that carefully laid plans to undermine and destroy me were being systematically carried out." However, according to Hull, Moley had overplayed his hand and both Roosevelt and the delegates had repudiated him. As the secretary saw it, Moley had pretended "to be my friend and loyal as well, while at the same time secretly sending back to Washington anything that might discredit me." Hull had tried to negotiate several minor agreements to salvage something from the London talks, but his chances were bleak: "According to all reports and indications, I have been spied on by subordinates from the time I left America."[44] In fact Hull greatly exaggerated the allegations of insubordination. Yet the secretary never forgot or forgave, and in years to come, whenever the discussion turned to Moley, Hull, whose use of profanity was well known, labeled him an "SOB."[45]

At almost the instant that Moley finished clearing off his desk, the secretary telephoned R. Walton Moore on September 19 to offer him the vacated slot of assistant secretary of state. Moore took the oath of office the next afternoon. Hull fondly memorialized his relationship with Moore: "He was a person of unusual ability and high purpose, a profound student of both domestic and international affairs, and possessed character and patriotism of the highest order."[46]

Tall, well built, and bald with gray-blue eyes, soft spoken with a slight drawl and a Southern sense of chivalry, Moore at seventy-four was a confirmed bachelor who had never learned to drive. He commuted to work in his chauffeured Packard, regularly arriving before 9:00 A.M. Moffat assessed his worth: "He is a delightful old gentleman . . . who was for many years a member of Congress where he served on the Foreign Affairs Committee. His approach to problems is very similar to that of the Secretary and I feel that the two together should make a congenial working team. In so far as I know, he is not being given any special duties but works on individual problems which may be referred to him."[47]

Moore was born on February 26, 1857, the oldest and only son among nine children. He grew up in a three-story colonial house with fourteen rooms on a hillside one block from the center of Fairfax, Virginia. His father served as a lieutenant in the Mexican War, and in the Civil War he was a major in the Confederate Army, assigned to the quartermaster corps. Although prosperous before the bloody conflict, by the end of the fighting, he had lost everything, including his slaves. When peace resumed, he quickly recovered by working as deputy clerk of the court in Fairfax and establishing his own successful law office. Moore's mother also had a distinguished lineage. Her ancestors had fought in the American Revolution, and one of them, Lewis Morris of New York, was a signer of the Declaration of Independence. His wife was related to another prominent family in that state, one that eventually included Franklin Roosevelt, a fact known to only a few. Moore sometimes chuckled privately that he served at the pleasure of a distant cousin.

Young Moore received an excellent education, first being tutored by his mother and then attending day school. In 1872 he enrolled in Episcopal High School, one of the best in the South, and he boarded there for five years. The academy's headmaster, Dr. Launcelot Minor Blackford, insisted that his charges practice their religion, learn academic skills, and understand the value of public service. Moore won a medal for debating, held down a starting position on the baseball team, and was well liked by his peers. After receiving his diploma, he attended the University of Virginia, where, by his own admission, he joined a social fraternity and led a "reckless life." Rather than complete college, he settled in his hometown and worked as the superintendent of the public high school while studying law in his father's office. After a year of reading law, he passed the bar in 1880, promptly started trying cases, and soon became active in local politics. Even though his county had a strong political organization, Moore carried the label of independent Democrat throughout his career. He was not beholden to any machine, owed no debts to any bosses.

As his legal practice flourished, so did his professional reputation. He capitalized on his good fortune by running for the Virginia senate in 1887 and won by a narrow margin. Although one of the youngest members of that body, he frequently spoke out on current issues and served on the finance committee. He decided not to run for reelection in order to devote full time to his law practice. His efforts resulted in his firm becoming one of the largest practices in the county, specializing in railroad law and eventually becoming counsel to the Railroad and Steamship Companies of the South. Acknowledging his professional standing, his colleagues elected Moore president of the state bar association in 1911.[48]

By the end of World War I he had grown tired of the legal grind. When a vacancy in the House of Representatives opened up in 1919, he was named to fill the seat and won elections to return him to it for the next decade. Just as he took up his duties, Moore recounted in his autobiography, Carlos Bee, a Texas representative "who was about the ugliest white man I ever saw," saluted Moore as "Judge." Moore asked why he had used that title and Bee replied, "'It is just a Texas habit. When we meet a very good-looking man we call him "General," and when we meet an ugly man we call him "Judge."' I at once said that I wanted to shake hands with the Chief Justice."[49] The nickname stuck for the rest of his life, causing many to assume mistakenly that he had sat on the bench.

As leaders on the Democratic side of the House, Moore and Hull became political allies as well as personal friends. Both were Southern lawyers with similar interests. Moore devoted his energies to international relations, joined the Committee on Foreign Affairs in 1923, and rose to become its second-ranking Democrat. He enthusiastically supported Wilson's efforts to join the League of Nations, American entrance into the World Court, Philippine independence, lower tariffs, and prohibition. At the same time he remained attentive to his constituents' needs, supporting, for example, the building of the Memorial Bridge to connect the Virginia suburbs with the capital. Poor health forced Moore to leave Congress in 1931. Although taking note of the despair caused by the Great Depression, he paid little attention to the 1932 presidential contest. He knew that neither party would fulfill its campaign pledges and thought that the only solution to the national dilemma was to form a coalition government along the lines of the British model. Questioning the abilities of both Hoover and Roosevelt, he wished for a candidate like Winston Churchill.[50]

After Roosevelt won, Moore regarded his election not as a Democratic triumph but as "a general expression of desire for a change based upon the universal depression and discontent." Personally he held Roosevelt "in high regard," but he doubted that anyone could bring about fundamental changes in the American economy. If the Democrats brought about a gradual recovery, that was all that could be expected. Only the exercise of extraordinary executive powers could prevent catastrophe. If this did not happen, Moore feared the formation of a new party composed of revolutionaries and radicals who would take control of the government as early as the next general election.[51]

By the spring of 1933 Moore had stopped being a bystander and had decided to look for a government position. Roosevelt's bold initiatives captivated him, but Moore still worried about the tremendously high unemployment level. The United States, he declared, must export more goods so as to be able to hire additional workers. As more and more positions in the State Department were filled and his name was repeatedly passed over, he became disenchanted, complaining that the major jobs went to a small coterie controlled by Postmaster General Farley and the Brain Trust. Yet, with his appointment as assistant secretary of state confirmed, his negative opinion of the selection process vanished. Once in office, he scrupulously guarded his friend Hull from various kinds of assaults, particularly while Hull was abroad. For example, when the Hearst press accused Hull of not being able to command his agency's affairs, it was Moore who refuted the allegations.[52]

Besides defending Hull, Moore helped shape such foreign policy initiatives as the recognition of the Soviet Union. Hull had briefly participated in the preliminary discussions from the middle of October 1933 until the beginning of November. He and Roosevelt differed sharply over the question of recognition. The State Department staff objected to taking the initiative. The White House, on the other hand, wanted to resume diplomatic ties and encouraged a national debate to reach a consensus on this issue. The secretary knew that he would be out of the country while much of the discussion proceeded, and he chose Moore to articulate the department's more cautious position. The secretary had Moore meet Maxim Litvinov's train at Union Station when the Russian negotiator arrived in the capital. During an early talk Moore jokingly invited the Soviet diplomat to go to church with him. Litvinov laughed and declined the opportunity.[53]

Roosevelt countered Moore's expected opposition by assigning William Bullitt to assist in the bargaining sessions because of his specialization in Soviet affairs and his advocacy of recognition. Bullitt was an enigma. His middle initial, C., stood for Christian—a description that his enemies had cause to question. A bon vivant in every sense of the word, well informed, highly intelligent, and in many instances incisive, Bullitt obscured these attributes by his limited grasp of nuance and his lack of tolerance and scruples. During the talks Bullitt and Moore worked closely together and became good friends. The pace of the discussions accelerated after Hull left the country, and on November 17, Roosevelt announced that the United States had opened diplomatic ties with the Soviet Union.[54]

Although Moore and Bullitt shared Virginia ancestry, Bullitt was a much younger man and of only medium height. Well traveled and an avid sportsman, he had a fit and distinguished appearance with fair skin and blue eyes, and, like Moore, he was practically bald. Bullitt had been born in early 1891 into an affluent and socially prominent Philadelphia family that traced its lineage back to George Washington. His family was extremely close and attended the Episcopal Church. As a young man he traveled extensively in Europe, and he spoke fluent French and proficient German. He attended the fashionable DeLancy School, where he won several prizes for both scholastic achievement and extracurricular activities. After receiving his high school diploma, he enrolled at Yale University, where he compiled an exceptional record, was named to Phi Beta Kappa, and served as editor of the *Yale News,* president of the dramatic society, and captain of the debate team. His classmates recognized him as the "most brilliant" senior in the class of 1912. He went on for a brief period to Harvard Law School but soon decided against a legal career, thus ending his formal education.

His background of privilege and achievement contributed significantly to the formation of Bullitt's personality. Unquestionably intelligent, self-assured, and a delightful host, he was as comfortable in a group as he was alone, and he remained loyal over the years to a wide circle of friends. He came from a well-to-do family, acquired expensive tastes, and could afford to indulge most of them. He appreciated classical music, particularly Mozart and Wagner, often led a chamber quartet, and frequently sang duets with his mother.

Yet these desirable attributes masked glaring weaknesses. The decisions that he made were black and white; he seldom compromised and was tenacious in battling his opponents. He had little patience for individuals who did not quickly comprehend his points; such people bored him and did not deserve his notice. If he felt that he was right, he followed his course wherever it led, no matter who was hurt, including himself. He was sometimes flamboyant and played the active, overly emotional romantic. This disposition led to exaggerations and gave free rein to an imagination that tended to embellish stories. His early dislike of the British, for example, grew with each minor incident over the years that gave him cause to turn distaste into hatred.

Under these circumstances, Bullitt had to find a job that permitted him to maintain his independence and creativity. He decided on newspaper work and became a reporter for the Philadelphia *Public Ledger.* He happened to be on vacation in Russia at the outbreak of World War I and filed stories of the spreading conflict. By 1917 he was respected for his insightful reporting and had won a reputation as an expert on European affairs. During this interim he married within his social class, while heading the *Ledger* office in Washington. During his tour of duty in the capital, Bullitt became friends with Colonel Edward House, President Wilson's confidential adviser. Their association brought Bullitt within the president's circle, and because of his deep interest in European affairs, he had joined the foreign service by the time the United States entered the war. He worked energetically in the European division and especially monitored the Bolshevik revolution. He doggedly endorsed a Soviet-American alliance, even though Wilson and his diplomatic advisers ignored the proposal.

Despite these rebuffs, Bullitt persisted in this recommendation. He attended the 1919 Paris peace conference as a diplomatic adviser, hoping to expand his role and helping develop a policy that would strengthen U.S.-Russian bonds. His chance to influence these relations emerged when Colonel House recommended him for a secret mission to the Soviet Union. At the age of twenty-seven, Bullitt slipped out of Paris in late February with instructions to investigate revolutionary conditions. But upon his arrival he tried to negotiate his own preliminary peace plan with the Bolshevik leadership based on the new regime's accepting the enormous czarist foreign debt and making territorial concessions. He returned to France with a draft of his plan, but once more Wilson paid no attention to his suggestions. Left with no recourse, Bullitt resigned, disappointed and disheartened.

Bullitt bitterly severed his diplomatic ties with the government, but he was not yet finished with the Wilson administration. When opponents in the Senate searched in 1919 for information with which to defeat the president's plea for the League of Nations, Bullitt freely stepped forward and gave damaging testimony before the Foreign Relations Committee against the president's concessions. His evidence was not crucial, but by demonstrating his willingness to inform on others and assist the Republican opposition, he proved himself indiscreet, erratic, and untrustworthy. He never understood the full significance of his decision to testify; nevertheless, it was a betrayal that many Wilson supporters refused to forgive.

For the next twelve years Bullitt absented himself from politics. For most of that time he lived abroad. He divorced his first wife in 1923; married Louise Bryant, widow of the American Communist John Reed, in 1923; divorced her in 1926; and took custody of their daughter Anne, his only child. He became known as a lady's man and had affairs with such well-known women as Eleanor "Cissy" Patterson, a wealthy mid-westerner who owned the *Washington Herald*. He also pursued his writing by publishing his only novel in 1926 and collaborating with Sigmund Freud five years later on a book about Wilson.

After over a decade of voluntary political exile, Bullitt reappeared by supporting Roosevelt's candidacy and contributing $1,000 to the nominee. The president-elect, impressed by Bullitt's knowledge of European affairs, dispatched him as an unofficial emissary to the Continent to examine the debt situation. Bullitt deliberately leaked word of his mission to the press and once again was the center of attention. After the inauguration many Democrats recalled his earlier testimony against Wilson; Phillips in particular resented him and had low expectations of his future worth. Roosevelt, however, swept aside these warnings and on April 20 appointed him a special assistant to the secretary of state, a position that did not require congressional confirmation.

Bullitt learned how to garner the support that counted most. The president already respected his brilliance. Bullitt went to the 1933 London Economic Conference attached to the U.S. delegation and there won Hull's confidence. Hull's opinion was reinforced when Bullitt and Moore became intimate, and Bullitt's ability to win these major supporters guaranteed him a prominent place in the State Department. Bullitt also happened to live at the Carlton Hotel, a situation that gave him additional opportunities to confer with Hull.

Because of this connection to the secretary and the confidence that Roosevelt had shown in Bullitt, he had been designated the first U.S. ambassador to the Soviet Union even before the recognition talks had been completed. Having fought in vain for a Soviet-American alliance under the Wilson government, Bullitt had dreamed about bringing the two giants closer together at a future date. By the end of 1933 he had helped to establish relations with the USSR and now had an opportunity to advance the cause about which he had preached for so long.[55]

Hull witnessed Bullitt's talents firsthand only at the start of their association, for when the secretary returned from England late in the summer, he had time to take part in the preliminary bargaining with the Russians. However, a more important task soon faced him: planning for the upcoming inter-American conference at Montevideo, Uruguay, toward the end of 1933. He recalled in his memoirs that many friends had warned him to stay in the capital, but that he had replied, "I feel I must go. We are going to start international cooperation right down here with our neighbors."[56]

This statement was another example of Hull's efforts to rewrite the past from his own perspective, for as the meeting in Uruguay approached, if he had had the choice, he would have stayed at home. The secretary initially viewed the trip as a goodwill gesture and yet another opportunity to promote his trade program. By late September, however, doubts about the success of the meeting had crept into his mind, and throughout October, at the urging of his chief advisers, he asked the president for a postponement. Roosevelt dismissed these objections, insisting that the secretary of state go and thereby, ironically, presenting him with one of his greatest triumphs. The president announced that Hull would be the first secretary of state to serve as a delegate to a Pan-American meeting while in office.

Hull worried that another diplomatic embarrassment would further lower his prestige. Some departmental personnel searched for excuses to avoid undertaking the mission, considering the chances of a productive gathering to be slim. This skepticism within the State Department might have been a blessing, for when the delegates were eventually chosen, they were primarily professional diplomats who were obliged to support Hull's proposals. Shortly before the U.S. delegation sailed from New York on November 9, Roosevelt announced that he had dispatched Hull to broaden hemispheric understanding. Two days later the delegation boarded the *American Legion,* a liner whose peeling paint was a metaphor for its owners' faltering financial condition.

Just before leaving, Hull contradicted the White House's earlier pronouncement by telling reporters that economic issues would play a major role at the conference, for he intended to call for a reciprocal trade agreement program. His public utterances, however, did not coincide with his private thoughts. Skeptical about the possibility of achieving substantial results because of the degree of hemispheric political and economic uncertainty, he planned to attend only a few sessions, appoint a replacement as chief delegate, and return home on a goodwill tour.

As an adviser, Hull had selected Ernest Gruening, a prominent newspaperman with experience in Latin American affairs. As Gruening later (and colorfully) recalled, Hull told him that the sole purpose of the conference was to make friends: "Ah'm against intervention . . . but what am Ah goin' to do when chaos breaks out in one of those countries, and armed bands go woamin' awound, burnin', pillagin' and murdewin Amewicans? How can I tell mah people we cain't intervene?" Hull worried that if he came out against intervention, the Hearst papers would attack him: "Wemember . . . Mr. Woosevelt and Ah have to be weelected."[57]

Before Hull arrived in Montevideo in late November, he had used his charm to win over the other delegates aboard ship. His attentiveness flattered them, and he decided to continue this approach upon his arrival. In so doing, he allayed Latin American suspicions, and the Latin Americans came to perceive Hull as a warm, sympathetic elder states-man. In contrast to the small delegations calling on the U.S. group, the secretary paid his respects accompanied only by an interpreter, James Dunn. Spanish names still proved an insurmountable obstacle for the secretary, though. He called the Chilean Foreign Minister, Miguel Cruchaga, "Mr. Chicago," and his Argentine equivalent, Carlos Saavedra Lamas, "Mr. Savannah."

Hull's style meshed well with his tactics. He knew that Argentina must come to support his trade resolution or his chances for broader international approval would be severely impaired. To win that nation's concurrence, the secretary needed to reach an accord with Saavedra Lamas—without question the strongest and most controversial personal-ity at the gathering, and the leader of the South American movement for closer ties with Europe. Easily recognizable by his five-inch-high, stiffly starched collar, he received from some delegates the sarcastic nickname John Collar. His hair and mustache were dyed red, and he was a chain smoker who would nervously puff a few times on a cigarette and then carelessly toss it over his shoulder without concern for where it landed. These idiosyncrasies aside, no one questioned his ability to carry his point in any arena.

Hull needed Saavedra Lamas's support, and the Argentine minister wanted the United States to sign his peace pact, an action that would give him greater prestige in the Western Hemisphere and within the League of Nations. Thanks to Hull's tact and perseverance the two men reached an agreement. Hull seconded Argentina's peace declaration, and when he introduced his trade resolution, Saavedra Lamas backed it.

Saavedra Lamas and Hull indeed triumphed, but their agreements were not the best-remembered act of the gathering; center state was taken by a nonintervention declaration holding that no American nation had the right to intervene internally or externally in the affairs of another. Representatives of the Caribbean and Central American nations dramatically brought this proposition before the meeting and used the session to denounce Yankee military occupations. Hull sat through the assault. Since he did not speak Spanish and refused to wear headphones, he understood only the broad outlines of what was said. Undaunted by the nationalistic rhetoric, he informed his audience that "no government need fear from any intervention on the part of the United States under the Roosevelt Administration." He received warm applause for his pledge and signed the declaration, with the reservation that his government must continue to observe its international treaty obligations.

When Roosevelt became aware of the steadily mounting degree of favorable publicity being accorded the conference, he wired the delegation to propose the immediate creation of an agency with $5 million in U.S. funding to erect radio stations and landing field lights on both South American coastlines. Hull rejected the suggestion because it smacked of "dollar diplomacy," an anathema to the delegates. He failed to mention that he was loath to give credit to the White House after it had tried to restrict his freedom of action.[58]

Roosevelt had given Hull permission to present his trade ideas at Montevideo, but after the secretary returned home, the president minimized the importance of Hull's resolution. Meeting with reporters the day after the secretary had first introduced his program, Roosevelt told them that the chances for the enactment of any general tariff proposals were remote for the next several months. The gulf between the two men was still broad, with Roosevelt concentrating on domestic considerations while Hull doggedly pressed for freer international trading.

After Hull returned to the United States, he bitterly complained about Roosevelt's unwillingness to give his blessings to the trade proposals. The secretary had hoped to do more, yet even as he was traveling to the conference the White House had refused his requests for added flexibility. Hull was disgusted and "sent word that there never had been anything more stupid than to send a delegation to the Pan-American Conference empowered only to propose to build a road."[59] He remembered the embarrassment he had suffered at the London conference. This would not happen again. Hull resolved not to "take a position unless we knew that the President fully approved. Otherwise we would invite overruling as in the case of the Montevideo Conference."[60]

The meeting adjourned on December 26, and Hull relished his victory. Before heading home, he declared with an air of self-congratulation that at the outset the "outlook could not have been more gloomy. . . . We have really had a one hundred percent conference—the best that has been held, according to the judgment of the veteran members."[61] In his closing radio broadcast, he claimed that the gathering marked the start of a new era in hemispheric relations by inaugurating the "good neighbor" policy.

Hull recognized his success and knew that he must build on it if the administration were to gain any political advantage. Shortly after resuming his routine in Washington, he wrote to diplomat Hugh Gibson: "I cannot impress on you too strongly the necessity for picking up the work where we left off at Montevideo and carrying it on successfully. It is only in this way and by constantly watching even the smallest causes for misunderstanding that we can firmly impress on our good friends to the South the real meaning and spirit of the President's good neighbor policy."[62] His subordinates noticed his improved disposition, but none was more pleased than his proud wife Frances, who echoed her husband's elation: "Our visit to South America is a dream to look back upon. Everything was so agreeable and so pleasant. The success of [the]

Conference [was] magnificent. . . . Makes us very happy to know we did our work well. Our trip back was perfectly delightful."[63]

Hull had unquestionably scored a badly needed personal triumph. Even though he had prevented a catastrophe at London, he had nevertheless been criticized by a press that questioned his value to the administration and wondered if he could even manage his own department. The secretary was unaccustomed to such assaults, for his congressional life had been confined to work on specific projects with limited press coverage. Now he was a world leader constantly in the spotlight, his every action or omission minutely scrutinized. His deflated ego had received a much-needed boost.

Although the secretary publicly praised Roosevelt's support, in private conversations he deplored the president's reluctance to promote his trade ideas. Even after Hull had been assured of the passage of his tariff resolution, the president had downgraded its value. When Roosevelt had tried hastily to introduce his communications proposal to the delegates, Hull had shelved it—conveniently forgetting that, had the president not demanded his attendance at Montevideo and permitted Hull the latitude to present his tariff proposals, he would have had nothing to condemn or cheer.

The secretary had undoubtedly accomplished a great deal on his first trip to South America, and that fond memory made him a firm convert to the building of better inter-American relations. Even though he understood neither Latin American customs or languages nor the complexities of Latin American negotiations with the United States, he did recognize that he had received plaudits from all quarters for his part in building regional goodwill, and he had no intention of allowing that momentum to sputter. Using his considerable political skills in winning congressional votes for hemispheric proposals, he promoted the mystique of the good neighbor and argued that regional cooperation benefited everyone. To be sure, he spoke most often in generalities, but few objected. Others had the specific knowledge to turn his vague promises into concrete commitments.[64]

Hull's victory rested on a special set of circumstances. He had seized the moment to present himself as a statesman who was sympathetic to Latin American feelings and had cooperated with Saavedra Lamas for the benefit of Argentina and the United States at a time when they had shared similar—or at least compatible—objectives. Hull never understood that this diplomatic success might not be replicable under different conditions. Nevertheless, during his Uruguayan trip the secretary had formed an unshakable mental image of how to bargain with Latin Americans. He never appreciated the fact that the Montevideo conference had been convened under unique circumstances. Thereafter Hull expected Latin American diplomats always to act in the same way, and when they did not he came to distrust them. It was a misconception that would lead to considerable misunderstanding.

Roosevelt, however, did not foresee future Argentine difficulties; seizing the moment, he preferred to build on the Montevideo success. After all, his diplomatic efforts during his first year in office had been far from impressive. He had failed to institute a consistent foreign economic policy and to comprehend the significance of the London Economic Conference. He had championed the cause of Russian recognition to improve commercial interaction without winning any business concessions in return from the Soviets. He had limited the secretary's trade options at Montevideo, and it was only when Hull had succeeded in winning Latin American support that Roosevelt had supported him.

Although the president's diplomatic maneuvers were confusing and largely ineffectual, he did win praise on December 28 when he spoke before the Woodrow Wilson birthday banquet. A huge crowd had gathered at the Washington Mayflower Hotel by the time the president started his speech at 10:30 P.M. He called for American cooperation with the League of Nations without having the United States join that body. He declared that everyone sought peace and promised ways to eliminate offensive weapons and aggression. He added that although Wilson had initiated an earlier nonintervention doctrine in Latin America, his effort had been premature. Hull had revived it at Montevideo and gone on to create a new spirit of cooperation. The president took the dramatic step of stressing that "the definite policy of the United States from now on is one opposed to armed intervention."[65]

Under Secretary Phillips had attended the affair and recorded in his diary that Roosevelt gave "a powerful speech, splendidly rendered and made a great impression on us all."[66] The Mayflower speech charted the future course for a considerable segment of American foreign policy. As a professional diplomat, Phillips understood this, and in all likelihood Bullitt and Moore took a similar view.

Hull on the other hand did not appreciate these nuances, for he was a novice, one who had been baptized at London and Montevideo on lowering trade barriers and constructing a world view based on a free trade philosophy. His first efforts in England to promote his cause had almost ended in disaster, whereas the Latin American mission had given him the chance to proclaim his crusade. Yet while in England he did not grasp the complexities of European diplomacy, nor did he comprehend the full significance of declaring an end to military intervention in Latin America. As usual he depended on specialists for explanations.

Although he depended on professional diplomats to handle detailed issues, Hull was developing his own skills for navigating through the political bureaucratic maze. First and foremost, he sought absolute loyalty and rewarded such men as Phillips, Moore, and Bullitt, in whom he recognized this trait. Those, like Moley, who chose to conspire against the secretary were purged from the State Department. The secretary never allowed for ideological differences; one was either with him or against him. Roosevelt, of course, was the exception. But Hull distrusted him because of his unilateral interference in foreign affairs and his refusal to provide unequivocal support for Hull's quest to lower trade barriers. Despite these problems with the president, Hull knew that he had to cooperate with the White House if he was going to succeed. Hull had worked with politicians throughout his professional life, and neither Roosevelt, Moley, nor anyone else would be allowed to tarnish his public image, encroach upon his department's perogatives, or interfere with his diplomatic initiatives. Hull may have been unsophisticated in foreign affairs, but he was a professional at flourishing in unfamiliar terrain.

# CHAPTER 3

# WELLES IN CUBA

WHILE REFUSING TO GIVE unqualified support to Hull in the Latin American arena, on April 6, 1933, Roosevelt personally appointed Benjamin Sumner Welles as assistant secretary of state for Latin American affairs. Although Welles, who preferred being called Sumner, had aspired to the under-secretaryship, he was satisfied with his appointment and looked forward to his new role. At forty, he was tall and thin, with a white mustache and matching temples, piercing blue eyes, and thinning hair. His wardrobe came from a Bond Street tailor. Energetic, ambitious, exacting, and intelligent, he was revered by his admirers as a well-educated, urbane, even brilliant diplomatic practitioner.[1]

Welles also had a darker side. To many he was overbearing; some actually feared him. He was stuffy to the point of pomposity and never neglected to punish those whom he felt had crossed him. His private life was markedly at odds with his public image. He engaged in clandestine bisexual behavior and hid it from his associates. On occasion, when intoxicated, he let down his inhibitions and propositioned Negroes for homosexual interludes. Of course the president had appointed the public

Welles, not the private one; indeed, in all likelihood, Roosevelt did not know about Welles's sexual preferences in the spring of 1933.

Of far greater concern to Roosevelt at the start of the New Deal was the decision to name an ambassador to Cuba because of the United States' enormous stake in that strategically located Caribbean island. Economic relations between the two countries had expanded rapidly beyond early colonial contacts because the island's inhabitants needed a wide variety of manufactured goods from the mainland. The United States had long been the largest consumer of Cuban sugar, much of it grown, processed, and transported by American companies. During and immediately after the Spanish-American War, U.S. troops had occupied the island, and before they withdrew the two nations had signed a treaty in 1903 empowering the United States to intervene militarily in the future should circumstances warrant. Thereafter, U.S. marines had landed twice, in 1912 and again in 1917; the American government had also intervened to supervise Cuban national elections in 1920.

American domination over its satellite state continued well into the twentieth century. When Gerardo Machado won the presidency in 1925, he initially gave his countrymen a period of stability and prosperity. After the Depression struck, however, political harmony within Cuba crumbled. Since Machado had taken credit for the boom, his opponents were only too ready to blame him for the bust. Totally autocratic, the Cuban president's response to opposition was a program of state-sponsored terrorism. Governing by decree, he closed universities and exiled enemies; many who remained were assassinated by the hated secret police. Revolutionaries united against this brutality and had become powerful enough by 1931 to stage a bloody, though abortive, uprising. The failure precipitated more murders by government forces, and as the rebels in turn retaliated against the dictator's henchmen the nation stumbled ever closer to civil war.

Although Machado had earlier enjoyed wide approval in the United States, at the start of the 1930s the American press began to report on the gruesome killings, the disappearance of students and university professors, and other atrocities, thus strengthening the opposition's cause. The Cuban ruler could not comprehend why the U.S. government permitted such accounts, which weakened his position and encouraged his

enemies. But he still had one major advantage. As long as he had the
military's loyalty, his political survival was assured.

Despite this precarious situation, Francis White, Welles's predecessor, actively sought the Cuban ambassadorship, believing that he had an
excellent chance for the post because of his distinguished career. He had
taken his foreign service examinations in 1915, passed them with high
marks, and, as a reward, been assigned to one of the choicest openings at
the Peking embassy. Only two others joined the diplomatic corps that
year, and by chance White happened to sail on the same ship with one of
them, with whom he talked frequently until the man disembarked at
Tokyo. White's traveling companion was Sumner Welles.

More by accident than by design, both White and Welles specialized
in hemispheric affairs. In 1927 White assumed the position of assistant
secretary of state for Latin American affairs in the Hoover administration. He received accolades for his leadership and remained at his desk
until the Democrats took office. Although he was a staunch Republican,
White believed that Welles's respect for his capabilities would supersede
partisan considerations and make him the frontrunner for the Havana
post. Secretary of State Henry Stimson had already lobbied the
president-elect on White's behalf, and he felt that Welles's influence at the
White House would assure him the Cuban slot.

As expected, Welles did indeed go to Roosevelt on White's behalf,
but the president refused to consider White and instead picked Welles
himself for the Havana job. Frustrated and angry over what he perceived
to be a betrayal, White complained bitterly to Secretary Stimson and
other friends that Welles had promised to support him for the Cuban
ambassadorship, only to grab the post for himself.[2] "I am exceedingly
sorry, but there is nothing I can do about it," was Welles's curt response
to White's disappointment.[3]

Turning from these unpleasant personal recriminations, Welles focused almost exclusively on Cuban matters. Shortly after being chosen
for the delicate assignment, he met with reporters and declared that he
expected to improve the island's economic and political conditions, while
also realizing the need to be flexible in dealing with its many deep-seated
problems. He had no predetermined proposals, but he planned to assist

the Cubans in solving their own problems within constitutional guidelines. If at all possible, he wanted to avoid military intervention.

Before taking office, Roosevelt had discussed the Cuban situation with Stimson, who wished to minimize the possibility of any American armed occupation because of the Cuban military's allegiance to the present regime. Roosevelt concurred, believing that the unrest could be calmed by a new commercial treaty. Even after he entered office, the president held to his superficial impressions. Hull also objected to any hint of intervention; the former senator's personal beliefs mirrored the strong opposition of most of his erstwhile constituents to sending American troops to fight in Cuba.[4]

Because of his solid reputation as a troubleshooter, it was Sumner Welles to whom Roosevelt turned to resolve the complicated hemispheric dispute.

Welles was born on October 10, 1892, in New York City and raised in Islip on Long Island. His family traced its lineage to the colonial era. Thomas Welles had emigrated from England in 1635 and later became governor of Connecticut. Welles's great uncle, Charles Sumner, was the famous Republican abolitionist senator from Massachusetts, and Welles was to follow in his family's distinguished tradition of public service.

Sumner was a frail child. His mother, the former Frances Swan, and Eleanor Roosevelt's mother were such close friends that when Eleanor's only brother Hall went away to school Sumner was his roommate. When Eleanor married, Sumner carried her wedding train as President Theodore Roosevelt walked his niece down the aisle. More important, Welles met Groton headmaster Endicott Peabody, who officiated at the wedding service. One year after the wedding, Welles entered Groton, where he, like Franklin Roosevelt, came under the headmaster's powerful influence. Like so many other students, Welles admired and respected the headmaster and stayed in contact with him long after graduation in 1910.[5] Welles later confided to his mentor that if he succeeded in his life's pursuits he believed that "it will be due very greatly to you and to my life at Groton."[6]

Welles accepted the rector's advice by attending Harvard after receiving his Groton diploma. He did not participate in any sports or join any social clubs while in college, but rather was known as "a fastidious dresser who wore stiff collars and a stickpin in his tie."[7] By his third year, he had studied economics and Iberian culture on campus; in 1913 he traveled abroad. After some big-game hunting in Africa and entertaining thoughts of enrolling at the École des Beaux Arts in Paris, he returned to Harvard to complete his degree and graduated in 1914.

One of his hunting companions, Nelson Slater, who had also attended Harvard, introduced Welles to his sister Esther, heiress to the family textile fortune. In April 1915 Peabody officiated at their gala marriage ceremony at Webster, Massachusetts, the Slaters' mill town. A special train brought in guests, including Governor David Walsh, and three thousand of the townspeople attended the wedding breakfast; it was a celebration quite in keeping with the social stature of the powerful families on either side of the aisle.[8]

Even before Sumner left on his honeymoon, he had already decided on a diplomatic career and had asked another prominent Harvard alumnus, William Phillips, for advice on how to join the foreign service and when to take the entrance examinations. Needing letters of recommendation, Welles approached then–Assistant Secretary of the Navy Franklin Roosevelt, who in the middle of March 1915 wrote the State Department that he had known the applicant "since he was a small boy and [had] seen him go through school and college and I should be most glad to see him successful in entering the Diplomatic Corps. He has traveled extensively, speaks several languages . . . and should give a very good account of himself in the service."[9]

With support from Phillips and Roosevelt as well as the proper preparatory school credentials and college training, Welles's success was assured. He passed the examination with the highest mark of those taking the test, an achievement that guaranteed him the best available entry post.[10] By late summer the newlyweds had boarded the S.S. *Mongolia* for Tokyo. Japan was an excellent station for a novice foreign service officer, and Welles looked forward to his future in America's diplomatic corps. He wrote Peabody during his first winter at his new post: "I have found my work most interesting and absorbing, and I hope the period of inertia in my life is past."[11]

While stationed in Japan, Welles decided to specialize in Latin American affairs, and when his tour of duty ended in 1917, he requested a transfer to a Western Hemisphere post. It was a decision that was to transform his life radically. No doubt his peers—other wealthy and ambitious graduates of Ivy League universities who had chosen the foreign service as a career and who lobbied for desirable assignments in Europe or Asia—considered a transfer to Latin America equivalent to a demotion. But Welles rejected this notion and set for himself a course that over the years would parallel the evolution of good neighbor diplomacy.

He and Esther arrived in Buenos Aires, Argentina, in 1918. Having already advanced two civil service grades, Welles eagerly set out to attain even higher goals, mastering Spanish, learning the local customs, and earning excellent ratings from his superiors. After almost three years in South America, he returned to the United States as assistant chief of the Division of Latin American Affairs at the young age of twenty-eight; the following year he became acting chief. During his stay in Washington, he focused his attention on the Caribbean and Central America, helping supervise the Cuban presidential election of 1920 and traveling to Haiti to improve commercial conditions and end the marine occupation of the island nation. He even tried to promote a regional conference of Central American nations to bring order to that chaotic region.

Sharpening his awareness of Latin American issues, Welles began to perfect his unique diplomatic style of personally assessing each nation's problems and then traveling to the trouble spot to solve them. Closely associating political unrest with economic instability, he stressed the need for the United States to serve as a trading partner with these economically dependent states, to encourage their prosperity and thus achieve political tranquility.

Despite his rapid advancement to chief of a division, Welles decided to leave the foreign service in the early spring of 1922 to demonstrate his opposition both to the Republican position on the high protective tariff (which he believed had destroyed inter-American commercial intercourse) and to the inefficiency he saw within the diplomatic corps. Although he had intended to pursue business opportunities in his native New York, within six months Secretary of State Charles Evans Hughes had persuaded him to become commissioner to the Dominican Republic. Hughes tempted Welles by telling him that his assignment was to be brief, conferring on him ministerial rank, and granting him direct access to the secretary. This additional authority and advancement convinced Welles to accept the offer. He hoped to complete his mission quickly, but his expectation was not fulfilled. He was to remain at his post for three years, during which time he sought to liquidate control over the tiny nation's finances, brought the occupying marines back to the United States, and served as a delegate to a conference of Central American states convened to formulate strategies for achieving political stability in that area.

Welles was not successful in these efforts, although a semblance of a constitutional government had returned to the Dominican Republic by the summer of 1925, when he again resigned from the foreign service. Although he had left his latest post without completing his appointed tasks, certain characteristic approaches to issues had emerged, and these would be hallmarks of his future career. He preferred to act independently with special directives from the secretary of state that furnished him with extraordinary authority beyond what a regularly accredited minister would receive.[12]

During his term as Dominican commissioner Welles also revealed one of his greatest faults—ignorance of or lack of sympathy with others' feelings. If he thought that someone in the State Department was likely to interfere with his policies, he would do all he could to bypass, remove, or simply ignore that individual. He seldom sought to understand or accommodate other viewpoints, especially once he had determined a course of action. After Welles took a position, issues became black and white; there were no shades of gray—and there was no turning back.

These extremes were increasingly reflected in his marital relations as well. While his professional standing rose steadily, his marriage crumbled. In late 1923 he and Esther divorced, at a time when marital disintegration almost inevitably brought a halt to any rising career. Esther took custody of their two young sons. The wreck of his family life attracted the cruel gossip of Washington society, for during the same year Senator Elbridge Gerry of Rhode Island, whom the columnist Joseph Alsop had described as "a pretty awful man by any standard," separated from his wife, Mathilde Townsend. Rumors lingered that Welles and Gerry's wife had had an affair that had led to the breakups of both of their marriages. When Welles married Mathilde in late June 1925, heads nodded smugly.[13]

Word of the scandal eventually reached the puritanical Calvin Coolidge, and two weeks after Welles took his second wife, Secretary of State Frank Kellogg received a message from the president instructing him to sever any government connection with Welles. Under Secretary of State William Castle hailed the decision: "I cannot but applaud the move although I think it should have come before rather than after he married the woman."[14]

Envy among Welles's detractors contributed to the malicious whispers that dogged the couple. Mathilde was the only child of an exceedingly wealthy family in Washington, who derived their fortune from the railroad industry. One of the best-known horsewomen in the capital, the tall blonde regularly rode high-stepping thoroughbreds down Massachusetts Avenue. Before her first marriage, rumors had frequently circulated that she was destined to marry into European royalty. She was heiress to a large block of Pennsylvania Railroad Company stock, and her wedding in the capital in 1910 was spectacular, with President William Howard Taft, his cabinet, and leading members of the diplomatic corps all in attendance. After her divorce from Senator Gerry thirteen years later, she went to Paris for a year, returned to Washington, and married Welles, eleven years her junior. Theirs was an inseparable bond: to their friends they appeared to act in unison.[15]

Not only did Mathilde support Welles emotionally, but her enormous wealth also sustained the regal life-style to which both were accustomed. During the winter, they resided in one of the most famous and palatial mansions in the city, which her parents had built in French renaissance style at the corner of Massachusetts and Florida avenues. The basement housed a heating plant, maintenance area, wine cellar, and food storage area; the first floor boasted a large entryway, a beautiful garden entrance, and lavish rooms for entertaining. On the second floor could be found a huge library, the dining room, many bedrooms, and an ornate ballroom that easily accommodated several hundred guests.[16]

To escape the capital's oppressive heat and humidity in the summer, the couple bought 255 acres in Maryland overlooking the Potomac River on a ridge eight miles from the Capitol. In 1928, on a site near the original plantation, Oxon Hill Manor, they built a reproduction of a colonial plantation that remains one of the finest examples of neo-Georgian architecture. A long driveway wound toward the tall brick pillars of an exquisite iron gate painted in white trim with the words "DIEU JE DOIS TOUT" ("I owe all to God"). Outside, there were elaborate terraces, elegant gardens, a kennel, a swimming pool, and a tennis court. The first floor featured a spacious foyer with Louis XV chandeliers hanging there and over the stairway. An intricately carved mantle and a black and white Italian marble floor formed the backdrop, and a large library and ballroom ran the complete length of the house. The upper floor housed six bedrooms with private bathrooms, fireplaces, and closets. The servants' wing was seventy-nine feet long, with large storage rooms, a wine cellar, and an incinerator. The kitchen, pantry, laundry, and additional servants' quarters were located on the ground floor.[17]

It was to such surroundings that Welles, out of government service, retired with Mathilde to the life of the gentry, members of the elite of the nation's capital and the landed Maryland aristocracy. He was not entirely idle, though, and in late 1925 he briefly considered working for Guaranty Trust Company as its banking liaison between Latin American governments and large financial institutions in the United States. Welles expressed mild interest in the post in 1926 and went so far as to meet with bank representatives, but by that summer he had decided against a full engagement in business.[18]

He was far more interested in winning the newly created State Department position of assistant secretary of state for Latin American affairs. During the spring of 1926 he corresponded about it with Norman Davis, then a New York financier associated with the House of Morgan on Wall Street, whom Welles had met when Davis was under secretary of state in the Wilson administration. Welles admired and respected Davis, a low-tariff Democrat from Tennessee with influential contacts in Coolidge's government, and he hoped that the former under secretary would assist him in his quest for the assistant secretaryship. The episode revealed Welles's naiveté about both politics and personal relationships, for he somehow reasoned that the post could be obtained without conflict or a political struggle.[19]

He told Davis, "I don't want to have any of my political friends take up the matter with the President since I have never in the past had any political backing either from one party or the other and I feel that any possible service by me in the future would be hindered were the question to take on a political aspect."[20] Welles need not have worried; Kellogg chose someone else. Welles never discovered that Coolidge had eliminated him, preferring instead to think that Senator Charles Curtis from Kansas was his nemesis. According to Welles, Curtis had asked Secretary Hughes in early 1925 to replace the general receiver of the Dominican Republic's customhouse with Thomas Kelly, who wanted the position not only for its $6,000 salary but also because of his doctors' advice that he needed to move to a warm climate for the sake of his health. Welles referred to Kelly as "one of Senator Curtis' leading henchmen," not conversant in Spanish or familiar with local customs. Under these circumstances Welles, who was in charge of Dominican affairs, resented the suggestion of Kelly and lobbied for the retention of the incumbent. Welles prevailed, even though Kelly did become deputy receiver. Welles also learned that Curtis, upon hearing Welles's unflattering evaluation, had vowed to have the commissioner removed from office.

When Coolidge approved every canidate nominated by his secretary of state to a panel of the Central American court with the exception of Welles, the latter immediately resigned as commissioner. He never knew that it was his divorce that had already turned Coolidge against him, and he continued to blame Curtis. Welles believed that he was the victim of an injustice, and in fact he was. But the Kansas senator was not the cause; Coolidge simply disapproved of anyone who was divorced.[21] Yet Welles's attack on Curtis may have had an additional effect that Welles did not expect. The senator was one of Washington's most influential political figures and may well have heard that Welles had accused him of political chicanery. If this had indeed occurred, Welles would have alienated not only Coolidge, but also the next vice-president of the United States.

With no realistic expectation of a diplomatic post, Welles turned to scholarship. The fruit of his labors was a two-volume history of the Dominican Republic published in 1928. In it he praised Hughes for defining the Monroe Doctrine as a hemispheric defensive measure and not a reflection of aggressive designs on the part of the United States. This did not mean that Welles repudiated the concept of American military intervention. He foresaw the occasional necessity of dispatching troops, but saw the strategy primarily as a way to protect lives, secure the defense of the Panama Canal, and deal with other emergencies. Even under these unusual circumstances, Welles believed that the United States needed to consult with the other American republics before it acted. Sending marines could only be a temporary solution, for Welles realized that the presence of American troops could never be a guarantee of long-term stability in Latin America. Welles also held that political tranquility depended on economic prosperity; to bring this about, he supported increased inter-American trading.[22]

At this time Welles also became active in the Democratic party, participating actively in Maryland politics, working for Alfred Smith's presidential candidacy, and contacting Roosevelt more frequently as a result of his work on Smith's race. Smith lost his bid, but the bond with Roosevelt grew stronger as Welles provided him with material on foreign affairs. To be sure, Welles and Roosevelt sometimes needed other Democratic spokesmen to articulate foreign policy issues. In early 1931, after Secretary Stimson attacked Wilson's diplomacy, they encouraged former under secretary of state Norman Davis to help draft the Democratic response in *Foreign Affairs*.[23]

Once Davis had agreed to the proposal, Welles played a major role in drafting the Latin American section of the article and also took the opportunity to clarify many of his own thoughts. He held that the U.S. position toward the other American republics had improved from 1913 through 1925 in terms of stability as well as goodwill toward the United States. Six years later, in contrast, the situation had become deplorable. Welles reiterated the point that the Monroe Doctrine, which he felt should be considered a multilateral policy, contained principles beneficial to both the Northern and Southern hemispheres. In practice it meant that the United States navy would defend both the Atlantic and Pacific oceans of the Americas, a strategy whose implementation required ready transit for American warships through the Panama Canal. Maintenance of hemispheric security therefore depended on the goodwill of all American nations, and armed intervention would never be welcomed.

Welles further wrote that the United States should send soldiers to Latin America only in the interest of self-preservation, broadly defined, and only after consultation with the other American republics. He affirmed: "If the equality of the Latin American republics with the United States as sovereign and independent powers is recognized, interference in their domestic concerns should be avoided to the same extent which the United States would demand that they refrain from interference in its affairs." He repeated his belief that restricting the flow of commerce damaged political stability and condemned Hoover for impeding hemispheric trade and for other inconsistent policies that retarded economic growth and assured political instability. Welles was delighted when the article appeared in July; future Democratic administrations, he declared, owed Davis a debt of gratitude.[24]

Welles also realized that, as the nation plummeted deeper into depression, Hoover would face an unprecedented struggle in winning reelection. He knew that Roosevelt was the probable Democratic choice, and once his nomination became a reality, Welles actively engaged in the national campaign from Maryland. He made a large contribution to Roosevelt's campaign and corresponded with Roosevelt's advisers concerning foreign policy issues. As the campaign drew to a close, Welles predicted that Roosevelt would be victorious because of his enthusiastic receptions at campaign stops and the positive responses that his speeches drew.[25]

Shortly after his election, Roosevelt wrote to Welles: "As you can imagine . . . I cannot ever express in writing my deep appreciation for all that you have done for me."[26] Basking in the glow of victory, Welles and Mathilde went to the White House for the inaugural dinner and reciprocated by inviting the Roosevelts to join festivities at their mansion on Massachusetts Avenue in mid-March. Welles had in mind to talk to the president-elect about the selection of foreign service personnel and Latin American diplomacy. He wanted to have some influence in choosing the next secretary of state, and he saw three forces exerting pressure not only on that process but on the making of other important assignments as well: those individuals whom Roosevelt desired, those whom the professional politicians recommended, and finally those whom the foreign service career officers hoped would continue in office.[27]

Roosevelt, on the other hand, had more pressing priorities for Welles to consider. Even before the election returns were in, Roosevelt had asked him to prepare a list of hemispheric problems and their solutions, and before the end of 1932 Welles sketched for the president-elect several inter-American issues that he believed the new administration should confront. Welles did not fully express his ideas until just before the inauguration, when he stressed that hemispheric matters "must be regarded as a keystone of our foreign policy." He called for frequent consultation and urged that Latin American relations be upgraded so that those nations would believe that the United States genuinely wished to improve relations. The Monroe Doctrine, he asserted, defended not only the United States but also the entire Western Hemisphere from attack. Such protection could be assisted by trade expansion, which in turn could be facilitated by reducing tariff barriers.

Welles contended that the end of military intervention was a cornerstone for these policies. Past American marine occupations in Central America and the Caribbean notwithstanding, Welles wanted the new administration to defend its citizens abroad with armed forces only if the citizens were in physical danger and anarchy was imminent. Except for such extreme circumstances, he was adamant that the United States must keep troops on its own territory: "I believe that the dispatch of armed forces of the United States to any foreign soil whatsoever, save for the purpose of dealing with a temporary emergency . . . , should never be undertaken by the American Executive except with the consent of the American Congress."[28]

Welles had favorably impressed the president, but others felt uncomfortable in his presence. Many influential leaders had grown to detest him, viewing him as pompous, self-righteous, and moralistic and a rigid egomaniac. He had a low, controlled voice, which he cultivated to heighten the impression of pomposity. He seldom laughed, and when he did he seemed to want to apologize for disturbing his normally solemn demeanor. Welles appeared to enjoy the idea that the troubles of the world somehow rested on his shoulders alone.

Welles's earlier diplomatic training and his relationship to Roosevelt compounded the problems that his personality caused. His authoritarian mannerisms and rapid advancement in his earlier diplomatic career spawned antagonism from those whom he outranked. His willingness to go directly to the highest possible authority and his unwillingness to solicit the opinions of his peers further alienated them. Just as Welles himself saw nothing in shades of gray, those who knew him either liked or disliked him, with no middle ground.

Fortunately for Welles, he and the president shared many similar views. Roosevelt respected the younger man's experience and ability to translate ideas into action; Welles reciprocated with genuine affection and admiration.

Thus it was that, having corresponded and talked with Roosevelt over a long period about foreign affairs, Welles was taking on the complicated assignment in Cuba with the White House's full support. He, his wife, a private secretary, and two servants arrived in Havana on May 7. Four days later he met with President Machado. After asking the Cuban leader to cooperate and suggesting a revision of the current commercial treaty, Welles gave the president a private letter from Roosevelt, which read in part, "I want you to know that he [Welles] is one of my very old friends, and as such has my confidence."[29] Machado would learn too late how heavily Roosevelt relied on this strong bond.

Welles carried several specific instructions from the president. First, the United States must refrain from any troop commitment. In order to guarantee internal peace, Machado must stop such heinous acts as the incarceration, torture, and execution of his adversaries. Once these measures were in place, Welles, at his sole discretion, would offer to mediate between the government and the rebel factions. These talks would, it was hoped, lead to a truce and then to free national elections without the threat of violence or intimidation. To improve the political environment, the United States would begin economic talks toward a new commercial treaty intended to stimulate bilateral trade.

Machado was at first oblivious to Welles's intentions, but after the two men conducted an exhaustive discussion on May 13, the ambassador's scheme surfaced. With no equivocation, Welles laid out his plan to replace the Cuban ruler with as little disruption as possible. The ambassador averred that the United States had the right to intervene militarily, but that no one wished to exercise that option. Instead, he continued, his government supported the idea of national elections in the autumn of 1934 and expected Cuba to work within its existing constitutional framework toward that goal. Welles volunteered himself as a mediator between the warring factions to halt any bloodshed, for without political tranquility, it was felt, the two nations would have no chance of economic improvement through any new commercial agreement.

Welles summarized the existing conditions for Roosevelt and pronounced them "both more precarious and more difficult than I had anticipated." He outlined his proposals and added that his most significant job was to bring about a conciliatory spirit. Machado, Welles claimed, had initially given the island good government, but the island's depression had by then erased his ability to rule effectively. He pointed out that the despot's "pathological obsession that only repressive measures, culminating in acts of hideous cruelty, could stifle that opposition, have fanned the flames of opposition into a detestation of the President's person which is unparalleled . . . in Cuban history." Despite the gravity of the present unrest, Welles gave the impression that he was in complete control of the situation, and he cautioned that any military occupation or overt diplomatic meddling would destroy the goodwill that Roosevelt was already generating.[30]

Throughout the remainder of May and most of June, Welles pushed for the government and its opponents to accept his mediation formula. His uncompromising support for continuing to keep the current administration in power gradually persuaded many political antagonists to negotiate under the ambassador's guidelines. His tireless efforts to win acceptance for mediation and refusal to accept defeat gave Cubans hope that they could negotiate rather than fight.

Roosevelt continually monitored Cuban conditions and wrote Welles on June 8 that the situation was "going as well as you and I could possibly hope for." Sixteen days later, he declared, "This is the first chance I have had to write you and tell you how proud I am of all that you have been accomplishing since you got down to Havana. I have been so taken up with the European situation that all I have been able to do in regard to Cuban affairs has been to read your dispatches and dismiss them from my mind for the very good reasons that you seemed to be getting the situation under control and to have the confidence of the people who count."[31] The president's words provided Welles with welcome encouragement, and he responded with absolute loyalty to Roosevelt. For each man, this was an ideal working arrangement.

Throughout July, Welles bargained with both sides to induce them to agree on the conduct of fair elections. Once that objective was reached, his task would be completed, and someone else could make certain that the agreement was followed, while he oversaw the proceedings from his office at the State Department. Believing himself to be on the verge of success, Welles at first neglected a labor strike in Havana that had begun in early August. Growing in momentum, it soon spread from a few industries to almost every segment of the city's economy, as a passive protest against tyrannical rule. By the seventh of the month, it had stopped everything. Transportation halted; food stores closed; nothing moved. The city was poised for the fall of the tyrant.

As the general strike intensified, Welles's reaction was to recommend Machado's immediate resignation to Roosevelt. If the president did not flee, the ambassador feared an outbreak of violence, and when sporadic fighting did in fact erupt, the dictator's first thoughts were of self-preservation. Machado openly rejected the mediation efforts, condemned the ambassador's interference, and indicated that, if necessary, he preferred armed intervention. Welles argued that the United States had one option: to withdraw recognition from the current regime and refuse to conduct official business until a stable government came into power. The ambassador forecast some disturbances as a result of this policy, but felt that they could be minimized if Roosevelt stationed two warships in Havana harbor.

From 1,300 miles away, the American president closely watched Cuban affairs during these hectic days. When the Cuban ambassador in Washington pressed him to disavow Welles's initiative, a determined Roosevelt expressed complete confidence in his emissary's ability and took the opportunity to lobby for Machado's resignation as a noble gesture to prevent starvation. If the dictator stayed and chaos erupted, he warned, the United States might be forced to land soldiers.

Pressure from the United States and long-standing enemies contributed to Machado's fall, but ultimately it was the withdrawal of military support that doomed him. His main ally having deserted him, the dictator fled the island on August 12. Cuba was at last free of his rule; now was the time for retribution, and the hunters quickly became the hunted. The United States worried about rioting and looting. The two destroyers that Welles had earlier requested finally arrived on August 14. Both Roosevelt and Hull stressed that these warships had been sent to Cuba as a precautionary measure to protect American lives and that there were no plans to deploy troops. Despite such assurances, this naval presence did influence those who monitored the ships at anchor; they were bound to have a stabilizing effect on the population.

The warships in the harbor, however, could not solve Cuba's domestic turmoil, a fact that Welles understood. The instant that Machado fled, Welles began his search for a suitable successor. Within a day, he had tapped Carlos Manuel de Céspedes, a former Cuban ambassador to the United States whom Welles had recommended for the presidency in 1920, and who, according to Welles, "had the great advantage of being regarded as thoroughly impartial by everyone in Cuba."[32]

With Céspedes in power as provisional president and order being restored, Welles had reason to be satisfied, for he had accomplished his mission with minimal bloodshed. The State Department was also optimistic. Edwin Wilson, who worked on the Latin American desk, expressed the optimism shared by those in his division that everything had "turned out wonderfully well. We are of course not out of the woods yet, but it looks very much better than it did a few days ago."[33]

Welles assessed the continued need for his presence in Cuba on August 19 and concluded that the situation had stabilized enough for him to be replaced by September 1. He was convinced that the new government had popular backing, and with the move toward national elections proceeding well and negotiations for a commercial treaty under way, Welles wished to resume his duties as assistant secretary to prepare for the upcoming inter-American conference in Uruguay. He had another pressing reason for wanting to leave: certain Cuban politicians had accused him of having had a direct hand in making Céspedes president, and although Welles had vigorously denied these accusations, he knew that the charge—an accurate one—was spreading. Since he had an "intimate personal friendship" with Céspedes and his cabinet, he noted, "I am now daily being requested for decisions on all matters affecting the Government of Cuba." Although not yet under direct attack for this questionable association, Welles did not want this kind of relationship between Cuban officials and American ambassador, whoever he might be, to continue. The next ambassador, Welles believed, would have to stay out of the spotlight.[34]

Later Welles bitterly protested to Samuel Inman, a prominent Latin American journalist in the United States, "I had no more to do with the selection of Doctor Cespedes as Provisional President of Cuba than you did." After all, reasoned Welles, when the mediation talks began, the political leaders needed an "honest, high-minded, non-political" individual to head the government after Machado resigned. Not many fit these requirements. Céspedes had been identified as a primary candidate in early June, and by late July most of the opposition forces had come to support his candidacy. "The Department of State and myself had absolutely no connection whatever with the selection of Doctor Cespedes, directly or indirectly, and I feel that, in justice to our policy in Cuba, in justice to the parties responsible for the selection of Doctor Cespedes, and in justice to the Secretary of State and myself, that misapprehension should be most decidedly corrected."[35]

His lack of candor over the genesis of the new regime notwithstanding, almost from the moment of Céspedes's accession, Welles had labored to consolidate the president's political power by restoring order with the placement of warships, winning needed allies from among the various political groups, asking Roosevelt for a treasury loan to provide greater economic stability, and initiating negotiations toward a trade treaty. Yet despite all of these efforts and much to his own chagrin,

Welles had come to admit to himself that Céspedes was an ineffective leader who did not inspire confidence. The sooner elections were conducted, the sooner Cubans could choose a new president. This would not be Welles's responsibility, of course, for he was due to resume his duties in Washington by September.

The timetable for national elections abruptly changed on the evening of September 4, when a group of noncommissioned officers led by Fulgencio Batista deposed their superiors and took command of the armed forces. Inspired by the news, student groups raced to join the revolt, and the combined strength of these diverse forces was enough to take control of the presidential palace and topple Céspedes and his inept government. The ease with which Céspedes surrendered his office shocked Welles. Forgotten were his earlier criticisms of the ineptitude of the interim president, for the conspirators had, in a seemingly bloodless revolt, destroyed the constitutional order that Welles had so strenuously labored to preserve. Since the warships that had been dispatched in August had by then departed, Welles asked Roosevelt to return two to Havana and send one more to the strategic port of Santiago. The ambassador warned the State Department, "The action taken has been fomented by the extreme radical elements."[36] Because the previous Cuban administration was unwilling to move against the rebels, he anticipated that the public would renew its general strike and that anarchy would ensue.

On the morning of September 5, Welles phoned Hull to tell him that the extremists and noncommissioned officers had occupied the presidential palace. The calm that hung over Havana was deceptive, he cautioned, for chaos could break out at any moment. Under these conditions, the presence of United States warships in the harbor was essential to maintain order. Hull listened to Welles's bleak evaluation, but reacted with his customary caution by seeking first to consult with the other American republics.

That afternoon Welles was on the phone again with the secretary, asserting that Céspedes's backers were calling for the United States to land troops, an action the ambassador favored: "Our policy would simply be on the grounds of protection of the American Embassy and the protection of American nationals."[37] This rationale masked Welles's driving desire to restore the toppled government of his creation, for he knew that without a troop deployment the Céspedes regime was doomed. Hull, as was his habit, wanted to consider other options, but Welles emphasized the necessity for prompt military action.

Despite Welles's call to arms, in the end Hull and others persuaded Roosevelt that the administration should reject his recommendations. Unless the embassy was in actual physical danger, no troops should land, for in Hull's view a marine occupation would "provoke trouble rather than quiet trouble." Welles's caution that the revolutionaries could not maintain the peace went unheeded, and Hull further distanced himself from his subordinate by declaring that "unless there is physical danger to you folks in the Embassy" the administration would not intervene.

In his communications with Hull, Welles never mentioned the highly nationalistic program of the new government, the violent punishment of Machado's henchmen, the failure of Céspedes to inspire public confidence, and the restoration of the country's political and economic stability. He exaggerated the extent of civil disorder and refused to admit that neither a general strike nor a massive pro-Machado uprising had materialized. Even though he seemed outwardly to accept the administration's position against intervention, and despite stressing his personal abhorrence of such a strategy, he nevertheless wanted Washington to keep open the option of sending in troops. Beneath his apparent resigned acceptance of having been rebuffed, Welles was bitterly disappointed that his advice had been rejected. The continuity of constitutional rule on which he had staked his career had disintegrated in a matter of days. Welles—ever quick to preceive a slight—viewed the Cuban revolt as a personal affront to his skills as a diplomat.

While Welles grappled with this turn of events, Roosevelt and Hull on September 6 and 7 instructed the ambassador to remain strictly neutral in the battle for political control in order to avoid any possibility of American military intervention. The United States would not land marines unless it had a compelling reason to do so. Welles could not reverse this directive, but he did persuade Hull to withhold recognition of the new government until stability had been restored. To Hull the request seemed logical and appropriate, but Welles knew the devastating consequences that it could have on those in authority in Cuba. Without diplomatic ties, the new government had no chance of conducting normal relations with its most important neighbor. Who would judge when peace had been restored? Welles, of course. Although Welles withheld from his superiors the implications of this decision, Hull eventually comprehended the difficult and uncomfortable position into which the ambassador had placed him.[38]

Welles intended nonrecognition to be the lever with which he would pry the new regime from power. He argued that Roosevelt and Hull should consider Céspedes as the rightful constitutional ruler, one who had been ousted by mutinous soldiers. Proceeding from this assumption, the ambassador outlined his interventionist rationale for his superiors in Washington. The United States, he insisted, had an obligation to keep troops in Cuba only until the deposed Cuban officers could train troops loyal to them. To carry out this policy, the United States would need to deploy a considerable military contingent in the Cuban capital and smaller contingents in other strategic ports. The only disadvantage he saw to this approach was that the government would "incur the violent animosity of the extreme radical and communist groups in Cuba who will be vociferous in stating that we have supported the Cespedes Government because that Government was prepared to give protection to American interests in Cuba and that our policy is solely due to mercenary motives."

Welles went on to dismiss these hypothetical complaints by pointing out that opposition groups had always attacked American motives. He stretched his logic by reasoning even further: "Since I sincerely believe that the necessity of full intervention on our part is to be avoided at all hazards, the limited and restricted form of intervention . . . would be infinitely preferable." Céspedes had been illegally removed, and the United States was therefore duty bound to restore him. Welles concluded, "The landing of such assistance would most decidedly be construed as well within the limits of the policy of the 'good neighbor' which we have done our utmost to demonstrate in our relations with the Cuban people during the past 5 months."[39]

Roosevelt gradually rejected these arguments owing to the enormous opposition at home to a military expedition abroad. The president had polled his cabinet and found it overwhelmingly opposed to intervention unless such action was absolutely necessary. Most members of the press and Congress also objected vigorously and vocally. Hull, whose personal opposition to armed intervention was of long standing, shared these views. But neither the president nor his secretary of state saw any inconsistency in withholding recognition. They did not at first associate a refusal to grant diplomatic ties with any form of intervention. Roosevelt would watch and wait. Until Welles approved the new Cuban leadership, the status quo would prevail.

To combat nonrecognition, on September 10 the revolutionary junta selected Dr. Ramón Grau San Martín, a university professor, to serve as provisional president. This appointment signaled the creation of a centralized authority and a consolidation of power. Welles realized this and took the opportunity to attempt to build a coalition government that included all factions. Preoccupied with negotiating this political compromise, he failed to see that in the wake of Machado's departure the various parties had become unable to agree on anything. Welles was still convinced that by playing a central role he could bring the politicians back to the bargaining table and establish the eventual national elections that he so coveted. Welles could not adapt to the changed circumstances, however, and he soon came to represent the polarization between the past and present in Cuban politics. His first role had been as the manipulator who overthrew the tyrant; next he had crowned the successor and tried to prop up his government. After the sergeants' revolt, his primary objective had been to replace the revolutionary regime with the traditional leadership. Once Roosevelt and Hull rejected armed intervention, Welles had sought to make Grau and his followers bend to the American embassy's will. The new Cuban administration desired Welles's approval, but to Welles it symbolized the fall of the old regime and the advent of a burgeoning nationalism. In this explosive climate, Welles understood that no one would agree to any compromise; each group would appeal to its own particular constituency.

Since Grau and his followers could not reach any accord with their opponents, political stability was merely a chimera. Welles never admitted to himself that he had been placed in an untenable position. Nor could he see that he had come to symbolize the past, while the newly installed Grau personified Cuban expectations of a brighter future.

These irreconcilable differences resulted in a shaky stalemate. The rivalry between Welles and Grau became more than a political struggle; it grew into personal bitterness and a battle of wills. By the end of September the unwholesome conflict between the American embassy and the Cuban government had become unbearable. Nevertheless, Roosevelt stood firm in his acceptance of the nonrecognition policy and declared that all the United States wanted was an orderly regime; when that appeared, diplomatic ties would be resumed. Roosevelt insisted that his administration would not intervene, never understanding that he was already meddling in Cuba's internal affairs.

In the midst of this political upheaval, Welles stumbled into an even more explosive situation. When the lease on his rental house expired on September 6, he moved into the National Hotel two days later. The hotel was one of Havana's finest and catered to many Americans. After the sergeants had taken control, several hundred officers had also made the hotel their headquarters because many of them had seen their own homes ransacked or feared for their lives if they returned home. The hotel had the added strategic value of being easily defensible. Yet Welles did not believe that the opposing military camps would actually fight on the hotel's grounds.

On September 8, after the new army leaders ordered a search of the property for arms, fighting almost erupted when the officers inside decided to resist the government's overtures. During this tense confrontation, Welles deliberately took a position in the middle of the lobby between the opposing forces, directly in the line of fire. He and Adolf Berle, a member of the Brain Trust and fellow New Yorker, sat on a long divan and calmly smoked cigarettes, discussing the value of Emily Dickinson's poetry and the natural beauty of the Berkshire Hills. When the commander of the government forces arrived, Welles arose, approached him, and advised him to use "discretion." The Cuban did not understand the meaning of the term, so Welles forcefully suggested that the troops should retire to avoid injuring or killing innocent civilians trapped in the building.[40]

Although the soldiers retired from inside the building, they still kept it surrounded to prevent the officers from staging a counterrevolution. Admitting to their precarious situation, these men approached Welles and asked him to intervene in order to gain time while they trained recruits who would be loyal to the old regime. Welles flatly refused. In so doing he seemed to be giving tacit support to the ousted military, but for reasons that had nothing to do with the two warring sides. He stayed because the National Hotel was American-owned and because his presence served to reassure U.S. citizens living there that they were safe. Had he left when the soldiers had first entered, he would have lost face by appearing to be afraid of the immediate danger, and he would have been criticized for his unwillingness to protect American lives. The uneasy standoff between the opposing military forces ended just before dawn on October 2, when shooting commenced. The initial fighting lasted a scant two hours; one section of the hotel was badly damaged. Welles negotiated a thirty-minute truce to remove civilians; the battle then continued into the late afternoon, when the defenders finally raised the white flag. By evening Havana was again quiet.

Welles warned that extreme elements of the Grau administration wanted to execute their captives. He vigorously lobbied against this action until Batista guaranteed their safety. The ambassador's critics later accused him of inciting the officers' revolt, but he denied these unfounded allegations, as did the officers. Nevertheless, his credibility had been further damaged. Not only was he forced to defend himself against untrue stories, but Hull also used the occasion, on October 5, to resurrect the Cuban recognition issue. The secretary argued that Grau had further consolidated his power by his victory at the National Hotel and in agreeing that the United States should reexamine its policy. Welles instantly managed to delay any attempt to alter his policy of nonrecognition.

Yet in his obsessive desire to form a coalition government, Welles behaved as though the hotel fighting had been inconsequential. He stubbornly held his ground and summarized his position on October 10: "To be quite frank, for the past four weeks existence has been unmitigated hell. The complexities seem to increase rather than diminish, and all that I can say at the present time is that the main objective—namely, nonintervention—has not been impaired. I am still hopeful that there is a possibility of a way being devised for a constructive program that will eventually get us out of the present unsavory mess into which Cuba has been plunged."[41] Welles still thought that he could find the solution to the island's political impasse. He refused to admit that his optimism was unfounded.

By the end of the month his inability to form a coalition government and the hostility he faced from his critics in the United States had begun to aggravate him. Welles saw "just as much graft going on at the present moment as there was during Machado's Government." The present rulers were personally profiting at the expense of the public and nepotism was widespread. He thought that Cuba still had honest administrators, and he rested his faith in their eventual restoration to office. The current bureaucracy was to his mind abysmal, composed with few exceptions "either of self-seeking, small caliber politicians, or fuzzy-minded theorists who have neither the training, the experience, nor the capacity to govern."

To answer the question of why he refused to recognize Grau, Welles replied that formal relations would give the regime "tremendous moral and financial support." If Roosevelt extended diplomatic ties to a regime that the ambassador felt represented a minority, the majority might never have free and impartial elections. Welles was immovable: "I believe that we owe it to the Cuban people not to assist in saddling upon them for an indefinite period a government which every responsible element in the country violently opposed, and which is opposed today by the laboring classes and by the farmers, as well as by the political parties and by the business interests." Welles knew his rigid stance might topple the administration, but he doggedly maintained that in the long run his decision would benefit bilateral relations. His perceptions, however, were by this time so distorted that he could not even bring himself to admit that Grau not only had survived the rebellion at the National Hotel but also was governing the island.[42]

If Roosevelt had wished, he could have replaced Welles for good cause at any time after the sergeants' revolt because Welles was scheduled to attend the Montevideo conference. Deeply disappointed that he was unable to attend, he expressed the sentiment on October 30 that "unless the immediate miracle which I am optimistic enough to believe is still possible, even in this modern world, takes place in Cuba, I shall have to stay here for a while longer."[43]

On the other hand, Under Secretary Phillips, who was temporarily serving as acting secretary, dreaded the thought of the ambassador continuing on his current course:

> Welles is doing no good in Habana; he has become so involved with the various political parties and is being so violently attack[ed] in the local press and otherwise that his presence there has no longer any "healing" effect. However, he is determined to stick it out and the President certainly has no intention of recalling him. I very much fear that the Cuban situation will boil over during the next two months while I am in charge of the Department and I am not looking forward to any such problem.[44]

Welles soon fulfilled Phillips's dire prophecy by telegraphing the State Department on November 13, requesting an urgent meeting with the president. Roosevelt approved the idea and decided to meet his ambassador at Warm Springs, Georgia, since he had already planned a vacation there. Welles left Havana on November 17 and two days later briefed the president on Cuban conditions. Early in the evening Roosevelt called Phillips and explained the situation from Welles's perspective. The president ordered Welles to consult with Phillips in Washington for several days and then return to Cuba for two weeks, at which point he would be replaced. Welles arrived at the department on November 20 and in spite of Phillips's pessimism drafted an American declaration that called on Cuba's political factions to establish a coalition government that had the support of the people. Welles adamantly insisted on this plan, believing that the United States had to clarify the fact that it would not recognize Grau's administration as presently constituted.

Phillips doubted the value of this action, but he was overruled. Welles completed the presidential statement by November 22 and late the following evening Roosevelt approved it. He told Phillips that if this clarification did not improve conditions on the island, the United States should consider withdrawing its embassy and having its citizens return to the mainland. The so-called Warm Springs declaration, which naturally mirrored Welles's views, was issued on November 24. The United States, it read, had not granted recognition to Grau because he did not represent the majority. The president hoped that the Cuban people would find solutions to their own internal problems and bring stability to their country. Once Cuba had a government based on popular support, the Roosevelt administration would grant diplomatic relations and proceed to negotiate a new commercial treaty. The communiqué also stated that Welles would briefly resume his duties in Havana until a successor was named.

Almost immediately upon his arrival at the end of November, Welles made one last desperate attempt to put across his political compromise. If he could not achieve his goal, he intended to leave within the allotted two-week time frame. On December 9 Phillips commented on this final diplomatic flurry: "Naturally Sumner feels that his prestige would be increased 100% if he could return to the Department after he had accomplished his own desire, which is to rid Cuba of Grau San Martin; otherwise he will return to the Department without the prestige of having accomplished anything."[45]

There was a brief moment when Welles thought that he had broken through Grau's intransigence and obtained his agreement to an acceptable coalition formula, but this hope collapsed on December 11 when Grau's followers rejected any compromise. The ambassador dejectedly admitted defeat and boarded his plane on the afternoon of December 13 with 500 well-wishers bidding him good-bye. He arrived at the State Department early on December 15 and immediately took the oath as assistant secretary of state for Latin American affairs.

Francis White condemned Welles's mission: "What outraged me was that Welles, for his own personal glorification, should pursue a thoroughly unsound policy simply because it was spectacular and gave him, he thought, a chance to enhance his own prestige." White believed that Welles's scheme to remove Machado had been disastrous. After White's own recommendations were discarded, he had refused to take any further part in Cuban matters, and Hull respected that wish. But Welles's ultimate failure still did not satisfy White: "The indignation that any man could and would use the opportunity he had for constructive work in a gamble on something which might have enhanced his personal prestige, has remained with me ever since I left home."[46]

As far as White was concerned, Welles had always been dishonest and had merely proved it during the Cuban fiasco. He never forgot or forgave Welles's intrigue over the Cuban ambassadorship and continued to attack Welles's actions in Cuba.[47] William Castle, a former Republican diplomat and a friend of White, shared many of his opinions. Castle heard rumors that Welles had told others in the administration that White was pro-Machado and confided to a foreign diplomat that as assistant secretary he was trying to help White even though the president wanted to fire him and that White had never had the slightest chance of becoming ambassador to Cuba even though the press had mentioned him as a serious candidate. However, these allegations appear unlikely to be true since Roosevelt had complimented White on his work and thus infuriated Castle, who believed that Welles had consciously plotted against White: "I think it is about time that fellow was shown up. Hull is a good man and ought not to have people of the kind around him." Castle also discovered through his contacts in the foreign service that Welles was already intriguing to take Phillips's place by having him assigned elsewhere.

Castle, furthermore, uncovered something so scandalous that, were it verified, it could destroy Welles's career. He had talked with another former under secretary of state, Henry Fletcher, who had "enough on Welles to blow him out of the water." Machado's foreign minister Orestes Ferrara was alleging that Welles had had homosexual relations while stationed in Havana. Castle cautioned: "I should not want to use it second-hand and should have to check up carefully. . . . Welles is the man in the Department who is closest to the President and if he should decide to exert his influence in that quarter it might be disastrous."[48] At that time, no one took up a crusade against Welles based on his alleged homosexuality. He was condemned solely for his policies.

In his memoirs Welles never discussed his personal life in Havana, preferring to concentrate on Machado's downfall, Grau's incompetence, and Roosevelt's leadership. He completely ignored his own call for troops and intimated that he too had always opposed any kind of armed involvement. According to his recollection, the main significance of his ambassadorship was the integral part he had played in the shaping of the good neighbor policy.

Far more fascinating and reliable than Welles's own reconstruction was the objective record of his behavior under stress. From May through

December, he wrote a tremendous amount of public and private correspondence and also had long recorded telephone conversations with
Roosevelt, Hull, Phillips, and others. Throughout his ordeal, he demonstrated the rigid, dogmatic, and opinionated characteristics that would
persist for the rest of his career. His stilted social manner and perception
of how a diplomat should behave, for example, caused him to risk his life
at the National Hotel because that was the way an ambassador ought to
act. He would risk death rather than weaken his machismo. He focused
on technical details, maintained a narrow focus, and spent day and night
making certain that every point was reported. While expending an
inordinate amount of time on trivial matters, he often missed the larger
picture.

The sergeants' revolt and the rise of Grau had surprised him. Forced
to swerve off his set path, he did not know how to respond. Out of anger
and frustration, he reverted to the solutions of his earlier years in the
diplomatic corps by calling for troops. Even when Roosevelt and Hull
refused, Welles continued to lobby for military intervention. Once he
realized that troop deployment was unlikely, he slanted his reports to
strengthen the case for maintenance of his nonrecognition policy. To him
nothing Grau did could justify diplomatic ties. When Welles finally felt
trapped, he used the only vehicle available to him, meeting with the
president at Warm Springs to plan and carry out a course of action.

Once Welles had established the parameters of his universe, he had
no room for flexibility. After Roosevelt and Hull forced him to abandon
military intervention in Cuba as a diplomatic option, Welles unequivocally accepted that principle for the remainder of his career and demanded strict adherence to that doctrine. The United States would not
land soldiers; there were no exceptions.[49]

Roosevelt, for his part, never worried about Welles's weaknesses, but
viewed him as a loyal follower who would carry out orders without
question. The president did not believe that the ambassador had taken
inappropriate action in Cuba; indeed he approved of every step short of
military occupation. Despite opposition by Phillips and without even
consulting Hull, the president endorsed the Warm Springs declaration
and allowed his ambassador, who was by then almost persona non grata,
to return to his station. Roosevelt thought in terms of generalities and

was always quick to draw the broad outline. For his part, Welles, never an originator, was the consummate professional technician who preferred to think in terms of specific problems that could be resolved based on presidential guidelines.

Ten years later, Roosevelt highlighted his administration's precedent against military intervention and ignored the complexities of nonrecognition: "Thousands of people pleaded with me to send troops to Havana." Refusing to heed their advice, in place of troops, he had sent "small ships" to transport United States citizens if they desired to leave. He had consulted with the other Latin American republics and assured them that as long as the revolution was confined to Cuban shores, the islanders could settle their own troubles. "As a result, the fire burned itself out and the Cubans and all other Latin Americans understood that dollar diplomacy and armed expeditions were at an end."[50]

Hull's recollections fifteen years after the events were quite different. He commissioned a special departmental study of Welles's conduct in Cuba to trace how the ambassador had promoted armed intervention and then contrasted this obnoxious and unsound advice with his own consistent stand against any military operation. He also falsely declared that he had agreed first to appoint Welles as assistant secretary and later to send him to Cuba.[51] Roosevelt had made these decisions; Hull had merely acquiesced.

Hull further asserted that he had always assumed "the responsibilities for all decisions," but the reality was far different. The secretary refrained from making any independent judgments during the crisis and left the formation of policy to Roosevelt and Welles. Hull consistently fought against intervention and intimated that he was unhappy with nonrecognition, but he never made a serious effort to overturn it or to criticize Welles. In fact, the secretary could not have played a large role in formulating policy toward Cuba, for he was traveling to London and Montevideo during much of the time when the crucial decisions were reached.

The slanted recollections of the principals do not detract from the reality: the Cuban episode was Roosevelt's first serious bilateral confrontation with a foreign nation. Although the president concentrated on domestic legislation, he also paid especially close attention to Cuban affairs and agreed to every ambassadorial suggestion short of sending troops, a decision that partially placated Hull. The secretary was not totally satisfied, however, because he could not shake Roosevelt's resolve to support Welles's stand against diplomatic recognition. Welles was not completely pleased either, for he had been rebuffed in his plea for a troop deployment. Nevertheless, the president professed faith in the ambassador's judgment, cordoned the island with warships, and rejected any request to extend diplomatic ties to Grau. Both Hull and Welles understood that the White House decided policy. Neither man was able to declare victory, but each perceived that he had the president's confidence. Feelings were soothed; loyalty had been preserved.

Yet Roosevelt had established a dangerous precedent by allowing Welles to speak directly to him on a regular basis. Hull had been absent much of the time during the Cuban crisis, and this situation permitted Roosevelt and Welles to bypass the State Department to arrive at their own independent decisions. Welles understood that this precedent gave him permission to go directly to the White House in the future, a practice to which Hull did not object, even though it deeply troubled him. The secretary of state was supposedly the chief policymaking officer in the State Department, but from the Cuban crisis onward, the White House placed that prerogative in serious jeopardy.

# CHAPTER 4

# THE BALANCE OF THE FIRST TERM

FROM 1934 TO THE END OF 1936, each of the significant characters who helped shape American diplomacy developed certain crucial personality traits while further defining his specific area of interest in foreign affairs. Roosevelt established himself as an activist president, and his promoters waxed ecstatic about the quality of his leadership in the Oval Office. They, of course, gave him too much credit, but he seemed successful enough to perpetuate the myth of his omnipotence. For example, Postmaster General Farley at the end of 1934 declared that Roosevelt looked "absolutely sure of himself—uncanny in his wisdom and judgment of things generally." His exceptional grasp of domestic and foreign affairs, Farley believed, would allow the president to lead the country out of the Depression. Roosevelt had grown in his job and carried out the enormous responsibilities of the White House with good humor and ever-increasing aplomb.[1] His detractors were relatively quiet, but some, like former under secretary of state William Castle, deplored the president's unpredictability. Roosevelt was always willing to experiment and take unconventional approaches. No one knew what he would advocate next, and Castle feared the unknown.[2]

Just as Castle distrusted Roosevelt, the president looked upon professional diplomats with deep suspicion. Regular reports flowed into the White House that, in his view, confirmed the unreliability of many in the foreign service. During a meeting with Canadian Prime Minister W. L. MacKenzie King in late 1935, Roosevelt claimed that the United States minister to Ottawa, Norman Armour, was "one of the very few of the diplomatic service who were really first-class men." The implication, of course, was that the president was skeptical about the usefulness of the career foreign service. Such prejudicial remarks lingered throughout his presidency because of Roosevelt's belief that the vast majority of diplomats held over from the Republican era were openly antagonistic to his New Deal.[3]

Such antipathy, however, did not inhibit Roosevelt from following through on his intention to play a paramount role in international affairs; in fact, it might have encouraged him. He had unilaterally set out to forge closer relations with the British and the French, but this initiative was quickly dashed by his fiasco at the London Economic Conference and the overwhelming desire of European leaders to keep the United States out of their affairs. The question of cooperation with the League of Nations further graphically illustrated Roosevelt's limitations. For example, he had wanted to ask Congress as early as 1933 to allow the United States to become a member of the World Court, but he waited until the first session of 1935, when obtaining the necessary two-thirds vote from the Senate seemed less of a hurdle, to present this proposal. Only a few senators had actually voiced any objections. In the absense of vocal opposition, the White House predicted easy passage, but Roosevelt had woefully underestimated the strength of his opponents. At the end of January 1936, after a bitter debate over foreign entanglements, the treaty lost by seven votes, thus handing the president another humiliation. Furthermore, he was left with no room for recriminations because he could not afford to offend those senators who had lined up against him. Some of them had voted for crucial New Deal domestic measures, and he would not risk the succesful passage of his recovery programs.

Even this debacle, however, did not prevent Roosevelt from speaking out against the growing cancer inside the Third Reich. Despite his warnings about Hitler's menacing militarism, the United States as well as the European community had refused to take any aggressive actions against the Nazis. When German troops marched into the Rhineland in 1936, the world watched passively. Yet the president was not willing to take a vigorous stand against the persecution of German Jewry. Although deploring this barbarism, he could not personally invite its victims to America at a time when the majority of its citizens opposed large-scale immigration. The United States, it was popularly felt, had enough economic problems without encouraging more people, in particular German Jews, to come here. But by the summer of 1936 Roosevelt had offered an alternative in publicly advocating the rebuilding of a Jewish homeland in Palestine and urging the British to ignore heavy Arab pressure to stop Jewish immigration.[4]

Although many were anxious about Nazism, far more abhorred Benito Mussolini's invasion of Ethiopia toward the end of 1935. The Italians fought with modern equipment, while the poorly trained and inadequately equipped Africans defended their homeland with the primitive weapons of their ancestors. The world read in horror as the fascists brutally obliterated organized resistance, and the fighting ended in the spring of 1936 when Addis Ababa fell.

This massacre faded from the front pages when the Spanish Civil War erupted that summer. The combatants in that conflict formed unofficial alliances: the government, with support from the French, English, and Russians, wore both democratic and communist labels; on the other hand, the Germans and Italians stood by Francisco Franco, who sided with the dictatorships. The bloodshed ceased when the rebels occupied Madrid in early 1939, a victory that gave added prestige to Hitler and Mussolini.

Comparatively few Americans paid attention to the worsening conditions in East Asia in 1933. The Japanese invasion of Manchuria in September 1931 startled the great powers; Tokyo's withdrawal in early 1933 from a dying League caused consternation; and the Emperor's abandonment of the naval limitation treaty in 1936 portended a new armaments race. Rather than take preventive measures to halt Japanese aggression, much of the Eurocentric world was content to look upon these worrisome happenings from afar and do nothing.

Roosevelt advanced several impractical schemes to stop global aggression. Collective action against Nazi rearmament by means of a blockade was not viable in the face of domestic opposition. The White House reacted sharply to the Italian invasion of Ethiopia and called for sanctions, yet most Americans would not approve of any forceful measures against Mussolini either. In the case of Spain, the president worried more about the conflict spreading into a wider European battleground than about his government's chances of preventing carnage on Spanish soil. As Japanese military expansion accelerated, Roosevelt offered no positive solution other than his demand for naval construction to check Tokyo's increased production of warships.

Instead of supporting measures to halt aggression, America's response to these international crises translated into neutrality legislation. When global aggression surfaced at the start of 1935, some favored allowing the president discretion in responding to developments, while others demanded rigid rules. Once it was clear that the latter view had prevailed, Roosevelt hopelessly tried to win concessions. But in late August he admitted defeat and signed an act that prohibited the United States from supplying belligerents with arms or contraband and forbade U.S. citizens from traveling in war zones or on belligerent vessels. The president believed that his signature would quiet congressional accusations that the bill was designed to expand his already broad discretionary authority. Since the law had only a six-month life, he hoped to reverse the congressional mood in the near future. His optimism was misplaced, however, for Congress would not succumb to his charms or his arguments. Upon the expiration of the act in early 1936, the White House took steps to modify it to permit greater presidential flexibility, but once again the administration failed to gauge the opposition's clout. Roosevelt did not win any major concessions and instead was forced to settle for a fourteen-month extension. Refusing to mount a protracted legislative battle over a losing proposition, the president once again conceded defeat.[5]

Roosevelt pledged not to repeat the same error of exaggerating his own abilities and underestimating the opposition's strength. He understood that any step, real or imagined, that would bring the country closer to another world war would face unrelenting hostility from Congress.

Roosevelt resolved not to stage a frontal attack against a superior political enemy; instead, he would probe its flanks until he sensed an advantage and only then would he strike. Although he at first did not fully comprehend the subtleties of political maneuvering, as the United States inched imperceptibly closer to war, he eventually hit upon the strategy of using initiatives within the Western Hemisphere as a method to reach beyond the Americas and yet minimize criticism. His opponents, who had targeted direct intervention in Europe and Asia as their battleground, ignored the president's sophisticated method of reaching the American people with his message of international cooperation through regional solidarity.

With the success of the Montevideo conference and his own nonintervention declaration during the Mayflower speech, the president took delight in the promotion of the good neighbor policy. In the summer of 1934 he visited the Caribbean, becoming the first American chief executive to travel to South America while in office. The tour focused attention on regional questions and demonstrated the priority he had accorded to improving inter-American affairs. Roosevelt maximized the value of the widespread news coverage of his first stop in Haiti by accelerating the pace of marine withdrawal from that country. He landed next in the colonial port of Cartagena, and he and his Colombian counterpart toured that city and exchanged pleasantries. This public relations effort was truly exceptional, considering that Cousin Teddy had boasted of taking the canal from the Colombians three decades earlier. Intent on improving relations throughout the region, Roosevelt then proceeded to Panama and announced his intention to discuss that tiny state's complaints of American abuses in the Canal Zone.[6]

The good neighbor policy had won widespread acceptance, and the president sought to extend the positive image of the United States in Latin America to the rest of the international community. For example, during a press conference on March 20, 1935, in response to a question on German rearmament, he declared, "I think we can only properly maintain the general principles of the good neighbor and hope that the American principle will be extended to Europe and will become more and more effectual and contribute to the peaceful solution of problems and, incidentally with it, as a very necessary component part, the reduction of armaments."[7] Few understood the nuances of the path that the president was taking. Toward the end of 1935 he spoke at the San Diego Exposition, pleading, "I hope from the bottom of my heart that as the years go on, in every continent and in every clime, Nation will follow Nation in providing by deed as well as by word their adherence to the ideal of the Americas—I am a good neighbor."[8]

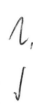

By the start of the new year Roosevelt was convinced that war in Europe was inevitable and that after the victorious dictatorships had carved up the Old World they would invade South America. There would come a time, not immediately, but within one or two generations, when an American president might have to repel an attack on Latin America.[9] That theme reached its logical conclusion on August 14, 1936, when Roosevelt gave his famous "I hate war" speech at Chautauqua, stressing his peace theme and reiterating the value of the good neighbor policy in the quest for tranquil relations among nations: "Yes, through-out the Americas the spirit of the good neighbor is a practical and living fact. The twenty-one American Republics are not only together in friend-ship and in peace; they are united in the determination so to remain." The president hoped to banish war forever from the hemisphere and dreamed of extending that vision worldwide.[10]

Although much has been made of Roosevelt's activist style and refusal to consult with his own diplomatic advisers, by the end of the first term the president had demonstrated that he was far more consis-tent than many of his critics thought. Above all, he would do nothing to jeopardize his New Deal programs. He needed as many votes as he could muster, and if this meant signing neutrality legislation, that was a price he was willing to pay. Despite this limitation, Roosevelt in those months was establishing trends in American diplomacy that would remain amaz-ingly constant for years to come: the embryonic beginnings of Anglo-Franco-American partnership; the immediate antipathy toward the Third Reich; the nascent attempts at improved relations with the Soviet Union; the use of the good neighbor concept, in the midst of powerful isolationist sentiment, as a way of forging a more aggressive inter-national commitment; and opposition to Japanese expansion in East Asia.

While the president was developing these innovative themes, Hull won plaudits as the conservator who made certain that the nation stayed true to its time-honored principles. In fact, though, the contrast between the two leaders was largely illusory. On the domestic front, the president was daring, willing to reach out for innovative solutions, and the public welcomed this approach to lead the country out of economic disaster. As for foreign affairs, Roosevelt realized that Americans appreciated the patience that the secretary had come to symbolize, and the White House benefited from this perception. Hull's imposing physical appearance and genteel Southern manners were comforting; here was reassurance of integrity, a man who promoted global peace and served his country with modesty and humility. His admirers clung to those admirable qualities.

Hull had spent decades learning the realities of political survival. Having built his career on following public opinion, not shaping it, his overriding goal was to avoid controversy. For him, analyzing all sides of an issue stifled action, and in many instances he purposely chose the least objectionable alternative as his best option for avoiding controversy. Whenever possible he would wait and see how future events unfolded before committing himself. By following the consensus rather than drowning in uncharted and hazardous waters, he had survived and flourished. Roosevelt promoted this image of Hull to his own advantage, openly praising the secretary's accomplishments and annually nominating him for the Nobel Peace Prize. The president knew that this pleased the secretary's ego; besides, Hull and his wife coveted the award for its cash prize of $40,000.[11]

Whereas the president's motives were self-serving, Postmaster General Farley was genuinely complimentary; Farley believed that the public revered the secretary as unquestionably the most respected member of the cabinet. Throughout Roosevelt's first term, he declared that Hull was "the most unselfish man" he had ever met and that he epitomized the loyal Democrat who provided the administration with the kind of leadership that regular party members cherished. Hull fervently worked to keep the United States out of European disputes, and, equally important, prevented the Brain Trusters from influencing Roosevelt. When the president asked for Hull's advice, he freely gave it; even if Roosevelt then chose another path, Hull would support the decision as long as the Democrats benefited.[12]

Although Senator Hiram Johnson had labeled Hull "a total loss," Republican outsiders like Stimson and Castle received confidential reports on departmental conditions from their friends inside the foreign service, and these former leaders agreed that Hull served a vital stabilizing function because he barred the fuzzy ideas of such New Dealers as Secretary of Agriculture Henry Wallace from the State Department. Hull had risen through the Democratic ranks and objected to those who gained entrance to the White House without first paying the required political toll. Although Castle criticized him for concentrating on trade matters and lacking a broader background in foreign affairs, the former diplomat also complimented Hull for being "a sweet person" who made "an excellent impression."[13]

The image of himself—as grandfatherly and conciliatory—was one that Hull welcomed, but at the same time, when he believed passionately in a project, he was capable of acting decisively, and this side of his nature was especially evident in his crusade to lower trade barriers. Demonstrating his determination in demanding reduced tariff duties, he spoke for a large following that had long yearned for a national champion. Before taking his cabinet post, Hull had believed that Roosevelt favored reducing trade barriers. Nonetheless, shortly after the inauguration, the president eliminated any legislative requests dealing with foreign commerce from his congressional agenda. When Hull tried to promote reciprocity agreements at the London meeting and again at the Montevideo conference, the White House minimized their significance.

Yet even in the midst of these stinging rebuffs, Hull's continual pressure for a new trade bill forced Roosevelt to relent by the end of 1933. With presidential acquiescence at the start of the new year (and during some of the worst Washington blizzards in over a decade), the secretary moved swiftly and energetically, sending the Reciprocal Trade Agreements Act to Congress in early March 1934. His congressional opponents were well organized and vocal, making the bill one of the most hotly contested pieces of legislation during the session, as antagonists attacked the fundamental concept of high versus low tariff barriers, while Republicans also warned that the measure was another vehicle for the expansion of executive prerogatives at congressional expense. The bill sought to remove tariff logrolling from the halls of Congress and gave the executive branch the privilege of negotiating reciprocal trade agreements that raised or lowered duties by as much as 50 percent. Because so many legislators were anxious about this added authority, when the bill eventually passed, its life was limited to three years. If Hull was unsuccessful in his crusade, his adversaries would then have an opportunity to cancel the program.

Hull never doubted the righteousness of his cause. Freer trade, he preached, assured economic recovery; he later added an additional theme: lower tariff barriers would stimulate international cooperation and reduce the political tensions that could result in warfare. The secretary left no room for debate within his department; no one dared to argue openly against the plan if he expected to retain his job.

The president signed the Reciprocal Trade Agreements Act in the summer of 1934, finally vindicating the perseverance of his secretary of state, who had almost single-handedly pushed this landmark legislation through Congress. The setting of duties that had traditionally consumed such an inordinate amount of legislative time ceased. Since the bill's passage, the executive branch has handled the technical issues it covers well enough that Congress has never again waged titanic battles over the passage of general tariff rate revisions. Upon the act's approval, Hull moved to put in place the infrastructure for its implementation, appointing Francis Sayre, Woodrow Wilson's son-in-law, to establish a trade agreements division within the State Department. The secretary also appropriated sufficient funding to staff the new division with three assistant chiefs, twelve officers, and fifteen clerks.[14]

The arguments against reciprocity did not shake Hull's devotion to his cause. By the time of Roosevelt's renomination, the Democratic platform included a plank, which the secretary had helped draft, claiming that the trade program was assisting domestic recovery and contributing to world peace. A year later Hull obtained the extension of the Reciprocal Trade Agreements Act (albeit without presidential endorsement), and three years later he won Roosevelt's blessings for yet another extension. Although the initial success of the program is still debated, its long-term effects cannot be doubted, for it has remained the cornerstone of American tariff policy since 1934.

Even though the legislation fundamentally changed the nature of trade negotiations, many questioned the worth of the reciprocity program in assisting domestic recovery. The most serious challenge came from foreign trade adviser George Peek, who advocated dumping U.S. surpluses on international markets to aid American farmers facing unfair competition from abroad. Those who supported Peek's theories thought that he symbolized a nationalistic approach in defending the domestic economy against foreign encroachment. If any international commercial bargaining was worthwhile, Peek felt, it should take the form of bilateral arrangements that exchanged an overabundance of American products for scarce foreign goods. These arguments directly contradicted Hull's philosophy, and the secretary came to view Peek's views as a personal affront, one that challenged the very foundation on which Hull intended to build a peaceful world. The two men clashed continually because of their fundamentally different economic theories, even though Hull never perceived a legitimate conflict. To him, Peek, like Raymond Moley, was disloyal, an antagonist who disrupted his department. From Peek's viewpoint, the roadblocks that the secretary put in his path only caused disillusionment and frustration, and it was in response to them that Peek resigned before the end of the first term.[15]

This episode demonstrated how Hull would rid his department of those whom he considered undesirable. He resented Peek, but did not openly confront him. Instead he rejected all of Peek's advice, and without any hope of obtaining a fair hearing, Peek resigned in disgust. Roosevelt had assigned Peek to the State Department, but the president never dared to risk the threat of Hull's resignation to retain Peek. Whenever Hull stepped forward to voice his displeasure in personnel matters, Roosevelt usually capitulated.

Hull also expended considerable energy on Asian issues, more or less by default, since no one else was interested or powerful enough to dominate policymaking for the region. Since Hull lacked any knowledge of the area, he initially depended on the chief of the Division of Far Eastern Affairs, the opinionated and domineering Stanley Hornbeck, to provide guidance. A Rhodes scholar who had received a doctorate from the University of Wisconsin, Hornbeck had traveled and taught in China before returning to the United States and lecturing at Harvard. In 1928 he became division chief and began to stamp his views on departmental objectives: he doubted the capabilities of the Chinese and at the same time opposed conciliation with the Japanese, unless there was a danger of provoking a military reaction.[16]

Hull initially followed these general outlines and relied on his own experience in inter-American affairs by referring the Asian combatants to the nonintervention principles adopted at the Montevideo conference as the foundation for peace. Just as the administration had renounced intervention in the Caribbean, the State Department expected Tokyo to follow the same policy in the Pacific. Under these guidelines the United States could not intervene in any dispute between China and Japan, for to do so would violate the spirit of the good neighbor.

Although the secretary was willingly drawn into Asian affairs, he refused to become involved in the persecution of German Jews and their emigration to the United States. Hitler had chosen the Jews as the scapegoat for Germany's troubles and advocated their removal from the Third Reich. But anti-Semites had preached these arguments for centuries, and German Jews had become accustomed to such rantings. Thus they continued their activities in the hope that, despite the call for pogroms, they could persevere and the Nazis would eventually disappear.[17]

Rabbi Stephen Wise, the most visible Zionist in the United States, had known Hull since the early 1920s and referred to him as "my dear Judge Hull".[18] By the summer of 1936, Wise and his followers were pressuring the secretary to lobby the British government against suspending Jewish immigration into Palestine. Arabs in Palestine had already staged a general strike, attacked Jews, destroyed their property, and assaulted English officials. Despite these difficulties, American Jews wanted their government to apply pressure on Whitehall to ignore the calls for closing the borders. Hull held private talks that summer with Wise—later requesting assurances that all records of their conversations had been destroyed. That was done, but Wise continued to press Hull to support Zionism and cautioned him that in the upcoming elections five million American Jews would be disappointed if their government did not assist their cause. Hull recognized this veiled political threat, but his refusal to become involved with Jewish matters did not stem from anti-Semitism; rather it could be traced to fear that allegations of his philo-Semitism would damage his future chances to run for the White House.[19]

In his entire public life, Hull never commented on his wife's religious heritage. Her grandfather was, in all likelihood, a practicing Austrian Jew, as was her father, Isaac, when he arrived in the United States at the age of nine. Isaac, even though he married a Christian, never abandoned Staunton's Jews. When they founded a synagogue in 1885, he sold ten dollars' worth of raffle tickets for the temple and, two years later, lent the congregation $200 to defray expenses at the cemetery. His brother Moritz was the secretary of the congregation for its first two years and continued as an active member. In 1925, the Temple House of Israel was built, and to this day the Jews from that region of the Shenandoah Valley practice their religion at this tiny, charming synagogue.[20]

In addition, Frances had three brothers, and one of them, Henry, married Sara Hertzberg, the daughter of a prominent Jewish family from Baltimore, who actively practiced her beliefs at a reform temple. Frances, who was quite fond of her brother, often visited him and Sara at their apartment on Lake Drive across from Druid Hill Park, an address that was in one of the most affluent neighborhoods in the city. Inside the apartment, Henry—who neither proclaimed nor concealed his faith—prominently featured a formal portrait of Hull as well as a caricature. These were only two displays of his closeness to his sister and her husband.[21]

Cordell feared that this Jewish connection made him vulnerable to attacks from anti-Semites, who would argue that his wife had forced him to support Jewish causes, and therefore that he had succumbed to un-American influences. Such charges were at that time not idle concerns and might cost him votes if he decided to seek the presidency. The Knights of the White Camelia, for example, in its August 15, 1936, edition of the *The White Knight,* published an article entitled "The Jew Deal," asserting that Roosevelt had allowed Jewish communists and socialists to control the federal government. Since Jews had already tainted Christian beliefs and white purity, the author asked: "Is this a 'new deal' or a 'Jew Deal'?" Hull, though not a Jew, would be part of this diabolical conspiracy because his wife was incorrectly characterized as a relative of members of the New York Jewish banking house of Kuhn, Loeb and Company. The author went on to charge that, through this firm, Frances had secretly contributed $60,000 to her husband's senatorial campaign in 1932. Through Hull's own fear of guilty association, Zionists secretly controlled the senator.[22]

If this were not worrisome enough to Hull, the August issue of the *American Bulletin* featured similar charges in an article under the title "Cordell Hull—Slave of Morgan and Jews." Its writer concluded: "Here then we have an example of American 'Statesmanship' of today. Men who are elected or appointed to an office of trust to represent the interests of the American people—the puppets of money magnates, betraying that office to satisfy the greed of the money changers."[23] Rather than reply to such outlandish accusations, Hull ignored them, hoping that they would disappear. In this instance, his political instincts proved correct. On the other hand, he was probably equally uncomfortable with Drew Pearson's very public praise of him in a nationally syndicated column later that summer, when Pearson—referring to Hull's summoning of the German ambassador into his office to protest Germany's treatment of its Jewish population—applauded the secretary's stand against "religious persecution or discrimination."[24]

Hull unquestionably followed the press with minute scrutiny and grew hypersensitive to any criticism. Hostile articles deeply disturbed him and he paid extraordinary attention to them, never forgetting the transgressions of their authors, especially those of the hostile Hearst chain.[25] The secretary agonized over unflattering columns and even his strongest supporters, like Farley, recognized this trait with regret: "If he were more forceful he undoubtedly could be of great aid to the Administration because of the prestige of his position, and the regard so many people have for him in this country."[26] A long-time Democratic ally, Ambassador Claude Bowers in Madrid, lamented the sharp contrast between Roosevelt and Hull. Both wrote to him, but the president answered candidly, while the secretary invariably chose to equivocate, refusing to act boldly.[27]

Adding to his feelings of inadequacy, the secretary often complained that Roosevelt ignored his advice and privately belittled him. Far more insulting was the president's habit, without directly mentioning the secretary, of condemning the State Department in public for its antiquated procedures and thus indirectly attacking the secretary's competence. These actions deeply offended Hull. He could never fully trust a president who could publicly embarrass him for no apparent reason. Above all else, the secretary dreaded this kind of insult.

Rather than assert many of his prerogatives, Hull continued to defer to the White House in crucial areas like the selection of personnel. Even after the London meeting, when he bitterly complained to the president about Raymond Moley's betrayal and insisted on the privilege of choosing future subordinates, this protest was confined during the first term only to Moore's hiring. Once his friend took office, the secretary reverted to his earlier posture of avoiding any involvement in picking his staff. The fact was that he abhorred deciding personnel matters and gladly delegated these responsibilities to others. Along with refusing to handle this duty, the secretary did not monitor his subordinates' White House visits. To be sure, Roosevelt encouraged the assistant secretaries to meet with him in the Oval Office; but Hull's failure to supervise his assistant secretaries lay with the secretary himself, for he did not relish regular sessions with the president for fear of rejection.[28]

Hull often spoke to Castle about his staff's loyalty, confiding that he trusted only a few individuals. His distrust permeated just about everything he did, and it was illustrated dramatically by his handling of sensitive private correspondence. He wrote letters on delicate topics to individuals in whom he seemed to have great confidence; but at the bottom of this correspondence, he occasionally added the directive READ AND DESTROY. Clearly, this material was intended only for the eyes of a recipient who was expected to shred the document after reading it. However, in the event that such a document ever reached other hands, Hull was protected—he carefully saved carbon copies for himself!

Hull limited his vacations for fear that a subordinate would misinterpret his policies and make major blunders.[29] Moore, though, was one of his completely trustworthy associates. He had declared his fealty to Hull in March 1936: "Without being controlled by my warm friendship for him, I am certain from what is being constantly stated in the newspapers and otherwise that he is regarded with great favor, not only by adherents of the Administration but by the public generally, and I rejoice at the opportunity of serving under him."[30]

The public was unaware of the secretary's insecurity; outwardly he was, as ever, calm and collected. Some mistook his demeanor as masking a mind engaged in cogent and incisive planning and perceived his indecision as a sign of thoughtfulness, but this was not the case. To those who hoped to slow rapidly changing international events, Hull personified an earlier era in which few pressing time constraints mattered. Unfortunately for those who clung to this antiquated view, world events would not adjust to the secretary's pace.

As noted earlier, his inability to act forcefully extended to fiscal affairs because he did not understand the budgetary process. For example, at a hearing before the House Appropriations Committee in early 1935, he made no opening statement, had no grasp of the facts and figures, and therefore was incapable of presenting an effective argument for increasing or even maintaining his department's current allocation. On one occasion, when his budget was reduced, he signed a letter of protest to the White House, but refused to present it to the president personally. Carr was astonished: "[Hull] seems amazingly diffident, lacking in courage or lacking in close relationship to President. Other cabinet officers demand things of the President. Why not he?"[31]

Throughout the summer of 1935, Hull considered resigning from the cabinet at the end of the first term. The secretary complained about the great physical strain of his office and the severe financial burden of his job. Besides, his predecessors had traditionally held office for only one term, and he did not wish to break with precedent. Frances, too, worried about her husband's hectic routine: "I often fear for his continued strength to cope with the many problems which increasingly come up."[32] Such international emergencies as the Italo-Ethiopian war and genocide in Spain added to her concerns, but her husband's health remained unimpaired. Short holidays helped, and once a year he left the capital for a month-long rest in the South so that his wife could visit family and friends.

Hull contemplated running again for the Senate because both he and his wife feared for their financial future if the Republicans recaptured the presidency. Frances now realized that Cordell could have remained in the

Senate for life, with a guaranteed salary, but instead had given up his situation in response to Roosevelt's solicitations. Throughout the fall and winter of 1935, his friend Judge James Gardenhire of Nashville explored the possibilities, and while the judge planned local strategy, the secretary talked to the senior senator from his home state, Kenneth McKellar, who appeared receptive to supporting Hull's candidacy. But at the end of the year, the secretary abruptly changed his plans. If the Democrats won the next national election, he would stay in the cabinet.[33]

After three years in office, Hull proudly listed his diplomatic accomplishments: the advancement of inter-American cooperation; the promotion of increased global cooperation by avoiding extreme nationalism or internationalism; and the creation of greater economic intercourse by lowering trade barriers and pursuing global peace. Hull skillfully hid his weaknesses. Americans saw his apparent strengths, and Roosevelt reinforced the perception of these with his guarded accolades. Hull's constituency implicitly trusted him for his staunch advocacy of traditional Democratic values, while his caution and suspicion of international conflict corresponded with the American mindset against foreign involvement. His indecisive nature was immaterial to foreign policy initiatives while the United States grappled with its domestic upheaval. Even to the skeptical mind of Secretary of the Interior Harold Ickes, Hull deserved to remain at his desk if Roosevelt won a second term.[34]

Although it was Hull who actively craved public approval, Under Secretary Phillips handled his own assignments without causing any ill will—a fact that was particularly remarkable owing to his delicate position of holding membership in the Republican party. An ideal second in command, he directed the daily departmental activities, attended the social engagements that the secretary so abhorred, monitored European affairs, and kept the secretary informed about major events. He avoided the spotlight and overcame the secretary's sense of inferiority with the outrageous flattery that many others in the department also used. Once Phillips wrote the secretary in London, "I miss you badly and never cease to regret your absence. The Department seems an unimportant place without you." A short time later, he pined, "I never cease . . . to wish that you were back again and sincerely hope that the Conference not go much beyond the end of July."[35]

Phillips helped the department achieve a relatively smooth routine by arbitrating internal disputes and preventing factionalism. He skillfully balanced two forces within the department: Hull, who personified the cautious political approach based on the Democratic imperative of retaining the presidency, and Phillips, who represented the professional diplomat, seeking to follow long-accepted principles of American foreign policy. Although the under secretary favored the latter view, he also acknowledged the power of party politics in shaping international relations. He lived in both worlds and survived because he overcame Hull's suspicious nature and enjoyed Roosevelt's blessings. Yet even with these accommodations, Phillips deplored Hull's inadequate preparation as an administrator, especially the secretary's laxness in allowing his assistant secretaries to visit the White House without his clearance. The latter trait was especially irritating to Phillips, who demanded strict adherence to the organizational chart from his staff.[36]

Since Hull avoided the growing agitation over German Jewish immigration, Phillips had to tangle regularly with the Labor Department over this issue. Despite Secretary Frances Perkins's best efforts to offer her assistance on humanitarian grounds, she, too, was concerned about adverse reaction from union and congressional leaders. The State Department's obstructionist practices made the achievement of any accommodation between the foreign service and labor officials hopeless. Very few, including Perkins, were willing to risk their prestige on such a volatile issue. Even powerful Jewish families within Germany agonized over whether to fight the Nazis or abandon a life-style that they had built from generation to generation.[37]

While Carr continued to formulate fiscal affairs, he also directed consular activities and followed the refugee policy advocated by Phillips. Carr knew how to tighten visa requirements, which was exactly what he tried to do, in most cases successfully. As long as entry into the United States for German Jews depended on the interpretation of the nebulous "likely to become a public charge" regulation by Phillips and Carr, the forces of restriction would rule over those of humanitarianism.

Exceptions occurred because George Messersmith happened to be consul general in Berlin when Hitler came to power. This American diplomat offered an early diagnosis of the Reich's growing cancer and then moved to Vienna to observe the Nazi party infect Austrian politics. He had joined the consular service in 1914 and vehemently worked against German infiltration of the Caribbean during World War I. Tough, strong-willed, and despised by the Nazis (who had erroneously labeled him a Jew), he was respected by his peers for his intelligence and vigor. Messersmith was meticulous and blunt-spoken, and he had no hobby except for his profession. His only recreations were mystery stories and Chinese checkers. He was the number one letter writer in the diplomatic corps, with correspondence that often ran to a dozen, single-spaced typewritten pages with several pages of postscripts. Messersmith lived to carry out his duties. His first objective was to protect American Jews, and next he enforced his country's immigration regulations by setting high standards for applicants.[38]

Assistant Secretary of State R. Walton Moore never concerned himself with visa questions. Above all, he made certain that the State Department did not take any precipitous action that could adversely affect the reelection of the national Democratic ticket. As a result, he thought foremost in terms of voters' preferences and therefore worried about immediate public reaction. As part of his political chores, Moore guarded the department from all attacks during Hull's absences and informed him of unfolding current events. For example, while the secretary was at Montevideo, Moore wired him about disturbing Hearst newspaper accounts that the president had lost confidence in Hull's abilities. Moore then worked energetically to dispel such rumors. His approach created friction within the foreign service since many career diplomats resented the fact that Moore decided policy matters based on how they affected voters, instead of on long-range considerations.[39]

Hull undoubtedly dismissed such complaints since he, too, appreciated the paramount necessity of ensuring a Democratic victory at the polls. Clearly, the secretary depended on Moore for his political savvy as well as his trustworthiness, for both men personified traditional Democratic values. Both also understood that their positions were rewards for their service to the party.

Moore, an astute politician, also served as the department's liaison to his former congressional colleagues. He helped guide the neutrality bills through Congress. As war drew closer, he watched the United States gradually align with the democracies, but he hoped to avoid war. He kept controversial opinions private, and like his boss, tried to maintain the appearance of impartiality.[40]

While Moore served the party and the secretary, Welles had broad powers in removing the last vestiges of United States intervention in the Western Hemisphere, and Hull relied on Welles's knowledge, expecting him to provide the technical skills necessary in carrying out the good neighbor policy. Welles showed Hull the respect due a secretary of state and was genuinely concerned about his superior's health.[41] When Mrs. Hull insisted that her husband take a three-week vacation, Welles heartily agreed because the secretary was "the hardest working man I know and he is compelled to take a real vacation if he is able to keep on efficiently with the work that he has to do." When the assistant secretary took a holiday in 1937, he wrote Hull to express his concern that his absence not cause any physical strain on him.[42] This did not mean that they were close friends. They never were, although the Hulls did attend some of Welles's social gatherings, and the men's wives had a cordial relationship. The assistant secretary's feelings for his superior did not appear contrived, and the secretary found Welles useful. At the end of the first term, there was no evidence of any serious friction between them; on the contrary, they complemented one another.

Nominally a Democrat, Welles never ran for public office and had no inclination in that direction, for his primary goal was to formulate an effective inter-American program. Both the president and the secretary understood that good neighbor diplomacy was winning a national following and that this support translated into votes at election time. With this reality in mind, Welles knew that he had wide latitude in building hemispheric solidarity; if that meant taking his proposals straight to the White House, he would not hesitate.

Not only did Welles have charge of inter-American affairs, but the secretary also used him as a liaison with those New Dealers who had business at the State Department. Since Hull disapproved of them, this was a chore gladly given to a subordinate, one who was eager to please the secretary. Although he welcomed Welles's association with the New Dealers, Hull was ambivalent over the close personal relationship between Welles and Roosevelt. The secretary accepted it because he grudgingly realized that this bond with the White House assured Welles a prompt and favorable hearing on hemispheric proposals that also added to the secretary's prestige. In addition, Hull realized that he could not dampen the friendship that had grown between the two men.[43]

Welles's wife Mathilde understandably could not imagine how the State Department could function without her husband's presence. Farley saw him as "a man of considerable ability." John Barnett, a prominent inter-American specialist, wrote Hull that he would "find him . . . a loyal and valuable assistant." Dean Acheson, who was a class behind Welles at Groton, offered another impression: "His manner was formal to the point of stiffness. His voice, pitched much lower than would seem natural, though it had been so since he was a boy, lent a suggestion of pomposity. Once, when a remark of my wife's made him laugh, he quickly caught himself and said, 'pardon me. You amused me.' Out of the office he could be a charming host and an appreciative guest."[44]

Moore expressed a far different opinion. From the first time he met Welles, Moore had developed an instant dislike for the man. With the exception of Moore, few bluntly warned Hull of Welles's unsavory character. From outside the foreign service, Castle admonished the secretary to watch his assistant secretary's ambitions and unreliability. Others concurred, but tried, at least superficially, to remain cordial, speaking only to close friends for fear of Welles's retribution. Although Hull listened to this advice, he recognized that it was at least partly motivated by jealousy and would make his own judgment. During the first term, the secretary had no cause for alarm.[45]

Part of the controversy that surrounded Welles could no doubt be traced to his opulent life-style. Senator Arthur Vandenberg and his wife Hazel attended their first dinner at the assistant secretary's mansion on Massachusetts Avenue in the winter of 1934. The Townsend estate, known as the "house with a hundred rooms," was the first home of its size and importance in the neighborhood. Hazel described it as "a real palace. . . . Simply the most elegant affair I have ever seen. The most gorgeous home I've ever seen."[46] Carr attended a New Year's party there at the end of the year. He, too, was impressed with the lavish setting "that would have done credit to England or France 100 years ago.

Beautiful young people, gay in their pretty gowns and graceful in their dancing." He also noticed a great deal of drinking, which continued throughout the weekend.[47] On several other occasions, Carr went to the Welles's summer estate, Oxon Hill Manor. On his first visit, he declared: "The house and grounds are magnificent, must have cost a fortune to develop them." The gardens, he noted, were beautiful, and the view of the Potomac River was superb.[48] Hazel Vandenberg also raved about a visit she made at the height of the summertime blooming: "everything just too beautiful for words."[49]

But during business hours Welles was anything but the solicitous host during meetings with his subordinates. He had a formal, even stuffy, exterior and greeted them by placing his fingers on the edge of his desk and bowing. He and his colleague would sit, discuss the topic at hand, and then expect to resolve the issue. After the meeting, Welles would write a memorandum on the conversation and take whatever action was deemed appropriate. Interestingly, such formality did not apply to Latin American guests, to whom he was warm and friendly. In short, Welles acted in the manner that each group expected of him: his associates anticipated a businesslike exterior, whereas Latin Americans expected a more overtly cordial welcome.[50]

Shortly after returning from Cuba, Welles was forced by a heart ailment to take a ten-day rest. Resuming his duties after that short break, he had a relapse and was forced to take an extended Florida holiday.[51] Upon his return, he proclaimed his complete recovery, but one friend thought otherwise: "he is overworking, as usual and as he always will until forced out by collapse."[52] Others noted signs of fatigue, but Welles stayed at his post and took occasional vacations in the summer. Extended leaves were impossible, for he insisted upon controlling everything under his supervision.[53]

Welles followed Roosevelt's and Hull's efforts to create a new spirit of hemispheric cooperation by reviewing agreements under which the administration had the right to interfere in domestic issues. For example, in the early 1920s the United States had signed an agreement with the tiny Central American countries that precluded diplomatic ties with a nation if its ruler had come to power as the result of a revolution. By the end of January 1934, that treaty had been canceled, and the United

States no longer had any obligation to defend existing regimes from their adversaries.

The assistant secretary also handled the delicate conversations that led to a new treaty with Panama. That small republic had been an American protectorate since achieving its independence in 1903 because Theodore Roosevelt had demanded control over a ten-mile-wide zone for an interocean canal. The United States built the canal, stationed troops and other personnel to manage it, sent marines to quell domestic disorders on several occasions, and actively intervened in local politics. When another Roosevelt entered the White House three decades later, he committed his government to revising the treaty that Cousin Teddy had signed in order to give the Panamanians greater authority over the canal's operations. After two years of intensive negotiations and adamant objections from the American armed forces, Panama signed a new agreement that gave it a larger share of the canal's revenues and, just as significant, eliminated the United States' privilege to intervene militarily in domestic matters. Both governments, at least in theory, were now responsible for the canal's defense.

Welles negotiated new agreements in the Caribbean by promptly withdrawing marines from Haiti and refusing to interfere with the growing repressive measures of Rafael Trujillo in the Dominican Republic. As long as the United States' vital interests were preserved, he believed that the State Department had no cause to intervene. Welles applied similar reasoning to Cuban matters. Once his nemesis Grau had left office in early 1934, Welles quickly saw to it that the new regime was recognized. With the restoration of diplomatic ties, he personally negotiated a new treaty that abrogated the Platt Amendment, meaning that American soldiers no longer had an obligation to keep the peace on the island.

Throughout this flurry of diplomatic activity, the Roosevelt administration was simply eliminating what was outdated and retaining what it considered to be crucial to its interests. What most did not comprehend was that the basic relationship of a superpower to its dependent client states remained unaltered. The public did not bother to analyze the nuances of the good neighbor policy, and Roosevelt certainly promoted it in simplistic terms. Few understood the complexities of inter-American affairs or how the president was using the policy to influence other international events. Of course previous administrations had taken unrelated regional actions, but none had woven them into a coherent pattern with broad governmental support. Under the New Deal, Welles painstakingly monitored and coordinated bilateral and multilateral activities and fit them into a neat mold. Observers seldom appreciated the scope of the entire orchestration, and neither the White House nor its Latin American beneficiaries, such as Batista, Somoza, and Trujillo, chose to alter that illusion. Nonintervention was never an absolute reality—merely an image that was useful in popularizing the good neighbor policy.[54]

Welles strengthened his standing with the secretary by promoting his reciprocity policy in Latin America. The United States sent a wide range of manufactured and agricultural goods to the South American republics, and they shipped noncompetitive farm commodities such as coffee and bananas to the north. Welles commended the secretary for establishing commercial interaction: "It struck a note of economic sanity when it was most needed. Even under the altogether abnormal conditions in which it operated, it was of material benefit to the United States and to the other co-operating nations."[55] The secretary realized that his assistant secretary was a firm adherent to the concept of lowering trade barriers and was his most productive subordinate in signing reciprocal trade agreements.

However, Welles sometimes crossed the imaginary line beyond which he could not act with his customary independence. Early in 1936 he put forth a proposal to make the Brazilian navy an auxiliary force to the United States fleet by selling that South American giant ten cruisers. He believed that Roosevelt and Hull had approved the transaction, but he failed to consult with his other State Department colleagues, who viewed the purchase as the start of a Latin American arms race that would bankrupt many of those countries. Joseph Green, the diplomat who was in charge of arms sales, frequently met with Welles, and they worked well face to face; but in this situation, Welles had acted alone. That unwillingness to work in concert with others gave his enemies the opportunity to urge the president to repudiate Welles's proposal. To Green the episode indicated that Welles was indulging "more and more

... in a tendency to act independently in pursuance of his own pet Latin American policies."[56] When the scheme was leaked to the press, opposition promptly surfaced, and the forebodings of Welles's colleagues were confirmed. Argentina announced its intention to purchase more naval vessels. That reaction hardened Hull's opposition to the plan, and the entire idea was temporarily abandoned. Welles learned a valuable lesson. He could remove troops from Latin America and dictate his division's daily routine, but once he acted beyond his regional responsibilities, he would need to consult with—and often obtain the permission of—others.

Yet as long as Roosevelt and Hull approved of his performance, Welles appeared to thrive under the tremendous stress that his supervision of every minute detail brought on. A driven man who felt compelled to complete every assigned task, when presented with a problem he would search for the right program within his well-defined area and would be responsible for supplying the corrective that could ultimately receive the "good neighbor" label. As a result of his accomplishments, the president and secretary acknowledged his value, and he savored their applause. Their praise, of course, reinforced his desire to work even more diligently, and this redoubled effort in turn evoked even more resentment and jealousy from his adversaries.

The person upon whom Welles depended most heavily in hemispheric matters was Laurence Duggan. Even though the new chief executive never knew him, Duggan and Welles had met at Roosevelt's home in New York shortly after the 1932 campaign at a reception that Duggan's parents, who labeled themselves liberals, attended as friends of the president-elect's family. Born on May 28, 1905, in New York City, Duggan was the son of a professor of political science at City College in New York. His mother Sara was active in social causes, such as the Negro Welfare League of White Plains. Duggan spent most of his childhood there, was enrolled in the nearby Roger Ascham School for his early education, and attended the White Plains Community Church, where people of many different religious beliefs came together under one roof.

After graduating cum laude in 1923 from Phillips Exeter Academy, he entered Harvard, where he served as class secretary and assistant manager of the football team before graduating with distinction. After his graduation, he worked as a book salesman for Harper Brothers, resigning in 1929, when his father, who headed the prestigious Institute of International Education, offered him the directorship of its Latin American division. Duggan learned to speak fluent Spanish and to read Portuguese, spent a considerable amount of time traveling throughout the Western Hemisphere to develop programs for the institute, and produced a report that recommended professional exchanges, scholarships for graduate students, and an increase in the number of English books translated into Spanish and Portuguese. Duggan also recommended that any proposals for exchange programs founded in the United States be made in a cooperative spirit, with emphasis on mutual benefits for the United States and Latin America.

After the completion of that project, he entered the foreign service in 1930 to specialize in hemispheric affairs. To improve his knowledge, he took postgraduate courses in history, government, and economics at George Washington University. Two years after he joined the diplomatic corps, he married Helen Boyd, a graduate of Vassar College, and they had four children. By the time Roosevelt entered the White House, Duggan was busy working to improve inter-American peace machinery, trying to end the chaotic conditions in the Dominican Republic, negotiating a new treaty with Panama, reexamining the United States' position toward its nonrecognition treaty with the Central American states, and seeking a consistent regional financial policy to protect American investments. His fervent commitment to improving inter-American understanding made him an immediate ally of Welles, and their relationship was helped by the fact that they shared similar backgrounds. Both had been born in New York City, had attended elite boarding schools, had graduated from Harvard, and came from families who had warm friendships with the Roosevelts. With his above-average height, glasses, and broad face with a wide nose, Duggan ultimately became Welles's alter ego, assuming his chief's role when he was unavailable. If anyone knew what Welles was thinking, Duggan did.[57]

Welles demonstrated his approval by promoting Duggan three times in 1935 alone, culminating in his appointment as chief of the Latin American division. Green commented on the rapid rise: "His career has certainly been meteoric, but every one recognized the fact that he was the ablest officer in Latin America and that if the new Chief was to be drawn from the present personnel of that Division he was the obvious man for the position. His appointment was generally approved, but I fear that it has created some jealousies which may make things difficult for him."[58] Few openly attacked Duggan's advancement because he was under Welles's protection, and Duggan did not hide his appreciation. After retiring from the foreign service, he paid tribute in the late 1940s to his superior as "a man who understood clearly the mistakes of our past policy and had definite ideas for building a new one." Welles, by Duggan's standards, fought bravely for better regional understanding when most diplomats ignored this hemisphere: "The Latin Americans recognized in him a kindred spirit with whom they could talk as friend to friend. He had infinite patience and tact and an unrivaled insight into their political problems."[59]

While Welles directed a variety of bilateral negotiations, he also prepared for the multilateral hemispheric peace gathering in Buenos Aires at the end of 1936 by setting the agenda and handling the preliminaries leading up to the conference. The president and his secretary of state also looked forward to this gathering for their own reasons: Hull remembered his triumph in the bleak days of 1933 and anticipated another victory, while Roosevelt, who recalled his limited role in the earlier meeting, had every expectation of playing a central part in this one. With expectations for a successful conference, the United States delegation left New York harbor on November 7 aboard the same ship that had steamed to Montevideo three years earlier. Once the delegates had settled into their quarters, Hull resumed his practice of meeting daily with his staff to discuss American proposals. After a smooth eighteen-day trip in fine weather, he arrived in Buenos Aires, still optimistic.[60]

While the delegation was at sea, Roosevelt, after his stunning reelection landslide, began to think about attending the meeting to give the opening address, in the hope of fostering improved regional relations and using the hemispheric forum as a vehicle to speak to the rest of the international community. German rearmament, the Italo-Ethiopian war, Japanese aggression, a dying League, and the apparent indifference of his countrymen to these grave dangers to world peace were all cause for apprehension. Additionally, his prestige in the Americas had dramatically risen during his first term, for his speeches as well as his deeds had been widely acclaimed, and he hoped that the hemispheric movement toward peaceful solutions to disputes would serve as an inspiration to the rest of the world.

When rumors of Roosevelt's possible attendance reached Argentina, President Agustín Justo extended an official invitation to the White House, and by November 16 Roosevelt had accepted. This was to be the first and only time that the president, Hull, and Welles would travel abroad and work together at an international meeting. Roosevelt left the White House the next day and on the following morning boarded the cruiser U.S.S. *Indianapolis* to enjoy an ocean cruise as a well-deserved relaxation after a strenuous campaign. He devoted the first phase of his trip to strengthening the bonds of hemispheric friendship with a demonstration of his personal magnetism. His cruiser entered Rio de Janeiro harbor on the morning of November 27, a day that the Brazilian government had declared a national holiday. Even though a steady drizzle was falling, Roosevelt insisted that his car remain uncovered in order to return the salutations of the huge crowds—including thousands of schoolchildren greeting the president with red, white, and blue banners—who lined his route. He spoke to the Brazilian congress, held a press conference, and attended a state banquet during his one-day visit.

On the last day of November, Roosevelt arrived in the Argentine capital. After coming down the gangplank, he illustrated his showmanship by vigorously shaking President Justo's hand and referring to him as *mi amigo;* his host warmly responded by giving his guest an *abrazo.* The enormous crowd watching their procession to the executive palace waved American flags and showered the presidential automobile with flowers. When the two leaders reached the palace, both appeared on a balcony facing the plaza. Roosevelt dramatically wrung Justo's hand while over 100,000 onlookers roared their welcome.

The Inter-American Conference for the Maintenance of Peace convened on December 1, and Roosevelt became the second American president to travel abroad to open a Pan-American gathering. His address was noteworthy on two counts: it was the last foreign policy statement of his first term, and he clearly aimed its message to the Old as well as the New World. By this time he had carefully connected regional cooperation within a broader international frame of reference. Besides minimizing Yankeephobia in Latin America, Roosevelt planned to speak out against warfare worldwide. Before leaving for Buenos Aires, he wrote Ambassador William Dodd in Berlin about his intention to use his hemispheric approach to influence European opinion: "That visit will have little practical or immediate effect in Europe but at least the forces of example will help if the knowledge of it can be spread down to the masses of the people in Germany and Italy."[61]

Others, troubled by Nazi militarism, also hoped that the president's message from the Americas would reverberate in Europe. Adolf Berle, who attended the meeting and assisted in drafting the presidential speech, noted that it was "addressed to Europe more than the Americas, for the conference, if it succeeds, is plainly a threshold to the possibility of dealing in Europe with the conference looking toward peace, but we are working against horrible odds in point of time."[62] The president reminded his listeners that the Americas were at peace while others fought, and he committed his administration to ensuring hemispheric order: "In this determination to live at peace among ourselves we in the Americas make it at the same time clear that we stand shoulder to shoulder in our final determination that others who, driven by war madness or land hunger, might seek to commit acts of aggression against us will find a Hemisphere wholly prepared to consult together for our mutual safety and our mutual good."[63]

Roosevelt's hope that his hemispheric message could be used as a vehicle to influence deteriorating conditions in Europe proved vain. Instead commentators focused on the festive atmosphere surrounding the presidential visit because it made for more exciting copy. Roosevelt, for instance, left the capital on December 2 in a driving rain that nevertheless did not deter large crowds from watching his departure. As if on stage, the president pulled a handkerchief in Argentine colors from his pocket and waved it, to the audience's delight.

He arrived in Montevideo the next day to another warm reception, and that stop completed his tour. The trip had not only provided excellent public relations for the United States but also further enhanced Roosevelt's personal popularity. Yet he still dreamed of extending his influence to other areas. At the height of his optimism, steaming homeward, he hoped that there would "be at least some *moral* repercussions in Europe."[64]

That never occurred. Indeed, as a prelude to the economic recession and political reversals that awaited him, on the return voyage Roosevelt experienced a personal loss. Gus Gennerich, his bodyguard and friend, died of a sudden heart attack. Gennerich had done far more than just protect the president; he had helped him dress and undress, had moved him in and out of automobiles, and was a favorite of the family. Someone new would have to assume that very sensitive role.

After Roosevelt's departure, the delegates began to act on the conference agenda. Even before Hull had arrived, American diplomats had warned him about Saavedra Lamas's renewed obstructionism. Ambassador Alexander Weddell in Buenos Aires reported "that any conference entrusted to the guidance of Saavedra Lamas will be handled with a maximum of ineptitude and a minimum of hope."[65] If the secretary believed that the rapport established in Montevideo with the Argentine foreign minister would ensure cooperation, he had grossly miscalculated. Saavedra Lamas consistently advocated Old World connections over an inter-American system led by the United States, and he wrote Hull before the conference suggesting increased economic ties as the main theme and opposing closer hemispheric political association. During a talk with Ambassador Bullitt, Saavedra Lamas declared that the Americas had nothing to fear from any non-American state, and that any conference declaration to the contrary would be misinterpreted on the continent as a step toward regional exclusiveness and away from universal understanding. The foreign minister's recalcitrance thinly masked his real dilemma. He had recently won the Nobel Peace Prize and was also the assembly president for the League of Nations. At the zenith of his fame, the egotistical Argentine had somehow to reconcile his allegiance to the League and Europe with the accomplishments to be expected from a regional gathering of which he was host.

Hull did not understand the political constraints that Saavedra Lamas faced; instead he proceeded on the belief that he had already struck one deal with the foreign minister and would do so again. On December 5 the secretary presented his "eight pillars of enduring peace" to the delegates, arguing that, since international law and cooperation were at their nadir, they needed revitalization through the reaffirmation of regional peace pacts. If war erupted outside the Americas, a common neutrality policy was essential. Within the hemisphere, each nation should educate its citizens concerning the evils of war. To encourage peace, the American republics must communicate frequently and hold regular meetings. Finally, since peace and prosperity were intertwined, Hull repeated his dream that his reciprocity program would lower trade barriers throughout the Americas.

However, those lofty principles did not translate into specific conference declarations, since any major resolution needed Saavedra Lamas's blessing. He rejected Hull's proposal for a permanent inter-American consultation committee to meet in the event of a military threat from outside the Americas, for such a body would exclude League participation. Hull unsuccessfully tried to appeal to the foreign minister's pride, but as one American, close to the delegation, wrote in frustration: "Everybody is disgusted with [Saavedra] Lamas, but no one seems willing to tell him where he ought to go!"[66] The Brazilian delegate finally offered an acceptable compromise, according to which the standing committee was eliminated in favor of voluntary consultation in cases of threats to peace. The secretary never publicly mentioned that Saavedra Lamas had humiliated him, but the foreign minister's actions had so shaken Hull that he briefly considered asking the Argentine president to replace his own foreign minister![67]

When the secretary left the capital, Saavedra Lamas further infuriated him by refusing to see his guest off at the dock. Hull took his actions personally, without appreciating Argentina's heritage of close European connections or its traditional stand as the leader in shaping South American diplomacy in direct opposition to United States hegemony. Instead, the secretary viewed Saavedra Lamas's intransigence in the light of his own political experience, and that simplistic view reinforced his resentment toward the foreign minister and ultimately extended it to include the ruling oligarchy.

The conference ended on December 23, and Roosevelt, eager to promote the spirit of hemispheric cooperation, complimented the delegation on a job well done. Hull, for his part, publicly exaggerated the accomplishments and hid his embarrassment over Saavedra Lamas's antics. He correctly gauged the heightened degree of positive inter-American comradeship, and capitalized on those advantages through the press, radio, and private conversations after returning to Washington.[68]

Welles viewed the conference results from a far different perspective. The meeting, he believed, marked a new epoch in Pan-American relations by laying the foundation for consultation and cementing firm regional bonds. The spirit of goodwill that the United States was cultivating could not be quantified, but it was already paying dividends. The growing cordiality among regional diplomats allowed the State Department to present its case about overseas aggression and its possible consequences for the Americas. The assistant secretary praised Hull's contribution: "The Buenos Aires Conference will always be one of my most thoroughly happy and satisfactory memories, due in very large part to the privilege I was afforded of working with you." Welles continued: "Your personal prestige on the Continent and the confidence which every one of the statesmen of the other American Republics [has] in you were, in my judgment, the chief factors contributing to the success which was achieved. Your generous words as to my own part are very deeply appreciated."[69]

Hull's bitterness over Saavedra Lamas's actions at the Buenos Aires conference and Welles's efforts to soothe those hurt feelings did not alter the fact that by the end of his first term, Roosevelt's vague allusions to the good neighbor policy in his inaugural address applied solely to the other American republics. The policy's success allowed the administration some flexibility in foreign affairs but did not seriously alter the traditional political relationships between the United States and Latin America. Nevertheless the administration recognized the value of its regional commitment and moved to maximize it.

Unable to play a positive role in European affairs, the president began to devise ways for the good neighbor to exert a global impact. Shut off from negotiating trade agreements in much of the world, the secretary welcomed Latin American participation in his reciprocity program. Welles encouraged that emphasis and also put his imprint on it by canceling interventions that had proven obsolete, in favor of other, more subtle, diplomatic acts that could accomplish the same desired ends. This concerted effort, more than anything, made the good neighbor concept unique to the Roosevelt era and allowed the president, his secretary of state, and the assistant secretary to act in concert, with each man receiving his own rewards.

Roosevelt, more than anyone else, provided the catalytic agent that linked European affairs with those in the Western Hemisphere, and by the end of his first term he had directed much of the diplomatic momentum that contrasted the growing movement for peace in the Western Hemisphere with the warfare raging in Europe and Asia. Unable to influence neutrality legislation at home or to have any significant impact on European and Asian events, the president began to formulate plans to build on the good neighbor policy and concurrently reach out to the rest of the world community.

Hull saw hope for international peace through the enactment of his reciprocal trade program, and he set out to sign as many agreements as possible. He also remained focused on improving hemispheric relations, for that arena had been the scene of his first major diplomatic triumph. Finally, he remained in command of East Asian affairs, a duty that fit well with his natural disposition to exercise extreme caution and if at all possible maintain the status quo.

As the secretary focused on those programs, Phillips watched the war clouds gathering over Europe while continuing to supervise day-to-day departmental affairs and acting as a buffer between Hull and Roosevelt. As long as Phillips remained in the middle, he could adjudicate disputes, and his solutions found general favor. Phillips also shaped policies in those areas that did not appeal to the president or the secretary. In the case of Jewish immigration from Germany, neither Roosevelt nor Hull wanted to fight for the refugees in the face of opposition from those who argued that they would take jobs from unemployed American workers. Phillips and Carr, as already noted, used this argument to restrict immigration while quietly expressing their anti-Semitism.

Moore, too, worried about the chaotic international situation, but he was even more concerned about how foreign policy affected domestic politics. His first priority remained the preservation of the stature of the president and keeping Roosevelt in the White House. Although Moore hated Welles, both were working toward the same objective. By concentrating on his regional mandate and fostering better relations, Welles provided a positive inter-American image for the administration and gave the president a forum within which he could speak to the rest of the international community.

These informal and unofficial assignments compartmentalized the State Department during Roosevelt's first term. With the world in the midst of a global depression, every government focused immediately on domestic survival, and diplomatic efforts were relegated to a secondary role. This set of circumstances may have helped the United States, which was not yet willing or prepared to move boldly in the international arena. Its citizens and their congressional representatives had shown an aversion to foreign entanglements. It was an antipathy that deeply concerned the Roosevelt White House, for the dictatorships and their expansionist tendencies would ultimately force the United States to react in order to preserve its very existence.

# CHAPTER 5

# THE BLOODIEST
# BUREAUCRATIC BATTLE

WHILE THE PRINCIPAL DIPLOMATIC ACTORS
in the administration were defining their roles in foreign affairs, Carr,
Moore, and Welles sank to the lowest levels of bureaucratic warfare
during the meetings of the Foreign Service Personnel Board, the body
within which the trio violently debated promotions, demotions, and
appointments. As each man battled for his own private agenda against
those of his rivals, their conduct periodically erupted into open confrontations. With so few openings available and merit increases growing ever
scarcer, the struggle for jobs and higher wages took on an even greater
significance among the three combatants.

Carr, whose primary objective was to upgrade the consular service
and the status of the career foreign service employee, chaired the committee. He was often distraught over the conduct of his two associates,
who frequently lobbied the White House directly for their favorites
behind his back. On one occasion Carr caught Moore going directly to
the Oval Office without Carr's permission and demanded an apology.

Moore continued to view his duties from a partisan perspective and
therefore emerged as the committee's Democratic watchdog. Anyone

speaking out was expected to toe the administration line; any Republican who voiced opposition to the New Deal would lose any chance of promotion. Moore also deplored moral indiscretions such as intoxication, and the price of such a transgression could also be one's further chances for advancement. Moore, having come to loathe Welles the moment they met, described him as "unethical" and a "poor thinker," and therefore refused to support almost all of his recommendations to the board.[1]

Of course, Welles had his own agenda, and he used his position to promote those whom he personally favored and punish those whom he believed disagreed with him. When he lost at board meetings, he went directly to the president to plead his case. Many career diplomats recognized how powerful Welles had become, and those who feared him disguised their distaste and pretended to be his allies rather than risk losing a promotion or suffering a demotion.[2]

The friction at board meetings started in early 1934 and continued unabated until the summer of 1936 when Under Secretary Phillips, having grown weary of his daily responsibilities, decided to leave his job and assume the position of American ambassador to Italy. Unbeknownst to him, this decision would trigger the bloodiest personnel battle at the State Department during the New Deal.

Once Phillips had announced his plans, Carr, Moore, and Welles all initiated campaigns to fill the vacancy. Rumors immediately circulated that Roosevelt wanted to appoint Moore, but before the announcement could be made, Welles learned of it, met with the president, and reminded him that if the job became available, it should go to him.[3]

Joseph Green, in charge of arms sales, reported on the evolving confrontation: "The smooth running of the Department is already greatly impaired by the serious disagreements and personal differences among Mr. Carr, Judge Moore and Sumner Welles. Each one of them is at daggers drawn with each of the other. The situation cannot be allowed to go on forever."[4]

Adolf Berle, a close friend from New York and an early member of the Brain Trust who had assisted Welles in Cuba, respected him and wrote the president at the end of June 1936 that Welles had strong political backing in Maryland and with the Eastern liberal establishment, adding an unwarranted and invalid assumption concerning the secretary's preference: "Both Sumner Welles and Cordell Hull consider that Sumner is entitled to it on all counts; and they are right. It is possible that Sumner would not care to remain if passed over. Were Hull otherwise constituted he would probably say so to you; but as you know, Hull does not make representations, especially just now."[5]

Carr had hoped that his longevity in the foreign service and his friendship with Louis Howe would make him a compromise candidate, but that chance vanished as Howe's health grew progressively worse. As the president's chief political adviser, he exercised considerable authority, but now this emaciated little man moved into the Lincoln Room at the White House and hoped futilely that his physical condition would improve. His final slide began in January 1935, and that summer he was transferred to Bethesda Naval Hospital, where he lingered until he died on April 18, 1936. However, Howe's death was not Carr's only liability. The assistant secretary had also made numerous enemies within the foreign service who saw him as too limited and as a relic of an earlier era.[6]

Some briefly included William Bullitt in their gossip about possible candidates, but he was quickly eliminated since many Democrats had never forgotten his disloyalty to Woodrow Wilson at the Senate hearings after World War I. They had already voiced their objections to any appointment for him at the start of the New Deal and would certainly oppose this promotion. In reality, Bullitt never coveted the under-secretaryship, for he had serious family problems. He had divorced Louise Bryant in 1930 because of her alcoholism and "cutting up." Six years later, after a bout of heavy drinking, she fell down a flight of stairs in a dirty little Left Bank hotel, suffered a fatal cerebral hemorrhage, and died a few days later in the American Hospital at forty-one. Her death left Bullitt with a daughter, to whom he was devoted.[7]

In addition to this personal tragedy, many disapproved of Bullitt's unprofessional conduct. Norman Davis, a Tennesseean and a roving ambassador for the State Department, had even more substantial reasons to be anxious:

> While Bullitt is a very brilliant and able man in so many ways, I fear
> that his feelings are so strong on certain subjects as to prejudice and

becloud his judgment. I have had several responsible persons tell me that for the past year he has been quietly conveying the impression that he is the spokesman for the President in Europe and that he deals directly with the President, without going through the Secretary of State. It is a tragedy and a disgrace that American representatives abroad do not pull together as a team for their country. We always seem to have some prima donna trying to play a personal role, which can be done only to the detriment of the United States.[8]

Others had also warned Hull that the ambassador was untrustworthy and refused to accept the secretary's cautious approach to international affairs. Bullitt regularly bypassed the State Department and communicated directly with the White House, a practice that Hull's allies in the department criticized. Castle talked to Hull about this unwholesome situation and believed that the secretary should not confide in Bullitt.[9]

Hull could have easily charged Roosevelt as an accomplice in this effort to bypass him. Rather than tell the ambassador to restrict his correspondence to official channels, the president encouraged this kind of direct access and in fact led Bullitt to believe that he was the White House's man in Europe. Bullitt took this cue as permission to transform the president's unofficial assignment into a bona fide mission. Regularly corresponding with Roosevelt on Soviet policy matters ranging from debts owed to the United States to Stalin's purges, Bullitt also made suggestions about American diplomatic activities throughout Europe and recommended individuals for diplomatic slots. While in Moscow, the ambassador tried to ingratiate himself with the president, as in this letter from the spring of 1934: "I should like to hear the sound of your voice and be with you for a few days. I don't like being so far away from you." Almost a year later, he continued in the same vein: "Bless you for your kindness to me when I was in America and for your friendship."[10]

Whatever his feelings regarding the under-secretaryship, Bullitt needed all the support he could muster, for his Russian assignment soon turned into a nightmare. Arriving in the Soviet Union in December 1933, he at first was optimistic about the chances for improving relations, for he still viewed Russia from the romantic perspective of his 1919 trip. But after he proved unable to settle the question of debts owed to American citizens and to check the spread of international communism, Bullitt's idealism quickly turned to disillusionment. He had hoped to win Stalin's confidence, but his inborn lack of tact made him ill-suited to deal with the dictator or his subordinates, and by the time Stalin began his brutal purges in 1935, the ambassador had turned against him and grown to despise his own post. By early 1936 Bullitt's residence had become a haven for anticommunist sympathizers, and his hosts initiated surveillance measures, checking his servants, tapping his phones, and screening every guest. Unable to function in this hostile environment, Bullitt left the Soviet Union with no significant accomplishments there to his credit.[11]

He sought another ambassadorial assignment and depended heavily upon Moore's assistance at the Personnel Board to win a desirable post. Bullitt's already warm friendship with Moore had deepened, and the ambassador signed letters to the assistant secretary "Yours affectionately" and extended "best wishes to your sisters and as always my deepest friendship." Moore replied with equal feeling, calling Bullitt "my dear friend" and protecting him from departmental criticism.[12] Bullitt also used Moore as a conduit to the White House. Since the ambassador trusted Moore and held him in the same high esteem in both personal and professional matters as he did the president, the assistant secretary became in effect a personal messenger for dispatches from Moscow that passed to the White House through Marguerite "Missy" LeHand, Roosevelt's private secretary. According to Roosevelt's eldest son James, she and Bullitt were romantically involved, and Bullitt had even promised to marry her.[13]

Bullitt returned to the United States in June 1936 to work on the presidential campaign and continued in that capacity until almost the end of the summer, when he took over as ambassador to France.[14] By the end of September he had already settled in Paris, and he reminded Roosevelt, "Please don't forget that before you and Cordell leave Washington [for the Buenos Aires conference] you must give Judge Moore the authority which he can have only if he is Under Secretary of State. A temporary position or Acting Secretary of State is no good."[15]

Roosevelt and Hull did not really seem to need this kind of prodding because they were already leaning toward Moore's appointment. During the summer of 1936 Roosevelt mentioned the position several times to Moore, and before the president left for Buenos Aires he confirmed his preference to Hull in Moore's presence by jokingly stating that he was thinking about appointing his distant cousin under secretary. The secretary facetiously replied: "That will be all right if he isn't too close a cousin."[16]

The speculation over the new under secretary temporarily faded into the background as the 1936 national conventions approached. The Republicans nominated Alfred Landon, the govenor of Kansas, to head their ticket based on a platform intended to appeal to those who detested the New Deal and its leader, whom they referred to as "that man in the White House." Two weeks later the Democrats met in Philadelphia. On Saturday evening, June 26, after a rainy day, Roosevelt spoke from the darkened end of the horseshoe at Franklin Field into the glare of spotlights, addressing over one hundred thousand of the party's faithful. With millions more listening on the radio, Roosevelt used his renomination address to denounce "economic royalists." Having established this theme for his campaign, the president unwittingly turned the contest into a referendum on the merits of the New Deal and himself. Although he did not fully understand all of the political dynamics he had set in motion, the election would provide a dramatic affirmation of his personal popularity.[17]

Contrary to his involvement in the 1932 campaign, in which he had played an active part, in 1936 Hull only attended the convention and assisted in several strategy sessions and some fundraising; as secretary of state, he clung to what he viewed as the traditional role of his office, which was to remain aloof and avoid energetic campaigning. Yet the secretary followed both campaigns closely and predicted a Democratic victory. Just after the results of Roosevelt's overwhelming landslide had been confirmed, he left for the Buenos Aires conference.[18]

During the campaign, Welles served as under secretary of state for Maryland within the Democratic party, vigorously sought financial contributions, and attended the national convention as a delegate from Prince Georges County. The electric atmosphere of the convention leading up to the president's renomination consumed him, and afterward he enthusiastically marched with his delegation, waving a flag, smiling, and slapping fellow delegates on the back. Celebrating at such a moment was of course entirely in character for most delegates, but this open display of emotion was quite unusual for Welles. When he noticed a member of the diplomatic corps observing his behavior, he promptly reverted to his customary ultrareserved demeanor. After the convention, Welles continued to work on the campaign while continuing his normal diplomatic activities and lobbying for Phillips's job.[19]

Even before Roosevelt's victory, Hull had decided to lead the United States delegation to the Buenos Aires conference and take Welles along as his second in command. Moore remained in Washington, and Hull gave him an obvious advantage in the selection process by making him acting secretary of state over Carr, who had seniority.[20] Despite the increased work load and his advanced age, Moore thrived on his added responsibilities and hectic schedule, arriving at his office before 9:00 A.M. and remaining until after dark, with but a few minutes to eat lunch at his desk. Nevertheless, he recorded on December 2, "I feel no sense of fatigue."[21]

As acting secretary, he witnessed the deteriorating conditions in Europe and Asia, worried about the danger they posed to world peace, and wished for a collective security effort in which the United States could participate, knowing full well that any possible American involvement would precipitate a storm of domestic protest. At the same time, Moore objected to the common hemispheric neutrality policy and disarmament proposals being advocated at the South American gathering, for he feared that those too might provoke public hostility.[22]

Yet even these anxieties did not dampen his exhilaration. Inside and outside the department, commentators speculated about Moore filling Phillips's slot, and the acting secretary of state confided to Ambassador Josephus Daniels in mid-November, "I can tell you confidentially that the President has more than once talked to me about the office of Under Secretary, but I begged him to do exactly what he thinks is best, without giving too much personal consideration to me. He is my very generous friend."[23] A few days later, he informed Ambassador William Dodd in Berlin, "I have reason to believe that I may become the Under Secretary, but I have quit predicting about anything."[24] Moore acknowledged the remote possibility of not getting the post, but he did not seriously believe that could happen.

Like Moore, Welles also assumed that he was the front-runner. Some inside the department understood that Roosevelt had promised Phillips's post to his protégé, and that if it was not offered, Welles would resign. The assistant secretary appeared to ignore the whispers to the contrary, for after his return from Buenos Aires, he spoke across the country about the conference's significance and highlighted the value of the good neighbor policy. Even without the formal title of second in command within the department, he began assuming more duties, and even critics like Castle, who disliked Welles, grudgingly conceded that he was doing a fine job.[25]

While Moore and Welles jockeyed for position, a more pressing domestic issue gripped the White House at the start of the second term. In his inaugural address, Roosevelt had recounted his grim vision of "one-third of a nation ill-housed, ill-clad, ill-nourished." His overriding interest focused on how New Deal legislation might alleviate these conditions, and on how the Supreme Court was consistently striking down those laws as unconstitutional. He had to find a means of halting this judicial obstruction. His solution remained a secret until February 5, when he outlined a bill that would reorganize the Supreme Court by allowing the chief executive to appoint six new judges to replace those who were then over seventy years old. The president never openly declared that his true purpose was to force the court to uphold his legislative program, but argued instead that his plan would lead to greater efficiency and reduced work loads for the overburdened judges. This proposal, which surprised the nation, was quickly labeled Roosevelt's "court-packing plan" and immediately drew an adverse reaction. The ensuing protracted and bitter debate proved that the president had grossly miscalculated on this initiative. The court proposal slowly died an unceremonious death that summer, but not before Roosevelt had squandered an inordinate amount of the enormous personal prestige he had built up during the campaign on an ill-advised and poorly conceived scheme.[26]

At the height of the court-packing debate, Roosevelt and Hull met for lunch at the White House on March 10 to discuss the choice of a new under secretary. Hull explained that he was "in a rather embarrassing position" because both Welles and Moore wanted the job. The secretary declared that Moore "was quite capable and despite his age has a very clear mind" and that Welles also was "very anxious" about the position. Hull's solution was to give the post to Moore "for a time" and then promote Welles after Moore had resigned to become "an adviser to the State Department." The secretary would make this offer to his friend, if Roosevelt would have Welles accept the arrangement; the president thought that he could "handle the matter" with Welles.[27]

Yet this compromise was never consummated, and in the meantime criticism multiplied. Castle, for instance, recorded that the president's inability to make a decision disgusted foreign service officers; the department's uncertainty over policy was becoming the butt of jokes. J. Butler Wright, a career diplomat, described in mid-March a department in which everyone was overworked "to the exasperation of many and the bewilderment of all. Your guess is as good as mine as to where and why it is held up and at the time of my departure no one seemed to know what the solution would be."[28]

Moore was growing impatient because he knew that Welles was vigorously lobbying against him. He had become frustrated and angry, especially since he had worked incessantly while Roosevelt and Hull were in South America. To give Moore's candidacy an additional boost, Bullitt returned from Paris in March, prompting speculation by some professional diplomats that his visit signaled a prominent role for the ambassador in this intrigue. Gossip momentarily intensified when Bullitt spent a week with Roosevelt in Warm Springs, followed by a trip to Washington for several days of consultations. However, he returned to France by the end of the month without receiving any indication as to who would emerge victorious.[29]

While Bullitt supported his friend, Drew Pearson was using his column, "Washington Merry-Go-Round," not only to advance Welles's candidacy but also to discredit Moore. Pearson, a powerfully built man with a thin face and a carefully groomed mustache, was just beginning his rise as a journalist with a national following. He never divulged his personal fondness for Welles or their long association. Born on December 13, 1897, in Evanston, Illinois, into a family with a Quaker heritage, Pearson was the first of four children. His parents moved to Pennsylvania when he was five, and his father Paul became a professor of public speaking at Swarthmore College. After Pearson's graduation from Phillips Exeter Academy in 1915, he entered Swarthmore and embarked on an outstanding collegiate career during which he edited the campus newspaper, earned letters in swimming and lacrosse, was named to Phi Beta Kappa, and delivered the valedictorian address in 1919. After completing his degree, he went to the Balkans to do relief work for the American Friends Service Committee and returned two years later to teach geography at the University of Pennsylvania and then at Columbia University. He also spent some time traveling in East Asia and India as a reporter. By 1925 he had decided to concentrate on a career in the news media, and in that year he married Felicia Gizycki, daughter of Eleanor "Cissy" Patterson, owner of the Washington *Herald,* one of the largest newspapers in the capital. During their short, stormy union, Pearson and Felicia had their only child, Ellen, in 1927; their divorce, a year later, precipitated a bitter custody fight for the child.

Pearson next moved to Washington, D.C., where he struggled as a reporter until the Baltimore *Sun* hired him as its correspondent in the nation's capital, specializing in American foreign policy with a Latin American emphasis. During this period, he and Robert Allen combined to publish anonymously *Washington Merry-Go-Round,* a commercially successful book attacking the Hoover presidency that was followed by an inferior sequel in 1932. After the books' authorship was discovered, Pearson was fired from the *Sun,* and although their second volume failed to sell well, the two authors decided to combine their talents on a newspaper column entitled "Washington Merry-Go-Round," which began publication in the winter of 1932. With its inception, the Pearson byline would be widely syndicated and read daily for over sixty years to come.

By the time Roosevelt entered office, Pearson was already considered an administration insider, having collaborated with Welles on a long, verbose foreign policy plank, which was essentially discarded, for the Democratic platform. Despite this slight, the president-elect invited the reporter to Warm Springs for advice on how to deal with the Washington press corps.[30] After the new administration entered office, the reporter and the assistant secretary remained close, and in April 1935 Welles asked Roosevelt and Hull to meet with Pearson, even though they resented certain of his articles and felt that the columnist was "impulsive and given to writing occasionally under the influence of superficial impressions." Welles urged both men to talk with Pearson, who actively supported them and the New Deal, but both the president and the secretary refused to follow Welles's advice. Even without Roosevelt's and Hull's blessings, Welles refused to end the relationship, "which existed long before I came back to the Department. I have invariably found him absolutely loyal, on innumerable occasions exceedingly helpful, and he is gifted with a very shrewd mentality." To avoid gossip, when the two men met, they did so discreetly, often at their homes.[31]

Without ever acknowledging this strong bond, Pearson prominently listed Moore's shortcomings in three columns in March 1937. The first pointed out that Roosevelt's court plan was designed to retire justices over the age of seventy, and that Moore was seventy-eight. The second alleged that Moore was desperate enough to ask Bullitt to plead with the president for his promotion. Moore had also erred by banning medical missions to Spain, and this miscue further hurt his cause. Finally, Pearson pointed out that neither the president nor the secretary knew about a credit to Italy that Moore had approved as chairman of the Export-Import Bank, and that that oversight "put a further damper on Moore's chances of becoming Undersecretary of State."[32]

Moore reacted angrily because Pearson's charges were entirely false. He had never asked for the position, he pointed out, but if it was offered, he intended to accept it. The fact that the post had been vacant for such a long period further infuriated him. Moore was convinced that Hull was responsible for this untenable situation since the secretary alone should have made the appointment. Hull was painfully aware that this unwholesome atmosphere was disrupting the smooth functioning of his department, but still the secretary refused to act.[33]

In the midst of this mounting friction and after almost ten months of uncertainty over filling the under-secretaryship, Senator Key Pittman, chairman of the Senate Foreign Relations Committee, introduced a bill in mid-April to revive the office of counselor to the State Department. Moore would assume that post, and Welles would become under secretary. Both men would have equal salaries and (at least for public consumption) equal responsibilities. Moore assumed that the bill had been introduced "to save my feelings" and believed that many senators viewed both promotions as part of a single package. If he were not advanced in rank, at least on paper, Moore reasoned, Welles would quite possibly have difficulties being confirmed by the Foreign Relations Committee. Senator Hiram Johnson considered Moore a close friend and wrote to him to solicit his opinion about this arrangement. Moore wanted to reply that he had never been consulted and was surprised by the legislation, but before mailing this response he showed it to Hull, who became aggravated. Although Hull told him to do whatever he pleased, Moore, not wishing to incur the secretary's wrath, rewrote his answer so as not to cause offense.[34]

On May 19 Roosevelt sent the two nominations to the Senate for confirmation, and they were promptly approved the following day. The president believed that, by promoting both candidates, he had discovered a solution that Solomon himself would have admired. Bullitt had hinted to Moore before flying to Paris that Roosevelt had hit upon a "clever method" of dealing with this ticklish issue, and Berle wrote Welles after the press release announcing both appointments that this action "would seem to indicate that the President has found an almost typical solution for the impasse."[35]

Even though his salary had been raised by $2,000, Moore preferred to remain an assistant secretary. Although initially considering resignation, he decided to stay at his desk because he found his work "congenial" and did "not wish to become entirely inactive." As long as his health remained intact, he would hold onto his existing assignment.[36] He had no idea what his new duties would entail, but he predicted that

> if Mr. Welles as Under Secretary is to have the same authority that those who have filled that office had, it will be in my opinion pretty bad for the Department. He is nominally a Democrat, excessively ambitious and autocratic, and notably unwise. He has always been very intimate with the President, and I hear that when he ascertained that the President desired me to become Under Secretary, he made a drive in his own behalf which caused a good deal of embarrassment.[37]

Moore described the events for Bullitt's benefit; after outlining the legislation, he complained, "Welles has won his fight with the President and the Secretary, and it is desired that I shall win the consolation race. 'Thus runs the world away!' I heard someone say that if Welles is to be Under Secretary, the logical thing would be to replace him as Assistant Secretary by his spokesman, Drew Pearson. They are two persons whom I hold in utter contempt."[38] Moore lambasted Pearson for using his column to boost Welles's candidacy and discredit Moore. He vehemently denounced Pearson's conduct and character, adding, "He would not hesitate to criticize his own mother if he thought thereby he would attract attention to his column." According to the counselor, Pearson had regularly visited the department, until his welcome had worn out. Moore was upset that Pearson had stopped coming in "after some of his blackguard articles [to] give me the opportunity to tell him what I think of him."[39]

After a month of reflection, Moore, recognizing that Welles was "a heavy fighter," began to appreciate the president's predicament.[40] An admirer of the president, Moore never blamed Roosevelt for appointing Welles; in fact, he and the president, Moore insisted, remained on amicable terms, and his esteem for the president had even increased. Moore convinced himself that Roosevelt was a great president and was embarrassed that in Welles he had had to select such an inferior candidate for the under-secretaryship. Moore was grateful for Roosevelt's friendship, for the president had always treated him "in my very numerous contacts with him in the most generous and often affectionate fashion." Although mistaken in his belief that Roosevelt and Welles were schoolmates, Moore correctly pointed out that Welles had participated in Eleanor and Franklin's wedding. In the face of such close family connections, Moore rationalized that Welles could be the White House's only choice.[41]

The same warm sentiments, however, did not extend to Hull. The struggle for the under-secretaryship unwittingly precipitated a breach between Moore and Hull, a festering sore that never healed. The counselor no longer felt the same affinity for the man directly responsible for his original appointment because Moore knew that Hull had had the authority to make the appointment and had refused to exercise his power. To Moore, the secretary's moral and ethical standards were placed in serious doubt: Hull had acknowledged his preference for

Moore without the slightest hesitation, but had "lacked the courage to have me appointed." Although Moore would always remain the trustworthy counselor, this knowledge was not enough to maintain the bonds of confidentiality between the two men, for they never again shared the same degree of intimacy. Hull thereby lost his closest confidant.[42]

When Frances Hull learned about Moore's accusations, she defended her spouse and argued that Moore had blamed Hull unfairly, because her husband had had nothing to do with Welles's appointment. Welles had won the position, she intimated, because he had gone directly to the White House, bypassing her husband entirely.[43]

Rather than concern himself with Frances Hull's excuses, Moore closely watched as Welles's power and prestige grew. All he had left were his burning hatred toward his antagonist and as much time as he wished to devote to the destruction of his enemy. As far as Moore was concerned, Welles had orchestrated his defeat. He never forgave Welles's perceived transgressions and spent the remaining years of his life searching for a vulnerable spot through which to ruin his rival. According to Moore, whose unquestioned distaste for the man had grown into a passionate hatred, Welles had become the very incarnation of evil.[44]

Not deigning to worry about the bruised feelings left in its aftermath, Welles celebrated his greatest triumph. Believing incorrectly that he had lost the job of assistant secretary for Latin American affairs in 1926 because of political pressure, he could now claim vindication. Welles had emerged as the number two man in the State Department, and he stood to gain far greater public exposure. He expected to serve those above and dictate to those below. Most important, in the secretary's absence, the under secretary became the acting secretary, thus commanding the department's entire apparatus. In his new position, Welles would not only formulate Latin American affairs, but also begin to expand his influence to European matters. To be sure, Welles was still a controversial figure: those who admired him applauded the appointment; those who despised him dreaded the future; and few took a neutral stance. If anything, time had accentuated his obsessive-compulsive character, and he was now even more driven to handle every task, even the most inconsequential matter, placed before him.

Somehow the story of the battle for the under-secretaryship—the open rivalry between Welles and Moore and the eventual resolution of the conflict—has ultimately been lost to history, submerged in the drama of the 1936 reelection campaign and the court-packing incident. No one except Hull has given the episode any significance in his writings. The secretary's recollections illustrate both the problems of writing a decade after an event and his attempt to gloss over his own glaring failures.

In the introduction to his memoirs, Hull pledged, "I have narrated events as I saw them and have drawn conclusions in the light of those events at the time. I have tried to be as frank, impartial, and accurate as is humanly possible."[45] Yet these pious and noble words did not apply to his truthfulness concerning the battle for the under-secretaryship. Rather than set down an accurate record, Hull placed the blame for this unpleasant struggle on others. He correctly recalled that once Phillips had left the department, Moore and Welles became the main contenders for the under-secretaryship. Hull admitted that he preferred his friend Moore, but he then declared that Roosevelt had "had the responsibility for filling the vacancy" and maintained that although he usually enjoyed making selections, he had "kept clear out of sight of this competition." The secretary falsely alleged that he "did not become an open partisan by making a recommendation to the President." Even with the intervening decade, Hull surely could not have forgotten Moley's firing, his demand to choose a replacement, and the fact that when he had first exercised that prerogative, it had resulted in Moore's appointment as an assistant secretary of state in September 1933. Hull, furthermore, had discussed Moore's promotion with Roosevelt at the White House luncheon of March 10. Even if we concede that Hull's memory had lapsed on these facts, it is unthinkable that he could believe his own memoirs that "Welles and Moore agreed to compromise": the two contenders barely spoke to one another. Hull concluded his summary with an even more outlandish claim: "So far as I was aware, there arose out of this situation no serious disturbance of my agreeable working relations with either Welles or Moore."[46]

This view might have been valid from the victor's viewpoint, but it was not so for Moore, who began to plant the seeds of discord against Welles. Although these did not bear immediate fruit, they did take root and begin to sprout. The antagonistic environment thus created provided the ideal climate for future intrigue. An administration in which the president enjoyed rivalries among his cabinet officials; a secretary of state who was incapable of supervising his subordinates; a controversial under secretary; and a counselor who was committed to his superior's demise—these potentially explosive ingredients needed only the proper catalyst to explode into catastrophe. That would take time, but Moore was willing to wait.

# CHAPTER 6

# REORGANIZING THE
# DEPARTMENT

AFTER THE ACRIMONIOUS STRUGGLE over the appointment of a new under secretary, how did the victor differ from his predecessor? William Phillips had held the post for three years and had developed his own unique style, founded on the clear premise that his first loyalty was to the foreign service and his second to the White House. He directed the daily routine of the department in the hope that he could improve the professionalism of the diplomatic corps. When he made decisions in regard to foreign affairs, he specialized in European matters because he had spent most of his career on the Continent. He was usually extremely reserved and seldom governed by prejudice, with the exception of his rigid stand against easing immigration restrictions. For one who claimed to be evenhanded, and who certainly hid from the public his opposition to the admission of German Jewish emigrés , this preoccupation certainly tarnished his judgment. Yet Phillips was generally known for being fair, not vindictive. Few if any of his peers ever commented on his style, and that probably suited him perfectly. He cultivated the image of a skilled administrator who did his job so well that officials simply accepted his decisions as matters of fact.

Welles also favored a career foreign service and fought for professionalism throughout his tenure, but beyond that point of agreement, his and Phillips's paths diverged. Welles was the subject of heated debate because of his peculiar habits. Some enjoyed his company, but many found him odd. Some feared him for his pettiness, unfairness, and arbitrary nature; others found him brilliant, charming, and loyal. The new appointee was the acknowledged diplomatic expert on inter-American affairs; however, when he tried to step outside that arena, competitors who had charge over other regions blocked him. After taking on his new duties, Welles moved into European affairs. Athough he had often traveled on the Continent since his childhood, he had not previously been identified with its diplomatic problems, nor had he needed to take a stand on the persecution of German Jews. Unlike his predecessor, Welles was not anti-Semitic, and that fact alone assured potential immigrants, at a minimum, of an impartial hearing.

Shortly after assuming his new position, Welles embarked upon a plan to reorganize the State Department, a task that only added to his mystique. As many anticipated, Wilbur Carr was at the top of the list for a transfer. He had already lost his credibility with the House Appropriations Committee chairman, Edward Taylor of Colorado, who disliked Carr so much that during the 1937 congressional session the powerful Democrat refused to allow him to testify.[1] Without any powerful allies, Carr felt abandoned, and he wrote in his diary, "I see nothing but blackness ahead. The actions of Welles and Hull . . . leave me no alternative but to believe that I am not trusted by them or the President and that a frame up is going on." His instincts were accurate, for that summer Hull appointed him minister to Czechoslovakia, and Carr, always the professional, went off to do his duty in Prague.[2]

By late July, George Messersmith had assumed Carr's duties, supervising fiscal affairs and handling consular, passport, and visa matters. Even though Carr approved of his replacement, Messersmith returned to Washington critical of his predecessor's leadership, especially his failure to increase the State Department budget and his inability to settle personnel disputes. Messersmith had the additional advantage of being a fresh face; he returned to the department without holding membership in any clique, and at the same time holding the respect of his superiors. He had met Hull in the 1920s and shared his beliefs regarding the expansion of foreign trade, a fact that pleased the secretary. Although he was outside the Welles circle, he and Welles shared a bond in despising Moore.

The new appointee immediately faced the limitations of a $16.6 million budget, which was still less than the one for 1932. To trim expenditures, he eliminated some overlapping duties, ordered career officers with lengthy stays in Washington to return to the field, and released forty to fifty diplomats from the government payroll. That left 713 foreign service officers, supported by more than 4,000 clerks.[3] Morale suffered because of the inadequate funding. When former Secretary of State Henry Stimson visited the department during Roosevelt's second term, he found his former colleagues fatigued, overworked, and pessimistic, and he worried about their effectiveness under these trying conditions. Stanley Hornbeck had watched these problems mount over twenty years and saw no signs of improvement: "Day after day, month after month, year after year, I have observed turning down requests in the Department and from the field for additional personnel and additional equipment; over and over I have observed the plea 'No funds' and the other plea 'No person available' (none that can be spared)."[4]

While Messersmith lived with this sort of grumbling, he also handled the emotional powder keg of the refugee explosion through the visa division. American Jews welcomed him as their defender. Had he not assisted them when he was consul general in Berlin and Vienna? Did he not speak out against the Nazi threat? The answer to both questions was yes, but Jews incorrectly presumed that he was philo-Semitic because of his unequivocal opposition to the Third Reich. To be sure, unlike Carr, Messersmith was not anti-Semitic. At the core of his beliefs was strict enforcement of the immigration laws; his main requirement in granting an emigré permission to enter the United States was that that person make a good citizen. He did not approve of the United States giving way completely to its humanitarian instincts out of fear that certain Jewish immigrants might be subversives planted by the Nazis, whose presence could disrupt "social harmony" and economic recovery. During a meeting with Jewish leaders in the spring of 1938, Messersmith argued that if refugees flocked here, a backlash might force harsher restrictions; his listeners agreed, and that ended the discussion for the remainder of his tenure at the department. Yet despite all of these limitations, more refugees came into the United States during his posting than at any other time during the New Deal.[5]

Another welcome addition in most eyes was G. Howland Shaw, who was transferred from Istanbul to the capital as director of personnel matters. Educated in a Jesuit school, in preparation for entering the priesthood, Shaw instead decided on a career in the foreign service. His selection pleased just about everyone; even Pearson, who was noted for his attacks on the incompetence of government officials, considered him one of the most brilliant men in the diplomatic corps. Bullitt concurred, imploring the president, "The morale of the Service is becoming more demoralized every day and nothing could turn the tide of discouragement so quickly and completely as his appointment."[6]

Along with these administrative reassignments, certain geographical responsibilities were consolidated. Robert Kelley, chief of the Eastern European Division, left his desk. Kelley hated the Soviet system and had become one of the outspoken leaders of the anti-Russian forces inside the department. Roosevelt wanted to improve bilateral relations with Moscow and worried that Kelley would sabotage those efforts. Not only was he removed, but Roosevelt also selected Joseph Davies, a wealthy contributor from Wisconsin and a strong advocate of closer relations with the Soviet Union, to serve as ambassador to Moscow.[7]

J. Pierrepont Moffat, who had received high marks for his knowledge of Western European affairs, absorbed Eastern Europe into his duties to create a new European Division. Hull and Welles liked Moffat, who came from a social register New York family and had graduated from Groton and Harvard, then decided to enter the foreign service as private secretary to the American minister to the Netherlands. In 1918 he had taken the foreign service entrance examination and passed it first in his class; nine years later, he married Ambassador Joseph Grew's daughter Lilla and continued his advancement through the ranks.[8]

The Latin American and Mexican sections were combined into the American Republics Division, and Laurence Duggan, Welles's most trusted associate in hemispheric matters, assumed its leadership. One of the youngest and ablest State Department officers, he was forever busy carrying out the under secretary's instructions. Indeed that was exactly what Welles expected, for the day after he became under secretary a departmental order was issued, declaring that all matters involving inter-American affairs were to be channeled through Welles's office.⁹ The under secretary did not hide these intentions when writing to Frank Corrigan, ambassador to Venezuela, on May 27: "My new duties will, of course, include continuing exactly as before in my relations with our inter-American affairs. To be quite frank with you, if they had not I would not have been interested in the position."¹⁰

Just as Welles protected his turf, Roosevelt continued to exert his influence over personnel matters. Bullitt remained in France as the president's chief adviser on European affairs. The excitement of Paris and his intimate connections with French leaders were invigorating, and he loved the balls, entertainment, and fine cuisine; he even employed his own chef. In addition to his residence in the embassy, the ambassador rented a chateau just outside of the capital and also kept a tiny Paris apartment with a small living room, a sleeping alcove, a tiny kitchen, and a spot for his Chinese manservant. It was to this pied-à-terre that he took his lovers, and the clandestine rendezvous was a poorly kept secret.

Bullitt frequently spoke with the president by phone, continuing to bypass normal diplomatic channels to communicate with Roosevelt on a multitude of subjects, some of which had little to do with his current assignment. He discussed domestic policies like his support for the federal housing program and voiced his disappointment over the defeat of the court-packing plan. He lobbied for diplomatic posts for his supporters and rejected a presidential suggestion to run for governor of Pennsylvania. Bullitt used his influence to obtain presidential audiences for visiting French dignitaries, and even went so far as to ask for advice on stamp collecting. Whenever he was in the United States, he visited with Roosevelt at the White House, Hyde Park, or Warm Springs, using these occasions to offer the president his firsthand observations and to strengthen his personal attachment to the White House. No wonder Bullitt came to believe that he alone was the president's spokesman in Europe.¹¹

The president depended a great deal on him to report on continental conditions, but this did not mean that Roosevelt blindly accepted these views; he was well aware of the ambassador's faults. First and most critically, Bullitt's deep hatred of communism and the Soviet Union clouded his judgment. According to the journalist William Shirer, French leaders admired Bullitt, but they, too, believed that his Russian phobias blinded him.[12] His obsession was never clearer than in the following dramatic warning:

> the so-called Soviet Government is a conspiracy to commit murder and nothing else. The Soviet Union is the base from which the conspirators operate and nothing else.
>
> I think Stalin intends to eat like a cancer into Europe . . . and that he hopes in the end that Germany will go Bolshevik and that he will then be able to "bolshevize" France and England also.
>
> [The Russian dictatorship] acts to spread the area in which it can murder persons whom we regard as decent, and extend its form of tyranny.[13]

Besides Bullitt, Roosevelt brought attorney Adolf Berle into the State Department as an assistant secretary in early 1938, to signal the re-emergence of the Brain Trust in shaping foreign policy. Berle had already assisted the president as a speech writer during his first term, and Roosevelt wanted to continue to use him in that capacity as well as for special projects. Hull also approved of Berle and later wrote that he had "splendid ability and excellent practical judgment." Moore shared his superior's feelings because of his admiration for Berle's exceptional legal and academic training. The under secretary also welcomed the choice of Berle, for they were close friends. Born in 1895, Berle had graduated from Harvard Law School at the age of twenty-one, the youngest graduate in its history. He had joined Louis Brandeis's law firm, without ever becoming a disciple of Brandeis's legal reasoning. During the Paris peace conference, he served beside Bullitt on the American staff. After his voyage home, he resumed his legal practice, taught at Columbia Law School, and married into a wealthy family. Along with his regular pursuits, he participated in local politics and crusaded for various causes, such as American Indian rights.[14]

Berle had learned how to attract enthusiastic support from those in authority but had the habit of disregarding the feelings of most of the associates who worked under him. To them, he was an enigma: an intelligent man, but one with no substance. He won promotions and recognition by knowing exactly how to ingratiate himself with those in power. One antagonist declared that he should be locked in a room and allowed to devote his energies to scholarship: "I think Berle is one of the smartest men alive and completely devoid of common sense and incapable of understanding or dealing with human beings." Despite such comments, Berle was to remain a powerful force within the administration during the remainder of Roosevelt's presidency.[15]

Hull exempted his own staff from the interference of Welles's reorganization efforts. Cecil "Joe" Gray, for example, served as the secretary's personal assistant. A soft-spoken Tennesseean, he was a brilliant organizer and a clear thinker who had served in Berlin and Vienna. Now he advised the secretary on European matters. The secretary also hired George Milton, an old friend from Tennessee with a long career in the newspaper business, as a special assistant to the secretary of state assigned to publicize the reciprocity program (and concurrently to explore Hull's presidential chances in 1940).[16]

James Dunn was another Hull intimate who was dependent upon him for promotion. The model modern diplomat who knew all the proper social graces, Dunn was born in 1890 into a wealthy New Jersey family and was educated privately without ever receiving a degree. He really did not need one, for at the age of twenty-four, he married Mary Armour of the Chicago meat-packing family. Dunn chose a career in public service by entering the diplomatic corps in 1920, ultimately advancing to the post of chief of protocol during the Hoover administration.

After Hull became secretary, Dunn supported him against Raymond Moley at the London Economic Conference and then served as the secretary's adviser and translator at the Montevideo conference. In 1934 Dunn became Hull's special assistant and the next year he took over as chief of the Division of Western European Affairs. During the reorganization of 1937, he won the crucial position of political adviser on European affairs. Throughout his career, Dunn was rewarded for his loyalty, not his intellect. He did not need brilliance, for he knew how the flatter Hull outrageously, and as a result he became a member in good standing of the secretary's "croquet clique."[17]

Hornbeck remained at the head of the Far Eastern Division as second in command to Hull, who looked upon this region as his special province. As the second term progressed, Hornbeck gradually became more militant in his advice to halt Japanese aggression by defending Chinese sovereignty. Somehow the State Department never acknowledged the inconsistency of trying to avoid confrontation with Tokyo while simultaneously coming to the defense of Peking. The administration condemned Japanese advances and applauded Chinese tenacity without seriously weighing the outcome of these antagonistic positions. As long as the secretary was at his desk, Welles was excluded from Asian affairs, but when Hull left the capital the under secretary sometimes tried to influence decisions in that region as well.[18]

As for Moore, with no one to protect him, his earlier prophecy that he would be pushed aside if he lost the competition for the under-secretaryship came true. Even the advancement in rank was only an illusion. He was not consulted in the reorganization, and the new under secretary purposely relegated the office of counselor to a minor role dealing with legal, arms control, and aviation issues. Colleagues quickly noticed a change in Moore's mood; he had quickly become an old man, one who ignored his tasks and had lost his vitality. His pessimism became steadily more pronounced.[19]

By the winter of 1937, Moore's feelings toward Welles had degenerated to the point that the counselor sarcastically remarked that they were "not at all intimate." Moore disapproved of the departmental reorganization and the men chosen as political advisers, but his continued presence in the department still provided him with the opportunity to erode the under secretary's authority. Moore continually warned his allies that Welles's direct access to the Oval Office gave the under secretary countless chances to advance unsound policies. He believed that the folly of Welles's recommendations would eventually surface, but he also realized that until then, the under secretary would continue to exercise enormous power. "I am satisfied that by his untiring persistence he has acquired great influence with the President," Moore stressed, "more influence than the Secretary himself, whose judgment the President does not trust to the extent generally supposed."[20]

Moore never forgave Hull's behavior during the under-secretaryship struggle; he perceived that their close association had disintegrated to the point that Hull was distant because of his refusal to take responsibility for making the selection. Rather than take command now, the secretary deferred to Welles.[21]

Moore's melancholy deeply touched Bullitt, and on November 3, 1937, he wrote the president about the counselor's plight: "Inasmuch as he is the only man in the Department who sincerely and completely loves you and would gladly stand up against a wall and be shot to help you, I should hate to see that happen for your sake; and I should hate to see that happen for his sake as I am deeply fond of him." If Roosevelt would not come to Moore's defense, Bullitt was convinced that his friend at least needed some activity if he was to thrive; otherwise Bullitt was certain that Moore would resign. The ambassador suggested several assignments for the counselor, such as acting as liaison between the foreign service and Congress, reinstatement of his position on the Personnel Board, or supervision of the Eastern European Division. While Hull was in Buenos Aires, Bullitt reminded Roosevelt that Moore had done an admirable job as acting secretary, "and to be reduced now to a post which is somewhat less than that of the negro messengers in the halls of the Department is necessarily very discouraging."[22]

But these pleas accomplished nothing. Moore and Bullitt remained close, but the extent of their contact and correspondence dramatically declined. Moore occasionally wrote and complimented the ambassador on the excellent job he was doing, and Bullitt replied in kind and warned of the impending European war clouds. Their connection was disintegrating because of Moore's inability to find an avenue to communicate through departmental channels. On July 19, 1938, Bullitt lamented, "I really miss you and miss your letters." How could Moore respond? His enemies had slowly eroded his responsibilities, and everyone in the department who was knowledgeable understood that.[23]

As Moore's decline became more pronounced, Welles's name became more visible; as a result, he gained wider recognition among the media and those who followed international events. The president occasionally criticized Welles, complaining that he was "fundamentally a 'career man.'" But such mild slaps aside, the president was comfortable working with Welles, for he took broad, vague ideas and shaped them into specific programs. Their interchange brought the two into closer contact: Welles became a familiar figure at the White House, and Roosevelt, in turn, was a welcome guest at social gatherings of the Little Cabinet (composed of members of the subcabinet) at Welles's estates.[24]

Although the reorganization was not totally of Welles's orchestration, he took much of the credit for instituting the reforms. Shortly after Welles's promotion, Laurence Steinhardt, ambassador to Peru, wrote that the under secretary was increasing departmental efficiency and that the positive atmosphere was "extraordinary," since he was clearing out the "deadwood" by insisting on merit advancements. As far as the ambassador was concerned, "the more I see of Sumner Welles the better I like him."[25] The following spring, Moffat expressed his approval, for the department was "chugging along pretty satisfactorily, and the feuds that tore it apart a year or two ago have entirely disappeared." Moffat did not specifically mention the role that Welles had played in creating a more conducive working environment, but many others within the department hailed his leadership.[26] Ambassador Davies called him "an indefatigable worker" who made incisive suggestions, and Ambassador Claude Bowers, who would be transferred from Spain to Chile in 1939, liked his superior, even though he was "a bit stiff."[27]

Pearson openly favored his friend, informing readers on September 13, 1937, that "Welles is a man of decision, broad ideas, and an acute understanding of human nature." The new appointee and Hull saw "eye-to-eye so closely that a well-trained team is now running the foreign affairs of the United States." As a result, the State Department was "functioning more efficiently and more humanely than at any time in years." In a later article he painted Welles as the model British diplomat, from his tendency to dress in three-piece suits and sport a walking cane to his outward demeanor, but he asserted that Welles's shyness and aloofness hid admirable qualities. When that veneer was pierced, Pearson claimed, Welles could laugh at or even tell a good joke. Pearson did note two major faults in Welles: he was not a good judge of people and he was exceedingly overworked.[28]

Many, however, were ambivalent toward Welles. Postmaster General Farley's relations with him were "all right" during their interaction at cabinet meetings and White House events, and they also discussed political appointments for Marylanders and commented on local elections. Even though Farley did not speak to the under secretary about foreign policy, he conceded that Welles was Roosevelt's closest diplomatic adviser. Yet even with this grudging admission, Farley could not "make up my mind about Sumner Welles." Some diplomats labeled him "very competent," but Farley perceived a "pompous sort of man," one who remained difficult to analyze. Concluded Farley, "I don't feel at ease in his presence."[29]

Many echoed this uncomfortable feeling. Secretary of the Interior Harold Ickes, for example, described the under secretary as "a man of almost preternatural solemnity and great dignity. If he ever smiles, it has not been in my presence. He conducts himself with portentous gravity and as if he were charged with all the responsibilities of Atlas. Just to look at him one can tell that the world would dissolve into its component parts if only a portion of the weighty secrets of state that he carries about with him were divulged."[30]

Despite such disparaging remarks, Welles was unassailable because he had the White House's confidence, and no one questioned the fact that Roosevelt dipped his hand into diplomatic affairs at will. The president constantly listened to warnings about the disloyalty of the diplomatic corps. Ambassadors like Daniels and Dodd, staunch southern Democrats, repeatedly warned the White House that many foreign service officers despised the New Deal philosophy and were trying to limit its effectiveness abroad. Ambassador Bowers agreed. These influential party regulars believed that wealthy career diplomats were contemptuous of real democracy, and since so many of these men occupied critical posts, they were compromising the effectiveness of the New Deal.[31]

Congressional criticism, especially from those members who served on the Senate Foreign Relations Committee, also aggravated White House suspicions. In the summer of 1936 Senator Pittman, for example, described some cavalier behavior by the department's staff during testimony before his committee, reminding Hull that he had to stop this unacceptable behavior. Two years later Senator Theodore Green, Democrat of Rhode Island, declared that improved methods of communication like the telegraph and the airplane had reduced the value of foreign service officers because most major decisions were now relayed from Washington and not left to the diplomat in the field. On April 4, 1939, Senator Joseph Guffey of Pennsylvania warned Hull that during trips to Europe over the preceding two years, he had discovered that "a number of our career men are pro-Fascist and Anti-Roosevelt." Some individuals at the State Department—like Welles, Dunn, Moffat, and Green—were, Guffey proclaimed, "reactionary in heart and are only giving lip service to you and the President."[32]

Roosevelt was receptive to these warnings because he himself had had long-standing doubts about the career foreign service. These in turn led him to develop his own goals, outlining broad objectives and attempting to achieve them in his own ways, which were admittedly often circuitous. In East Asia, he tried to limit Japanese expansion and bolster Chinese defenses. In Europe, he pushed for closer Anglo-French bonds and displayed open hostility toward the Nazis. In the Western Hemisphere, he championed the good neighbor policy and simultaneously used the concept of the pax Americana (under which the Western Hemisphere was kept secure from any foreign invasion) to move boldly in the international arena.

Early in the second term, Japan's expansionism briefly held center stage. Although the White House generally followed the State Department's strategy for peace in Asia, the president occasionally longed for a more vigorous approach. Despite this hope, he realized that forceful measures were impossible. Many domestic critics had already insisted that the United States completely withdraw from Chinese affairs, and the few who held opposing views did not have enough of a following to press for action. When the Japanese staged a minor clash at the Marco Polo Bridge in July 1937 as the pretext for attacking and capturing Peking, Roosevelt's timidity momentarily disappeared: he began to consider force and started to use the term "quarantine." He even entertained the idea of drawing a line in the Pacific to halt Japanese trade and military expansion.[33]

On October 5, in the heartland of noninterventionism, Roosevelt spoke in Chicago of his indignation toward the dictators' warlike tendencies. He did not single out any one nation and refused to point directly at the Rising Sun. Instead he called for all peace-loving nations to move in unison against aggressors, suggesting the vague concept of a quarantine as a means of preserving international order. Public reaction to the address was generally favorable. Within the State Department, Hull and many others expressed their delight, and White House mail and phone calls strongly supported the presidential initiative. Given the public's interest in the quarantine speech, reporters questioned Roosevelt about specific details, but he refused to respond definitively and abandoned the idea just as quickly as it had been raised.[34]

Why did Roosevelt respond negatively when so many had reacted positively? He may not have correctly gauged the extent of his support, and instead may have paid far greater attention to those few congressional and administrative leaders who expressed their hostility to his idea. In this instance, the president may have simply overestimated the power of his adversaries and thereby missed an opportunity to give followers the chance to pursue the quarantine idea. Or, as he was often prone to do, he may simply have noted the favorable reaction to his quarantine idea for use at a later time.

At the end of the year, Japanese military aircraft, stationed in China, attacked the American gunboat U.S.S. *Panay*, resulting in two Americans being killed and fifty wounded. Roosevelt at first considered an armed response, but Hull counseled restraint, demanded restitution, and quickly negotiated a settlement. Cries for war were nonexistent; some Americans even seemed to accelerate their demands for a total withdrawal from East Asia. The last thing the United States wished to provoke was war in the Pacific.[35]

Another reason why Roosevelt may not have pursued the quarantine idea was that East Asia was not the primary focus of his attention as he shifted his energies to the threat of war across the Atlantic. His European strategy rested on three basic assumptions: stronger ties with the British, French protection of the Continent, and the need to counter German aggression.

The president pushed for an Anglo-American partnership throughout the 1930s, as historian Richard Harrison has shown, but improved relations failed to materialize because Prime Minister Neville Chamberlain, who entered office in the spring of 1937, ruled out American collaboration and instead favored an alliance with the Italians and reconciliation with Germany. Roosevelt was blinded to this opposition by the encouragement of English friends who preached greater cooperation between the two major English-speaking nations. As early as 1933, visiting British statesmen called on Roosevelt to consider a great-power summit, and at the end of his first term he again toyed with the idea, reasoning that if five or six world leaders could meet sometime in 1937, something positive was bound to result.[36]

When the president suggested this idea to Welles, it was his cue to turn the concept into a reality. In a memorandum dated October 6, 1937, Welles outlined a proposal for a preliminary meeting to agree on the principles for peace to be followed by a conference. Twenty days later, the under secretary added a dramatic touch by recommending that on Armistice Day, November 11, the president invite the international diplomatic community to the East Room of the White House, where he would make a plea for disarmament and economic stability to prevent future warfare and then formally call for the conference. Hull's response was skeptical, pointing out that the dictators had rejected the peace treaties already in force. He therefore vetoed the plan, but by January 1938 he had agreed to reverse his position under the condition that the State Department be allowed to consult with the British and the French before the announcement of any peace conference. Foreign Secretary Anthony Eden responded enthusiastically; however, Chamberlain still adamantly opposed a powerful American presence in European affairs.[37]

While Roosevelt probed for ways to forge Anglo-American ties, his antipathy toward Hitler grew. Drawing a sharp distinction between the current Nazi barbarism and traditional German values, he yearned for a return to the days of Bismarck, with their emphasis on strong family ties, moral upbringing, and respect for property rights. In their place, he was witnessing the rebirth of militarism as the Nazis absorbed Austria into the Third Reich early in 1938. Although the Munich agreement provided a brief respite, by the end of the year Czechoslovakia had virtually vanished as a sovereign state.[38]

The president also watched as Hitler gradually disenfranchised Germany's Semitic population. By chance, several American Jews had become a conspicuous part of the New Deal coalition: Henry Morgenthau, Jr., served as treasury secretary; Bernard Baruch, the industrialist, was an unofficial adviser; and Judge Samuel Rosenman was a presidential speech writer and confidant. Besides these prominent men, who received regular press coverage, other less well-known Jewish politicians and influential federal civil servants, among them Herbert Feis in the State Department and Abe Fortas in the Department of the Interior, gave the illusion to some that the administration favored Jews. In fact, this was untrue, but anti-Semites nevertheless referred to Roosevelt as "Rosenfeld" and the New Deal as the "Jew Deal," giving greater credence to this myth.[39]

When a distraught Polish Jew fatally wounded a diplomat at the German embassy in Paris, Nazi Propaganda Minister Joseph Goebbels unleashed the Kristallnacht, the Night of the Broken Glass. On the night of November 9–10, 1938, mobs murdered almost a hundred Jews and tormented thousands more; synagogues and Jewish-owned buildings were burned to the ground; over seven thousand businesses were destroyed; and thirty thousand Jewish men were sent to concentration camps. As the final insult, the Nazis demanded economic payment from the Jewish community for the damage that they had inflicted.[40]

On humanitarian grounds, this terror appalled Roosevelt. Although he would not push to increase immigration quotas, he welcomed eminent Western European Jews to the United States and authorized the issuance of thousands of visas with the expectation of granting them to Jews. The president also recalled the American ambassador from Berlin as a protest to focus immediate attention on Hitler's brutality and on the need to convene an international refugee conference at the French resort town of Evian-les-Bains. Thirty-two governments sent representatives, but no nation, including the United States, was willing to permit large-scale Jewish immigration; Americans were far more concerned about protecting their jobs from unwanted immigrants than about granting them safe harbor.[41]

Although the president was sympathetic to the plight of Jewish refugees, he was far more concerned about Nazi penetration of the Americas. In the summer of 1938, he warned Canadian Prime Minister W. L. MacKenzie King that German and Italian infiltration into South America might serve to foment revolution. To prevent such fifth-column activity, Roosevelt made hemispheric defense a top priority. When, for example, a reporter questioned him on this subject at a press conference on November 15, the president replied that technological advances over the last several years had significantly altered American strategy in the Western Hemisphere. Technical breakthroughs in military aircraft now exposed the Americas to attack from abroad, and Roosevelt intended to ask for congressional appropriations for measures to prevent any invasion by foreign forces. He extended this argument to his private talks as well. Germany would try to build bases in South America, and the Japanese would reach out farther into the Pacific. Since the British had moved slowly to counter what he viewed as a very real threat, the United States would be potentially vulnerable to Axis penetration from Latin America, and Roosevelt would have to guard energetically against that possibility.[42] Once Hitler dominated Europe, the president charged, he could force any Latin American country trading with the Continent to become economically dependent on Germany, and this threat struck at a fundamental United States principle: European political expansion in the Western Hemisphere was prohibited under the Monroe Doctrine. The message was clear: Germany now menaced the sacred principle of Fortress America.

Rather than confiding in Hull, Roosevelt deprecated him. In October 1937 the president told Interior Secretary Ickes that the White House "would have to take the ball way from Hull." Several months later Roosevelt informed Berle, "Hull was magnificent in principle but timid." Farley learned from the president that he was "very fond" of the secretary, but that Hull was a "free trader at heart and for that reason his views could not be accepted in their entirety." Hull heard this criticism, agonized over the display of presidential disfavor, and later bitterly recalled that the president "seemed to take a boyish delight in seeing two of his assistants at odds; he would say, 'Settle it between yourselves,' or simply let the controversy go on without taking a hand to solve it."[43]

Roosevelt sometimes provoked conflict within his cabinet and, as we have seen, encouraged officials to usurp Hull's powers regarding foreign affairs. Yet when the secretary protested vigorously enough, the White House generally yielded and forced others to retreat. Hull never appreciated his political might and the fact that Roosevelt could not afford to remove him from office. Hull could have exerted greater pressure on behalf of his causes, but he hardly ever chose that course. He refused to act positively and allowed others to bypass him and to lobby for their own causes. When ambassadors like Daniels, Joseph Kennedy (ambassador to Great Britain), and Bullitt made requests, Hull usually permitted them to go directly to the White House without his permission because he considered them presidential selections and did not want to risk being overruled because of what he perceived as their persuasiveness inside the Oval Office.[44]

Following the presidential example, some of the secretary's most adamant opponents accused him of stupidity and of fanaticism on the question of free trade. Encouraging their attacks was the fact that, when Hull did make public pronouncements, they were often vague and without substance, in order to save him from the need to take controversial positions. Senator Johnson called the secretary a "dumb Dora." Even crueler comments came from Raymond Moley, who labeled the secretary "a complete, ignoramus [sic]" before dismissing him as "plain and petty."[45]

Several of Hull's cabinet colleagues argued constantly with him. Ickes, who had initially admired Hull, had reversed his opinion by the summer of 1938. The Interior Department had agreed to sell helium to the Nazis but had later decided to cancel the purchase. The State Department argued that Ickes should honor his original commitment. This disagreement damaged the working relationship between the two agencies and sparked Ickes's attacks on Hull. The interior secretary could not understand how the State Department could run effectively while it tried to force other agencies to follow its unsound policies.[46]

But Ickes was a minor annoyance to Hull compared with Henry Morgenthau, Jr. Born in 1891, he was descended from German Jews who had immigrated to New York City. After becoming financially successful as a publisher, he turned to agriculture and bought a large farm near Roosevelt's Hyde Park home. The two men met in 1914 and became close friends and Democratic allies. Morgenthau went so far as to back his neighbor in every one of his political campaigns. He was initially disappointed that the president did not make him a cabinet member, but that changed in 1934 with his appointment to head the Treasury Department. Morgenthau became only the second Jew to reach that rank; coincidentally, it was Theodore Roosevelt, Franklin's cousin, who had chosen the first Jewish cabinet member: Oscar Straus, secretary of commerce.[47]

Morgenthau followed most of the president's policies and was especially vocal in regard to Nazi tyranny and the State Department's failure to counter it. With the exception of State Department economic adviser Herbert Feis, who happened to be the highest-ranking Jew in the foreign service, and Welles, Morgenthau generally detested working with those in the foreign service; he also objected to Hull's obsession with the reciprocity program and his willingness to accept incompetent advice from career diplomats who did not recognize the dangers of Axis aggression. Morgenthau, by 1938, had encouraged Roosevelt to supply needed capital and credits to East Asia and Latin America in order that those regions could resist the dictatorships' efforts at foreign economic penetration. Hull, on the other hand, refused to move energetically in this direction, instead choosing to deliver what were seen as pious speeches.[48] Speaking for the Treasury Department, Assistant Secretary Harry White wrote his superior on March 30, 1939, "So long as foreign policy is permitted to develop within the confines of the State Department hierarchy, so long will it be a do-nothing policy."[49]

Several cabinet members listened to Hull's frequent complaints about the president and other interlopers. The secretary told Farley that Roosevelt did not consult him enough or ask his advice on tax matters, a topic on which the secretary considered himself an expert. Hull felt that the White House ignored many of his diplomatic recommendations, and he even told Morgenthau that Roosevelt had inhibited his ability to carry out diplomatic initiatives.[50]

However, these gripes never reached the American public. Hull maintained his image as the second most influential figure in the administration and as the Democrat who personified party unity. If the secretary cherished anything above all else, it was his national prestige. He seldom lost control of his temper in public and thus gave the impression of strength, of being a leader always in command. To Hull, that perception was crucial. Indeed many viewed the secretary as a great man who was a stabilizing force within the administration. Messersmith lauded his role in the establishment of the good neighor policy and the passage of the reciprocal trade agreements program; Farley declared that the secretary performed exceptionally well, and that the public held him in the highest esteem. Other proponents were glad that their standard-bearer kept the New Dealers from dominating the government. Even the Republican vice-presidential candidate in 1936, Frank Knox, supported Hull's leadership. Journalist William White labeled Hull "honest, brave and wise."[51]

Hull's advancing years did not seem to interfere with his busy schedule because he maintained his strength by carefully budgeting his time. After returning from South America in the middle of January 1937, he spent most of his time at the office, continued the informal Sunday gatherings with his associates, and limited his outside engagements. When he took vacations, they lasted only a week. By the end of the year, however, Hull was complaining of the long hours required to deal with recurring emergencies: "I am working sixteen and eighteen hours a day without even any let-up over the week-end. In these circumstances, I feel obliged to conserve my strength to meet the ever-increasing demands upon me."[52]

These long hours had started to exhaust him by early 1938, and during most of March he rested in Florida, supposedly because of a cold. Shortly after returning to the nation's capital, Frances Hull expressed concern over her husband's physical condition and complained about the individuals in the administration who had caused the strain: "No use killing himself. It is not what *he does* that is hard, but what *others do*." On April 15, Hull left for Pinehurst, North Carolina, ordered by his doctor to take a vacation, only to return to Washington in early May to respond to press reports about his impending resignation by immediately issuing a statement that the gossip was ridiculous.[53]

The secretary was extremely sensitive to such rumors, and his anxiety over media attacks grew more pronounced as he daily followed newspaper accounts of State Department activities, especially those by Pearson. Former Hoover diplomat William Castle believed that the reporter made life miserable for the secretary by attacking his staff and policies, and at the same time praising Welles. James Dunn intimated to Castle that Welles and Pearson were more than just chums—that their relationship was much more intimate. Castle dismissed the inference and argued that Hull should insist upon a total break between Welles and Pearson, for the former under secretary was undoubtedly funneling material to the journalist. The secretary, argued Castle, needed to force the issue because Roosevelt depended on Hull's political backing; the secretary could demand just about anything he wanted, but refused to stand firm.[54]

Hull controlled his long-simmering animosity toward Pearson until early May 1938, when he claimed that the State Department's "pro-Nazi career boys" had illegally approved a shipment of airplane parts to Germany. The reporter as well as other lobbyists demanded that Hull halt the sale until the attorney general could determine if it were legal. At a press conference on the sixth, Hull spoke for over an hour, suspended a long-standing rule that forbade direct quotations unless his staff could check a reporter's copy, and periodically directly addressed Pearson, who replied and so turned the meeting into a debate over the legality of the sale. The secretary was clearly angry and declared that his associates had been "criminally libeled." This especially applied to the accusations of disloyalty that had been hurled at Moore. Hull was well aware that Moore had suffered from Pearson's charges in 1937 that Moore was too old for the under-secretaryship. The State Department, according to an agitated secretary of state, had not violated any laws, nor did any of his subordinates have pro-Nazi leanings.[55]

That night in his syndicated newspaper column, Pearson repeated the charge that the State Department had violated the law by assisting German rearmament. In fact, he privately considered taking the unprecedented action of hiring an attorney to file an injunction against the department to stop all arms sales to Germany, and by the middle of the month he had publicly announced that he was contemplating suing Hull to resolve the issue. Pearson felt that the government had never been challenged about violating treaties: "The State Department during the some 13 years I have covered it has remained a little sacrosanct air-tight vacuum, beyond the pale of the law and impervious to legal steps when it violates a law or a treaty." By the end of the month, Pearson had decided not to pursue legal action and moved on to other topics, but Hull never forgot the incident. From the moment that the reporter accused his department of a Nazi bias, he was persona non grata. Yet this display of wrath did not seem to bother Pearson. He not only refused to apologize, but also confronted the secretary at his own press conferences and continued writing inflammatory columns.[56]

Hull could not physically stand this kind of tension. It aggravated the congestion in his lungs, and he took several short trips during the fall of 1938. Fortunately for him, he embarked for a hemispheric conference at Lima, Peru, in late November and did not return to the United States until early January. This relaxing journey gave him the opportunity to enjoy a pleasant cruise and to spend several winter months away from the usual bleak Washington weather. In addition, he received an enormous amount of favorable publicity for his efforts on behalf of the good neighbor policy, and his participation at the conference gave him valuable exposure. While the ship was at sea, Hull continued his habit of working out the conference agenda in pleasant surroundings.

The delegation arrived at its destination on December 7, two days before the conference opened. Hull attended very few social functions, went to bed at 10:00 P.M., and arose the next morning at 9:00 A.M. If any of the delegates stayed out late for state dinners or to socialize, the secretary did not directly rebuke them, but he let them know of his disapproval. During the conference, he sat through the sessions without any earphones, even though he could not understand any foreign language! When addressing the proceedings, he spoke in generalities and depended on others to translate his pronouncements into concrete proposals. The exception was his forceful, indeed overzealous, advocacy of his reciprocal trade agreements program. The main controversy at the conference centered on the United States' proposal to keep non-American states from endangering this hemisphere, and the Argentine delegation caused Hull his greatest difficulty. But as Christmas Eve approached, the delegates, wanting to adjourn with a meaningful declaration, reached a consensus. The declaration that was agreed upon stated that the American republics would oppose any kind of attack from a non-American state; if any one were threatened, the act would be a signal for immediate consultation. Although this declaration did not go so far as some might have wished, it did inch the cause of solidarity forward. The Declaration of Lima, issued in late December, became a reality, a reflection of hemispheric unity and the United States delegation's quest to condemn foreign aggressors.[57]

Samuel Inman, a Latin American specialist who served as an unofficial adviser to the delegation, expressed ambivalent feelings about Hull's capabilities, wondering if the secretary wanted to be the next president. Hull certainly looked the part, with his grave, sincere manner and gray hair; but he had spent thirty years in Washington without gaining a cosmopolitan perspective or losing his small-town Tennesseean mentality. Hull's concept of right and wrong, to Inman, was rigid: "Truth, pay debts, demand respect." He was humble, spoke only one language, and had simple tastes. Such a man did not belong on the bridge of a battleship barking commands. Inman concluded his portrait: "The world is in a trouble[d] state. Hull knows how to save it. That is the serious business that overwhelms him."[58]

While Hull concentrated on Asian and Latin American affairs, William Dodd was finishing his diplomatic assignment to Germany. Born in North Carolina just after the Civil War, Dodd had graduated from Virginia Polytechnic Institute, continued on for a doctorate from the University of Leipzig, and then returned to the South, to a teaching position in Virginia that lasted for eight years. In 1908 he accepted a professorship at the University of Chicago, specializing in Southern history. While focusing his energies on scholarly pursuits, he also entered Democratic politics and identified with Woodrow Wilson's progressivism.[59]

During the 1932 convention and the subsequent campaign, Dodd actively supported Roosevelt. A close friend, Daniel Roper, the incoming secretary of commerce, had recommended Dodd for the ambassadorship to Germany, but unfortunately for Dodd, he was ill equipped to serve as the American representative to what he considered a pariah nation. He abhorred Nazi policies, spoke openly against them, and hoped that America would take a vocal stand against Hitler and all that the Third Reich represented. As the ambassador became more vehement in his opposition, his usefulness, such as it was, disintegrated because the German foreign ministry almost completely ignored him. The ambassador also expressed his distaste for professional diplomats like Welles.

Dodd had met the assistant secretary "of doubtful Cuban fame" and learned that he was "the owner of a mansion in Washington which outshines the White House in some respects and is about as large." Such pretensions appalled Dodd, who protested to Hull about the selection of "millionaires who speak no language but their own and know little of the real history of the countries to which they are appointed." The ambassador did not specifically mention Welles and did not advocate banning all men of wealth from the foreign service, but he was disappointed that so many career diplomats were so exceedingly rich, worked on frivolous projects, lacked energy, and spoke only English. Dodd suggested that the foreign service should have a limit of no more than two millionaires in service at any one time—and Welles fit into that odious category.[60]

Even though Roosevelt had promised to keep Dodd in Berlin until March 1938, he was recalled early. He erroneously presumed that Welles had instigated this change and complained to the White House about the under secretary's interference. The president, who had personally initiated and approved the action, never corrected Dodd's misconception.[61] As a result of his perceived grievances against Welles, Dodd became his enemy, declaring that Welles stood for everything the ambassador opposed. The under secretary lived in an opulent fashion, spent twice what Hull did, and gave extravagant parties. When Dodd read that Roosevelt had spent a summer Sunday at Oxon Hill Manor, Welles's suburban estate, he expressed surprise and lamented, "Politics is a strange game, even with a real man like Roosevelt." Dodd urged Moore to tell him what Welles intended to do now that he controlled the selection of embassy personnel, and the counselor implied that the under secretary was responsible for the rejection of the ambassador's policies, an allegation that only reinforced Dodd's charge that "Welles was opposed to me and everything I recommended."[62]

Dodd returned to Washington armed with Moore's information that Welles personally disliked the ambassador and had ignored his advice. Moore had further encouraged Dodd in his belief that the under secretary had forced his retirement. It was under these circumstances that Dodd wrote Roosevelt on December 23, 1937, to express his disgust for the manner in which Welles had engineered his removal and his anticipation for a meeting at the White House at which he could defend his actions and attack the under secretary's dishonorable conduct. When his presidential audience came in late 1938, Dodd vented his anger against Welles.[63]

In Dodd, Moore had a willing coconspirator who wished to discredit the under secretary. However, instead of joining forces with Moore, upon his return to the United States in early 1938 Dodd immediately launched a speaking tour to warn against the rising might of the Third Reich. But shortly after his campaign began, personal tragedy struck. Dodd's wife of thirty-seven years died, and this loss slowly sapped his will to live. By that winter he was sixty-eight years old and had developed a progressive paralysis that attacked his ability to speak and swallow. In his weakened mental and physical state, on the evening of December 5, he was driving near Petersburg, Virginia, when he struck a four-year-old girl. He fled the scene and was later arrested for hit-and-run driving. The incident made the headlines in the United States, and the German press used the event to malign the ambassador and counteract his avowed antipathy toward the Reich.[64] Although the child eventually recovered, Dodd was forced to plead guilty and to pay a fine and the girl's hospital bills. Humiliated and in financial difficulties, and with his health rapidly deteriorating, he entered Georgetown University Hospital for observation. But there was no cure for his ailments, and he was released to return home. Moore visited him in the winter of 1939 and "found him in a pitiful state. He was unable to talk and had to communicate with me by using a pad and pencil, and he was unable to take any nourishment except through a stomach tube. It is one of the saddest things I have known."[65] Dodd died early in the next year, ending his suffering and removing from the scene an ally upon whom Moore could have depended to help drive Welles from office.[66]

Yet Dodd's passing did not end Moore's campaign. He continued to condemn Welles for pushing Dodd aside and to look upon Hull as a tragic figure who lacked the moral fiber to select the under secretary of his choice. Without allies, Moore had to find new plotters or else wait for Welles to make a significant blunder. The under secretary's eccentricity alone would not be enough to drive him from office.

Roosevelt paid no attention to this intrigue. At the beginning of 1939, he was working to align America with France to stop Nazi expansion in Europe. The French air ministry had already agreed to send French airmen to accompany American pilots on training exercises in Douglas DB-7 attack bombers, and in early January 1939, one of these airplanes crashed near Los Angeles, injuring a Frenchman. To prevent an embarrassing investigation of this incident, the president called several senators from the Military Affairs Committee to the White House to answer questions about the episode. They met on the last day of the month, and Roosevelt used the occasion to convince his guests that the best way to protect the Americas was to assist the Allies. Even within that context, he swore that the administration would never again send American troops to Europe. Despite that pledge, reporters soon learned that the president had also declared, "the frontiers of the United States are on the Rhine." The repercussions of this leak were devastating. The White House characterized the charges as lies, and, far more damaging, Roosevelt was never again so candid in discussing military strategy. Indeed, he became so suspicious that in the summer and fall of 1940 he had his White House press conferences and other conversations secretly recorded.[67]

Bullitt supported the president's proposals but nevertheless admired German military power; he also loved French culture and disapproved of the British diplomatic interference on the Continent that had forestalled Franco-German reconciliation. He was a poor forecaster of the European military situation in that he overestimated the strength of both French and German forces, and these predictions brought him into direct conflict with those who argued against negotiations with the Nazis, advocated stronger Anglo-American bonds, and held different views about the military balance in Europe. Bullitt desperately tried to draw the United States closer to the French, and by the summer of 1939 he felt that Germany was preparing to start a European war. The United States, Bullitt proposed, should send supplies, not troops. He saw his work in Paris as at an end and wanted the president to appoint him either secretary of war or secretary of the navy.[68]

Hull's recurrent illnesses prevented him from participating in many of the European decisions. Some, like Feis, noticed that the secretary's strength was fading; his age was becoming apparent and he now depended on others to accomplish routine tasks. The number of informal

Sunday gatherings with his closest advisers dwindled, a further sign of the secretary's failing health. Periodic influenza epidemics that struck Washington were cause for tremendous consternation. That February, his wife Frances, who also had followed a hectic schedule, "fell victim." She recovered, but was nevertheless "very weak and miserable." Her husband took ill in the middle of the month. Still in bed in early March, the Hulls decided to go to Florida to recover.[69]

Moffat saw the secretary after his return and commented that although Hull looked "much better after his rest," he continued coughing. Pearson spotlighted the secretary's weariness on March 24 in the "Washington Merry-Go-Round." Hull was being seen less and less at his desk because he was almost sixty-eight and in poor health. Welles had assumed most of the secretary's duties and was running the department: "The real fact is that the Secretary of State never was very active except in pushing his trade treaties, and recently he has drifted even more to the side-lines." Hull continued to be upset at other cabinet members like Ickes and Morgenthau and close White House advisers like Harry Hopkins for trying to influence foreign policy at the expense of the foreign service. Some believed that his resignation was imminent, or that he wished to serve on the Supreme Court.[70]

On August 1, the secretary traveled to White Sulphur Springs, West Virginia, for another rest. By then, he had developed a routine that he was to maintain for the remainder of his tenure. When taking extended leaves, he received a daily pouch of dispatches, had a special telephone line run to his hotel room, and each morning received briefings from Welles. He kept in constant touch, but had to rely on his under secretary to an ever-increasing degree. No one connected these trips, or his symptoms, to an active case of tuberculosis compounded by a mild form of diabetes.[71]

This was especially remarkable because tuberculosis—caused by airborne tuberculosis bacilli inhaled into the small tubes of the lungs— was such a dreaded disease. The infected were considered not merely victims, but carriers of death. A tuberculosis victim had to make the decision of whether to admit openly to having the illness or to live in secrecy because of the stigma associated with it. Carriers sometimes lost their jobs or were forced to leave their families for years to recuperate—if they survived. Elaine Redfield, a New Yorker who was a senior at Wellesley College in the fall of 1937, was diagnosed with tuberculosis, hospitalized, and sent to a sanitarium in Colorado. After several years of rest, her tuberculosis was arrested; yet she was never allowed to say that she was cured. Looking back on her struggle more than fifty years later, Redfield claimed, "TB was like AIDS is today. There was no cure for what you had. People were afraid of it. They were afraid of you."[72]

As Hull's health deteriorated, Welles spent more time as acting secretary and assumed even greater responsibilities. During those intervals professional diplomats like Moffat, Berle, and Feis thought that Welles's long-range views tended to prevail. When Hull was at his desk, domestic considerations pressed by Moore and others seemed to supersede strategic planning. When the domestic advocates won, they tended to weigh their actions in terms of how many potential votes in the next election they might have gained or lost. As a result, these politicians-turned-diplomats delayed their decisions, preferring above all to be cautious. These distinctions were not sharply accentuated in the second term because Hull and Welles seemed to agree and work together on most issues. Farley watched both men interact and, at least at the start of 1939, believed that they cooperated. Some rumors about discord between them surfaced in the spring, but these quickly disappeared. By the beginning of the following year, the postmaster general had begun noting a gradual shift. Even though Hull resented Roosevelt's confidence in Welles, the secretary refused to "call for a showdown" because he was "a good party man."[73]

At the end of March, Berle noticed some friction between the two. Their relationship had become strained because the under secretary went "frequently to the White House and is considered a thoroughly capable man. Hull tends to be silent, cautious and quiet." The secretary's associates also resented Welles's growing power and did whatever they could to discredit him. When the secretary, for instance, was absent during the Munich crisis, Welles's statement on this conflict made the headlines. To inflate the secretary's stature and minimize the under secretary's, Hull's supporters falsely declared that the secretary had written the document. These kinds of petty jealousies created antagonism, and Berle lamented this because "the men complement each other completely; and it is essential that they work together in complete confidence."[74]

That winter even Pearson conceded that Hull and Welles sometimes quarreled, but remarked that this was not an uncommon occurrence in Washington. They naturally did have differences, "but on the whole they are good friends." According to Pearson, they were "a unique couple. He [Hull] is slow, cautious, drawls out his sentences with a homely Tennessee accent. Welles is quick, imaginative, not afraid to probe a difficult situation, bites out his conversation with an inclusive Harvard accent. The two supplement each other beautifully." Another point was also plainly evident. Hull did not appreciate Welles's newly won fame.[75]

Although the secretary might have had some doubts, he and Welles, out of sheer necessity, cooperated during this period. Their cooperation was based on a certain degree of trust and a division of functions. Both men promoted hemispheric solidarity and reciprocal trade agreements. Besides these common interests, each had his own special responsibilities: the secretary was concerned with events in East Asia and his own political future at the 1940 Democratic convention, while the under secretary handled inter-American and European matters and the departmental routine. No one recognized the extent of Hull's physical incapacity, and Welles unwittingly assisted in the deception. He had assumed Phillips's bureaucratic and policy roles, carried them out conscientiously, and made certain to prove his loyalty. During the secretary's absences, Welles stepped into the role of acting secretary and carefully abided by his superior's wishes. As long as Welles followed these practices, the State Department operated smoothly.

During the hot, humid summer of 1939, Hull began his vacation on the first of August, leaving Welles in charge. The acting secretary was anxious about the impending war and canceled all leaves. The State Department prepared for a possible wartime emergency by drafting a neutrality proclamation and taking other measures. Roosevelt shortened his vacation in Hyde Park by a day and had returned to the capital by the twenty-third; Hull came back the next day.[76] As the European war was about to erupt, Berle confided to his diary, "In this kind of a contingency, the American public trusts Secretary Hull: and nobody else will do."[77]

German troops stormed across Polish borders on September 1, and World War II began. The United States, as anticipated, declared its neutrality, and the American agenda centered on two recurring themes: protecting the Americas and freedom of the seas. Immediately after the commencement of hostilities, the State Department still gave the illusion of carrying on business as usual. The shocking collapse of Polish resistance had radically altered the face of Europe, but it had hardly dented the traditional American diplomatic routine. The foreign service still emphasized the reporting of current events and, thus narrowly focused, its members sometimes missed pertinent long-range trends.[78]

The real state of affairs in the department was quite different from the public's perception. Future secretary of state Dean Acheson recalled "a department without direction, composed of a lot of busy people working hard and usefully but as a whole not functioning as a foreign office. It did not chart a course to be furthered by the success of our arms, or to aid or guide our arms. Rather it seems to have been adrift, carried hither and yon by the currents of war or pushed about by collisions with more purposeful craft."[79]

Acheson's memory might have been faulty when he reported that no one was steering the ship of state. Those who worked in the diplomatic corps at secondary levels often were not privy to major decisions. Indeed, sometimes the rank and file purposely chose to ignore directives from above. The president still was the originator of policy and now took action to promote an Allied victory while the secretary, wary as ever of the untested, preferred to move more cautiously. When the White House needed to take urgent steps, it simply bypassed him and acted independently or went directly to Welles to present an idea that Welles, the consummate technician, could then mold into a workable form.

By the start of the European war, these lines of communication provided a method of checks and balances. When Roosevelt moved precipitously, Hull invariably called for restraint. If he judged the call warranted, the president listened. If not, he turned to Welles, who at worst would be a sympathetic listener or at best would turn the idea into a practical plan. The career officials who offered opinions to their superiors continued to exert their influence through normal channels. What Acheson had observed was an organization that received most of its critical commands from above, and as a consequence had lost its initiative to the White House, to a secretary of state who did not know fully how to mobilize his own bureaucracy, and to an under secretary who gladly took direction from the Oval Office. To magnify the problem, neither Roosevelt, Hull, nor Welles systematically outlined his agenda, and without a clearly defined written or oral record to follow, subordinates did not have proper guidance. Ironically those at the top preferred this management style in order to maintain control; unfortunately for those below them, the last thing diplomats needed at the start of a global conflict was to have to guess at their own government's intentions.

# CHAPTER 7

# THE WELLES MISSION

FROM THE ONSLAUGHT OF the European war in the fall of 1939 to the beginning of the next year, Roosevelt responded vigorously. Although he certainly never claimed to be mimicking Woodrow Wilson, the parallels between the two presidents are too striking to be overlooked. During World War I, Wilson took absolute personal control, bypassed the State Department by using private emissaries like Colonel Edward House, favored his own intuition, ignored the advice of his own secretary of state, and went directly to his constituency through the media and his oratory. At the beginning of World War II, Roosevelt drew upon his own unique experiences as Wilson's assistant secretary of the navy by recalling Germany's war zone around the British Isles, acting as a military strategist, moving to modify the neutrality legislation to give himself greater latitude, and trying to mute those adversaries who loudly decried White House efforts as the opening drive in United States participation on the Allied side.[1]

Just after the fighting erupted and before the belligerents had a chance to bring their struggle to the Western Hemisphere, Roosevelt seized the occasion to declare the Americas as falling outside the war zone. Simultaneously he directed Assistant Secretary of State Berle to search for precedents in support of the concept of a security zone that the United States navy would patrol. Berle found that several Latin American nations had proposed such a concept during World War I in order to keep warring vessels from threatening inter-American shipping lanes. "This," the assistant secretary thought, "was logical and necessary under existing situations. It does really change the status of the New World; a kind of *pax Americana.*"[2]

Because of the range and speed of contemporary military aircraft, the president argued that the traditional three-mile limit of international law was obsolete. He therefore unilaterally extended the protected area to one varying in width from three hundred to one thousand miles by personally outlining a security zone with the assistance of the State Department's geographer. To make certain that the belligerents respected it and to emphasize the United States navy's readiness to defend the Americas, he organized a naval patrol to report and track any intruding vessel. In addition to this initiative, Roosevelt called Congress into special session on September 21 to revise the neutrality legislation. The initiative succeeded largely through his ability to draw upon bipartisan support for revision, particularly from those Republicans who vocally favored the Allies. The White House stressed insulating the Americas from attack, avoiding foreign confrontations, minimizing any emphasis on Allied assistance, and allaying congressional fears about the expansion of executive prerogatives. Even with these assurances, however, the revised neutrality act did not grant credits to purchase supplies; it merely allowed belligerents the right of cash-and-carry. But since the British controlled the seas, the bill was in reality a form of indirect aid.[3]

While the president was acting forcefully, Hull's outlook on the outbreak of war was much bleaker. He feared the destruction of the Anglo-Franco forces, the Nazi and communist domination of Europe, and the ascendancy of the Japanese in East Asia. His friend and newly appointed assistant secretary, Breckinridge Long, commended Hull for his "fine character" but worried about his indecisiveness and his limited knowledge of European affairs.[4]

In addition to Long's professional concerns, Hull's health had further deteriorated. By the end of November 1939, he needed an extended vacation, and even upon his return, Duggan noted that the secretary "looked extremely tired."[5] At the start of the new year, he suffered a relapse of his tuberculosis, and by the end of January he was bedridden, allegedly for a head cold and possible influenza. Frances, his dutiful protector, hid his real disease from the newspapers, for she and his physician knew that his tuberculosis was growing progressively worse.[6]

Hull's incapacitation made Welles acting secretary, and Long observed that Welles was "crowded to death" by the additional work load caused by the European fighting; Berle commented that the under secretary was "now stoked above the gunwales with work." Welles conceded that he was overcommitted and usually had "to cancel even those few engagements that I make to undertake addresses outside of Washington." Overwork led to fatigue, and Duggan noticed how Welles's own health was worsening. On January 23 and 24, 1940, Welles, like his superior, was confined to bed. The cold weather in the capital added to the misery. Nine inches of snow had piled up in the streets, and the thermometer read ten degrees above zero in the morning and lower at night. Since Hull was restricted to his apartment, the flu-ridden under secretary hurried to resume the duties of acting secretary. To Frances, this created an untenable situation, for she did "not want it thought that the Department can't run while Welles is away."[7]

Neither illness nor the weather prevented Welles from carrying out White House initiatives, for shortly after the president proclaimed his neutrality zone for the Americas, Welles drafted telegrams calling for an inter-American consultative meeting at Panama to approve the concept. After an agenda had been quickly approved, Welles sailed from New York on September 15 to lead a delegation to a hemispheric conference that was to open eight days later. Since Argentina and the United States had similar objectives in this situation, cooperation replaced controversy, and the neutrality zone that Roosevelt had already championed won acceptance as the Declaration of Panama in late October. Welles had accomplished his objective. He received praise from Drew Pearson, who pointed out that, although Welles had been working on inter-American conferences for years, this was the first time that he had chaired a delegation to cement hemispheric solidarity.[8]

Hull, however, vehemently disagreed with the neutrality zone concept. He questioned its legality; since it violated international law, the belligerents would never adhere to it. The secretary later recalled, "The hemispheric neutrality zone was frankly an experiment. It was the idea of the President, seconded by Welles."[9] When representatives of the Latin American Division and the navy pointed out the flaws in the plan, Hull readily concurred. Anxious over a possible public outcry, he stressed the fact that the neutrality zone was a hemispheric arrangement and did not have the force of a treaty, and that under these conditions the United States did not have to confront any belligerent if it entered the patrol area. In private, the secretary's anger grew so intense that he briefly considered filing a formal protest with Roosevelt. As Berle listened to the secretary's outrage, he lamented, "It was the old task of trying to accommodate the Secretary's ideas to those of the President and Sumner."[10]

During the early days of the fighting, Anglo-American relations remained strained because the British, who controlled the sea lanes, would not respect any vaguely drawn neutrality zone unless American military vessels kept German shipping out of the entire Western Hemisphere. The administration refused to accept that responsibility, and occasional English attacks on German freighters within the announced boundaries created Anglo-American friction. Despite these difficulties, the interpretation of the security zone gave rise to correspondence between Winston Churchill and Roosevelt. As cabinet minister in charge of the admiralty, Churchill wrote the president on October 5 that the British understood why the United States wanted to keep belligerents from the Americas, but that he wanted the United States to patrol the zone more effectively to make sure that the idea would work.[11]

The most famous violation of the security zone occurred in mid-December 1939, when three of His Majesty's warships trapped the pocket battleship *Admiral Graf Spee* in Montevideo harbor; for several days, journalists rushed to Uruguay to report on the impending naval battle. Rather than fight or surrender, the captain of the *Graf Spee* ordered the vessel's destruction in midchannel and then committed suicide. Opponents of the zone used this spectacular event to ridicule the "chastity belt," but was that conclusion warranted? Although the British protested alleged violations of the zone, they were at once the worst offenders and its chief beneficiaries. Hitler's admirals rightly pointed out that the zone hindered submarine operations and asked for permission to launch U-boat attacks within the forbidden region, but the Führer, preferring not to provoke an incident, rebuffed them. The effectiveness of the neutrality zone was unquestionable, and it also clearly demonstrated how Roosevelt had intentionally shut Hull out of White House plans and how much the president depended on Welles to make them operational.[12]

While Roosevelt initiated measures for hemispheric defense and neutrality revision, the Nazis, shortly after the collapse of Polish resistance, took diplomatic steps to entice the president to act as a peace mediator. Hull and several chief assistants feared that Roosevelt would accept this role at an inappropriate moment, for under the present circumstances the secretary thought that mediation would fail, embarrass the Allies, and damage American prestige in Europe. At first, Roosevelt concurred and turned down the suggestions, but by the beginning of 1940 he had begun to reassess his position. Historian Wayne Cole has given probably the most logical rationale for this change of attitude. The prospect of a negotiated peace was the president's best response to calls from isolationists to use mediation as a way to settle the war; furthermore, by serving as a mediator Roosevelt would take the charge of warmongering out of the arsenal of his political opponents.[13]

Others, like Ambassador Joseph Kennedy in Great Britain, clamored for presidential action to reestablish peace. William Davis, an American businessman with contacts in the German government, talked to Nazi leader Hermann Göring about the prospect of the White House acting as a mediator. James Mooney, a General Motors executive with influential contacts inside the Third Reich's hierarchy, also searched for a path to peace. King Leopold of Belgium saw the president as the only hope to halt the fighting. While these individuals called for mediation, the United States revived the idea of a peace gathering by sending out invitations to forty-six neutral nations to exchange views that might lead to their assuming a role as a mediator in a peace settlement.[14]

Faced with this growing pressure for White House involvement, Roosevelt reevaluated his options. He wanted to avoid coming under domestic attack for interfering in the European conflict, and at the same time he did not intend to be charged with refusing to assist the peace process. The Allies also needed time to establish defenses in order to demonstrate that the Nazis could not continue their victories. If the British and French could not reverse German gains, the president foresaw two dismal possibilities: an ultimate triumph of the Third Reich or a protracted war that the Allies would win. In either case, the Continent would be devastated economically.

To accommodate both foreign and domestic critics, in January 1940 the president began to consider sending a special emissary on a European mission. Even if the chance of peace was remote, he thought, the United States should still attempt to assist the forces of reason. Besides, the White House was receiving contradictory information from Europe, and Roosevelt needed a clearer picture before taking definite action. During the middle of March, the president reflected on his reasons for initiating the mission; he believed that the mission might postpone or even prevent an expected Nazi spring offensive and thus give the Allies more time to achieve military preparedness. Since Roosevelt already knew the French and British positions, visits to those countries were merely window dressing. However, the president did not understand where Hitler and Mussolini stood and therefore believed that he would gain valuable insights from discussions with those leaders.

Yet, at the very moment he was contemplating his next move at the start of 1940, the American ambassadors accredited to Great Britain, France, and Germany were away from their posts. Roosevelt had already pulled the American ambassador from Berlin as a protest against Nazi brutality toward Germany's Jewish inhabitants; Bullitt had spent Christmas vacationing in Africa before returning to Paris; Kennedy had returned to the United States for medical treatment. Even though these men were readily available for consultations, the president never sought their advice about the impending mission.[15]

Bullitt was particularly distraught by this slight because of his perceived role in American foreign policy. When, for example, James Farley had toured Europe in the summer of 1939, he had declared that Bullitt "impressed me beyond expression." The postmaster general had discovered that the ambassador had "listening posts" throughout Europe and knew everything that was occurring. Farley felt that Bullitt was unquestionably the best American representative on the Continent: a solid, mature, good-humored, and energetic professional. Although the New Yorker greatly admired Hull, Farley believed that Bullitt had direct links to the White House and phoned Roosevelt without consulting the secretary. The ambassador, after all, was the president's man in Europe.[16] Of course that was the impression that Bullitt intended to create, but he was also becoming annoyingly cavalier in his contacts with the Oval Office. On January 30, 1940, in anticipation of the president's fifty-eighth birthday, he telegraphed "Missy" LeHand about his return to the United States for a probable cabinet appointment, making an irreverent request: "PLEASE PAT GOD FIFTY-EIGHT TIMES ON HIS BALD SPOT FOR ME AND GET HIM TO ISSUE THAT SUMMONS WHICH HAS NOT YET ARRIVED. LOVE. BILL."[17]

Ambassador Kennedy was simply ignored. James Reston, who had been stationed in England for the *New York Times* after the fighting broke out, distilled the reasons for the president's neglect. Kennedy, according to the journalist, was a womanizer whose romance with movie star Gloria Swanson was common knowledge. His poor judgment and intemperate statements caused further embarrassment. He, for instance, blamed "the Jewish conspiracy" for the international crisis and further argued that once the British had drawn the United States into the war, Germany would lose and economic chaos would result, until the Soviets filled the vacuum as the predominant power in postwar Europe. Reston succinctly summarized Kennedy's flaws: "He couldn't keep his mouth shut or his pants on."[18]

On February 1, Roosevelt summoned the British ambassador to the United States, Lord Lothian, to the White House and told him that as president he wanted to satisfy himself and the public that the United States had done everything it could to end the war. Therefore he had decided to send a representative to Europe to determine if a peaceful solution were possible. If not, Roosevelt would be able to brand the Nazis aggressors and declare unequivocally that they were the obstacle to peace.[19]

Ambassador to Cuba Sumner Welles and President Franklin D. Roosevelt taking a drive during their meetings at Warm Springs, Georgia, in November 1933 to discuss the Cuban situation. *(National Archives.)*

Secretary of State Cordell Hull (second from right) and his wife Frances (far right) with Senator Joseph Robinson and Mrs. Woodrow Wilson at Roosevelt's fifty-third birthday party in January 1935. *(Franklin D. Roosevelt Library.)*

Cordell Hull's birthplace in Byrdstown, Tennessee, in the northern part of the state. *(William Brinker.)*

Cordell Hull (front row center) poses with a foreign service officer training class in April 1937. Also shown are Wilbur Carr (left of Hull) and R. Walton Moore (right of Hull). *(Franklin D. Roosevelt Library.)*

The Old Executive Office Building, referred to as the State, War and Navy Building in Roosevelt's time and situated next to the White House. *(Barbara Gellman.)*

Ambassador William Bullitt (center, smiling) at the Warsaw airport in November 1937. *(Franklin D. Roosevelt Library.)*

Franklin Roosevelt with (left to right) his staff—Margaret "Missy" LeHand, Marvin McIntyre, and Grace Tully—in November 1938. *(Franklin D. Roosevelt Library.)*

Ambassador to Italy William Phillips (left), Ambassador to Germany Hugh Wilson (center), and Marvin McIntyre in November 1938. *(Franklin D. Roosevelt Library.)*

Secretary of State Cordell Hull and Under Secretary of State Sumner Welles arriving at the Capitol to testify before a House Foreign Affairs Committee hearing in June 1939. *(Franklin D. Roosevelt Library.)*

Columnist Drew Pearson *(Hessler, Lyndon Baines Johnson Library.)*

Cordell and Frances Hull with Postmaster General James Farley (right) at the Jackson Day dinner in January 1940. *(Franklin D. Roosevelt Library.)*

The First Methodist Church in Jasper, Alabama, at the time of the funeral of Speaker of the House William Bankhead in September 1940. Note the ramp provided for the presidential car, so that Roosevelt would have only a short distance to the church. *(Franklin D. Roosevelt Library.)*

Franklin and Eleanor Roosevelt returning to the White House after his third
inauguration in January 1941. *(U.S. Information Agency.)*

Sumner Welles's "summer cottage" in Bar Harbor, Maine. *(Barbara Gellman.)*

The Townsend mansion in Washington, D.C., former residence of Sumner and Mathilde Welles. It is now the Cosmos Club. *(Barbara Gellman.)*

The Wardman Park Hotel in Washington, D.C., Cordell Hull's residence from 1941 until his death in 1955. It is now part of the Washington Sheraton hotel. *(Manny Gochin.)*

Sumner Welles aboard the H.M.S. *Prince of Wales* during the Argentina conference in August 1941. *(Franklin D. Roosevelt Library.)*

Franklin Roosevelt extending the Lend-Lease Act in March 1943. Lend-lease administrator Edward Stettinius, Jr., is second from the right. *(Franklin D. Roosevelt Library.)*

Franklin Roosevelt meeting with Canadian Prime Minister W. L. MacKenzie King in August 1943. *(Franklin D. Roosevelt Library.)*

Franklin Roosevelt (seated in jeep) with Secretary of State Edward Stettinius, Jr. (holding his hat), Soviet Foreign Minister Andrei Vishinsky, and British Prime Minister Winston Churchill at Saki airport in Yalta in February 1945. *(Franklin D. Roosevelt Library.)*

Franklin Roosevelt with Ambassador to the Court of St. James's John Winant (left of Roosevelt), Edward Stettinius, Jr., and presidential adviser Harry Hopkins aboard the U.S.S. *Quincy,* bound for the Alexandria conference in February 1945. *(Franklin D. Roosevelt Library.)*

On February 9, 1940, the president, acting as his own secretary of state and without consulting Hull, announced that Welles would visit Italy, Germany, France, and Great Britain to report on current conditions. He was not to make any proposals or commitments, merely gather information for Roosevelt and Hull. An earlier draft of this statement had declared that the emissary would explore peace possibilities. In all likelihood, this passage was deleted to minimize domestic objections to any form of involvement in the fighting. That afternoon, at a cabinet meeting, the president stated, "I am telling the foreign nations that anything that Welles learns while abroad is going to be given only to myself. But the Secretary of State and myself may get together some dark night in secret to talk it over." What he did not tell his listeners was that only the British government had been so notified, and that at that moment he did not even know if his envoy would be welcomed in London or the other capitals.[20]

Welles's selection was the logical outcome of a succession of White House assignments. First, he had been especially chosen to go to Havana in 1933; in late 1937 and early 1938, he had released the trial balloon for a peace conference; and now he was off to Europe to see if a peace meeting was possible. In addition, each September since becoming under secretary, he had gone to Lausanne, Switzerland, for his annual holiday. While there in 1938, he took the opportunity to visit French leaders and Bullitt; the following fall, he briefly stopped off in London for discussions with British officials. Already acknowledged as the department's Latin American expert, Welles intended to wear the same badge for European matters.[21]

The under secretary was also spending more time with the president searching for ways to solve European problems. As early as July 1937, Welles had written his former headmaster, Endicott Peabody, to warn him about the explosive Old World powder keg. The United States, according to the former student, had to avoid foreign confrontation, but its government simultaneously had the obligation to shape public opinion so that the administration could "legitimately cooperate with other nations in averting a new catastrophe."[22]

Welles's selection as the American representative was not certain at the outset, for Roosevelt had omitted any name in an earlier draft of the press release. When the press received the announcement, the under secretary was recuperating from influenza. Yet despite his weakened condition, he personally notified the four embassies of his mission and insisted on briefing the ranking diplomat at each. The French representative was ill, but Welles still demanded to see him. Although the German chargé d'affaires was not at his embassy, his valet was dispatched to retrieve him so that the under secretary could meet with him.[23]

Foreign press reaction was mixed. The Allies were apprehensive that the United States would promote peace proposals in such a way that their resolve would be fractured. If the British and French refused to bargain with the Axis, that apparent inflexibility would damage their cause in the United States. The Italians, on the other hand, welcomed the visit, and once they accepted the Nazis promptly agreed. The greatest animosity came from the Russians, who had been excluded from the tour and who attacked the entire concept as the prelude to American interference and warmongering. Roosevelt had probably rejected the idea of a stop in Moscow because he was outraged by the Soviet invasion of Finland. Welles had earlier recommended going even further by considering breaking off diplomatic relations with Moscow as a dramatic deterrent to German and Japanese extremists and to indicate just how far the United States would go to oppose aggression.

The announcement of the mission also brought an immediate domestic response. Hull had had no inkling of the mission, and Kennedy was humiliated because the president was sending an envoy to assess a situation that he was in part responsible for evaluating. Others declared that the idea was an administration ploy designed to win votes from peace activists in the 1940 election, while some commented favorably on the idea as a way to search for a compromise to stop the fighting. A few withheld judgment until the conclusion of the trip.[24]

Welles's selection startled Senator Johnson, who thought that the mission was "a coolly calculated scheme to take us further in . . . easing us a little bit forward to war." The senator knew the under secretary well and considered him "a stuffed shirt, but with a certain ability, and a great deal of experience." Cyril Wynne—who had been Johnson's best friend in the foreign service before committing suicide with a .44 caliber revolver—had characterized Welles "as a 'rat,' with all a rat's cunning."

Johnson concluded that the president and his closest associate at the State Department were using their skills to draw the United States closer to an Anglo-American alliance.[25]

Bullitt, who had flown to the capital just after the announcement, was livid, but because of a far larger issue. Welles's selection, according to the ambassador, had led him to conclude that the under secretary had violated the unwritten delegation of duties as to the shaping of United States policy in Europe. During a conversation with Roosevelt, Bullitt exploded when the president claimed that Welles had sold him on the idea because peace groups would welcome this gesture as an administration attempt to seek an end to the war. The president soothed Bullitt's hurt feelings and bought his silence by implying that he had a chance at filling the upcoming cabinet vacancy as secretary of the navy. But Bullitt demonstrated his opposition to this diplomatic action by vacationing at the Jupiter Island Club on Hobe Sound in Florida and refusing to return to Paris until well after Welles had completed his journey.[26] He still tried to disrupt the mission clandestinely by planting a front-page story on February 14 in the *Chicago Tribune* entitled "Welles' Peace Trip Scuttles Peace at Home." The story alleged that Hull and ambassadors Bullitt and Kennedy were all "furious" over Roosevelt's failure to consult them.[27]

The secretary publicly denied the allegation by stating first that he and the president fully cooperated on diplomatic matters, and second that he regarded Welles "as one of my most trusted personal friends and loyal co-workers, and it is always in that spirit that we discuss the various phases of our duties and problems. I do not think a more capable person could be sent upon the proposed European mission than Mr. Welles." By acting independently, the president had placed Hull in the awkward position of having to lie; the truth was that Roosevelt had never informed him about the mission.[28]

The secretary had successfully hidden his feelings from the public, but Maxwell Blake, American minister to Morocco, expressed the anger that many who supported the secretary felt. In fact Blake was aroused enough to inform a British colleague that any peace effort at that time would fail, and that it "could only do harm and bring ridicule upon the United States Government." In addition, he claimed, Welles wanted to become the next secretary of state; to accomplish this objective, he was willing to damage the State Department by bringing in "his own cronies" to promote his policies, and to constantly undercut Hull, who "disliked and despised" him. While this kind of gossip followed Welles, he concentrated on his final preparations by discussing the British situation with Kennedy and Italian affairs with Assistant Secretary Long, former ambassador to Rome. Bullitt, of course, was conspicuous by his absence.[29]

Shortly after those briefings, Welles boarded the luxury liner *Rex,* along with his wife Mathilde; Reekes, his personal English valet; Moffat, chief of the European Division; and a young foreign service officer, Hartwell Johnson, who served as secretary. Except for the first stop, no one knew the rest of the itinerary, and the true purpose of the mission came under suspicion when Myron Taylor, president of U.S. Steel Corporation, sailed on the same ship. Roosevelt had chosen him as a special representative to the Vatican with the rank of ambassador in order to obtain information on papal diplomacy and to place pressure on Mussolini to remain neutral. Since Welles and Taylor were traveling on the same ship, their association led to the mistaken speculation that their assignments were somehow connected, and throughout the mission, in the absence of regular press releases by Welles or the State Department, reporters consistently filed stories that had no relation to fact.[30]

While Welles was steaming toward his destination, the Italians were preparing their welcome, flattered that their country was to be the first stop. Even given this apparent honor, however, the state-controlled press was still guarded about the possibility of a successful visit. After the delegation arrived in port at Naples on the morning of February 25, it quickly headed for the train station, decorated with flowers and red carpets, where William Phillips, now the American ambassador, met the group that boarded a private railroad car for the three-hour ride to Rome. When the train reached the capital, Welles stepped out to receive an elaborate floral display and the greetings of a large, friendly crowd. The fascist government had supplied the party with a limousine, which deposited its passengers at the Hotel Excelsior, one of Rome's oldest and finest. At this point reporters expected a statement but the envoy refused, thereby earning the name "Sumner the Silent"—a title that stuck throughout his travels.[31]

Welles adhered to the same format during the rest of his journey. He did not communicate with the American embassy in a given city until his arrival. (In fact, Phillips had heard about the visit from an Associated Press dispatch, and Alexander Kirk, chargé d'affaires in Berlin, found out about the trip quite by accident.) Upon reaching his destination, Welles minimized his social engagements, met with embassy personnel, and had the ranking American official accompany him on his interviews. The envoy met with the chief diplomatic official of the host country and explained that he had no proposals to offer, but rather had come to listen to his views on ways to bring about a lasting peace. After the official had expressed his viewpoint, Welles would have an interview with the chief of state. To each leader he carried a personal letter from Roosevelt. There was one obvious snub: the president sent no message to Hitler, the dictator who, Roosevelt claimed, had caused the bloodletting.[32]

During the first meeting, which took place with Count Galeazzo Ciano di Cortellazzo, the Italian minister for foreign affairs and Mussolini's son-in-law, Welles met with Ciano for one and a half hours on the morning of February 26 at Chigi Palace in a hall hung with beautiful tapestries. Each man impressed the other. Although Ciano looked older than his thirty-six years, he was charming, spoke excellent English, and openly discussed his country's interests. Both governments, the foreign minister suggested, should adopt a common neutrality policy and increase bilateral trade. He made no secret of his dislike for the Nazis or his hatred for the German foreign minister, Joachim von Ribbentrop, for the Germans had taken their Italian allies for granted, and so offered an insult to Italian national honor. Although friction was evident between the Axis partners, Ciano discouraged peace proposals. Italy wished to remain neutral until the opportune moment, and when it arrived the fascists intended to play a prominent part in any peace conference.[33]

Late that afternoon Welles and Phillips went to see Mussolini at the Palazzo Venezia. The two Americans entered the same side door that the Duce used, went up to the second story in a small elevator, and walked down a long corridor to a reception room where Ciano again greeted them. The trio passed through the Hall of the Grand Fascist Council to the dictator's office, "Sala Mapa Mondo," an extremely long room furnished with only a desk at one end and a small reading lamp to illuminate the vast space. Mussolini's cordial welcome was somewhat surprising, since the Duce had refused to see the ambassador since February 1938 as a protest against American policy toward his regime. The dictator's appearance startled the emissary, for Mussolini's poor health made him look like a man older than his fifty-six years. Later Welles somehow attributed his appearance to the fact that he had just recently taken a new, young mistress. The under secretary presented Mussolini with a letter from Roosevelt asking for a meeting in the near future, an initiative that clearly pleased the recipient. Their discussion, at first, focused on increasing bilateral trade and reduction of armaments. When Welles asked what would be necessary to ensure a lasting peace, Mussolini replied that the Germans would demand the retention of Austria and Poland and a restoration of those among their colonial possessions that had been lost in World War I. As for Italy, the Duce wanted unrestricted access to the Mediterranean Sea, something the British now prevented. After he finished, Welles asked if under the present conditions there could be peace between the Allies and the Axis. Mussolini replied affirmatively, and he urged Welles to return after completing the rest of his journey to discuss the possibilities for peace.[34]

According to Phillips, the interviews went well, and the mission was "exceedingly helpful" because the ambassador had reestablished U.S. contact with Mussolini, who had been impressed by Roosevelt's letter. The under secretary's "friendly approach" toward Ciano and Mussolini had helped promote better relations and established a conducive atmosphere within which to conduct bilateral relations after Welles's departure. The Italian version of the meeting was somewhat different. First, the Duce felt that any hope for a restoration of peace lay in providing Germany with *Lebensraum* (living space) and colonies. He intimated that Italy expected to play a prominent role in any peace conference, and that it would charge for services rendered. After these political problems were solved, economic cooperation would follow. The under secretary had talked about a bilateral trade agreement and offered to include American recognition of Italy's Ethiopian conquest as a part of a larger settlement. Neither these suggestions nor the force of Welles's personality impressed Mussolini.[35]

While the Nazis courted their fascist ally, Welles left Rome by train on February 28 and rested for a day in Zurich. Throughout most of his trip from the Swiss frontier to Berlin, the blinds to his carriage were drawn shut. Before he had even crossed the border, secret agents were watching him; and once they were on German soil, a foreign service officer accompanied the Americans.[36] Although the frigid landscape was hidden from the delegation's sight, William Shirer, an American reporter stationed in the German capital, experienced that winter as the worst in that nation's history. The rivers and canals were frozen solid for three months. Since the British had cut off shipments of coal for heating, to Shirer "life became a struggle to keep warm—and dry."[37]

Up to the moment of his arrival, Welles was uncertain of his reception, for the Nazis had never accepted the stated purpose of the mission for fear that rumors of peace would diminish the public's will to fight, thus weakening resolve. The foreign office, furthermore, worried that the United States might entice the Italians to join in mediation efforts. Despite such trepidation, Chargé Kirk learned that the highest-ranking officials would meet with Welles, in an attempt to improve the dismal relations between the two countries.[38]

Welles arrived early on the morning of March 1 at the Friedrich-strasse station and drove down Unter den Linden to the Hotel Adlon. He had lived in Germany as a child and still understood the language, although he no longer spoke it fluently. He had not seen the capital since the Depression. From his hotel room, he looked across the snow-covered Pariser Platz, a sight he had first seen as a young boy. After settling into his quarters, he scanned several local newspapers, becoming dismayed at the lies that the Third Reich's propagandists apparently expected their readers to accept. Despite his incredulity, Welles was faced with an opportunity not previously given to any foreign diplomat. He was about to gain a unique inside view of the Nazi leadership—a prospect that was particularly amazing since the Reich's leaders so distrusted American motives. Hitler had personally written the directive on how to deal with Welles, but his further order to talk sparingly was ignored. However another instruction, that the Czech and Polish questions were not to be discussed, was strictly followed. The Nazis tried to convince Welles that the United States had nothing to fear from their victories; quite to the contrary: America would have freedom of the seas without British interference. Each government officer reiterated the same themes: the Reich would be victorious on the battlefield; it was the Allies who had declared war; Germany wished for nothing beyond peace and guarantees from Allied threats of annihilation; Germany hoped for improved trade. The plight of Germany's Jews was never addressed, nor was Welles aware that that very day Hitler had given the orders for the simultaneous occupations that spring of Denmark and Norway.[39]

At noon, Welles and Kirk went to see Ribbentrop. It was an interview notable on two counts: it was the first time the chargé had ever met the foreign minister, and it was to be the most distasteful conversation of the entire trip. The German chief of protocol escorted the Americans to the foreign office, where every official wore a uniform. Ribbentrop received them at the door to his office; although he had an excellent command of English, he chose to speak German through an interpreter. The session lasted almost three hours, and the contrast with the warm atmosphere that had prevailed at the Rome talks could not have been more obvious. Ribbentrop was not concerned about accommodation; instead he treated Welles to a discourse on how the United States was responsible for deteriorating bilateral relations, on Germany's role in Europe since Hitler's coming to power, on the English rejection of the Third Reich's peace feelers, and on the need to ensure security for Germans living in central Europe. The national socialists, who numbered among their members the vast majority of the German people, would never accept the Allied pledge to destroy Hitlerism; Ribbentrop declared that the achievement of peace was impossible except through a military triumph.

Welles, having spelled out the reason for his mission, listened to Ribbentrop's rambling, not wishing to jeopardize his meeting with Hitler the next day. Although the envoy tried to remain silent, he was compelled to point out that the strained bilateral relations were due to Germany's treatment of its minorities and to unfair trade practices. What most disturbed Welles was Ribbentrop's declaration that Germany wanted a Monroe Doctrine for central Europe. Welles objected that a German Monroe Doctrine should not be intended to limit trade or imply political domination, nor should it be synonymous with the concept of spheres of influence; the foreign minister should pick a better example.

Welles later evaluated Ribbentrop as "one of the weirdest individuals in history" and described him as a man with "a completely closed mind. It struck me as also a very stupid mind. The man is saturated with hate for England, and to the exclusion of any other dominating mental influence." The German interpreter, who was present at most of the talks, expressed his opinion that the American emissary was unyielding; the Germans did not have confidence in his objectivity because he echoed Roosevelt's bias toward the Allies and antipathy toward the Third Reich.[40]

Early that evening, Welles met with his German counterpart, State Secretary Ernst von Weizsäcker, who had originally served in the Germany navy before transferring to the recently completed chancellery on the Wilhelmstrasse. Welles learned that no diplomat was to mention peace, and that if any step in that direction were possible, Mussolini's influence on the Führer would be beneficial. But Welles would have to speak directly with Hitler because Ribbentrop would disrupt or block any negotiations.[41]

At noon on March 2, several foreign service officials, dressed in military uniforms, came for Welles at his hotel and escorted him and Kirk to the chancellery. The building was spartan, with walls and halls of white marble and an entryway that looked more like a prison courtyard. As Welles entered, soldiers snapped to attention and gave him the Nazi salute. The Führer greeted him pleasantly, but with great formality, while an interpreter and Ribbentrop watched silently. Hitler looked well and spoke exceptional German, so polished in fact that Welles was able to follow every word. During the one-and-a-half-hour conversation, the under secretary repeated his basic question about how Germany expected to establish a durable peace and emphasized that the Duce thought that peace was achievable. The United States had no proposals but instead wanted to hear Hitler's ideas. Roosevelt was willing to help on trade matters and the limitation of armaments, but any peace had to be a just one. The dictator emphasized that the British had called for the destruction of national socialism, an impossible demand given that the German people were united behind the Nazi regime. Hitler promised that his country never again would be surrounded by its enemies, and that until security was guaranteed, the fighting would continue, no matter how much he personally wished to reduce armaments. He also insisted on fairer international trading practices toward his country, while at the same time maintaining its economic supremacy in central Europe. Finally, he demanded that the colonies taken from Germany at the end of World War I be returned. After the meeting, Welles reflected on his "very cordial" talk with Hitler and the favorable impression the dictator had made on him.[42]

On the following morning, Welles spoke with Rudolf Hess, deputy Führer and head of the national socialist organization, for an hour at party headquarters. The under secretary later described him as "devoid of all but a very low order of intelligence. His forehead is low and narrow, and his deep-set eyes are very close together. He is noted for his dog-like devotion to Hitler." Several youthful Nazi party members stood in the background while Hess repeated the themes that all Germans supported Hitler and that peace would only be guaranteed by the ultimate German military victory.[43]

Following this interview, Welles and Kirk immediately drove for about one and a half hours through a heavy snowstorm to see Field Marshal Hermann Göring at his palace, Karinhall. The estate had originally been a log cabin used for hunting trips. It had been built north of the capital, at the entrance to a national game preserve, and was guarded by a series of gates controlled by electric eyes. Welles's car moved silently and alone along the snow-blinded road, and they arrived at noon. The building they entered was enormous. To Welles, it was also "incredibly ugly," just like the gluttonous Luftwaffe chief, about whom Welles later recollected, "His thighs and arms are tremendous, and his girth is tremendous." During a three-hour talk, they sat in low easy chairs in front of an open fireplace while the snowstorm outside thickened in ever greater gusts. The field marshal told his listeners that Germany was better prepared to fight now than it had been during World War I, reiterating the point that the Allies wished to destroy national socialism, and that under that threat peace was impossible. Although the Reich intended to play the dominant role in central Europe, Göring assured Welles that the regime had no interest in the Americas.[44]

After the emissary returned to Berlin, Kirk held a tea at his home. There Welles talked with Dr. Hjalmar Schacht, past minister of economics and president of the Reichsbank, and currently minister without portfolio. An admired and respected economist of the 1920s and a leading architect of German rearmament in the 1930s, he had grown disenchanted with the Nazi party and become associated with the resistance movement, although he was never part of its inner circle. Schacht informed Welles that the leading generals were ready to oust Hitler, if they could win Allied assurances that Germany would maintain its supremacy in central Europe. The economist felt that the movement was gaining momentum, and he told the envoy that Hitler was the "greatest liar of all time" and that he was "a genius but an abnormal, a criminal genius."[45]

Welles left the Third Reich the next day, but before boarding a special salon car to Paris, he rested two days in Switzerland to reflect on his visits to Berlin and Rome. While in both capitals, he had continually heard remarks about territorial readjustments and political security, and he had also learned that the Fascist and Nazi hierarchies completely dominated the thoughts of their people. No matter how repugnant Welles found them, they ruled absolutely. He unrealistically perceived the possibility that Ciano could keep Italy from joining forces with the Germans, and at the same time realized that Schacht had exaggerated any hope of revolt, for as long as the Nazis felt that the Allies intended to destroy them and had a powerful military force to defend themselves, internal opposition to the Reich would remain silent.[46]

On the morning of March 7, Welles reached Paris, the city where he had lived during part of his earliest childhood. He vividly remembered such sights as the gardens at the Luxembourg Palace. From all appearances, the capital seemed normal, except for the presence of a large number of uniformed soldiers and ramparts of sandbags. He immediately drove to the Ritz. Since Bullitt had stayed away from his post, Robert Murphy, counselor to the embassy, accompanied him. The press had already speculated about the mission being the prelude to a peace gathering, and the government had tried to squelch such accounts because it feared giving any encouragement to pacifist and appeasement elements. At least for public consumption, the government would fight on until the final victory.[47]

The envoy's first call was at the Elysée Palace that afternoon to meet President Albert Lebrun, who, at sixty-nine, was a pathetic figure.

Lebrun, growing senile, recalled past German invasions and their effect on France's demands for territorial security from its menacing neighbor; for Welles, ever the technician, the security theme resurfaced.[48]

After that interview, secret service agents escorted Welles directly to see Prime Minister Edouard Daladier, who was waiting at the Ministry of National Defense. The envoy presented a presidential message, and the two men then conferred for two hours about the difficulty of achieving any peace settlement under the current conditions and about the need for American assistance. The prime minister feared that Hitler intended to dominate Europe and annex Alsace-Lorraine into the Reich. If an end to the fighting was to be at all conceivable, his country needed real security, which might be obtainable by destroying offensive weapons and creating a European aviation police force to halt aggression. Although the United States would not become actively involved in the war, Welles pledged that the administration would willingly participate in peace talks; even the Duce had agreed to assist in negotiations in deference to the friendly Franco-Italian relations. Mussolini, responded Daladier, had behaved well during the Munich crisis, but he had a tremendous problem with the Duce's anglophobia. The two men extended their discussions over dinner, with several other influential government officials in attendance. To Welles, these conversations were most encouraging. He had the distinct impression that the French government was willing to bargain with the Reich; what mattered the most was how to guarantee French security.[49]

On the following day Welles met with the presidents of the French Senate and the Chamber of Deputies, Jules Jenneney and Edouard Herriot, both of whom were in favor of maintaining a valiant front and fighting on until Germany's collapse. Later Welles lunched with Paul Reynaud, minister of finance, who in Welles's estimate had the best grasp of French foreign affairs. Reynaud regretted not having declared war at Munich, but past mistakes could not correct current conditions. If his country had security through an effective international air force, he would favor an end to the fighting. While Welles was maneuvering for peace proposals, German Propaganda Minister Joseph Goebbels falsified a photograph of Welles and Reynaud to show a map of central Europe with Germany bounded between the Rhine and the Oder and divided into northern and southern states, thus supposedly proving allegations that the Allies intended to partition the Third Reich. For his last interview, Welles paid a courtesy call on the former prime minister, Léon Blum, who was living in retirement, apart from the current political upheaval. The Nazis also turned the Welles-Blum meeting to their advantage, condemning Welles for seeing a Jew. For the first time and at first hand, the under secretary witnessed the deeply rooted strand of French anti-Semitism.[50]

On the sunny Sunday morning of March 10, the French government had a military escort fly Welles to London. As in Paris, aside from the large number of uniformed military personnel in evidence, the city did not seem to be on a wartime footing. Even before the plane touched down, Lord Lothian had advised his government to treat Welles with great courtesy, even though the foreign office felt that the United States would argue for a negotiated peace because of British vulnerability. The press reflected the cabinet's anxieties and warned that the Americans could potentially split Allied unity and strengthen Hitler's resolve. As a result, British reporters minimized the visit's importance. Lothian had informed Prime Minister Chamberlain of the proposed trip in early February, and by the time the envoy reached London, the prime minister was relieved to learn that Welles was not bringing any peace offering with him. Chamberlain had held his post since May 1937; although seventy-one, he was still physically powerful and looked younger than his years, his hair dark except for traces of white across his forehead. The prime minister replied that his government would cooperate, but cautioned that its announcement would create sensational coverage in the news media and would hold out false hopes for peace. Nor was he eager to negotiate with the United States, because he had never sought close Anglo-American ties in his career. Hitler could not be trusted, he asserted, and any possibility of ending the war had to begin with the restoration of Poland. This was an extremely unlikely event, he felt, for the Nazis were firmly ensconced and did not intend to end the fighting. To bolster German morale, Third Reich propaganda was disseminating erroneous information about Allied objectives for destroying the Fatherland. Even though frequent rumors of a German spring offensive crossed his desk, Chamberlain would not be rushed into negotiations unless he felt they would culminate in a lasting peace.[51]

Welles next met with the tall, thin, and imposing Lord Halifax, secretary of state for foreign affairs, at his office in the late afternoon of March 11; the meeting lasted less than an hour. The envoy continued his routine by bringing along the senior United States representative, Ambassador Kennedy, who had returned to England just five days earlier and whom Welles considered a friend and ally. Rather than request British views on the chances for peace, as had been his custom, Welles summarized his perception of the current situation: first, the German people believed that the Allies wished to destroy national socialism; second, an armistice was impossible; third, if peace were obtainable, the way to lasting security lay through disarmament and an international air force; fourth, the United States would assist in reducing weaponry and in economic reconstruction. Finally, Welles noted that he thought that Mussolini would indeed participate in settlement negotiations. Halifax responded by declaring that although his government had no intention of annihilating Germany, he had no confidence in Hitler or his promises; therefore, as long as the Nazis ruled, he did not see any likelihood of peace. If any negotiations were to move forward, the prerequisite was the restoration of Polish sovereignty.[52]

Welles and Kennedy next paid a courtesy call on the king and queen at Buckingham Palace and then went to 10 Downing Street, where they met Chamberlain at 6:00 P.M. As usual, Welles handed him Roosevelt's personal message, but he then changed his regular presentation by outlining a tentative peace plan. He prefaced his proposals by declaring that before the United States acted, it would consult the British. Under Welles's plan, Germany would agree to pull its troops out of Poland and part of Czechoslovakia; rapid disarmament would take place, highlighted by the destruction of offensive weapons and the creation of an international air force; while these negotiations were taking place, the warring armies would remain mobilized and the Allied blockade would hold fast. To encourage the momentum toward peace, the United States would aid in disarmament discussions and provide economic assistance. Although the acceptance of these proposals was unlikely, Chamberlain did not categorically reject them. Instead, he and Halifax, who had joined the group, declared that no plan would work as long as Hitler stayed in power. Without trust, they felt, talk of disarmament was useless, and the only alternative was to fight the Nazis. Welles implied that this might be the last hope for any bargaining because Chargé Kirk had learned that the Germans planned to launch their great offensive that April. The prime minister dismissed this intelligence report, replying that none of the previous rumors of Nazi assaults had materialized, and he wondered if the Reich would renew the fighting now that the Allies were fully mobilized. Chamberlain later reported to his cabinet that Welles had recommended that the Allies leave Hitler in power, and said that this condition would be acceptable if there could be general disarmament and an international air force to prevent future German aggression. The United States would assist in disarmament and economic reconstruction, but it would not participate in any guarantees to European security. Chamberlain again ignored these suggestions because of his perception of the Nazi mentality; the best chance for peace still rested with Allied military strength.[53]

That evening Welles dined with Halifax and several other influential government officials in his apartment at the exclusive Dorchester Hotel; after eating, they exchanged a wide range of views in the drawing room. Most wished to dismantle the Third Reich; others backed the British war cabinet's avowed stand that Hitler must be defeated, and a few were opposed to the policy of total victory.[54]

Before the start of his second day of consultations, Welles visited his personal tailor in Hanover Street and ordered a half dozen suits. With that task completed, he went to see the Labor party's leader, Clement Attlee, who called for Hitler's defeat but would only support a peace initiative based on real security. Welles then called on the spokesman for the Liberal party, Sir Archibald Sinclair, who demanded the eradication of Nazism.[55] Late that afternoon, the emissary saw Anthony Eden at the Dominions Office. Eden admired the under secretary and wrote at the end of 1938, "Of all contemporary Americans, Mr. Welles seemed to me to have the widest knowledge of European problems, together with a lucid mind which I grew to respect."[56] When Welles saw Eden during this visit, the envoy declared that Eden "was as charming and agreeable as always." Yet despite their mutual respect, it was clear to Eden that a military solution was essential: "Mr. Eden's conviction is that nothing but war is possible until Hitlerism has been overthrown."[57]

Winston Churchill reiterated that theme when Welles next met with him for almost two hours at the Admiralty. The American found the future prime minister "sitting in front of the fire, smoking a 24-inch cigar, and drinking a whiskey and soda. It was quite obvious that he had consumed a good many whiskeys before I arrived." The first lord of the admiralty was adamant in his belief that the Nazis must be annihilated, viewing the conflict as a fight to the finish. Peace propaganda in the United States, he asserted, had harmed Allied objectives for defeating Hitler. Militarily, the British were improving: the convoy system was functioning well now that the Allies had learned how to counter the threat of the U-boat. The chief danger now came from the airplane, but Churchill confidently predicted that the Allies would also meet that challenge.[58]

Welles's round of meetings continued on the morning of March 13, when he saw the former prime minister, David Lloyd George, for the first time since 1927. Although the man who led the British through World War I was seventy-seven, during their two-hour chat, he lucidly presented his view that the Germans already dominated central Europe, and that his government was therefore fighting a lost cause.[59]

That evening Welles returned to Chamberlain's official residence and was escorted to the cabinet room, which ran across the back of the house on the ground floor. A green baize table filled most of the small room, and only Welles and Kennedy were present along with the prime minister and Halifax. Chamberlain saw the political situation in Europe as having improved since the Russian conquest of Finland; the Soviets were now free to concentrate on their border with Germany. In addition, Mussolini had decided to remain neutral, a fact that further isolated the Reich. Under the existing circumstances, the prime minister would only consider negotiating with Hitler after the Nazis had taken concrete steps to disarm and renounce the spoils of war. The British especially demanded Polish and Czechoslovakian freedom and equivalency between Axis and Allied military might. The Nazis would have to grant freedom to their subjects by eliminating the Gestapo and ending persecution. If the Germans agreed to these terms, they would be demonstrating a complete reversal of past policies, and this, according the Chamberlain, would frankly be a miracle.[60]

Welles listened to the differing British viewpoints, and in his own dispatches conveyed the impression that the British were willing to negotiate to a far greater extent than was the reality. The envoy promised that Roosevelt would be the sole judge when it came time to make a public statement about the possibility of peace talks. Before returning to Italy, Welles promised to inform the British of what Ciano and Mussolini had said. Welles left London on the morning of March 14 in yet another snowstorm. Perhaps it was a harbinger of the chances for peace.[61]

Oblivious to British intransigence, Welles flew to Paris and met with Reynaud for several hours. Churchill had already seen the Frenchman two days earlier to try to strengthen his will to continue the fighting; however, these arguments could not dissuade Reynaud from considering a negotiated peace, and Welles viewed this meeting as a poignant example of the fact "that the great key problem today was security and disarmament." Before boarding his train, the envoy talked with the Italian ambassador in France and told him that his upcoming discussions with Mussolini could be decisive because immediate action was imperative.[62]

While Welles was in London, Ribbentrop took his own diplomatic initiative by arranging a hasty visit to Rome to prevent any deal with the United States that might cause a breach between the dictators. Hitler actively sought to curry the Italian dictator's favor with a long, cordial letter and an exchange of views on the American mission, while the German foreign minister used the occasion to brag that France would crumble under the military weight of German forces within three or four months, a prophecy intended to stiffen Mussolini's resolve. At the same time, he encouraged the Italians to undertake a rapprochement with the Russians. Welles could propose nebulous benefits of future bilateral cooperation, but Ribbentrop painted a glowing picture of how Germany's partner would share in the spoils of conquest, even resurrecting the glory of the Roman Empire. But these grandiose images did not budge Mussolini from his resolve to remain neutral.[63]

By the time Welles returned to Rome on March 16, spring had arrived, and at 9:00 A.M. in this inviting atmosphere he met with King

Victor Emmanuel. At the age of seventy, the king had great confidence in Mussolini and in his negotiating abilities at any peace conference. The titular ruler also expressed his disapproval of communism. Welles noted that although Russia had great defensive capabilities, it did not have an offensive capacity. The Allies, on the other hand, were ready to fight but were not intransigent; they needed real guarantees of security and had stressed that they had no intention of annihilating Germany.[64]

One hour later Welles, accompanied by Phillips, met with Ciano to reiterate the key issues of security and disarmament. The Allies were willing to bargain, Welles said, but they also had definite goals. He described Hitler and Göring as moderates who mistakenly could only see a military solution. Although Mussolini, according to Ciano, was leaning toward the Reich, he himself doggedly held to neutrality, and his government favored a peace treaty under which the four great European powers would declare that if one were attacked, the remaining three would join together to repulse the aggressor.[65]

That evening the American representatives again talked with Mussolini, who looked well and received them warmly. Welles repeated his list of issues critical for peace and intimated that Italy would play a crucial role in any bargaining. Mussolini reiterated his territorial concerns and also emphasized Hitler's demand for *Lebensraum*. If the Reich did not receive it, an invasion would follow quickly. Mussolini expected to see Hitler in several days and promised to take up these subjects with him.

Welles was not empowered to act, but he promised to call Roosevelt that evening to see what the United States was willing to do to assist in any peace talks. When Welles phoned the president, Roosevelt rejected any involvement in Hitler's peace proposals and ordered the envoy to reiterate the fundamental security issues and the fact that the Allies' purpose was not to destroy the German people. To reinforce his position, on March 16, Roosevelt publicly stated that he could not condone Hitler's military conquests, and that the United States sought peace based on moral values, not military conquest. When the emissary told Ciano at dinner about his conversation with Roosevelt, the foreign minister concurred with the president's prudent course. Ciano would wait for the imminent meeting of Axis partners and then determine his next move; in the meantime, he expressed his desire to strengthen United States ties and again put forward his idea of a four-power security pact.[66]

Mussolini and Hitler conferred at the Brenner Pass on March 18 at 10:00 A.M. According to Ciano, the German dictator had scheduled the meeting two days earlier because he had not seen Mussolini since Munich and wanted to discuss current affairs. In good physical condition and mental spirits, the Führer did most of the talking, without specifically mentioning any peace initiative or the Welles mission. Instead, he appealed to Mussolini's dream of a new Roman Empire by holding out the fruits of military victory. Hitler did not insist upon an Italian declaration of war owing to the Duce's rigid stand for neutrality. No concrete agreement was signed, but the discussions drove Mussolini inexorably closer to his partner.[67]

While the dictators conferred, Welles had a fifty-minute audience at the Vatican with Pope Pius XII, who lamented that any peace negotiations at the present time would be "impracticable"; he had recently seen Ribbentrop, who had reiterated his belief in Nazi invincibility. With the Nazis preaching such military sermons, the leader of the Catholic church saw no immediate end to the fighting. No attack would occur for at least a month, he believed, and in the interim he hoped that the United States would keep Mussolini out of the conflict, for most Italians opposed involvement. But if the Duce did decide to join in the fighting, the Pope doubted that any serious opposition would surface.[68]

The meeting at the Brenner Pass and Welles's visit to the Holy See encouraged the American press to speculate about the significance of both events happening concurrently. Hull worried about the erroneous rumors of an American peace initiative so much that on March 18 he obtained presidential approval for a press release emphasizing the fact-finding nature of Welles's mission. Welles, according to Hull, was not acting as a mediator between the belligerents, nor drafting any peace proposals. This denial came out one day before Herbert Matthews published an article in the *New York Times* claiming that the Germans had given Welles an eleven-point peace plan, one that included a role for the Holy Father. Welles contacted Matthews, declaring that his story did not contain "one solitary vestige of truth," and he even issued a press statement denying that he had received, presented, or offered any peace plan; he was merely collecting information to give to Roosevelt and Hull.[69]

To avoid any more undue publicity, Welles met privately with Ciano for lunch at the Golf Club outside Rome, where Ciano freely related the substance of the Brenner Pass talks and confirmed that Mussolini had refused to budge from his neutrality stance. Even though Ribbentrop had pressed for war, Ciano felt that the Führer would shortly make efforts to win a negotiated settlement. The Western Front was quiet, and the Italians did not expect any change, thus allowing Ciano more time to prevent the Duce from entering the conflict and giving the United States an opportunity to assist in peace efforts.[70]

On this guarded note, Welles completed his European mission and left from Genoa the next day—with at least one offer of $50,000 for the rights to the story of his trip. He had spent twenty days shuttling across Europe and divided his time almost equally between Italy, Germany, France, and England; after reviewing the situation, he submitted his findings to Hull and Roosevelt. He reported that Italy was the linchpin for peace in Europe. He reasoned that Mussolini, "a man of genius" but "at heart and in instinct an Italian peasant," enjoyed power and dreamed of reconstructing the Roman Empire, and at the same time admired Nazi military might. If the German conquests continued, Mussolini undoubtedly would join with Hitler; to prevent this, the United States had to strengthen relations with Italy to improve prospects for peace. This thin thread of optimism, though, would be insufficient to stop the fighting. The only way to avoid catastrophe was through bold leadership, and any peace plan would have to come from outside Europe. Germany under the national socialists lived as "people on another planet. To them lies have become truth; evil, good and aggression, self-defense. But yet, back of all that, their real demand is security, the chance to live reasonably happy lives, and peace." The Allies under those circumstances should not bargain with a regime and a dictator that they could not trust. Welles concluded, "What is imperatively required is statesmanship of the highest character, marked by vision, courage and daring." The United States and the other neutral nations, especially the American republics, had to take the lead in any movement toward peace; once this momentum accelerated, Mussolini and the Vatican would add their support.[71]

After reading this report, Roosevelt thanked Welles for his efforts, but the president minimized any immediate prospects for peace. If and when the outlook improved, Welles's information might prove useful. Despite this pessimism, Roosevelt, Hull, and Welles met with British Ambassador Lothian during the first week of April, at which meeting Welles warned that German propaganda was concentrating its efforts on the purported Allied goal of dismembering the Reich. When the president urged the British to deny those charges, the ambassador refused to recommend any such declaration.[72]

Roosevelt also summarized the report for MacKenzie King. The visits to England and France had been "most satisfactory," even though Churchill drank excessively. Still, the president did not think that the Allies were proceeding quickly enough in their military preparations. Ciano favored the Allies, but Mussolini, who dictated policy, was mesmerized by Nazi military superiority. Both Italians had treated Welles cordially, but the Duce had refused to make any war commitments. This open, conducive atmosphere contrasted markedly with that in Germany, with Ribbentrop's extreme rudeness and Hitler's argument for total victory.[73]

Hull never commented publicly on the mission or its consequences, but he later conceded that the under secretary had presented "a superb report of his conversations." Since a satisfactory conclusion depended on the United States and other neutrals preparing a plan of security and disarmament that the belligerents would accept, he did not expect a successful outcome. Neither the Americans nor anyone else had the ability to interrupt the fighting. Much of what Hull sensed had merit, but he was deeply upset that Roosevelt had never discussed Welles's mission with him before its announcement. Even though the secretary acquiesced to it after the fact, he blamed Welles for initiating the mission. Of course, the secretary ignored two major factors: first, he had been at his apartment during the genesis of the visit and had been physically unable to discuss the matter with the White House; second, Roosevelt had undoubtedly remembered the secretary's role in torpedoing the earlier peace conference initiative in 1937 and, more recently, his objection to the security zone.[74]

The Welles trip did not alter the course of European events. Italy still hoped for United States cooperation, and Phillips initially found a welcome reception at the Italian foreign office. But without any definite proposals, doors began to shut. Relations with the Nazis never improved, nor did there ever appear to be any expectations that a better understanding would be forthcoming. The British were relieved that the drive for "peace at any price" had been crushed, and Ambassador Lothian thanked Hull for squelching this harmful rumor. The French, already deeply divided, waited for the Nazis' next move.[75]

The under secretary had grossly misinterpreted British resolve. Chamberlain and Halifax never bluntly rebuffed Welles, but they clearly believed that any chance to end the fighting depended on a complete Nazi reversal. In a memorandum dated March 18, Sir Robert Vansittart, the permanent under secretary of state in the British foreign service, was far more direct, calling Welles "an international danger." Disarmament was impossible until the Nazis' removal, "but Mr. Sumner Welles' chief crime towards common sense and humanity is that he has now gone so far as to want us to make peace with Hitler." This, according to Vansittart, was sheer lunacy; the Allies had to state without any equivocation that they would not negotiate with Hitler. Roosevelt was risking the defeat of the democracies in order to win the presidential election scheduled for later that year.[76]

In fact not only did Welles fail in London, but his visit to France also had disastrous consequences. Although a senior American representative usually accompanied Welles, Ambassador Bullitt had been conspicuously absent, to register his protest against the mission. Bullitt felt grievously injured that the president had not consulted him about the idea, especially since he had been in the United States lobbying for French military assistance during the formulation of the proposal. Even though the ambassador had promoted Moore's candidacy for under secretary, he had not joined in the counselor's vendetta against Welles, nor had Welles challenged Bullitt's special role at the White House. Moreover, Bullitt perceived himself, not Welles or anyone else, as the president's man in Europe. Outraged that Welles had violated an unwritten division of function to boost his already inflated ego, rather than returning to Europe in time for the Welles visit Bullitt vacationed in Florida. With the mission in progress, he talked to Henry Wallace about Welles and his associate Berle, whom the ambassador sarcastically referred to as "Little Adolf." Welles, concluded Bullitt, had seriously imperiled Allied morale by undertaking the mission. According to the ambassador, if he had learned about the trip in advance, he would have had it canceled, and Welles knew it. Although the ambassador could not actively consort with Moore to plot Welles's downfall from afar, this incident brought Bullitt vocally out against the under secretary, who was now, in his view as well, the enemy.[77]

Just before returning to Paris, Bullitt learned that the Nazis had captured Polish diplomatic documents during their conquest and had published them in New York under the title *The German White Paper.* Some material implied that he had promised that if the French and British guaranteed Polish borders, the United States would quickly enter the war on their behalf. The ambassador vigorously denied these allegations and even had the French premier write Roosevelt denying the allegations. But the damage was done, the document seemingly offering further proof of Bullitt's unwillingness to follow orders and his tendency to make imprudent statements.

Bullitt resumed his post near the close of the "phony war" and almost immediately began reporting on the German occupation of Norway and Denmark. Early on the morning of April 9, the Nazi ambassadors to Oslo and Copenhagen demanded acceptance of occupation forces. Denmark succumbed immediately, and although the Norwegians fought valiantly, they were no match for the Germans. While Bullitt filed his dispatches, he also speculated that Mussolini might move against Yugoslavia or Greece, and he used that possibility to paint Welles's visit in the worst possible light. Without any prospect of peace, the ambassador wrote Roosevelt on April 18 that French politicians still had not forgotten the mission because Welles had "eulogized" Mussolini. Bullitt warned that the Duce could not be trusted and should not be promoted as the arbitrator of European politics. The ambassador also inferred that the envoy's belief in German invincibility had led the Allies to think that the president concurred, and that the Allies should negotiate a peace to give the Reich control of central Europe. As a result of Welles's statements, both Bullitt's and Roosevelt's popularity and prestige plummeted in France because Welles and Roosevelt had left the impression that Britain and France should stop fighting and allow Mussolini to serve as the European peace broker. Welles had praised the Duce, and the French defeatists used this fact to help sue for peace. The ambassador was furious: "I have been highly restrained in this report since certain of the remarks which have been made to me have been violent in the extreme. Now let's forget the matter for good."[78]

Bullitt wrote Moore the same day about the chaos in France's internal politics. The armed forces were in disarray, but were nevertheless trying desperately to drive the Nazis back. In the midst of the blitzkrieg, the mistresses of the two French government leaders played a bizarre role, and within this context, he described the nature of the Daladier-Reynaud rivalry: "The lady love of each hates the lady love of the other, and from your experience as an old roué, you know that venom distilled in a horizontal position is always fatal."[79]

After the Wehrmacht swept across the Netherlands and Belgium, Bullitt started to anticipate the collapse of French resistance. With the British evacuation of Dunkirk, the ambassador worried about the French government's withdrawal from Paris. Just as he had exaggerated in his analysis of the Welles mission, Bullitt's anti-Russian bias now led him to report events that had never occurred. According to the ambassador, the communists "will seize the city, and will be permitted to murder, loot and burn for several days before the Germans come in."[80] As the swastika moved closer to being raised over the French capital, Bullitt could not resist another derogatory reference to Welles's admiration of the Duce: "To believe that the Government of the United States will be able to cooperate with Mussolini is as dangerous to the future of America as would have been the belief that our Government could cooperate with Al Capone."[81]

With the occupation of Paris rapidly becoming a reality, Bullitt decided to stay there to help prevent panic. French resistance had almost disintegrated, and on June 10, Italy entered the war against the Allies. Four days later Nazi soldiers captured Paris, causing the United States ambassador to fear for his personal safety as well as anticipate possible atrocities. These anxieties ceased, however, when the occupation forces quickly guaranteed order.[82] Hull directed Bullitt to follow the French government into exile to exert influence on it, but the ambassador decided otherwise. Hull later recalled in his memoirs, "Bullitt was both capable and sincere. And, having the courage of his convictions, he naturally did not hesitate to proclaim and pursue them."[83] Bullitt had also demonstrated that he would listen to his own conscience no matter what his superiors urged.

Bullitt's decision to remain in Paris was his most controversial act. Both the president and the State Department issued orders for him to leave, but Roosevelt gave him discretionary authority—which he naturally interpreted as leave to follow his own instincts. He wanted to act heroically and was even prepared to die. Other American ambassadors to France had stayed at their posts when Paris was threatened, and he believed that he would also save lives by remaining at his station to stop the Nazis and communists from plundering the city. After the Germans had assured order, Bullitt left the city on the last day of June for Vichy. His messages reflected the chaos within government circles and also French bitterness over British attacks on French warships in order to keep them from German hands. The collapse of the French republic on July 10 was Bullitt's signal to leave the country. He headed for Madrid the next day and flew from Lisbon to New York four days later.[84]

He hoped for another job in the administration helping to prepare for the inevitable war against the Nazis, having already discussed with Roosevelt the possibility of becoming secretary of war or of the navy. If neither of these positions proved available, he would probably have to settle for another diplomatic assignment. But it was Welles who, with Roosevelt's consent, approved most diplomatic appointments, and Bullitt, who was an ambassador without a post, now had to go through a superior whom he had openly belittled. Not only had the ambassador written critical dispatches about the value of Welles's mission, but by the time Welles returned from Europe, the under secretary knew of Bullitt's hatred for him.[85] Interior Secretary Ickes, a trusted confidant of the ambassador, supplied his own negative assessment: "I would think more of Sumner Welles if he could put a little feeling into a discussion now and then, especially when undoubtedly he has strong feelings. But he is glacially toplofty even when he is engaged in a fight."[86]

Despite such personal attacks, Welles stuck to his rigid policies, such as trying to increase coal exports to Italy as a means of blocking closer bonds with Germany. He indiscreetly confided to Morgenthau that

Mussolini "was the greatest man that he ever met."[87] On the eve of the collapse of French resistance, Welles played a prominent role in the American appeal to keep the Duce out of the war. Even after Italian troops had marched onto French soil, the under secretary vainly asked Roosevelt to exclude a phrase condemning Italy for stabbing its neighbor in the back from his commencement address to the University of Virginia at Charlottesville, from whose law school his son Franklin Jr. was graduating. Welles still wanted to keep open a channel to the Duce.[88]

While Welles focused his attention on rapidly changing worldwide conditions, Hull was concerned with his own image problems and the under secretary's growing importance. He was angered over the publication of the *American White Paper*. Written by two young newspapermen, Joseph Alsop and Robert Kinter, who had relied heavily on Berle's private diaries for an inside look at the State Department since the Munich crisis, the book suggested that the United States was being drawn into the war despite its neutrality policy. Hull felt that the reporters made him appear a hillbilly with limited common sense, needing to take direction from others. He complained about the book to Farley, who started to chuckle, whereupon the secretary exclaimed, "Kwist! Jim, you don't know what it is to have trouble."[89]

While the secretary sought to plug the leaks in his department, he faced a far larger emerging problem. Hull was starting to feel that his under secretary was usurping his authority and was becoming the president's closest foreign affairs adviser. The seed of disloyalty had already been planted and needed only nurturing to germinate. At that moment Hull did not entertain the notion that Welles had betrayed him, for the secretary had no concrete evidence of this. After all, it had been Roosevelt who had selected Welles for the Panama conference and the European trip.[90]

Berle heard rumblings of Hull's disenchantment and tried to bolster the secretary's ego. Others suggested that the three men worked well together. Roosevelt led; Welles took the generalities and molded them into practical programs; Hull provided the brake when the other two acted precipitously. In the middle of March, Assistant Secretary Long talked with Hull about his feelings concerning Welles: "[Hull] is very fond of Welles and appreciates his ability. However, Welles thinks so fast and moves so rapidly that he gets way out in front and leaves no trace of the positions he has taken or the commitments he has made, and the Department is sometimes left in the dark as to his meanings and actions. He acts independently and forgets to tell the Secretary." Hull worried about this unwholesome situation. Furthermore, although they worked well together, Hull disapproved of Berle and Duggan, who considered themselves part of an organization directed by Welles and not responsive to orders delivered through regular departmental channels. Hull expected the under secretary to call frequently at the White House about day-to-day departmental matters and Latin American affairs. However, he did not specialize in European or East Asian topics "and it was those fields which now occupied the public thought and in which he thought he should be in entire control subject only to the President. He felt that there should be a united front by the Department and an agreement here before things went to the President."[91]

As Welles tried to supervise his multiplying functions, Hull was trying to understand the crosscurrents of a changing world. While attempting to adjust to the international scene, he also had to confront growing criticism about his conduct of foreign affairs. Stimson complained that the secretary did not control his subordinates. Earlier he had applied effective brakes against hasty decisions, but currently he spent too much time on reciprocal trade agreements and allowed Roosevelt the latitude to take unwise actions like the Welles mission and the enactment of the security zone.[92]

Ickes concurred in his lack of respect for Hull's abilities, claiming that the State Department had become "a conglomeration of ambitious men consisting mainly of careerists who, because they are career men, feel no obligation to follow Administration policy. I believe that, in substance, it is undemocratic in its outlook and is shorn through with fascism." The foreign service, he complained, was "divided into cliques and factions, with each strong subchief running his show more or less to suit himself and reporting to the President." Welles and Berle were both ambitious and arrogant; Castle still had the allegiance of many Republicans in the department. Since the secretary refused to decide personnel matters, Roosevelt did so. According to Ickes, Hull concentrated instead on futile protests against the dictators and on his trade agreements, with limited benefits. "As I remarked to the President on one occasion, with the world in a turmoil they were like hunting an elephant in the jungle with a fly swatter."[93]

During a conversation with Farley in mid-May, Hull conceded that Roosevelt did not confide in him, whereas he frequently met with Berle and Welles. When, on June 13, the president, seconded by Welles, considered sending supplies to the French military, the secretary was frightened. He did not want to leave any impression that the United States was about to declare war and he was also disgruntled that Welles had sided with the president. Berle watched Hull and Welles closely during these conversations. The assistant secretary commented that Hull acted slowly, whereas Welles moved quickly. In the case of supplying the French with arms, the secretary's advice not to send them prevailed. Hull was

> a realist. He was afraid, of course, that the President's impassioned pleas, and the emotion of the situation might lead to the sending of some message which the French would interpret as a commitment to immediate intervention; which would lead them, accordingly, to con-tinue to fight, in the hope of help which would never arrive; and thereby place on this government the responsibility for killing hundreds of thousands of men who otherwise might live.[94]

The arms never arrived, and the United States avoided a potentially explosive situation. Hull, in this case, had acted prudently, and yet he could not fully grasp the momentous changes during the first six months of 1940 that were radically altering the face of Europe. Between the collapse of Polish forces under the onslaught of the blitzkrieg to the fall of France by the end of June, the United States' primary effort to seek peace was the Welles mission, and its bleak results demonstrated the inherent limitations placed on American diplomacy.[95]

Roosevelt had single-handedly initiated the idea, and it was a poorly conceived, planned, and prepared mission. Prior consultation with the Europeans had been restricted to Great Britain, and the United States did not know how the three other countries would react. The president had sent personal letters to each head of state except Hitler—the one leader whom it was most necessary to influence if peace were to be achieved.

The stated objective of the mission was to collect information, but no one believed that explanation, and the press continually reported rumors that led to sensational expectations of peace talks. The president had probably chosen Welles for the mission because Roosevelt trusted his friend's judgment, but Welles exceeded his orders by erroneously believing that he could act as a mediator, an initiative that Roosevelt instantly squelched. Welles also had great difficulties dealing with reporters during his travels, and without adequate briefings from the envoy, the journalists who followed him regularly filed incredible accounts of events.

Welles was a technician, not an innovator, and he was a poor judge of character. He made outlandish and indiscreet remarks about the abilities of Mussolini. Impressed by his reception in Rome, he overestimated the power of the Italians to affect the course of the war. Depressed by the environment in Berlin, Welles took an instant dislike to his Nazi hosts, and they reciprocated in kind. His stop in Paris presented a confusing picture of French politics and the uncertainty of fighting the aggressor. Bullitt's conspicuous absence further weakened his position in talks with French politicians. Rather than listen to all the parties before reaching any tentative conclusions, by the time he reached London he had moved from the collection of data to the promulgation of a vague, naive peace plan. Chamberlain and Halifax, instead of unequivocally rejecting any compromise with Hitler, gave Welles some reason to believe that under certain conditions, no matter how remote, they would be willing to negotiate. Reality only came crashing back in when Welles and Roosevelt talked by phone and the president crushed any possibility of United States participation in peace talks.

Almost from the onset of the trip, Roosevelt listened to a constant stream of complaints from Hull about unfounded rumors of an American peace plan, and the president therefore had to reassure the public of the trip's avowed purpose. When Welles presented his report, urging direct American action, Roosevelt and Hull were unwilling or unable to follow that advice. Even if they had, by then the course of European events was at the mercy of the Nazis, not the United States.

The mission did provide some useful information concerning European conditions, but its benefits were vastly overshadowed by its contribution to a further strain in relations with Hull and its creation of an irreparable breach with Bullitt, who openly and vocally condemned Welles for encroaching on forbidden territory. The ambassador's perception of Welles's dishonor and Moore's animosity had by then coalesced into a powerful force poised to attack the under secretary. Hull did not go nearly that far, but he had started viewing Welles as a competitor.

Bullitt had opened up more than just a personal breach with Welles. The ambassador had irritated the president by refusing to follow White House dictates and by becoming too impertinent. Roosevelt had had few intimate advisers throughout his career, and he quickly became suspicious of those who presumed that they were indispensable and did not show the proper respect for the occupant of the Oval Office. Raymond Moley and George Peek were excellent examples of men who had felt that they had the president's blessings, only to find themselves first frustrated and ultimately abandoned.

These new circumstances at the highest level of government and the events surrounding the fall of France dramatically altered the personal relationships among those who formulated American foreign policy. Roosevelt took a greater diplomatic role, using Welles to carry out his directives. Hull's physical condition had worsened and so had his temperament as far as White House interference in foreign affairs and its dependence on Welles were concerned. Moore stood on the sidelines, a bystander without any ability to influence policy determinations. With Bullitt on his way home, Moore now had a willing coconspirator in his plan to destroy Welles, the man who had ruined his career.

# CHAPTER 8

# THE SPHINX, HULL,
# AND THE OTHERS

EVEN BEFORE WELLES HAD LEFT for Europe, many Americans had already begun speculating on the possible connection between his mission and the presidential election of 1940. With the national nominating conventions coming up that summer, some wondered if the trip was an administration ploy to give Democrats an opportunity to wear the peace-party label.

Would Roosevelt break the tradition established by George Washington of retiring after two terms in order to try for a third? Early in 1937 he had emphatically told Prime Minister MacKenzie King of Canada that he would not run, and late the following year he expressed his weariness and fatigue over the midterm elections. He was looking forward to a long rest, and Senator James Byrnes of South Carolina believed that the president would retire and that he longed for a suitable successor to continue the New Deal. But in the summer of 1939 even an experienced politician like James Farley was not privy to Roosevelt's intentions. The president was as communicative as the Sphinx.[1]

Privately, Roosevelt encouraged others to seek the nomination. Harry Hopkins, his friend and confidant, was a possibility, but a divorce, a stomach operation, and an extravagant life-style soon eliminated him from consideration. Henry Wallace momentarily hoped for a chance, but his flirtation with mysticism and past Republican connections removed him. Even Harold Ickes dreamed of receiving consideration, but ultimately came to the painful realization that any chance he had was extremely remote. Paul McNutt, former governor of Indiana, started to campaign, but his efforts ended in failure. These and other Democratic contenders all went to the Oval Office looking for support; some sparked lukewarm interest, but none ever found the elusive formula that could bring him to the convention as the front-runner. Roosevelt and the New Deal had become synonymous, and no one could take his place.[2]

Although Roosevelt tried to persuade several prominent New Dealers to run for the presidency, the most popular choices within the party were all Democratic regulars—men such as Vice-President John Nance Garner, Postmaster General Farley, and Secretary Hull—who were close personal friends and political allies. To them and others among the party faithful, it seemed that the New Deal leadership should relinquish power to a "true" Democrat, and Garner, Farley, and Hull each had the qualifications to assume the presidency. Each agreed with that assessment and, to varying degrees, hoped to take the presidential oath of office.

Garner was the oldest. Born in 1868, he had grown up in Texas, studied law, and settled in Uvalde, a small frontier town west of San Antonio. He rose to become its leading citizen, as an attorney, banker, and real estate investor. Elected to the state legislature in 1898, he won his first congressional contest three years later. He served in the House of Representatives until his rise to Democratic minority leader; when his party gained the majority, he was elected speaker of the House, becoming known as one of the most respected and influential members of that chamber. When his state delegation and the Hearst newspaper chain championed a run for the White House in 1932, the speaker emerged as a viable candidate.

Garner had not known Roosevelt well until after the start of his battle with polio. From the time of Roosevelt's reemergence in national politics until the 1932 convention, Garner met periodically with him during his travels to Washington or on his way to Warm Springs. This cordial relationship and the New York governor's strong showing in the primaries convinced the Texan to release his delegates on the fourth ballot, a step that assured Roosevelt the nomination and guaranteed Garner the second spot on the ticket. Both men had maintained a friendly rapport throughout the first term, but their relationship dramatically soured during the second because the vice-president opposed the court-packing plan, deficit spending, and what he viewed as foolish executive appointments. Their relationship soon deteriorated to such a low point that each often made snide remarks about the other, and eventually they preferred not to be seen together.

At the age of seventy-two, the vice-president had not expected to mount a vigorous campaign for the nomination, but he would not disappoint the loyal followers who had backed him over four decades. In 1939, when Garner thought that Roosevelt might seek a third term, his attitude visibly changed, and he actively sought the nomination to stop any third term momentum. By mid-December, he had publicly declared his candidacy and had persuaded the Texas Democratic convention to endorse him. Yet even the enthusiasm of his most avid supporters could not hide many of Garner's weaknesses. He chewed tobacco, drank heavily, and gambled large sums on high-stakes poker. Some believed that he had more than good luck in these games—that they were a clandestine way to pay bribes to secure the vice-president's political favors. These suspicions, along with his advanced age, such regional biases as opposition to civil rights legislation, and his association with the high-protective-tariff wing of the Democratic party, all hurt Garner's chances for winning the nomination. If these problems were not enough, his own state delegation was deeply divided. Sam Rayburn, majority leader of the House, spoke out for his friend, but a young Lyndon Johnson, elected to the House in 1937 as an avid New Dealer, favored the president.[3]

Although these troubles hurt Garner's chances, his greatest and most insurmountable hurdle was Roosevelt himself, who refused to pass the party standard on to an adversary intent on dismantling the foundations of the New Deal. Probably echoing the president's thoughts, Secretary Ickes labeled Garner a "traitor." Of course, the antagonism between the two highest elected officials in the country created embarrassing situations; just before Christmas 1939, for example, Roosevelt sarcastically commented on Garner's announcement for the presidency at a cabinet meeting: "I see that the Vice President has thrown his bottle—I mean his hat—into the ring."[4]

James Farley embarked on a far different course in his quest for the White House and ultimately grew even more disillusioned than Garner. This large, jovial man had been born some thirty-five miles north of New York City on May 30, 1888. Raised in a poor Irish Catholic setting, he became a staunch Democrat. At the age of twenty-three he was elected town clerk of Grassy Point. From that beginning, he rose to the post of county party chairman and later became a member of the state assembly and chairman of the New York State Boxing Commission. During the 1920s he backed Al Smith's attempts for the presidency, and although these bids failed, Farley gained national prominence and the necessary experience to direct Roosevelt's victorious campaigns as chairman of the Democratic National Committee. His reward was retention as party chairman and appointment as postmaster general.

For eight years he held both positions, and when the president confidentially told him of his plans to retire, Farley decided to try for the nomination. Since he had planned the strategy for two triumphant presidential races, he was confident that he could do the same for his own campaign. He was well known, popular, and in control of the party apparatus. Roosevelt, however, saw Farley as an adequate postmaster general, but did not believe that he had the intellectual capacity to serve in the White House. At first, the president encouraged Farley to run for the New York governorship in 1938 to gain experience in a major elected office. When the postmaster general rejected that advice, the president raised Farley's Catholicism as a political liability, since no member of his religion had ever won the presidency, including fellow New Yorker and friend Al Smith. But Farley minimized the issue's importance, believing that the party machinery at his command coupled with his positive image would bring victory. He also poined out that, should Roosevelt decide to step down, he could depend on Farley to continue the New Deal.

Yet, after Farley ignored Roosevelt's warnings, the president used other channels to discourage him. After a visit at the White House in the summer of 1939, George Cardinal Mundelein of Chicago spoke with

Farley about the upcoming campaign. At the conclusion of their conversation, the cardinal announced his support for a third term and objected to a Roman Catholic once more raising the religious issue in national politics.[5]

Neither Farley nor Garner ever heeded Roosevelt's objections. Nor could they mount any serious challenge, because the president minimized the former's intelligence and detested the latter. Since neither man had a chance of winning Roosevelt's endorsement, both eventually became bitter enemies of the president and critical of the New Deal and the chief executive's power. They were not alone, for they represented many regulars inside the party who expected to be heard but were denied that privilege.

Hull alone had the best chance to succeed Roosevelt. In fact, he had had presidential aspirations since the election of 1928. When the draft for his nomination that he had expected after Al Smith faltered never materialized, Hull waited for the appropriate moment to make another try. That chance occurred in the summer of 1937, when his Tennessee backers formed a presidential committee. The secretary discouraged this well-intentioned but premature effort, but he did not extinguish their fervor; he merely wished to pick the appropriate time to announce his candidacy. In the meantime, as secretary of state he could concentrate on diplomatic issues, and this was where many Americans preferred him to stay: he shared many of their values, and they felt safe with the secretary at the helm of the foreign service. Hull himself was content to remain the elder statesman who had come to symbolize the United States' commitment to a peaceful world by speaking out about the possibility of joining the League of Nations (albeit under a more "palatable" name at a later date), worrying about deteriorating global conditions, and labeling the dictators "international gangsters." Throughout the second term, Hull placed special emphasis on reciprocal trade agreements as a panacea to resurrect domestic prosperity and lessen the threat of war. He expected to capitalize on his positive public image and economic philosophy as the cornerstones for his bid to win the Democratic presidential nomination by hiring his close friend George Milton in September 1937. As a special assistant to the secretary of state, Milton was to form the Economic Policy Committee as a front for the secretary's upcoming campaign, preach the reciprocity faith, and thereby win converts to Hull's presidential crusade.[6]

By May 1939, Hull had closely connected trade and peace during a speech before the Foreign Affairs Council in Chicago, further warning his listeners that domestic recovery and global war were interrelated. The United States needed to interact commercially abroad if it were to solve its own economic problems, and the only way to keep out of war was to maintain world peace by promoting international commercial intercourse. The secretary urged worldwide financial cooperation and claimed that the United States had started down that path through the reciprocity program, "which has already demonstrated its effectiveness as a powerful instrument of action in that direction; by being ready to extend our policy and action along every practicable line that holds a promise of strengthening the foundations of peace through mutually advantageous economic relationships among nations."[7]

Throughout 1939 many prominent politicians anticipated Hull's nomination. Farley and other influential leaders had no doubt of Hull's chances for victory, even with such shortcomings as poor public speaking, advanced age, and an evident lack of charisma. Even the Republican candidate in the last election, Alf Landon, considered Hull a formidable opponent. Within the State Department, Berle, Messersmith, and Bowers saw him as the party's best choice, and at the beginning of 1939 Welles surprised Farley by coming out in favor of Hull and opposing Hopkins, Wallace, or Ickes. Welles stuck to that path even when New Deal adviser Thomas Corcoran solicited him to join the third-term movement; Welles believed that the president wished to retire and had already anointed Hull as his heir apparent.[8]

Even though Moore opposed the secretary's nomination, he still acknowledged Hull's many attributes. Hull, wrote Moore, was "a man of very impressive personal appearance, and of very excellent manners. No one can see him or meet him without being prepared to rate him highly. Beyond that he is a man of strictest integrity, who is deeply concerned about what is occurring in the country and about its future, and he is most industrious in promoting and advocating the policies in which he has faith." Moore recognized that Hull was the spokesman for low-tariff Democrats, and he reasoned that by decreasing trade restrictions, economic relations would improve. That improvement would in turn bring forth international cooperation, and the secretary was "passionately in favor of bringing about a more peaceful world."[9]

Yet in the midst of this growing support for his candidacy, Hull was extremely distraught over press reports about his failing health. Moffat, in late March 1939, had noticed that the secretary was much improved after his rest but remarked that he was "still coughing." Whenever critical issues like Munich and the outbreak of the European war arose, some media spokesmen would note that Hull was absent from his post. The secretary was convinced that columnists were trying to discredit him at the upcoming convention, and he was chagrined that his friends did not refute these accusations.[10]

Hull faced another liability to his possible nomination: Frances's ethnic background. That summer Ickes thought that his colleague might become the compromise candidate for the Democratic party, but he noted that, among his many shortcomings, Hull was not a New Dealer, and that "Mrs. Hull is Jewish, which is not a political asset, even in free America, at this time."[11] By the end of the year, Hull had heard vicious gossip about his wife's ancestry, and some had already started spreading anti-Semitic rumors. Although he did not believe that they would interfere with Hull's nomination, Farley commented that Hull "would not have his wife humiliated no matter what the stakes; that Mrs. Hull's happiness means more to him than anything else."[12]

Reporter Mary Johnson of *Time* went to Frances's birthplace in 1939 to investigate her religious background. In his *Who's Who* biography, Hull had listed her last name as Whitney, which was not her maiden name. The family doctor in Staunton said that she was a practicing Presbyterian, but her brother admitted that some of their relatives were Austrian Jews. As the nominating convention approached, the reporter requested additional information; aware of the political stakes, both Frances and her brother refused to speak further to the press. Yet their reticence did not prevent the publication of an article asserting that Frances came "from an old Jewish family in Staunton," a statement that the Hulls never challenged.[13]

Although the secretary worried about his health and his wife's Jewish heritage as barriers to the nomination, he also knew that the shortest route to the White House was via Roosevelt's endorsement; in fact, the president often appeared sympathetic to Hull's candidacy. In October 1938 the president told him that he could expect to receive the nomination. On a drive to the opening of the professional baseball season in April 1939, Roosevelt reiterated this preference for Farley's benefit. Roosevelt also conceded that the secretary had the confidence of the American people. When the president nominated Hull for the Nobel Peace Prize in late 1939 for his efforts in promoting the good neighbor policy and lowering tariff barriers, and, for the first time, announced his support for the reciprocity program in early 1940, these gestures of support delighted Hull and strengthened the bonds between the two leaders.[14]

Despite Roosevelt's apparent vote of confidence, Hull also heard of complaints from the Oval Office. Roosevelt thought that the secretary was too old and had proved to be a poor administrator who had difficulty making decisions. His single-minded commitment to the reciprocal trade program created doubts that he had the requisite broad range of skills to serve in the Oval Office. Since it would not solve the international crisis, Roosevelt's verdict was that Hull had spent too much time on this trivial pursuit.[15]

Nevertheless, the secretary was gaining momentum for his candidacy, and the embittered Garner and Farley recognized that their breach with the president was irreversible. Without any chance of winning the nomination, Garner publicly opposed a third term for Roosevelt, and declared that, if offered the opportunity, he would not again run on the ticket. For Garner it was a win-win situation. By entering the primaries on his own, he would please his followers; when he lost, he would retire to his farm in Texas. Farley, who had also turned against Roosevelt, could not understand why the president opposed his candidacy; he was determined to fight for the nomination. As long as the White House remained silent, Farley thought that he still had a chance, but this hope collapsed when Ernest Lindley, who had close ties to the president, published an article in the spring, reporting Roosevelt's assertion that Farley could not win because of his Catholicism. Although the president belatedly denied making this statement, Farley knew that bringing religion directly into the campaign had destroyed his presidential ambitions.[16]

Realizing the impossibility of winning the top spot, Farley shifted his energies to gaining the vice-presidency. At fifty-two years of age, he could run for the White House four years hence, and now, by maneuvering to control sufficient delegates to the convention, he could still assure himself the vice-presidential prize. That plan would work as long as Roosevelt followed through with his retirement, but when the president discouraged Berle from writing speeches for Farley in spring 1940, he finally understood the depth of Roosevelt's opposition. Abandoned by the man whom he had helped elect, Farley became a bitter antagonist. No longer did he seek approval from the "Boss." Instead, he entered the New Hampshire and Massachusetts primaries and won enough delegates to have his name placed in nomination at the convention. As it neared, he wondered if Roosevelt had reversed his earlier course and had decided to run after all. If he had, Farley would have his name presented to the delegates as a symbolic gesture against the third term, leave the cabinet, and resign from the party chairmanship.[17]

As Farley's and Garner's aspirations plummeted at the beginning of the new year, Hull's aspirations rose when Drew Pearson published the first article in the United States declaring that Roosevelt had chosen him as the Democratic nominee. Walter Winchell, a well-known columnist, predicted the secretary's nomination in early 1940; a month later the Washington *Post* declared Hull the White House's preference. In late April the North Carolina state convention believed that Roosevelt favored his secretary of state. The postmaster general now sought to combine forces with the secretary by promoting the idea of a Hull-Farley ticket. Some public opinion polls briefly indicated that Hull was even more popular than the president, and although he publicly denied any presidential ambitions, he did nothing to interrupt the momentum building in his behalf, nor would he oppose a draft.[18]

Rather than campaign actively, the secretary continued to work for the renewal of the reciprocity program as the foundation of a better world and as his vehicle to the White House. He sermonized about international trade leading to peaceful relations while the Axis forces swallowed Europe. Yet the contradiction between what Hull dreamed and what was actually occurring did not bother his followers, who focused on their candidate's ability to shape foreign policy in a troubled world. Hull rejected preparations for global warfare, preferring to imagine that the path to peace lay through the acceptance of the reciprocal trade agreements program. When his cherished legislation finally came up for a congressional vote in the spring of 1940, the secretary marshaled all his forces for its passage—for the first time with the president's blessings. Even though the congressional debate was bitter, the bill passed, and that was enough for Hull; the victory vindicated his life's work. Even if the idea of lowering trade barriers during wartime was frankly impractical, the secretary had at least kept its spirit alive, and he intended to use lowering tariff rates as a main theme of his anticipated presidential campaign.[19]

No one was more effusive in his congratulations than Francis Sayre, who had served under Hull for seven years working on the reciprocity program, and now connected its passage with a bid for the presidential nomination: "He has a native strength, a clarity of judgment, and an utter sincerity which often remind me of Lincoln. He is so free from personal ambitions that I am convinced he will in no way seek the Presidency nor even accept it unless a determined drive is made upon him by his friends."[20]

Economic adviser Herbert Feis was far less sympathetic as he watched the secretary cling to this theme and surround himself with advisers who all preached to the same choir. "This group," Feis asserted, "thought or considered that activities in this field could have far more decisive influence in the increasingly critical international situation that was developing than I did; they very often impressed and bothered me as rather ill-informed enthusiasts." The same criticism also came from Ickes and Morgenthau, who minimized Hull's capabilities and complained about his ineptitude. Hull, in turn, oftentimes blamed prominent New Dealers for encouraging unsound foreign policy initiatives, constantly griped about their unwanted entries into foreign affairs, and expressed anxiety over the White House's independent initiatives.[21]

Welles presented another problem by winning headlines from the Panama conference and the European mission. Even though he sometimes acted as a welcome brake on unwise initiatives, the general impression, no matter how unfair and unfounded, was that Hull was losing control of his own department's direction. In fact, the reality was far more dangerous: the diplomatic corps was gradually splitting into two distinct factions, with Hull relying on his own close associates, and Welles on his.[22]

The under secretary did not comprehend the consequences of this growing schism. Instead, he was busy returning to his normal duties after his sojourn in Europe. He was preparing for the renewal of the Reciprocal Trade Agreements Act, and he was facing criticism from those within the State Department, like Herbert Feis, who accused him and the president of "rather half-baked and dangerous" initiatives.[23] Still believing that Roosevelt intended to retire and orchestrate Hull's nomination, Welles met Berle late in the evening of May 8 at the exclusive Metropolitan Club, a short walk from the White House. After rapidly downing four Scotches, the under secretary predicted that Roosevelt would wait until the last possible instant and then commit to Hull. If he won the general election, Norman Davis, a close diplomatic adviser and personal friend from Tennessee, would become secretary of state, and Welles would be dismissed.[24] Even in the face of such a bleak prediction, Welles worked energetically throughout the summer, while Berle watched and commented, "Sumner is still working like a beaver."[25] He also carried on with his fashionable social engagements, hosting periodic parties at his magnificent estate. On vacation, he no longer traveled to Switzerland, but instead traveled to his thirty-eight-room "summer cottage" in Bar Harbor, Maine.[26]

Hull was obviously distraught over the relationship between Welles and Roosevelt, but he did not confront either of them. No matter how upset he was, he would not quarrel with the man in the White House whose support he so desperately coveted, and his patience seemed to be having the desired results. During April the president reiterated to Farley that Hull would be his successor; several days later, the president sat next to Frances Hull at a White House banquet and told her to get used to these affairs, for her husband would be the next president. Some voters favored a drive for a popular draft, but Frances, knowing Cordell's plans, tried to discourage her hometown press by denying that her husband was a candidate.[27]

At the end of the month, Roosevelt met with Prime Minister King and declared that Hull "commanded the greatest respect of the party."

His weaknesses were overzealousness on trade matters, his advanced age, and his lack of familiarity with domestic politics. But despite these faults, "he was decidedly the best of all." King reported to Hull that Roosevelt had tapped him as the successor, and that reassurance pleased the secretary. Even with this knowledge, he did not declare his intentions, but the prime minister perceived that Hull was a candidate with powerful support within both political parties.[28] As late as June 20, Roosevelt reasserted to Hull his backing for the secretary as the Democratic nominee.[29]

While Hull seemed to be inching toward the nomination, others within the party, such as Ickes, opposed him because of his obsession over lowering tariffs and his apparent inability to cope with the worsening global situation. Eleanor Roosevelt, among others, questioned the secretary's commitment to New Deal programs. Most simply wanted to maintain their influence within the administration, and to do so they hoped to maintain the status quo.[30]

The drive for a third term began in earnest at the end of October 1939, when Secretary of Agriculture Henry Wallace told a Berkeley, California, audience that Roosevelt should run again. This trial balloon was the first partisan speech in the upcoming battle for the nomination, but the president seemed uninterested. At the start of 1940, he appeared ready to end the strain of eight years in office by stepping down to write his memoirs. Farley reported that the president had lost "his usual vigor"; his color was bad; he complained of colds and sinus trouble, and his family wanted him to retire.[31]

Farley's wishful thinking did not take into account certain subtle signs of change at the White House. In mid-February, for the first time, Berle saw indications that Roosevelt might run again because Democratic leaders were pressuring him in that direction. Far more worrisome, the president was growing anxious about European conditions; if the situation worsened, he might seek the nomination in order to protect national security. By the end of April, Roosevelt still was not feeling well and seemed to look forward to the end of his term; however, there had been a noticeable shift in attitude; he would not rule out the possibility of running again. With the Nazi spring offensive and the impending collapse of France, Roosevelt's resolve not to seek a third term seemed to be wavering.[32]

In the midst of this European crisis, Roosevelt made headlines on June 19 by announcing the appointments of Republicans Frank Knox and Henry Stimson to the cabinet as secretaries of the navy and war, respectively. Some Republicans called their acceptance of the posts a betrayal, while staunch Democrats deplored the decision. The president, who had been considering this bipartisan step for some time, thought that bringing these prominent Republicans into the administration would offer a symbol of national unity in the midst of Allied disaster.[33]

Many Republicans viewed the action as an unwelcome political diversion, intended to draw attention away from their convention, which opened a mere two days later in Philadelphia. When the Republicans finally made their selection, many New Deal antagonists went away disgruntled. Wendell Willkie, a utility executive who had voted for Roosevelt in 1932, won on the sixth ballot.[34]

Sometime between Willkie's nomination and early July, Roosevelt decided to shatter American political tradition by seeking a third term. The balance had been tipped by his dislike for the Republican standard bearer, the fall of France, Hull's weaknesses, his own ego, or perhaps some combination of all of these factors. In any event the president, having charted his course, now had to inform the Democratic pretenders to his throne.

Hull learned of the about-face at a luncheon meeting on July 3. At the start of their conversation, the president downplayed the idea of another term and then went on to list the secretary's strengths and weaknesses. As he spoke, Hull instinctively noticed a change in the president's tone and intuitively understood that Roosevelt would run for a third term. Under those conditions, the secretary denied any interest in seeking the nomination, assuring the president that the convention would quickly renominate him. Upon leaving the White House that afternoon, Hull had no doubt that Roosevelt had abandoned him. The president had gambled successfully that Hull would instantly retreat. The secretary might want to live in the White House, but he would never fight for the privilege, and that was the hunch on which Roosevelt had counted.[35]

The following day, the president met with Farley at Hyde Park and told him of his intention. Appalled by what he considered the president's devious tactics, the postmaster general was crushed. Shortly after their talk, Farley flew to Chicago in preparation for the Democratic national convention, knowing that his political aspirations were ruined. White House strategists intended to stage a spontaneous demonstration to give Roosevelt the nomination by acclamation, and in the face of such a show of enthusiasm by the party faithful, the president would "reluctantly" agree to run.[36]

In the midst of this political maneuvering, Farley opened the convention on the morning of July 15 at Chicago Stadium. Speaker of the House William Bankhead of Alabama took the gavel as temporary chairman, a privilege won by his long and faithful service as former chairman of the powerful House Rules Committee and currently as speaker. At the peak of his career but weakened by a series of heart attacks, Bankhead gave a keynote address stressing unity, hoping that the speech would propel him into the vice-presidency. But his efforts had just the opposite effect, for the address was dull and uninspiring, and it effectively ended any serious support for Bankhead in the second spot on the ticket. The following evening Senator Alben Barkley of Kentucky took the podium and read a letter from the president stating his intention to retire. The stunned delegates sat in confused silence. Then someone shouted over the loudspeaker, "*We want Roosevelt.*" The gallery, packed with loyal Chicago Democrats by Mayor Ed Kelly, immediately joined in the chorus, and soon the entire floor of the convention had begun demonstrating for the president.[37]

Farley watched the pandemonium and was particularly amazed by the actions of one participant: "As the delegates filed past the platform in a joyous snake dance, my eyes popped in surprise to see the austere, impeccable Under-Secretary of State, Sumner Welles, joggling along. . . . Welles' creased trousers were getting a collection of wrinkles and his collar was wilting. He was going through the motions, but his wan smile was ample evidence that he was not really enjoying himself."[38]

The next day's result was anticlimactic. Although Farley, Garner, Hull, and several others received token votes, Roosevelt's victory was overwhelming. Farley, as party chair, then faced the unpleasant duty of calling for unity and having the convention unanimously endorse its candidate. The delegates next had to select a running mate. Roosevelt had already pleaded with Hull to take the vice-presidency, but he vigorously refused: "No, by God!" With the secretary out of contention, the president insisted on naming Henry Wallace, an act that almost caused a party rebellion. The delegates did not especially care for him to begin with, and even more, they resented him being forced upon them. "Dear old Will," as Roosevelt called Bankhead, refused to step aside in the face of the president's preference and consequently became a rallying point for dissidents; but when the votes were tallied, Wallace was victorious by a margin of two to one.[39]

As for Farley and Garner, after eight years of serving in the New Deal, they left unceremoniously and disillusioned. Roosevelt asked Farley to remain as Democratic National Committee chairman, but he, as anticipated, declined the invitation. Ed Flynn immediately replaced him, much to Farley's surprise. Garner remained in the capital, not even bothering to attend the Chicago convention. After it adjourned, he vacationed in Texas until the Senate reconvened and filled out the balance of his term. Neither man was ever called upon to return to government service.[40]

Angered by Roosevelt's decision to run and frustrated that he had lost any hope of residing in the White House, Hull momentarily contemplated resignation, but he decided to remain as a patriotic obligation. As soon as Roosevelt had been renominated, the secretary congratulated him and left for an inter-American conference scheduled to begin on July 18 in Havana. Once the meeting convened, Hull hoped to take the lead in shaping its resolutions. The meeting was notable for the establishment of a hemispheric trusteeship that would consider questions relating to European possessions in the Americas, and for its final declaration, known as the Act of Havana, which provided the machinery for a committee to resolve possible problems over the transfer of European colonies. Although the body never acted, this accord showed the willingness of the American republics to take steps toward hemispheric defense.[41]

After the meeting, Hull briefly returned to Washington, D.C., on August 1 for a long talk with the president and then left for a vacation. He had been working steadily since the start of the year with only brief periods for rest. His deteriorating health, coupled with the hot summer weather, necessitated a twenty-day stay in the cooler climate of White Sulphur Springs. Although a direct phone line from his room to the State Department kept him abreast of daily events, in general he followed the accepted treatment for consumption: complete bed rest.[42]

William Bullitt did not have an opportunity to see the secretary. He boarded Pan American's *Dixie Clipper* in Lisbon on July 15, 1940, but the plane was forced down in the Bahamas with engine trouble and did not land at La Guardia Field in New York until five days later. At an impromptu press conference, he spoke to reporters for twenty minutes, proclaiming the continued recognition of Vichy without having first cleared his remarks with the State Department or the White House. The next day the headlines read, "FRANCE OF PETAIN IS NO FASCIST STATE." A police motorcycle escort with sirens screaming, running red lights at fifty miles per hour, rushed him to Pennsylvania Railroad Station, where he had to wait nearly half an hour before leaving for Philadelphia to spend a weekend with his family. After a pleasant holiday, he proceeded to the White House for dinner with Roosevelt, and then the two men traveled to Hyde Park to continue their discussions of European conditions. There they formulated the theme of the speeches that Bullitt would give during the pending presidential campaign, warning the public of the Nazi menace and suggesting that the only way to prevent this danger from spreading to the Americas was through the rendering of all possible assistance to the British.[43]

Before making his first speech, Bullitt lunched with Welles (who in Hull's absence was acting secretary), seeking approval of its contents. On August 18 the ambassador told the American Philosophical Society audience of 4,000 at Independence Square in his home town that the United States faced great peril. Bullitt lectured his listeners that "the United States will not go to war, but it is equally clear that war is coming towards the Americas . . . I am certain that if Great Britain is defeated, the attack will come."[44] While Bullitt was speaking out in favor of the Allied cause, he was also lobbying for a cabinet post in order to remain in the United States to take charge of raising his teenage daughter. Roosevelt balked at any thought of giving him that rank, for he believed that Bullitt talked too much. Indeed, Bullitt now had the audacity to recommend himself as the next secretary of the navy, suggesting that the president remove Secretary Knox and appoint him ambassador to Great Britain.[45]

In the midst of the presidential campaign, Speaker Bankhead interrupted his legislative duties on September 11 to travel to Baltimore for the opening of the Democratic campaign in Maryland. Minutes before a scheduled radio address, he was discovered unconscious on the floor of his hotel suite. When his daughter Tallulah, a movie and stage star, learned of his collapse, she chartered a plane and rushed to his side, but by the time she arrived he had already been transported to Bethesda Naval Hospital, critically ill. He died there on Sunday, September 15, at the age of sixty-six, of a stomach hemorrhage. The following day his body lay in a gray casket against a backdrop of lilies and palms at the marble podium in the well of the House. Following that chamber's tradition of naming a successor before conducting the funeral service, the clerk of the House swore in Sam Rayburn of Texas. At the end of the services, Hull, who had counted Bankhead as a friend, went over to the family to express his condolences.[46]

As a tribute to Bankhead and in added recognition of the South's pivotal role in the Democratic party, Roosevelt took the unprecedented step of ordering his entire cabinet to attend the funeral in the speaker's home town of Jasper, Alabama. Late that afternoon, the Southern Railway Company ran two special trains, one bearing a large congressional delegation, the family, and the casket and another carrying the president and his party. Hull was one of the few cabinet members who remained in Washington, but Welles substituted for him at the services. Many newspapermen, broadcast journalists, and photographers accompanied the procession.[47]

Accustomed to traveling by train, Roosevelt had had the Pullman Company lease a specially designed car to the government for one dollar a year. Armor-plated and bulletproof, it had a reinforced steel frame, bedrooms, bathrooms, and a sitting room. Since the president lived in a ramped environment, secure bars had been mounted on the walls as well as the back platform, and an elevator had been installed at the end of the compartment to accommodate his wheelchair.[48]

After a day's journey, the party arrived in Jasper, a town of 5,000 whose population had quickly swelled to over 35,000 as crowds strained to get a glimpse of its distinguished guests. The temperature was over ninety degrees in a region that had not seen rain in over a month. Several thousand people watched the full-dress affair from outside the First Methodist Church at the peak of the afternoon heat. Mourners were packed inside the old three-story structure, where conditions were made even more unbearable because of the oppressive heat. All the local Protestant ministers took part in the tasteful, short services. After the local clergy had finished, the chaplain of the House, Reverend James Montgomery, spoke extemporaneously for about forty minutes in the oppressive heat, raising the audience's temperature almost off the gauge. At the end of the ceremonies, the president hurried to his train and headed back to the capital.[49]

On the return trip, Welles had dinner with Wallace and John Carmody of the Maritime Commission; the under secretary drank quite heavily and spoke indiscreetly of his admiration for Mussolini and the Brazilian ruler Getulio Vargas. After this conversation, he retired to his private Pullman compartment.[50] Welles returned to his departmental duties the next day; overwhelmed with work, he wrote, "The present situation is such that I fear it is out of the question for any of us to leave Washington for long during the months to come." He also kept abreast of Maryland politics and actively tried to encourage state officials to campaign energetically for the president.[51]

Hull reluctantly spoke out in favor of Roosevelt's reelection in the face of partisan Republican attacks on foreign policy. At the end of October, the secretary formally endorsed the president by informing a radio audience that he was preventing war, not leading the nation into it. Roosevelt was an experienced leader at a time when the United States could not afford to stand idly by for two and a half months of uncertainty if Willkie triumphed. On the day before the balloting Hull went even further by introducing the president over nationwide radio as an additional testimonial and offering a response to the Republican assaults on American diplomacy.[52]

Even with Hull's support for the incumbent, the differences between Roosevelt and Willkie on foreign policy issues were inconsequential. Both favored alignment with the British as the best way to keep American shores safe from German infiltration. Each had pledged to keep the

United States out of war, but neither was candid about the possibility of American participation. Both painted themselves into a corner with promises of avoiding confrontation when they knew that such a pledge could not be guaranteed. Although Roosevelt ultimately won by a comfortable margin, those who pressed to keep American troops at home did not trust his assurances. As long as the European war raged, they lobbied vigorously against any foreign entanglement.[53]

Had Hull resigned at the end of the second term, he could have taken pride in the passage of the reciprocal trade agreements program, the evolution of good neighbor diplomacy, careful supervision of East Asian policy, and the maintenance of an uneasy peace in a world bent on going to war. Hull remained in office in order to guarantee those policies, but at the same time he had to face certain inevitable changes. First, the secretary advocated caution. Such was his nature, and Roosevelt's antagonists depended on him to do so. The philosophical differences between the two were clearly articulated and acknowledged. But how could Hull continue to practice restraint in the midst of global upheaval and in direct opposition to the White House's propensity for action?

The answer, of course, was that Roosevelt ignored much of the secretary's advice and used Welles increasingly to carry out White House initiatives. What Roosevelt failed to realize was that Hull no longer coveted White House support. Thanks to the president, the secretary had lost his last chance to run for the Democratic presidential nomination. During the period before Roosevelt had decided on a third term, Hull had periodically voiced his displeasure over Welles's close ties to the Oval Office, but in spite of this uneasiness the secretary and the under secretary maintained a working relationship. It did not ensure harmony, but the State Department's machinery continued to function. Yet despite appearance of a relatively smooth operation, the difference between Welles and Hull were gradually growing more distinct. At least to the secretary, they were moving from a source of annoyance to one of deep-seated aggravation.

This emerging friction did not initially disrupt American policies as the administration continued on its slow course toward an Anglo-American alliance, advocating opposition to Axis aggression, hemispheric solidarity, and maintenance of the status quo in East Asia. The basic lines of authority were still in force, and as long as they were undisturbed, United States diplomatic initiatives would follow a clearly charted path.

In many ways, Roosevelt, Hull, and Welles had taken on the characteristics of chess pieces, each holding enormous power unique to himself. Roosevelt could move in any direction and had supreme control. Hull had less mobility, but still had considerable strength. These two superior pieces in turn restricted Welles's options, but he had enormous latitude. The rules were sometimes relaxed, but the game of diplomacy could continue infinitely, with no one gaining a decided advantage or conceding any move. One absolute rule, however, applied solely to the under secretary. He could not afford to make a wrong move. Since he and his two superiors had worked together for eight years and knew each other's tendencies, a misstep seemed highly unlikely. Nevertheless, the possibility, no matter how remote, was still part of the game, and Welles knew that if Hull ever found an opening, checkmate would be guaranteed.

# CHAPTER 9

# AN INCREDIBLE SET OF CIRCUMSTANCES

EVEN BEFORE ROOSEVELT had defeated Willkie, the president had prioritized his diplomatic objectives; they would remain remarkably consistent until the end of 1941. Above all else, he fervently fought to keep the nation out of the war, remembering the death and destruction of World War I as well as the disillusionment over the League of Nations after the bloodletting had ceased. If the United States were forced into the fighting, the president would stand by the British and his "Europe first" strategy; despite some confusing signals, he sold military preparedness in the North Atlantic to the American people by championing the cause of hemispheric defense and assisting the British as a second line of defense against the Third Reich.

These trends came into sharp focus at the height of the 1940 presidential campaign when Roosevelt risked his reelection chances by entering into negotiations with Churchill to decide on a formula according to which the British would lease some of their Western Hemisphere bases in exchange for outmoded American destroyers. When the two countries announced an executive agreement at the beginning of September 1940, the United States emphasized the substantial benefits of the British concessions for hemispheric security; although some public outcry of warmongering surfaced, Roosevelt had acted to supply the Allies with equipment without shedding American blood.[1]

This agreement was a harbinger of the closer Anglo-American co-operation that came about when Roosevelt concocted another scheme that pushed the rationale of the destroyer deal one step nearer to outright belligerency. The United States would now lend the Allies essential war materiel, and in return they would lease strategic British bases in the Americas to the United States. During January 1941 the Treasury Department drafted the lend-lease bill and sent it to Congress, emphasizing its self-defense aspects and arguing that by helping the British, the United States was, in effect, defending the Western Hemisphere. Although the congressional debate was ferocious, the legislation passed and received a presidential signature in mid-March. More than ever, the U.S. government had sided with the Allies and moved the nation another step closer to armed confrontation.[2]

The Anglo-American alliance was moving along an irreversible path, and even the Nazi invasion of Russia on June 22 could not change the signals. While most of his advisers counseled restraint, Roosevelt offered aid to the Soviets almost immediately after the Wehrmacht's massive onslaught on the enormous Russian front. According to the president, everyone who fought the Third Reich—and that included the Communists—deserved assistance. Despite dire forecasts from General George Marshall that the Soviets would not withstand the German assault past November or December, the president lobbied and gradually won approval for long-term aid to the belligerent nation.[3]

The existence of another front added a new feature to Roosevelt's strategic thinking, and it also firmed his resolve to meet with Churchill at Argentia harbor in Placentia Bay, Newfoundland. In early August, Roosevelt left the capital, ostensibly to fish off the New England coast. He did just that for a few days, but then secretly boarded the U.S.S. *Augusta* for a rendezvous with Churchill aboard the battle cruiser *Prince of Wales*. At the end of their first meeting, the two leaders issued a joint Anglo-American declaration, known as the Atlantic Charter, in which both democracies called for an end to Nazi tyranny and rejected any territorial gains for themselves. The charter pledged that all peoples had the right to choose whatever form of government they wished; it reaffirmed freedom of the seas while encouraging improved trade and improved economic standards; and it advanced a permanent world organization to maintain world peace.[4]

The destroyer deal, the lend-lease program, and the Atlantic Charter were all interrelated. Herein lies one of Roosevelt's greatest strengths: he was able to frame broad guidelines for policy and action yet stay focused upon the task at hand. He took charge of the Anglo-American partnership and never deviated from that controlling theme. Yet herein also lies one of the president's greatest weaknesses: he would set forth ideas without explaining them to the American diplomats whose task it was to institutionalize presidential initiatives. Rather than follow traditional practices, the White House turned to a group of personal assistants who were unquestionably loyal but who had no organizational structure within which to sustain long-range objectives.[5]

Harry Hopkins typified Roosevelt's haphazard management style. On May 10, 1940, the day that the Nazis invaded the Low Countries, Hopkins dined at the White House, fell ill, stayed overnight—and remained a guest in the Lincoln Room for the next three and a half years, serving as the president's constant companion and personal emissary. For example, it was Hopkins who went to England for six weeks in January 1941 to meet with Churchill and assess the chances of British survival. By the conclusion of the mission, Hopkins and the prime minister had become friends, and the American had committed himself to British assistance and the destruction of Hitlerism. Upon returning from London, he turned those objectives into reality by serving as lend-lease administrator; while spending most of his time on shipping military supplies, he also helped arrange the first summit and met with Stalin to ascertain his wartime needs and to determine if the Russians would survive.[6]

To assist him in these complex efforts, Hopkins recruited Averell Harriman, who became an influential liaison between Roosevelt and Churchill. In mid-March 1941, Harriman flew to London to expedite lend-lease aid, then attended the summit. That fall he went to Moscow to negotiate a military assistance package. Given the nature of his assignments, he also emerged as advocate of the Anglo-American alliance and the defeat of Nazism.[7]

While personal representatives like Hopkins and Harriman carried out White House initiatives, Roosevelt also still depended on the State Department. Even though Hull was crushed that Roosevelt had abandoned him for the presidential nomination, the secretary remained a central character in the formulation of certain American diplomatic affairs. James Dunn, who had become an intimate adviser and personal friend, reflected the secretary's shifting moods when he told friends in early October 1940 that Hull had accomplished his objectives and was going to resign because of his opposition to the third term and the president's preference for Welles. But this opinion started to change as the contest reached its finale; if Roosevelt asked Hull to stay in the cabinet, he would continue on, viewing it as his patriotic duty.[8]

Hull of course did just that, and he became even more fixated on defending his department from such perceived incursions as Secretary of the Treasury Morgenthau's encroachment into foreign affairs, conveniently forgetting to mention the Treasury Department's crucial cooperation on many questions involving foreign economic policy. The idea that support was expected without being appropriately recognized irritated Morgenthau: "I will never forget the tongue lashings that I have had from Mr. Hull about how I want to run his department and the sarcasm and everything else."[9] Indeed, once provoked, the secretary of state had a reputation for having the foulest mouth in Washington, a fact that Pearson confirmed for a national audience: "When the Secretary of State really gets wrought up he lets loose with the most vitriolic tongue-lashing of anyone in the Roosevelt Administration. All the feudal instincts of the Tennessee mountains come to the surface."[10]

Hull also worried about internal divisions. Never confident in his position, he regularly expressed his suspicions. During a meeting with Herbert Hoover, Hull confided to the former president that he distrusted most of his personnel.[11] This general feeling of uneasiness applied particularly to Welles, whom Hugh Cummings, Jr., one of Hull's most trusted aides, attacked during a luncheon on October 18. The response was triggered by administration critic William Castle's comment that women found the under secretary desirable. Cummings responded that Welles was "queer and exaggerated in everything he did, personal and physical as well as mental."[12] This unwholesome atmosphere led Hull and his immediate staff to establish several informal lines of communication that all bypassed Welles, even though all correspondence was supposed to go through the under secretary's office before reaching the secretary's. Of course such tactics were not unusual, for circumventing the proper channels was an acceptable New Deal practice—one that Roosevelt himself had taken to new heights.[13]

Despite such bureaucratic intrigue, Hull continued with his affairs as if the third term had been an acknowledged reality long before the campaign. The secretary held weekly news conferences at noon in his private office, with its ceiling fans and latticed swinging doors, to present his global views before about a dozen reporters, peppering his remarks with stories from his days in the Tennessee mountains. The reporters, who sat on the three black leather couches arranged around the secretary's desk, would listen as he carefully dissected an issue and then, at the conclusion of his monologue, took the position that appeared most convincing. To protect himself from possible gaffes, Hull enforced a rule that no one could quote anything that he said until his assistants had cleared the text of the articles.[14]

By thus avoiding controversial positions, Hull maintained his positive image, reassuring the public that the American government was searching diligently for global peace. As long as the secretary stayed in the administration, he would fight against United States involvement in foreign wars and speak out for the restoration of international tranquility. In addition, even though the European conflict had restricted international commerce, he continued to advance the cause of lower tariffs through his cherished reciprocal trade agreements. These vague, general declarations were in fact what his countrymen yearned for, and they truly hoped that Hull could achieve his unrealistic goals.

Along with personifying broad support for American peaceful intentions, Roosevelt used Hull to maintain the status quo in East Asia. Although the president never considered the Japanese navy a serious threat to the United States, he wanted to avoid war in the Pacific or at least postpone it until the United States was well prepared. Hull had taken charge of Asian affairs almost at the start of his tenure, and he emerged as the administration's leading proponent of trying to check Japanese expansion.

While the public followed Hull's attempts to seek peace in the Pacific and promote international trade, some within the administration saw a far different person. Sometimes his faulty recollection of departmental decisions embarrassed him. One example of this problem was the establishment in 1938 of the Standing Liaison Committee (SLC), which brought together the seconds-in-command of the state, war, and navy departments to coordinate hemispheric military planning. Welles had set up the SLC with the secretary's full knowledge, but by the time Henry Stimson became secretary of war and questioned Hull about the SLC having too much responsibility, Hull had forgotten about this committee. Embarrassed by his failure to follow the SLC's deliberations, Hull formed a group consisting of himself, Knox, and Stimson to meet on a weekly basis to plan strategy.[15] The secretary of war was elated: "We have gone a long step towards regularizing a very haphazard situation which has been brought up apparently by Sumner Welles' activities."[16] The arrangement did not always function harmoniously, but it did help the secretaries occasionally present a united front to the president.

Welles recognized Hull's discomfort but was unable to allay his uneasiness. After all, Welles was the diplomat closest to the president and had the most responsibilities in the State Department. He saw Roosevelt daily, met with foreign diplomats, and served as liaison to the military. When the secretary left for extended periods, Welles became acting secretary. To emphasize the secretary's prolonged absences, Welles confined his own vacations to two weeks in early spring.[17]

As he had done since the end of 1933, Welles continued to direct hemispheric affairs, ranging from multilateral concerns like inter-American defensive preparations to bilateral relations with each of the American republics. Without understanding the full implications of Roosevelt's general guidelines, he provided the connection between hemispheric security and the necessity for equipping the British. If the Americas were to be safe, then the British would have to act as the first line for hemispheric defense, and more than anyone in government Welles advanced that position.

The president also placed Welles in charge of Russian affairs, a job that he reluctantly accepted because of his long-standing opposition to the communist regime. With the signing of the Russo-German non-aggression pact, Stalin's seizure of Polish territory, and the attack on Finland in 1939, American-Russian relations had slipped to their lowest point. It was to show his disapproval of recent Russian incursions that Welles excluded Moscow from his European mission. Yet despite these strained relations, the under secretary consented to hold regular talks with the Soviet ambassador and slowly began working toward improved relations. Throughout the winter of 1940 and the spring of 1941, Welles speculated about Russian objectives, noting particularly that the Soviets on the one hand were encouraging the Japanese to fight the United States and on the other were supplying Germany with raw materials for its military forces. Although Welles provided intelligence to the Russians regarding an impending German invasion, as late as May 19, the under secretary predicted that the chance of Hitler attacking Stalin was only one in a hundred.[18]

Welles handled yet another sensitive assignment for the White House: the issue of refugees. American Jews had overwhelmingly voted for Roosevelt in 1940, even though he had never satisfactorily addressed the question of the refugees' plight. Although the president granted visas for special humanitarian reasons, he also restricted immigration to prevent possible spies and saboteurs from entering the United States. As an alternative, he proposed refugee resettlement efforts in Alaska, Africa, and Latin America. Meanwhile, his wife Eleanor had also received direct appeals from prominent Jewish leaders to help save emigrés' lives; such pleas went from her to Franklin to Welles, who was known to be sympathetic. When Welles did not respond quickly, the First Lady prodded him into action.[19]

While Welles was overwhelmed with his expanding duties, Moore was relegated to minor assignments. Pushed aside after Welles became under secretary, the counselor at first felt abandoned. To him, a European war was unlikely because the nations of the Continent were not "crazy enough to engage in a major conflict."[20] He gradually changed his opinion and began to press the administration to preach the democratic faith over the evils of dictatorship, but as destructive forces mounted in

Europe and Asia any hope for world disarmament faded from reality. Moore had tried to maintain American neutrality, but he slowly came to favor selling supplies to the Allies and grew even more pessimistic about heading off a European confrontation.[21]

For a brief moment, however, optimism about the future returned to Moore. His fondest memory was of an airplane trip to Great Britain in the summer of 1939, when at the age of eighty, he was a passenger on the first Pan American Yankee Clipper to fly via the northern route to Europe. It was an adventure that temporarily reinvigorated him. The flight left from New York on the afternoon of June 24 and made stops at New Brunswick, Newfoundland, Ireland, and England, covering a total of 7,000 miles over a week-long excursion that he thoroughly enjoyed.[22]

However, his positive attitude quickly evaporated upon his return, for by that winter, he had decided to resign at the completion of Roosevelt's second term and was making preparations for his departure. Now over eighty, he saw his life drawing to an end; disheartened by the outbreak of the European war, he seemed even more weary. Around him he saw evidence that his suggestions were no longer being taken seriously. Hull concentrated on the reciprocity program and East Asia, which left Welles to run the department with the assistance of Berle and Messersmith. At another time, Moore would have cared about being pushed aside, but now he no longer could.[23]

Adding to his somber mood, he bowed out of playing an active role in the election because his younger sister Jennie, who had served as his official hostess, had had a serious stroke, the result of high blood pressure. During her recuperation at home, she took a turn for the worse and died in November 1940. Saddened by her death, Moore had expected to resign, but when Hull decided to remain, he persuaded Moore to continue at his job despite his growing melancholy and infirmities: "I am simply too old to indulge any ambition or desire to hold office."[24] Roosevelt's victory had heartened him, as did Hull's decision to remain in office. Moore had talked to Frances Hull; she wanted her husband to "lead an easier life," but had "made up her mind that he should not give up the Secretaryship." At least that would prevent Welles's promotion to the post.[25]

Bullitt mirrored many of Moore's concerns. Now that the ambassador had returned to the United States and had been relieved of his diplomatic post, the two friends regularly communicated. They found themselves agreeing that it was Welles who was responsible for their diminished status. In a sharp exchange with Roosevelt, Bullitt expressed his displeasure about his reduced standing. Although this outburst did not appear to create an irreparable breach with the White House or end his speeches on behalf of British aid, it did serve notice to the president that Bullitt would not work with Welles.[26]

Adolf Berle remained at his post and routinely assisted both Hull and Welles on numerous projects. Whenever Roosevelt chose Berle for special assignments, he made certain to inform the secretary of his actions. Aware of the growing distance among the three, Berle also tried to act as a mediator between Roosevelt, Hull, and Welles so that they might maintain a smooth working relationship. Sometimes Berle succeeded, but more often, he could do little but watch as the breach widened.[27]

At the start of the European war, Breckinridge Long joined the department as an assistant secretary of state. Dean Acheson described him as "a gentleman of the old school—spare, courteous, and soft-spoken." Extremely wealthy, he had bought a magnificent estate called Montpelier at the top of a knoll in Laurel, Maryland, where he had raised thoroughbreds during the late 1920s. He knew how to enjoy life.[28]

A descendant of two distinguished border state families, Long had been born on May 16, 1881, and was raised in St. Louis, Missouri. He studied with private tutors before attending a public high school. Following a family tradition, he entered Princeton University in 1899 and graduated in 1904. He went on to study at the Washington University school of law and was admitted to the Missouri bar two years later. He became a candidate for state assembly on the Democratic ticket in 1908, but placed a distant eighth. Neither his political nor his legal career flourished, but his marriage to a wealthy socialite in 1912 allowed him to devote most of his energies to politics. After giving a large amount of money to Woodrow Wilson's reelection campaign, in 1917 Long was appointed third assistant secretary of state, in charge of fiscal matters and Far Eastern affairs. A confirmed Wilsonian, he resigned in 1920 to run for the Senate, campaigning on behalf of the League, and lost badly; he tried again two years later and was defeated in a bitter contest, which ended his desire for elective office. He still remained a major Democratic donor, however, and his hefty contribution to the Roosevelt campaign as well as his service as floor manager at the convention resulted in his appointment as ambassador to Italy from 1933 to 1936, when he resigned due to illness.

Although Long wanted to return to the administration shortly after his recovery, Roosevelt did not recall him to government service until September 1, 1939, when he was made special assistant secretary of state in charge of war emergency matters. Hull considered Long an ally and had at first coaxed him out of retirement to advance his own presidential aspirations; but by the end of the year Long had agreed to assume George Messersmith's duties, such as enforcing the immigration laws, after Messersmith assumed the ambassadorship to Cuba. Long had no training in immigration policy, but like the president he feared the penetration of spies. Reflecting the wishes of most Americans, he zealously strove to prevent foreign infiltration by reducing the number of immigrants entering the United States.[29]

While the new State Department appointees were adjusting to their assignments and the rapidly changing world conditions, the *New York Times,* in the middle of November 1940, broke the news about secret Anglo-American negotiations with the Spanish regime. The British had asked "El Caudillo," Francisco Franco, to remain neutral, and to ensure his cooperation they wanted the United States to supply him with a million tons of wheat and gasoline credits for an undisclosed sum. During the first two weeks of December, several newspaper articles reported that the United States had agreed to grant Spain large credits for foodstuffs and gasoline, in the range from $100 million to $260 million, to keep Franco from joining the Axis. In December, Hull confirmed that talks were under way, but without having achieved any conclusive results thus far.[30]

While the *Times* concentrated on the potential deal, "some of the highest officials of the State Department" were talking to Drew Pearson about internal feuding over the proposal; he had also formed close bonds with some of Hull's competitors, such as Harold Ickes, Harry Hopkins, and Henry Wallace. Pearson had not learned about the disagreement from Welles, but he did confirm the story, and on December 20 the "Washington Merry-Go-Round" published allegations that State Department officers had serious differences over the credit to Spain. Hull and James Dunn of the "croquet clique" favored it, but Welles had consulted Roosevelt, who had "radically modified" the proposal. Hull exploded over the article because of the attack it represented on Dunn and because of the embarrassment that Pearson had caused him in May 1938 over American munitions sales to Germany.[31] Hull also cursed out "Welles in his most picturesque and forceful Tennessee language, blaming Welles for giving me [Pearson] the story."[32]

On the day after the article appeared, the secretary held a press conference to repudiate the story. Forgetting his statement in early December, he declared that he had never discussed a $100 million credit and sent off a letter to United Features Syndicate, Inc., which represented Pearson's column, demanding an immediate retraction because the article contained "deliberate misrepresentations."[33] Welles, in an official response to the columnist, sided with Hull because no one, according to the under secretary, had ever even considered, let alone made, such a proposal. Hull and he agreed on Spanish policy, Welles maintained, and he further asserted that he had never discussed this matter with Roosevelt; thus, the column was false, and the erroneous impressions it created should be corrected. The under secretary appealed to Pearson's sense of patriotism: "At a critical moment in the history of the United States like the present it is particularly regrettable that the people of this country should be led to believe that there exist between the higher officials of the Department of State disloyalties, controversies, and fundamental differences which do not in the remotest sense exist."[34]

To protect his friend, Pearson retracted the allegation that Welles had appealed to the White House to have the credit proposal modified, but he still insisted that Welles had opposed the idea while Hull supported it. The reporter deeply regretted that Welles had come under attack and claimed to have learned that certain State Department officials were conspiring against him. For example, after Welles and Pearson had had lunch at the Mayflower Hotel, the secretary's allies told Hull

about the meeting, implying that the under secretary was providing
Pearson with classified material. To prevent such an impression, Pearson
suggested that they should simply not talk about foreign policy issues in
public in the future.[35]

On the morning of December 28, Pearson published another story
that claimed that Hull had taken exception to an article saying that
Welles had rejected Dunn's proposal for a $100 million credit to the
Franco government. The American Red Cross, instead, had sent supplies
to Spain as an outright gift, and that had ended the matter. Pearson
added, in an attempt to repair the gulf that he had helped create, that
"the differences between Hull and Welles were . . . friendly, and of the
healthy variety necessary when important questions of policy are at
stake."[36]

Welles held a press conference the same day to assert that the article
was false and that Dunn was indeed part of the State Department team.[37]
To soothe Hull's hurt feelings and retain his post, Welles also issued a
glowing tribute to the secretary, denying any friction:

> I think it would have been humanly impossible for two people, over a
> period of eight years, to agree more consistently and thoroughly than
> Mr. Hull and I have done. There has never been the slightest important
> difference of opinion between us, and so far as I am personally con-
> cerned I think it would be impossible for any man in my position, who
> has been so closely associated with the Secretary—who has had the
> opportunity of being associated with a man of his extraordinary moral
> courage and consistency, and I think an almost unique intellectual
> integrity—to have anything except very deep devotion for him.[38]

Hull remained unconvinced, still believing that Welles had leaked the
columnist the story. As a result of these rumors, Pearson had heard
whispers that the secretary had even contemplated removing his chief
assistant and making him ambassador to London. Roosevelt had gone so
far as to make the offer, but Welles had declined because his wife
Mathilde had feared that the sound of exploding bombs would ruin her
husband's health owing to his fragile nerves.[39]

While Hull and Welles were patching up their differences, Pearson
issued a retraction only because of his friendship with Welles. The

admissions that the reporter had made concerning the under secretary's actions were startling: "Actually Welles does go over Hull's head all of the time and did so in the case of the Spanish credit. Maybe I was wrong in denying this part of the story, but Welles told me he was in the toughest spot of his entire professional career."[40]

While half-truths and rumors festered beneath the surface of the daily routine, Pearson's column had almost caused an irreparable breach in the State Department. But nothing was as potentially explosive as the shocking, unconfirmed whispers that Welles had made homosexual advances to several Negro porters on the train ride back from the Bankhead funeral in September 1940. As this gossip filtered back to the Oval Office, Roosevelt, on January 3, 1941, ordered General Edwin "Pa" Watson, the president's military aide and confidant, to summon J. Edgar Hoover, director of the Federal Bureau of Investigation (FBI). According to Watson, the president assigned the bureau the task of "handling a very delicate and confidential matter" that concerned Welles's behavior on that train trip; Roosevelt desired "a full and thorough investigation" and wanted a report as soon as possible.[41]

Toward the end of his career as assistant secretary of the navy, Roosevelt had investigated other charges of homosexual conduct. At the beginning of 1919, authorities at the naval station in Newport, Rhode Island, learned about a group of homosexuals on the base who were labeled the "Ladies of Newport." A vice squad was established, and Roosevelt quickly took charge of the investigation in late March; by the end of the next month, the ring had been destroyed. Overzealous in his efforts to stop perversion at Newport, Roosevelt went so far as to authorize the use of vice squad decoys. When this practice was revealed during the highly publicized trial that followed, severe criticism was aimed at the navy, forcing the convening of a separate court of inquiry in early 1920. When Roosevelt testified, he misled the committee about his detailed knowledge of and supervisory role in the scandal. The panel did not seriously challenge him, but when its findings were released in March 1921, they contained a mild rebuke of Roosevelt, declaring that he had acted unfortunately and had been ill advised.

The episode did not end there. A Senate naval affairs subcommittee convened early in 1920 was not nearly so forgiving. Of the three members of the body, the two Republicans asserted that Roosevelt had perjured himself, while the lone Democrat called the report an unjusti- fied partisan attack. Roosevelt maintained his innocence and denounced the majority's verdict. The report tarnished his public image only tempo- rarily. Nevertheless he was clearly on record as opposed to homosexual- ity in his department, and he had also established the lengths to which he would go to eradicate it.[42] To Roosevelt, homosexuality was immoral, and he would expend every effort to ferret out offenders and expel them from government service.

Two decades later, it was a different Roosevelt who had to deal with allegations of Welles's homosexuality. The president ordered the FBI into the case, and Welles received far different treatment. Hoover appointed Edward Tamm, his top assistant, to investigate because he thought that the under secretary might be "susceptible to blackmail." Because of who was involved and the nature of the accusations that were being investi- gated, the inquiry fell within the Official/Confidential (OC) file. The OC designation was special, for it was reserved for information—such as that dealing with homosexuality, alcoholism, and extramarital affairs among the wealthy and powerful—that the director deemed most sensi- tive. The investigation was unusual for another reason: the possibility of prosecution never arose. If FBI agents had been gathering evidence for a criminal trial, they normally would have taken signed affidavits under oath; instead, the agents took unverified "statements" from several porters. This was particularly significant since Welles's behavior possibly constituted a criminal act.[43]

On January 23 the agents submitted their findings to the director regarding the "allegations of irregular personal conduct" by Welles, including the interviews with the porters and their signed statements. One glaring omission was puzzling: the under secretary himself had not been interrogated. The investigators had tracked Welles's activities after leaving the dining car until he retired to his private Pullman compart- ment; they had determined that sometime after reaching his sleeping quarters, he had begun to ring his service bell. When a Negro porter answered, the drunken under secretary offered him money to commit homosexual acts. The shaken attendant rejected this proposition, but his rebuff did not stop Welles from repeating his call several times. Only when none of the porters would accept his advances, did the buzzing finally stop. The next afternoon the train pulled into Union Station as though nothing unusual had occurred.[44]

On January 29 Hoover took the report to the White House, where he met with Pa Watson, Postmaster General Frank Walker, and Rudolph Forster, a senior presidential assistant. All agreed that the director should brief the president in private. Hoover provided the president with copies of the affidavits, a short summary of the report, and confirmation of Welles's homosexuality from his agents' interviews. The director had concluded that "Welles had propositioned a number of the train crew to have immoral relations with them." The president listened but did not ask Hoover for his advice, nor did the director offer any. That ended the discussion; the president never again spoke with the FBI director about this topic.[45]

If Roosevelt was not sufficiently distraught over this embarrassment, Hoover added that Bullitt also knew about the incident and was spreading the story. In the middle of January, Senator Burton Wheeler, Democrat of Montana, indignantly told a reporter about Bullitt's "vicious story." The senator had also learned that Bullitt had refused to confront Roosevelt with this "bad news" because anyone who did "would get his own legs cut off." To avoid White House wrath, Bullitt wanted Moore or Colonel Edmund Starling of the Secret Service to present this explosive information to the president.[46]

When a reporter informed Welles about Bullitt's allegations, the under secretary considered asking the Secret Service to investigate the accusations, but instead went to see the attorney general to confirm that Bullitt was circulating news of "some 'terrible' incident" to senators, congressmen, and newsmen. Although Welles was not able to ascertain the contents of the story, he admitted that "he had been drinking rather heavily and was no doubt considerably under the weather. . . . He had been taken sick early in the morning and had taken a sleeping pill and had sent for some coffee from the dining car as he had a heart attack [*sic*] and that coffee was the only thing which relieved it, but beyond that he did not recall any other thing happening." The under secretary had completely blocked out from his mind the indiscreet references to Mussolini's greatness and the homosexual advances allegedly made to the porters on the train.[47]

Bullitt had most likely heard about Welles's behavior from Southern Railroad executives after returning to Philadelphia on September 21, 1940, for the University of Pennsylvania's bicentennial anniversary. Not only was Philadelphia Bullitt's hometown, but it was also the site of the company's headquarters. A railroad executive had probably shown him one of the porters' affidavits describing Welles's deviant behavior. Bullitt now had the evidence with which to drive Welles out of office.[48]

Bullitt hastened to share the affidavit with Moore, who, after reviewing it in early January 1941, decided to write the president or go to the White House personally. Moore cryptically wrote his coconspirator: "I am all in a fog as to what should be done in respect to the particular matter we discussed."[49] But Moore never followed up on his intentions because soon thereafter he contracted pneumonia. Although he showed gradual signs of improvement, he was too weak to continue his duties, and he submitted his letter of resignation to Roosevelt on January 27, giving his failing health as the reason and adding, "I could have had no higher privilege and honor than to serve under your great leadership." He appreciated the personal kindness that the president had displayed, and noted that "Secretary Hull, by his unvarying friendly and helpful attitude, has placed me under obligations which I can never forget." The president responded with compassion, refusing to accept the resignation and hoping instead that Moore would be able to return to his duties.[50]

This kind message arrived just before Moore slipped into a coma on February 5; three days later he died at his home in Fairfax. A few days later, there was a brief service without a sermon at Truro Episcopal Church, where Moore had served on the vestry. Six neighbors bore his casket; flowers darkened the church altar; mourners crowded pews and aisles. Those who could not get inside the church overflowed into the churchyard. Roosevelt sent a personal message and a wreath of deep pink carnations. Hull, Berle, and Acheson paid their last respects, as did many members of the diplomatic community. Bullitt called at Moore's home before the burial and was present at the graveside service. The counselor was buried at Fairfax Cemetery on a hillside next to the graves of his mother and father.[51]

Hull mourned his death in a press release: "His loss was . . . a personal one to me, and his passing has deprived the Department of one of its most valuable and inspiring officers."[52] Hugh Wilson, a prominent Republican diplomat who had worked with Moore, expressed his condolences to the family. To Wilson, the counselor was in spirit a peer of such great Virginia statesmen as George Washington, Thomas Jefferson, and John Marshall: "I talked more political philosophy with him than I did with any man in the Department, and my affection and admiration of his character and method of thought, grew with each interview."[53] The *Washington Evening Star* devoted an editorial to Moore's passing: born to power and prestige and loved by his friends, he was a Virginia gentleman in the true sense of the word. Until the end he had been physically active and mentally alert, and had had a youthful outlook.[54]

It is curious that Moore's significance has been almost totally erased from the history of New Deal diplomacy. There are few if any memorials to the man. His family home still stands at 3950 Chain Bridge Road, a busy thoroughfare in the center of Fairfax. After the city council agreed to restore the house, his heirs deeded it and lot just over an acre in size to the city in 1972 to serve as a park and a memorial to Moore. Eleven years later, the council members voted to return the gift because the rehabilitation costs had skyrocketed. Moore's descendants then turned the building into professional offices, but there is still a "Moore House" sign hanging in front and another sign on the porch that marks the home as part of the city's historical walking tour.[55]

Leaving the home and driving several miles to the west, a visitor would arrive at the cemetery where Moore is buried, in the family plot amidst relatives dating back to the Civil War. On his headstone, is carved Psalm 37, verse 37:

> MARK THE PERFECT MAN
> AND BEHOLD THE UPRIGHT,
> FOR THE END OF THAT MAN
> IS PEACE.

When Moore died, Bullitt lost his best source of information in the department, his strongest supporter, and a potential messenger to carry to the president the news of Welles's sexual transgressions. The ambassador was unaware that the president had already read an FBI report documenting Bullitt's attack on Welles. Once Roosevelt knew about this, his cordial relationship with Bullitt began to deteriorate. In early March, after speaking with him, Secretary Morgenthau told Roosevelt that "what Bullitt really wants is to work for you, Mr. President—to be at your side." The president replied, "Well, I just don't have anything definite to offer him now."[56]

Bullitt's last hope of remaining a presidential adviser evaporated on April 23, 1941, during an interview with the president shortly before noon. After a preliminary chat about the best way to defeat Hitler, Bullitt launched into his main reason for coming. Just before Moore had died, he had made Bullitt promise to hand over to the president certain documents about Welles's homosexual activities that he had never had the opportunity to deliver personally. Bullitt then gave Roosevelt a single affidavit. After reading the first page, the president acknowledged, "I know all about this already. I have had a full report on it. There is truth in the allegations."

Stunned by this admission, Bullitt recalled Moore's contention that keeping Welles on opened the way to criminal charges or blackmail by foreign governments and that it could quite possibly menace the presidency by provoking "a terrible public scandal" that would undermine the confidence of the American people in Roosevelt's leadership. Roosevelt declared forcefully that no newspaper would publish anything about this sordid affair, nor would anyone insist on a criminal action. Besides, he had hired a bodyguard to prevent Welles from propositioning anyone else. Bullitt shifted to another argument, claiming that Hull knew about the incident and "considered Welles worse than a murderer." Bullitt added that since the under secretary controlled appointments and transfers, knowledge of his homosexuality could damage diplomatic morale. Bullitt reiterated his fear that if a hostile power were to blackmail Welles, he could become a traitor, a possibility that the president had considered but for which he offered no solution. Bullitt wondered why Welles was so indispensable. How could the president ask Americans to fight for decency against the Axis while condoning the leadership of "a criminal like Welles"? Bullitt ended his interview with an unwise ultimatum. Although he hoped to work with Roosevelt against Hitler and for wartime preparedness, he would not serve in the State Department until Welles had been dismissed. On that note the conversation ended.[57]

Bullitt expected to receive Roosevelt's reply within a few days, but it was not forthcoming. He never understood how his campaign against Welles had jeopardized his relations with the White House, nor how much he depended on Roosevelt's protection. Without presidential support and recognition of his ability to provide useful data on European conditions, Bullitt would not have received his appointments to the Soviet Union and France. His breach with the White House opened wider that July when Marguerite "Missy" LeHand, Roosevelt's private secretary, suffered a paralyzing stroke that slowly sapped her strength. She died three years later. She had been with Roosevelt during his fight against polio, lived in a bedroom adjoining his at the governor's mansion in Albany, shared meals with the family, and enjoyed the longest relationship with the president outside of his immediate relatives. She alone called him "F.D." She controlled his business day and decided whom he saw. Bullitt had an intimate relationship with "Missy," and she may even have contemplated marriage. After her hospitalization, this bond was broken. Bullitt had no one else close to the president to take his side.[58]

Despite his brilliance and personal courage, Bullitt's assertions were suspect. He had a venomous tongue, was widely known for spreading vicious rumors about his opponents, and hated the under secretary. Many Democrats had never forgotten Bullitt's betrayal of Woodrow Wilson, and even after a two-decade interval, the ambassador's vitriolic assault against Welles seemed to follow the same pattern of disloyalty. To lend credibility to the charges against the under secretary, Bullitt needed a well-respected man like Moore to lead the attack. Harole Ickes gladly joined in the intrigue as a way of discrediting the State Department and learning firsthand about the scandal, but he had no intention of openly challenging Welles. The ambassador stood alone in the vanguard without any powerful allies, and that was an extremely uncomfortable position.

In all probability, Hull did not know about the accusations of Welles's homosexuality until that spring. He and his wife were far more consumed with their own more mundane problems. After more than two decades of marriage, much to Frances's delight, the Hulls had moved from the Carlton Hotel to take up residence in apartment 400G at the Wardman Park. According to Hazel Vandenberg, Frances was a "swell person," and this was her first real home since her marriage. She hired a professional decorator from Richmond, Virginia, to furnish her new home, and compared to their first apartment, this one looked much more elegant.[59]

Although overjoyed with her new surroundings, Frances worried constantly about her husband's worsening health. His Sunday meetings at the department grew infrequent, and he was absent from work almost three months in 1941. By spring his tuberculosis had spread markedly throughout the right lung, and his symptoms included an almost constant fever, blood in his spittle, and aggravated coughing. At home on June 22 during the Nazi invasion of Russia, Hull was told by his physician to leave the capital the next day to begin his therapy at White Sulphur Springs. Hull agreed and remained there until late July. With relaxation, his temperature returned to normal, and he regained lost weight. Upon his return to Washington, his health was much improved.[60]

In the middle of his recovery, Frances wrote Norman Davis of her husband's steady improvement and her hope that this vacation could be extended even longer. Cordell had started working again. He had a direct line to the department, instructed that papers be sent to him regularly, "and [had] talks [with] Sumner each day," for indeed the under secretary was the vital link between the department and Hull. Frances's compassion for Mathilde Welles showed in her description of his condition: "Sumner is tired out and looks terrible." When Frances returned to the capital, she immediately noticed Welles's fatigue, but she worried far more about her own spouse when she realized that if Welles were to recuperate from his extraordinary work load he would have to leave Hull alone in charge: "Too bad Cordell will have to take on double duties when he returns to the heat of Wash[ington]."[61]

Hull's return to the capital was greeted by rumors that he was losing the confidence of the White House. Even though he frequently spoke with Roosevelt on the phone, he saw the president on an irregular basis. Yet even with these real and imagined difficulties, Roosevelt continued to acknowledge Hull's importance. According to Roosevelt, the secretary acted slowly, but he prepared meticulously.[62] Canadian Prime Minister MacKenzie King lavished praise on Hull after a meeting that spring: "I was immensely impressed with his clear comprehension of the whole situation. I felt that he has been the real directing force behind the President; that it was his policies that have been shaping America's policies. That he was a really great man."[63]

Most observers glossed over Hull's weaknesses; he not only remained the second most influential political figure in the country, but was even gaining in popularity. When Assistant Secretary Long talked to presidential assistant Pa Watson late that summer, Watson condemned Welles for trying to "take over" Hull's responsibilities. As far as Watson was concerned, the secretary was "the best thing in the Cabinet and the greatest strength to the Administration." If Welles did not stop usurping Hull's prerogatives, said Watson, the secretary "had got very provoked and threatened to resign." Neither Watson nor Roosevelt wanted that to occur.[64]

Roosevelt paid little attention to Hull's concerns over the perceived extension of Welles's authority. The secretary's ego had been deeply wounded, and this applied particularly to the outcome of the first summit in the summer of 1941. Hull expressed his displeasure over the results, particularly Great Britain's refusal to promote freer trade. He also believed that the president's selection of Welles only confirmed widespread suspicions and gossip that the secretary no longer controlled his department's activities. To put the best possible face on a dismal situation, Hull's position was that had he been asked, he would have certainly allowed Welles to attend the meeting because Churchill had brought Sir Alexander Cadogan, the British equivalent to the American under secretary.

Hull openly vented his frustration over the close association between Roosevelt and Welles to Assistant Secretary Long, who came to realize the extent of this resentment on August 11. To Long, Hull and Welles were two men of quite different temperaments. Welles showed little emotion, especially when he made a deliberate effort to conceal his feelings. Otherwise, "Welles was daring, thorough, quick thinking, clear headed—but possibly a little on the too daring side in an effort to do whatever the President says even if not thoroughly considered." Hull, in contrast, was "wary, scrupulous in exploring all the ground around, slow to come to conclusion, less clear in preliminary thought, critical of any proposal which he assumes responsibility for—even the President's— and not lacking in courage to present his different advice to the President or other proposer." His cautious nature was often misconstrued as diffidence or indecisiveness. Long concluded, "Naturally, two such different temperaments have some little difficulty in reconciling themselves in continuous contacts—but one would have to be very well acquainted with either *and* very observing to discover evidence of antagonism. Each is a gentleman and would respect the position of the other."[65]

Roosevelt believed that he could manage Hull's discomfort with Welles, but the same could not be said for his relationship with Bullitt. Roosevelt sought to redirect Bullitt's energies away from personal rivalry and in a more productive direction. On November 18, 1941, the president invited him to lunch to review the situation in Africa, the Middle East, and East Asia. Roosevelt wanted an eyewitness account and asked Bullitt to travel to those regions as his personal representative, with ambassadorial rank. Roosevelt, according to Bullitt, acknowledged that "Welles would do everything possible to knife me in the back," and the president pledged to prevent this by channeling any communications through naval codes to prevent any leaks to Drew Pearson. Bullitt insisted on two other conditions: he would control his own itinerary and route. Roosevelt agreed, and Bullitt immediately began making plans for his departure.

Before leaving, he gave Ickes two memos on Welles's sexual habits, alleging that the under secretary had been "showing bad symptoms again recently." Bullitt also might have instigated a malicious campaign against the under secretary. Rumors resurfaced at about that time about his "queer" activities during his ambassadorship in Havana. Gossip about homosexual advances he had supposedly made during a train ride to Chicago late in the year appeared. Allegations emerged that A. Philip Randolph, the president of the porters' union, had written the State Department to demand Welles's resignation.

In early December, Bullitt informed Hull, who heartily concurred, about his mission. They agreed that the ambassador would receive his orders through James Dunn, whom the secretary trusted absolutely. After completing his business in Washington, Bullitt departed for his assignment.[66]

While most of his reports were well thought of, many of Bullitt's personal principles were not. Former under secretary Castle watched Bullitt's activities on behalf of the Democrats and remarked on his double standard. On the one hand the ambassador called for Christian ethics and high moral standards in the fight against the Axis; on the other he flaunted his mistresses. In the years during which Bullitt had lived in Europe, he had been well acquainted with a variety of sexual appetites. His marriage to his second wife Louise illustrated his tolerance, for she enjoyed a bohemian life-style for years; she also engaged in heavy drinking and took drugs.[67]

A further example was provided by the case of Carmel Offie, Bullitt's most trusted subordinate since 1933. Born into an Italian immigrant family in Pennsylvania, Offie worked his way through business college and entered the government as a stenographer. He later took a post at the United States embassy in Honduras and was transferred to Moscow. Offie was superb at shorthand and typing, clever and discreet, and completely loyal to Bullitt, who had him transferred to Paris. There he relied on him for everything from looking after his health to taking his voluminous daily dictation to serving as his smoking and chess partner. After Bullitt left government service, Offie remained in the diplomatic corps to serve in Italy during the war and then hold a post in the occupation government in Germany. In 1947 he joined the Central Intelligence Agency and a year later became the deputy in charge of the office of policy coordination. Offie's career ended abruptly in 1953 when the Washington, D.C., police arrested him on charges of immoral loitering. As close as he and Bullitt were, the ambassador had to have been aware of Offie's homosexuality, yet it obviously did not interfere with their friendship.

Offie was a close friend; Welles was an enemy. That distinction was sufficient for Bullitt; anything that rendered Welles vulnerable to attack was fair game.[68]

Bullitt was not the only person who considered Welles an enemy by the end of 1941; Hull was driving in the same direction. However, he was unaware of the under secretary's homosexuality. Moore knew, but he had died, and Bullitt no longer was able to use him as a willing accomplice. The president had even more detailed knowledge than Bullitt, but Roosevelt depended on Welles to carry out White House directives. The haphazard diplomatic organization chart that the president had drawn was still blurred, but the alignment of characters was becoming more rigid. The unknown factor was what Hull would do when the gossip surrounding Welles's homosexuality finally reached the secretary's ears.

# CHAPTER 10

PROVOKING WAR

ROOSEVELT MANEUVERED THROUGH the individual minefields that he had planted from the start of the New Deal to assure himself control over his appointees, but by the end of 1941 he was suffering the consequences of the growing antagonism that Hull and his staff were heaping on Welles and his supporters. Somehow these opposing factions kept working to meet the challenges of a chaotic world, and at the same time, the president kept both groups' attention focused on the larger picture. Roosevelt thought in terms of global strategy, and nothing—including the State Department's internal feuding, in large part allowed to simmer owing to White House directives—would prevent the president from moving ahead on his course, indirect though it might appear on occasion.

During the first term, shut out from positive actions in Europe and Asia, Roosevelt had haltingly attempted to project the good neighbor's spirit of cooperation as an example that the rest of the world could emulate. By his second inauguration, the president was seeking to safeguard the Western Hemisphere from the venality of the Third Reich. Toward the close of his second term, Roosevelt made a subtle yet decisive switch in his emphasis by placing assistance to the British ahead of hemispheric preparedness. This shift to Anglo-American cooperation relegated East Asian policy to an even lower priority.[1]

The president also relied heavily on the Monroe Doctrine to rationalize support for the British. The idea that the Americas were forever closed to foreign colonization had become an established principle of American foreign policy by the turn of the twentieth century, and Roosevelt constantly invoked the Monroe Doctrine to convince his countrymen of the good neighbor's value and of how the British were protecting the Western Hemisphere against the Nazi threat.

Roosevelt combined the Monroe Doctrine with his unique understanding of military affairs. He was the catalytic agent who adroitly advanced the concepts of the good neighbor and British cooperation against the Third Reich through the concept of hemispheric defense. Undoubtedly remembering his first federal post as assistant secretary of the navy and his role during World War I, he recognized, at least partially, that the United States had declared war on Germany then as the result of its submarine attacks. If that had occurred in World War I, could a similar set of circumstances be duplicated over two decades later?[2]

Roosevelt's domestic political opponents also remembered what had driven the United States into World War I and staunchly protested against an Anglo-American alliance in fear of drawing the United States into another European conflict against Germany. The president understood this antagonism and sincerely tried to search for ways short of war to placate isolationists and deflect charges of warmongering. Thus, after the fall of France, Roosevelt repeatedly emphasized defensive, not offensive, measures; he sought to project the image of protecting the Americas from the Nazis, who might invade the Americas by using aircraft carriers, build secret Latin American bases to attack the Panama Canal, or enlist fifth-column infiltrators to topple existing governments and establish puppet regimes.[3]

As Roosevelt pursued this zigzag course and the United States drew ever closer to war, Hull grew increasingly uncomfortable, since he viewed his primary task as preventing any such occurrence. He objected to the neutrality zone so much that he considered filing a protest with the

White House. As the president strengthened his ties with the British through the lend-lease program, the secretary not only worried about isolationist opposition but also feared that his diplomatic initiatives were losing force. Finally he was anxious that Roosevelt had ignored his counsel in favor of Welles's unconditional support.

Hull had reason to be anxious. Welles was reaching the pinnacle of his influence. Toward the end of 1941, his critics were seemingly losing ground in their bureaucratic battle to unseat him: Moore had died; Hull's spreading consumption increased his unwilling dependence; and Bullitt was traveling overseas. In the power vacuum that Hull's withdrawal created, it was Welles more than anyone else in the State Department who took vague presidential guidelines and turned them into concrete plans. Roosevelt had bestowed a tremendous amount of trust on Welles, something that the president shared with only a select few. At the start of the New Deal, he had limited Welles to Latin American affairs. After assuming the under-secretaryship in 1937, Welles had continued to advance the cause of inter-American cooperation; in addition, the president had sent him on a European mission, placed him in charge of Russian affairs, and made him chief liaison between the White House and the State Department. Welles continued to supply specific proposals to flesh out the broad outlines dictated in the Oval Office; as always he chose to follow, not to originate.

Roosevelt gladly supplied the direction. For example, during late April 1940, the president talked with MacKenzie King about stopping the Third Reich from expanding into the Americas. Since the Nazis had military superiority, particularly air power, the president was taking Hitler's aggression more seriously with each passing moment. To prevent an Axis victory, the United States had to draw closer to the British.[4]

Public opinion, something that Roosevelt carefully monitored, was already moving on a parallel course, as indicated by a *Fortune* magazine poll published during June. The poll showed that 40 percent of those surveyed had conceded the Reich's conquest of Europe and now overwhelmingly backed defensive measures to protect the Americas. Two-thirds of the respondents wanted to assist the Allies, as long as American troops were not sent to Europe. If Germany was victorious, almost four-fifths of the sample thought that the Nazis would extend their influence to South America and over 60 percent of those surveyed believed that they would try to seize hemispheric possessions. After that had been accomplished, almost half felt that the Axis would attack the United States.[5]

After the Germans crushed French resistance, Secretary of War Stimson and Secretary of the Navy Knox almost guaranteed an Anglo-American bias within the cabinet. Both preached Allied assistance as the first line of defense for the Americas to keep Hitler confined to continental Europe, where he would either lose the war or sue for a negotiated peace. If the Germans conquered the British, Stimson and Knox assumed that the Third Reich would seize the British fleet and eventually invade the Americas.[6]

Along with the assistance to Great Britain that the war secretaries advocated, Roosevelt used the neutrality zone patrolled by the United States navy as an offensive weapon against the Nazis by reducing the area that His Majesty's Navy had to monitor. To make the patrol effective, the president worked directly to mobilize the navy and then turned to Welles to coordinate activities among the departments of state, war, and navy. With this machinery in place, Roosevelt anxiously watched the effectiveness of the naval patrol in keeping belligerents away from the Western Hemisphere. Whenever the navy did not deploy its warships quickly enough or the State Department did not act promptly, Roosevelt responded impatiently: the warring parties had to recognize and respect the legality of the security zone, and the president expected it to be enforced.[7]

The president, even in his first term, had considered several options to prevent any foreign power from transferring its hemispheric territory to a non-American nation, a violation of an implied corollary that the United States had added to the original Monroe Doctrine. After the fall of Denmark, the administration gave more serious thought to the no-transfer issue when the British secretly sent a small military detachment to the Dutch West Indies to prevent German sabotage of the oil refineries at Curaçao and Aruba. The United States objected to the occupation for fear of setting a precedent that would encourage the Japanese in the Dutch East Indies. However, when the Dutch government-in-exile specifically asked for British protection, the United States, bowing to the unofficial Anglo-American understanding, ended its objections.[8]

Congress addressed the no-transfer issue by passing a resolution in June 1940 that forbade any transfer of European colonies in the Americas, and when Welles drafted a similar declaration for a specially convened inter-American conference at Havana that August, the delegates promptly voted their approval. The signals were clear. If the Nazis and their allies had invasion plans, the American republics would join together to repulse any European colonization attempts.[9]

The United States was particularly concerned about territories that might possibly fall under the Monroe Doctrine. For example, the Netherlands claimed sovereignty over Greenland. Although the president did not expect to seize the island, he wanted to make certain that the Nazis could not station troops there either. After all, the American patrol was reaching out toward Greenland. Iceland came under a similar, although more elastic, interpretation because of its enormous strategic significance. Traditionally, the Monroe Doctrine had been associated with areas near American shores. If Greenland was a stretch, Iceland was literally off the map, for it did not fall within any geographical definition of the Western Hemisphere. But under the unique set of circumstances prevailing in the summer of 1940, the no-transfer principle was applied in a political, not a geographical, context. Thus it was that Iceland, for the first time, became part of the Americas.[10]

The president also worried about economic penetration of the Americas by the Axis. Once the Reich controlled the Continent, it could force Latin America to trade on terms unacceptable to the United States; this action could potentially create a breach in hemispheric solidarity. Roosevelt refused to accept this possibility and briefly considered the establishment of a regional customs union. Although such a drastic step proved unnecessary, since the United States, practically speaking, already controlled much of the commerce in the Americas, this initiative did illustrate the extent of the president's commitment to keep the Nazis away from the Americas.[11]

While Roosevelt was advancing his wide-ranging initiatives to assist the British, he was also carefully scrutinizing polls, such as the one compiled by Hadley Cantril for the Gallup organization in November to be sure that the American people were heading in the same direction as their elected leader. The poll indicated that 85 percent of Americans favored aid to the British, but that if supplying such aid meant the risk of war, the percentage plunged by 35 points. However, if the Nazis attacked South America, two-thirds of those surveyed were willing to fight.[12]

Without any doubt, by the end of 1940, Americans overwhelmingly favored assistance to Great Britain, as long as there was no risk of American military involvement and that the aid was closely tied to hemispheric defense. The president had combined inter-American solidarity with aid to Britain and headed down several crucial, irreversible paths. First, he had emphasized Hitler's tyranny and aligned his administration with that of Churchill, forming a bulwark to keep the Nazi scourge from spreading across the Atlantic Ocean to the Americas. Second, he had effectively cloaked the neutrality patrol and the no-transfer resolution with the mantle of the Monroe Doctrine, thus strengthening the Allies and damaging the Axis on the high seas without precipitating extended domestic debate. Domestic opponents attacked Roosevelt for drawing nearer to the British, but they could not figure out a way to detach the issue of hemispheric security from that of collaboration with the British. Roosevelt was an experienced swimmer—one who never swam directly against the current, but instead chose a longer, slower, diagonal course. Isolationists realized that Churchill and Roosevelt were pulling together, and that their strokes were growing stronger. Opponents could chart the president's course and note his increasing speed, but they could not reverse his path.

Even though the democracies were joining forces, Roosevelt as well as his military leaders recognized that the United States was as yet woefully unprepared for war. To emphasize this weakness, when the annual budget for 1941 went to Congress, 60 percent of it was allocated for defense, and even that figure was seen as inadequate for future production and manpower requirements. In addition, the United States armed forces were not ready to fight and needed more time to train. Roosevelt unquestionably understood those prerequisites for mobilization and moved energetically toward that objective.[13]

As the president lobbied for massive military spending, he also turned the United States into the so-called arsenal for democracy. Churchill had already bluntly informed him that Britain had almost depleted its resources. The implication was obvious: without American aid, Allied resistance might disintegrate. Roosevelt regularly pounded away at the need to assist the British, always carefully coupling the issue with inter-American security. Addressing the annual awards dinner of the Academy of Motion Picture Arts and Sciences in late February 1941, he stressed the good neighbor spirit and the extension of national defense to the entire Western Hemisphere: "We can no longer consider our own problem of defense as a separate interest. It involves the defense of all the democracies of all the Americas—and therefore, in fact, it involves the future of democracy wherever it is imperiled by force or terror."[14]

By the spring of 1941, an overwhelming majority of his constituents supported this initiative, and a Princeton University opinion poll confirmed how strongly the public had come around to share Roosevelt's views. Four-fifths of the survey respondents believed that if any European power attacked Latin America, the United States should forcefully expel the aggressor. Almost three-quarters believed that the United States would fight in a European war and that if the Third Reich vanquished the British, American citizens would be affected. Almost 70 percent now wanted the British to win, even at the risk of war.[15]

As the battle for Britain raged, Roosevelt attempted to aid the Allies by enlarging the security zone in the North Atlantic. By mid-April he had announced the extension of the security zone to longitude 25°W, placing Greenland and Iceland within the neutrality patrol. A few weeks later, he extended it farther out into the Atlantic and deployed additional naval vessels. Privately, the president informed Churchill that the American navy would monitor Nazi movements and pass this intelligence on to the British.[16]

Not only did Roosevelt extend the zone, he concurrently agreed to escort convoys, couching this hostile action in terms of the Panama Declaration's intent that the security zone serve to defend American neutrality. Convoying was an act of war, according to the president, whereas he had only agreed to an inter-American neutrality patrol.

Recognizing this semantic subterfuge, Secretary Stimson urged the president to tell the public his true intentions.[17]

But Roosevelt refused to take a frontal approach. Instead, at a press conference on April 25, he defended the patrol concept and lectured reporters: "Now this is a patrol, and has been a patrol for a year and a half, still is, and from time to time it has been extended, and is being extended, and will be extended—the patrol—for the safety of the Western Hemisphere."[18] The patrol, which originally extended as far as 1,000 miles in some places, under new presidential orders stretched 2,000 miles into the Atlantic. Roosevelt simultaneously added to the list of those possessions falling under the no-transfer principle by proclaiming Greenland part of the Americas, with the approval of a congressional resolution and without even asking for inter-American consent. The United States would hold the island in trust for Denmark until its occupation ceased. For the first time during the war, the United States had expanded the territorial limits of the Monroe Doctrine.[19]

These tactics inextricably linked hemispheric security with opposition to the Nazi conquest of Europe; Roosevelt's grand strategy of disrupting the Nazi war machine was understated but always understood. The president even considered measures to prevent the German occupation of the Azores, the Cape Verde Islands, and North Africa. Several times, he discussed the vulnerability of South America with Secretary Ickes, pointing out that the distance from Dakar to the Brazilian bulge was only 1,600 miles, and that with one refueling, German bombers could drop their deadly cargoes and return to North Africa.[20]

Roosevelt seized any opportunity to accuse the Third Reich of trying to penetrate the Americas. After Rudolph Hess parachuted into Scotland on May 10, the president promptly wrote Churchill about the potential value of the deputy Führer, mentioning the Reich's plans for the Americas in regard to "commerce, infiltration, military domination, encirclement of the United States, etc. . . . If he says anything about the Americas in the course of telling his story, it should be kept separate from other parts and featured by itself."[21]

Later that month, a German submarine sank the United States freighter *Robin Moor* in the South Atlantic, outside the neutrality zone.

In doing so, the Germans had violated the long-cherished American principle of freedom of the seas. There were no deaths, nor was there any public outcry. Rather than breaking off diplomatic relations, the president called the attack an act of piracy and demanded compensation from the Reich. In retaliation, he froze Axis assets and ordered all German consuls and staffs out of the United States.[22]

On May 24, the German pocket battleship *Bismarck* broke out into the Atlantic and steered toward the Americas. Some feared that it would attack hemispheric shipping lanes, but the British spotted the battleship two days later, crippled it with a depth charge, and sank it the following day. Assistant Secretary Berle concluded from this battle that as long as the United States had an adequate air force, a naval invasion of the Americas was impossible.[23]

Roosevelt disagreed. He again involved the hemispheric connection in an emotionally charged radio speech delivered on May 27 before an assemblage of Latin American diplomats and their families at a black-tie affair for the governing board of the Pan American Union in the East Room of the White House.[24] Proclaiming an unlimited national emergency in the face of aggression, he called for accelerated defensive measures, a halt to German economic penetration, and the prevention of fifth-column movements. British warships guarded American shores, but such defense was insufficient to the president, who cautioned his radio audience, "Adolf Hitler never considered the domination of Europe as an end in itself. European conquest was but a step toward ultimate goals in all the other continents. It is unmistakably apparent to all of us that, unless the advance of Hitlerism is forcibly checked now, the Western Hemisphere will be within range of the Nazi weapons of destruction." The audience applauded politely and then moved out to the south lawn for a private party.[25]

The day after the address, when opponents accused the president of leading the nation into war, he backed away from his bellicose tone. Admiral William Leahy, ambassador to Vichy, thought that this speech was tantamount to a declaration of war against the Axis and that it signaled "the certain eventual defeat of Hitlerism." Secretary Ickes was far less convinced; to him the president was not being aggressive enough. The American rearmament program was lagging badly because the nation was still insufficiently aroused to the Nazi menace. The status quo had not changed.[26]

In fact, neither Roosevelt nor Hitler wanted to heighten tensions between their two countries. The president had to move carefully, making certain of majority support, and he was also painfully aware of his military deficiencies. The Führer recognized that he had to keep the United States out of the war; Hitler refused to antagonize Roosevelt because he had secretly drawn up plans for the invasion of the Soviet Union and needed to concentrate all his efforts on that titanic effort.

Launched on June 22, Hitler's attack on Russia dramatically changed the complexion of the war. Secretary Stimson argued that the possibility of a Nazi invasion of the British Isles had evaporated overnight, as had any chance of the occupation of Iceland and North Africa. He urged that the United States use this unexpected respite to strengthen its military position in the Atlantic.[27]

As acting secretary of state, Welles spoke for the White House by immediately drafting a press release. In it he declared that Hitler's assault upon Russia was another example of his treachery, and that although the United States condoned neither communism nor nazism, the administration would support the Russians, for "Hitler's armies are today the chief dangers of the Americas."[28] Six days after the invasion, Welles predicted that the Third Reich would crush Russian resistance. Yet this warning illustrated his misunderstanding of Russo-German relations by its erroneous conclusion that recent communist activities in Europe and Molotov's unsuccessful diplomatic trip to Berlin had encouraged Germany's decision to attack. The under secretary did not comprehend how deeply seated was Hitler's hatred for communism or how longstanding and fervent was his commitment to destroy the Soviet Union.[29]

When former ambassador to the Soviet Union Joseph Davies saw Welles for lunch on July 7, they discussed Russian affairs; after the meeting, the ambassador recorded in his diary, "Welles has a mind like a Swiss watch. He is a thoroughgoing individualist, a democrat, and naturally hostile to Communism, but he is heart and head in this fight to save this country from the menace of Nazi victory." Both men agreed that since Stalin was fighting Hitler, the Russians were indirectly defending American shores. When Davies's book *Mission to Moscow* appeared late in the year, the ambassador projected the Russians as sympathetic partners who were fighting on the side of the Allies, and American readers appeared to accept that reasoning.[30]

Bolstered by support for the Russians, Welles now felt confident that Roosevelt would lead the United States into the conflict, but "before going to war there must be intermediate steps." One was the occupation of Iceland.[31] When the Danes had asked Welles on February 19 if their island was considered to lie within the Western Hemisphere and thus protected under the Monroe Doctrine, he had answered affirmatively, and on July 7, 4,400 marines occupied the island—a deployment based squarely on the premise of inter-American security. Although Iceland was crucial to the North Atlantic trading route to Britain, the concept of self-preservation was still far more palatable to the American public than aid to the British. Roosevelt had also failed to divulge publicly that the security zone now covered four-fifths of the Atlantic Ocean.[32] At a press conference the next day, he admitted that although the island might fall outside the Western Hemisphere, it was nevertheless "terribly important to Hemispheric defense."[33]

The aviator Charles Lindbergh worried about this American armed occupation of European territory. Even though the American public might be led to think otherwise, Lindbergh knew that Iceland was a part of Europe and realized that the U.S. troop deployment might lead to war. This was a danger Roosevelt had not told his constituents about. Lindbergh wondered, "Will Germany pick up the gauntlet we have thrown down? We have now entered her declared war zone for the avowed purpose of getting war supplies to England."[34]

Lindbergh did not know that Nazi naval commanders had already asked the Führer for permission to occupy Iceland, the Azores, and the Canary Islands to forestall the de facto establishment of United States protectorates. But Hitler had refused to entertain their plans until Russia surrendered. As long as the Russian campaign continued, the Third Reich would not provoke American forces. Indeed, after the U.S. occupation of Iceland, he ordered his submarines out of nearby waters to prevent any possible incidents.[35]

However, Hitler's preoccupation with the Eastern Front did not affect Roosevelt's militant actions. When the president asked Congress toward the end of July to extend the Selective Service Act, he directly linked the Nazi conquests with protection of the Americas: "Each elimination of a victim has brought the issue of Nazi domination closer to this hemisphere, while month by month their intrigues of propaganda and conspiracy have sought to weaken every link in the community of interests that should bind the Americas into a great western family." The United States, Roosevelt contended, had to honor its commitments under the good neighbor policy, and in these perilous times, Americans had to be prepared to make sacrifices.[36]

While the United States was moving forward with its own domestic priorities, Anglo-American military strategy played a paramount role at the Atlantic conference in August 1941, at which both leaders agreed first to the defeat of Hitler and secondarily to delay a war in the Pacific as long as possible. The president also promised to escort British convoys through the neutrality zone and search out and sink U-boats. Without acknowledging the obvious, the United States had moved another step closer toward belligerency against the Third Reich. The initial response to the Atlantic Charter was not impressive. When asked by reporters if it meant war, Roosevelt denied it. Yet this response satisfied neither his opponents, who only grew more suspicious about his motives, nor the British, for the United States had still refused to join in the fighting. However, Churchill and Roosevelt parted friends.[37]

By taking Welles to the conference, Roosevelt exposed his under secretary to military planning as well as broad diplomatic strategy. Always the State Department specialist in hemispheric matters, Welles had gained ascendance over Soviet policy and now was privy to Anglo-American collaboration.

By the fall of 1941, the diplomatic connection between the Americas and the European war had become even more pivotal. On September 4, a British patrol plane spotted a U-boat and radioed its location to the U.S.S. *Greer,* a lone destroyer carrying mail to Iceland. The warship tracked the submarine for several hours; when the *Greer* would not attack, the bomber dropped its depth charges. Believing that the warship had attacked, the German commander fired two errant torpedoes, and the destroyer retaliated with several depth charges before proceeding to its destination. The White House received a summary of this incident, in which the navy acknowledged that the U-boat could not identify its attacker.[38]

Roosevelt had scheduled a fireside chat for September 8, but the death of his mother Sara one day earlier had caused the postponement of the broadcast to September 11. When the president spoke to his radio audience, he unequivocally declared that the Nazis were trying to end freedom of the seas. He deliberately failed to mention that the *Greer* was radioing the U-boat's position to a British warplane that had dropped depth charges and that the submarine did not know who had attacked it. Instead he painted an ominous picture: "For with control of the seas in their own hands, the way can obviously become clear for their next step—domination of the United States—domination of the Western Hemisphere by force of arms. Under Nazi control of the seas, no merchant ship of the United States or of any other American Republic would be free to carry on any peaceful commerce, except by the condescending grace of this foreign and tyrannical power." Roosevelt also claimed to have uncovered several German plots to overthrow Latin American regimes and to have found several secret Nazi landing fields within striking distance of the Panama Canal. If anyone still doubted that the Third Reich was threatening the Americas, here was the irrefutable proof. To prevent any such threat, the president had decided to deploy United States naval and air patrols to defend freedom of the seas. "Our patrolling vessels and planes," he declared, "will protect all merchant ships—not only American ships but ships of any flag—engaged in commerce in our defensive waters. They will protect them from submarines; they will protect them from surface raiders." Under the guise of hemispheric protection, Roosevelt had announced to the world that he had agreed to the warlike act of convoying Allied shipping.[39]

A month later, a large wolf pack of German U-boats attacked a convoy protected by the destroyer U.S.S. *Kearny,* which was struck by a torpedo. Its crew suffered the first eleven casualties of this undeclared ocean war. Toward the end of the month, the president, in his Navy Day speech, claimed not only that the Nazis had killed American seamen, but also that he had uncovered a secret German map on which South America and the Panama Canal were divided up into five vassal states. The Third Reich promptly denied the charges. When reporters asked

Roosevelt to produce the map, he refused, claiming that the notations on it might reveal his source. In fact the president need not have feared identifying any one individual, because several maps outlining the Nazi conquest of the Americas had already been published in newspapers. Claiming that the German government was responsible was at best irresponsible, and at worst deceitful.[40]

After Roosevelt's charges concerning the secret map failed to excite his constituents as he had hoped, the president appeared resigned to the fact that a war declaration was impossible. When, on the last day of October, the U.S.S. *Reuben James* was torpedoed and sank with the loss of more than a hundred men, the president made no demands, not even for severing relations. Instead, he concentrated on repealing the neutrality legislation. After an acrimonious congressional battle, he accomplished this objective in mid-November. Throughout the rest of the month and the first week of December, he considered expanding United States naval forces even farther into the Atlantic and also increased expenditures for military forces. As previously, these limited responses disappointed his ardent supporters, while his enemies feared that they represented additional steps toward intervention. In reality, the president of the United States was provoking war. But as Frank Freidel, one of Roosevelt's most knowledgeable biographers, has shown, the president still hoped that the nation's involvement would be limited.[41]

Roosevelt had accurately read the sentiments of his constituents. Before he could even think about asking for a declaration of war against the Nazis, he had to have unanimity. Even the constant equation of the Third Reich with the forces of evil would be insufficient to push the United States into the conflict. Even though most Americans accepted the premise that Hitler would challenge the very existence of the United States, they were unwilling to join the Allies. Before the inevitable confrontation, Roosevelt emphasized several recurrent themes: the Nazis were chiseling away at hemispheric freedoms; U-boats were restricting commercial sea lanes; spies were infiltrating Latin American governments; and German agents were priming their puppets to overthrow current regimes.

To the president, these were real dangers that threatened the Americas, and he made certain to preach this sermon to receptive parishioners.

The Nazi dictatorship was no match for British democracy, and the Third Reich's claim to western hemispheric colonies was anathema under the Monroe Doctrine. Roosevelt continually stressed these dangers in his speeches, and Welles devoted his energies to making certain that the Nazi menace never reached American shores.

# CHAPTER 11

# HULL LOSES CONTROL

DECEMBER 7, 1941, A DAY THAT still lives in infamy, has had such an enormous impact on the course of United States history that views of its significance have become dramatically skewed. Americans, fixated on that Sunday morning in the Hawaiian islands, ask not how fortunate or how brilliant the Japanese attack plan was, but how United States military forces could have failed so abysmally. Some have chosen an erroneous, simplistic answer: conspiracy. They claim, without any documented evidence, that Roosevelt clandestinely assisted in the "sneak" attack by concealing knowledge of the Japanese plans from the military commanders at Pearl Harbor; yet, over half a century after the fact, no one has uncovered any verifiable proof to confirm that allegation.[1]

The latest twist to this conspiracy theory is the assertion that Roosevelt has been unjustly convicted of the Pearl Harbor disaster because he would never have allowed his beloved navy to be annihilated. The president, at last, is declared innocent, and the real villain is revealed to be Winston Churchill, who had broken Japanese secret codes and thus learned about the surprise attack, but refused to inform the Americans in order to coerce them into joining the war. In *Betrayal at Pearl Harbor,* James Rusbridger and Eric Nave—without the benefit of newly declassified British navel intelligence that states categorically that Churchill did not know about a surprise attack on Pearl Harbor—conclude: "Roosevelt was thus deceived by Churchill, who took a ghastly gamble to bring America into the war in a manner that would sweep aside all opposition."[2]

After more than fifty years, Americans have singled out Pearl Harbor for reverent ceremonies, while the memory of the undeclared naval war in the North Atlantic had dimmed. The concept of hemispheric defense and its use in forging the inter-American coalition during World War II have been virtually forgotten. But in late 1941, the vast majority of Americans ignored the Pacific, their attention riveted on the menacing events unfolding in Europe. Principally responsible for this attitude was Roosevelt himself, who concentrated his diplomatic and strategic efforts on the machinations of Hitler and Mussolini; when the president paid attention to the Pacific at all, it was only as a momentary distraction from the parts of the larger European puzzle.[3]

To illustrate the secondary status of East Asian matters before the Pearl Harbor disaster, one need only recall that from the commencement of the New Deal Roosevelt provided no leadership in that region. He did not appoint a specialist to head the Far Eastern division of the State Department, nor did he take a personal interest in the area. Filling this void, Hull began to coordinate Pacific policy. As Jonathan Utley has shown, by the end of the first term, he jealously guarded this prerogative, and the career diplomats in the division relied on him for protection and continuity in Asian matters. In addition, the secretary's style was ideally suited for this mission; he would neither appease nor provoke, and his caution was just what the president wanted.

Although the State Department's avowed position was the preservation of peace, its policies were inconsistent with that lofty goal. Hull did not realize that his efforts, rather than discouraging conflict between the United States and Japan, were encouraging the two nations to drift slowly toward confrontation. He hoped to maintain order in East Asia as part of his commitment to resolving problems using the rules of international law and avoiding armed force. On the one hand, the United

States tried to minimize friction with Japan by advocating tranquility in the region, and Hull personally tried to reduce animosity by refraining from branding the Japanese aggressors. On the other hand, the administration insisted on supporting Chinese sovereignty through continued diplomatic recognition of the Chungking government led by Chiang Kai-shek, and even provided token financial aid to support him.

American diplomacy, therefore, worked against Japanese expansion. Throughout the 1930s Tokyo used force to gain entry into China, and the outbreak of the European war gave the aggressors an added opportunity to pressure the British and French into withdrawing their soldiers from the Pacific. Hull resented this bullying tactic and warned the Japanese that such provocative actions could damage relations between their governments, but such meaningless threats did not deter the Japanese from pursuing their military conquest of mainland China and extending their domination to the surrounding area.

Hull was equally concerned about Japan's emphasis on the East Asia Co-Prosperity Sphere, intended to make Tokyo the center of the region's commerce and finances. Such a restrictive economic policy ran directly contrary to the secretary's trade program. By the start of World War II, he had explicitly linked lower tariffs with political stability. Japan sought to limit commercial intercourse, and Hull naturally opposed this antithetical position, as did the American lobbyists who pressured the administration to reduce trade with Japan because of its reliance on military might. Pro-Chinese and anti-Japanese groups staged marches on Washington and held demonstrations in major cities in favor of economic sanctions against Tokyo as their way of protesting against aggression. However, this was the extent of their agitation; they were not willing to risk war.[4]

Hull and Roosevelt argued against sanctions, for the two countries had a commercial treaty. But when it came up for renewal in the summer of 1939, the administration gave notice of its intent to cancel as a means of applying pressure on Tokyo to reverse its militaristic practices. When the Japanese ignored the warning, the United States let the treaty expire in early 1940. Even then Roosevelt did not apply sanctions, but instead only permitted a moral embargo on aircraft and its supplies. The threat of future trade reductions, the president hoped, might inhibit Japanese expansion.

While the president wished for a relaxation of tensions, the secretary worried about the creation of a Japanese puppet regime in Nanking at the start of 1940. Without the possibility of an American military response, Hull threatened economic coercion to show his displeasure. This strategy, coupled with the huge cost of stationing soldiers in China and the large concentration of Russian troops billeted across the border, would, he was certain, force the Japanese to reevaluate their position. Instead, German victories in Europe that spring proved far more significant than the American bluff; the Japanese now demanded concessions in the East Indies from the Dutch, who had lost sovereignty to the Nazi conquest. This vacuum aggravated the growing divergence between Washington and Tokyo.

The provocative actions of the Japanese, accelerated by the fall of France, touched off even more pointed demands for an Allied withdrawal from the Orient, for the Japanese asserted that their special regional role obligated them to guard against anarchy. Once again the United States called for restraint in the face of the Japanese drive to push into southeast Asia. Hull's strategy of keeping the government in Tokyo guessing about American economic sanctions was ineffective, however. Uncertainty only led to frustration and weakened moderate factions while hardening the resolve of the pro-Axis forces. He also failed to consider the military realities of a nation preparing for the domination of East Asia. Somehow the secretary believed that warfare could be avoided by using everything from military threats to commercial cooperation.

When Japan, Germany, and Italy signed the Tripartite Pact on September 27, 1940, Americans came to view the dictatorships in Europe and Asia under one name: the Axis. Believing that each member of the trio was equally abhorrent to democratic values, many Americans argued that the British were the first line of defense, followed by the Chungking government. If the United States did not accept this reasoning, it would be surrendering to Japanese intimidation and betraying Chiang Kai-shek. By early October, Hull worried about a Japanese declaration of war on the British and a military push into southeast Asia.

Roosevelt added more confusion by his ambivalence: although British assistance was paramount, he did not want a confrontation with the Japanese, but neither did he fear one.[5]

At the beginning of 1941 the hostility between the United States and Japan momentarily slackened while the secretary tried to work out a peaceful resolution with the newly appointed Japanese ambassador to the United States, Kichisaburo Nomura, based on a restoration of Chinese sovereignty, noninterference in southeast Asian matters, acceptance of freedom of trade, and the maintenance of current borders. Although these measures seemed quite reasonable to the United States, they ran contrary to the will of a Japanese government intent on dominating the region.

Hull was perplexed, but at least one observer mistakenly thought that the secretary was in control. When Canadian Prime Minister Mac-Kenzie King met with the secretary in late April, he seemed optimistic, compared to the president, about the prospects for peace. To achieve his goals, Hull recommended an Allied blockade of Germany while attempting to keep peace in the Pacific.[6]

In actuality, the secretary did not recognize the inherent political conflict. Rather than work within a realistic context, Hull chose to adopt the futile posture of trying to split the Axis partners by encouraging the moderates in Tokyo against their militaristic foes. He even tried to convince Ambassador Nomura that his government should withdraw troops from most of China, but this approach, too, was not feasible. Hull could not comprehend that his opposition to Japanese predominance in Asia would eventually lead to war. The secretary did recognize that Japanese expansionist goals and his position were in direct conflict, but he could not find a way to ease this friction. Instead he spent the entire year seeking a means to drive the militarists out of power. To capitulate to them would only lead to an acceleration of military aggression and ultimately to a major war.

In addition to his growing pessimism over international conditions, the secretary's own health was steadily deteriorating. His tuberculosis had grown worse, and other complications, including his diabetes, retarded his healing powers. His throat had become so inflamed that his doctor prescribed a narcotic* to soothe the rawness and thereby reduce coughing.[7]

While the secretary was recovering, Welles temporarily directed East Asian affairs. Although Welles had started his career in Japan, Hull had specifically excluded him from making decisions in the Pacific except when the secretary was absent. Even in those situations, adherence to Hull's intentions was assured because the career diplomats in the Far Eastern division guaranteed continuity. Before the Nazi invasion of the Soviet Union, Welles concluded that Stalin was encouraging the Japanese to fight the United States. In fact, the Japanese were acting more aggressively and, according to Welles, were trying to reach some accord with the communists. Once the Germans attacked the Soviet Union, the Japanese waited to see the outcome before taking any independent action.[8]

Roosevelt followed Hull's cautious guidelines, for the longer the talks continued, the more the war in China would sap Japanese resources and provide time for American military preparation. The president reluctantly ordered Welles, in early July, to promulgate an order freezing Japanese assets in the United States. Always the same theme surfaced: keep the peace in the Pacific while focusing on Allied assistance in Europe.[9]

Hull approved of these positions, and after his recovery in early August he worked tirelessly to prevent war. Throughout the fall, he vainly tried to negotiate an accord. He was at first unaware that by September the Japanese had secretly begun planning for the inevitable conflict with the United States. Once the United States had broken the Japanese secret codes, the administration became aware of the quickening pace of Japan's military preparations. Roosevelt and Hull realized that their enemy would strike somewhere in the Pacific, but the unanswered questions were where and when. Physically drained, Hull had

---

*Hull claimed that he took a morphine solution; however, almost every ear, eye, nose, and throat specialist whom the author consulted said that he probably took cocaine or codeine; most dentists concurred with this opinion. For an example, see William Brinker to author, Dec. 19, 1991, Gellman Papers.

by then not rested for over four months; he endangered his health even more in his search for a way to slow the momentum toward war, but to no avail. Near exhaustion by November, Hull met regularly with the Japanese envoys at his office and even extended those unproductive conversations into the night at his apartment. He began holding secret discussions with Stimson and Knox, focusing on the extreme danger in the Pacific, and told a press gathering how precarious conditions had grown. He did not divulge the precise reason for this opinion, but other high officials in the administration who were reading the Japanese intercepts—which were referred to by the code name Magic—also predicted an imminent attack.[10]

Still Roosevelt stalled for more time. When the Japanese sent Saburo Kurusu, a professional diplomat, to join Nomura in the Washington negotiations in mid-November, the president was skeptical but thought of an interim accommodation. As long as conversations continued, the United States bought time to prepare for the fighting. Bedridden on November 27 and 28 and then again from December 1 to 3, Hull remained at his apartment, closely watching the worsening situation. He was disappointed that his talks with the Japanese envoys had not resulted in any workable solution. His staff continually monitored Japanese movements in the Pacific, and on December 4 United States naval forces reported a Japanese fleet steaming toward the Gulf of Siam.[11]

Hull faced another insurmountable hurdle in the procedure that he followed in reviewing the Magic intercepts. The messenger who brought them typically arrived unannounced. The secretary then interrupted whatever he was doing, read the raw translations with the runner at his side, and returned the documents to him after he had completed his review. The State Department did not keep any copies. Given this haphazard procedure and the fact that the secretary was ill, he could not have possibly comprehended the full importance of the decrypts under consideration, or how each day's documents related to earlier ones. Hull faced the impossible task of concentrating on a myriad of seemingly unrelated documents at a time when he was having difficulty even getting out of bed.[12]

On Sunday, December 7, the secretary went to his office at the request of the Japanese diplomats, who had scheduled a meeting for

1:00 P.M.; the session had to be postponed for over an hour because their staff had trouble decoding a message from the Japanese foreign ministry declaring war on the United States. During this delay, Roosevelt phoned Hull to inform him of the surprise attack on Pearl Harbor. When the Japanese envoys saw the secretary at 2:20 P.M., shaken by their betrayal, he pretended to skim their note, dismissed its contents as falsehoods, and ordered them out. Tokyo had planned to have its message relayed just before the assault on Hawaii, but by the time the emissaries left the State Department, the two nations had already been at war for more than an hour.[13] After dismissing them, Hull went into "a towering rage," calling them "scoundrels and piss-ants."[14]

The next day Roosevelt asked for and received a congressional resolution calling for war on Japan. While the United States eagerly anticipated sending troops to the Pacific, the administration remained at peace with Italy and Germany until December 11, when Hitler finally declared war against the United States. At last the president had the opportunity to ally with the British, but not because of an incident in the Atlantic; the fuse had been ignited on the other side of the globe. No longer confined to the role of impatient observer, Roosevelt now was the commander in chief, rallying his countrymen in the struggle to destroy the Axis. His wheelchair, so long hidden from public display, now came to symbolize his commitment as well as his limitations. When visiting soldiers in the veterans hospitals, he would wheel himself in, to let them see how he functioned despite his handicap.[15]

Hull's responded far differently to the opening of hostilities. Distraught over the failure to prevent war and weakened by the spread of tuberculosis, he overreacted to unfounded rumors alleging that he had caused the fighting, intimating that he had somehow withheld from the military information on an expected attack on Pearl Harbor. The secretary vehemently resented and vigorously denied these unsubstantiated charges of a diplomatic conspiracy to hide crucial data.

During the fighting, the War Department held hearings on this sensitive and emotional topic.[16] In mid-November 1945, a joint committee of Congress on the Investigation of the Pearl Harbor Attack opened hearings. Hull was the third witness; he appeared on November 23 before a standing-room-only audience to vindicate himself of any wrongdoing by delivering a twenty-five-thousand-word statement justifying his department's actions. During his testimony, he told the committee of his warnings to the cabinet of the likelihood of a Japanese attack, but no one ever mentioned Pearl Harbor as a potential target. When asked specifically about the false accusations that he was responsible for the bloodshed, Hull trumpeted, "I stood under that infamous charge for months," but every reasonable person, he declared, knew that these were lies. Hull finally had the chance to clear his name and was applauded for his efforts. When the committee released its findings, it exonerated him of any wrongdoing.[17]

Yet even at the end of 1941, these unfounded charges had not seriously damaged Hull's national popularity; in fact, it soared. When Harold Hinton, a prominent newspaper columnist and admirer of the secretary, published the first biography, Welles wrote in a glowing foreword, "Cordell Hull is the least self-seeking man I have ever known." Hull allowed others to take credit for such initiatives as the good neighbor policy, the reciprocal trade program, and the preservation of peace:

> If this is the faith we are fighting for, Cordell Hull is one of its leading apostles. For years no man on earth has labored more diligently or more sincerely to perpetuate that philosophy and to prevent the retrogression to the level of savagery at which the world finds itself today. His name is written high, and will remain high, on the list of those who have kept alight the flame of civilization in the new Dark Ages which have come upon us.[18]

Vice-President Wallace reaffirmed that tribute. Hull, more than anyone, was responsible for improved inter-American relations, along with many other diplomatic successes. From the vice-president's perspective, the secretary was praiseworthy as a leader who was "characterized by fairness, a straight forward manner and simple dignity, qualities which have won for him the sincere respect and admiration even of those who have not always agreed with his views."[19]

Publicly, the president exaggerated Hull's importance; privately, Roosevelt insulted him by questioning his competence. Other critics inside the administration, such as Treasury Secretary Morgenthau, concurred and interfered in foreign affairs, trying to dilute the State Department's powers. Interior Secretary Ickes, another member of the White House inner circle, constantly impugned the competence of Hull and his staff. Hull's reluctance to make decisions particularly irritated Ickes: "I do not doubt Hull's sincerity but the fellow just can't think straight and he is totally lacking in imagination. He makes no move until his hand is forced and then it is too late to be effective."[20] Associate Justice Felix Frankfurter, who frequently spoke with those close to the Oval Office, was so disappointed with the State Department that he initiated a campaign to replace Hull with Dean Acheson, who was then in charge of economic matters. Acheson had originally entered the administration early in the New Deal and was one of the few men whom Roosevelt had personally fired. Acheson now returned to government service, supposedly because Frankfurter had lobbied for his appointment; Acheson would report faithfully to his mentor to make certain that the associate justice's opinions were taken into account in policy decisions.[21]

Even more damning than these voices was the indictment of presidential speech writer Robert Sherwood. According to this insider, who undoubtedly mirrored some of Roosevelt's hostility, Hull looked upon any attack on his department as a personal affront. He crusaded for the good neighbor policy and the reciprocal trade agreements program, but that was all. To get things done, the president turned to those who moved decisively, for Hull was always cautious:

> He was extremely jealous of his reputation as one officer of the Administration who had been guilty of no conspicuous blunders and who had been spared the criticism lavished on all the others, including the President himself. However, in times of desperate emergency when drastic action had to be taken quickly, Roosevelt was bound to become impatient with anyone whose primary concern was the maintenance of a personal record of 'no runs—no hits—no errors.'[22]

Nowhere did the failure to communicate become more flagrant than during the most insignificant diplomatic squabble of the war: the St. Pierre–Miquelon incident. Although most of the attention devoted to French colonies focused on the West Indies, France's oldest and smallest possessions in the Western Hemisphere lay twelve miles off the southern coast of Newfoundland, near the entrance to the Gulf of St. Lawrence. The three tiny islands of St. Pierre, Grande Miquelon, and Petite Miquelon had a population of about 4,400 who relied on fishing to eke out its existence. But the Allies were far more concerned with the islands' strategic location, which made them possible U-boat refueling stations, and with the fishing trawlers that daily went out to sea, which could easily provide information on convoy movements. St. Pierre, in addition, had a powerful radio transmitter that could be used to relay weather reports and other classified information to the enemy.

Both Vichy and the Free French squabbled over ownership of these islands. The current administrator of the islands favored Vichy Premier Henri Philipe Pétain, and his German wife provided additional evidence of Nazi bias. The majority of the residents, on the other hand, seemed to support Charles de Gaulle and his Free French forces. In early 1941 the Free French considered occupying the islands, and that fall the authorities, with the assistance of a visiting Vichy warship, suppressed a revolt.

Two days after Pearl Harbor, Admiral Emily Henri Muselier of the Free French arrived in Newfoundland to consult with the American and Canadian governments about seizing the islands and placing them under the banner of the Free French. Having received the anticipated Allied approval, he fully intended to fulfill his mission, but unfortunately for Muselier, Hull and Roosevelt vetoed his plan for an invasion. When their objections reached de Gaulle, he overruled them, and on his own initiative ordered a military assault.[23]

In the midst of this wartim intrigue, Churchill arrived for his first state visit to Washington on December 22 to discuss Allied military strategy and draft a broader statement of democratic wartime principles. He would remain three weeks as a guest at the White House, turning the second floor into his command headquarters. Upon the completion of their talks, Roosevelt and Churchill released the Declaration of United Nations, which pledged no separate peace and the final defeat of the Axis forces and secretly agreed that Germany would be conquered first and that defeat of the Japanese would be relegated to a secondary priority.[24]

As the Anglo-American discussion were beginning, Admiral Muselier slipped out of Halifax harbor with three corvettes, a submarine, and

360 sailors and marines for the 365-mile journey to St. Pierre. On the following day, he signaled London about his plans. Even at that moment they were not a well-kept secret, for some newspapers had already published rumors of a possible assault. Thanks to a sentry who had retired early, the invaders landed undetected on Christmas Eve and quickly secured the islands without any bloodshed. On Christmas Day, the admiral held a plebiscite that went overwhelmingly for de Gaulle.

Here was the first Allied victory! It was front-page news, along with the tragic surrender of Wake Island. While the public, at least, cheered this tiny triumph, Hull was livid. He feared that the invasion would create the excuse Vichy needed to merge its fleet with that of the Nazis. In an unfortunate choice of words, the usually circumspect secretary at a press conference demanded a withdrawal of the "so-called Free French" soldiers. The United States and Vichy had entered into an agreement under which its American possessions would remain neutral during the war, an understanding this attack had violated. Hull privately asked the British and the Canadians to intercede, but they refused, and de Gaulle's troops stayed in place, much to the secretary's chagrin.[25]

Churchill's and MacKenzie King's denials of support were just the start of Hull's humiliation. A small event had exploded into the headlines, and the secretary's imprudent response had been magnified out of all proportion. Some press commentators relentlessly lampooned him, sarcastically branding him the "so-called secretary of state" of the "so-called State Department"; some even called for his resignation. As the reporting on Hull's unpopular action intensified, he asked for presidential backing, but Roosevelt also rebuffed him. Robert Sherwood regarded the affair as nothing "more than an isolated flea bite." The president treated the matter lightly, while his secretary fumed: "As an elder statesman and a figure of great dignity, Hull had established for himself a position that was almost sacrosanct. It was bewildering as well as infuriating for him to find himself the target of the kind of insults and gibes to which many of his colleagues in the Administration had long since become accustomed."[26]

Roosevelt and Churchill downplayed this episode, but Hull never forgave de Gaulle, for causing his humiliation, or Churchill, who made the situation worse by giving an inflammatory address before the Canadian Parliament on December 30 in which he praised de Gaulle, denounced Vichy, and criticized the State Department. Hull perceived this as yet another example of Churchill's duplicity. Others quickly forgot the incident, but during the first two weeks of 1942, the secretary was the target of a continuous bombardment from the media, and he allowed this minor event to fester into a major defeat.[27]

Hull's diplomatic miscue coincided with his worsening health problems. When MacKenzie King saw him at the end of 1941, he sadly commented that Hull "was very tired and very worn."[28] Greatly fatigued and nervous, he at one point momentarily forgot his new address at the Wardman Park Hotel, and during much of January, he was physically unable to go to work, so that he remained at his apartment much of the time.[29]

Assistant Secretary Long recorded the following in his diary on January 13: "Hull is worried. His status is clouded. He is cleaning out his desk. For several days he has unostentatiously—almost secretly—been getting out, and mostly into wastebaskets, the papers accumulated through years in the drawers of his big desk. He is awfully disappointed—and expecting the worst." Roosevelt, Long continued, refused to support Hull in his struggle against de Gaulle, and this demonstrated "that his relationship to the President has undergone a very definite change for the worse." During Churchill's talks in Washington, the prime minister objected to any statement in favor of Hull's cherished reciprocal trade program, and this devastated the secretary: "His trade agreements—as expressions of his economic philosophy—are the base on which rest his whole foreign activity. Without that base the structure falls. And Churchill has kicked the base out from under—for without England's cooperation the world phase of its operation ceases." As a result of these actions, Hull looked "tired, thin, disheartened and has no present zest for his work. He is awaiting the blow." At any moment the president might replace him.[30]

But Long misjudged the president; Roosevelt would not relieve his most popular cabinet member, who still symbolized stability to many Americans and remained an elder statesman within the Democratic party. However, Hull's physical condition had deteriorated so much that, on January 16, he penciled out a letter of resignation on the grounds that during the first half of 1941, "I was hopelessly overworked and was obliged to take a long rest." Now he had to retire: "It has been a rare privilege to work with you during past years. I pray that you may have the health and strength to keep your great fight against the Axis Countries."[31] But after finishing the draft, he returned it to his desk. He could not leave office during the darkest days of the war; his patriotic duty far outweighed his illnesses and even the humiliation that he had suffered.[32]

Because of the extreme physical strain under which he found himself, Hull was unable to supervise the inter-American response to Pearl Harbor. By December 9, 1941, most Latin American republics had already agreed to call for a conference to discuss the attack and its consequences, and although the majority of the Latin American nations had declared war on or at least broken off diplomatic ties with the Axis, Argentina, Brazil, and Chile remained neutral. With Hull too sick to travel, Welles was the logical choice to send to the conference at Rio de Janeiro.[33] He understood the importance of his mission, and on January 7, 1942, wrote, "With the attack of Japan on the United States and the declarations of war by Germany and Italy the defense of the hemisphere has passed definitely to a stage of action."[34]

Assistant Secretary Long concurred. The Japanese were moving on Manila and had shockingly illustrated the vulnerability of the United States; the Germans were pushing deeper into Russia, and the British were barely surviving. Since these Axis victories gravely damaged the image of the Roosevelt administration, Long believed, "The result is a loss of prestige on our part. The invincibility of the United States is being questioned by the world. The effect of that on the coming Rio Conference may be of the first importance. We *have* to be impressive there."[35]

Welles set out an agenda for the meeting, and just before flying to Rio on January 9, he talked to the president about a strategy for preserving hemispheric solidarity. Welles arrived at the Brazilian capital during a thunderstorm, but even the driving rain did not dampen a hero's welcome. From the airport he was rushed to the Copacabana Palace, while large crowds cheered along the route; Welles immediately saw

President Getulio Vargas, who offered his wholehearted support to the delegate from the United States.[36] Argentine and Chilean views were still clouded, but the under secretary was optimistic: "the general atmosphere is excellent."[37]

When the conference opened on January 15 in the middle of a hot, humid Latin American summer, Welles addressed the first session by recounting the treacherous deeds of the Axis and its goal of world domination. The Western Hemisphere was fighting for survival, and the United States had pledged to assist its Latin American allies in their efforts to defeat the common foe; to demonstrate solidarity, the assembled nations must sever diplomatic bonds with the dictatorships. On the same day, Welles received a telegram from the department reflecting its inflexible position: "In the Department from Secretary Hull down the feeling is in accord on the belief that rather than a compromise formula a breach in unanimity would be preferable. The Argentines must accept this situation or go their own way and in the latter event reliance may be placed upon the overwhelming public feeling in Argentina to supply the corrective."[38] Ever since Argentine Foreign Minister Saavedra Lamas had insulted Hull at the Buenos Aires meeting in 1936, Welles believed, the secretary "had already become almost psychopathic" when dealing with Argentina. Roosevelt knew of this resentment and "occasionally, in the spirit of sheer mischief he sometimes showed, goaded Mr. Hull when the question of Argentina came up."[39]

This rigid stance proved unnecessary during the early stages of the talks, for both the Argentine and Chilean delegates seemed willing to accept an unequivocal pronouncement severing diplomatic relations with the Axis. Welles single-handedly directed the negotiations along the lines of the basic outline formulated in Washington, calling for an immediate rupture, and then relayed the results to the State Department. He thought that he had achieved his goal. On January 21, broadcast journalist Eric Sevareid, in a radio broadcast from Rio de Janeiro, predicted that Argentina and Chile would agree to sign the declaration, but Welles had no comment. For the first time since his arrival, he went to bed early, a very tired but extremely satisfied man. By the next day, the excitement of Sevareid's news flash had begun to evaporate as rumors surfaced that Argentina might renege on its pledge of support. In fact, its president refused to follow his foreign minister's recommendation to sign the declaration. When Welles learned of this reversal, he immediately moved to counteract its harmful effects.[40]

While Welles tried to determine how best to respond to the Argentine rejection, he did not immediately inform Washington of this crisis or his potential options. Hull happened to be listening to an evening radio news broadcast on January 23 at his apartment when a reporter at the conference claimed that Argentina had reversed its course, preventing the severance declaration from being approved and forcing the United States to suffer a terrible diplomatic defeat. Without first confirming with Welles what had actually occurred, Hull exploded. He did not understand that the delegates had merely modified the proposal from one calling for an absolute break in diplomatic ties to a recommendation for severing relations in order to accommodate the Argentine foreign minister.

But in the secretary's eyes, this was the final betrayal. The Japanese envoys had lied to him; he had been accused of helping to precipitate the Pearl Harbor attack; and the Free French had humiliated him over the St. Pierre incident. These events coupled with his worsening physical condition had driven him to the brink of resigning, but he had stayed on as a patriotic duty. Now, barely one week later, Welles had allowed Argentina to dismantle United States policy. The under secretary, before having a chance to defend himself, had been indicted, tried, convicted, and sentenced for disloyalty.

Infuriated by the news reports, Hull placed urgent calls to Berle and Duggan, and once they had joined him at his suite, he phoned to awaken Welles, who had just gone to sleep at midnight after staying awake for forty-eight hours, and tore into him with a profane tongue lashing. Without any introduction or permitting the under secretary an opportunity for explanation, the secretary accused him of undermining the department's position by acting independently and without authority in arriving at this precipitous and unilateral decision. The United States had now lost its leadership position in the Americas as well as internationally. Welles strenuously disagreed, for the president, he claimed, had indeed given him permission to act unilaterally. Hull demanded that Roosevelt confirm this and had the president join the heated conversation. After listening to both arguments, Roosevelt sided with Welles.

Once more the president had rejected his secretary's advice. Hull could not repudiate what his under secretary had done without resigning. Dismissing that alternative, the secretary resolved to force Welles from office.[41] Berle, who was at Hull's apartment, realized that this exchange had done irreparable harm: "For it is obvious that now there is a breach between the Secretary and Sumner which will never be healed—though the Secretary will keep it below hatches to some extent. Life in this Department under those circumstances will be about as difficult as anything I can think of."[42]

Without knowledge of this violent exchange, the delegates approved the compromise formula of "recommending" a break in relations with the Axis on January 26, two days before adjournment. Hull had been wrong in his prediction of doom, for the meeting was extremely successful. Welles succeeded in broadening hemispheric solidarity, and by the end of the gathering nineteen of the twenty-one nations had severed relations with the Axis; they would cooperate with the United States throughout the war.[43]

In terms of personal relations, however, the resulting cost was staggering. Hull had tolerated Welles's close relationship with the president as long as no blatant sign of disloyalty surfaced and because Welles was productive. The explosion over Rio radically changed all that. Hull's declining health and other setbacks had put him in a foul mood, and he was inclined to lash out at someone. The under secretary was available and vulnerable, and the secretary finally had an opportunity to take out the frustrations over Roosevelt's refusal to support him that he had so long repressed. By confronting Welles over the events at Rio, Hull was also lashing out at the White House. The secretary now placed Welles in the same category as Moley and Peek. Both had been untrustworthy and had been forced to resign. The secretary now intended to maintain a perfect score by forcing out his under secretary, but any intrigue leading to his removal would have to wait until Hull's physical condition improved.[44]

From mid-January until early February, the secretary spent most of his time at his apartment waiting for Welles to return to the United States to assume the duties of acting secretary. Almost immediately after Welles returned, Hull went to Miami, accompanied by his wife and his doctor, who personally supervised his care for a week and then returned to his Washington practice, while his patient remained in Florida for almost three months.[45]

Just before Welles took over as acting secretary, Berle commented on February 1 about Hull's dismal appearance and his relationship to Welles. The assistant secretary did not think that the under secretary was disloyal. The real issue was who made foreign policy: "the Rio incident did raise a square question as to who is the real Secretary of State. In cabling the President in defense of his course, Sumner intimated that there had been a major decision of policy which he had agreed on with the President without reporting to Secretary Hull." At least he had no recollection of any conversation. Berle hoped to restore cordial relations between his two superiors, but this proved difficult: "Sumner is really preserving a direct line of power through the White House, irrespective of the Secretary; the Secretary will be satisfied with nothing less than cutting that off. The difficulty is that no single human being could cover all the ground; and the Secretary is slow in making up his mind . . . in situations that call for rapid action. But his judgment is far better than Sumner's. Sumner, on the other hand, will move like a shot in all situations. It is essential that the values of both be preserved."[46]

Berle dreamed the impossible. Hull could no longer tolerate his chief subordinate, who he was now convinced was disloyal. Not only was Welles untrustworthy, but Bullitt was also spreading renewed rumors of the homosexual incident on the train. This combination was ample cause for dismissal. Unfortunately for Hull, no matter how much he resented Welles, he still needed him; yet it was a dependence that the secretary refused to concede.

Roosevelt had been transformed in the public's eyes from Dr. New Deal to Dr. Win the War. This monumental switch in emphasis certainly transcended the feud between Hull and Welles. Although the president himself was in many ways responsible for his secretary's insecurity as well as the under secretary's open access to the White House, Roosevelt never encouraged the two men to improve their relationship. He hated personality disputes in which he was caught in the middle, but time and again it was he himself who created the antagonism. In the dispute between Hull and Welles, Roosevelt certainly had played a major part in causing the breach, and the situation could only deteriorate. While Roosevelt and Welles steadily grew closer, Hull's influence at the White House slipped. At first this proved merely embarrassing; eventually, it became a major point of contention. Hull was now a part-time secretary of state, and Welles had become a marked man.

# CHAPTER 12

# WORKING FOR VICTORY

Hull's collapse went unnoticed as the magnitude of American military losses during 1942 mounted. Not only had the Japanese assault decimated United States armed forces in the Hawaiian islands, but the Rising Sun quickly crushed American resistance in the Philippines as well. In Europe the Wehrmacht was still on the offensive against the Russians and at times appeared on the verge of annihilating them. In North Africa, Field Marshal Erwin Rommel's tanks pushed the British so far into Egypt that they threatened the Suez Canal. Creating further havoc, Hitler unleashed his U-boats within the Atlantic neutrality zone; a relatively small group of experienced submarine captains named this period the "happy time," because they sank almost 400 ships with a loss of over 5,000 lives. In sheer numbers, the loss added up to the worst United States maritime disaster on record.[1]

In the midst of this carnage, Roosevelt rallied his countrymen and exercised a degree of power never seen before or since over the political, military, social, and economic aspects of American life. Comfortable with making complex bureaucratic decisions, he now used the experience he had gained in World War I to ensure that the United States would be victorious in World War II in the quickest time frame and with the fewest casualties. Although the American military in the Pacific had little to celebrate in 1942, Lieutenant Colonel James Doolittle's bold air strike on the Japanese home islands, the triumph at the battle of Midway, and the costly American landing at Guadalcanal that secured the U.S. presence in the Solomons all boosted American morale and demonstrated the vulnerability of the enemy's armed forces. Many had argued that the surprise assault on Pearl Harbor dictated a massing of American forces against the Japanese before turning to Europe, but Roosevelt held firm to the path that he had taken since the rise of Nazi Germany: Hitlerism was the most serious danger, and therefore the United States would stick to a "Europe first" strategy.

Roosevelt confirmed this commitment during a conversation with Canadian Prime Minister MacKenzie King at the end of 1942. As president, he would do whatever was expedient to achieve that goal, and he expected the other members of the administration to emulate him. Rumors of food shortages along with public and military discontent in Germany were spreading, and this growing dissatisfaction suggested that the Third Reich might be overthrown in the near future. To hasten its decline, Roosevelt had to forge an unbreakable alliance with Britain, Russia, and China; once they had crushed the Nazis, the Japanese would quickly succumb.[2]

Although Roosevelt was unrealistic in trying to turn the Chinese into a major power in the Pacific to achieve these objectives, he was much more successful in cementing the Anglo-American alliance by taking Churchill into his confidence and making him a partner in the war effort. The president provided unconditional military assistance to the Soviet Union in order to help it repulse the invader along its enormous front; Roosevelt also tried without success to comply with Stalin's request to open a second front as soon as possible with an invasion across the English Channel. To reduce military pressure on the Russians, the president pressed for a North African assault, successfully landing troops there in early November with relatively little resistance and beginning the campaign to expel the Italian and German armies from that continent.

The president used Harry Hopkins like a junior partner to complete these critical tasks. When necessary, it was he who prodded the War Department into action, shaped the Anglo-American command system, promoted unconditional aid for the Soviets, and helped in determining lend-lease allocations. Never known as a military strategist, Hopkins did recommend General George C. Marshall to lead the invasion of Europe and eventually succeeded in promoting an uneasy partnership between the president and the general. Hopkins also enthusiastically supported the "Europe first" strategy, a prompt cross-channel invasion, and the North African landing. Like the president, Hopkins recognized that United States troops would have to fight and die to defeat the Axis.[3]

These issues consumed most of Roosevelt's attention; other topics became secondary. That reality did not translate well for the Jewish victims of Hitler's terror, for the president never understood the scope of the tragedy that was unfolding in occupied Europe. Jewish questions rarely reached the Oval Office, and when they did, they were quickly and superficially resolved. As for the president's personal views, he was not philo-Semitic, and the prominent Jews who held powerful positions in his administration were really political eunuchs, without independent political bases of their own. That was a major reason why German barbarism against European Jewry was not addressed. Reports of Nazi atrocities against the Jews appalled the president, but the Nazis' sadism also extended to slavs, gypsies, homosexuals, and prisoners of war. To Roosevelt, the Third Reich had to be annihilated; that strategy alone would halt Hitler's reign of terror. Indeed, in Roosevelt's voluminous correspondence with Churchill, neither man ever touched on this subject in any meaningful way. They, as well as the rest of the world, failed to realize that Hitler had made the final solution a matter of policy; few outside of the Third Reich ever imagined that any regime could actually create "death factories."[4]

While Roosevelt paid scant attention to the destruction of European Jewry, he continued to devote some time to good neighbor diplomacy by giving speeches calling for inter-American cooperation, lecturing reporters on the benefits of Latin American friendship, and entertaining a constant progression of rulers from the other American republics throughout the war. The president talked with them, dined with them, and invited them to stay overnight at the White House; then they would be moved over to Blair House to discuss bilateral issues with representatives of the State Department. These displays cost little and strengthened goodwill throughout the Americas.[5]

As central as Hull had become to America's commitment to hemispheric solidarity, he was effectively removed from the conduct of foreign affairs at the start of hostilities. After the bitter exchange over the Rio resolution, some wondered if the secretary and Welles would ever be willing to speak to one another again, let alone cooperate in shaping a united foreign policy. On February 1, Assistant Secretary Berle wrote, "Sumner gets back tomorrow and there is likely to be a considerable amount of trouble."[6] That explosion never took place because by the time Welles returned the secretary had left for Miami without ever confronting his nemesis.[7]

With Hull absent, Welles immediately stepped into his familiar role as acting secretary and established the guidelines for the wartime bureaucracy. Even though very few major personnel changes occurred within the diplomatic corps, more than 2,500 civil servants were employed at the State Department, working Monday through Friday from 9:00 A.M. to 5:30 P.M. and from 9:00 A.M. to 1:00 P.M. on Saturdays. To prevent duplication in this vastly expanding organization, Welles set up his own watchdog committee and also served as the departmental liaison with the armed forces.[8] He paid a high price for this exhausting routine; during a cabinet meeting in early March, Attorney General Francis Biddle noticed that "Welles looked terribly worn, almost like a skeleton, his bones sticking out."[9]

Besides physically running this burgeoning bureaucracy, Welles, following the tone that Roosevelt had implicitly dictated to the State Department, reinforced the president's overall strategy by handling crucial secondary matters. Few, if any, understood to what extent the president relied on the under secretary to carry out these missions and to provide diplomatic counsel for major presidential decisions, for it was he who followed Roosevelt's grand strategy and translated much of it into sound proposals.

Acknowledged as the department's Latin American specialist, Welles understood South American conditions and, during the war years, outlined regional policies. With the exception of Argentina and Chile, every Latin American republic had broken off relations with the Axis in early 1942, and they too would eventually follow their neighbors. The Americas had united as never before and would go even further in forging regional bonds. To accomplish this goal, Welles aligned Brazil with the Allies and sought to neutralize any potential danger from Argentina. He formulated his post-Rio programs so as to isolate the Buenos Aires government so that it could not rely on any Latin American allies to crack the foundations of hemispheric unity. To assure the success of this policy, Welles assisted Chile in easing wartime economic dislocation and concurrently applied mild pressure to its government to sever relations with the Axis. When this subtle persuasion failed to bring forth the desired corrective, the under secretary bluntly warned the Chileans that financial aid would be withheld until diplomatic ties with the enemy had been broken.[10]

When these measures proved ineffective, Welles spoke before a Boston audience on October 8, 1942, to thank most of Latin America for its cooperation. Argentina and Chile were the exceptions. There Axis agents still conducted subversive activities and were responsible for the sinking of Allied shipping. He then declared: "I cannot believe that these two republics will continue long to permit their brothers and neighbors of the Americas, engaged as they are in a life and death struggle to preserve the liberties and the integrity of the New World, to be stabbed in the back by Axis emissaries."[11] This public condemnation of Chile and Argentina created controversy. Some argued that this kind of coercion violated the good neighbor spirit, and others who opposed Welles's leadership saw the address as another example of his unwise decisions. Yet most, including the under secretary's closest hemispheric adviser, Laurence Duggan, applauded this initiative because they saw it as another necessary step to drive the enemy from the Western Hemisphere. Although the Chileans openly protested against this overt pressure, they too understood the message and broke relations three months later.[12]

Along with his long-standing regional interest, the under secretary regularly conferred with the Soviet Ambassador, Maxim Litvinov, who had arrived in the United States at the end of 1941. Welles, like the president, became a leading proponent of lend-lease. He shared Roosevelt's overly optimistic view of American-Soviet cooperation, but also still shared some of the doubts of the department's Russian experts about the value of unconditional assistance to the Russians. By the summer of 1942, Welles had become convinced that the Soviets would repel Nazi aggression and guard against a possible Japanese invasion of Siberia. What worried him was the possibility that Stalin was contemplating signing another separate peace treaty with Hitler, as the Russians had done in 1939.[13]

Welles also helped to shape United States policy toward Vichy. When criticism of American collaboration with the Pétain government erupted, the attacks sometimes mistakenly focused on the role of the State Department. In reality, the president dictated the general guidelines, but he implied through his press conferences that real blame rested with the diplomatic corps. Despite this unfair impression, the under secretary led the fight for Roosevelt's policies, reflected the administration's hope of keeping Vichy as neutral as possible, and concurrently made certain that French possessions in the Caribbean stayed out of Nazi control.[14]

Welles also emerged as the most sympathetic administration figure in hearing complaints from American Jews. From the summer of 1940 through 1941, the under secretary talked with and wrote to Jewish leaders in the United States about such nebulous proposals as an inter-American Jewish conference and a Jewish military unit to assist the British in the Near East. However, none of these issues was carefully examined, and nothing concrete was ever accomplished.[15]

Despite Welles's hectic schedule after Pearl Harbor, a variety of Jewish leaders were ushered into his office to offer suggestions and voice their concerns. He also pressured the British to end restrictions on immigration to Palestine and to ease their opposition to an independent Zionist state. After Whitehall objected to these proposals, Welles blamed British intransigence for the failure to create a Jewish homeland.[16]

Yet these squabbles seemed insignificant when news of the wholesale murder of thousands of Jews began filtering back to the State Department. In May 1942, the Jewish underground in Warsaw reported that seven hundred thousand Poles had been exterminated, but when the British, Poles, and Jews held a press conference several months later to confirm the story, it received only marginal press coverage. Since many doubted the veracity of these accusations, the World Jewish Conference (WJC), which had established its center of operations and intelligence-gathering efforts in Switzerland, set out to prove that the allegations were true. Gerhard Riegner, representing the WJC, in Geneva, confirmed them and notified WJC president Rabbi Stephen Wise in late August. Wise, in turn, sent this information to Welles on September 2 and asked him to investigate on his own.[17] Welles did so, and on November 24 he met with Wise to acknowledge that European Jews were indeed being systematically murdered. The under secretary then declared, "For reasons that you will understand, I cannot give these [facts] to the press, but there is no reason why you should not. It might even help if you did." Wise accepted that advice and publicized the atrocities, but the Allies did not respond. The slaughter of Jews was lost in the midst of enormous military casualties.[18]

Welles did undertake one new project that consumed an inordinate amount of his time: the evolution of a new League of Nations. During the fall of 1939, the State Department, under his guidance, formed a committee to study prospects for reestablishing a peaceful world. Welles did not concentrate on this topic until after the Nazis had attacked the Soviet Union. On July 22, 1941, for example, he began to highlight the subject by informing an audience that, after the fighting had ceased, any future world would require security. The League of Nations had failed because it had been unable to exercise any coercive authority when seeking solutions to problems arising among warring nations. A global association had to be built to resolve conflicts, abolish offensive and limit defensive weapons, and monitor compliance.[19]

On November 11, 1941, standing in front of Woodrow Wilson's tomb, the under secretary continued his advocacy, stressing that Wilson's vision had been for the United States to play a major international role after World War I. Americans had rejected this advice, and as a consequence the Axis powers had emerged to spread their odious political ideologies around the world through conquest. Once these doctrines were repudiated, the United States would be forced to assume a greater international commitment to prevent any repetition of these events. In anticipation of that day, Welles appointed the Advisory Committee on Postwar Foreign Policy to plan for a new world organization. Leo Pasvolsky, an economist who had served as a special assistant to the secretary since 1936, would play a leading role researching solutions to postwar problems. The committee gradually mushroomed to forty-eight members, eleven from the State Department and the remainder from

Congress and other public and governmental agencies. A multitude of issues, such as alternatives to the League, territorial boundaries, postwar security, and economic transition, eventually came under discussion.[20]

While exploring these topics, Welles continued to offer other suggestions, such as one on May 30, 1942, recommending a United Nations police force to keep order and provide a permanent system of global security. This body could also become the foundation for an international association to preserve peace and deal with postwar reconstruction. To allay Latin American anxieties over the elimination of the inter-American regional system in favor of a universal one, Welles pledged,

> I cannot believe the peoples of the United States and of the Western Hemisphere will ever relinquish the inter-American system they have built up. Based as it is on sovereign equality, on liberty, on peace, and on joint resistance to aggression, it constitutes the only example in the world today of a regional federation of free and independent peoples. It lightens the darkness of our anarchic world. It should constitute a cornerstone in the world structure of the future.

Addressing a United Nations rally in Baltimore in the middle of June, Welles further claimed that the inter-American system, as well as the rest of the Allies, would embrace a postwar organization before the end of hostilities to provide a bridge for the transition from war to peace.[21]

These speeches, according to Welles, served to educate the American people. Writing to poet Archibald MacLeish on August 13, the under secretary highlighted this point: "I am only an amateur politician and therefor[e] I may be wrong. But if one can judge by the temper of the American people during the Civil War, they fight better when they know for what they are fighting and when that 'common hope' is responsive to their own aspirations and to their own idealism, and when they believe that its realization will make for the security of their country, their children and their faith."[22]

The under secretary gave two more major speeches in November and December about the eventual Allied victory and potential postwar problems. Welles rhetorically asked what would have happened if Wilson had joined the League. Having rejected that course of action, Americans were now paying for that costly blunder, and those who opposed the League again were fighting to prevent any postwar international cooperation. The United States was coordinating its programs with many nations to fight the war; after its end, the United States should certainly have the sense to work with its allies to preserve peace by ensuring against any future catastrophe.[23]

Arthur Sweetser, a prominent international advocate for a global association, applauded Welles's efforts and reminded him of the necessity for a universal body that would encourage regional cooperation to assist the world community in stopping starvation, controlling the production of armaments, and providing equality of economic opportunity. Sweetser had carefully listened to Welles's speeches as well as those of other administration spokesmen, and he worried about the wide divergence of opinions within the government. He feared that this lack of clarity could create problems in the formation of a new global association. When he saw Welles toward the end of 1942, they discussed this lack of consensus, and Welles promised to talk with Roosevelt and Hull about precise guidelines and the need for greater publicity.[24]

Welles did not explain that the president's purposeful silence was partially based on the humiliating defeat that the Cox-Roosevelt ticket had suffered in the election of 1920 by supporting the League issue. The president had also witnessed the Senate's rejection of the World Court during his first term and the continuing opposition to international collaboration almost up to the moment of the United States' entrance into the war. The president, according to the under secretary, was moving toward the concept of another global organization and had ordered Welles to speak out on these postwar topics in order to educate the public instead of making the gross miscalculation that Wilson had made when he unilaterally negotiated the League of Nations and came home with an unwanted fait accompli.[25] There were, however, times when Roosevelt wished that Welles would pay less attention to the League issue, and in late November he expressed his irritation that Berle and the under secretary "have been acting as impresarios and have been talking too much post-war stuff."[26]

Such mild criticism did not detract from Welles's high marks for his overall performance. Norman Davis, a friend to both Hull and Welles,

declared that "the State Department is run better than any other department of the government." The diplomatic corps faced criticism for its
inability to coordinate foreign affairs, but it was the president who had
caused a great many of these troubles by acting independently and not
consulting or even reporting to the State Department.[27] Former ambassador to Moscow Joseph Davies recorded in his diary that spring, "I am
always impressed with Welles' ability and high-mindedness. He is always
tolerant and fair." During the darkest days of the war, Welles, as the
acting head of the State Department, had effectively placed it in a state of
wartime readiness.[28]

Despite such accolades, Welles could not forget how enraged Hull
had been over the events at the Rio conference. The two men had since
had time to compose themselves, but Welles was well aware of how the
secretary had forced Raymond Moley and George Peek to resign. The
under secretary had no doubt that his job, like those of the earlier
dissenters, was in jeopardy. Aware of his precarious position, he nevertheless relegated his personal insecurities to a secondary place while
concentrating on the struggle against the Axis.[29]

Rumors of Hull's impending resignation occasionally surfaced while
he was resting in Florida. When the media speculated in late February
about Hull's departure, Roosevelt told reporters that the story was
ridiculous; the secretary was simply taking a well-deserved rest because
of illness. As far as the president was concerned, "There is no thought
about his being ousted from the Cabinet, or resigning, or anything
else."[30] Berle also learned that Associate Justice Felix Frankfurter was
continually lobbying to place Dean Acheson in the secretaryship, but
that intrigue would fail because there was no semblance of truth to the
gossip.[31]

The secretary admitted that he "had been very tired and was suffering from nerve fatigue." To cure it, he and his wife went to Miami for "a
complete rest."[32] He had shown remarkable improvement, but the un-
favorable gossip still disturbed Mrs. Hull.[33] Although her husband was
gradually improving, she wrote a friend, "I dont [sic] think any one
realizes the terrible condition Cordell was in when we left Washington
and in fact some time before. He frightened me to death, and it actually
turned my hair white. Never have I seen one's nerves affected so

strangely. He had a narrow escape." She had harsh words for those White House advisers who ridiculed her husband: "These 'squirts' in the 'New Deal' would like to drive him out. . . . I am so afraid Cordell will over do when he gets home if he continues on in his position." While she longed for the tranquility of her husband's retirement, he slowly began to show marked improvement with no intention of quitting.[34]

Hull's deteriorating physical condition never affected his popularity; in fact, Farley still attributed the smooth running of the State Department to Hull's leadership and believed that the secretary was the only government official who had the confidence of the American people. Fellow Tennesseean and roving ambassador Norman Davis wrote, "Hull is a real statesman and a genuine and unselfish patriot. He is one of the wisest and finest men I know." Vice-President Wallace concurred and hoped for the secretary's prompt return.[35]

Isaiah Berlin, a British diplomat, who had gained a prominent place in the capital's social circles with his brilliance and wit, agreed. According to him, Roosevelt had contributed to the secretary's standing by continually praising him in public, and that only enhanced his carefully nurtured image. Now Berlin thought that the secretary's position was unique in American society:

> Hull is held both by country and by press in higher respect than any other Cabinet officer or member of Congress. He is to the average American the most distinguished living embodiment of traditional American virtues and his prestige and influence derive not merely from his office but from conviction which he inspires in a large section of United States electorate that it is his wise and moderating influence alone which acts as a brake upon impulsive extravagances of the New Deal. His words are consequently listened to with a respect and attention almost as great as that accorded to the President.[36]

After an almost three-month leave, Hull returned to Washington on April 20 well rested; to prevent overexertion, his doctor put a stop to the informal Sunday meetings of the secretary's advisers and reduced his social obligations. Yet even with these limitations, the secretary tried to reassert his control over foreign affairs by responding to the challenges from those who held powerful positions outside the State Department.

For example, in March, while he was away, Vice-President Wallace had gone to the White House to insist that the Board of Economic Warfare (BEW), which he chaired, be given permission to make foreign economic decisions without prior State Department approval. Welles argued against this, but Roosevelt overruled him and let the BEW act independently.[37]

Whereas Welles did not have the political clout to countermand Wallace's actions, Hull had a national following, second only to the president's. He went to Roosevelt and renewed objections to the BEW functioning outside diplomatic guidelines. Wallace again complained about undue diplomatic constraints, but Hull held firm, and Roosevelt reversed himself, ordering Wallace to submit his plans to the State Department.[38] After the vice-president lost this bureaucratic struggle, Farley asked the secretary how he had accomplished this feat. Hull replied, "I used old fashioned methods. I gave him plenty of rope."[39] That was his style. Sooner or later his enemy would err; the time to strike was at that moment when his antagonist was most vulnerable.

The vice-president also stepped enthusiastically back into the international arena by endorsing Welles's call for a new world organization and arguing for a lasting peace based on worldwide economic cooperation. The United States, he reasoned, could only prosper through universal collaboration achieved by acting collectively against aggressors.[40]

The vice-president's entry into this same arena bothered Hull, but Wallace was a mere annoyance compared to Treasury Secretary Morgenthau. Years later, Hull recalled, "Morgenthau often interfered in foreign affairs, and sometimes took steps directly at variance with those of the State Department. Since there was frequently a connection between foreign and financial affairs, he had in his hands monetary weapons which he brandished in the foreign field from time to time, often without consulting the State Department."[41]

During the time that Hull was absent, the treasury secretary, for instance, successfully lobbied the president to freeze Argentine assets in the United States. When Hull returned, he objected to this form of economic coercion because it ran contrary to his view of hemispheric solidarity. He also could have added that he resented any Treasury Department interference. Roosevelt was well aware of Hull's distrust of Morgenthau, and he bowed to the secretary of state in this case, for he would not condone fighting within his cabinet over such a relatively trivial matter. The president told Morgenthau on May 14 that he could study Nazi subversion in Argentina and throughout the Americas, but could not impose any economic restrictions on the Buenos Aires government.[42]

But this mild rebuke did not lessen Morgenthau's concern over espionage in South America or reduce his influence. On the following day, the president explained to his friend that he was carefully monitoring the situation; he also provided a perceptive glimpse inside his own character: "You know I am a juggler, and I never let my right hand know what my left hand does. . . . I may have one policy for Europe and one diametrically opposite for North and South America. I may be entirely inconsistent, and furthermore I am perfectly willing to mislead and tell untruths if it will help win the war."[43]

In many ways Roosevelt indeed performed like a juggler, and the cases of the BEW and the freezing of Argentine funds demonstrated how carefully Roosevelt manipulated Morgenthau and Wallace in particular. They could act up to a point, but only until Hull vigorously asserted supremacy on behalf of his department. Hull had presented an ultimatum to the president as a last resort, and when Roosevelt knew that Hull would not be pushed any further, he relented. The president did not follow the same course in the matter of military strategy; from that arena, the secretary of state was almost completely eliminated.

Hull tried to regain some initiative as the chief administration spokesman on foreign affairs by preparing his own statement on an international organization. This proved frustrating, since Welles and Wallace had already brought the subject of a postwar international organization into the global spotlight. They had talked about saving the world by policing the globe and caring for its inhabitants. These goals, according to the cautious secretary, were unrealistic and impractical; yet Hull needed to articulate a dramatic alternative to this view on the postwar world.[44]

Instead, on July 23, he delivered a carefully worded, lackluster address to a nationwide audience, trying to capture the majority's backing and to offend as few as possible. Once the Allies proved victorious, they should supervise the Axis governments until their pacific intentions were documented. To provide an orderly enforcement of law, an international court of justice would also be necessary. Also included was yet another plea for his reciprocal trade program.[45] Senator Harry S Truman, Democrat of Missouri, wrote his wife Bess, "Listened to old man Hull on the radio and he made a good speech too but sounded as if he was about to lose his upper plate every once in a while."[46]

Behind this speech was Hull's fear that the Democrats would suffer a fate similar to Wilson's if the party acted imprudently. The secretary, however, was too pessimistic. He had not accurately gauged by how much public opinion had changed, for by the summer of 1942, almost three-fourths of those surveyed favored the United States' joining a world organization after the war.[47]

Sweetser, who interviewed the secretary two weeks after the address, came away with a clear understanding of what Hull really believed in the privacy of his office, where he had candidly expressed his views on the establishment of a world organization. Hull recalled his defeat in 1920, when voters had turned against the League, the Democratic party, and him; that bitter experience still lingered in his mind, and for that reason he was unreceptive to the concept of any global association. Furthermore, he was disillusioned about any possibilities for creating such an international body, believing that, in all likelihood, the administration would be swept out of power in the next general election. Once the war ended, the secretary predicted that the American people would revert to the same complacency that had prevailed after World War I, and if Roosevelt pushed too hard for postwar cooperation the Democratic party would be rejected at the polls. Sweetser concluded dejectedly, "He felt that the only way was to go very gradually and cautiously and not risk another debacle and disillusionment." The secretary further was "very cautious, even discouraging, regarding the future, notably as regards post-war reaction, development of the United Nations."[48] For more than a year after this discussion, Hull avoided any discussions of specific postwar matters and resented anyone in the administration who encouraged a future League.[49]

This glaring neglect did not trouble Hull, who began reminiscing about and memorializing his accomplishments during an interview with the journalist Louis Fisher in the late summer of 1942. The secretary told his guest that he had championed independence movements and the recognition of new governments. Hull erroneously recalled favoring Russian recognition and the adoption of good neighbor diplomacy in 1933; he accurately remembered working to keep peace with the Japanese until the very last moment. After the Allied occupation of North Africa, Hull spoke with MacKenzie King and argued that, as secretary, he had shaped the best possible policy in regard to the Vichy government, and that by dealing with French collaborators, he had saved American lives and worked out a plan to keep the French fleet out of the hands of the Germans. He blamed the British for supporting de Gaulle, who had damaged the American diplomatic effort, and in this situation he vastly overestimated his own impact.[50]

The American public was generally uninformed about the struggle within the French factions over control of North Africa. Instead, Americans riveted their attention on a far more spectacular event at the start of 1943. Roosevelt, flying for the first time since he had traveled to the Democratic convention in 1932, secretly boarded a plane to meet Churchill at Casablanca. The president was the first chief executive to fly, the first to leave the country in wartime, and the first since Abraham Lincoln to visit an active combat area. Such a dramatic opportunity undoubtedly appealed to him. Roosevelt and Churchill used this occasion to discuss the invasion of Sicily. Once it was conquered, Anglo-American troops would force Italy to surrender while preparing for the main cross-channel operation. The prime minister argued in favor of postponing the French landings until 1944, but the president held firm for an earlier date because he did not want the Mediterranean fighting to interfere with the establishment of the second front.[51]

At the last press conference of their meeting, Roosevelt surprised Churchill by declaring that the Axis would have to accept unconditional surrender. The president believed that this measure would forever end any claim of betrayal. Germans had argued during the peace negotiations in the final days of World War I that they really had not lost the war, and the president wanted to avoid use of a similar tactic by the Nazis. Roosevelt had been considering this idea since the spring, and he reaffirmed the concept several months later for two reasons: he admired General Ulysses S. Grant, who had demanded unconditional surrender from General Robert E. Lee, and he saw a parallel between depriving the South of the ability to wage war and doing so with the Third Reich.[52]

After returning to the White House, Roosevelt actively began to plan for the postwar world. When British Foreign Secretary Anthony Eden came to the United States in mid-March, the president talked about a peacekeeping committee to be composed of the United States, Great Britain, Russia, and China. These four powers would assure the peace, and a general assembly would arbitrate international disputes. By the next month, Roosevelt was confident enough in the public mood to encourage further debate and to share some of his thoughts with the columnist Forrest Davis in an interview published by the *Saturday Evening Post.* Davis reported that Roosevelt favored global cooperation based on the inter-American model because it had worked so successfully. Of course, the president had his concerns, the most pivotal of which was whether Stalin would cooperate.[53]

In order to assure Soviet cooperation, the president asked Ambassador Litvinov on May 5 to arrange a meeting with Stalin in late July. He assured the ambassador that neither the Americans nor the British would defend Polish interests; that a committee meeting in London would discuss unresolved issues; and that France should not be one of the four great powers. When the new Soviet Ambassador, Andrei Gromyko, saw Roosevelt at the end of July, the president reaffirmed his desire to meet with Stalin to exchange views. Roosevelt also believed that as soon as the Allies landed in Italy, that nation would quickly surrender, and he had sent Churchill a message about inviting the Soviets to participate in discussions of the Italian situation.[54]

While the president concentrated on the major war issues, in early 1943 Welles continued to focus on postwar concerns, wanting them addressed promptly. The United States' error in judgment in refusing to join the League of Nations could not be repeated, for the Allies had to band together to structure an enduring peace. At present the American republics had developed a viable regional association, and if the Americas could solve their hemispheric problems, the rest of the world should follow this successful model. This was the path, according to Welles, that would turn military victory into a lasting peace.[55]

In late May, Churchill invited Welles, Wallace, Stimson, Ickes, and Senator Thomas Connally to the British embassy for lunch to discuss an international association that would be directed by a supreme world council made up of the United States, Great Britain, and the Soviet Union. Three subordinate regional councils would include the nations of Europe, the Americas, and the Pacific. Welles thought that the United States would follow those general guidelines, but he also wanted to include China at the upper level, and he suggested that all other nations should participate at the regional level. At the end of the month, Welles delivered an address at Southern Negro College in Durham, North Carolina, calling for a halt to aggression, disarmament, a world court, freer trade, and an end to racial and religious persecution in the new global order. By the start of July, Welles had completed his blueprint for a new world organization. During a transition period, the four major world powers would act to preserve peace. The new international body would be divided on a regional basis, with the United States, Great Britain, China, and Russia each supervising its own region. If any regional group could not resolve a particular problem, it would come before an executive body with the power to take military action.[56]

Besides looking into the postwar future, Welles was concerned with the shifting battlefronts. In early 1943, he sat in his office and talked to Louis Fisher, occasionally taking a cigarette from the silver cigarette case in his breast pocket. The under secretary predicted that Roosevelt would lead the Allies to a military victory and that his charisma would guarantee domestic approval. The British, according to Welles, concentrated on Europe because of the constant fear that the Russians and the Germans would sign a separate peace. In East Asia, the Japanese were making significant concessions to their Chinese puppets, while the nationalist government of Chiang Kai-shek was in disarray.[57]

As for Soviet affairs, Welles worked diligently to supply the Russians with lend-lease aid, and he also tried to resolve territorial questions and to promote the postwar international organization. He also followed the president's dictate that the United States must establish a sound, friendly working relationship with the Soviet Union, and he encouraged a Roosevelt-Stalin meeting. Before returning to Moscow that spring, Ambassa-

dor Litvinov met with Welles to say good-bye and admit that he had lost
Stalin's confidence. All recommendations from the embassy were being
dismissed, and Litvinov was returning to Moscow to convince Stalin that
he must commit his administration to closer ties with the United States.
But Litvinov was pessimistic about his chances for success and assumed
that he would be replaced. Furthermore, he was not optimistic about
prospects for a meeting between the two leaders because Stalin would
not be willing to leave Moscow long enough to travel to a location
convenient for both men.[58]

Litvinov provided a detailed and fascinating perspective on the
United States diplomatic landscape for his Soviet superiors in early June,
warning them that the American public was ignorant about the Russian
people and was disconcerted with the Soviet government because it had
refused to discuss postwar problems. Such attitudes only served to
isolate the Soviet Union and forge stronger Anglo-American bonds. To
counteract this momentum, Litvinov wanted to mount a public relations
campaign, establish a permanent Soviet-American commission to discuss
mutual problems, and become actively involved in postwar discussions
and debate.

Litvinov had difficulty analyzing American policy in detail, but he
attempted to outline the general trends. Between the wars, the United
States had dominated Latin America through the Monroe Doctrine, had
had hazy relations with Europe, and had opposed Japanese expansion in
China. The nation had also exhibited powerful isolationist sentiment,
and because this feeling was so pervasive, Roosevelt had made many
concessions to its followers. Nazi advances in Poland and the collapse of
France had allowed him to shift toward internationalism, and after the
Pearl Harbor attack the isolationists had wanted to conquer Japan; to
placate them, the president had sent a considerable military detachment
to East Asia. Even with this large troop allocation, Roosevelt had followed a "Europe first" strategy. He had wanted to open up the second
front in Europe as early as possible, but strategic plans were made in
London, and Churchill had dissuaded Roosevelt from this strategy
owing to the insurmountable transportation problems of crossing the
English Channel. Instead the president had decided to invade North
Africa as a way of bringing American troops into the fighting. The

Russian ambassador did not think that the Americans were stalling, but that the isolationists were working for an early peace even if it damaged British and Russian interests. To prevent such an occurrence, his government would immediately have to exert enormous pressure to open the second front.

As for the American leadership, Litvinov did not understand Anglo-American motives and was not privy to British and American discussions. Roosevelt, with support from Morgenthau, Ickes, and Coordinator of Inter-American Affairs Nelson Rockefeller, made most policy decisions, including the call for the unconditional surrender of the Axis, strengthening bonds with China to keep it in the war, and playing an active part in the formation of a peaceful postwar world. As for the role of the State Department, according to Litvinov, Hull was old and only connected to the White House through the Democratic party. His assistants acted independently because of their personal wealth, and they often haggled among themselves. Berle, for one, maintained ties with the most reactionary European political emigrés through the representatives of the exiled governments, much to Litvinov's chagrin.

Even though American motives were difficult to discern, Roosevelt was more receptive to Soviet-American understanding than any other influential American, but Litvinov warned that the president's attitude had recently changed for the worse because he was upset and disappointed by the Soviet refusal to discuss current and postwar problems. He would not oppose Stalin's objectives in the Baltic and Poland if they did not hurt his reelection efforts, nor would he drop out of the war. But if an isolationist won the 1944 election, such an exit was possible.[59]

Although Litvinov's call for closer bilateral ties met with resistance in both countries, the under secretary faced no opposition to the administration's unequivocal commitment to hemispheric solidarity. He still directed bilateral relations with each American republic. When Latin American leaders visited the United States, it was he who arranged for them to met the president, and after that formality, he also handled the substantive talks. When a revolt in Buenos Aires toppled the Argentine government on June 4, 1943, the under secretary did not interrupt diplomatic relations, for he hoped that the new rulers would break relations with the Axis. This did not occur, but Argentina's internal upheavals did not disrupt inter-American solidarity. Welles had constructed an alliance that served the Allies well throughout the crucial period of the war, and one obstinate nation could not dismantle it.[60]

Welles also continued to supervise the U.S. visa policy that had reduced immigration to American shores to a trickle. When the British restricted refugee resettlement in Palestine, the State Department concurred. Both Allies echoed similar sentiments: the quicker the Nazis were defeated, the faster Jewish suffering would end. Anglo-American representatives met in Bermuda in the spring of 1943 to discuss the plight of the refugees, and at the conclusion of their meeting gave the false impression that the Allied governments were already doing everything possible to aid the Jewish exodus from Axis-controlled territories. This reassurance quickly evaporated as reports of atrocities increased and the State Department demonstrated a singular lack of compassion.[61]

As for Hull, he once again shepherded the renewal of the Reciprocal Trade Agreements Act through Congress. In many ways, this was a symbolic gesture in the middle of the war, but the secretary was looking toward future peaceful international commerce. After some heated debate, the legislation passed in June, and once again the cherished principle of reciprocity had been reaffirmed. Otherwise, he spoke, as always, in generalities. When Litvinov visited him in early May, the secretary called for Soviet-American cooperation, but he never talked about specific issues like the structure of a postwar international organization. When he saw Gromyko in mid-July, Hull invited the new ambassador to visit whenever he wished, but he did not mention any definite agenda.[62]

From the United States' entrance into the war until the summer of 1943, the Democratic administration mobilized its resources to defeat the Axis. The president controlled military strategy and those foreign policy objectives that directly influenced the battlefronts; he depended primarily on Hopkins to assist the White House in these crucial matters. Welles provided additional support, especially in his bilateral negotiations with the Russian ambassador. However, the under secretary played a much more critical role in running the State Department bureaucracy, handling secondary matters such as making certain that Latin American governments believed that hemispheric solidarity remained an administration priority, and working for a postwar international organization.

Hull, for his part, served as a positive image of America's commitment to a democratic world and as the administration's spokesman for lower tariff barriers after the war. Each had his own specific areas of interest, and together the trio charged with shaping American foreign affairs laid the essential foundation for defeating the Axis.

# CHAPTER 13

## RUINING WELLES

WHILE ROOSEVELT DROVE TO mobilize his countrymen to defeat the Axis, Hull had emerged as a part-time secretary of state, excluded from the war councils, brushed aside by the White House, and disgruntled over his lack of control within his own department. But he seemed oblivious to the fact that his political decline was attributable to his worsening physical condition. The secretary considered any taint on the foreign service to be a personal affront that had to be repelled, and in order to maintain some semblance of control he was ready to defend his department from incursions by Henry Morgenthau, Henry Wallace, Harry Hopkins, or any other intruder.

Hull, furthermore, never totally accepted Roosevelt's thrust because of the rage he had aimed at Welles. Instead, the secretary launched a concerted attack against his chief assistant on three grounds: first, he was a homosexual and therefore an embarrassment (or worse) to the State Department; second, he acted irresponsibly in making foreign policy decisions; and third, he had proven disloyal. Upon returning to his office in late April 1942, Hull confided to his friend Breckinridge Long private discussions that he had had with Roosevelt and Welles about the homo-sexuality charges. The discussions reassured Hull, causing him to ques-tion the truthfulness of the allegations—but he was ready to make contingency plans just in case.[1]

Toward the end of June, Hull met with Welles concerning the consid-erable attention that the under secretary had drawn to his postwar planning speeches. Roosevelt, according to Welles, had encouraged members of the administration to make postwar policy statements as trial balloons in order to gauge the public's reaction. Welles asserted that he was not charting any new policy courses, but that he would submit his speeches to Hull for advance review, if he so desired. The secretary also objected to Welles's depiction of the United States as eventually policing the world and caring for its people; those concepts ran contrary to the secretary's practical approach of solving current problems and not peer-ing too far into the future.[2] Assistant Secretary Berle thought that even though Welles had made some excellent points, it should have been Roosevelt or Hull who made them. But they had not, and as a conse-quence, "there is . . . an increase in tension between Mr. Hull and Sumner. I don't know what the end of all this will be; it was forecast at the Rio Conference."[3]

Long, too, was troubled, for Hull was "irritated and nervous—almost agitated. Said he could no longer trust Welles—he was laying plans for himself, was making speeches without approval and with an illusory consent 'weasled' . . . out of the White House." The secretary was unfamiliar with many departmental procedures and decided to handle ambassadorial discussions, a function that nominally fell under Welles's supervision. He was also suspicious and angry that others, such as Wallace, were trying to usurp his duties: "It is an odd humor for him to be in. He is nervously tired and lacks something of his fire and perspi-cacity—though he never was decisive. Tenacious to an idea—yes—but very, very awfully slow at decision."[4]

Bullitt added to the friction. At the time of the Rio conference, he had been a special presidential emissary to the Near East and had not returned to New York until the end of January 1942, too late to commis-erate with Hull over Welles's alleged transgressions at Rio, for the secretary had already left for Miami. Although Bullitt did not have a chance to confer with Hull, the envoy did have an opportunity to tell Harold Ickes about Welles's disgraceful performance. The secretary of the interior had already heard Bullitt's criticism of Welles's diplomatic gaffes and his homosexuality. As a result, Ickes perceived that Roosevelt was driving the former ambassador out of the government because of his erratic behavior and his attacks on Welles.[5]

With no new assignment from the White House into which to channel his positive energies, Bullitt openly campaigned to remove Welles and his followers from office. When the ambassador saw the vice-president, for example, Bullitt bitterly explained that he had had to move his offices out of the State Department because Berle had supposedly photostated some private correspondence and refused to destroy it. When Bullitt had demanded Hull's intervention, the secretary had admitted that he had no control over Welles's or Berle's actions, and that was when Bullitt had left. He also had spoken with Hull and his wife, who, according to the ambassador, declared that "Welles was worse than a murderer" because of his homosexual conduct. Bullitt deplored this: "the President was weak in not firing Welles at once."[6] When these stories filtered back to the Oval Office, Roosevelt, on April 8, decided to limit the damage by offering Bullitt another overseas mission to the Near East, but he declined in favor of a specific job with a definite purpose. The president promised to consider this request, but nothing concrete ever came of it.[7]

While anxiously hoping for a presidential appointment, Bullitt intensified his attacks on Welles by using social functions as forums. During trips to the capital, the former ambassador shared the quaint Georgetown house of his closest adviser, Carmel Offie, himself a homosexual, who had assisted Bullitt since 1934.[8] At a small dinner party given on May 20 for Vice-President Wallace, Attorney General Francis Biddle, and their wives, Offie began telling anecdotes. One involved the rise of Batista in Cuba and a request by the admiral commanding U.S. naval forces that Welles recognize the Cuban military ruler. The ambassador stood erect, and with great pomposity responded in his deep, pontifical voice: "I will not shake hands with that nigger." When Offie vividly described Welles's extreme distaste at shaking hands with a "nigger," Wallace glanced at Bullitt, remembering his stories of the under secretary's sexual proclivities toward male Negroes, and found him laughing hilariously.

Another incident that the gathering found amusing was Welles's visit to Bullitt at the American embassy in Paris just before the Munich conference. While they were talking, Offie interrupted to see if they wanted more Scotch and soda—which both men were freely imbibing—at which point he overheard Welles tell Bullitt, "I have always admired you. You are the most distinguished member of our career service. I trust that you will do me the honor of calling me Sumner and that I may have the privilege of calling you Bill."

Biddle mentioned that Welles had recently talked to him about possible appointees to a committee, and that the attorney general had suggested, "Why I think Bill would be excellent on that committee." Welles angrily declared that he would not consider Bullitt for any post because of the scurrilous rumors that he was spreading.[9]

Although this kind of occasion gave Bullitt an opportunity to smear his enemy, the episode also demonstrated his greatest liability: he talked too much, too indiscreetly, and to an extreme. His poor taste was a mild embarrassment. Alone he was annoying, even troublesome. But when Hull decided to supply the needed punch, he called on Bullitt for the knockout combination that would ultimately interfere with the administration's successful prosecution of the war effort.

Bullitt knew that the president disapproved of these attacks, but the ambassador somehow clung to the expectation that he would receive a major executive appointment. Writing the president on June 13, Bullitt began to realize that he had fallen from grace: "I do not care about anything except helping to beat Hitler and the Japanese. If there is anything I can do with you or for you, I want to do it. If there is nothing, I must try to serve in other ways."[10] Nine days later, Secretary of the Navy Frank Knox made him a special assistant secretary to the navy and sent him to England to work on the North African invasion. For the remainder of the summer, Bullitt dealt with vital military issues rather than fomenting dissension inside the State Department, for he was too far removed to plot against Welles.[11]

However, Bullitt's departure did not end Welles's troubles. By late summer, Hull had linked Welles's perceived disloyalty to the gossip about his homosexuality. The secretary mentioned this delicate situation to Long in July, and by the fall, it had crescendoed. Returning from a cabinet meeting on September 11, Hull confided to Long that he had investigated the stories about Welles's alleged homosexual conduct, and that although he had no documentary proof, he now believed the rumors.

Long, for his part, had "too much confidence" in Welles to accept the gossip; in addition, he remembered how similar unfounded charges against Senator David Walsh, Democrat of Massachusetts, who chaired the Naval Affairs Committee, had almost destroyed him. In May the press had reported that New York City detectives and naval intelligence officers had raided a Brooklyn brothel for homosexuals that was reputed to be a haven for Nazi spies. They had learned from the manager that Walsh was an occasional customer and that he had met with a known German agent there several times. Roosevelt had no sympathy for homosexuals in general and Walsh in particular: if the senator were guilty, he should commit suicide. Without knowing that J. Edgar Hoover had had the brothel under surveillance for months, Roosevelt ordered a full FBI investigation. After a lengthy interrogation, the manager recanted his identification, and FBI agents later located another suspect who not only matched the senator's description but also had been at the brothel on the dates in question. Walsh was exonerated, but not before Hoover had accumulated an eighty-five-page "Official and Confidential" file containing other derogatory material on the senator.[12]

Hull was afraid that the press might publish a story about Welles that might stain the State Department's reputation, or even worse, since Welles was so close to the White House, impair the president's prestige. Uncertain about how to proceed, the secretary asked Long for advice, and he suggested that the secretary pointedly give Welles a chance to refute the allegations. Long refrained from mentioning that he had already spoken with Welles on several occasions about these charges as early as that spring, and that the under secretary had vehemently denied them, holding Bullitt responsible for spreading the vicious gossip. Long was sympathetic, for he believed Bullitt to be dishonorable and unreliable, but the former ambassador had placed Welles in an impossible position: "there was nothing one could do. To deny the story publicly would be to add to its currency and would detract from his dignity by mentioning or alluding to a filthy scandal." Long had no easy answers, but it was clear that something had to be done before Welles suffered "serious consequences."[13]

In the midst of the quandary over how to respond to these unsavory charges, Hull left Washington on October 2 for a seventeen-day vacation at his wife's home in Staunton. During his absence, Welles gave his speech before an audience in Boston attacking Chile and Argentina for not breaking off relations with the Axis, and by his return Hull had bitterly condemned Welles in private discussions with his associates for taking this initiative without prior consultation. Mimicking those who attacked Welles's judgment, Hull argued that the address had violated the good neighbor spirit and signaled the possible resumption of Yankee imperialism.[14]

Welles's speech prompted Hull to arrange a secret meeting at his apartment with J. Edgar Hoover on Saturday, October 24. In the privacy of his home, Hull lectured the FBI director on Welles's "headline hunting" and his improper speeches, especially the recent statements on Chile and Argentina. In the secretary's eyes, "this matter had been entirely and grossly mishandled" because Welles had not consulted him, and the results might be disastrous. Hull also told the director that Mrs. Hull had heard several senators' wives discussing Welles's homosexuality at tea parties and talked at length about the gossip circulating in the capital. The secretary understood that the FBI had investigated these charges over a year ago and asked for a copy of the report in order to evaluate the evidence. Hoover admitted conducting an investigation at the request of Pa Watson and having transmitted the findings to Marvin McIntyre, the presidential appointments secretary. If Hull wished to read the file, he required White House permission. The secretary promised to contact either McIntyre or Roosevelt because "the situation was of a character that there might eventually be some publicity of considerable embarrassment unless some steps were promptly taken."[15]

Without ever actually reviewing the file, Hull now had verified its existence, knew where to find it, and strongly suspected that the documentation would confirm the truth of the allegations. Armed with this information, the secretary eventually secured a copy of the file.[16] Even before reading the narrative, he had become openly abusive of Welles's reputation, to the point of referring to his chief subordinate as "my fairy."[17] When talking to Nelson Rockefeller, the secretary regularly belittled Welles for five, ten, or twenty minutes at a time by referring to him as "that polecat in the next room" and proclaiming that "he wasn't going to get into a public pissing contest with a polecat." On the other hand, Rockefeller, during interviews with Welles, never heard him criticize his superior.[18]

Unbeknownst to Hull, the FBI added a bizarre element to its investigation. Friends of a well-known Philadelphia racketeer who was imprisoned and trying to win a pardon had learned about the Welles scandal. Toward the end of 1942, his associates considered sending a letter to Roosevelt, threatening that if no pardon was forthcoming, they would release sensational material on the under secretary. But before the plan could be carried out, the convict died in jail, and nothing ever materialized. Other unconfirmed reports of Welles's alleged homosexual propositions periodically surfaced. According to one source, several FBI agents covered the under secretary twenty-four hours a day, and one of these guards had followed Welles on a train ride to Warm Springs, where the agent caught the under secretary and a Negro train employee in a compromising act. Hoover later commented that rumors like these would make the 1944 presidential campaign the dirtiest ever.[19]

During the winter of 1942–1943, tensions inside the State Department grew dramatically worse. Although Hull looked old and frail, he acted quite energetically in his crusade against his disloyal subordinate. The secretary and his wife, according to Bullitt, complained that things were happening in the department of which the secretary had no knowledge, and that Welles's errors in judgment and sexual misconduct further upset them. However, the secretary still refrained from asking Roosevelt to fire the under secretary. At the end of the year Hull lunched with Canadian Prime Minister MacKenzie King. The two men discussed several diplomatic problems, but the secretary was particularly worried about the rampant factionalism within the State Department. Hull had tried for some time to eliminate this kind of unhealthy competition, but the White House, he claimed, refused to cooperate in ending the intrigue.[20] Adding to these problems was Welles, who maintained an exhausting schedule, was "completely swamped under present conditions," and hardly had any time "except for urgent and immediate business."[21]

Roosevelt conveniently forgot his responsibility for creating this unwholesome rivalry. From the very start of the New Deal, he had welcomed Welles as well as others to come to the White House and present their ideas that could contradict the secretary's. The president was at last paying the price for his divisive management style. Already known for his antipathy toward the diplomatic corps, he was growing terribly frustrated with the Hull-Welles powder keg. That summer he remembered that as far back as 1932 he had intended "to clean up the State Department," but "Hull had not done a thing." Those accusations grew more caustic in late November 1942, when the president complained, "Cordell was absolutely helpless as an administrator and . . . he claimed he didn't have any control over his own department." Roosevelt also berated Welles and Berle for being publicity-hungry bureaucrats, but he never acknowledged that, as president, he had permitted this unconventional structure to flourish.[22]

At the beginning of 1943 the situation had deteriorated to such an extent that Berle lamented in his diary, "The antagonism between Secretary Hull and Mr. Welles makes a good deal of difficulty; the Secretary resents Sumner's going to the White House too much but as he does not go very much himself, this leaves the President at the mercy of unskilled advisers."[23]

In early March, Bullitt provided yet another example of his talent for sowing dissension by suggesting that the United States should negotiate points of disagreement with the Soviets before the fighting stopped. He warned that if this did not occur the United States would lose whatever bargaining position it had and the communists would come to dominate postwar Europe. He pressed his position in a memorandum to his superior, Navy Secretary Knox, resurrecting fears of Soviet aggression after the Nazi collapse. If the United States did not act quickly to gain concessions from the Soviets, Bullitt predicted, American forces might have to fight the Japanese alone. Secretary of War Stimson read Bullitt's arguments but dismissed them on the grounds that the United States had to cooperate with Stalin. When Drew Pearson learned about Bullitt's recommendations and Stimson's rejection of them, he exposed the disagreement in the "Washington Merry-Go-Round."[24] Bullitt promptly phoned Stimson to ask him to issue a denial, but he balked: "I realize what a preposterous thing it was for me to have my time taken up with this wretched, selfish, disloyal man's troubles. He has gotten into this mess himself by virtually being disloyal to his chief."[25]

Whereas Bullitt was blackballed from government service, Roosevelt generally simply ignored Hull. The president, for example, did not inform the secretary about the Casablanca conference until just before his departure, and he took along Harry Hopkins, deliberately snubbing the State Department. When Roosevelt announced the unconditional surrender pledge, Hull was not consulted and merely rationalized it as a military decision, albeit one with tremendous diplomatic implications.[26]

Despite the constant bypassing of his office, Hull's popularity with the American people soared. If Bullitt had his way, the secretary should fire Welles, Berle, and Acheson; with them gone, Hull should appoint individuals in whom he had confidence.[27] At the end of January, Bullitt presented his case to the White House: "Hull has an old line American wisdom which is so great that I have not known him to go wrong once in the past ten years on a fundamental decision. Moreover, his prestige in the nation is unique. He is far more trusted than any other member of your administration. And he has an influence with the Senate which is very great and will be vital in obtaining the consent of the Senate to postwar agreements."[28]

In public, Roosevelt continued to rely on Hull's great prestige, but in private, the president still belittled him and single-handedly directed wartime policy. Humiliated by the executive decision to eliminate him from military strategy discussions, Hull had decided to confront Roosevelt upon his return from North Africa in order to force a showdown over Welles's dismissal. However, he did not present this demand in the form of an ultimatum, and as long as Hull did not give Roosevelt this distasteful choice, the president postponed any decision.[29]

Yet even if the president had accepted Hull's request, the secretary still needed Welles. Hull, for example, left his office for a week in mid-February looking pale and coughing badly. He returned for a brief period and on the twenty-fifth headed for Palm Beach, Florida, for a longer rest with his wife. He was not only physically ill but also distraught over recent press criticism of American decisions made in North Africa in dealing with the various French factions.[30]

Before leaving the capital, Hull had wired British Foreign Secretary Anthony Eden to delay a trip to the United States for several days to coincide with his return from Florida. Eden replied that this was impossible, and Welles informed Hull that he and Roosevelt would handle the discussions so that the secretary could complete his rest. Upon receiving the message on March 12, Hull lost no time in booking passage on the evening train to Washington to meet with Eden on March 15.[31] During the ensuing discussions, Eden noticed the friction between Hull and Welles: "Their relations were vinegar, although the Secretary of State when speaking of his Under-Secretary in his absence was acidly correct."[32] Just before Eden returned to London at the end of the month, the secretary gave a dinner party for the foreign secretary at which Welles was not present. The British statesman preferred to work with Welles and believed that Roosevelt held the same opinion. Eden liked Hull, but he disapproved of his obsession with the reciprocity program and his pursuit of private vendettas, such as his hatred of de Gaulle.[33]

Eden's criticism was mild compared to that of Felix Frankfurter, who repeated his call to replace Hull with Acheson. The associate justice knew that the secretary was often sick, away from his desk, and incapable of supervising his staff. Frankfurter acknowledged that the secretary would not resign, but noted that as long as Welles continued to function well, the State Department operated efficiently. The columnist Walter Lippmann concurred and argued that Hull should retire to let Welles assume command. Even if the rumors of his homosexuality were true, he would still be an improvement over Hull.[34]

Hull became even more agitated when, on April 8, Pearson published a devastating column calling for the secretary to leave office. Hull was determined to remain for two reasons: first, Congress was at that time debating the renewal of the reciprocal trade agreements program, and second, his wife opposed his retirement. The truth, according to the reporter, was that the secretary simply did not have the physical strength to stay in office. In 1942 alone, he had been out of Washington for six months, and he continued to miss some time each week. There had been a time when he had conducted daily press briefings, but currently weeks passed without any contact with the media. But Hull would continue "until the last horn blows." Welles, by comparison, took on even more duties that brought him into daily contact with the White House. When the president had a question, he usually talked directly to the under secretary, who seemed instantly to know the answer. Welles also had given the recent foreign policy addresses, and Roosevelt had specifically asked him to speak before the *Herald-Tribune* forum on current and postwar diplomacy.[35]

Hamilton Armstrong, editor of the prestigious journal *Foreign Affairs,* was an audience for another of Hull's harangues, declaring that Welles had inspired the "scavenger" columnist Pearson to write that Hull was only a nominal cabinet official, and that by encouraging this kind of journalism, Welles was guilty of treachery. Armstrong disagreed and lamented that during "the greatest war in the history of the world, it is too awful to have the head of the premier department of the government suspect disloyalty on the part of his subordinates." If Hull suspected betrayal, he should take action instead of choosing to wait: "he is a great believer in giving people rope enough to hang themselves. . . . Hull is notoriously one of the most sensitive and suspicious people who ever held office."[36]

Once again upset by the alleged disloyalty of Welles, Hull now actively searched for coconspirators with whom to plot against the under secretary. In late April, Hull met with Attorney General Biddle to ask him to go to the White House to have Welles fired, but Biddle refused. When Biddle later talked to Ickes, they agreed that if Hull forced the issue, Roosevelt would have to relieve Welles. Even though Welles carried on most of the departmental business, Hull had a powerful national following, and the White House needed that political clout.[37]

The secretary also contacted Leo Crowley, who had served as chairman of the Federal Deposit Insurance Corporation and later as alien property custodian. A devout Catholic who had been a successful Wisconsin businessman, he had become a powerful Democrat in the administration, had gained a reputation as an adroit manipulator of patronage, and was known as a man with many congressional supporters.[38] Biddle also pointed out that Crowley had worked for the attorney general and "was very skillful at settling rows and cleaning up messes."[39] He also was friendly with James Byrnes, who had unofficially won the label "assistant president" for his work in domestic affairs and who had talked with Hull many times about the allegations against Welles. One afternoon, Roosevelt asked Byrnes for his advice, and the former associate justice replied that if Welles were being unjustly accused, the president should stand by him, but if the allegations were valid, Welles should go. Roosevelt then admitted, "I believe Hull's statement is correct."[40] Byrnes now knew that the accusations were based on fact.

As the rumors of Welles's homosexuality spread to a wider audience, it was clear that eventually someone antagonistic to the administration would hear about the scandal. Senator Ralph Owen Brewster, Republican of Maine, was that man. Never a major political force, he was known for his opposition to the New Deal and his assignment on the Senate Special Committee to Investigate the National Defense Program, better known as the Truman committee, which had gained a national recognition for exposing wrongdoing in wartime procurement contracts.[41]

Armed with some details concerning the 1940 train episode, Brewster called on J. Edgar Hoover on April 27, asserting that "thoroughly reliable sources" had informed him that the FBI had investigated "certain alleged disgraceful actions upon the part of" Welles. The senator even declared that he had the names of the FBI agents and those whom they had interviewed. He then stated "that the information was so shocking that he had not discussed this matter with any one but had come directly to see [Hoover] in order to determine whether or not any such investigation had in fact been made by this Bureau." Hoover admitted making a report on the incident but told Brewster that if he wanted more information, he should see Hull, who was well acquainted with the charges. Without knowing that the secretary himself had choreographed these very steps, Brewster followed Hoover's lead and talked to Hull, who confirmed the story and in turn blamed Roosevelt for refusing to remove Welles. Since the president would not act, Brewster next went to Biddle to find out why. If nothing would be done, the senator, as a member of the Truman committee, threatened to launch an inquiry into these allegations. With the real possibility of a public exposé, the attorney general promised to take up the matter with Roosevelt.[42]

Biddle scheduled an appointment with Pa Watson on Monday, May 3. Now that a congressional adversary knew about the incident, the president had to take measures to prevent it from becoming public knowledge, even though that would involve the painful and disagreeable task of firing Welles. Even though the under secretary was the only member of the diplomatic corps who both fully understood foreign affairs and had the trust of the White House, the greater political reality made those advantages meaningless. If Brewster pursued his inquiry, it would pose a major liability for the Democratic ticket in the 1944 campaign.[43]

The president had heard that Bullitt had spread rumors about Welles's homosexuality, and he asked him to come to the White House for a meeting with his press secretary, Stephen Early, on May 5 at 11:00 A.M. When they met, Early accused Bullitt of talking with Hull and others about Welles's conduct; Bullitt responded that he had discussed the subject three times with the president and would only take up this issue with him. Early disregarded this response and alleged that Bullitt had turned over documents on the train incident to Eleanor "Cissy" Patterson, the publisher of the Washington *Herald*, a charge that Bullitt branded "a complete lie." Toward the end of the meeting, the ambassador cautioned Early to remind Roosevelt that Welles "would be his Achilles Heel, and that he must dismiss him both for his own good and for the good of the country." After giving that advice, Bullitt admitted that he and the president had moved from a cordial to a distant relationship but said that he had no regrets; he had done his duty, while Roosevelt had closed his mind and surrounded himself with "yes men." Early agreed that even though the president wished to silence the gossip about Welles's sexual habits, they were about to become public. The meeting ended on this somber prediction, and so did Bullitt's service at the White House.[44]

The next day the attorney general discussed the Welles matter with the president. By that time, Biddle had already spoken with Truman, who had promised to keep the entire affair out of his committee's deliberations. Crowley had seen the Republican leaders, and they promised not to bring up the subject either. The President "was very much relieved and grateful."[45]

These White House tactics did not impede Hull's momentum in removing Welles. The Hulls invited Farley to dinner at their apartment on May 8. Hull was in good physical condition, but he was still distressed over his treatment by Roosevelt and Welles. The secretary expected to remain at his post until failing health dictated retirement. Disturbed by the wide spread of the homosexuality gossip, the Hulls understood that several embassies had now learned of the story, and they feared that if the rumors spread much further, newspaper coverage could not be far off. Hull had informed the president about these possibilities, but Roosevelt had refused to fire the under secretary. The Hulls were even more pessimistic because they now believed that the Republicans would win the 1944 presidential election.[46]

To undermine Welles's authority, Hull began that spring to insist that every crucial departmental matter come across his desk, instead of his subordinate's. When, in the middle of June, Welles went to New York to complete negotiations with the Bolivian president that had begun in Washington, Hull demanded to know why he had not been advised of them so that he could participate. When Hull interrogated Harley Notter (who served as one of the department's representatives on the postwar committee for a new international organization) about Welles's central role, the secretary became angry and threatened to attend those meetings. Prior to that conversation, the secretary had ignored the committee's deliberations.[47] When Berle anticipated traveling to England for bilateral talks, Hull objected to what he considered independent action. By the end of June, Hull was frustrated with Welles's disloyalty and his unfair treatment at the hands of the White House. He was disappointed at not receiving proper credit for his work on the trade agreements, the good neighbor policy, and other policies, but, according to Farley, the secretary was "determined to sit it out."[48]

In a talk with Morgenthau on July 9, Hull painfully conceded that since Pearl Harbor, Roosevelt had not consulted him on major foreign policy issues, "and I just don't know what's going on and the President won't let me help him." Hull, who asserted that he himself made no mistakes, compared himself favorably to Welles, who made several major blunders. Under his system of scorekeeping, Hull could not conceive why Roosevelt favored the under secretary over him on foreign policy questions.[49]

Roosevelt's insensitivity to Hull's real and imagined complaints made Hull hate Welles all the more. Since Hull could not directly attack the president, the secretary went after his most vulnerable confidant, and he chose the period after Congress adjourned that summer to make his move. When the under secretary went on a brief vacation from July 8 through 12, Hull seized the opportunity to meet with Brewster and Bullitt to plot against Welles. The secretary also spoke with Long about the possibility that foreign governments that had learned about Welles's homosexuality might try to blackmail him. Hull was further agitated over the under secretary's contacts with the White House; the secretary thought that the results of these conferences went unreported to him, and he resented being uninformed.[50]

Hull met with Roosevelt for lunch on July 16, probably to discuss Welles's resignation. By that time, the president knew that Bullitt's charges were widespread and that if the under secretary resigned, Brewster would not bring the sordid episode before the Truman committee. The secretary seemed confident that he had finally triumphed toward the end of the month, when Berle reported that Hull was "in excellent form; he seemed to think that matters were beginning to clear up."[51]

To place even more pressure on the president, Hull asked Arthur Krock, the powerful Washington bureau chief for the *New York Times*, to write a front-page article on the many bureaucratic conflicts in the government, especially the State Department. According to the reporter, Hull was virtuous whereas Welles had emerged as a bitter rival who was trying to oust his superior. This kind of inappropriate behavior disrupted the smooth running of international affairs.[52]

While Roosevelt was responding to the assault against Welles, he was also preparing for the Quebec conference. When Churchill had arrived at Hyde Park on August 12 for preliminary discussions, he was unaware of Roosevelt's predicament concerning Welles, possibly because Hull was also a houseguest. Roosevelt did divulge that he and the secretary would leave New York on Sunday for a brief trip to Washington and then head for Canada, without explaining the reasons for this decision.[53]

That Monday, August 15, Roosevelt lunched with Hull at the White House and later summoned Welles. According to the secretary's memoirs, the president told Welles that Hull had demanded his removal. To soften this painful blow, the president, with Hull's concurrence, offered Welles a roving ambassadorship to Latin America or a special assignment to the Soviet Union. After completing his task, Welles would then quietly leave government service. With this distasteful duty done, the president left for Quebec.[54] After the White House interview, Welles immediately returned to the State Department, where he confronted Hull. The secretary admitted asking the president to remove Welles, but steadfastly maintained that Roosevelt had concluded that the homosexual gossip would "explode in Congress with great damage to the State Department." The secretary held out the special mission as an opportunity for Welles to continue serving his country. The under secretary then rose, went over to Hull's desk, shook hands, and left. From that moment forward, they never again spoke to one another.[55]

Hull had won. "I never saw him in a better humor," Farley reported after a meeting late Tuesday morning. The secretary "appeared to be very happy over his own situation because it looks to me, as if he is going to get clear on the Welles situation and he said he felt that within a few days everything would be all right."[56] On the following day, Hull left the capital with his chief adviser, James Dunn, for the two-day journey to Quebec, the only wartime gathering that the secretary and the president ever attended together. Hull undoubtedly believed that Welles would remain as acting secretary during his absence, consider his options, and accept the secretary's offer. What other choice did he have?[57] Satisfied with his accomplishment, the secretary turned to the upcoming conference at Quebec. He had gotten rid of his enemy and had done it quietly. Why should he not be satisfied?

CHAPTER 14

# RESIGNATION

HULL HAD ASSUMED THAT WELLES would follow the carefully written script that the secretary had provided, but, deviating from the plot line, Welles rejected the idea of a farewell mission and submitted a formal letter of resignation to the White House on August 16, 1943. He thanked Roosevelt for his many kindnesses and promised that, if needed, he would gladly advise the president on foreign policy matters in the future. He then enumerated the three reasons why his resignation was imperative: first, ever since the explosion at Rio, Hull had wanted to fire him, and this vendetta had climaxed in the present ultimatum; second, because Roosevelt needed Hull's powerful congressional support, the president had to accede to Hull's demand; and third, the press was starting to print stories about discord within the diplomatic corps, and the focus on Welles had turned him into a political liability.[1]

Roosevelt did not immediately accept Welles's resignation, nor did the president ever release the contents of the letter. While he was considering how to respond, Welles met with Vice-President Wallace five days later about the resignation and the alternative of a special mission to

Moscow. Wallace urged Welles to accept the mission out of loyalty to the president; the Russian situation was so precarious that Welles also had a patriotic duty to defuse a future war. The under secretary replied that Hull listened to his staff, who argued for conditional aid, whereas Welles advocated the White House position of assistance with no strings attached. Furthermore, he disagreed with those of Hull's advisers, such as Leo Pasvolsky, who supported a universal approach to the international organization; Welles urged that the organization have a strong regional component. Finally, the under secretary characterized his superior as an inept leader, one who could not or would not make decisions, with the result that he followed public opinion instead of shaping it.[2]

The next day, Sunday morning, August 22, Welles called Assistant Secretary Berle to an afternoon meeting at the State Department. By the time Berle arrived, Welles had already phoned Hull in Quebec, and they had agreed that the secretary would announce the resignation at the appropriate moment. Berle tried to persuade Welles to remain until Hull's return, but he had decided to leave immediately after clearing out his desk and dictating farewell letters. According to Welles, there would be "a week of unpleasant and difficult comment then complete obscurity." The left-wing press would attack the State Department over his ouster, and the "liberals" might make him their hero. The two men then said good-bye as the sun was setting on the empty building in which Berle now temporarily served as acting secretary.[3]

That night Welles had dinner with Drew Pearson, who had already heard about the resignation. The reporter recommended that Welles remain loyal to the president but refuse any diplomatic assignment because Hull would sabotage Welles's negotiations; therefore any mission was doomed to failure. The columnist reminded his friend that appointees such as Moley, Peek, and Bullitt, who had tried to retain their influence after being forced out, soon lost the president's respect, whereas those such as Acheson, who left office with dignity, later rejoined the administration with honor. Welles should wait; after all, Hull might retire in the near future.[4]

Exhausted and embittered from his ordeal, Welles left the hot, humid capital for the natural beauty of Mount Desert Island, Maine. Welles's thirty-eight-room "summer cottage" was just outside Bar Harbor, located on the northeast side of the island; from it he enjoyed a breath-taking, panoramic view of Frenchman Bay. Ironically, even there he could not escape from a Hull. Captain Samuel Hull, a sea captain, had established a settlement at Bar Harbor around 1789 and had become the most important citizen of the village; Welles happened to live on Hull's Cove.[5]

While Welles traveled north, Berle started work on Monday, August 23, without telling anyone about his new duties. He did cancel a press conference, but no one noticed anything unusual. It was not until the next day that someone asked about Welles's whereabouts. Berle replied that the under secretary was ill and had gone to Bar Harbor for several days of rest. Speculation about Welles's removal had already begun circulating in the press. Some intimated that the Hull-Welles personality conflict had necessitated the latter's departure; others chose to emphasize the roving ambassadorship to the Soviet Union; a few even mentioned irreconcilable differences between the two men over Soviet policy as the proximate cause for the resignation.[6]

Pearson and Wallace also discussed the effects of Welles's departure. The vice-president believed that the under secretary's resignation would be a serious loss to the diplomatic corps and that Latin American envoys especially would be shocked. Wallace hoped to convince Welles to reconsider his decision and accept the Moscow mission. Pearson disagreed, reiterating his belief that Hull's hatred for Welles would compel the secretary to make certain that any assignment would climax in failure.[7]

Hull returned from Quebec on the afternoon of August 25 to face reporters' inquiries about Welles, but he never made any public statement on this subject. Outwardly, the secretary showed no emotion over the emerging storm of press commentary; privately, Hull's deep-seated bitterness hardened as the attacks against him intensified. Many papers, such as the Baltimore Sun, rallied to the secretary's defense, as did Arthur Krock in the New York Times. They accepted the basic line that Welles had emerged as a disorganizing influence and had had to be terminated; furthermore, Roosevelt had had to respect Hull's wishes because of his powerful congressional connections. Krock purposely minimized the factionalism within the department and claimed that the foreign service was united behind Hull.[8]

Those who had heard about the charges of homosexuality reacted with a wide variety of viewpoints. Assistant Secretaries Berle and Long, Vice-President Wallace, and others believed that Bullitt had lied about Welles being a homosexual. Pearson, for example, had known about Bullitt's accusations since the early spring of 1942, but he had dismissed them as malicious falsehoods intended to discredit the under secretary. The reporter, in fact, went so far as to claim that he had been acquainted with Welles for years, and that as a young man he had been regarded as somewhat of a ladies' man. William Castle heard the rumors, but did not want to precipitate a scandal by firing Welles and make him a martyr in the cause of American-Russian cooperation. In the end, he had become a martyr, but for the wrong reasons, just as Castle had predicted. Those who advocated stronger ties with Stalin used Welles's ouster as a means of attacking the professionals who opposed closer links with the Soviet Union. Ickes read the early editorials that roundly criticized Hull; Welles surely had not been well liked, but, the secretary of the interior conceded, the under secretary had run the State Department smoothly. The general impression that the foreign service was a poorly managed bureaucracy had been further reinforced.[9]

Pearson was now poised to use his considerable skills in defense of his friend. According to David Brinkley, then a young journalist in the wartime capital, Pearson at that time was one of the most highly paid persons in his profession. Even though much of what he wrote was inaccurate, he had become a national celebrity by helping to send several crooked public figures to jail, and when officials attacked him, a skeptical public rallied around him rather than around government spokesmen.[10]

The reporter had no idea how overly sensitive Hull was to press criticism, but R. Walton Moore had certainly made the secretary cognizant of Pearson's attacks during the battle over the under-secretaryship. Moore came to realize that as long as the columnist did not go after Hull directly or question his competence, Pearson was not a threat. But this view changed dramatically after the exchange over the armament sales to Germany in 1938, when Pearson had directly challenged Hull. He was thereafter lumped in with the secretary's antagonists. If this were not sufficiently damning, Pearson had directly attacked Hull and his staff regarding the possible credit to Spain at the end of 1940. As a result of that article, Welles had almost been fired and had been forced to state publicly that Pearson was a liar. Hull thereafter linked Welles with Pearson's columns and unfairly accused his subordinate of leaking classified information. After the Rio conference, the "Washington Merry-Go-Round" columns were interpreted to be further evidence that Pearson and Welles were plotting to destroy the secretary. On September 17, 1942, Hull illustrated how far his hatred had come when he asserted that Pearson "makes it a business of disseminating false statements about me and about the Department. This he has done for many years, and why any newspaper uses his stuff I cannot understand."[11]

When Pearson came to the defense of Welles after his resignation, according to Hull, he supplied conclusive proof that Welles and Pearson spoke with one voice. Pearson was not the impartial, unbiased observer that he loudly proclaimed himself to be. Instead, without ever acknowledging his friendship, the columnist openly favored Welles over Hull; at least in this instance, Pearson violated the canons of his profession.

Beginning on August 26 and continuing daily through the end of the month, Pearson not only questioned the secretary's competence but also credited Welles as the president's primary adviser in foreign affairs, especially in regard to the good neighbor policy. Welles had left the department, according to his friend, to satisfy Hull's whim and those around him who had vehemently fought the under secretary's efforts to forge closer ties with the Soviet Union: "Therefore, the exit of one of the few liberals in the State Department, leaving a battery of Soviet-haters behind, is not going to help things at a time when Russian relations remain on tenterhooks." Pearson feared that Welles's ouster signaled a purge of the liberals, and that anyone who supported him was in danger of losing his position.[12]

On the last day of the month, Pearson concluded his assault by pressing his charge of a conspiracy and the threat of being fired. Those who favored de Gaulle and Loyalist Spain were placing themselves in jeopardy. For the first and only time in print, Pearson obliquely alluded to the real cause of Welles's resignation: "Today, stories of divorce, domestic infelicity and sex rumors have been spread regarding certain progressive members of the State Department whom it is out to purge.

Once these stories circulate to enough people through the gossip under-ground, the target of the gossip is told by his superiors that his usefulness is over and he must resign."[13]

In the middle of this seemingly unceasing press attack, Hull became so agitated over allegations of his anti-Soviet attitude that he went so far as to call the Justice Department to ask Attorney General Biddle to indict Pearson for libel on the grounds that he had falsely accused Hull of being anti-Russian. Biddle never even tried to have the reporter prosecuted because the attorney general knew—as Hull the former judge should also have known—that there was no sound legal argument upon which to draft a complaint.[14]

Roosevelt joined the spectacle at the end of the month. After the Quebec meetings, he took a train to Hyde Park, rested until August 29, and was back at the White House the next day for lunch with Hull.[15] The secretary reminded Roosevelt that the reason for sending Welles to Moscow was to avoid a "public sensation over his resignation." Yet these conditions had changed materially when he began "to martyrize himself" and to talk with his friends about being "the victim of ill treatment." Hull would no longer sanction the mission, unless Welles repudiated those stories and declared his loyalty to the administration.[16]

On the same day, Hull also attacked Pearson at a press conference for alleging that he and other high State Department officials wished for "the Soviet Union to be bled white"; these accusations were "monstrous and diabolical."[17] Roosevelt, at his August 31 press conference, also lashed out at Pearson. Although declining to comment on the Welles resignation, he denounced the reporter as "a chronic liar in his columns" who had unfairly accused Hull of anti-Soviet practices. Such misinfor-mation was detrimental to the war effort.[18]

The replies to Pearson's charges effectively ended his media cam-paign. His syndicators refused to allow him to answer the administration's counterattack and went so far as to censor his columns. Maybe, as Pearson suspected, they feared litigation, or possibly the government pressured them to stop the columns. But Pearson's biographers offer another reason. The government barrage had embarrassed him and had lowered his readership. He therefore looked for and soon found another story to draw attention away from the Welles episode. During a radio broadcast, he informed his listeners that General George Patton had slapped a soldier. The army at first denied the incident but eventually admitted that Pearson's report was accurate. This new story line succeeded beyond all expectations; the Welles matter was forgotten.[19]

Pearson knew that Hull had partially attributed Welles's removal to him, but he had no idea to what extent. The secretary had confided in Walter Fitzmaurice of *Newsweek* that the under secretary had inspired a series of articles that Pearson had printed in early 1942 about the removal of four cabinet members who were over seventy. Fitzmaurice relayed this conversation to Pearson who in turn wrote Welles, "I realize that I was the source of some of the friction, and that was why I have stayed away from you so consistently in the last two years. But I did not realize that Mr. Hull blamed everything I wrote on you."[20]

The reporter was just now realizing the extent of his role in the Welles-Hull feud, and at the start of September the situation seemed to be growing even worse. Hull was calling his old friend James Byrnes almost daily because the secretary was angry that Welles, in the adjoining office, had not been "kicked up stairs" weeks ago. Newspapers were indirectly alluding to the homosexual rumors, and the Truman committee might yet start an investigation. The secretary also wanted "this fellow" to "issue a sweeping statement correcting the lies that have been told by his friends about the attitude of the department as to Russia." These issues were becoming very serious. Byrnes concurred and promised, "I am confident I can get Hull to help instead of hurt the situation." The "assistant president" further argued that Welles should go on the mission to Moscow. During this trip, Roosevelt would have sufficient time to consider whatever future plans he had for Welles. In all likelihood, after his return, he would "voluntarily take himself out of the picture."[21]

J. Edgar Hoover had his own concerns, after receiving a Los Angeles field report about a conversation among three suspected Communist sympathizers in the movie business. One claimed that the FBI director had told him about the well-known immorality of Welles and that an Eastern senator who was a member of the Truman committee had read the FBI report and was mobilizing twelve to fourteen senators to demand Welles's resignation. FBI agents in Hollywood questioned the man about the assertion that he had received his information from the director. When confronted, he denied ever speaking to Hoover about Welles, and this closed the case in regard to Hollywood and the FBI.[22] Without even acknowledging his own vital role in this episode, Hoover wrote the attorney general, "I thought you would be interested in this matter, since it does clearly indicate how vicious rumors can be circulated."[23]

While the FBI director indignantly accused others of spreading false rumors, throughout September reporters discussed every conceivable explanation for Welles's removal, except his sexual preference. Pearson, of course, led the assault on Hull, declaring on September 10 that the secretary had given Roosevelt no choice but to fire Welles. The president had suggested a Russian mission, but Welles had refused on the grounds that Hull would prevent any worthwhile results from being achieved.[24] Most commentators attributed Welles's ouster to the clash of personalities between him and Hull, and to a great extent that interpretation was accurate. The secretary was famous for getting even; here was another instance where he had gotten his man. But according to most writers, the pair had made an excellent team; it was too bad that Welles was gone. He was especially needed at a time when careful planning was so essential.[25]

Others, such as Krock, applauded Welles's removal. He had become a disruptive influence, they said, and his absence would allow the diplomatic corps to function more smoothly. Secretary of War Stimson congratulated Hull on getting rid of an untrustworthy subordinate. Yet Stimson still could not make his colleague take command of his department. Instead, Hull continued to concentrate on media attacks on his various policies. The secretary of war provided an excuse: Hull "is very abnormally sensitive and he has palpably slowed up in his mental work of handling such matters. I hope that it is only temporary and that it will be remedied now that he is free from the harassing differences between him and Sumner Welles."[26]

Roosevelt also expressed his opinion: Welles and Hull were often of like mind. The friction between them had arisen because Welles spoke more often and more clearly, but made the critical error of never showing his speeches to his superior. On September 7 the president told Wallace that Hull was upset, and that as president, he was having a difficult time "keeping the Old Boy sweet." Hull was receiving unfair criticism, and Roosevelt had a duty to keep the secretary in office "for the general welfare of the country." [27]

Within the State Department, Berle was distraught over his friend's departure and hoped that Welles would still take the Russian assignment. Long, however, complained about the numerous newspaper reporters who had flocked to Bar Harbor to talk with Welles. After their interviews, many of the reporters filed dispatches hostile to the administration, greatly distorting the direction of American foreign policy and impugning Hull's leadership.[28]

Josephus Daniels, former American ambassador to Mexico, was disgusted by the entire escapade. He had close political ties to Hull, having even proposed him for the presidency in 1928. After assuming his ambassadorial post in 1933, he had worked with Welles and respected "his ability and forcefulness." Daniels did not know all the facts, but he intended to learn the truth. He concluded, "It is distressing and disturbing that in these war days public men cannot adjust their differences if they cannot agree both on the same way."[29]

In the midst of this turmoil Welles traveled to Hyde Park on Sunday, September 20, to meet with Roosevelt. The president still tried to persuade Welles to accept the trip to Moscow; Welles would only promise to consider the offer.[30] By the next day Welles had memorialized his decision in two letters. The first went to Hull, informing him that Pearson's articles had not been instigated or inspired by Welles, for he would "not stoop to tactics of this character." He had only seen the columnist four times in the preceding two years and always in the presence of others. When Pearson had initially heard about his resignation, Welles had asked him not to write about it: "During the past ten years of my official life I have talked frequently with many members of the press. There is not one of them who can truthfully say that in any conversation I have ever had with them I have ever referred to you except with the utmost loyalty."[31] Welles addressed his other letter to Roosevelt. In it he refused the Moscow mission because of Hull's deep-seated personal hatred: "From what you have told me, Secretary Hull's feelings with regard to myself—unjustified as they are—would make any such relationship impossible. He would be constantly imagining that I was threatening his legitimate jurisdiction, or undermining his authority, and [the] possibility for the success of what you desire accomplished would be seriously jeopardized."[32]

Four days later, Roosevelt returned to the White House and met with Hull before lunch. That afternoon, the president announced that Welles was leaving the State Department owing to his wife's poor health. The president had changed the draft of the press release wording from merely regretting the resignation to a text accepting it "with deep and sincere regret."[33] The president had lost the services of his most trusted adviser in the State Department. With Welles gone, Roosevelt had no further reason to consult a bureaucracy that he had intuitively abhorred since the days of World War I. Normally, he released letters of resignation to the public, but he did not do so in this case. Following the White House example, Welles refused to comment. Although now out of government service, Welles still occasionally met with Roosevelt, who persisted in offering him the Moscow mission. Welles continued to decline, reiterating his belief that Hull would veto whatever he tried to accomplish.[34] The president finally relented, but after a meeting in early October at the White House, he wrote, "I do hope that when you get back to Washington you will come to see me. There are many things I want to talk over with you."[35]

Such prominent administration figures as poet and Librarian of Congress Archibald MacLeish, tariff specialist Charles Taussig, and Treasury Secretary Morgenthau sent their regrets.[36] Particularly touching was a letter from Justice Frankfurter:

> No one who has followed events even from the side-lines can be ignorant of the weight you threw in the direction of the forces that seek to shape a better world. Those forces can ill spare the understanding and the disciplined pursuit of reason and fair dealing that you would have brought toward translating gracious generalities into working arrangements. Even out of office your powers will . . . make themselves felt. . . . But I cannot forego a word of deep regret at your leaving.[37]

As for Bullitt, his role in this sordid episode effectively finished his government service. Castle, speaking as an outsider, declared that Bullitt had "a rotten character."[38] From within the administration, Long assumed that Bullitt's whispering campaign had been "a malicious lie. . . . Bullitt is a person without honor, in my eyes. I have known him a long, long time and know him well but I have *never* had any confidence in him. And—he wanted Welles' position."[39]

Louis Wehle, a close adviser to Roosevelt at the start of the New Deal, who had first introduced Bullitt to the presidential candidate, defended Bullitt's actions and saw nothing wrong with having him fill the now-vacant under-secretaryship. Welles "was impossible as a member of the organization, and his vulnerability to foreign duress was so certain that informed persons everywhere would have to admit that it was even the duty of one in possession of the facts (and with courage enough to do so) to help rid the Government of his presence."[40]

Roosevelt certainly did not share Wehle's opinion, and with the withdrawal of White House favor, Bullitt lost any remaining political clout. When he contemplated running for governor of Pennsylvania in 1942, Democratic Senator Joseph Guffey openly declared his opposition and wrote on March 8, 1943, "Bill Bullitt was wrong in Russia—was wrong in France. . . . He has evidently fallen from the good graces of some of our friends."[41] In a desperate effort to gain some Democratic support, Bullitt sought James Farley's assistance, but the former post-master general had no influence over Pennsylvania politicians.[42]

Shut out of national and state politics, Bullitt opted to run for mayor of Philadelphia, a city that had traditionally been a bastion of Republicanism. He announced his candidacy in mid-July 1943 and easily won the Democratic nomination. However, his campaign proved a fiasco because it lacked direction and he projected the image of being a social snob. Five days before the fall election, Republicans published a thirty-page pamphlet entitled "Who is William C. Bullitt?" This devastating indictment pointed out that he had never paid state property taxes and had not lived in the city since his boyhood, merely using the exclusive Rittenhouse Club as a mailing address in order to be registered as a voter. He had divorced his first wife, who was a pillar of society, written a scurrilous book about Philadelphia life-styles, and married the widow of the communist John Reed, the only American buried in the Kremlin.

Under the Roosevelt administration, Bullitt had promoted recognition of the Soviet Union and was sympathetic toward the communist regime. The Republicans additionally accused him of damaging American preparedness by allowing the French to purchase United States military aircraft. They repeated his expression of admiration for Pétain and recalled that he had remained in Paris after the French government fled; the implication was that he had countermanded Hull's orders and, because of his admiration for Hitler, helped the Nazis gain control of Paris. The authors also alleged that Bullitt had praised the kaiser during World War I and broke Wilson's trust at the end of the fighting. To reinforce the claim of Bullitt's Nazi sympathies, the pamphlet—in a blatant display of guilt by association—prominently featured a picture of the ambassador standing next to Hermann Göring.

If these transgressions were not enough to turn voters against him, his antagonists also painted Bullitt as anti-Negro in colored neighborhoods and anti-Semitic in Jewish areas. They warned Irish voters that if Bullitt were victorious, he would fill city jobs with Jews. The writers did not worry about consistency, only playing on voters' fears. Bullitt cried foul and asked Roosevelt to write a letter denouncing the outlandish charges, but even this was not enough to provide him with a credible showing. He lost in a landslide.[43]

The former ambassador had been humiliated, but even this outcome did not bring Welles back to the president's side. Berle realized that Welles's removal was "pure tragedy. As the Department became too small for both Sumner Welles and Secretary Hull, the difficulties of all of us were extreme."[44] In specific terms, the void that Welles left signaled a massive bureaucratic disruption, for he had directed the daily departmental routine for over six years. During that period, Hull and Welles had each favored certain employees over others. What was going to happen to the under secretary's followers, to their morale, and to the department's overall efficiency?

Inter-American affairs represented another major concern. Welles had been in charge of hemispheric matters for ten years, and Berle warned Hull that the resignation would cause significant uneasiness in Latin America. Since Welles was closely identified with the good neighbor policy, should not the administration reaffirm its support for the policy?[45]

Questions about the postwar international organization also created uncertainty. Hull had been angry at the under secretary's central role in discussions of the matter, but he had not taken any part in them himself. Who was now going to direct the studies leading to a new association, and who was going to speak about the multitude of concerns sure to arise after the fighting stopped? Bilateral negotiations had been seriously impaired by the open controversy in the press over Welles's position in favor of collaboration with Stalin, while Hull and his followers had been labeled anti-Soviet. Since the under secretary had directed Soviet-American policy for the last three and a half years, who would replace him, and what would be the future course of American diplomacy in that region?

Finally, Jewish leaders had seen Welles as a sympathetic supporter. When he resigned, Rabbi Stephen Wise thanked him: "Your vision and your wisdom, your courage and effectiveness cannot long be lost to the American people, which cherishes your service, as my fellow Jews in all free lands will, when the whole story can be told, bless your name."[46] Those accolades were welcome, but Rabbi Morris Lazaron, a prominent anti-Zionist, had a more immediate problem. He knew Assistant Secretary Long, "but somehow I don't feel the same warmth and understanding in my talks with him as I have always felt with you." Whom should the rabbi see to fill that void?[47]

Hull did not have the answers to any of these questions, nor could he physically fill the vacuum. From his selfish perspective, he had finally achieved a momentous victory by ridding the department of Welles. Yet the secretary had not considered the short- or long-range repercussions of his actions. In his own view, he had solved a pressing problem, and he now had the fortitude to endure and persevere. With Welles gone, Hull was in sole command, but unfortunately for him, he had never been able to take advantage of this situation.

Even though Hull never admitted the fact, everyone suffered from Welles's departure. Hull had conspired against Welles without considering the adverse outcome, and he now shared the blame for it. Roosevelt no longer had a trustworthy loyalist in the foreign service who would faithfully carry out his directives. Although the charges of immorality had immediately precipitated his ouster, his greatest professional failure was his unwillingness to share information with his subordinates. When he left, the work of a decade went with him. No one remained to carry out his duties, for only he knew the full extent of his responsibilities.

Long cogently summed up the impact of Welles's dismissal: "The Administration has suffered, the White House has suffered, the State Department has been seriously affected and Welles has been put under a dark cloud from which he may not emerge." Roosevelt had wanted to keep Welles in office, but Bullitt's insidious tongue drove him out. "But the world will soon march by the little tragedy and it will be smothered in the dust of rapidly succeeding events."[48] Indeed that was exactly what occurred, as reports of Allied advances soon pushed this episode from the limelight.

Welles could not and would not directly attack his superior in public. From early in his career, he had demonstrated his commitment to the professionalism of the diplomatic corps; he had refused to apply political pressure to retain his post during the Coolidge administration, and he had never wavered from that approach. Thus, just as he had been unable to retain his assignment two decades earlier, he once again walked away from the State Department without retaliating and never again did what he did best: serve his nation in the diplomatic arena by providing specific implementation of the general policy guidelines set out by the White House.

# CHAPTER 15

# HULL'S LAST YEAR

WITH WELLES'S DEPARTURE, the most direct link between the White House and the State Department had been shattered. Roosevelt knew that Hull had orchestrated the under secretary's removal, and as a result, the president did not deviate from his previous course of seldom seeking the secretary's advice, and he occasionally ridiculed Hull in the presence of others to demonstrate his displeasure. Hull cringed at these embarrassing remarks, but he never demanded an end to them. Although the secretary had rid the foreign service of Welles, he had no plan of action to capitalize on the under secretary's exit, nor did he have anyone ready to assume that pivotal position. In fact, the loss of Welles forced Hull to assume direct command of his own bureaucracy, and by doing so the secretary graphically demonstrated both the limited extent of his skills and how physically impaired he had grown.

The advertisement Hull might have run in seeking to replace the most influential American under secretary of state of the twentieth century might have read: "WANTED: skilled diplomatic technician able to work closely with the leaders of the Grand Alliance, with a superior grasp of inter-American affairs, committed to improving Soviet-American relations, possessing the trust of the American Jewish community, and in the vanguard for a new world organization." The under secretary had typically been chosen from among candidates who had already served in high diplomatic positions, in order to provide continuity and experience. Using those standards, the possible candidates narrowed to Breckinridge Long and George Messersmith; those who had applauded Bullitt's efforts in the ouster of Welles also quietly advanced the promotion of the former ambassador.[1]

On September 21, 1943, James Byrnes, who answered directly to the Oval Office, wrote the president that if he were still undecided, Edward Stettinius, Jr., would be an excellent selection because he was a loyal Democrat, who had "not been very active politically . . . would not antagonize any particular group," and as lend-lease administrator had "demonstrated executive ability" in working with foreign governments. Byrnes reminded the president that the original lend-lease bill had passed only after acrimonious debate, but that under Stettinius's guidance, the agency had functioned so smoothly that Congress had recently unanimously approved its extension.[2] Harry Hopkins enthusiastically seconded the nomination, for with Stettinius as second in command at the State Department, Hopkins would replace Welles as the liaison between the White House and the State Department.[3]

Four days after Byrnes had made his suggestion, Roosevelt announced the appointment of Stettinius as under secretary of state, commending him for his "broad experience" in working with the Allied governments, and noting that his business acumen "splendidly equipped him for his new post."[4] With the exception of insiders like Byrnes and Hopkins, most commentators and administration officials were shocked at the news because Stettinius lacked diplomatic training. But such an unexpected selection was consistent behavior for a president who was furious that Hull had placed him in the position of having to replace Welles, but who could not directly retaliate against a well-respected secretary of state because the White House needed him to popularize its foreign policy initiatives. What the president did was the worst possible thing at the worst possible time. The White House continued to make the major decisions and relegated Hull, his advisers, and their recommendations to second-class status. Welles alone had been capable of putting

White House proposals into practice, and without his presence, the president accepted the untested assumption that Hopkins would supervise Stettinius's activities.

How qualified was Stettinius for this post? He had been born on October 22, 1900, in Chicago, Illinois, where his father was a partner in the banking house of J. P. Morgan and Company. The son was sent to private school and attended the University of Virginia from 1919 to 1924, leaving without receiving a degree. Although Stettinius never graduated, he did learn the necessary skills for advancement in the business world. Handsome and gracious, by the age of thirty-one he had become a vice-president at General Motors, and seven years later he became chairman of the board of U.S. Steel. After the European war began, Stettinius left private industry at Hopkins's urging, joined the administration as chairman of the War Resources Board, and next served as head of the lend-lease program with Hopkins, assisting in the dispensing of vital war supplies. Stettinius handled this position competently, for he was well suited to it as an organizer who could put essential services in place and as a compromiser who could win approval for the allocation of materials to Allied nations.[5]

After the announcement of the new appointment, Welles came to Stettinius's assistance by telling the press that he wished his successor well and thought that Stettinius would do a fine job.[6] This well-meaning gesture, however, was meant strictly for public consumption, for after the war Welles expressed another opinion: "devoid of any knowledge of international relations or even of modern history and lacking the personal qualifications desirable in so high an office, Mr. Stettinius, it was painfully evident from the outset, could play only a meager part."[7]

Hull conceded that he had had nothing to do with the appointment. Quite frankly, he did not care; anyone would be an improvement over Welles. Nevertheless, he too applauded the selection and later claimed to have "a high regard for Stettinius on account of his extensive business experience, his fine character, and his belief in the principles and policies President Roosevelt and I were supporting. He made a splendid showing as Under Secretary."[8] During their first conversation on October 4, Hull told Stettinius about the scandal that had consumed his predecessor, but this initial confidence did not provide admission into the secretary's "croquet clique." Hull never fully utilized Stettinius's skills, explaining that the under secretary "was a very decent fellow," but "entirely inexperienced in foreign affairs except in the domain of Lend-Lease and could not be expected to advise the President."[9]

Diplomats like Ambassador Claude Bowers in Chile compared both under secretaries and reached the expected conclusion that Welles had been the better one: "No man in Washington understood so perfectly or sympathetically the problems of Latin America, and no one was so familiar with the personnel and the psychology of the various nations."[10] Others, without attacking Stettinius, held Welles in such high esteem that his successor could not avoid starting off an inferior even before he had had an opportunity to prove his worth. Nelson Rockefeller, who served under Stettinius, added the observation that his superior had an attractive personality but was insecure in a job for which he was untrained.[11]

Drew Pearson tried to create added friction by spreading rumors that James Dunn had become "the most powerful man in the State Department" and that Stettinius was "a mere figurehead with no power or influence whatsoever—except over the negro messengers who hate him profoundly."[12] The reporter even accused Hull in the "Washington Merry-Go-Round" column of distrusting Stettinius because the secretary had ordered his subordinate not to speak with the press after returning from London. Stettinius had, and as a result Pearson claimed that the two officials were "in about the same pistol-drawn position as Hull was with former Undersecretary Welles." Neither the secretary nor the under secretary answered the charges; instead, they had Arthur Krock write an article about their harmonious relations.[13]

Thus, even before Stettinius had had an opportunity to establish his credentials, he was receiving low marks without being given the proper tests. No one pointed out that the president was growing progressively more incapacitated from his heart condition, that Hopkins would shortly undergo major surgery, and that Hull was succumbing to his spreading tuberculosis. Despite these various debilitating factors, every member of this trio traveled abroad at the beginning of Stettinius's tenure, leaving him to function as acting secretary without any guidance almost immediately after assuming his new duties. Now he had to handle discussions with ambassadors, act as liaison with the White House, attend cabinet meetings, hold press conferences, and perform numerous other official functions. These were enormous responsibilities to be assigned to a man who admittedly was not conversant in diplomatic matters and who was already being criticized for his shortcomings.[14]

If these were not hurdles enough, Hopkins, who was supposed to assist Stettinius with his White House relations, never really did so. In reality, Hopkins was unavailable for consultations with the under secretary because part of the time Hopkins was out of the country. In addition, during the first half of 1944, his intestinal problems became so severe that he required major surgery on March 29 and was unable to return to work until Independence Day; even then, he did not regain full strength until November.[15]

Hull also exacerbated this difficult situation because he was not conversant with Welles's administrative and policymaking responsibilities and because his physical condition had worsened materially. Four days after Hull met with Stettinius in early October, the secretary traveled to Hot Springs, West Virginia, for an eight-day vacation. In defending his turf, he had grown extremely weary—yet he now left a novice in charge of running the State Department.

By the time he returned, Hull had decided to lead the United States delegation to the Moscow conference rather than allow Welles to attend. At almost seventy-two, Hull was so adamant about personally representing the United States that he did not consult his doctor Matthew Perry or his wife, or let his claustrophobia shake his determination. The mere thought of flying caused Hull "the most extreme mental anguish,"[16] but his boiling hatred of Welles transcended his fear of small, enclosed spaces. Hull left the capital from Washington National Airport at noon on October 7 on the first leg of his journey. While boarding the four-engine transport, he looked around at the tiny compartment and thought, "Oh, what the hell!"[17] For most passengers, the trip proved monotonous, but not for Dr. Perry, who observed his patient coughing up a good deal of blood during the first several days of the journey.[18]

His coughing had stopped by the time he landed in the Russian capital on October 18. Now he had to face Soviet negotiators in the midst of Moscow's winter weather; adding to his fatigue, the meetings commenced on the evening of his arrival. But Hull was well prepared because he brought the detailed position papers that Welles had drafted![19]

Although most of the discussions served as the prelude to a meeting among Roosevelt, Churchill, and Stalin to be held at Tehran, each foreign minister advanced his country's main causes during the talks. Hull argued for a four-power declaration in favor of a postwar international organization. Vyacheslav Molotov pressed to shorten the war against Germany and argued for an early second front with the invasion of France. Anthony Eden called for a European advisory commission to supervise the captured Italian and other Allied-liberated territories. On October 31, the last day of the meetings, Stalin, who was in a cheerful mood, gave a banquet in the Hall of Catherine the Great at the Kremlin. In order to conserve his strength, this was the only social gathering that Hull attended. He sat on the dictator's right in the chair of honor and was astonished when Stalin, without asking for anything in return, leaned over and voluntarily informed the secretary that after the fighting in Europe had ended, the Soviet Union would declare war against Japan. This unanticipated, unilateral declaration ended the conference on a positive note of closer Soviet-American solidarity.[20]

Hull was so excited over Stalin's unsolicited offer that not even the foul weather delaying his takeoff until November 3 could dampen his enthusiasm. He was pleased yet exhausted. During his strenuous journey, he had lost ten or twelve pounds because he was unaccustomed to Soviet food and could not get a supply of fresh milk. Despite these problems, Dr. Perry did not notice any negative effects, and within months Hull had regained the lost weight. His military transport plane touched down in Washington on November 10 to a president and a special congressional delegation prepared to pay homage. Even before Hull's victorious return, the president, without giving specific details, had told correspondents that the secretary had accomplished a great deal by highlighting the fight for unconditional surrender and the four-power momentum toward a postwar international organization.[21]

The day after Roosevelt had greeted Hull as a hero at the airport, they lunched and chatted briefly about the mission. Roosevelt was pleased that Hull had persuaded the Soviets to endorse the four-power declaration to collaborate in postwar security matters; the secretary's triumph dovetailed with White House goals. Hull had finally spoken out unequivocally in favor of a global association and Soviet-American friendship. What better personal example did Roosevelt have to warm congressional and public sentiment for these controversial goals than Hull's endorsement? The White House also realized that, with the 1944 presidential campaign approaching, the Democrats would have to speak out in favor of these issues before the Republicans seized either one or both for themselves.[22]

The day following his return, Hull became the first secretary of state to speak before a joint session of Congress. He reported on his successful journey and, indulging in a bout of wishful thinking, told his former colleagues that "there will no longer be need for spheres of influence, for alliances, for balance of power, or any other of the special arrangements through which, in the unhappy past, the nations strove to safeguard their security and promote their interests."[23] Hull was incredibly naive about the Soviets and their supposed willingness to cooperate. He had never taken a serious interest in Soviet-American relations and did not understand their complexities. In fact, he believed that the communists were "like your country cousins come to town a little slow but well worthwhile." Stalin had assured him that he would not sign a separate peace treaty with the Axis, and Hull expected the Soviets to "cooperate in the future."[24]

After enduring years of ridicule for being a free trader and being ignored by the White House, Hull had finally succeeded beyond his imagination. He became a national hero, receiving overwhelming praise for his deft diplomatic maneuvering and for creating a great-power alliance. In the midst of his euphoria, Hull falsely claimed that he had always expected to head the delegation, and that nothing would have kept him from attending. He added a cryptic, sinister note during a meeting with Ambassador to Venezuela Frank Corrigan: "The attempts to sabotage my mission were dastardly."[25] The inference was that Welles had been the potential saboteur, but when several reporters correctly credited Welles with drafting the meeting's proposals and asked for the secretary's comments, Hull refused to reply.[26]

Despite this success, Roosevelt did not begin to reach out to Hull for advice. Instead, on the day before the president left for Tehran, he spent the morning in his White House bedroom with none other than Welles to brief him on the objectives of his journey. After dark on the evening of November 11, without advising Hull as to the upcoming agenda or taking along any senior member of the diplomatic corps, the president and Hopkins drove to the marine base at Quantico, Virginia, boarded his private yacht, and steamed out to the point at which the mouth of the Potomac River spilled into the Atlantic Ocean. By dawn, the president had boarded the mighty battleship *Iowa* and was heading for Cairo. During the stopover in Egypt, Roosevelt held talks with Churchill and Chiang Kai-shek to bolster Chinese morale. Although the president's seeming attempt to make China a major postwar power irritated the prime minister, Roosevelt had no illusions as to Chiang's abilities to fight or govern.[27]

After completing these discussions, the president was driven to the airport on the morning of November 27, boarded his plane, and waited for the fog to lift. Within an hour, the pilots were cleared for takeoff. As the plane cleared the haze, its passengers adjusted to the brilliant sunlight as they flew east to Iran; the president was on course for his first meeting with Stalin.

When the formal meetings opened on November 28, the president chaired the talks without any fixed agenda, to allow the participants to discuss freely any issue that they wished to raise. The three leaders agreed to a cross-channel invasion no later than spring 1944, and Stalin reiterated his pledge to join in the fight against Japan. In addition, Roosevelt convinced the other two to support the idea of an international organization. Churchill and Roosevelt also urged Stalin to open discussions with the exiled Polish government in London, for the dictator had backed Polish communists. That issue was left unsettled, as was the question of German reparations. The Big Three had not resolved every problem, but the president came away from the conference with positive feelings about his direct negotiations with the Soviet ruler. He recognized that he and Stalin were realists and therefore believed that they could reach a satisfactory accommodation. At least for the moment, the Grand Alliance appeared to be marching toward victory; Overlord, the planned military invasion of the Continent, was moving toward a projected May debarkation date.[28]

With the temperature hovering near zero, Roosevelt returned to the White House from his long journey on December 17, after having traveled over 17,000 miles and been away for five weeks. He was well tanned and looking refreshed; his only problem seemed to be a persistent cough. Undoubtedly he owed his healthy appearance at least in part to his satisfaction over his mission; he optimistically told the assembled politicians who greeted him upon his arrival and other subsequent listeners that the journey had succeeded beyond his expectations. That afternoon, the president told his cabinet that he and Stalin had gotten along "admirably," and he complimented Hull for laying that foundation. The president had doubts about British cooperation, fearing more trouble in the postwar world from the British than from the Soviets. Churchill, for example, wanted to keep the Chinese weak in order to exploit their markets, and when Roosevelt had asked him to return Hong Kong to Chiang after the war, Churchill had merely grunted. The president also mentioned the possibility of dividing Germany into seven parts and recorded his belief that Charles de Gaulle was losing support within the Free French forces.[29]

Even though the president looked upon the Tehran meeting as a milestone, Hull considered his talks at Moscow far more significant, and during December the Hulls held a series of social gatherings at their apartment to advance their views. MacKenzie King came for dinner early in the month and listened as the secretary charged the New Deal "polecats," with having conspired, with Welles's active connivance, to remove him from office for more than a year. But Hull had remained in control, and he now predicted that the war would continue through the next year.[30]

Several days later, the Hulls invited James Farley to their home. He had already spoken by phone to the secretary in late November about his achievements in the Soviet Union, and now Farley's admiration for Hull soared even higher: "as a result of all this he will go down in history as probably the greatest Secretary of State of all time."[31] Farley closely observed the secretary during their December chat: "I have never seen him in a better frame of mind." Hull talked at great length about Welles's removal and asserted that he had worked out the foreign ministers' agenda months in advance and won more concessions from the Soviets than had the British. Farley was elated: "The thing which impressed me more than anything else was the fact that Mr. Hull has come into his own in his position of Secretary of State and I could see by his attitude that is exactly how he felt."[32]

At a dinner party just before Christmas, Hull saw in Arthur Krock of the *New York Times* another opportunity to vent his frustrations over the events of the preceding several years. Hull recalled that when he would leave town, Welles would give unauthorized speeches. He had warned Roosevelt that a coalition among Welles, Henry Wallace, and Wallace's chief assistant, Milo Perkins, could commit the administration to making reckless and impossible pledges. From these false premises, Hull concluded that Welles, Wallace, and other New Dealers had tried to undermine his programs. As a reward for joining forces with the Wallace faction, Welles, according to Hull, had also expected to replace him, and in an effort to gain more support, the under secretary had cultivated certain media figures by giving them confidential information and placing them on State Department committees. Hull then indicted, convicted, and sentenced Welles for conspiring with Wallace and Perkins in the Board of Economic Warfare's preemption of foreign economic policies.[33]

Most of the charges that Hull hurled against Welles and his alleged allies were unfounded. The under secretary certainly wanted to advance, but he knew that Hull would have his cabinet position for as long as he wished to remain in office. The other accusation, of conspiracy, was ludicrous. If anyone was adept at plotting, it was the secretary, and at the same time, he also knew quite well how to protect his prerogatives.

While the secretary reviewed the state of his affairs, Stettinius chose the modernization and reorganization of the inefficient and cumbersome State Department bureaucracy as one of his immediate priorities. Rather than use foreign service experts to assist in the evaluation, he brought in three special assistants who were personally loyal to him, but who shared his inexperience in international affairs. Under a cloak of secrecy, the investigators identified many glaring weaknesses in the existing system. The assistant secretaries unquestionably carried heavy work loads, but nothing compared to the burdensome duties that overwhelmed the under secretary. This examination led to the combination of some functions; new posts were created; more specialists were assigned to the geographical divisions; a committee to review the thrust of major policies and address postwar considerations was established. Some continued to carry out their existing responsibilities under different titles. Possibly the most significant innovation was the recognition of the need for a positive public relations effort and the necessity of keeping Americans informed regarding foreign affairs.

Yet even with these good intentions, when Stettinius formally announced the department's reorganization on January 15, 1944, it was clear that the under secretary's associates had examined the existing organization hastily, without either comprehending the peculiarities of departmental operations or consulting with those who did. A number of embarrassing gaffes resulted. Officers who had to sign documents and contracts were eliminated, with no replacements being designated. The Division of Near Eastern Affairs was changed to the Office of Eastern and African Affairs; an order had to be issued to correct the name to the Office of Near Eastern and African Affairs. The office charged with reviewing structural problems had been dismantled, and so the best place to correct many of the new mistakes had itself vanished. Officials continued to operate without legitimate authority under the new organizational chart, and morale in the department slipped badly. These problems were all eventually solved, but the suspicion created by the manner in which the reorganization had been accomplished caused lingering distrust between the professional diplomats and Stettinius's staff. As a consequence, whenever career officials could make Stettinius look incompetent, they did.[34]

The president further confused the situation because he did not make any effort to define Stettinius's role or offer him any meaningful support, nor did he have the time to conduct training sessions. After all, he made the primary diplomatic decisions, and he expected his orders to be followed. If Stettinius had any questions, Hopkins was supposed to be available to advise his friend; but at the beginning of 1944 he was confined to the hospital.

While Hopkins struggled to regain his health, Roosevelt looked fit and rested, but in this instance appearances were deceiving. A severe case of influenza contracted on the return trip from Iran sapped the president's strength into January 1944. No longer was he partly independent; he was now truly crippled. Everything was done for him; he depended more and more on advice from his staff. His personal physician, Admiral Ross McIntire, did not seem overly concerned with his patient's worsening condition, but others around the president noticed his deteriorating health and put pressure on him to get a complete physical. These concerns grew so incessant that, in late March, Roosevelt was driven to Bethesda Naval Hospital for an examination supervised by a young cardiologist, Dr. Howard Bruenn. The results gave genuine cause for alarm. The president was suffering from hypertension, hypertensive heart disease, signs of congestive heart failure, dangerously high blood pressure, anemia, and arteriosclerosis. To ameliorate his patient's symptoms, Dr. Bruenn recommended extended bed rest of at least ten hours a day, limited cigarette smoking, and a bland diet. To minimize the president's coughing, he prescribed codeine, and for the heart condition, digitalis. Roosevelt accepted most of this medical advice without ever inquiring why Dr. Bruenn had been consulted or why he had recommended that course of treatment. Possibly he was fatalistic; maybe he did not want to know, or, even more worrisome, maybe he understood far more than he admitted.[35]

Melancholy may have contributed to his physical decline, for he may have been going into clinical depression. Many of those closest to him, such as his political confidant Louis Howe, his bodyguard Gus Gennerich, and his mother Sara, had died. "Missy" LeHand, his private secretary since the years in Albany, had suffered a stroke that would shortly end her life. Welles had been disgraced, and Hopkins was slowly wasting away from intestinal malfunctions. Roosevelt's marriage to Eleanor had evolved into more of a merger, and whatever sexual bond may have existed had vanished after the Lucy Mercer affair at the end of World War I. Eleanor's friendship in the middle of World War II with the youthful Joseph Lash offended the president, but Eleanor ignored her husband's feelings and remained devoted to the much younger man.

The president reacted to this relationship and to the absence of female companionship by having Anna Roosevelt Boettinger, his daughter, move into the White House to try to make her father's schedule more pleasant. But the president pushed his daughter's loyalty beyond accepted limits when he asked if she objected to his inviting Lucy Mercer

Rutherford (she had in the meantime married an elderly widower named Winthrop Rutherford) to dinner at the White House. Anna agreed, but she knew full well that he had long ago promised Eleanor never again to see Lucy. To improve his health, the president accepted an invitation from the industrialist Bernard Baruch to visit his plantation in South Carolina; Roosevelt also knew that Lucy lived nearby. He left the White House on April 8 with only a few aides, including Admiral McIntire. Dr. Bruenn traveled to the estate nine days later, and his examination showed that the president was still suffering from high blood pressure. He had also had two serious gallbladder episodes, and these forced the president to extend his vacation until early in May.[36]

Even before the president traveled to the South, Hull's advocacy of another diplomatic post for Bullitt had aggravated Roosevelt. The secretary and the former ambassador met on the morning of February 1 to discuss Soviet-American relations. The former ambassador wanted the president to send Stalin a message about future collaboration because American public opinion was turning against the communist policy in Poland. Bullitt believed that it should be made clear to Stalin that if the Soviets did not reverse their attempt to turn that country into a communist satellite, U.S. cooperation would cease. The secretary thought that this reasoning favorably impressed Roosevelt, but as yet he had not made a firm decision.

Far more critical to Bullitt, the secretary recounted a recent White House conversation during which Hull had asked Roosevelt to appoint Bullitt to "a position of real importance." Hull had stressed that he "had been sitting on a keg of dynamite for two years and that anyone who had helped get Welles out of the picture had performed a great public service. . . . I told the President that it was criminal for a man of Welles' habits to hang himself around our necks and hang on when he knew that the exposure of his behavior would blow the Administration into the air." Roosevelt had inquired, "Well, what kind of a job can we put Bill on?" Hull had replied that he should be appointed ambassador-at-large in North Africa and the Middle East. With this exchange, the secretary believed that the president "had gotten over the top of the hill of his rage" over the Welles episode, and that Bullitt should expect a reply within a week.[37]

Later the same day, the secretary spoke with Roosevelt, anticipating approval for Bullitt's ambassadorship; instead, the president rejected any appointment. When Hull pressed the issue, Roosevelt responded, "Why not Minister to Saudi Arabia?" Hull knew that the offer would be unacceptable to Bullitt. He also informed Bullitt of his intention to remain in office until the end of the third term in order to improve Soviet-American friendship and to build congressional support for the world association. The White House had hampered both efforts by refusing to consult with or even inform Hull of the results at Tehran and the contents of communications among the three world leaders. The secretary was distressed; he "had never known the President to be so aloof."[38]

In a last desperate attempt to influence Roosevelt, Bullitt had dinner the next day with Admiral William Leahy, the principal military adviser in the White House. Bullitt explained that he wanted to help shape the postwar world, but realized that since the Welles scandal "his relations with the President have been strained to say the least." The admiral listened, but he never acted on Bullitt's behalf.[39] The former ambassador next went to Stimson for an army commission, but he was denied it "because Bullitt had never been loyal to anybody that I knew whom he had had as a colleague. To my surprise the President at once agreed and said that he never had been." Roosevelt declared his opposition to having Bullitt playing any role in the administration and thereafter would not even allow him to visit the White House. Never again would he be called to government service.[40]

After this final rejection, Bullitt asked Charles de Gaulle for a commission in the Free French army, a request the general promptly approved. Bullitt received the rank of commandant in the infantry, equivalent to the rank of major in the U.S. Army. He sailed for Europe and landed in the south of France to a warm reception. When Paris was liberated on August 25, Bullitt unlocked the American embassy's gates. He enjoyed his tour of duty and wrote his brother, "This decision to go into the French Army was good. Indeed, I don't see why I never thought of becoming an army officer."[41]

While Bullitt was delighting in the romance and drama of the fighting in early 1944, the secretary was suffering from growing fatigue. He was plagued by a severe cough, and he battled a low-grade fever each afternoon. To improve his condition, Dr. Perry ordered two weeks of bed rest, and to guard against further complications, on February 9, Hull traveled to Palm Beach, Florida, for a month of relaxation.[42] While on vacation, he and former ambassador to Russia Joseph Davies talked about the cross-channel invasion and Big Three unity as well as Hull's complaint about Roosevelt's neglecting to consult him about military plans. Rather than admit to being ignored, Hull attributed this slight to the president's preoccupation with the war effort. He "spoke also, very frankly, of the stress of mind he had suffered for some years because of what he called 'lack of loyalty in the Department,' and the sniping of some commentators and others, inspired by his enemies."[43] When Hull returned to work on March 10, the president greeted him at a cabinet meeting by poking fun at his department's outmoded practices and at how he used Arthur Krock to write articles favorable to the foreign service. The president relished needling Hull, who was in no mood to be the butt of presidential humor in front of his colleagues.[44]

The secretary faced much deeper problems within his own organization. He appeared unwilling to deal with many substantive diplomatic issues, such as the department's response to the destruction of European Jewry. Hull had consciously turned away from the refugee question, whereas Welles had at least been sympathetic to those problems, although he had seldom had sufficient time to make a sustained effort in addressing them. After Welles left office, Hull continued to avoid them. When Rabbi Stephen Wise, for example, asked for an interview in early September 1943, Hull declined because of a scheduled "much needed rest." In fact he postponed that vacation in order to orchestrate Welles's demise, but he made no attempt to reschedule with the rabbi. Hull also refused to meet with those in the foreign service who specialized in this subject and had the files on refugee matters routinely routed away from his desk.[45]

Hull's handling of refugee matters bothered Treasury Secretary Morgenthau, but, as the highest-ranking Jewish appointee in the government, he had at first scrupulously stayed away from these topics rather than face charges of religious bias. He was an American Jew, not a Jewish American. He was also initially unaware of the magnitude of the Third

Reich's crimes. After Welles left office, Rabbi Wise, Morgenthau's private secretary (who was an orthodox Jew), and three Christian lawyers on his staff prodded him to examine the State Department's actions concerning the Final Solution. Once Morgenthau had reviewed the data that his staff had gathered, he angrily denounced Hull for his ineptitude and declared that if he "were a member of the Cabinet in Germany today, you would be, most likely, in a prison camp, and your wife would be God knows where" because she, the treasury secretary believed, was Jewish. With the complaint thus drawn, Morgenthau demanded a meeting with Hull in mid-December to allow the secretary to answer the charges of wrongdoing, but at the meeting Hull was so poorly prepared that he was unable to introduce four of the five State Department refugee experts. This pathetic confrontation had the expected result: Morgenthau decided to petition the president to take refugee matters away from the State Department and place them under his command.[46]

Morgenthau presented his indictment to the White House on January 17, 1944. Roosevelt read the charges and realized that the State Department's value had been placed in serious jeopardy. He sensed that the American mood toward the destruction of European Jewry had changed in favor of rescue. Morgenthau's evidence of diplomatic ineptitude gave the president added impetus to take action, and he gave the treasury secretary permission to establish a new rescue agency. The War Refugee Board was formally created on January 22 to assist Jews in their escape from the Nazis. The board's efforts were commendable, but it was a prime example of too little, too late.[47]

Although Hull had almost totally abdicated his humanitarian duty toward European Jewry, he did try to supervise Latin American affairs; however, he seldom looked beyond the broad, vague principles, such as nonintervention and lowering trade barriers, that he had advocated since the start of the New Deal. Welles, after all, had filled in the details in that domain for over a decade, and once the United States had entered the war, he had even expanded his responsibilities to include military and economic assistance, while Hull had reduced his involvement and paid almost no attention to inter-American affairs. Under these circumstances, Latin American representatives had naturally gravitated even more toward the under secretary.[48]

Several prominent New Dealers doubted that Hull could fill the void left by Welles's removal. Ambassador Bowers asserted, "There is a general fear through South America that the passing of Welles from the Department means less interest in South America in Washington, and even a change, if not abandonment, of our 'good neighbor policy.'"[49] Vice-President Wallace expressed his fear that since Latin American assistance was no longer crucial, the United States would neglect regional concerns.[50]

Without firm direction, the hemispheric solidarity that Welles had so painstakingly constructed began to crumble. He had jealously guarded that region as his own private preserve, and Hull disapproved of any "Welles men" like Laurence Duggan continuing the under secretary's policies. As a result, long-established guidelines such as the nonintervention declaration started to unravel. Duggan wondered if Hull would take command. He was known for his attendance and successes at inter-American meetings, but his last appearance had been at the Havana gathering in the summer of 1940. Since then, regional leaders had seen little of him, especially after Pearl Harbor.[51]

When a military coup d'état in Bolivia overthrew the existing regime on December 20, 1943, Hull, convinced of the new leadership's pro-Nazi connections, unilaterally refused to grant recognition and ignored the practice of hemispheric consultation that Welles had scrupulously cultivated. This precipitous decision quickly proved unpopular and provoked adverse reaction. The United States did finally grant recognition in the summer of 1944, but not before the State Department had sustained a loss of prestige.[52]

Hull directed Argentine relations even less skillfully. Welles had isolated that South American nation from influencing most of its neighbors to adopt a policy of neutrality during the war. Once he left office, opposition forces in the administration, spearheaded by Morgenthau, intensified efforts to punish Argentina for its Axis sympathies. These sentiments won additional converts when the regime was accused of conspiring to promote the Bolivian revolt. Without Welles to argue against retribution, these allegations—combined with Hull's humiliation at the hands of Saavedra Lamas during the Buenos Aires conference a decade earlier—turned U.S. policy from one of toleration to one of confrontation. When Argentina's military forces staged a bloodless coup d'état in late February 1944, the State Department seized this occasion to recall its ambassador and break off relations. Nelson Rockefeller, who had started his government career as an inter-American specialist, watched these events unfold, "was completely disgusted with Hull," and later recalled that Hull "was paranoid" when dealing with Argentine affairs.[53]

Once again the United States acted alone without any call for hemispheric consultation. However, unlike the Bolivian case, this time Argentina's strong economy and military might undercut United States pressure. The State Department withdrew its ambassador and enforced mild economic sanctions, but these measures did more to embarrass Hull than hurt the Argentine rulers. If the secretary were to be effective, he would require British acquiescence, but the British placed their need for South American meat and wheat ahead of bending to Hull's desires.[54] Mildly annoyed, on February 19 Roosevelt wished "Argentina would behave itself!"[55] He realized that the fascist-oriented Argentine military regime interfered with inter-American solidarity and hurt the forces of democracy, but that the Allied response was limited by British reliance on imported Argentine foodstuffs. The president routinely condemned the Argentine fascist regime but characterized the country's people as democratic, somehow trying to draw a distinction between the military dictatorship and its subjects. His lack of consistency illustrated how badly he missed Welles's counsel in resolving hemispheric issues.[56]

Duggan, Welles's closest associate, opposed Hull's nonrecognition policies, and he was soon condemned for allegedly supplying Welles and other critics with classified material. Once the secretary had convicted Duggan of disloyalty, his value to the diplomatic corps ceased, and he was forced to leave his post in July 1944. In his letter of resignation, Duggan graciously thanked the secretary for giving him the opportunity to occupy a position of importance in shaping hemispheric decisions. He had traveled to many regional meetings and conferred with numerous Latin American leaders: "To you, Mr. Hull, I shall always be grateful for the confidence you placed in me and which made all of this opportunity possible."[57] With Duggan and Welles gone, Latin American representatives feared that they had lost the two most powerful advocates of the good neighbor policy.

The secretary was far more successful in the formation of the international organization. Under the Welles proposal, regional bodies such
as the inter-American system played an integral part, whereas Hull's
model, as drafted by Leo Pasvolsky, relied on a universal framework,
with Latin America no longer at the core. Hull, Pasvolsky, and his staff
had changed Welles's emphasis and had drawn up a brief outline calling
for an executive council with military power, a general assembly consisting of all nations to discuss disputes, an international court, and social
and economic agencies.[58]

In the debate over the new world order, Congress trusted Hull far
more than Roosevelt. To reinforce that belief and avoid a repetition of
the bloody battle between the Senate and Woodrow Wilson over the
League of Nations, Hull formed the Committee of Eight, with Thomas
Connally, chairman of the Senate Foreign Relations Committee, as chair,
three other Democrats, three Republicans, and one Progressive. They
met with Hull for the first time at the end of April 1944 with the
admonishment to keep their proposals confidential. They then received a
copy of the State Department draft. The outline's provision for the right
of veto and exclusion of mention of an international police force pleased
the committee; even the most committed isolationists could subscribe to
these proposals. Roosevelt added his public support for a postwar world
order and declared to reporters on Memorial Day that he appreciated the
spirit of senatorial cooperation.[59]

Although Hull was pleased with this favorable momentum toward a
world association, he was now regularly reading Welles's objections to
State Department policies in the media and was powerless to censure his
former subordinate's actions. Even more infuriating, Welles stayed in
close contact with Roosevelt and Wallace, lending credence to the gossip
that Welles would try to return to the diplomatic corps after Hull retired.
To his further chagrin, Welles had emerged as an instant celebrity; his
public profile was highlighted even more by the enormous amount of
attention that the media lavished upon him. Within less than a month
after leaving office, the former under secretary had spoken before an
audience of a thousand at the Waldorf-Astoria Hotel in New York City
on the twenty-fifth anniversary of the founding of the Foreign Policy

Association. During his address he called for presidential leadership in hemispheric affairs and a four-power agreement for an international organization, with an executive committee and regional bodies reporting to it.[60]

Welles had been actively involved in the planning for a world body since 1939, and after leaving government service he continued to discuss the concept with Roosevelt. Throughout the spring of 1944, Welles stressed the need for an operational international organization, not just a temporary great power alliance. To guarantee full participation, the governing body should work harmoniously with regional groupings like the inter-American system. When the department shifted its thrust to a universal body with minimum importance given to regional associations, Welles nevertheless asked his followers to back the secretary's general proposal. He disagreed with this change in emphasis and attacked Hull for his failure to consult with Latin America over the provisions of the outline, but he believed that even those problems were insignificant given the real possibility of finally establishing a viable replacement for the League of Nations.[61]

Welles accentuated Hull's hemispheric inadequacies by serving as a constant reminder of how much Latin American diplomats relied on the former under secretary and of how much the president missed him. Welles, according to the secretary, used the public platform to attack his policies. In one article Welles recalled his fruitless advocacy of a non-recognition policy in Cuba during 1933, and on May 10, 1944, he suggested that the same logic applied to Argentina: "Non-recognition in order to exert political pressure is always sterile."[62]

Yet these remarks were mere irritants to Hull compared to his discovery that Welles was writing a book about his years in the State Department. To complete it quickly, he had stopped most of his writing for newspapers and canceled many of his speaking engagements. By the end of 1943, he and his wife were living in Palm Beach, Florida. They had arrived during a terrible cold spell, and Mathilde had been confined to bed due to illness. While caring for his wife, Welles finished his manuscript, and they returned to Oxon Hill Manor to await publication. During the interim, journalists continued to interview him, and he resumed work on his newspaper columns and speaking engagements.[63]

*The Time for Decision*, which was dedicated to Mathilde, was published in the summer of 1944. The book's main theme was that Welles and Roosevelt had directed foreign affairs; Hull received only one passage in praise of his work on reciprocal trade, and Bullitt was not mentioned at all. The study was divided into three parts. In the first, Welles discussed European history starting with World War I, reviewed his mission in 1940, and ended with a summary of United States diplomacy prior to Pearl Harbor. The second part dealt with the past and future of Latin America, Eastern Europe, the Near East, Japan, Asia, the Soviet Union, and Germany; the third was a plea for the United States to join a world organization and play a vital role in shaping international affairs.

An immediate best-seller and a Book-of-the-Month Club main selection, the book sold approximately half a million copies. Reviewers praised it as "mandatory reading," a "must" book, "well written," and "unquestionably one of the most important books of the day." Some criticized the prose, and Berle disapproved of the Soviet section, but they were in the minority.[64] Secretary of War Stimson, who disliked Welles, was surprised by what he read: "It is highly interesting and written in very good taste. I have not run across anything yet which seems to me erroneous in fact or in policy, which indicates that it is a good book."[65]

Hull was terribly shaken and objected to the inference that Welles and Roosevelt had excluded him from the making of foreign policy.[66] Pearson, in the "Washington Merry-Go-Round," magnified this resentment by reporting that Mrs. Hull had expected her husband to be vilified: "However, to be ignored is worse than being criticized, so Mrs. Hull complains bitterly about the Welles book."[67] The secretary chafed at these attempts to embarrass his wife and was further enraged when Mathilde Welles started her own campaign of social ostracism against Frances. According to Welles's wife, Mrs. Hull pretended to be a friend while attacking Sumner behind his back, and it was this duplicity that had been responsible for his removal.[68]

The secretary retaliated with venom and malice. Shortly after James Reston wrote a column in the *New York Times* regretting Welles's departure, the secretary called him into his office and gave him "a thick FBI report alleging homosexual charges against Welles." By giving Reston privileged FBI documents, Hull, the attorney and former judge, was of course violating the law. When the reporter asked Hull if he would accept responsibility as the source of this explosive material, he declined. He was, he replied, merely doing Reston a favor by supplying him with the facts about Welles. Reston took the information to his superior, Arthur Krock, for review, and Krock sent the file to the paper's New York City headquarters. Not one word of it was ever printed.[69]

While Hull waged his private vendetta, Roosevelt concentrated on winning the war. With the successful landings at Normandy and the securing of the beachhead, the Allies had finally established the second front, creating instant euphoria. After a brief respite, the president resumed what had become his normal pattern of settling disputes between the British and the Soviets, mediating disagreements over the composition of the Polish government, and negotiating with Chiang over the course of the war on mainland China.[70]

Not only did the president refuse to consult with Hull on these critical diplomatic matters, but the secretary was not even given the courtesy of having prior notice of the impending Allied invasion of Europe. He also was spending more time at his apartment and was conducting much of his business over the phone. When time permitted, he took brief vacations, including a week's visit in early June to Hershey, Pennsylvania. During that trip, Roosevelt and Churchill secretly agreed to a three-month trial period during which the Russians would control Bulgaria and the British would supervise Yugoslavia. This step did not mean that the United States had sanctified postwar spheres of influence, but it did illustrate how easily the president was willing to take politically delicate steps in Hull's absence. Roosevelt never did inform the secretary of this White House decision; only by chance did Hull learn of it.[71] Some accused him of not directing foreign affairs, and Assistant Secretary Long concurred: "The impression was growing."[72]

Intense fighting was not only confined to the battlefields that summer, for the American political parties were preparing for their national conventions. Hull was determined not to allow the postwar international organization to become a partisan issue, and on June 15 the White House released the broad outline of the State Department proposal. With the Republican convention two weeks away, the secretary had made a brilliant tactical move, for at that point all the opposition could do was accept or reject the administration's recommendation. The secretary also worked within the internationalist wing of the opposition party to garner support for the Democratic blueprint. Although he was unable to win ratification, the Republican platform was not hostile to the proposal, and the party's presidential nominee, Thomas Dewey, refrained from making postwar cooperation a campaign issue. As the Democrats prepared for their convention, the president made his expected decision, one week before the start of the convention in mid-July, to run for a fourth term. Once again, he asked Hull to be his running mate, and for the last time, the secretary declined.[73]

The Soviet ambassador to the United States, Andrei Gromyko, watched the upcoming election and reported to Moscow on July 14 that he hoped Roosevelt would defeat Dewey, for Dewey represented a return to isolationism. Currently, Roosevelt, Hull, and the congressional majority favored assisting Russia in the defeat of the Nazis, while the Catholic Church and American Poles attacked Russian motives. Although the United States and the Soviet Union had serious disagreements, the two great powers had to reach an accommodation. After the war, the United States would remain powerful, supporting Western Europe while opposing neo-fascist governments, and expanding its international economic influence. The Russians would need American trade, financial credits, and scientific and technical assistance.[74]

While the Russian ambassador expressed cautious optimism for the future, Hull was driving in the same direction because he needed Soviet support for the future global association. As Stalin's armies pushed deeper into Eastern Europe that spring, Hull was asking Great Britain, the Soviet Union, and China to comment on the draft proposals for a charter. Late that summer, he proposed talks on the future international organization to be held at Dumbarton Oaks in Washington. Almost immediately after this announcement, leaks surfaced about the absolute veto and the omission of mention of an international air force. Dewey, disturbed by the rumors of a great power alliance to coerce smaller nations, spoke out publicly on August 16 for equality for all nations and won widespread media praise. Hull reacted angrily the next morning, calling the charges unfounded, and then invited Dewey to confer with him in the spirit of bipartisanship. The presidential contender appointed John Foster Dulles to represent him, an act that thrust Dulles into the national spotlight. When he and Hull met, they agreed to keep the upcoming talks out of the campaign. It was the first time that two spokesmen for presidential candidates had reached an accord to remove a major foreign policy issue from a presidential campaign. The secretary had once again accomplished what he did best: avoiding controversy by seeking a political compromise to eliminate potential conflicts. Hull gave the opening address at Dumbarton Oaks on the morning of August 21, stressing the need to have force available to preserve peace. The secretary then left the proceedings in the hands of Stettinius as head of the American delegation, but scrupulously kept the Committee of Eight informed, recognizing the importance of making certain that the Senate was apprised of the substance of the discussions.[75]

While Hull concentrated on Dumbarton Oaks, the president conferred with Treasury Secretary Morgenthau, who had just returned from England, about British fears of a possible postwar German military resurgence. Roosevelt responded by declaring that he would forestall such an abhorrent possibility by using the might of American armed forces. Impressed by that militant stance, the secretary formed a treasury committee to develop a plan for postwar Germany. Roosevelt wanted that nation to suffer, and Morgenthau obliged him by advocating truly spartan measures. Stimson, however, wanted to act carefully before destroying any key industrial regions, such as the Saar and the Ruhr. Without having made any decision, Roosevelt, weary and nursing a cold, traveled to the second Quebec conference in mid-September; Morgenthau arrived several days later to present his proposal to divide Germany into three zones and destroy the industrial installations in the Ruhr, thereby transforming the Third Reich into a pastoral country. Hull had originally approved the initial concept, but Stimson, who had always opposed it, won out over Hull. When the proposal was leaked to the newspapers, it was attacked as too harsh and liable to stiffen German resistance to the point of fanaticism.[76]

The controversy over the dismemberment of Germany never became an issue in the national campaign because Dewey had chosen other themes: age, health, and leadership. Roosevelt had stronger ammunition by trading on his prestige as commander in chief, the victories in the field, and a prosperous economy. Both parties advocated postwar collaboration and called for an expanded U.S. role in foreign affairs. Voters had far more fundamental instincts; they preferred Roosevelt's long record of experience to that of an unknown.[77]

Canadian Prime Minister MacKenzie King visited with the president on September 11 and noticed that his friend had lost thirty pounds and that his face looked thinner, "quite drawn," and "his eyes quite weary." Not only was he gaunt, but he looked "distinctly older and worn. I confess I was just a little bit shocked at his appearance."[78] Yet within two weeks, Roosevelt's looks had dramatically changed. He seemed healthy and gave one of the best performances of his presidency in the famous Fala speech, in which he sarcastically resented his adversaries' attacking not only his immediate family but even his dog. While a partisan Democratic audience howled with approving laughter, few noticed that for the first time Roosevelt spoke sitting down, without the use of leg braces.[79]

Although the president's health had become a hotly contested issue, only a very few knew of Roosevelt's complaints of headaches, chronic fatigue, loss of appetite, temporary memory lapses, and intellectual impairment. Admiral McIntire's elimination of exercise had weakened his muscles, and this made him even more dependent on his valet for a variety of nursing care. The president was no longer merely paralyzed by his polio; he was losing the fight against the disease. When the admiral declared that his patient was in good health, he was either lying or guilty of incompetence.[80]

During the last two weeks of the campaign, Roosevelt shed any doubts about his health, invoking all of his political skills and also enjoying some luck. The headlines on October 20 proclaimed that General Douglas MacArthur had invaded the Philippines with light casualties, and naturally, as commander in chief, Roosevelt benefited from that victory. The next day he was driven through New York in a heavy rain storm with the automobile's top removed. Crowds estimated at between one and three million greeted him warmly, and that night he gave a masterful speech before an appreciative Democratic audience. Throughout the remainder of the campaign, he continued his energetic schedule, seeking to negate any charges of physical impairment.[81] During the contest, he had come to detest Dewey, and the fact that the challenger did not concede until very early on the morning after election night further irritated him. As the president went up the steps to the second floor at Hyde Park to go to bed that night, he snidely remarked, "I still think he is a son of a bitch."[82]

Hull followed most of the campaign from his apartment, making two partisan statements praising the president and endorsing his reelection. Although most Americans expected Hull to stay in office, he had notified the president on several occasions that spring of his intention to resign owing to ill health. Roosevelt refused to accept this intention, insisting that Hull remain to serve as the U.S. delegate to the San Francisco meeting for the establishment of the international organization.[83]

Hull acceded to the president's wishes and also remained to work against the German dismemberment proposal. When Pearson attacked him and Stimson on September 21 on this issue, the secretary was furious. Five days later, Assistant Secretary Long recorded the secretary's anger: "[He] is in the worst humor I have ever seen him. He is worried sick and has not slept for two or three nights and finds it impossible to get this off his mind. He feels that it is a repudiation and that it has placed him in a position which he may not for very long be able to maintain. . . . He feels that a rift between him and the President has become real and that his position under these circumstances may not long be tenable."[84] Three days later the secretary spoke to Roosevelt about his opposition to the dismemberment proposal, and on October 1 he personally handed the president a memorandum enumerating his reasons, forcing Morgenthau to concede defeat; Roosevelt promptly withdrew his earlier support.[85]

The spectre of Sumner Welles also haunted Hull, who seemed to be consumed by his foe's every real or imagined action. The secretary's extreme sensitivity turned Welles into a villain, out of office but not out of the Hulls' lives. The secretary even erroneously accused him of leaking classified documents to Pearson and took every word that Welles uttered as a personal affront, even when he offered prudent advice. The former under secretary endorsed the general framework of the Dumbarton Oaks proposal, but complained that the smaller nations needed a larger voice. He argued for a stronger regional character for the organization, according to which each member should select its representative for the executive council and maintain peace within its area. He warned against a great power alliance since its viability would be brief. These recommendations, especially the regional emphasis, were in contradistinction to Hull's views.[86]

Hull spent "restless nights" over what he perceived as Welles's activities to undermine the department's declarations. The secretary had allegedly discovered that his enemy was holding frequent meetings with hemispheric diplomats, and one South American representative told Hull that Welles was in effect running a second State Department with Roosevelt's blessings, "and that more reliance was being placed upon what was going on at Mr. Welles' residence than what was going on at the State Department."[87]

When the former under secretary voiced his opposition to the department's Argentine nonrecognition policy as being ineffective, weakening hemispheric solidarity, and promoting the fascist regime, Hull exploded. When Welles called for an inter-American gathering to discuss such postwar concerns as future economic plans, dialogue concerning Dumbarton Oaks, and Argentina, the secretary stubbornly refused to consider its viability.[88]

In fact Hull opposed just about anything that Welles favored, and as a consequence, even his best recommendations were dismissed. He did not understand that he was contributing to the fragmentation of hemispheric solidarity by raising Hull's ire. Welles knew something was wrong and was extremely anxious about the future of the good neighbor policy, warning Ambassador Corrigan "that, if we continue our present course for much longer, not much will remain."[89]

The secretary, too, was worried, but his concern was that Roosevelt had refused to listen to his counsel because Welles was going to replace him. Hull confided to Morgenthau that Welles's admirers were criticizing him with the White House's blessings; furthermore, the secretary could not trust his advisers because they, especially Duggan, were all loyal to Welles—who was telling everyone not to listen to Hull because after the election Welles would be back at the department.[90]

Hull's fears were unwarranted and unfounded. He had offered his resignation since spring, and the president had repeatedly rejected it.

Hull was too valuable to the reelection campaign because the public revered him, and Roosevelt recognized that reality. Just before the campaign began in earnest, the president told Wallace that Hull would remain because he "was an old dear and he [the president] could not bear to break his heart."[91]

Roosevelt apparently was unaware how close Hull was to collapse. When Farley saw the secretary for an hour on September 29, he "was pale and drawn and nervous." His throat was so sore that he could not deliver any speeches. Roosevelt continued to bypass him and consult Welles; therefore, as soon as possible after the election, Hull would leave. He told the former postmaster general, "Jim, I am through."[92] Hull saw Krock the same day and lambasted the president for neglecting him. He angrily claimed that the president "was basing his hope for re-election on a foreign-policy record which I personally made—often after talking the President out of 'some folly.'"[93]

On October 1, the secretary went for the last time to the White House, where he convinced the president to repudiate Morgenthau's plan. This was his "last important item of business in his office. I was now on the verge of the collapse that necessitated my resignation."[94] The very next day, on his seventy-third birthday, Hull was confined to bed. His heart and digestive tract were fine, but his tuberculosis had worsened, and he was running a temperature in the afternoon. He had difficulty speaking and complained of toothaches, and for the first time, his doctor found blood in his urine.[95]

Restricted to his apartment, Hull invited Frank Walker, the postmaster general, to visit him on the evening of October 13. During their meeting, Hull recalled that a medical specialist had warned him against a Senate race in 1932 because of a spot on his lung and a mild case of diabetes, but that his private physician encouraged him to run. His health had been fine up until the negotiations with the Japanese before Pearl Harbor. By then, his lung condition had deteriorated, and he suffered so much that his doctor had prescribed narcotics to soothe the pain in his throat. His health had improved until that spring, when he admitted undergoing considerable stress. Now his diabetes had reached an advanced stage, and his lung had gotten much worse. Hull then lost control and began to cry. He wanted the president to know that Berle,

Long, and Acheson were going to draft a foreign policy statement proclaiming his views, and although he had been named to lead the American delegation to the San Francisco conference that was to complete the negotiations for the postwar international organization, he could not complete that mission. He hoped that the press would not discover the gravity of his illnesses, for he might never work again or even leave his bed.[96]

Hull had been so skillful at hiding his infirmities that on the following day Dewey publicly pledged, that, if elected, he would offer Hull a diplomatic post. Hull responded by pledging his loyalty to the current Democratic administration, prompting the following remarks from British diplomatic observer Isaiah Berlin: "Hull's name is still the greatest symbol of sound foreign policy in either party and both sides naturally wish to buttress themselves with his prestige."[97]

Hull was by then unable to conduct business or even function normally. Frances worried about her husband's loss of appetite and inability to sleep owing to a persistent cough. She was so concerned about his health that she made him promise to go to the hospital, and on October 20 he entered Bethesda Naval Hospital, where doctors found that his heart was strong, his tuberculosis had spread to both lungs, and two badly infected teeth had to be extracted. No one at that time predicted that his recovery would take seven months.[98]

The initial draft of the State Department press release dealing with Hull's hospital stay, according to Dean Acheson, "raised serious doubt that he [Hull] would ever come out." In order to assure the public that Hull would return to his office and thus not diminish his value to the presidential campaign, diplomats Acheson and Joseph Grew prepared an innocuous and misleading statement declaring that Hull was going into the hospital for rest and a medical checkup. Most Americans believed that the secretary would remain at his post after the election until the new international organization had become firmly established. Roosevelt had gone to the hospital on November 15 to see how Hull was progressing, with no intention of replacing him. If Hull could not continue, Roosevelt at least wanted him to remain in office until the end of the third term.[99] Hull simply could not comply, and Frances agreed. That was crucial, for as Joseph Davies pointed out, she was his "spark plug," as she had been "throughout the Welles situation."[100]

Hull sent his letter of resignation on the grounds of ill health to the White House on the afternoon of November 21, but he promised to be available for public service after his recovery. During the almost twelve years of his association with Roosevelt, Hull claimed that

> our personal relations have been uniformly and invariably agreeable and that, by our joint efforts, many difficult tasks growing out of the foreign relations of this country before and during this war have been brought to partial or full completion; many great questions have been faced successfully; and many forward movements of surpassing importance to friendly relations among nations have been instituted.

He had hoped to work on the transition from war to peace, particularly the foundation of the international organization, but since he was now bedridden, Roosevelt would have to continue without him.[101]

Roosevelt responded the same day, accepting the resignation and making a gracious gesture by offering to delay the announcement until the end of the third term. The president began:

> Your letter of this afternoon has hit me between wind and water. It has been very sad for me even to contemplate the ending of our close relationship during all these twelve years. It is not merely that our personal relations have been so uniformly and invariably agreeable, or that our joint work has borne true success in so many fields, as it is the personal feeling of not being able to lean on you for aid and intimate interchange of thought.

When the San Francisco conference convened,

> I shall continue to pray that you as the Father of the United Nations may preside over its first session. That has nothing to do with whether you are Secretary of State or not at the time, but should go to you as the one person in all the world who has done the most to make this great plan for peace an effective fact.[102]

Hull had always taken exception to the president's earlier claims that the White House directed foreign affairs, but Roosevelt's letter pleased him because, according to the secretary, this time the president complimented his work at the State Department and, for the first time, called Hull the "Father of the United Nations"—an undeserved acknowledgment that has stuck to this day.

On November 27, Roosevelt announced Hull's resignation "with very great regret, deep regret." Secretary of the Interior Ickes, who minimized his colleague's worth, did not feel that this was a great loss, for Hull had been a poor secretary of state, although he did have fine personal qualities, such as steadfastness and objectivity. Stimson, however, spoke for the vast majority when he claimed that Hull's exit was a tremendous blow. Even his nemesis Saavedra Lamas declared that Hull had helped shape the good neighbor policy, forged continental solidarity, fought for reciprocal trade, and worked for the nonintervention principle. Farley, who had visited his friend at the hospital, exaggerated Hull's importance and deprecated the president's. Roosevelt had taken "for himself all the credit, as if he had directed the Department's policies, whereas, we who were close knew that Mr. Hull was a potent force, dictating all the State Department's activities."[103]

The British embassy provided its evaluation on December 2. The vast majority of editorials, most broadcasters, and both houses of Congress eulogized the secretary's character and judgment,

> which had made him for so long the symbol of traditional American virtue, the possessor of attributes which many Americans instinctively think with pride as the national character at its best and finest. There is no doubt about the unanimity and sincerity of this nationwide outpouring of homage and personal regret at the retirement of this widely admired and indeed much beloved figure, whose very tartness and obstinacy have contributed to the image of him as a Grand Old Man, the father of the new American foreign policy, in whom almost infinite trust was reposed by the average unsophisticated American citizen.

Hull would continue as an elder statesman and a presidential adviser on the formation of a world council. That was a fitting climax to a distinguished career.[104]

Graham Stuart, in his history of the State Department, probably provided the most favorable insider assessment: "Hull was a great

Secretary of State, a great statesman, but, above all, a great man."
Having led the foreign service through the war years, when Roosevelt
temporarily ruled "as an absolute dictator," Hull's achievement was all
the more noteworthy. To the end of his career, he never openly attacked
the president, and as a staunch Democrat and a patriotic American, he
loyally supported his party by staying at his post. He successfully struggled to establish the reciprocal trade agreements program, an action that
to its advocates meant lowering trade barriers and to its antagonists
meant stripping away tariffs that protected domestic businesses. That
was the "monument to his name."[105]

Others, however, provided far harsher assessments in hindsight.
James Roosevelt claimed that his father had never respected Hull and
had therefore ignored him. Career diplomat Robert Murphy agreed and
added that Hull's national prestige had forced the president to have him
remain in office.[106] Acheson saw the estrangement between the two
leaders as having devastating consequences. Since Hull refused to assert
his authority, the State Department did not participate in major wartime
decisions, and this void created uncertainty in formulating postwar
policies:

> Largely detached from the practicalities of current problems and power
> relationships, the Department under Mr. Hull became absorbed in
> platonic planning of a utopia, in a sort of mechanistic idealism. Per-
> haps, given the nature of the current problems, of the two men, and of
> the tendency to accept dichotomy between foreign and military policy,
> this would have occurred in any event. But it accentuated the isolation
> of the Secretary and the Department in a land of dreams.

Acheson exaggerated, but the president clearly did not consider his
secretary of state to be his principal adviser on foreign affairs.[107]

Hull also commented on his lack of influence and the reasons behind
it. Before Pearl Harbor, he had sat on the government's war council and
participated in its decisions, but immediately after the United States
entered the conflict, he was excluded from military conferences. When
the president and Hopkins traveled to Casablanca, Cairo, and Tehran,
Hull stayed at home. During Churchill's visits to the White House, the
prime minister and the president, along with Hopkins, charted military

strategy by themselves. Hull did not even know about the extent of casualties at Pearl Harbor until reporters informed him, and he was unaware of both D-Day and the Manhattan Project until after the fact. Roosevelt's mode of operation during the war was the most frequently mentioned reason for excluding the secretary: the president handled military matters owing to his role as commander in chief and so did not require the State Department's opinion. The secretary added that whenever he had asked for specific information, Roosevelt had always honored those requests—an assertion that was quite simply untrue. Hull could rationalize the reasons for this neglect, but these were only a façade. In reality, he was terribly shaken by the White House's failure to consult.[108]

Despite the recognition of the tenuous ties between the State Department and the White House, the end of Hull's tenure created a feeling of uneasiness. His overwhelming popularity had rested on a carefully crafted and cultivated image symbolizing traditional American values that the public revered, and it believed that Hull had played a major role in the conduct of wartime diplomacy. Yet behind this public persona lay a terribly insecure man who had been relegated to lowly standing in the Oval Office. In a multitude of ways, his career was that simple and that complicated.

# CHAPTER 16

# ROOSEVELT'S LAST MONTHS

ONLY A HANDFUL OF PEOPLE knew the extent of Hull's total collapse. Although his tuberculosis responded positively to treatment, he suffered from night sweats. Even if he were asked to recommend his successor, he asserted, "I would have had no voice in it anyhow, and no suggestion from me was wanted or would be effective— probably to the contrary."[1] The one unspoken exception was that Hull so despised his former second in command that the secretary "was willing to take any other man than Sumner Welles."[2]

Ambassador Claude Bowers in Chile lamented that if only Welles had backed Hull's policies, he would have succeeded him as secretary of state. Josephus Daniels, who had retired from his ambassadorship in Mexico, added, "[Welles] is a very able man, and it is a misfortune that at this time our country should not have the benefit of his experience and his world knowledge."[3] Welles, in fact, longed to return, but he realized that he never stood the remotest chance because "the scandal mongers" would continue to spread stories about his homosexuality. Permanently exiled from government service, Welles made his widest impact that winter from his Palm Beach home by working on a radio program, starting a foreign affairs magazine, and editing a series of books for Harvard University. He also lobbied ardent New Dealers like Henry Wallace and Archibald MacLeish, who remained in the administration, to advance "liberal" causes.[4]

With Welles excluded, the main contenders for the secretaryship narrowed down to James Byrnes and Edward Stettinius. The former had powerful congressional support, while the latter was under secretary. Some believed that Harry Hopkins had lobbied for his protégé Stettinius as a way to limit the influence of the Southern wing of the Democratic party, for those like Hopkins who had intimate links with the New Deal fought to maintain their White House power over party regulars, personified by politicians like Byrnes. By making the State Department a New Deal appendage, Hopkins hoped to minimize the importance of Southern Democrats in Congress and in the executive branch.

Roosevelt eliminated any doubt over the succession by summoning Walter George of Georgia and Thomas Connally of Texas, the Democratic leaders of the Senate Foreign Relations Committee, to the White House on November 27, 1944, and presenting them with Stettinius's promotion. Both were stunned and disappointed that Byrnes had been passed over, but neither voiced any serious objection. After all, Stettinius was the president's natural choice because Roosevelt intended to continue to operate as his own secretary of state and did not want to face Byrnes's strong opinions. Stettinius was convenient and would continue to carry out White House directives with Hopkins providing supervision.[5]

Roosevelt had dramatically altered the traditional role of the diplomatic corps; its assigned mission to shape foreign policy had now crossed over to the White House. Hull, Moore, Welles, Duggan, and Bullitt were gone, while the man who appointed them remained, and he, more than anyone else, was responsible for the turbulence and disruption at the State Department. Career diplomats still handled their daily duties and made recommendations based on reports from around the world. On major decisions, rather than having them submit proposals for the president's approval, this process was reversed. The White House routinely took independent action and instructed the State Department how to respond. Whether the diplomatic corps understood the consequences of these actions or not was immaterial; the White House had become the final initiator and arbitrator of foreign policy.

The president governed from the top of the pyramid and continually overestimated his abilities to make any decision that appealed to his fancy. He never memorialized his grand design with anyone, and that glaring flaw in his personal style of constructing American foreign policy caused havoc. Since he did not have the time or the inclination to follow up each one of his instructions, he expected Stettinius and his staff to fill in the specifics without clearly enunciated guidelines. One key result of this poorly conceived management style was that fourth-term Vice-President Harry Truman was never consulted about foreign affairs; therefore, he would be woefully unprepared to direct American diplomacy if he were forced to assume the presidency.

Roosevelt's management style was not an issue during Stettinius's Senate confirmation hearings, at which he was approved with only one dissenting vote. He seemed an adequate choice because of his familiarity with the diplomatic corps and his ability to maintain good congressional relations. Professional diplomats also welcomed his appointment because Stettinius had come to rely on them to make policy recommendations, a fact that pleased the professionals.[6] The relatively smooth hearings, however, did not translate into enthusiastic support for the new appointee. Although he did not have many outspoken opponents, several influential politicians seriously questioned his qualifications. Treasury Secretary Morgenthau thought that Stettinius would fit the job description of a "good clerk"; Interior Secretary Harold Ickes thought that Stettinius did not have the appropriate training or intellectual depth; Senator George was even more derogatory in labeling the secretary "a nice enough lad if not too bright."[7]

Stettinius did not appear to warrant such pessimistic comments because, in many ways, he was ideally suited to manage a rapidly expanding bureaucracy. To cope with this growth, he almost doubled the size of his staff and brought in a multitude of consultants for special assignments. These adjustments were long overdue. For example, in 1939 the State Department had 974 employees and by 1945 it had 3,767, an increase of almost 400 percent. During the same period, the number of foreign service personnel jumped from 3,730 to almost 7,000.

The budget had risen to $50 million.[8] Joseph Davies, former ambassador to the Soviet Union, anticipated that the new secretary would do a creditable job, but that professional diplomats would cause friction: "Little men, who got into the saddle by fishing in the troubled waters of the Hull-Welles quarrel, are persistent and shrewd. Some of them are fine, but they generally are of a caliber that is governed by abstractions. The facts of life they cannot access. If they had to earn a living most of them would starve."[9]

Stettinius disagreed with these negative remarks because he heavily relied on advice from career officers. At the same time, he shocked Washington circles by firing Assistant Secretary Adolf Berle when the latter was in the middle of an international aviation conference. Breckinridge Long, suspected of anti-Semitism and tired of refuting these charges, retired, as did G. Howland Shaw. In their places, Stettinius announced his team in early December. Of the previous high-ranking appointments, only Dean Acheson remained, to handle congressional relations. Joseph Grew, a professional diplomat, moved into the under secretary slot. James Dunn, a long-time adviser to Hull and another career official, continued to direct European affairs. Nelson Rockefeller, whom Roosevelt had personally tapped, supervised Latin American matters. William Clayton, a Texas businessman who had made a fortune in cotton, concentrated on international economic issues. Julius Holmes, who had twenty years' experience in the diplomatic corps and later became president of General Mills of Brazil, worked on administrative matters. Archibald MacLeish, poet and librarian of Congress, directed public affairs. The press reacted immediately by dubbing the group six millionaires plus a poet; others scored them for their close connections with Wall Street and the career foreign service. When a reporter questioned the president on their qualifications as New Dealers, he responded that they were expected to follow orders; he did not worry about their political philosophy.[10]

Grew's appointment was central. He had graduated from Groton and had entered Harvard two years before Roosevelt. They became friends, and since Stettinius was away from the capital much of the time during his tenure, Grew often went to the White House as acting secretary and worked well with the president.[11] The new under secretary also enjoyed pleasant relations with Stettinius, who had hoped "to bring new blood into the old Department and to sweep away some of the cobwebs." He expected Grew to become his partner, and when Stettinius was traveling, Grew acted with full authority, a fact that he truly appreciated: "In all my service in Washington I never saw the Department better organized than during the Stettinius regime."[12]

While Stettinius was adjusting to his new role, Roosevelt was becoming deeply concerned over the direction of Soviet-American relations. Ambassador to Russia Averell Harriman, who had been appointed to Moscow in late 1943, initially thought that the United States could cooperate with Stalin, but that view slowly changed as communist forces swept across Eastern Europe. George Kennan became counselor to the embassy in the summer of 1944 and reinforced the ambassador's growing trepidation. Kennan had long held that the Soviet system was antithetical tooAmerican democracy, and he also stressed that Stalin's motives, especially in regard to the liberation of Poland, were antagonistic to those of the United States. To impress upon the president the gravity of his concerns over the future of Soviet-American solidarity, Harriman returned to the United States in October, just before the presidential election, to warn Roosevelt that cooperation with Stalin would be extremely difficult because the dictator supported communist regimes in Eastern Europe based on repressive measures like the use of secret police.[13]

Whereas Harriman and Kennan were skeptical about working with the Soviets, most State Department professionals accepted the importance of Soviet-American collaboration as advanced by Roosevelt, Hull, and Welles. Charles "Chip" Bohlen typified their position. Having entered the foreign service in 1929, he became a Soviet specialist and spoke Russian fluently. Hopkins had met him in late 1942 and was impressed by the younger man's ability to get along with people and his knowledge of the Soviet Union. They talked further during the journeys to and from the Tehran conference, and in early 1944 Bohlen was appointed head of the department's Soviet section; by the end of the year, he had moved up to serve as the department's official liaison with the White House.[14]

Before Roosevelt acted, he took both viewpoints into consideration, understanding that he had to deal cautiously with Stalin and concurrently recognizing that solidarity was critical in winning the war. While both sides continued to argue over the best approach toward Soviet policy, two days after his fourth inauguration, the president secretly left the White House for the second Big Three meeting in Yalta, to confer on military strategy to end the war and on the transition toward the postwar world. Along with the president, the American delegation included Stettinius, Pa Watson, and Byrnes; Hopkins had previously flown to London, Paris, and Rome to prepare for the talks and resolve as many problems as possible before they commenced. In early February the delegation arrived at Malta, where the Anglo-American military chiefs decided their strategy in the closing months of the European fighting.

Roosevelt then took off on the flight to the Crimea. Turbulence made the trip uncomfortable, and thus when the plane touched down at Yalta, the president was exhausted. Despite his weakened physical condition, his health was not a major factor at the conference, even though he worked long hours and sometimes ignored his rest periods in order to finish that day's business. He had every intention of serving as the facilitator between Stalin and Churchill. To the president, nothing was more important than the Anglo-American alliance, and concurrently he pressed diligently for cordial relations with the Soviet Union.

The conference opened on February 4 in the late afternoon, and although disagreements sometimes arose during the sessions, in general a spirit of cooperation prevailed; each leader promoted his own specific proposals but was open to compromise. The president put forth the latest form of the proposal for a future world organization, and Stalin ended the stalemate over the impasse that had arisen at Dumbarton Oaks by accepting the American veto formula. The Soviets also reduced their earlier demand for all sixteen of their republics to be seated in the general assembly to three. As for the Polish question, Roosevelt had to answer to an anti-communist, Polish-American constituency, and therefore he advanced the cause of Polish political self-determination in the face of Soviet occupation. Stalin insisted on having a Polish neighbor that was sensitive to Soviet fears; the long common border between the two countries would never again become the staging area for an invasion. Unable to resolve the vast gulf that separated them on this issue, the three leaders passed a nebulous proposal according to which Poland and the rest of liberated Europe would hold free elections. To soothe Churchill's ego, he was granted an occupational zone for France in Germany, and all agreed to create a special commission to study German reparations. In East Asia, Churchill and Roosevelt conceded the Soviets use of the Manchurian railway as well as occupation of the Sakhalin and Kurile islands to protect the approaches to the Soviet harbor of Vladivostok in return for Stalin's pledge to declare war against the Japanese.[15]

At the conclusion of the talks, the Big Three left the Crimea on February 11, optimistic that they had strengthened the Grand Alliance. On the return voyage, Roosevelt began preparations for a report to Congress on the success at Yalta. But this positive atmosphere disintegrated when Pa Watson suddenly died from a heart attack; in addition, Hopkins had become so ill that he was confined to his cabin until reaching Algiers, where he left the presidential party to fly to the Mayo Clinic. Deeply upset by Watson's passing, Hopkins's incapacitation, and his own exhaustion, Roosevelt disembarked at Newport News, Virginia, at the end of February and immediately returned to the White House.

On March 1, he went before Congress for the first time in two years to report on the results of his travels, and observers witnessed a spectacle that they had never before seen. Rather than walk with the aid of his steel braces, the president was rolled into the House chamber in a wheelchair and transferred to an armchair to address his audience. Many who witnessed this startling event also noticed his drawn appearance and an unusually poorly delivered speech, during which he slurred his words and on several occasions seemingly lost his place in the text. To excuse these lapses, he mentioned his paralysis for the first time and alluded to the strain caused by his long journey.[16]

While the public riveted its attention on the presidential address and daily reports from the battlefields, hemispheric affairs slipped from the front pages, and, without Welles's driving presence, were eliminated as a major diplomatic imperative. Those who had been closely associated with the former under secretary were systematically reassigned or fired.[17] Unfortunately for many of them, the new assistant secretary of state for Latin American affairs, Nelson Rockefeller, made job security precarious: "when I entered the State Department . . . we cleared out most of the people who were there [in the Latin American division]. . . . There were a hell of a lot of them [homosexuals] there. We got them out."[18]

Welles watched the departmental purge and the disintegration of the good neighbor policy in sorrow, declaring that it was "going to hell" and that his twelve years of work were "being lost." Despite such pessimism, he continued to speak out for hemispheric unity, urging governmental loans and the infusion of private capital to assist Latin American economies. By adopting these practices, the United States would aid industrialization and raise living standards throughout the Americas.[19]

Rockefeller hoped to reinvigorate the good neighbor spirit by embracing the call for an inter-American conference. No regional gathering had been convened since the Rio meeting in early 1942, and despite increasing Latin American pressure for one, Hull had effectively blocked it. Hemispheric statesmen wanted to voice their preference for the continuation of the inter-American system, whereas those who surrounded Hull promoted a more universal concept. Rockefeller embraced hemispheric solidarity, gained Stettinius's approval for another meeting, and then won presidential support.[20]

While the top American diplomatic leaders were in Yalta, Rockefeller independently arranged an agenda for the inter-American meeting, to be held outside Mexico City at the Chapultepec Castle. It opened on February 21, with Rockefeller and the Latin American delegates united on regionalism at the same time as Stettinius and his staff were flying from the Crimea, where they had vigorously advanced a global model. Stettinius's staff successfully prevented any open debate concerning universalism versus regionalism, but the United States could not prevent the Latin Americans from voicing their opposition to weakening the inter-American system. The Act of Chapultepec demonstrated their resolve, for the declaration guaranteed that the regional system protected any members from aggression by their neighbors.[21] Ambassador George Messersmith, stationed in Mexico, participated in his delegation's debates, favored inter-American understanding, and sadly lamented that "Stettinius was . . . completely beyond his depth."[22]

Roosevelt did not play any significant role in the drama unfolding in Mexico. The day after addressing Congress on the results at Yalta, he headed for Hyde Park for a week of relaxation and then returned to the

White House to concentrate on the final military campaigns of the war. He also started to search for ways to achieve a lasting peace. Chiang Kai-shek and his communist foes needed to cooperate; Stalin had to compromise over the composition of the Polish government; the role of the Allied forces in Italy had to be clarified; and the White House had to sell participation in the world organization to the American people.[23]

Attorney General Biddle met with the president twice in the first half of March; he commented that the "President looked thin, brown and well." Two weeks later, Biddle still thought that Roosevelt "looked well, but thinner"; he was tired and planned to travel to Hyde Park and then Warm Springs "for a rest."[24] During a visit to Washington on March 9, Canadian Prime Minister MacKenzie King talked with Eleanor, who admitted that her husband was tired from his Yalta trip. King saw the president on several occasions during his stay and "felt compassion for him. He looked much older; face very much thinner, particularly the lower part." The Canadian realized that Roosevelt was ill, but commented that he had not become nearly so unattractive as recent uncomplimentary photographs suggested: "he has lost a certain merriment, looks older and wearier, but has a certain firmness, which might carry him along for some time." The two leaders also discussed Roosevelt's reluctance to attend the opening ceremonies at the San Francisco meeting. Instead, he hoped to substitute Hull if he were well enough to travel, for his name symbolized global cooperation, and the new world body would have added stature if the former secretary were the first president of the security organization.[25]

On the evening of March 13, King and Roosevelt had dinner at the White House. The president's daughter Anna served as hostess, and she confided to the Canadian guest that her father "missed his old friends" like "Missy" LeHand and Pa Watson. Before sitting down to eat, the president introduced the prime minister to Lucy Rutherford, identifying her as a relative from South Carolina; King described her as "a very lovely woman and of great charm" and "exceptionally fine character."[26] Although Franklin had promised Eleanor in 1918 never to see Lucy again, the president had blatantly broken that pledge. After she had left their employment, she had served as governess for the children of Winthrop Rutherford: handsome, wealthy, and thirty years her senior. They eventually married, and she became a stepmother to his five children, including one girl and four boys. Winthrop and she formed a loving union and had a daughter. As he slowly began to deteriorate physically, Lucy painstakingly devoted much of her time to making him comfortable until his death as well as caring for the children.[27] Eleanor did not know that her husband had invited Lucy to the White House. Yet those unmentioned meetings did not disturb Franklin's outward relationship with his wife; that Saturday, Franklin and Eleanor celebrated their fortieth wedding anniversary at a small family luncheon.[28]

The complexities of Franklin's private life did not interfere with his command decisions. During the final months of the war, a faction within the German hierarchy made overtures to British and American agents in Switzerland about surrendering. When Stalin learned about this activity, he accused Churchill and Roosevelt of purposely excluding him from those talks. The president vigorously denied the charge and chose to treat this exchange as a minor disagreement. He intended to cooperate with the Soviets in the future, but at the same time stick to a firm course for the present.[29]

By the end of March, the president was extremely tired and had lost his appetite. Once more, he traveled to the South to take the mineral waters of Warm Springs, Georgia. Seldom did he take Eleanor on these trips, for she disliked the region, but to him, April in Georgia was one of the most picturesque times of the year. Nestled at the foot of an incline was the Little White House, and guests stayed at the two cottages to the right and left of the president. Besides bathing, Roosevelt often cruised over the narrow, winding roads to admire the cultivated land and breathtaking scenery from his own specially built car, with its hand-operated shift and brakes.

Upon his arrival, his spirits seemed to improve from the wholesome and invigorating climate. He had invited his cousins Laura Delano and Margaret Suckley to join him. Lucy arrived at the end of the first week in April with Elizabeth Shoumatoff, who had already gone to the White House shortly after the Casablanca meeting to paint Roosevelt's portrait, and who had now been hired to do a watercolor of the president. When she started her work on the afternoon of April 10, she painted an ill man. Posing continued the next day, and in the late afternoon Franklin and

Lucy drove to his favorite spot overlooking the valley. When they returned for dinner with their guests, who included Treasury Secretary Morgenthau, Lucy sat to Franklin's right, and they chatted pleasantly throughout the meal.

On the morning of April 12, Roosevelt was sitting in his favorite brown leather chair in the living room, posing for Elizabeth. He looked healthy and was doing his "laundry," the name that he had given to the process of signing papers and the period of waiting for the ink to dry. Lucy and the two cousins talked, while Elizabeth painted ten feet away from the president. She constantly looked up at her subject. As lunchtime approached, the Filipino butler entered and started setting the table. Roosevelt pulled out a cigarette and announced that he would pose fifteen minutes longer; that would end the day's session. Elizabeth continued to paint and noticed that Roosevelt had suddenly raised his right hand and passed it over his forehead several times. At 1:15 P.M., he fell forward and lapsed into unconsciousness without saying a word.[31]

Dr. Bruenn was immediately summoned and diagnosed that his patient had suffered a massive cerebral hemorrhage. For the next several hours, the physician treated the dying president, but at 3:35 P.M., he stopped breathing, and Bruenn pronounced him dead. Shaken and in a state of hysteria, Lucy quickly packed and departed along with Elizabeth. As they approached Macon, Georgia, a flag was lowered to half staff; the news of Roosevelt's death had been released, and Lucy sobbed for the rest of the drive back to her home.[32]

Shortly after Roosevelt died, his corpse was placed in a casket draped with an American flag and loaded onto the last car of a train supplied by the Southern Railway Company (the same company that had carried Speaker Bankhead's body to Alabama and brought Welles back to the capital), leaving from Georgia and slowly heading north for Washington. Eleanor sat with her husband's coffin on the slow, painful trip to the capital. He had become an instant martyr, a symbol for victory. At the same time, as the train rolled northward, Eleanor struggled with the fact that Franklin had invited Lucy to Warm Springs. He was a national hero, but to her, he had broken a sacred pledge made decades earlier.[33]

When the train reached its destination, services were conducted in the East Room of the White House late in the afternoon of April 15. Most in attendance stood, for there were few chairs, and those who could not cram into the room listened to the simple ceremony over a loudspeaker placed outside. After the funeral, dignitaries and friends filed past the flag-draped coffin to pay their last respects. Once the official ceremony had concluded, the casket was placed on another train headed for Hyde Park, where Roosevelt was to be buried next to his parents in the rose garden. He had last visited his home in late March and now made his final journey. On Sunday, April 18, he was interred with an assemblage of family and close friends looking on. At last he was at peace.[34]

As the news of Roosevelt's passing spread, condolences poured in from all corners of the world. Hull issued a press statement from his hospital bed:

> No greater tragedy could have befallen our country and the world at this time. His inspiring vision, his high statesmanship and his superb leadership were factors without which the United Nations could not have come to the present phase of the war with victory just in sight. That leadership is gone, but his vision and the spirit of his statesmanship must continue to inspire us for the crucial task which even now is before us, the task of building a world peace. Mankind will be vastly poorer because of his passing.[35]

Welles released his tribute: "A tower has fallen. A star has set. . . . Our hearts are heavy today because of the gallant leader we have lost. No man in our nation's history has done more for our country."[36]

Joseph Davies was far more eloquent than either Hull or Welles. Roosevelt's death, he wrote in his diary, "was the greatest and most costly of war casualties." The capital was numb. Unfortunately for the president, he had not lived to see victory and the advent of an effective international peacekeeping organization, but he "went suddenly and without pain. He was at his zenith. For two years, he had held the Grand Alliance together." Roosevelt, he wrote, "will be the martyred leader of the democratic forces of the world, who actually gave his life for the cause. For that is what he did. And for that, he will be remembered more vividly and more warmly than any of the Big three, so far as the conduct of the war and its victory goes in this Second World War. And he was our American President!"[37]

Roosevelt had died before laying the foundation and constructing the framework of his postwar policies. Indeed, just before his death, he had been finishing a draft of his Jefferson-Jackson Day address, in which his theme was confidence: "The only limit to our realization of tomorrow will be our doubts of today." The passage hauntingly echoed the exhortation of his first inaugural: "the only thing we have to fear is fear itself." He thus ended his presidency on the same note that he had opened the New Deal.[38]

No one with sufficient stature or knowledge was prepared to assume his mantle. At a time when coordination was an imperative, he did not share with any staff member or confidant his outline for the future, and that failure to confide in anyone was his greatest shortcoming, something that even today that detracts from Roosevelt's legacy. If he was, as James MacGregor Burns calls him, a soldier of freedom, he certainly wears some tarnished medals. He understood the issues and the direction that he wished to pursue, but he did not know how to maintain the allegiance of the men who surrounded him. He was one of the few presidents who bonded world history to that of the United States, but he did not recognize that such a continuity was based on sharing information so that programs could become institutionalized. He led his nation to global prominence, and along the way he became a towering international figure. However, those who served under him in shaping foreign affairs developed enduring hatreds that prevented them from cooperating for the rest of their lives in helping to formulate American foreign policy.

# CHAPTER 17

# THOSE WHO SURVIVED

IN THE SEEMINGLY COUNTLESS studies on Franklin Roosevelt, his own enormous contribution is invariably the centerpiece, for he is an almost omniscient and omnipresent figure in American history. In large part because of this emphasis, the significance of others has been shamefully glossed over or grossly distorted. Harry Truman and Edward Stettinius, for example, supposedly carried on Roosevelt's policies, but they were simply men of lesser caliber. Neither man's good intentions are questioned; the crucial issue is how they could make decisions on matters in which they were but novices, substituting for the martyred, mature professional. Truman and Stettinius, of necessity, had to rely on each other, and both had stepped into their jobs without proper training. Few have pointed out that this was not their fault; the blame rests squarely with Roosevelt, the man who selected both of them for their positions.[1]

Immediately after Truman assumed the presidency, he openly admitted that his predecessor had not discussed foreign affairs with him; therefore, the inexperienced president would have to depend on his diplomatic advisers for guidance. With this seemingly logical decision, the new president had instantaneously altered the course of how the United States had decided many major diplomatic issues since the start of the New Deal. Until Roosevelt died, the president had personally determined the direction of American diplomacy and then told the State Department how to react. Truman reversed the practice; he made policy after consultation with his foreign affairs experts.

Truman made another political decision at the beginning of his presidency that had far-reaching consequences for the conduct of American foreign affairs. Since he had moved from the vice-presidency to the White House, he was acutely aware that the secretary of state was next in the line of succession. If Truman died, he wanted an heir who had a popular following and who had served in Congress. Those criteria, by definition, disqualified Stettinius. Rather than keeping this decision secret, Truman told enough people to expect Stettinius's resignation in the foreseeable future that this action soon became the subject of Washington gossip and effectively made Stettinius a lame duck.[2]

Others worried about his abilities for a multitude of reasons. On the day after the president expired, Senator Arthur Vandenberg, Republican of Michigan, expressed his reservations about Stettinius: "Up to now he has been only the presidential messenger. He does *not* have the background and experience for such a job at such a critical time—altho[ugh] he is a *good person* with every good intention and high honesty of purpose. *Now* we have *both* an inexperienced President *and* an inexperienced Secretary."[3] Secretary of War Stimson doubted that his congenial cabinet colleague could manage his subordinates: "It probably cannot be helped because Stet.[tinius] is inexperienced and has no background on those matters. Although well intentioned, he is not very firm in his decisions and character, and the result is that we have been called in on several issues in which, while we have some military interest, we are being made to take a very predominant part."[4]

Nelson Rockefeller, who already held Stettinius in low esteem, recalled that he "was a terrific hand-shaker, but he just simply could not make a big decision." He "was lost as soon as Roosevelt died." He "carried out Roosevelt's plans, Roosevelt's concepts, they were Roosevelt's emissaries, and when Roosevelt wasn't there, it's like pulling the plug out of the light, the light goes off."[5] Even if Stettinius had wanted to answer these charges, he was unable to defend himself because he had gone to San Francisco to prepare for the upcoming conference to establish the United Nations, but that did not alter the fact that overnight he now was responsible for making global decisions of a sort that he had previously discussed firsthand with Roosevelt. Few thought that Stettinius was capable of handling that enormous weight.

Truman never took advantage of the secretary's background, but instead followed an independent and uncharted path. Ambassador Harriman returned from Moscow on April 18 to brief the White House on his anxieties about Soviet expansionism by advising the president to be firm with Stalin, if the two nations were to cooperate. When Soviet Foreign Minister Vyacheslav Molotov met Truman at the White House several days later on his way to San Francisco, the president ended Roosevelt's posture of unconditional cooperation by speaking sharply to Molotov, demanding that Stalin adhere to the Yalta accords in regard to free elections in Eastern Europe.[6]

This unpleasant exchange with Molotov did not bode well for the San Francisco conference. Truman, aware of great public pressure to continue with the commitment for a world organization, stuck to Roosevelt's scheduled opening of the United Nations conference on April 25, 1945. As a symbol of continuity, Stettinius led the U.S. delegation. Once Molotov arrived, he attacked the seating of Argentina and demanded the admission of Poland's procommunist government. These issues were promptly resolved, as were most amendments to the Dumbarton Oaks proposals, but Molotov's refusal to accept the veto formula for the security council created an irreconcilable impasse, and without agreement on this vital question a successful conclusion was in doubt.[7]

To solve this problem and prepare for the next Big Three meeting, Truman sent Harry Hopkins on a mission to Moscow to mend the breach, for he best embodied Roosevelt's approach. Hopkins met with Stalin and Molotov on May 25 in a congenial atmosphere. The dictator reversed his foreign minister's stand and agreed to support the U.S. veto proposal at San Francisco after Hopkins appeared willing to allow the Soviets some latitude in handling the composition of the Polish government. Although many disputes remained, Hopkins left Russia on June 7 encouraged that Stalin would cooperate in the postwar period.[8]

The agreement over the veto formula ended the stalemate at San Francisco, and the signing of the United Nations Charter occurred on June 24, marking the beginning of the new world organization and also the termination of Stettinius as secretary of state. He had already submitted his resignation upon Roosevelt's death, and Truman accepted it the day following the signing ceremony. More than ever, Truman intended to name his own successor, and his choice as secretary of state was James Byrnes.[9]

On July 2, Hopkins resigned from government service for two reasons: he knew that continued stress would ruin his health and he was financially insecure. To remedy the latter situation, he took a job as mediator for $25,000 a year and also negotiated a large literary advance to write his memoirs. He never had an opportunity to finish them because the intestinal ailments that had plagued him for so long finally consumed him, and he died on January 29, 1946, at the age of fifty-five.[10]

Whereas Hopkins's vital role in the Roosevelt administration has been carefully and sympathetically documented by the award-winning playwright Robert Sherwood and the historian George McJimsey, Edward Stettinius, Jr., has been virtually ignored. After the founding of the United Nations, he served as U.S. representative to the Security Council and then returned to Virginia, where he was chosen rector of his alma mater. He followed a hectic schedule, traveling, lecturing, and completing a book on the Yalta conference. In the spring of 1949, his doctors ordered him to reduce his activities owing to a weakened heart, but it was already beyond repair, and he died during the last week of October, nine days after his forty-ninth birthday.[11]

Stettinius lasted seven months as secretary of state and a year as under secretary. He attended the Yalta, Chapultepec, and San Francisco conferences. In addition to participating in those crucial meetings, he led the State Department as it moved from the era of global combat to that of the embryonic United Nations. His role as the transitional figure who replaced Welles and then Hull has never been fullly explored. In the relatively short span of his life, he occupied a central position in the deliberations of the Grand Alliance, but rather than view him from that challenging vantage point, historians have granted him the dubious distinction of being the least-known secretary of state in the twentieth century. When he is mentioned at all, authors tend to highlight his negative image instead of evaluating his accomplishments.

Stettinius, in fact, was a manager accustomed to receiving instructions and faithfully carrying them out. Once Roosevelt died, he was not given the opportunity to assume the awesome responsibility of serving as chief foreign policy adviser to Truman. This outcome seemed at least superficially to validate the verdict of Stettinius's inadequacies, but no one has taken into consideration the fact that Roosevelt did not have any expectation of allowing Stettinius to take an independent course, nor has anyone acknowledged the vast differences in leadership style between Roosevelt and Truman. No one has tried to place Stettinius in the proper perspective; he deserves better.

Hull left a far different legacy. Shortly after his resignation, he was given a very small room on the seventeenth floor of the tower at Bethesda Naval Hospital. He never admitted publicly to having tuberculosis. By the 1940s more people were dying of it than of any other contagious disease, and it was only during the winter of 1944 that doctors finally began to use medication effectively to combat the illness. At first, Hull saw only his wife, the president, a select group of friends, and State Department personnel, but by the end of January 1945, he was sitting up in bed and reading for about two hours a day.[12]

Hull finally started walking on March 9; the following day, MacKenzie King came to visit an exhausted friend, with "his eyes filled with tears" and "a leather-like appearance," who spoke about "suffering from diabetes" and who mentioned some trouble with his lungs. Hull reflected on his career, taking credit for the success at the Moscow conference, the preparations for Tehran, the Dumbarton Oaks talks, and building momentum for the world security organization. As the prime minister prepared to leave, Hull pressed their hands tightly, told his guest to guard his health, and "broke down" as his wife comforted him. Afterwards, King was moved to write in his diary that the secretary was "perhaps the greatest of the men of the U.S., so far as its foreign policy and shaping of world affairs was concerned. . . ."[13] By mid-April, James Farley saw an improved patient who was still bedridden, but well enough to criticize the president's "cronies whom he took on trips who just 'yessed' him." Hull refused to follow that course, preferring to offer prudent advice, and thereby preventing Roosevelt from making grave diplomatic blunders.[14]

Unable to attend the San Francisco conference, he took the honorary title of senior delegate and spoke nightly to Stettinius. The former secretary tried to advise his successor, but this proved difficult. Without acknowledging Hull's sickness and his inability to understand the complexities of an international gathering 3,000 miles away, Ambassador George Messersmith, who also was receiving treatment at the hospital (for an intestinal disorder) and oftentimes was in Hull's room, listened to the conversations and lamented, "The trouble was that at San Francisco as elsewhere, Stettinius was dealing with matters in which he had no adequate preparation and in which he had no background nor experience, and by the very nature of his position was required to make decisions."[15]

What bothered Hull the most during the proceedings was that Argentina was admitted as a member. He hated the Argentine government for its fascist sympathies and the embarrassment that Saavedra Lamas and other Argentine diplomats had forced him to endure. After Argentina was seated, Hull singled out Nelson Rockefeller as the culprit who had pushed through Argentine admission, leading the U.S. delegation into believing that Roosevelt had approved the idea. As far as Hull was concerned, the president supported the State Department's policy opposing Argentine participation at San Francisco, and therefore Rockefeller had lied about Roosevelt's intentions. The former secretary grew to despise Rockefeller so much that after the meeting ended and he asked for an interview at the hospital, Hull flatly refused.[16]

The debate over the value of regional organizations also troubled him because he wanted the universal body to settle hemispheric disputes. In early June, he commented that the Latin American delegates were "a perfect illustration of the proposition that your friends are more dangerous sometimes than your enemies." Although Latin America comprised twenty of the fifty nations attending the gathering, Hull bluntly pointed

out, "How many divisions can they send to the Pacific; How many can
the Russians send?" Despite this sarcastic outburst, the former secretary
eventually accepted the regional concept and applauded the draft of the
new world charter.[17]

Long before Hull left the hospital to return to his apartment in the
first week of July, tributes started to mount. In 1944 the Variety Clubs of
America conferred upon him their Humanitarian Award; the foreign
service presented a bust of him to the State Department; Congress and
the Tennessee legislature made similar gestures. He was particularly
pleased when Truman presented him with the Medal of Merit in 1947
for his accomplishments as secretary of state.[18]

Although these accolades were gratifying, the Hulls had lobbied for
the Nobel Peace Prize above all else since the first term, and no one tried
as hard as Frances to advance her husband's cause. Writing to George
Milton, on May 14, 1937, she vented her frustration: "It is not square or
right." Others, including the president, were now backing his selection;
she applauded their efforts and absolutely did not want Cordell to know
about this confidential correspondence: "He would not like it. I *never* do
anything he disapproves of, but I feel this treatment so keenly—the *worst
yet.*" He had worked for peace at the London Economic Conference and
the ones at Montevideo and Buenos Aires: "I get tired of letting some one
constantly steal Cordell's thunder." He deserved the prize.[19] That dream
was finally realized in December 1945, but he was too ill to travel to
Sweden to accept his long-coveted honor.[20]

In September 1946 Hull returned to the hospital because of his
diabetes and tuberculosis. He steadily showed signs of improvement
until October 1, when he suffered a minor stroke that temporarily left
him disoriented and irrational. Recovery was slow. He was allowed to
see his wife, who had a nearby room, to interact with the medical staff,
and to listen to the radio, but his doctors prevented him from even
reading newspapers. During much of 1947 his doctors concentrated on
his diabetes, and by the spring they had controlled it. They next turned
to the tuberculosis that caused daily rises in his temperature along with
a mild cough. Not until July was he able to sit up in an easy chair, and a
month later he was allowed up for an hour and a half a day.[21]

Hull's memoirs took from 1946 to 1948 to complete, but he was unable to play a major role in this long, arduous task because of his various ailments. Although the dedication of the book is to his wife, he paid special tribute to his ghost writer, Andrew Berding, an old friend and newspaperman who was educated at Oxford University in modern history and had covered the State Department for the Associated Press. He started work on this gigantic project with three research assistants in 1946, and with permission from Hull's doctors in September 1947, Berding started to spend one hour a day, three days a week, reviewing material with him: "Without him this book would not have been written. I owe to him a lasting debt of gratitude." Hull certainly did, for *The Memoirs of Cordell Hull* belonged more to Berding than to the secretary.[22]

For the first time, Hull offered the public a glimpse into his opinions of Roosevelt, calling him "one of the greatest social reformers in our modern history" for having advanced individual freedoms; but concurrently, Hull contended, the president was "oftentimes an extreme, liberal in his views." As for his leadership during the war, he was an outstanding commander in chief who used military strategy to strengthen diplomatic maneuvering, and he "had no contemporary rival in political skill."[23]

Hull also filled his recollections with descriptions of the way he would have liked events to have taken place rather than they actually did. The descriptions of his relationships with Welles, Moore, and others have never been challenged. The value of his presence at meetings such as the London Economic Conference, the Montevideo gathering, and his mission to Moscow has not been carefully reviewed. His criticism of the security zone has been widely accepted, and its benefits to the British navy have been minimized. Hull's claim to be the Father of the United Nations has been vastly exaggerated, but no one has bothered to rebut it.

Hull had left a record of his achievements and was not troubled by inconsistencies and inaccuracies that sometimes approached the outlandish. He had avoided the refugee issue to hide Frances's Jewish heritage; although an overwhelming number of authors writing about the Final Solution lambaste the State Department, they avoid charging the secretary with negligence owing to his wife's ancestry. The memoirs go even further by categorically rejecting allegations of indifference: "The results accomplished by the State Department, up to the time of the creation of the War Refugee Board, at least equaled those of all other countries combined, and that some hundreds of thousands of Jews are now alive who probably would have fallen victim to Hitler's insane enmity had not the Department begun so early and so comprehensively to deal with the refugee problem."[24]

After the publication of his memoirs, Hull watched events from the sidelines, except for unusual circumstances. After his retirement, he and Dean Acheson developed "a real friendship," and Hull sent a copy of his memoirs to Acheson, inscribed "with warmest friendship." Acheson regularly visited his former superior at the hospital and at his apartment, where they would reminisce and discuss current affairs. In December 1950, while Acheson was secretary of state, powerful lobbyists pressured Truman to fire him for being "soft" on Communism. Unannounced, Hull was driven to the State Department basement garage, stayed in his automobile, and asked to see Acheson before he left on a trip abroad. By the time Acheson reached the basement, everyone in the building knew about Hull's presence, and he announced to all that Acheson was his friend and wished him "good luck and bon voyage." Everyone understood why Hull was there: he did not forget his friends.[25]

Hull's admirers wished to create a lasting memorial with the establishment of the Cordell Hull Foundation for International Education. Harvis Branscomb, chancellor of Vanderbilt University, proposed the idea to Hull on March 17, 1951. Branscomb regarded Hull "as the greatest citizen of the State [Tennessee] since Andrew Jackson." Its congressional delegation had endorsed the concept because he was an internationally known statesman, and any memorial to his ideals should concentrate on the Americas. The foundation would have two main objectives: to provide scholarships primarily for Latin American exchange students to study at Nashville, the state capital, and to construct a headquarters at the University Center to serve as a base for instructional programs dealing with the Western Hemisphere. The former secretary responded favorably on April 4, giving his approval and replying that he was honored to have his name associated with the project. He also thought that the inter-American emphasis was desirable because of the common hemispheric heritage against such threats to liberty and freedom as the communist menace.[26]

The foundation received its Tennessee charter and began operations in May, with the expectation of becoming a multimillion dollar enterprise, competing with the Rhodes and Rosenfeld scholarships. The trustees and sponsors included such prominent members of the Roosevelt administration as James Farley; Myron Taylor, American representative to Pope Pius XII; and Assistant Secretary of State William Clayton. Yet the foundation's lofty hopes were never matched with money because Hull refused to endorse the effort enthusiastically. The foundation floundered and moved its headquarters from Nashville to New Orleans, Louisiana, in early 1954 to merge with International House, an organization that promoted the port's commerce and Latin American student exchange. The foundation still exists, but its current activities are as foggy as Hull's lack of motivation.[27]

Ill health may have dampened Hull's interest, for he now spent most of his time in the hospital. Complications caused by his diabetes and tuberculosis, along with a series of heart ailments, regularly forced him back for treatment, and occasionally, as in September 1952, he went on the critical list, only to rebound and return to his apartment. He read a great deal, listened to the radio, looked at television, and enjoyed seeing old friends who visited on his birthday. When able, he took daily strolls with his wife and periodically stopped to watch a tennis match.[28]

This pattern changed in the spring of 1954. Frances had often visited her home town of Staunton, where she had been closely associated with the founding of the Woodrow Wilson Rehabilitative Center during World War II and had helped to establish the Woodrow Wilson Birthplace Foundation. This time she arrived with a nurse on March 23 to recuperate from a recent attack of pneumonia, but three days later, at 11:30 A.M., she suffered a fatal heart attack and died within the hour. Her congregation paid its highest respects by interring her in a crypt beneath Washington's National Cathedral.[29]

Until Frances's passing, Cordell had at least been alert, but with her gone he became a semiinvalid, cared for by a niece. Exactly one year after her death, he suffered a major stroke and was once more placed on the critical list; instead of rebounding, he lapsed into a coma on July 21 and never regained consciousness. Two days later he died quietly at 9:00 A.M.[30]

President Dwight Eisenhower ordered the flags on all U.S. government buildings lowered to half staff until Hull's interment "in solemn tribute to this great American statesman." Condolences poured in from around the globe, including those from foreign ministers Eden in London and Molotov in Moscow. Secretary of State John Foster Dulles praised him, and former Secretary of State Acheson claimed, "He was in a very true sense the father of the United Nations and the Reciprocal Trade Act to which he gave his complete and single-minded devotion."[31] On July 26, 1955, over 2,000 mourners attended a ceremony at the National Cathedral at which the dean of the church, who had shortened his vacation to fly back in order to officiate, presided. Dulles and Acheson, along with contemporaries like Farley and William Castle, sat in front of the flag-draped coffin surrounded by floral arrangements. Hull was then laid to rest in a crypt beneath the church next to his wife, an honor granted only to individuals who had performed special services to God and mankind; he joined other famous Americans like Woodrow Wilson, Admiral George Dewey, and Secretary of State Frank Kellogg.[32]

Tennessee has not forgotten him. In Carthage, the town where he was raised, there are a Cordell Hull motel, dam, and lake. At his birthplace in Byrdstown near the northern border of the state, there is a marker that gives directions to his home, a modest one-story wooden building. The house has been fenced off with a sign identifying Hull as the "Father of United Nations." This tribute distorts Hull's role in the founding of the United Nations, but in many ways it also demonstrates yet again his lifelong ability to make illusion into reality.

While Hull was being honored and memorialized, Welles's early years of retirement took a similar path. His health was fine, although his workload was so heavy that he had difficulty fulfilling his obligations. He gave a series of lectures in Canada, spoke throughout the United States, and received numerous offers to write articles and books.[33]

Even before Roosevelt's death, Welles had anticipated the international mood for the upcoming San Francisco gathering. He anticipated that Stalin might gain an advantage over Roosevelt at Yalta, but hoped that the Big Three would reach an agreement on the Dumbarton Oaks proposals. To achieve global stability, the United States had to join an effective international organization and needed Latin American support at the meeting. Welles broadcast for four and a half hours on the issues in the charter and became a special commentator, with a daily fifteen-minute radio program to report on the day's proceedings. He did not attend the conference for fear that if he promoted anything, the United States might have to oppose it for that sole reason. During the sessions, he called for the new body to have the ability to solve disputes. He opposed the veto but recognized that the Senate would not pass the charter if that provision were deleted. Each of the five major powers had to have an absolute veto right to maintain unity; however, once the United Nations had been in existence for a decade, its inadequacies, including the constraints caused by the veto, could be amended by a constitutional assembly.[34]

From late in 1946 until the end of 1947, Welles broadcast an NBC series entitled "Your United Nations" to win public acceptance for the organization. He urged locating its headquarters in New York City, served as honorary president of the American Association for the United Nations, Inc., and insisted that the United States fully commit to the organization. He wanted the general assembly to discuss colonialism and exploitation and called for an end to imperialism. To Welles, the only hope for an enduring peace was a universal agency that could impose collective security. He encouraged the inter-American system to return to the spirit of the good neighbor and to play a major role in the United Nations. If the Truman administration did not act to solve hemispheric social and economic inequities, anarchy might result. He also championed freedom of information throughout the Americas so that there would be a free exchange of ideas.[35]

As part of his international commitments, Welles accepted the presidency of the Wendell Willkie Memorial Freedom House, located in New York City, which had been founded to counter totalitarianism and stimulate the free communication of ideas. On October 7, 1945, on the anniversary of Willkie's death, Welles spoke before two thousand people and dedicated a nine-story building in Manhattan to support organizations like the Anti-Defamation League, B'nai B'rith, the National Association for the Advancement of Colored People, and the World Student

Service Fund. In fact, as many as ninety agencies used the premises for meetings.[36]

He also turned to writing *Where Are We Heading?* in 1946. In the book he lamented Roosevelt's death as a national tragedy and a watershed event in foreign affairs. If he had only lived, the current global instability would not exist. Under Truman, the United States did not clearly understand the political realities of international relations, and this especially applied to atomic diplomacy.[37]

The former diplomat also spoke out forcefully against other concerns, such as the return to the high tariff. Even though the Republican party had switched to a policy of international cooperation, this did not mean that its members supported lowering trade barriers. If the United States was going to remain powerful, foreign economic policy had to dovetail with political objectives, and Truman had to extend the reciprocity program. In regard to Soviet-American collaboration, Welles had worked closely with Roosevelt to encourage closer ties and concurrently made Stalin aware that the United States expected good-faith bargaining and adherence to treaties. Welles still wanted to seek an accommodation between the two superpowers, for he believed that that was the only way to ensure peace.[38]

Welles also became passionately involved with the creation of a Jewish homeland in Palestine; he insisted that Roosevelt had supported turning the British mandate in Palestine into a United Nations trusteeship. As early as April 1945, he openly called for the end of British rule in favor of an international force to allow large numbers of Jewish refugees to settle there. He hoped for Arab cooperation, but if that was not forthcoming, he suggested that unrestricted immigration proceed under military supervision. To demonstrate his commitment, he accepted the chairmanship of the American-Christian Palestine Committee of Maryland, an organization that Rabbi Stephen Wise had formed in late 1942 to assist European Jews, end the British mandate, and support the state of Israel. Welles thought that the world owed Europe's displaced Jews a homeland in Palestine, and to guarantee that objective the United States and the United Nations should provide whatever armed forces were necessary.[39]

By 1947 Welles had evolved into an active Zionist, and although he opposed extremist tactics, he exerted pressure to accelerate rescue and resettlement activities on behalf of European Jewry. On April 22, he made a startling admission. As early as 1938, he had hoped to resettle Jews outside Axis-controlled territory and send them to the Americas, Australia, Africa, and Palestine. He had never anticipated the horrors of the Final Solution, and the world was now in debt to the survivors. The only option, since the United States, the United Nations, and other countries had refused to act, was to open Palestine to what remained of European Jewry and sponsor the creation of Israel.[40]

Welles worked tirelessly in this cause. At the start of 1948, he hoped that the General Assembly would help defuse the dangerous situation in Palestine by debating the matter. He even wrote a scathing attack on Truman's refusal to support Israel in *We Need Not Fail,* claiming that Roosevelt was a Zionist who had expected to settle the Palestine question after the end of the war. The nation would have been founded and the United Nations police force would have guaranteed the peace, and Welles was disappointed that Truman had not followed that direction. The United States needed a democratic ally in the Middle East, and Israel would become that bulwark. On May 14, when the state of Israel became a reality, Welles congratulated Rabbi Wise on their victory. To acknowledge Welles's many years of service, the American Jewish Congress honored him in November for his courageous support in favoring immediate United States recognition for Israel.[41]

Welles's spirits at the end of the year took a disastrous turn. To combat chronic insomnia, he often took nocturnal walks. One evening while on such a walk, with the temperature at fifteen degrees above zero, he felt a chest pain and hurried back to the estate. In his haste, he made a wrong turn in the darkness and fell into a creek. Somehow, he managed to climb out, staggered onto the snow-covered field, and fainted with his clothes frozen to his body. He lay there for several hours before a passerby returning from morning church services spotted him. Suffering from severe exposure, he was rushed to the hospital and treated for frostbite of his hands and toes; several digits had to be amputated. The police conducted an investigation and concluded that there was no evidence of foul play. Vicious rumors about the incident started to spread. Some whispered that he had become drunk and had gone out in search of sexual adventure. They said he had seen a Negro male cutting across his property and had propositioned him. Instead of accepting his offer, the man had knocked Welles unconscious on the frozen turf near the house.[42]

The truthfulness of this story is immaterial. What is crucial is the indisputable fact that Welles had become seriously impaired. After the ordeal, Pearson used his column to appeal to Hull to permit Welles to return to the diplomatic corps. Whenever his name was mentioned for an appointment like commissioner to Palestine or troubleshooter in Indonesia, Hull vetoed the idea. As a result, the columnist believed that Welles would never receive any post. Because of Hull's having blackballed him, Pearson continued, Welles had had insomnia, had taken some sleeping pills, had gone for a night walk in a state of sheer exhaustion, and had collapsed. Hull, looking down from his hospital room "could have concluded . . . that he 'got his man.' Or could it be that Mr. Hull at long last will say that an old score is now more than settled, that peace is more important than personalities; so let bygones be bygones."[43]

Not only was Hull unforgiving, but homosexuality linked with the communist menace had become a national obsession. Republicans like Francis White and J. Reuben Clark actively connected Welles's homosexual behavior with Secretary of State Acheson and other government officials. Clark contended that more people were growing skeptical of and resented the State Department's policies because the many "fairies" in the capital were causing havoc. Labeled deviants, homosexuals in government became scapegoats for such demagogues as Senator Joseph McCarthy, Republican of Wisconsin, who charged the State Department with being a haven for communists and homosexuals. Somehow these immoral and unstable people had infiltrated the government and thus become susceptible to blackmail by Russian spies, making themselves national security risks.[44]

Some activists in the gay and lesbian movements assert that it was this hysteria that caused the change in the Presidential Succession Act of 1886 from president, vice-president, secretary of state, and then the rest of the cabinet to the line of succession that became effective in 1947:

president, vice-president, president pro-tem of the Senate, speaker of the House, and then secretary of state. The change was intended, they claim, to diminish the likelihood of a homosexual reaching the White House. According to the activists, Congress knew about Welles, and how close he might have come to the Oval Office if Roosevelt and Truman had died and Welles had been appointed secretary of state.[45]

Once Welles's homosexuality and poor health had eliminated him from being offered any diplomatic assignment, his only recourse was to become a commentator. He recognized that the Truman administration had focused almost exclusively on the Soviet Union, Europe, and East Asia. This meant that the inter-American system was being overlooked, and the result was growing dissatisfaction with the United States throughout Latin America. To change this perception, the United States had to extend the Marshall Plan to this hemisphere.[46]

When Pearson saw him in the summer of 1949, Welles had lost thirty-five pounds and aged ten years; his doctors had recently declared him well enough to travel and ordered complete rest to regain his strength. He and his wife booked passage on the French liner *DeGrasse* to Europe for a planned two-month vacation; they left New York on July 7 and arrived in Switzerland twelve days later. During the crossing Mathilde contracted peritonitis, an inflammation of the lining of the abdominal cavity. Upon reaching Lausanne, she refused to undergo surgery and died on August 7. The following day she was cremated, and a week later Welles traveled to Washington to place her ashes in the family mausoleum at Rock Creek Cemetery. When her will was probated, it was revealed that she had left the bulk of her $1.4 million estate to him.[47]

Her death ended twenty-four years of marriage, and this tragedy combined with his own infirmities presented a dismal picture. Pearson saw Welles that fall and described his friend's condition: "Sumner Welles is in terrible shape—his wife dead, his big toes gone, some of his fingers off. He has no interest in life, won't see his friends, can't sleep at night. I'm afraid he wants to die."[48]

The reporter did not know that Welles had a compelling reason to live. Before Mathilde's death, Hull had published his memoirs, and she had insisted that her husband answer that prejudicial account. That pledge, plus Welles's hatred of Hull, was more than sufficient motivation for writing the new book.[49] Too him, autobiography was the ultimate test of an author's worth. In Hull's memoirs, "the psychopathic vanity, the pettiness, and the venom and inarticulate incapacity which operated behind the saintly mask and the assumed modesty that so long misled the general public are bound to be apparent to any thinking readers of what he may write." Welles realized that Hull's memoirs purposely belittled any of Welles's achievements. The secretary, for example, took credit for the Cuban mediation in 1933, whereas Welles maintained that Hull did not have "the foggiest idea of what was going on in Cuba."[50]

His flirtation with death and his wife's sudden passing postponed any literary project, but as early as October 1948, he anticipated writing the book because "of my fear that some recent books giving grotesquely distorted versions of President Roosevelt's handling of many vital problems might so crystallize public opinion here and abroad that the subsequent writings of more impartial historians would not erase the initial impact of these smears."[51] Welles worried that the attacks on Roosevelt's diplomacy might be accepted, and "I am one of those who are convinced that the stature of Franklin D. Roosevelt will not shrink, but will rather grow, with the passage of time."[52] Welles was certain that without the president's effort on behalf of the United Nations, war between the Soviets and the West would have been inevitable.[53]

Welles wrote Samuel Rosenman, one of Roosevelt's favorite speech writers and confidants, on June 17, 1949, to express his anger over the secretary's memoirs. Welles expected the "diatribe against myself," but he deeply deplored and would "never forgive . . . his [Hull's] consistent effort . . . to make it appear that in his conduct of foreign affairs President Roosevelt always failed when Mr. Hull was not in agreement with him and that the President's only successes were those instigated by or approved by Mr. Hull." Welles hoped that historians would seek the truth, and he intended to "offer our testimony now before the Roosevelt haters and the psychopathic egotists have hammered into the public consciousness a picture that is wholly false."[54]

Late that year, Pearson dined with Welles for his birthday and reported that although he was in poor health, he was lucid and looked better than at any time since his wife had died. The reporter admitted that his friend "has plenty of faults and is a difficult man at times to get along with, but he has a perspective far beyond anyone else I have known in the State Department." Both the United States and Welles would have profited had he not had to resign from office.[55]

Although Welles was lonely and drank to excess, he was now concentrating on completing his manuscript. He harbored no bitterness against Roosevelt because the president needed Hull's congressional skill to move the United Nations charter through the Senate. In the summer of 1951 Welles published *Seven Decisions That Shaped History*, a thinly disguised, self-serving attempt to justify his actions and an attack on Hull's memoirs. Unlike his earlier books, in which Welles had ignored the secretary, this time he openly attacked Hull for his overly cautious positions, which had resulted in the State Department following instead of initiating foreign policy. Welles at last had the last word and castigated his former superior's judgments at length, but the book was so poorly written and such a partisan response to Hull's mammoth project that reviewers generally panned it.[56]

While Welles was finishing this, his last book, he had begun dating a wealthy, divorced socialite, Harriette Post, the daughter of a founder of the New York Stock Exchange. In early 1952 they assembled a small gathering of friends at her home on Fifth Avenue in New York City and got married.[57] By this time he had lost his appeal as a public speaker; John Metcalfe, president of National Lecture Management, declared that May that he "had to drop Sumner Welles from the list of its lecturers; the reason—Welles' drunkenness and homosexuality. Welles is said to have started drinking like a fish. Combined with the homosexuality, the other vice often makes Welles entirely unfit for the lecturing."[58]

With a new circle of friends and a permanent change of residence, Welles spent most of his time in New York and decided to sell the palatial Oxon Hill Manor. On February 1, 1953, an art enthusiast bought the 250-acre tract with the intention of making the home into a private museum and subdividing the rest of the land for homes with a yacht harbor and a country club. Welles also sold his huge, imposing mansion in Washington to the Cosmos Club, a social club incorporated in the late nineteenth century by individuals active in science, literature, and the arts. Members are chosen because of their achievements, and the club holds a wide range of cultural events, including lectures, forums, concerts, art exhibits, and literary dinners.[59]

By the end of 1953, Pearson believed that Welles was "now almost a forgotten man." He lived almost exclusively on his wife's estate in New Jersey and at her home in New York. He still maintained vacation retreats in Bar Harbor, Maine, and Palm Beach, Florida, but they were used sparingly. The change in life-style seemed to improve his health, and by the end of 1954, Pearson commented that Welles seemed "in pretty good health." Four years later, the reporter noted that his friend could hardly walk without the use of a cane, and although he was more coherent than he had been in many years, the columnist lamented that he was: "Completely sober, but looked like a ghost."[60]

Truman Capote, in the May 1976 issue of *Esquire,* described a chance encounter with Welles in the 1950s. If this disgusting, vivid description did not reach enough of an audience, *Answered Prayers,* a Book-of-the-Month Club selection in 1987, repeated the same lurid passage:

> It was after midnight in Paris in the bar of the Boeuf-sur-le-Toit, when he was sitting at a pink-clothed table with three men, two of them expensive tarts, Corsican pirates in British flannel, and the third none other than Sumner Welles—fans of *Confidential* will remember the patrician Mr. Welles, former undersecretary of State, great and good friend of the Brotherhood of Sleeping Car Porters. It made rather a tableau, one especially *vivant,* when His Excellency, pickled as brandied peaches, began nibbling those Corsican ears.[61]

On September 24, 1961, at sixty-nine years of age, Welles died at the Post estate after a brief illness. A short, private service was followed by cremation and a memorial service in Washington. Another eulogy took place at St. Bartholomew's Protestant Episcopal Church in Manhattan; Welles's widow, his two sons, and old friend Adolf Berle were among those in attendance. Under Secretary of State Chester Bowles declared, "His passing will be mourned throughout all the Americas." Pearson added a column extolling his many contributions.[62] Echoing such brief praise, Welles's contributions have been largely ignored in the intervening years, with the exception of a few scholarly articles and dissertations.

The Cosmos Club still occupies its magnificent, stately mansion. Up until 1988 the club excluded females, but thereafter it ended its discriminatory practices. Welles is acknowledged as a previous owner, but his importance in the life of the capital is glossed over. The elegant parties and other social functions there are forgotten, but stories are still recounted that, long after her mother's death, Mathilde never allowed anyone in her mother's bedroom and that she pulled down her sheets each night.[63]

Oxon Hill Manor and its surrounding acreage were not developed. By the early 1970s, the mansion had sunk into a terrible state of disrepair. The first floor was not used, and the second story served as a dormitory for several tenants, with unsightly locks haphazardly screwed or nailed into each ornate door. Finally in 1978 the Maryland legislature appropriated $300,000 for restoration and rehabilitation. A three-year facelift began, and the following year the first floor was completed and opened to the public. The standard rental fee for an evening is $3,000. Currently, weddings, receptions, meetings, art shows, and other varied programs are held at the manor. For example, on August 2, 1994, the Democratic National Committee celebrated President Bill Clinton's birthday with a $1,000-a-couple party. These activities keep the operations going on a self-sustaining basis, although more funds are needed to complete the refurbishing.[64]

A few old-timers in Oxon Hill still tell stories about the strange happenings while Welles lived there. Neighbors ordered their children to avoid walking across the property for fear of the weird events at the manor. Some believe that FBI agents killed one or more Russian spies in Mathilde's bathroom and secretly buried them somewhere on the property. Others claim that pornographic photographs of Welles with other males were discovered in the trunk of his automobile. These are unproven allegations, but the paintings of boys, nude and seminude in Greco-Roman garb, that once hung in what was Welles's study are still on the walls, lending credence to the tales of his sexual proclivities.[65]

As for the summer house in Bar Harbor, with its breathtaking view of the ocean, it was sold and razed after Welles died. His next-door neighbor had firsthand knowledge of Welles's homosexuality and serious drinking problem. The neighbor declared that "he was as queer as a three-dollar bill." Welles entertained frequently, drank too much, and propositioned Negro taxicab drivers. Sometimes after he became intoxicated, "his valet and butler chased after him with a net to stop him from accosting us."[66]

There are no monuments or tributes to acknowledge his many worthwhile accomplishments, while the taint of his homosexuality lingers. In the late 1970s *Parade,* a Sunday magazine that reached millions, published a question and answer column. Someone inquired which secretary of state had made homosexual advances to railroad porters. The reply was cryptic: "he was no secretary of state, he was an undersecretary of state. No charges were ever preferred against him. The vicious story, which may or may not have been true, was circulated by William Bullitt. . . . There is no point in identifying the individual involved. He gave this country long years of expertise and honorable service."[67]

Ironically, Bullitt was named. As Roosevelt had declared, "Poor Sumner may have been poisoned but he was not, like Bill, a poisoner."[68] Bullitt never understood that his crusade against Welles doomed his own political future. Many supporters of the League of Nations never forgot Bullitt's treacherous conduct against Woodrow Wilson during the Senate debates, and the attack on Welles graphically confirmed his unsavory reputation. Yet this did not deter Bullitt from his myopic vision of events. He acted in accord with his own special ethical code. He did not consider his secret apartment in Paris, where he had amorous encounters, immoral or unethical, and he was unconcerned with Carmel Offie's homosexuality or with rumors about his own romantic interludes with men.

Bullitt never doubted his righteous mission, but he was hampered by failing health. At the beginning of 1945, he was hit by an automobile, leaving his left leg, hip, back, and ribs injured. He later had spinal fusion, but this operation did not correct the conditions that left him semi-crippled, forced him to use a cane, and in later years caused him great difficulty in walking. During his recuperation, the Allies completed their conquest of the Third Reich, and so ended this quixotic figure's military career.[69]

He spent most of his later life in Paris, living at his tiny apartment on the Rue de Ponthieu. To keep his United States residency active, he used the Rittenhouse Club address in Philadelphia, for the family estate had been torn down to make way for two large apartment complexes facing the square. During his self-imposed exile, Bullitt published *The Great Globe Itself,* which condemned Roosevelt's last months in office. Bullitt contended that a sick president had damaged American interests at Yalta, and that although Roosevelt was spared the consequences of his actions, others now had to stop the spread of communism.[70]

Although Bullitt's warnings received a lukewarm response in 1946, the public was far more receptive to similar arguments as the Cold War grew hotter. Just as Bullitt had turned against Wilson after World War I, the former envoy attacked Roosevelt in two *Life* articles during August and September 1948. Everyone wanted to believe in Stalin's good intentions, but the former ambassador claimed that the American people were duped: "So most Americans preferred the agreeable lie to the upleasant truth; and while our fighting men were winning the war our government went blithely on losing the peace." He painted the president in the worst possible light, arguing that Roosevelt should have forced the Soviets to sign accords favorable to U.S. interests before releasing lend-lease assistance. The White House, Bullitt concluded, did everything to please the Soviet Union and rewarded its sympathizers within the administration. At Yalta, Roosevelt surrendered Poland, gave the Russians three votes in the General Assembly of the United Nations, and weakened American power in East Asia. When the president returned from the Crimea, he was greeted "amid the almost unanimous applause of his bamboozled fellow countrymen." Truman then entered the Oval Office without understanding the dire consequences of Yalta. Bullitt warned: "We face today a struggle not for security but for survival."

The former diplomat conveniently overlooked his own ardent advocacy of U.S. recognition of the Soviet Union shortly after World War I. Although he later claimed opposition to extending diplomatic relations in 1933, his lapse of memory cannot change his unbridled enthusiasm for this step. He also ignored his recommendation for an accommodation with the Nazis in the late 1930s as a barrier against Russian expansion and dismissed his questionable initiatives as American ambassador to France during the fall of Paris. His refusal to present the complete picture illustrated one of his greatest faults. Others, never he, were always to blame.[71]

In the late 1940s Bullitt vigorously spoke out against the communist menace. He supported the Truman Doctrine, but did not think it went far enough. After becoming disenchanted with Democratic positions, he supported Dewey for president in 1948 and changed his party affiliation to Republican in the hope of becoming under secretary of state in the new administration. Although Truman's upset victory disappointed the former ambassador, he did not waiver from his anticommunist stand. A staunch admirer of Chiang Kai-shek, Bullitt called for American intervention in restoring the Nationalists on mainland China, and during the Korean conflict he joined those who promoted a sea blockade against the Chinese communists in order to limit their military and economic influence on the fighting.[72]

Many agreed with Bullitt about the Soviet threat, but few, if any, understood his most bizarre postwar enterprise, the release in early 1967 of *Thomas Woodrow Wilson,* authored by himself and Sigmund Freud. He and Freud had met and became friends in the mid-1920s when the famous psychiatrist had treated him for self-destructive behavior. They both detested Wilson and collaborated on a psychoanalytical study of him, completing a draft in the early 1930s, with Freud writing the introduction and Bullitt the rest of the text. The manuscript was revised in 1938, but the authors agreed to wait until Mrs. Wilson had died before publishing it. The project lay dormant for almost three decades, long after her death. When the book was finally released, its theses embarrassed psychoanalysts. According to the coauthors, Wilson had repressed his rage against his religious father and transformed him into a deity. This strong-willed reverend had turned his son into a passive, feminine personality, and these character traits accounted for the president's alleged religious fanaticism. The study was Freud at his worst, and his followers kindly refer to it as "an embarrassing production."[73]

Bullitt missed this controversy, for he was dying of chronic lymphatic leukemia, which had first been diagnosed in late 1946. Over the next twenty years, this horrible, incurable disease wrecked his body, and in early February 1967 he booked passage to fly back to the United States to die. Unfortunately for him, he was too ill to travel and had to cancel his flight. On February 15, at the American Hospital outside the French capital, he died at the age of seventy-six with his daughter at his side. His body was flown to Philadelphia, and on February 20 services were held at the Holy Trinity Episcopal Church off Rittenhouse Square. His immediate family attended, as did such dignitaries as James Farley and Richard and Pat Nixon. As the American flag–draped coffin was carried from the church, the several hundred mourners sang "My Country 'Tis of Thee."[74]

Berle did not pay his respects, but vividly recalled Bullitt's campaign against Welles and recorded in his diary, "Bullitt was a flashing, effective, ego-filled, knight-errant. What it all came to in addition to human progress, I don't know. Sentimentally I found it difficult to forgive his destruction of Sumner Welles, who also went bitter and died in his bitterness."[75]

Pearson never forgave Bullitt and used his death as the occasion to repeat an earlier column. In it, he recounted the story of the ambassador's request for Roosevelt's endorsement in his 1943 mayoralty bid. The president refused: "If I were St. Peter and you and Sumner Welles should come before me seeking admission into the Gates of Heaven, do you know what I'd say? I would say: Bill Bullitt, you have defamed the name of a man who toiled for his fellow man, and you can go to Hell. And that's what I tell you to do now."[76]

If Bullitt had to face judgment by a jury of his contemporaries from the New Deal, the verdict would be mixed. Without any doubt, Roosevelt, Welles, Berle, and Pearson would sentence him to damnation in Hell, while Hull, Moore, and others would welcome Bullitt into Heaven. Robert Murphy, a career diplomat who served with Welles and Bullitt, speculated on one of the New Deal's great might-have-beens:

> I am convinced that if the President had kept the ardent support of these two positive personalities during his last two years, when his health declined so disastrously, American postwar policies would have been shaped much more realistically. Bulllitt, in particular possessed a cool, clear awareness of Russian aims which might have proved invaluable to Roosevelt at Teheran and Yalta, and later to President Truman at the Potsdam Conference.[77]

What if Roosevelt, Welles, and Bullitt had joined hands in the closing days of World War II? Would that have influenced the decisions made at

Yalta or assisted in postwar planning? These "what ifs" never happened because personal animosities erected impenetrable barriers. Instead of working together for the common good of mankind, the factions personified by Hull and Welles set out to destroy each other, and in the process consumed themselves. At a moment in history when the world united against the Axis and the evil that it came to represent, American diplomatic leaders could not rise above their emotions to join forces for the common good. Somehow, because of and in spite of these complex characters, the United States survived.

Hull, Welles, and these other significant figures are occasionally subjects for historical discussion, and yet they are distant names, seldom recognizable, even though their most significant causes are still being hotly contested. Hull's crusade for freer trade is a subject of ongoing debate, with the enactment of the North American Free Trade Agreement and the General Agreement on Tariffs and Trade. Welles's goal of stronger hemispheric bonds is still elusive. Batista left Cuba decades ago, but Fidel Castro has assumed many of his predecessor's dictatorial powers and has caused considerable consternation among those dedicated to the building of inter-American solidarity. Bullitt's recommendation for carefully considered negotiations with the Soviet Union is a recurrent theme; even with the chaos and confusion sparked by the recent collapse of the Russian empire, many observers who think like Bullitt still worry about a possible resurgence of the USSR.

Far more than any of these men, Franklin Roosevelt is associated with the New Deal and the defeat of the Axis in World War II. His birthplace in Hyde Park, New York, sits on thirty-three acres, and on April 12, 1946, the first anniversary of his death, the home was formally dedicated to the American people, to be administered by the National Archives and Record Service. There are no spectacular signs at the entrance, but just about everyone in the surrounding area knows where the home is located. Arriving at the turnoff, one travels down the long driveway leading up to the Franklin D. Roosevelt Library. From there one can walk to the rose garden, the nearby graves of Franklin and Eleanor, and, a little farther off, the house where he was raised.[78]

Approximately 120,000 visitors—of whom 60 percent were over sixty and had lived through the New Deal—went through the Little

White House at Warm Springs, Georgia, in 1986. This unpretentious six-room white clapboard cottage, completed in 1932 at a cost of $8,713.14, now serves as the centerpiece of the four-thousand-acre Georgia State Park. It remains exactly as it was the day Roosevelt died. The fireplace with some partially charred logs, Elizabeth Shoumatoff's "Unfinished Portrait" standing on the easel, and his specially designed wheelchair are haunting reminders of his presence.

The president used this rural residence as the headquarters of the Warm Springs Foundation, which was established in 1927 to search for a cure for polio. Although the United States, through vaccination, has nearly eradicated the disease, it still causes serious problems in developing nations. In the summer of 1988 the trustees of the foundation turned over its assets of $1.2 million to the University of California at Irvine to establish the Roosevelt Endowed Chair of Rehabilitative Medicine in order to attract a physician with national stature and to continue research into the worldwide eradication of polio. There is some irony in the foundation's move to the Irvine campus, for it rests in the middle of Orange County, one of the most conservative bastions of Republicanism in the United States.[79]

The homes and open spaces that surround Hyde Park and the Little White House are reminders of how Roosevelt lived. His presidency ranks with those of Abraham Lincoln and George Washington, and yet, whereas the latter two have national holidays dedicated to their memory, Roosevelt does not. His birthday is not celebrated as part of Presidents' Day, nor is any other day designated in his memory. Until recently, the only monument to his presidency in Washington, D.C.—a city filled with epic statues—was a tiny carved stone on a small plot of grass at the back of the National Archives that was dedicated twenty years after his death. The inscription records that in September 1941 Roosevelt called Supreme Court Justice Felix Frankfurter to the White House and said that if any memorial to him were to be erected, he wanted it placed exactly on that spot. Even if that conversation did take place—and there is no record that it ever did—far less significant figures in American history have commanded far greater recognition.

This inconspicuous marker might have neatly wrapped up the story of a lesser figure, but the leitmotivs of Roosevelt's life were controversy and change. In September 1991 the initial phases of site preparation and construction for the Franklin Delano Roosevelt Memorial commenced, at an estimated final cost of $52 million. Located on over seven acres near the Cherry Tree Walk by the Tidal Basin, the memorial will join those of Washington, Jefferson, and Lincoln. This ambitious project will have four outdoor galleries, one devoted to each of Roosevelt's terms. Quotations reflecting his titanic struggles, from the Great Depression to the closing days of World War II, will be carved into the granite walls. Bronze images of Franklin and Eleanor, as well as others depicting significant events, are currently being sculpted by famous American artists. The FDR Memorial Commission has invited Americans to contribute to the capital campaign: indeed this is the first time since the construction of the Washington Monument in the 1880s that the public has been actively solicited for direct contributions to a presidential memorial. The monument is expected to be completed by late 1996.[80]

It is already the topic of heated debate. Advocates for the disabled are angry that any mention of the president's paralysis has been excluded. They argue that this is a historical aberration, while the commission holds that its treatment is consistent with Roosevelt's own approach to his disability during his lifetime. Some complain that the project is too costly and ostentatious, while many others defend it just as it is. Antagonists argue that "that man in the White House" who created the welfare state does not deserve such a tribute, while proponents just as vehemently rally to the cause of liberalism. If Franklin Roosevelt were alive today and a reporter were to ask him for his comments, he might well behave once again like the Sphinx, offering nothing but a cryptic chuckle as the controversy swirled around him. He would feel right at home.

# NOTES

## CHAPTER 1: THE CHIEF SETS THE TONE

1. Daniels diary, Oct. 6, 1943, Box 14.

2. Ward, "House at Hyde Park," 41–50.

3. Ward, *Before the Trumpet*; Freidel, *Rendezous with Destiny*, 3–118.

4. Davis, *The Beckoning*, 15–167; Isaacson and Thomas, *Wise Men*, 47–50; Alsop, *"I've Seen the Best of It,"* 19 and 54–59; Ward, *First Class Temperament*.

5. Lash, *Eleanor and Franklin*, 1–220.

6. Rollins, *Roosevelt and Howe*, 3–380 and 454.

7. Freidel, *The Apprenticeship*, 139–333 and *The Ordeal*, 135–241.

8. Shoumatoff, *Unfinished Portrait*, 84; Ward, *First Class Temperament*, 29.

9. Gallagher, *Splendid Deception*, xiii–xiv and 16–154; Mark Renovitch, principal audiovisual archivist at the Franklin D. Roosevelt Library, to author, Dec. 30, 1994, Gellman Papers.

10. Freidel, *The Triumph*, 3–371; Farley, *Behind the Ballots*, 58–154.

11. For a few of those who find consistency in Roosevelt's diplomatic efforts for different reasons, see Dallek, *Franklin D. Roosevelt*; Kimball, *The Juggler*; Heinrichs, *Threshold of War*; Marks, *Wind over Sand*.

12. King diary, Nov. 8 and 9, 1935; Welles, *Seven Decisions*, 43; Dallek, *Franklin D. Roosevelt*, 59; Davis, *New Deal Years*, 201–13; Farley, *James Farley Story*, 103; Hull, *Memoirs*, 2:1057; Gallagher, *Splendid Deception*, 76–77 and 106–12; Alsop, *"I've Seen the Best of It,"* 136.

13. Lash, *Eleanor and Franklin,* 220–27; Shoumatoff, *Unfinished Portrait,* 72–79; MacMillan to Pearson, Aug. 16, 1968, Pearson Papers, G 242, 2 of 3.

14. Nixon, *Franklin D. Roosevelt,* 1:20.

15. Moffat to White, Apr. 7, and Moffat to Wilson, Apr. 22, 1933, Moffat Papers.

16. Roosevelt, "Our Foreign Policy", 573–86; Cole, *Roosevelt and Isolationists,* 3–6; Dallek, *Franklin D. Roosevelt,* 23–24.

17. Stimson diary, Jan. 9, 1933, vol 25; Culbertson to Davis, Jan. 9, 1933, Davis Papers, Box 9; Carr diary, Feb. 21, 1933, Box 4; Feis, *1933,* 80.

## CHAPTER 2: ENTER HULL

1. Stuart, *Department of State,* 315–16.

2. Nixon, *Franklin D. Roosevelt,* 2:435–37; Freidel, *Launching the New Deal,* 355–57; Weil, *Pretty Good Club,* 24–25; Breitman and Kraut, *American Refugee Policy,* 28–29.

3. Freidel, *Launching the New Deal,* 137–47; Nixon, *Franklin D. Roosevelt,* 1:17.

4. Castle to Wilson, Feb. 10, 1933, Wilson Papers, Box 1.

5. Wehle, *Hidden Threads,* 129–31; Freedman, *Roosevelt and Frankfurter,* 108–9; Farley, *Behind the Ballots,* 75–128 and 204–6, and *James Farley Story,* 18, 25, and 37.

6. Memorandum on Hull, Oct. 15, 1933, Farley Papers, Box 37.

7. Stimson diary, Feb. 25 and 26 and Oct. 18 and 19, 1933, Vol. 26.

8. Burke, *Diary Letters of Hiram Johnson,* Vol. 5, Jan. 21 and Feb. 26, 1933.

9. Lipscomb to his brother, Nov. 27, 1933, Pearson Papers, F 155, 3 of 3, Hull, Cordell #2.

10. Hull, *Memoirs,* 1:3–163; Hinton, *Cordell Hull,* 1–217.

11. Milner diss., "Cordell Hull," 98–99.

12. Grollman diss., "Cordell Hull," 4–27; Milner diss., "Cordell Hull," 123, 195–99, 205, and 315–16.

13. Milner diss., "Cordell Hull," 266.

14. *Staunton Daily News Leader,* Apr. 16, 1940, and Mar. 26, 1954, Gellman Papers; telephone interview with Edward and Tae Bonfoey (Francis Hull's niece), Aug. 1, 1990; MacMaster, *Augusta County History,* 44, 57, 71–73, 76, and 78.

15. Watters, *History of Mary Baldwin College,* 559; William Pollard, College Librarian, Mary Baldwin College, to author, Aug. 9, 1990, Gellman Papers.

16. *New York Herald Tribune,* Mar. 24, 1954; *New York Times,* July 24, 1955; Hull, *Memoirs,* 1:93 and 178; Milner diss., "Cordell Hull," 267–69.

17. Memorandum on Hull, Mar. 24, 1936, Farley Papers, Box 39; Moore autobiography, 129, Gellman Papers; Phillips Papers (Columbia Oral History Collection); Spaulding, *Ambassadors,* 252; Cole, *Roosevelt and Isolationists,* 35; Graebner, *Uncertain Tradition,* 184–209; Clausen and Lee, *Pearl Harbor,* 198.

18. Milner diss., "Cordell Hull," 305–7, 363–71, 380, 400–4, 425, 447–48, 453–54, and 460–62; Cook, *Eleanor Roosevelt,* 1:346.

19. Grollman diss., "Cordell Hull," 21–81; Rollins, *Roosevelt and Howe,* 221, 228, 313, 318, 330, 336, 340–41, 344, and 370–71.

20. Moore autobiography, 125–26, Gellman Papers.

21. Hull, *Memoirs,* 1:105–54; Milner diss., "Cordell Hull," 464–68; Krock, *Memoirs,* 160–61; Roper, *Fifty Years of Public Life,* 290–91; Milton to Hull, Jan. 24, and Milton to Rogers, Feb. 6, 1933, Milton Papers, Box 12; Dodd to Hull, Feb. 11, 1933, Dodd Papers, Box 41; Castle diary, July 30, 1934; 1934 and 1935 Calendars, Reel 37, and 1936 Calandar, Reel 38, Hull Papers.

22. Hull, *Memoirs,* 2:1255; King diary, Nov. 8, 1935; Cordell Hull medical records, Oct. 20, 1944, Gellman Papers.

23. Cordell Hull medical records, Oct. 20, 1944, Gellman Papers; Caldwell, *Last Crusade,* 5–9.

24. General Service Administration, *Executive Office Building,* 1–91; "Washington Merry-Go-Round," Sept. 13, 1937; Alsop, *"I've Seen the Best of It,"* 137.

25. 1933 Calendar, Hull Papers, Reel 37; memorandum from Gosnell, Jan. 23, 1947, Welles file; Ellis, *Republican Foreign Policy,* 39–52.

26. Green to Moffat, Oct. 12, 1935, Moffat Papers; memorandum on Hull, no date, Pearson Papers, F 155, 3 of 3, Hull, Cordell #2.

27. Hull, *Memoirs,* 1:90, 168, 177, and 179.

28. Hooker, *Moffat Papers,* 113.

29. Moore autobiography, 130–31, Gellman Papers; Welles, *Seven Decisions,* 61.

30. Hooker, *Moffat Papers,* 108.

31. Carr diary, Mar. 20, Box 5, and Oct. 9, 1933, Box 4; Crane, *Mr. Carr of State,* 311–14; memorandum by Pearson, 1933?, Pearson Papers, F 155, 3 of 3, Hull, Cordell #2.

32. Hull, *Memoirs,* 1:160–61.

33. Phillips, *Ventures in Diplomacy,* 3–187; Phillips Papers (Columbia Oral History Collection); Lash, *Eleanor and Franklin,* 190–91; Overaker, "Campaign Funds."

34. Memorandum on Phillips, Dec. 20, 1934, Farley Papers, Box 37.

35. Breitman and Kraut, *American Refugee Policy,* 28, 29, 34, and 37; Crane, *Mr. Carr of State,* 309–10 and 326; Stuart, *Department of State,* 312.

36. Crane, *Mr. Carr of State,* 310–17; Stuart, *Department of State,* 311–14 and 326–27.

37. Breitman and Kraut, *American Refugee Policy,* 28, 30, 32, 33, 36, and 37.

38. Ibid., 12–17 and 35–37.

39. Clapper diary, 1933, Box 8; Stimson to Hoover, July 31, 1933, Stimson Papers, Reel 85; Freidel, *Launching the New Deal,* 454–69; Israel, *Nevada's Key Pittman,* 131–32; Alsop, *"I've Seen the Best of It,"* 100.

40. Hull, *Memoirs,* 1:255.

41. Bullitt, *For the President,* 35.

42. Fecher, *Diary of H. L. Mencken,* 60.

43. Daniels diary, June 15, 1933, Box 6, and Bingham to Daniels, Aug. 25, 1933, Daniels Papers, Box 698; Stimson to Hoover, July 31, 1933, Stimson Papers, Reel 85; Cole, *Roosevelt and Isolationists,* 51–64; Freidel, *Launching the New Deal,* 363–65 and 470–95; Hull, *Memoirs,* 1:256–68; Crane, *Mr. Carr of State,* 321–22.

44. Hull to Phillips, July 11, 1933, Hull Papers, Folder 62.

45. Memorandum on Hull, July 23, 1939, Farley Papers, Box 44; Carr diary, Aug. 27, 1933, Box 4.

46. Hull, *Memoirs,* 1:301–2.

47. Moffat to Montgomery, Sept. 30, 1933, Moffat Papers.

48. Moore autobiography, 1–86, Gellman Papers.

49. Ibid., 87.

50. Ibid., 89–110.

51. Moore to Walton, May 4, 1933, Gellman Papers.

52. Ibid.; Moore to Hull, Nov. 27, 1933, Hull Papers, Box 35.

53. Moore to Walton, Nov. 14, 1933, Gellman Papers.

54. Farnsworth, *William C. Bullitt,* 89–115; Orville Bullitt to author, July 9, 1976, Gellman Papers.

55. Carr diary, Nov. 17, 1933, Box 4; memorandum on Bullitt, May 1, 1933, Farley Papers, Box 37; Bullitt, *For the President,* 158–59; Farnsworth, *William C. Bullitt,* xxxvi-xvi and 4–88; Freidel, *Launching the New Deal,* 106–8; Overaker, "Campaign Funds"; Hull, *Memoirs,* 1:296; Martin, *Cissy,* 9–371; Roosevelt, *This I Remember,* 170.

56. Hull, *Memoirs,* 1:317.

57. Gruening, *Many Battles,* 159.

58. Memorandum by Pearson, 1933?, F 155, 3 of 3, Hull, Cordell #2, and memorandum on Montevideo, 1934?, F 155, 3 of 3, Hull, Cordell #1; Gellman, *Good Neighbor Diplomacy,* 21–27.

59. Memorandum on Hull, Apr. 12, 1934, Milton Papers, Box 15.

60. Crane, *Mr. Carr of State*, 322.

61. Hull to Daniels, Dec. 19, 1933, 710.11/1900, Record Group 59, National Archives, Washington, D.C.

62. Hull to Gibson, Feb. 9, 1934, Hull Papers, Box 36.

63. Frances Hull to Inman, Feb. 18, 1934, Inman Papers, Box 14; "Washington Merry-Go-Round," Jan. 30, 1934.

64. Moffat to White, Feb. 6, 1934, Moffat Papers; Hull to Gruening, Feb. 7, 1934, Hull Papers, Box 36; Hull to Daniels, Oct. 2, 1934, Daniels Papers, Box 750.

65. Rosenman, *Public Papers and Addresses,* 2:545.

66. Phillips diary, Dec. 28, 1933, 117.

## CHAPTER 3: WELLES IN CUBA

1. Graff, *Strategy of Involvement,* 27–29; memorandum on Welles, May 1, 1933, Farley Papers; Carr diary, Jan. 9, 1933, Box 4.

2. Carr diary, Apr. 21, Box 4; White to Dodd, June 16, 1933, F. White Papers; Moffat diary, June 22, 1933, Stimson to Frankfurter, Apr. 21, 1933, Frankfurter to Stimson, Apr. 18, 1933, Stimson to White, Nov. 14, 1933, Stimson Papers, Reel 85; Mishler diss., "Francis White," 3–338.

3. Welles to Pearson, June 7, 1933, Pearson Papers, F 33, 2 of 3.

4. For complete citations for this chapter, see Gellman, *Good Neighbor Diplomacy,* 17–21, and *Roosevelt and Batista,* 9–74.

5. Welles, *Time for Decision,* 109–10; Lash, *Eleanor and Franklin,* 571; "Washington Merry-Go-Round," Oct. 14, 1939; Graff, *Strategy of Involvement,* 1–3; Alsop and Kinter, *American White Paper,* 3; U.S. Department of State, *Foreign Relations,* 1940, 1:91; *Baltimore Sun,* Nov. 9, 1941; *New York Times,* Jan. 9, 1952, 24; *Time,* Aug. 11, 1941, 11; Hanson diss., "Sumner Welles," 30–39.

6. Welles to Peabody, Jan. 4, Peabody Papers.

7. *Time,* Aug. 11, 1941, 11.

8. Graff, *Strategy of Involvement,* 2–4; Roosevelt and Brough, *Rendezvous with Destiny,* 57; Hanson diss., "Sumner Welles," 39–46.

9. Welles to FDR, Mar., and FDR to Welles, Mar. 15, 1915, FDR Group 10, Box 81, File: Patronage-General, 1913–1920, Franklin D. Roosevelt Library, Hyde Park, New York.

10. Graff, *Strategy of Involvement,* 4; Mishler diss., "Francis White," 34 and 36; Alsop, *"I've Seen the Best of It,"* 20.

11. Welles to Peabody, Dec. 7, 1915?, Peabody Papers; Hanson diss., "Sumner Welles," 51–64.

12. Graff, *Strategy of Involvement,* 5–20; Welles to Davis, Aug. 6 and 29, 1921, and Davis to Welles, Aug, 19, 1921, Davis Papers, Box 63; Welles to Peabody, Nov. 19, 1925?, Peabody Papers; Hanson diss., "Sumner Welles," 65–208.

13. Graff, *Strategy of Involvement,* 19–21; Moore autobiography, 119, Gellman Papers; *Baltimore Sun,* Apr. 4, 1933, and Aug. 9, 1949; Alsop, *"I've Seen the Best of It,"* 23–24.

14. Castle diary, July 14, 1925.

15. *Washington Star,* Feb. 18, 1940, and Aug. 8, 1949, Gellman Papers.

16. *The Cosmos Club,* pamphlet, Washington, D.C., Gellman Papers.

17. Oxon Hill Manor Foundation, *Oxon Hill Manor* (PS Enterprises, Inc., 1979), 1–13, Gellman Papers.

18. Davis to Welles, Sept. 2, 1925, and Apr. 22 and 28, 1926, and Welles to Davis, Nov. 9, 1925, and Apr. 25 and 29, and May 24, 1926, Davis Papers, Box 63.

19. Welles, *Seven Decisions,* 20–21; Cole, *Roosevelt and Isolationists,* 65–66.

20. Welles to Davis, Apr. 29, 1926, Davis Papers, Box 63.

21. Davis to Welles, Apr. 30 and May 7, 1926, and Welles to Davis, May 4, 1926, Davis Papers, Box 63.

22. Welles, *Naboth's Vineyard,* 2:900–37.

23. Graff, *Strategy of Involvement,* 24; Welles to Robbins, Feb. 10, 1953, President's Personal File 2961; Welles to FDR, Feb. 17, 1931, Box 177, FDR: Papers as governor, Franklin D. Roosevelt Library, Hyde Park, New York; Welles to Davis, Feb. 14, 17, and 21, and Apr. 6, 1931, and Davis to Welles, Feb. 19, 24, and 25, and Apr. 3, 1931, Davis Papers, Box 63.

24. Welles's draft of article, Apr. 6 and June 26, 1931, Davis Papers.

25. Welles to Davis, Oct. 22, 1933, Davis Papers; Overaker, "Campaign Funds," 782; Berle and Jacobs, *Navigating the Rapids,* 71.

26. FDR to Welles, Nov. 19, 1932, President's Personal File 2961.

27. Welles to Davis, Nov. 19, 1932, and Mar. 20, 1933, Davis Papers, Box 63; Welles to FDR, Dec. 19, 1932, Official File 470; Welles to FDR, Jan. 23, 1933, President's Personal File 2961.

28. Nixon, *Franklin D. Roosevelt,* 1:18–19.

29. FDR to Machado, May 11, 1933, Official File 470.

30. Nixon, *Franklin D. Roosevelt,* 1:134–42; Welles to Pearson, May 17, 1933, Pearson Papers, F 33, 2 of 3.

31. Roosevelt, *F.D.R.,* 1:350 and 354; Welles to Pearson, June 7, 1933, Pearson Papers, F 33, 2 of 3.

32. U.S. Department of State, *Foreign Relations,* 1933, 5:358–59.

33. Wilson to White, Aug. 18, 1933, F. White Papers.

34. U.S. Depatment of State, *Foreign Relations,* 1933, 5:367–69.

35. Welles to Inman, Oct. 30, 1933, Inman Papers, Box 13.

36. U.S. Depatment of State, *Foreign Relations,* 1933, 5:379.

37. Ibid., 5:385–86.

38. Ibid., 5:386–87.

39. Ibid., 5:396–98.

40. Schwarz, *Liberal,* 122.

41. Welles to Gibson, Oct. 10, 1933, Gibson Papers.

42. Welles to Inman, Oct. 30, 1933, Inman Papers, Box 13.

43. Ibid.

44. Phillips diary, Nov. 6, 1933, 18.

45. Ibid., 80.

46. White to Stimson, Nov. 26, 1933, Stimson Papers, Reel 85.

47. Wright to White, Jan. 9, 1934, and Cintas to White, Dec. 7, 1934, F. White Papers; Castle diary, Apr. 17, 1935.

48. Castle to White, May 23, 1934, F. White Papers; Castle diary, May 22 and July 8, 1934; This information was confirmed by the author through two separate interviews.

49. Welles to Pearson, Dec. 31, 1943, Pearson Papers, F 33, 2 of 3; Shapiro, *Neurotic Styles,* 23–53.

50. Roosevelt, *F.D.R.,* 2:1445–46.

51. Memo from E. Wilder Spaulding, Aug. 28, 1941, Folder 146, Box 49, Hull Papers; Hull, *Memoirs,* 1:313.

## CHAPTER 4: THE BALANCE OF THE FIRST TERM

1. Memorandum on FDR, Dec. 20, 1934, Farley Papers, Box 37.

2. Castle diary, Jan. 10, 1934.

3. King diary, Nov. 8, 1935.

4. Breitman and Kraut, *American Refugee Policy,* 18, 27, 48, and 223; Freidel, *Rendezvous with Destiny,* 111–12.

5. Dallek, *Franklin D. Roosevelt,* 70–72, 75–77, 85–86, 101–10, and 117–21.

6. Gellman, *Good Neighbor Diplomacy,* 38.

7. Presidential Press Conference, Mar. 20, 1935, Reel 3.

8. Rosenman, *Public Papers and Addresses,* 5:412.

9. Phillips diary, Mar. 20, 1935; Roosevelt, *F.D.R.,* 1:487; Nixon, *Franklin D. Roosevelt,* 3:152–56 and 372; Ickes, *Secret Diary,* 1:312, 479, 494, and 514.

10. Nixon, *Franklin D. Roosevelt,* 3:379.

11. Ibid., 3:577–78; Frances Hull to Milton, May 14, 1937, Milton Papers, Box 20.

12. Memorandums on Hull, Dec. 20, 1934, Box 37, May 15 and July 3, 1935, Box 38, and Mar. 24, 1936, Box 39, Farley Papers; Phillips, *Ventures in Diplomacy,* 90.

13. Castle diary, Mar. 29, 1934; Stimson to Hoover, June 26, 1934, Stimson Papers, Reel 87; Burke, *Diary Letters of Hiram Johnson,* Vol. 6, Feb. 10, 1935.

14. Stuart, *Department of State,* 318; Burke, *Diary Letters of Hiram Johnson,* Vol. 6, Feb. 25, 1934.

15. Gellman, *Good Neighbor Diplomacy,* 25, 45–48, 93, and 161; "Washington Merry-Go-Round," Mar. 6 and Apr. 4, 1935.

16. Thomson "Role of Department of State," 82–91.

17. Yahil, *Holocaust,* 15–122.

18. Wise to Hull, Dec. 11, 1922, Wise Papers, Box 78–14.

19. Nixon, *Franklin D. Roosevelt,* 3:352–54, 359, and 369–70; Feingold, *Time for Searching,* 198 and 212; Hull to Wise, Sept. 2, 1936, Box 122–3, and memorandum of Wise's visit to the secretary of state, July 11, 1937, Wise Papers.

20. Visit to Staunton, Virginia, by author, Aug. 1, 1990; Young to author, May 9, 1991, Gellman Papers.

21. Telehone interview with Philip Heller Sachs, attorney for the Henry Witz estate, Baltimore, Maryland, July 25, 1994, Gellman Papers; Castle diary, Apr. 8, 1938.

22. "The Jew Deal," Aug. 15, 1936, Pearson Papers, F 155, 3 of 3, Hull, Cordell #1.

23. *American Bulletin,* Aug. 11, 1936, 4; Pearson Papers, F 155, 3 of 3, Hull, Cordell #1; Feingold, *Time for Searching,* 190–91.

24. "Washington Merry-Go-Round," Aug. 16, 1936.

25. Hull to Gardenhire, Sept. 18, 1935, Hull Papers, Folder 85.

26. Memorandum on Hull, Mar. 24, 1936, Farley Papers, Box 36.

27. Bowers to Daniels, Mar. 22, 1937, Daniels Papers, Box 790.

28. Phillips diary, Jan. 3, 1935; Castle diary, Jan. 31, 1937; Crane, *Mr. Carr of State,* 324.

29. Castle diary, July 30, 1935.

30. Moore to Bullitt, Mar. 31, 1936, Moore Papers, Box 3.

31. Crane, *Mr. Carr of State,* 325.

32. Frances Hull to Breckinridge, Apr. 28, 1934, Breckinridge Papers, Box 18.

33. Carr diary, Oct. 22, 1936, Box 5; Gardenhire to Hull, Aug. 28 and 30, 1935, and Jan. 3, 1936, Hull to Gardenhire, Aug. 21 and 31, Sept. 4 and 10, Oct. 7, and Dec. 30, 1935, and Hull to Daniels, Sept. 28, 1935, Hull Papers, Box 36; Hull, *Memoirs,* 1:855; Castle diary, Oct. 3, 1935; Farley, *Behind the Ballots,* 221.

34. Memorandum by Hull, Jan. 21, 1936, Carr Papers, Box 5; Daniels to Dodd, Sept. 19, 1935, Daniels Papers, Box 712; House to Dodd, July 21, 1936, Dodd Papers, Box 49; Hull to Milton, Sept. 13, 1935, Milton Papers, Box 18; Bullitt, *For the President,* 180; Ickes, *Secret Diary,* 2:3; Acheson, *Present at the Creation,* 9–10.

35. Phillips to Hull, June 30 and July 7, 1933, Hull Papers, Reel 34.

36. Memorandum on Phillips, May 15, 1935, Farley Papers, Box 38; Davis to Moffat, July 29, 1936, Moffat Papers.

37. Breitman and Kraut, *American Refugee Policy,* 19–27; Chernow, *Warburgs,* 365–457.

38. Gellman, *Roosevelt and Batista,* 178–79; Breitman and Kraut, *American Refugee Policy,* 40–50.

39. Moore to Hull, Nov. 27, 1933, Hull Papers, Box 35.

40. Phillips, *Ventures in Diplomacy,* 90; Green to Moffat, Apr. 22, 1936, Moffat Papers; Moore to Hull, Dec. 29, 1933, Hull Papers, Box 35; memorandum on Moore, July 22, 1935, Farley Papers, Box 38; Moore to Mary McCanlish, May 4, 1933, Gellman Papers.

41. Welles to Hull, Jan. 25, 1935, Hull Papers, Box 37.

42. Welles to Hull, Sept. 7, 1937, Hull Papers, Folder 100.

43. Castle diary, Aug. 31, 1934; Welles to Berle, Aug. 12, 1934, Berle Papers, Box 12; Welles to Hull, Oct. 31, 1934, Hull Papers; Phillips Papers (Columbia Oral History Collection).

44. Castle diary, July 28, 1934; memorandum on Welles, July 22, 1935, Farley Papers, Box 38; Barnett to Hull, Jan. 18, 1934, Hull Papers, Box 35; Acheson, *Present at the Creation,* 12.

45. Moore to Hull, Nov. 27, 1933, Hull Papers, Box 35; Moore autobiography, 118, Gellman Papers; Castle diary, May 21, 1934.

46. Mrs. Arthur H. Vandenberg diary, Feb. 17, 1934, Vol. 4.

47. Carr diary, Dec. 31, 1934, Box 5.

48. Ibid., June 9, 1934, June 6, 1936, and June 12, 1937.

49. Mrs. Arthur H. Vandenberg diary, June 2, 1940, Vol. 8.

50. Rockefeller interview, Aug. 11 and 12, 1976, Gellman Papers.

51. Phillips diary, Jan. 14, 1935, 611–12.

52. Flexer to Lane, Mar. 24, 1935, Lane Papers, Box 10.

53. Green to Moffat, Oct. 12, 1935, and Sept. 12, 1936, Moffat Papers.

54. Gellman, *Good Neighbor Diplomacy,* 29–40; Welles to Pearson, Dec. 31, 1943, Pearson Papers, F 33, 2 of 3.

55. Welles, *Seven Decisions,* 11.

56. Green to Moffat, Apr. 22, 1936, Moffat Papers; Gellman, *Good Neighbor Diplomacy,* 128–29.

57. Gellman, *Good Neighbor Diplomacy,* 15; Welles et al., *Laurence Duggan,* vi–vii and 3–4.

58. Green to Moffat, Nov. 25, 1935, Moffat Papers.

59. Duggan, *The Americas,* 60.

60. For details of the conference, see Gellman, *Good Neighbor Diplomacy,* 61–67; "Washington Merry-Go-Round," Dec. 3, 1936.

61. Roosevelt, *F.D.R.,* 1:625.

62. Berle to Taussig, Dec. 1, 1936, Taussig Papers, Box 21.

63. Rosenman, *Public Papers and Addresses,* 5:604–10.

64. FDR to Sweetser, Dec. 9, 1936, Sweetser Papers, Box 4.

65. Weddell to Hull, Oct. 12, 1935, 710.Peace/10 Record Group 59, National Archives, Washington, D.C.

66. Inman to his wife, Dec. 15, 1936, Inman Papers, Box 14.

67. Gellman, *Good Neighbor Diplomacy,* 67.

68. Ibid., 67–68.

69. Welles to Hull, Jan. 19, 1937, Hull Papers, Box 40.

## CHAPTER 5: THE BLOODIEST BUREAUCRATIC BATTLE

1. Moore to Daniels, Nov. 14, 1935, Daniels Papers, Box 787; Castle diary, Oct. 25, 1935; Carr diary, Feb. 28, June 6, and July 6, 1934, and Jan. 10 and July 24, 1935, Box 5; Crane, *Mr. Carr of State,* 318.

2. Crane, *Mr. Carr of State,* 327; Castle diary, Sept. 4, 1934, Jan. 1, 1935, and May 2, 1936.

3. Hickerson to Moffat, Aug. 25, 1936, and Green to Moffat, Sept. 12, 1936, Moffat Papers; Moore to Bullitt, Oct. 3, 1936, Moore Papers, Box 3; Phillips, *Ventures in Diplomacy,* 88; Castle diary, Dec. 29, 1936.

4. Green to Moffat, Sept. 12, 1936, Moffat Papers.

5. Berle and Jacobs, *Navigating the Rapids,* 110.

6. Rollins, *Roosevelt and Howe,* 432–49.

7. Shirer, *Twentieth Century Journey,* 446–47.

8. Davis to Hull, Apr. 13, 1937, Hull Papers, Folder 98A.

9. Castle diary, July 30, 1935, and Oct. 5, 1938; memorandum on Bullitt, Sept. 1, 1936, Farley Papers, Box 40; "Washington Merry-Go-Round," July 10,

1936; Carr diary, July 3, 1936, Box 5; Murphy, *Diplomat among Warriors,* 28, 29, and 32–33; Farnsworth, *William C. Bullitt,* 155–69.

10. Bullitt, *For the President,* 87 and 106, also see 82–85, 88, 95–97, 103–5, 111–13, 115–17, 121–26, 130–31, and 144–46.

11. Castle diary, Dec. 3, 1934; memorandum on Bullitt, Dec. 19, 1935, Farley Papers, Box 28; Orville Bullitt to author, July 9, 1976, Gellman Papers; Farnsworth, *William C. Bullitt,* 116–54; Isaacson and Thomas, *Wise Men,* 158–66.

12. Bullitt, *For the President,* 98 and 152, also see 77–81, 86, 102, 105–8, 134–35, 141, 146, 161, and 163.

13. Various conversations between author and James Roosevelt, 1978–89; Roosevelt, *This I Remember,* 170.

14. Bullitt, *For the President,* 157–58, 163, and 167–69; Farnsworth, *William C. Bullitt,* 154.

15. Bullitt, *For the President,* 176.

16. Moore autobiography, 115, Gellman Papers.

17. Farley, *James Farley Story,* 62 and 64–65; Dallek, *Franklin D. Roosevelt,* 124–32.

18. Memorandum on Hull, Apr. 29, 1936, Box 39, and Aug. 19 and Sept. 25, 1936, Box 40, Farley Papers; Hull, *Memoirs,* 1:485–87.

19. Welles to Lane, Aug. 11, 1936, Lane Papers, Box 13; Davis diary, Dec. 15, 1936, Box 3; Castle diary, Sept. 14, 1935, and July 23, 1936; memorandums on Welles, Mar. 7 and May 7, 1936, Farley Papers, Box 39.

20. Moore autobiography, 115 and 120, Gellman Papers; Castle diary, Nov. 6, 1936.

21. Moore to Lane, Dec. 12, 1936, Lane Papers, Box 14.

22. Moore to Dodd, Aug. 31, 1936, Dodd Papers, Box 49; Moore to Davis, Nov. 20, 1936, Davis Papers, Box 40; Moore to Bullitt, Jan. 22, 1937, Moore Papers, Box 3.

23. Moore to Daniels, Nov. 13, 1936, Daniels Papers, Box 752.

24. Moore to Dodd, Nov. 19, 1936, Dodd Papers, Box 49.

25. Welles to Peabody, Feb. 8, 1937, Peabody Papers; Welles to Corrigan, Feb. 10, 1937, Corrigan Papers, Box 10; Castle diary, Mar. 21, 1937; Moore autobiography, 121–22, Gellman Papers; Dunn to Moffat, Dec. 19, 1936, Moffat Papers; Welles, *Seven Decisions,* 8.

26. Moore to Lane, Feb. 26, 1937, Lane Papers, Box 14; memorandum on FDR, Mar. 7, 1937, Farley Papers; Farley, *James Farley Story,* 72–81; Welles, *Seven Decisions,* 7–8; Freidel, *Rendezvous with Destiny,* 221–57.

27. Memorandum on undersecretary position, Mar. 10, 1937, Farley Papers, Box 41.

28. Castle diary, Feb. 20, 1937; Wright to Lane, Apr. 19, 1937, Lane Papers, Box 15.

29. Kiley to Lane, Mar. 19, 1937, Lane Papers, Box 14; Moore autobiography, 121, 122, and 133, Gellman Papers; Bullitt, *For the President,* 195, 208–9, 211, and 214–15.

30. Abell, *Drew Pearson Diary,* xii-xiii; Moore autobiography, 120, Gellman Papers; Pilat, *Drew Pearson,* 76–136; Klurfeld, *Behind the Lines,* 3–68; Martin, *Cissy,* 207, 227–30, 239, 248–49, 295–97, 312–13, 362, and 425–27.

31. Welles to Davis, Apr. 5, 1935, Davis Papers, Box 63.

32. "Washington Merry-Go-Round," Mar. 3, 17, and 26, 1937; also see Castle diary, Dec. 11, 1936.

33. Moore to Dodd, Mar. 20 and 29, 1937, Dodd Papers, Box 51.

34. Moore autobiography, 122–24, Gellman Papers.

35. Ibid., 122; Berle to Welles, Apr. 21, 1937, Berle Papers, Box 26.

36. Moore autobiography, 124, Gellman Papers; Moore to Lane, May 22, 1937, Lane Papers, Box 15.

37. Bullitt, *For the President,* 214; Burke, *Diary Letters of Hiram Johnson,* Vol. 6, July 8, 1936, and Vol. 7, Sept. 30, 1939.

38. Bullitt, *For the President,* 211.

39. Moore autobiography, 117, Gellman Papers.

40. Ibid.

41. Ibid., 113, 122, and 126.

42. Ibid., 122, 125, and 127.

43. Carr diary, Aug. 19, 1937, Box 5.

44. Moore autobiography, 120, Gellman Papers.

45. Hull, *Memoirs,* 1:viii.

46. Ibid., 509–10.

## CHAPTER 6: REORGANIZING THE DEPARTMENT

1. Crane, *Mr. Carr of State,* 328–29.

2. Ibid., 329; Carr diary, May 24, 1937, Box 5.

3. Stuart, *Department of State,* 329; Stiller, *George S. Messersmith,* 103–5.

4. Hornbeck to Stimson, Mar. 7 and 8, 1939; Stimson Papers, Reel 97.

5. King diary, Nov. 17, 1938; Stiller, *George S. Messersmith,* 34–95, 123, 124, and 132; Wyman, *Paper Walls,* 221.

6. "Washington Merry-Go-Round," Sept. 13, 1937; Bullitt, *For the President,* 212.

7. "Washington Merry-Go-Round," Sept. 13, 1937; Dallek, *Franklin D. Roosevelt,* 144–45.

8. Hooker, *Moffat Papers,* v–vi and 1–4.

9. Schoenfeld to Steinhardt, Dec. 15, 1937, Box 19, and Duggan to Steinhardt, Apr. 14, 1938, Steinhardt Papers; memorandum by Gosnell, Feb. 2, 1948, Welles file.

10. Welles to Corrigan, May 29, 1937, Corrigan Papers, Box 10.

11. Bullitt, *For the President,* 203, 209, 212, 214–17, 223–29, 232–33, 240, 244–54, 256–64, 267–71, 278–83, 302–3, 305–17, 323–26, 332–36, and 338.

12. Shirer, *Twentieth Century Journey,* 444.

13. Bullitt to Loy Henderson, Nov. 1, 1939, Henderson Papers, Box 6.

14. Memorandum on Hull, Jan. 25, 1938, Hull Papers, Box 42; memorandum on Berle, Mar. 22, 1938, Farley Papers, Box 43; Moore autobiography, 135, Gellman Papers; Berle and Jacobs, *Navigating the Rapids,* 129, 135, and 148–49; Ickes, *Secret Diary,* 1:693; Schwarz, *Liberal,* 16–113; Hull, *Memoirs,* 1:495.

15. Long diary, Nov. 8, 1939, Box 5; Wallace diary, Feb. 6, 1940, Box 4; Moore to Borchard, Nov. 3, 1942, John Moore Papers, Box 82; Burlingham to Davis, Feb. 8, 1942, Davis Papers, Box 3.

16. Richard Harrison, "Roosevelt vs. Hull: Conflicts of Personality and Substance in Making American Foreign Policy in the 1930s," 30–31, Gellman Papers; Stiller, *George S. Messersmith,* 27 and 73–74.

17. Block, *Current Biography 1943,* 181–82.

18. Utley, *Going to War,* 3–22 and 47–48; "Washington Merry-Go-Round," Sept. 10 and 27, 1937.

19. Moore autobiography, 134, Gellman Papers.

20. Ibid., 126; Moore to Dodd, Nov. 12, 1937, Dodd Papers, Box 51.

21. Moore autobiography, 113 and 124, Gellman Papers.

22. Bullitt, *For the President,* 229.

23. Ibid., 206, 218, 222–23, 277, and 285–86.

24. Berle and Jacobs, *Navigating the Rapids,* 151; Castle diary, June 18, 1938; Davis to Gibson, Jan. 8, 1938, Davis Papers, Box 26; Sherwood, *Roosevelt and Hopkins,* 63.

25. Berle diary, June 18, 1937; Moffat to Doyle, Apr. 25, 1938, Moffat Papers; Schoenfeld to Steinhardt, Aug. 2, 1937, and Steinhardt to Schoenfeld, Aug. 4, 1937, Steinhardt Papers.

26. Moffat to Doyle, Apr. 25, 1938, Moffat Papers.

27. Davies, *Mission to Moscow,* 373; Davies to Welles, Mar. 22, 1939, Davies Papers, Box 9; Bowers diary, Mar. 10, 1939.

28. "Washington Merry-Go-Round," Sept. 13, 1937, and Oct. 14, 1939.

29. Memorandums on Welles, July 30, 1937, Box 41, and June 8, 1938, and Jan. 10, 1939, Farley Papers, Box 43.

30. Ickes, *Secret Diary,* 2:351.

31. Daniels to Bowers, Sept. 6, 1938, and Bowers to Daniels, Aug. 16, 1938, Box 732, and Bowers to Daniels, Oct. 25, 1938, Box 791, Daniels Papers; Bowers to Dodd, Nov. 3, 1938, Dodd Papers, Box 56.

32. Pittman to Hull, July 7, 1936, Box 39, Welles to Hull, Aug. 17, 1938, Folder 107, and Guffey to Hull, Apr 4, 1939, Folder 115, Hull Papers.

33. Dallek, *Franklin D. Roosevelt,* 146, 151, and 153–54; Welles to Rosenman, June 17, 1949, Rosenman Papers.

34. Rosenman, *Public Papers and Addresses,* 6:406–11; Dallek, *Franklin D. Roosevelt,* 148–49; Hooker, *Moffat Papers,* 153.

35. Welles to Rosenman, June 17, 1949, Rosenman Papers; Welles to Lazaron, June 14, 1940, Lazaron Papers, Box 9; Welles, *Seven Decisions,* 13; Utley, *Going to War,* 24–48; Burke, *Diary Letters of Hiram Johnson,* Vol. 6, Feb. 19, 1938.

36. King diary, Mar. 5 and 6, 1937; Harrison, "United States and Britain," 25–33, Gellman Papers; Rock, *Chamberlain and Roosevelt,* 1–50.

37. Graff, *Strategy of Involvement,* 189–98; Rock, *Chamberlain and Roosevelt,* 51–77.

38. Offner, "Roosevelt, Hitler, and the Search," 611.

39. Schwarz, *New Dealers,* 128–31; Morgenthau, *Mostly Morgenthaus,* 315–17; see Herzstein, *Roosevelt and Hitler;* Hand, *Counsel and Advise,* 140–41 and 233; Stephen Schuker to author, Dec. 11, 1990, Gellman Papers.

40. Dawidowicz, *War against Jews,* 100–2.

41. King diary, Nov. 17, 1938; Wyman, *Paper Walls,* 43–63.

42. U.S. Department of State, *Foreign Relations,* 1938, 5:38–9; King diary, Aug. 18 and Nov. 17, 1938.

43. Ickes, *Secret Diary,* 2:221–22; Berle and Jacobs, *Navigating the Rapids,* 151; memorandum on Hull, Dec. 11, 1937, Farley Papers, Box 42; memorandum by Pearson, June 15, 1939, Pearson Papers, F 155, 3 of 3, Hull, Cordell #2; "Washington Merry-Go-Round," Apr. 21, 1938; Hull, *Memoirs,* 1:598.

44. Hooker, *Moffat Papers,* 196–98.

45. Castle diary, May 25 and 27, 1938, and July 28, 1939; Buell to Milton, Mar. 29, 1939, Milton Papers, Box 26; Ickes, *Secret Diary,* 2:419 and 558; Israel, *War Diary,* 1–2; Fecher, *Diary of H. L. Mencken,* 127; Burke, *Diary Letters of Hiram Johnson,* Vol. 6, Feb. 19, 1938.

46. Ickes, *Secret Diary,* 2:388; Bullitt, *For the President,* 267–71.

47. Morgenthau, *Mostly Morgenthaus,* 215–75.

48. Memorandum by Gosnell, Feb. 2, 1948, Welles file; Morgenthau to FDR, Oct. 17, 1938, Morgenthau Papers, Box 1, presidential diaries; White to Morgenthau, Mar. 31, 1937, H. White Papers, Box 6; Blum, *Morgenthau Diaries,* 1:452 and 485 and 2:58.

49. White to Morgenthau, Mar. 30, 1939, H. White Papers, Box 6.

50. Morgenthau diary, June 1, 1938, Box 127; memorandum on Hull, Jan. 3, 1938, Farley Papers, Box 42.

51. Hull, Messersmith Papers, 2:22, Box 9; Knox to Hull, Oct. 12, 1937, Hull Papers, Box 42; White to Milton, Aug. 16, 1939, Milton Papers, Box 85; Berle and Jacobs, *Navigating the Rapids,* 242.

52. 1937 Calendar, Hull Papers, Reel 38; Hull to Inman, Dec. 14 and 21, 1937, Inman Papers, Box 14.

53. Frances Hull to Milton, Apr. 14 and May 11, 1938, Milton Papers, Box 25; 1938 Calendar, Hull Papers, Reel 38; Hull, *Memoirs,* 1:581–82 and 615.

54. Stimson diary, Mar. 24, 1938, Vol. 28; Castle diary, June 18 and July 15, 1938, and Apr. 13, 1939; memorandum by Pearson, no date, Pearson Papers, G 236, 1 of 3.

55. "Washington Merry-Go-Round," May 5, 1938; *New York Herald Tribune,* May 7, 1938.

56. "Washington Merry-Go-Round," May 8, 1938; Pearson to Carlin, May 19, 1938, various newspaper clippings, G 210, 2 of 5, G 136, 3 of 3, and memorandum by Pearson, Nov. 7, 1939, F 155, 3 of 3, Hull, Cordell #2; Lerner, "Behind Hull's Embargo," 607–10.

57. Gellman, *Good Neighbor Diplomacy,* 74–79.

58. Memorandum, Cordell Hull, Inman Papers, Box 36.

59. Dallek, *Democrat and Diplomat,* 3–285.

60. Dodd and Dodd, *Ambassador Dodd's Diary,* 94; Dodd to Hull, Feb. 15, 1937, Hull Papers, Folder 97.

61. Dallek, *Democrat and Diplomat,* 286–317; Dodd and Dodd, *Ambassador Dodd's Diary,* 421, 434, and 443.

62. Dodd and Dodd, *Ambassador Dodd's Diary,* 421–22 and 427.

63. Ibid., 445; Dodd to FDR, Dec. 23, 1937, Dodd Papers, Box 51.

64. Dallek, *Democrat and Diplomat,* 318–31; Bullitt, *For the President,* 232–33.

65. Moore autobiography, 144–44 1/2, Gellman Papers.

66. Dallek, *Democrat and Diplomat,* 332.

67. Clifford, "Note on the Break."

68. Brownell and Billings, *So Close to Greatness,* 198–240; Boswell diss., "Buddha Bill," 51–148; Rock, *Chamberlain and Roosevelt,* 100–63.

69. Cordell Hull medical records, Oct. 21, 1944, Gellman Papers; memorandum on Pasvolsky, Apr. 8, 1953, Feis Papers, Box 17; Frances Hull to Steinhardt, Feb. 27, 1939, Steinhardt Papers; Berle and Jacobs, *Navigating the Rapids,* 197–98; Buell to Milton, Mar. 29, 1939, and Milton to Buell, Mar. 30, 1939, Milton Papers, Box 26.

70. Hooker, *Moffat Papers*, 235; "Washington Merry-Go-Round," Mar. 24, 1939.

71. 1939 Calendar, Hull Papers, Reel 38; Hull, *Memoirs*, 1:615 and 654.

72. *Orange County Register*, Mar. 16, 1994, 1 and 10.

73. Castle diary, Oct. 31, 1937, and Sept. 19, 1939; memorandum on Hull and Welles, Jan. 10, 1939, Farley Papers, Box 43.

74. Berle and Jacobs, *Navigating the Rapids*, 205–6.

75. "Washington Merry-Go-Round," Oct. 14, 1939.

76. Moffat diary, Aug. 18, 1939; Hooker, *Moffat Papers*, 245–50, 252–56; Graff, *Strategy of Involvement*, 254–58.

77. Berle and Jacobs, *Navigating the Rapids*, 242.

78. Hooker, *Moffat Papers*, 259–62; Gellman, *Good Neighbor Diplomacy*, 82–83.

79. Acheson, *Present at the Creation*, 38.

## CHAPTER 7: THE WELLES MISSION

1. Link, *Wilson the Diplomatist*, 22 and 27.

2. Berle and Jacobs, *Navigating the Rapids*, 245.

3. U.S. Department of State, *Foreign Relations*, 1939, 5:35; Dallek, *Franklin D. Roosevelt*, 199–205.

4. Israel, *War Diary*, 1–2.

5. Duggan to Daniels, Nov. 25, 1939, Daniels Papers, Box 736.

6. Berle and Jacobs, *Navigating the Rapids*, 186 and 270.

7. Ibid., 278 and 285–87; Israel, *War Diary*, 36; Welles to Lazaron, Dec. 7, 1939, Lazaron Papers, Box 9; Burke, *Diary Letters of Hiram Johnson*, Vol. 7, Jan. 26, 1940.

8. Gellman, *Good Neighbor Diplomacy*, 83–85; "Washington Merry-Go-Round," Oct. 14, 1939.

9. Hull, *Memoirs*, 1:690.

10. Berle and Jacobs, *Navigating the Rapids*, 263.

11. Rock, *Chamberlain and Roosevelt*, 1:209–46; Kimball, *Churchill and Roosevelt*, 26–27.

12. Gellman, *Good Neighbor Diplomacy*, 88–91.

13. Moffat diary, Oct. 5 and 9, 1939; Hooker, *Moffat Papers*, 272; Cole, *Roosevelt and Isolationists*, 331–45.

14. Berle and Jacobs, *Navigating the Rapids*, 284; Dallek, *Franklin D. Roosevelt*, 206–8 and 216.

15. Abell, *Drew Pearson Diary*, 540; Welles, *Time for Decision*, 73–74; Reynolds, *Anglo-American Alliance*, 69–72; Israel, *War Diary*, 64.

16. Trip to Europe, July-Sept. 1939, Farley Papers, Box 44; Farley, *James Farley Story*, 192–95.

17. Bullitt, *For the President*, 402.

18. Reston, *Deadline*, 68–70.

19. Welles to Pearson, Feb. 25, 1948, Pearson Papers, G 87, 3 of 3; Woodward, *British Foreign Policy*, 1:165.

20. Woodward, *British Foreign Policy*, 1:165; U.S. Department of State, *Foreign Relations*, 1940, 1:4; Hilton, "Welles Mission," 101–2; U.S. Congress, *Hearings*, pt. 1:547; Wallace diary, Feb. 9, 1940, Box 4.

21. Berle and Jacobs, *Navigating the Rapids*, 140 and 186; *New York Times*, Feb. 10, 1940; Welles, *Time for Decision*, 122, and *Seven Decisions*, 13; Graff, *Strategy of Involvement*, 232.

22. Welles to Peabody, July 9, 1937, Peabody Papers.

23. Pearson to Welles, Feb. 15, 1940, Pearson Papers, F 33, 2 of 3; Ickes, *Secret Diary*, 3:138; Berle and Jacobs, *Navigating the Rapids*, 280; Graff, *Strategy of Involvement*, 264–65; Wiebel thesis, "Strange Odyssey," 48, Gellman Papers.

24. Castle diary, Feb. 18, 1940; Rock, *Chamberlain and Roosevelt*, 276–78; Beschloss, *Kennedy and Roosevelt*, 191–98 and 204–5; Welles, *Time for Decision*, 74–77; Wiebel thesis, "Strange Odyssey," 44–45 and 49–50, Gellman Papers; Graff, *Strategy of Involvement*, 275–76; Hooker, *Moffat Papers*, 280–81; Hilton, "Welles Mission," 94; Moore to Sayre, Feb. 28, 1940, Moore Papers, Box 25.

25. Burke, *Diary Letters of Hiram Johnson*, Vol. 7, Sept. 30, 1939, and Jan. 26 and Feb. 10, 1940.

26. Castle diary, Feb. 13 and 21, 1940; Wallace diary, Mar. 1940, Box 7; Bullitt, *For the President*, 398, 402–3, and 406; Murphy, *Diplomat among Warriors*, 35–36.

27. *Chicago Tribune*, Feb. 16, 1940; Israel, *War Diary*, 58.

28. U.S. Department of State, *Foreign Relations*, 1940, 1:8.

29. Joe Gascorgne to Jock, Mar. 12, 1940, Gellman Papers; Rock, *Chamberlain and Roosevelt*, 276.

30. Wiebel thesis, "Strange Odyssey," 105–6, Gellman Papers; Hooker, *Moffat Papers*, 146 and 292; Hilton, "Welles Mission," 105–6.

31. U.S. Department of State, *Foreign Relations*, 1940, 1:7; Graff, *Strategy of Involvement*, 279–82; Hilton, "Welles Mission," 97; Hooker, *Moffat Papers*, 292–93.

32. Wiebel thesis, "Strange Odyssey," 57, Gellman Papers.

33. U.S. Department of State, *Foreign Relations*, 1940, 1:5 and 21–27; Welles, *Time for Decision*, 78–82; Gibson, *Ciano Diaries*, 212.

34. U.S. Department of State, *Foreign Relations*, 1940, 1:27–33; memorandums on mission, Mar. 12 and Apr. 22, 1940, Pearson Papers, F 33, 2 of 3; Welles, *Time for Decision*, 83–88.

35. U.S. Department of State, *Foreign Relations*, 1940, 1:12–13; Phillips, *Ventures in Diplomacy*, 150–51; Gibson, *Ciano Diaries*, 212; Muggeridge, *Diplomatic Papers*, 337–38; Wiebel thesis, "Strange Odyssey," 88, 91–92, 103–6, and 171, Gellman Papers.

36. Wiebel thesis, "Strange Odyssey," 57, Gellman Papers; Welles, *Time for Decision*, 89.

37. Shirer, *Twentieth Century Journey*, 475.

38. U.S. Department of State, *Foreign Relations*, 1940, 1:8 and 10; Hilton, "Welles Mission," 98–99.

39. Welles, *Time for Decision*, 109; Wiebel thesis, "Strange Odyssey," 58–60, Gellman Papers; Bullitt, *For the President*, 406–7.

40. U.S. Department of State, *Foreign Relations*, 1940, 1:33–41; memorandums on mission, Mar. 12 and Apr. 22, 1940, Pearson Papers, F 33, 2 of 3; Welles, *Time for Decision*, 90–98; Graff, *Strategy of Involvement*, 282; Wiebel thesis, "Strange Odyssey," 11, Gellman Papers; Weitz, *Hitler's Diplomat*, 3–234.

41. U.S. Department of State, *Foreign Relations*, 1940, 1:42–43; Welles, *Time for Decision*, 99–100.

42. U.S. Department of State, *Foreign Relations*, 1940, 1:43–50; memorandums on mission, Mar. 12, Apr. 22, and June 25, 1940, Pearson Papers, F 33, 2 of 3; Welles, *Time for Decision*, 101–9; Wiebel thesis, "Strange Odyssey," 62 and 74, Gellman Papers.

43. U.S. Department of State, *Foreign Relations*, 1940, 1:50–51; Welles, *Time for Decision*, 110–11.

44. U.S. Department of State, *Foreign Relations*, 1940, 1:51–56; Welles, *Time for Decision*, 112–20.

45. U.S. Department of State, *Foreign Relations*, 1940, 1:56–58; Wiebel thesis, "Strange Odyssey," 108–26, Gellman Papers.

46. Hooker, *Moffat Papers*, 294; Nicolson, *Harold Nicolson*, 2:63.

47. U.S. Department of State, *Foreign Relations*, 1940, 1:56; Hilton, "Welles Mission," 96–97; Hooker, *Moffat Papers*, 296.

48. U.S. Department of State, *Foreign Relations*, 1940, 1:58–59; Welles, *Time for Decision*, 121.

49. U.S. Department of State, *Foreign Relations*, 1940, 1:59–67; Wiebel thesis, "Strange Odyssey," 134–35, 152, and 154, Gellman Papers.

50. U.S. Department of State, *Foreign Relations*, 1940, 1:61–71; memorandums on mission, Mar. 12, 1940, Pearson Papers, F 33, 2 of 3; Reuth, *Goebbels*, 266; Welles, *Time for Decision*, 26–130; Webster, *Pétain's Crime*.

51. Hooker, *Moffat Papers*, 297; U.S. Department of State, *Foreign Relations*, 1940, 1:1–4 and 14–15; Reynolds, *Anglo-American Alliance*, 80–88; Welles, *Time for Decision*, 180; Rock, *Chamberlain and Roosevelt*, 264–79.

52. U.S. Department of State, *Foreign Relations*, 1940, 1:72–74; Welles to Pearson, Feb. 12, 1945, Pearson Papers, F 33, 2 of 3; Welles, *Time for Decision*, 130; Hooker, *Moffat Papers*, 298.

53. Rock, *Chamberlain and Roosevelt*, 270–72.

54. U.S. Department of State, *Foreign Relations*, 1940, 1:74–80; Reynolds, *Anglo-American Alliance*, 286–88; Welles, *Time for Decision*, 130–32.

55. U.S. Department of State, *Foreign Relations*, 1940, 1:80–83; *Newsweek*, Mar. 15, 1940, 28.

56. Eden, *The Reckoning*, 48.

57. U.S. Department of State, *Foreign Relations*, 1940, 1:83.

58. Ibid., 1:84–85; Rock, *Chamberlain and Roosevelt*, 272–73.

59. U.S. Department of State, *Foreign Relations*, 1940, 1:85–86.

60. Ibid., 87–90; Reynolds, *Anglo-American Alliance*, 82–83.

61. Welles, *Time for Decision*, 134; Rock, *Chamberlain and Roosevelt*, 273–74.

62. U.S. Department of State, *Foreign Relations*, 1940, 1:91–92; Welles, *Time for Decision*, 134–35; Wiebel thesis, "Strange Odyssey," 164, Gellman Papers.

63. U.S. Department of State, *Foreign Relations*, 1940, 1:89 and 95–100; Welles, *Time for Decision*, 135–36; Weitz, *Hitler's Diplomat*, 234–36.

64. U.S. Department of State, *Foreign Relations*, 1940, 1:92–96.

65. Ibid., 1:17–18 and 96–99; Muggeridge, *Diplomatic Papers*, 359–60; Gibson, *Ciano Diaries*, 222.

66. U.S. Department of State, *Foreign Relations*, 1940, 1:100–6; Hull, *Memoirs*, 1:739; Wiebel thesis, "Strange Odyssey," 161–65, Gellman Papers; Gibson, *Ciano Diaries*, 222.

67. Gibson, *Ciano*, 224; Wiebel thesis, "Strange Odyssey," 101–2, Gellman Papers; Welles, *Time for Decision*, 137–41.

68. U.S. Department of State, *Foreign Relations*, 1940, 1:106–9; Welles, *Time for Decision*, 142.

69. U.S. Department of State, *Foreign Relations*, 1940, 1:18–19; *New York Times*, Mar. 19, 1940; Hull, *Memoirs*, 1:739.

70. U.S. Department of State, *Foreign Relations*, 1940, 1:110–13; Welles, *Time for Decision*, 143–47.

71. Memorandum on mission, Apr. 22, 1940, Pearson Papers, F 33, 2 of 3; U.S. Department of State, *Foreign Relations*, 1940, 1:113–17.

72. Ibid., 1:20; Woodward, *British Foreign Policy*, 1:171.

73. King diary, Apr. 23 and 24, 1940.

74. Hull, *Memoirs,* 1:740 and 2:1628.

75. U.S. Department of State, *Foreign Relations,* 1940, 1:19–20; Wiebel thesis, "Strange Odyssey," 166–69, Gellman Papers.

76. Bullitt, *For the President,* 404–5.

77. Wallace diary, Mar. 1940, Box 7.

78. Bullitt, *For the President,* 409–10.

79. Bullitt to Moore, Apr. 18, 1940, Moore Papers, Box 3.

80. Bullitt, *For the President,* 441 and 448.

81. Ibid., 445–46.

82. Ibid., 415–31, 462–63, 466, 469, 474, and 476–80.

83. Hull, *Memoirs,* 1:791.

84. Bullitt, *For the President,* 439–93.

85. Berle and Jacobs, *Navigating the Rapids,* 311; Berle to Stimson, Mar. 20, 1940, Stimson Papers, Reel 100.

86. Ickes, *Secret Diary,* 3:273.

87. Ibid., 3:464.

88. Berle and Jacobs, *Navigating the Rapids,* 301, 322, and 325; Wallace diary, Apr. 3, 1940, Box 7; Welles to Bowers, May 10, 1940, Bowers Papers; Graff, *Strategy of Involvement,* 314–17.

89. Schwarz, *Liberal,* 133–34; Farley diary, Apr. 9, 1940, Box 45.

90. Farley diary, Mar. 8, 1940, Box 44; Berle diary, Feb. 17, 1940, Box 211; Ickes, *Secret Diary,* 3:138; Berle and Jacobs, *Navigating the Rapids,* 293; *Baltimore Sun,* Feb. 19, 1940.

91. Israel, *War Diary,* 67.

92. Stimson diary, May 8, 1940, Vol. 29.

93. Ickes, *Secret Diary,* 3:216–19.

94. Farley, *James Farley Story,* 232–33; Berle and Jacobs, *Navigating the Rapids,* 323–24.

95. Offner, "Appeasement Revisited"; Hilton, "Welles Mission," 94 and 120; Wiebel thesis, "Strange Odyssey," 181 and 184, Gellman Papers; Graff, *Strategy of Involvement,* 305–6.


## CHAPTER 8: THE SPHINX, HULL, AND THE OTHERS

1. Farley diary, Mar. 5, 1937, and Nov. 17, 1938, memorandum on election of 1940, July 23, 1939, Farley Papers, Box 44; memorandum on the election of 1940, Byrnes Papers.

2. McJimsey, *Harry Hopkins,* 3–124; Watkins, *Righteous Pilgrim,* 677; Lash, *Dealers and Dreamers,* 352–54 and 364–65.

3. Memorandums on Garner, Farley Papers, Nov. 22, 1937, Box 42, Dec. 7 and 12, 1938, Box 43, and July 6, Oct. 20, Nov. 30, and Dec. 22, 1939, and Jan. 7, 1940, Box 44; Berle and Jacobs, *Navigating the Rapids*, 304; Farley, *James Farley Story*, 205–8 and 217–22; Timmons, *Garner of Texas*, 1–271; Hardeman and Baem, *Rayburn*, 229–39.

4. Watkins, *Righteous Pilgrim*, 676; Ickes, *Secret Diary*, 3:95.

5. Memorandum on 1940 election, Farley Papers, Dec. 7, 1939, Box 42, Mar. 21 and Aug. 25, 1938, Box 43, July 7, 12, and 25, Oct. 20 and 27, and Nov. 30, 1939, and Jan. 2, 11, and 31, and Mar. 8, 1940, Box 44; Berle and Jacobs, *Navigating the Rapids*, 274; Farley, *James Farley Story*, 153, 173–77, 184–88, 223–29, 238–39, 244, and 248–56; Farley, *Behind the Ballots*, 1–369; Watkins, *Righteous Pilgrim*, 677.

6. Hull, *Memoirs*, 1:855–56; King diary, Mar. 5, 1937; Richard Harrison, "Roosevelt vs. Hull", 30–32, Gellman Papers.

7. Speech by Hull, May 28, 1939, Davis Papers, Box 27; Moore to Sayre, Dec. 8, 1939, Moore Papers, Box 25.

8. Bowers diary, July 14, 1939; Landon to Inman, Aug. 26, 1939, Inman Papers, Box 14; Messersmith to Burlingham, July 13, 1939, Messersmith Papers, No. 1259; King diary, Nov. 17, 1938; Ickes, *Secret Diary*, 2:555; Bowers, *My Life*, 295–96; memorandum on Welles, Farley Papers, Jan. 11, Box 43, and Nov. 29, 1939, Box 44; Farley, *James Farley Story*, 164–65; Berle and Jacobs, *Navigating the Rapids*, 194, 195, 197, 206, 216, 224, 227–28, 234, and 270.

9. Moore autobiography, 128, Gellman Papers; Moore to Sayre, Feb. 28, 1940, Moore Papers, Box 25.

10. Hooker, *Moffat Papers*, 235.

11. Watkins, *Righteous Pilgrim*, 677.

12. Memorandum on Hull, Dec. 8, 1939, Farley Papers, Box 44.

13. Memorandum on Mrs. Hull, 1940, Pearson Papers, F 155, 3 of 3, Hull, Cordell #3.

14. Memorandum on election of 1940, Mar. 7, 1937, Farley Papers, Box 41; Roosevelt, *F.D.R.*, 2:972–73.

15. Hull, *Memoirs*, 1:855–57; Farley, *James Farley Story*, 230; Roosevelt, *This I Remember*, 213; King diary, Nov. 17, 1938; memorandum on election of 1940, Mar. 7, 1937, Box 41, Jan. 10, Box 43, and May 30, 1939, Box 44, Farley Papers; Ickes, *Secret Diary*, 2:555 and 3:68; Farley, *James Farley Story*, 113; Burke, *Diary Letters of Hiram Johnson*, Vol. 7, Apr. 6, 1940.

16. Memorandums on 1940 election, Jan. 2, 3, 7, 11, and 31 and Mar. 8, 1940, Box 44, and June 21, 1940, Box 45, Farley Papers; Berle and Jacobs, *Navigating the Rapids*, 304; Farley, *James Farley Story*, 225–29.

17. Memorandums on election of 1940, Apr. 30, May 6, 17, and 28, and June 14, 1940, Farley Papers, Box 45; Farley, *James Farley Story,* 223–24, 236–38, and 244; Berle and Jacobs, *Navigating the Rapids,* 294.

18. Memorandum on election of 1940, June 21, 1940, Farley Papers, Box 45; Moore to Sayre, Apr. 16, Box 19, and Moore to Bullitt, Apr. 26, 1940, Box 3, Moore Papers; Berle and Jacobs, *Navigating the Rapids,* 288; "Washington Merry-Go-Round," Jan. 2, 1940; Hull, *Memoirs,* 1:856–57.

19. Memorandums on Hull, May 9, 1940, Apr. 5, 1941, May 8, 1943, and Apr. 18, 1945, Farley Papers, Box 45; Sayre to Hull, Apr. 10, 1940, Hull Papers, Box 46; Farley to Sayre, Feb. 8, 1940, Sayre Papers, Box 4; Farley to Bowers, May 15, 1940, Bower Papers; Farley, *James Farley Story,* 232–33 and 244; Hull, *Memoirs,* 1:746–50 and 855–58; Alsop and Kinter, *American White Paper,* 83; Burke, *Diary Letters of Hiram Johnson,* Vol. 7, Apr. 6, 1940.

20. Sayre to Farley, Apr. 8, 1940, Sayre Papers, Box 4.

21. Memorandum by Pasvolsky, Apr. 8, 1953, Feis Papers, Box 17; memorandums on FDR, July 23 and Dec. 8, 1939, Jan. 3 and Mar. 7 and 9, 1940, Box 49, and May 17, 1940, Box 45, Farley Papers; Wallace diary, Mar. 1940, Box 7; Farley, *James Farley Story,* 208–9; Berle and Jacobs, *Navigating the Rapids,* 225–26, 291, 307, and 314–15; Pickersgill, *MacKenzie King Record,* 1:109; Dallek, *Franklin D. Roosevelt,* 217; Watkins, *Righteous Pilgrim,* 676.

22. Moore to Sayre, Dec. 8, 1939, Moore Papers, Box 25; Moffat diary, Apr. 26, 1940; Stimson diary, May 8, 1940, Vol. 29; Berle and Jacobs, *Navigating the Rapids,* 323–24; Ickes, *Secret Diary,* 3:216–19; Farley, *James Farley Story,* 233; memorandum by Pearson, 1940, Pearson Papers, G 236, 1 of 3.

23. Stimson diary, Vol. 29, May 8, 1940.

24. Memorandums on Welles, Jan. 11, 1937, Box 43, Nov. 29, 1939, Box 44, and May 9, 1940, Box 45, Farley Papers; Berle and Jacobs, *Navigating the Rapids,* 199, 206, 224, 227–28, 270, 306, and 311; Farley, *James Farley Story,* 164–65.

25. Berle and Jacobs, *Navigating the Rapids,* 325.

26. Welles to Lazaron, Oct. 1, 1940, Lazaron Papers, Box 13.

27. Hull, *Memoirs,* 1:856; *Staunton Daily News Leader,* Apr. 16, 1940, Gellman Papers.

28. Pickersgill, *MacKenzie King Record,* 1:108, 111, and 113.

29. Hull, *Memoirs,* 1:858.

30. Ibid., 1:855–56; memorandums on Hull, June 21 and 28, 1940, Farley Papers, Box 45; Lash, *Eleanor and Franklin,* 616; Berle and Jacobs, *Navigating the Rapids,* 288; Welles, *Time for Decision,* 61.

31. Berle and Jacobs, *Navigating the Rapids,* 225–26; Farley, *James Farley Story,* 208–9; memorandum on election of 1940, Jan. 3 and Mar. 7, 1940,

Farley Papers, Box 44; Dallek, *Franklin D. Roosevelt*, 217; Burke, *Diary Letters of Hiram Johnson*, Vol. 7, May 27, 1939.

32. Memorandums on election of 1940, Mar. 9, 1940, Box 44, and May 17, 1940, Box 45, Farley Papers; Berle and Jacobs, *Navigating the Rapids*, 291, 307, and 314–15; Pickersgill, *MacKenzie King Record*, 1:108–9.

33. Timmons, *Garner*, 272; Farley, *James Farley Story*, 212; Clifford and Spencer, *First Peacetime Draft*, 63 and 66–67; Dallek, *Franklin D. Roosevelt*, 232; Morison, *Turmoil and Tradition*, 399.

34. Freidel, *Rendezvous with Destiny*, 342–43.

35. Memorandum by Hull, July 3, 1940, Hull Papers, Folder 135; Hull, *Memoirs*, 1:858–59.

36. Farley, *James Farley Story*, 248–56.

37. Ibid., 240, 259–64, and 271–82; memorandum on Bankhead, June 19–20, 1940, Farley Papers, Box 45; Hull, *Memoirs*, 1:861–62; McJimsey, *Harry Hopkins*, 129–31.

38. Farley, *James Farley Story*, 279–80.

39. Ibid., 293–95, 299–303, and 331; memorandum on Bankhead, Aug. 16, 1940, Farley Papers, Box 45; Pittman to Bowers, July 8, 1940, Bowers Papers; Ickes, *Secret Diary*, 3:286; Hull, *Memoirs*, 1:860–61; Byrnes, *All in One Lifetime*, 117–18, 120, and 124.

40. Memorandum on the election of 1940, Aug. 1, 1940, Farley Papers, Box 45; Timmons, *Garner of Texas*, 272–77.

41. Hull, *Memoirs*, 1:822 and 861; Gellman, *Good Neighbor Diplomacy*, 93–104.

42. 1940 Calendar, Hull Papers, Reel 39; Hull, *Memoirs*, 1:829, 834, and 862; Farley, *James Farley Story*, 330–31.

43. Bullitt, *For the President*, 267–71, 384–85, 454, 490–98, and 503; Ickes, *Secret Diary*, 2:388.

44. Bullitt, *For the President*, 502–3 and 505–6; Berle and Jacobs, *Navigating the Rapids*, 828.

45. Brownell and Billings, *So Close to Greatness*, 270–72.

46. Davis, *New Deal Years*, 537; Israel, *Miss Tallulah Bankhead*, 201–4; Bankhead, *Tallulah*, 247–48; Hardeman and Baem, *Rayburn*, 226 and 242–45.

47. *New York Times*, Sept. 15–18, 1940.

48. News release, Apr. 8, 1983, Southern Railway System, Washington, D.C., Gellman Papers; White, *American Railroad Car*, 370–71.

49. Official File 200, President's Trips (1940–45) 200, TTTT, Jasper, Alabama, Sept. 16, 1940, Franklin D. Roosevelt Library; *Montgomery Advertiser*, Sept. 18, 1940; *Birmingham News*, Sept. 16–18, 1940; Ickes, *Secret Diary*, 3:326–27; Gallagher, *FDR*, 97 and 173–74.

50. Wallace diary, Mar. 30, 1942, Box 13; Wallace Papers (Columbia Oral History Collection).

51. Welles to Daniels, Nov. 11, 1940, Farley Papers, Box 752.

52. Hull, *Memoirs,* 1:863–68; Berle and Jacobs, *Navigating the Rapids,* 344, 347, 351, and 387; Sherwood, *Roosevelt and Hopkins,* 185.

53. Divine, *Foreign Policy,* 3–89; Cole, *Roosevelt and Isolationists,* 395–405.


CHAPTER 9: AN INCREDIBLE SET OF CIRCUMSTANCES

1. Presidential Press Conference, Aug. 16, 1940, Reel 8; Rosenman, *Public Papers and Addresses,* 9:460–67; Conn and Fairchild, *Framework,* 51–62.

2. Freidel, *Rendezvous with Destiny,* 358–63.

3. Ibid., 373–76; conversation with Welles, Oct. 6, 1944, Fisher Papers; Biddle diary, Sept. 27, 1941.

4. Wilson, *First Summit,* 8–238.

5. Memorandum on State Department, Apr. 5, 1941, Farley Papers, Box 45; Hooker, *Moffat Papers,* 354; Israel, *War Diary,* 175–76.

6. Lash, *Eleanor and Franklin,* 504–6; McJimsey, *Harry Hopkins,* 129–92.

7. Abramson, *Spanning the Century,* 269–95.

8. Hooker, *Moffat Papers,* 332–33.

9. Blum, *Morgenthau Diaries,* 2:261; memorandum on Hull, May 10, 1941, Farley Papers, Box 45.

10. "Washington Merry-Go-Round," May 28, 1941.

11. Memorandums on Hull, Apr. 5 and May 10, 1941, Farley Papers, Box 45; memorandum of conversation, June 4, 1941, presidential diaries, Morgenthau Papers; Castle diary, Feb. 28, Mar. 5, and Oct. 18, 1941; Farley, *James Farley Story,* 340–43; Israel, *War Diary,* 175–76.

12. Castle diary, Oct. 18, 1940.

13. Welles file, memorandum by Gosnell, Feb. 2, 1948; Acheson, *Present at the Creation,* 15.

14. Reston, *Deadline,* 101–2; Alsop, *"I've Seen the Best of It,"* 138; Acheson, *Present at the Creation,* 20.

15. Stimson diary, Nov. 25, 1940 and Jan. 4, 1941, Vol. 31, and May 27, 1941, Vol. 34; Berle and Jacobs, *Navigating the Rapids,* 363; Morison, *Turmoil and Tradition,* 431.

16. Stimson diary, Jan 7, 1941, Vol. 31.

17. Moffat diary, Jan. 31, Apr. 3, and July 10–12, 1941; conversation with Welles, Mar. 26, 1941, Fisher Papers; Israel, *War Diary,* 179; Farley, *James Farley Story,* 343.

18. Conversations with Welles, Feb. 11, Mar. 26, Apr. 29, and May 19, 1941, Fisher Papers; Graff, *Strategy of Involvement*, 367–72; Hull, *Memoirs*, 1:812 and 2:967.

19. Feingold, *Time for Searching*, 212; Breitman and Kraut, *American Refugee Policy*, 230–38; Lash, *Eleanor and Franklin*, 575–78 and 636–37.

20. Moore to Dodd, Mar. 25, 1937, Dodd Papers, Box 51.

21. Castle diary, June 4 and July 3, 1938; Moore to Dodd, Sept. 1, 1938, Box 55, Nov. 8, 1938, Box 56, and Feb. 27 and Mar. 23, 1939, Box 57, Dodd Papers; Borchard to Moore, Feb. 7, 1939, J. Moore Papers, Box 76.

22. Livingston to Gellman, Oct 18, 1987, Gellman Papers; Moore autobiography, 151–55, Gellman Papers.

23. Moore autobiography, 155–57 and 165, Gellman Papers; Moore to Sayre, Dec. 8, 1939, Moore Papers, Box 25.

24. Moore to Sayre, Oct. 1, 1940, Moore Papers; Mary Livingston to author, Oct. 18, 1987, Gellman Papers.

25. Moore to Sayre, Nov. 18, 1940, Moore Papers, Box 19.

26. Bullitt, *For the President*, 502–12.

27. Welles file, memorandum by Gosnell, Jan. 23, 1947; Schwarz, *Liberal*, 114–75.

28. Acheson, *Present at the Creation*, 12.

29. Ibid., 13; Israel, *War Diary*, xi–xxiv, 1–49 and 179; Breitman and Kraut, *American Refugee Policy*, 237–39; Wyman, *Paper Walls*, 172–81, 184–91, and 192–205.

30. *New York Times*, Nov. 13, 1940, Folder 155, 3 of 3, Hull, Cordell #3, *New York Times*, Dec. 7, 1940, and NY *Times Herald*, Dec. 12, 1940, G 236, 1 of 3, Pearson Papers; for the diplomatic discussion of the proposed credit, see U.S. Department of State, *Foreign Relations*, 1940, 2:839–53.

31. Pearson to Welles, Dec. 26, 1940, and Pearson to Frantz, Jan. 8, 1941, G 210, 2 of 5, and Pearson to Green, Jan. 3, 1941, G 236, 1 of 3, Pearson Papers; "Washington Merry-Go-Round," Dec. 20, 1940; Abell, *Drew Pearson Diary*, xiii; Pilat, *Drew Pearson*, 161; Klurfeld, *Behind the Lines*, 59.

32. Pearson to Frantz, Jan. 8, 1941, Pearson Papers, G 210, 2 of 5.

33. Hull to United Features Syndicate, Inc., Dec. 21, 1940, G 210, 3 of 5, and Carlin to Godbey and Carlin to Hull, Dec. 31, 1940, G 236, 1 of 3, Pearson Papers.

34. Welles to Pearson, Dec. 22, 1940, Pearson Papers, G 210, 2 of 5.

35. Pearson to Welles, Dec. 26, 1940, Pearson Papers, G 210, 2 of 5.

36. "Washington Merry-Go-Round," Dec 28, 1940; Castle diary, Jan. 1, 1941.

37. Welles press conference, Dec. 28, 1940, Pearson Papers, F 155, 3 of 3, Hull, Cordell #3.

38. Hinton, *Cordell Hull,* 363.

39. Ickes, *Secret Diary,* 3:401; Castle diary, Jan. 1, 1941; Chapman to Pearson, Jan. 3, 1941, Pearson Papers, G 236, 1 of 3.

40. Pearson to Carlin, Jan. 3, 1941, Pearson Papers, G 210, 2 of 5.

41. Memorandum by Hoover, Jan. 3, 1941, Sumner Welles Federal Bureau of Investigation O.C. File, Washington, D.C., Gellman Papers.

42. Morgan, *FDR,* 234–45; Rollins, *Roosevelt and Howe,* 177–79.

43. Gentry, *J. Edgar Hoover,* 46 and 308–9.

44. Wallace diary, Mar. 30, 1942, Box 13, Wallace Papers and Wallace (Columbia Oral History Collection); memorandum by Hoover, Jan. 30, 1941, Sumner Welles Federal Bureau of Investigation O.C. File, Washington, D.C., Gellman Papers; D'Emilio and Freedman, *Intimate Matters,* 288.

45. Memorandums for Hoover, Jan. 23 and 30, 1941, Sumner Welles Federal Bureau of Investigation O.C. File, Washington, D.C., Gellman Papers; Hassett, *Off the Record,* 16; Gentry, *J. Edgar Hoover,* 309.

46. Memorandum for Hoover, Jan. 29, 1941, Sumner Welles Federal Bureau of Investigation O.C. File, Washington, D.C., Gellman Papers; Cole, *Roosevelt and Isolationists,* 17–19.

47. Memorandum by Hoover, Jan. 30, 1941, Sumner Welles Federal Bureau of Investigation O.C. File, Washington, D.C., Gellman Papers.

48. Orville Bullitt to author, July 9, 1976, Gellman Papers; author's telephone conversation with Marquis Child, June 17, 1976; Richard Harris, Public Relations Department of Norfolk Southern, to author, June 8, 1987, Gellman Papers.

49. Moore to Bullitt, Jan. 9, 1941, Moore Papers, Box 3.

50. Ibid. and Moore to FDR, Jan. 27, 1941, Moore Papers.

51. *Washington Post,* Feb. 11, 1941; *Evening Star* (Washington), Feb. 11, 1941, Gellman Papers.

52. *Washington Post,* Feb. 11, 1941.

53. Hugh Wilson to Hull, Feb. 10, 1941, Gellman Papers.

54. *Evening Star,* Feb. 11, 1941, Gellman Papers.

55. Historic American Building Survey Inventory, Apr. 11, 1957, "McCandlish House Gift," Nov. 11, 1972, *Northern Virginia Sun,* Mar. 26, 1969, City of Fairfax, Virginia, Office of Planning, *Special Report,* (July 1982), "G. Mason Bank May Purchase Historic House," Feb. 11, 1983, and "Fairfax City Gives Up Historic House," Sept. 29, 1983, Gellman Papers.

56. Memorandum, Mar. 6, 1941, presidential diaries, Morgenthau Papers, Box 4.

57. Bullitt, *For the President,* xi–xiii and 512–14.

58. Ibid., 587–18; memorandum on LeHand, July 9, 1941, Farley Papers, Box 45; Gallagher, *Splendid Deception,* 22; Roosevelt, *This I Remember,* 170;

many conversations between author and James Roosevelt (1978–89), who believed that Bullitt had seduced LeHand.

59. H. Vandenberg diary, Dec. 1940–June 1942, Vol. 9.

60. Hull, *Memoirs,* 2:967; Biddle diary, Oct. 10, 1941; Cordell Hull medical records, Oct. 20, 1944, Gellman Papers; 1941 Calendar, Hull Papers, Reel 39; Berle and Jacobs, *Navigating the Rapids,* 481; Moffat diary, June 26 and July 10–12, 1941; *Time,* Aug. 11, 1941, 10.

61. Frances Hull to Davis, July 17, 1941, Davis Papers, Box 27.

62. Hooker, *Moffat Papers,* 349–50; Farley, *James Farley Story,* 341 and 343; Morgenthau diary, June 4, 1941, Box 4, presidential diaries.

63. King diary, Apr. 17, 1941.

64. Israel, *War Diary,* 212.

65. Ibid., 210 and 214–15; Stimson diary, Aug. 19, 1941, Vol. 35.

66. Confidential source; Ickes diary, Nov. 23–30 and Dec. 1941, Box 8; A. Philip Randolph to author, July 18, 1976, Gellman Papers; Gentry, *J. Edgar Hoover,* 308; Bullitt, *For the President,* 528–45.

67. Castle diary, Jan. 7, 1941.

68. Brownell and Billings, *So Close to Greatness,* 149, 169, 176, 178, 182, 196, 211, 235, 261, 273, 286, 288, and 297–98; D'Emilio and Freedman, *Intimate Matters,* 288–95.

## CHAPTER 10: PROVOKING WAR

1. Freidel, *Rendezvous with Destiny,* 366–68.

2. Some of these ideas were developed earlier in Gellman, "New Deal's Use."

3. Presidential Press Conference, Feb. 19 and June 5, 1940, Reel 8; FDR to Bowers, July 12, 1940, Official File 303; FDR to Bowers, May 24, 1940, Bowers Papers; Stimson to FDR, May 18, 1940, Stimson Papers, Reel 101; Rosenman, *Public Papers and Addresses,* 9:184–87; Berle and Jacobs, *Navigating the Rapids,* 305.

4. King diary, Apr. 23 and 24, 1940; FDR to Bowers, May 24, 1940, and Welles to Bowers, May 29, 1940, Bowers Papers.

5. "Fortune Survey."

6. Stimson diary, Apr. 15, 1939, and Stimson to Eden, July 17, 1939, Reel 98, Stimson to Salter, May 18, 1940, Knox to Stimson, May 22, 1940, and Stimson to Knox, May 25, 1940, Reel 101, Stimson Papers; Knox to White, May 28, 1940, W. White Papers, Series C, Box 344; Knox to Ebert, Nov. 29, 1940, Knox Papers, Box 1.

7. Roosevelt, *F.D.R.,* 2:936–37 and 952–53; U.S. Department of State, *Foreign Relations,* 1939, 5:40.

8. Nixon, *Franklin D. Roosevelt*, 2:390 and 403–4; Roosevelt, *F.D.R.*, 1:607–8 and 2:871–72, 909, 1022–23, and 1162; Ickes, *Secret Diary*, 2:704–5; Logan, *No Transfer*, 309–13.

9. U.S. Department of State, *Foreign Relations*, 1940, 5:252–56; Israel, *War Diary*, 107; Berle and Jacobs, *Navigating the Rapids*, 330.

10. Presidential Press Conferences, Apr. 11, 12, and 15, 1940, Reel 8; Berle and Jacobs, *Navigating the Rapids*, 305–6 and 356–57; Israel, *War Diary*, 78–79; Roosevelt, *F.D.R.*, 2:1040 and 1142–43; King diary, Apr. 23 and 24, and May 24, 1940; memorandum by Berle, July 12, 1940, 710.11/2551, Record Group 59, National Archives, Washington, D.C.; Logan, *No Transfer*, 307–9.

11. Presidential Press Conferences, Jan. 12, Feb. 9, Apr. 18, May 30, and June 14, 21, and 28, 1940, Reel 8; Rosenman, *Public Papers and Addresses*, 9:158–62 and 273–74; Ickes, *Secret Diary*, 3:204.

12. "Americas Faces the War," Dec. 30, 1940, 740.0011 EW 1939/8035, and Rockefeller to Hull, Mar. 12, 1941, 710.11/2686 Record Group 59, National Archives, Washington, D.C.

13. Rosenman, *Public Papers and Addresses*, 9:1–10.

14. Ibid., 10:40–42.

15. Casey to Hornbeck, Apr. 17, 1941, 740.0011 EW 1939/10488, Record Group 59, National Archives, Washington, D.C.

16. King diary, Apr. 16 and 20, 1941; Kimball, *Churchill and Roosevelt*, 1:166; Blum, Morgenthau Diaries, 2:252; Roosevelt, *F.D.R.*, 2:1148–50.

17. Stimson and Bundy, *On Active Service*, 368–69; Pickersgill, *MacKenzie King Record*, 1:195–96; Ickes, *Secret Diary*, 3:491–92.

18. Rosenman, *Public Papers and Addresses*, 10:133; Ickes, *Secret Diary*, 3:503.

19. Presidential Press Conference, Apr. 15, 1941, Reel 9; Berle and Jacobs, *Navigating the Rapids*, 356–57; Rosenman, *Public Papers and Addresses*, 10:110; Roosevelt, *F.D.R.*, 2:1142–43.

20. Ickes, *Secret Diary*, 3:503.

21. FDR to Churchill, May 14, 1941, 740.0011 EW 1939/10944 1/2, Record Group 59, National Archives, Washington, D.C.; conversation with Welles, May 19, 1941, Fisher Papers.

22. Leahy diary, June 14 and 21, 1941, Box 10, pp. 69 and 71; Freidel, *Rendezvous with Destiny*, 372.

23. Berle and Jacobs, *Navigating the Rapids*, 370; Sherwood, *Roosevelt and Hopkins*, 294–96; Freidel, *Rendezvous with Destiny*, 371.

24. Sherwood, *Roosevelt and Hopkins*, 296–97.

25. Rosenman, *Public Papers and Addresses*, 10:181.

26. Leahy diary, May 28, 1941, Box 10, p. 63; Sherwood, *Roosevelt and Hopkins*, 298; Ickes, *Secret Diary*, 3:526–27.

27. Stimson to FDR, June 23, 1941, Stimson Papers, Reel 104.

28. Welles statement, June 23, 1941, 740.0011 EW 1939/12385a, Record Group 59, National Archives, Washington, D.C.; Welles, *Time for Decision*, 171.

29. Conversation with Welles, June 28, 1941, Fisher Papers.

30. Davies, *Mission to Moscow*, 488; MacLean, *Joseph E. Davies*, 7–79.

31. Conversation with Welles, June 28, 1941, Fisher Papers; Stimson to FDR, June 23, 1941, Stimson Papers, Reel 104.

32. Memorandum by Berle, July 12, 1940, 710.11/2551 and memorandum by Welles, Feb. 19, 1941, 710.11/2679, Record Group 59, National Archives, Washington, D.C.; Stimson and Bundy, *On Active Service*, 373; Gannon, *Operation Drumbeat*, xvii and 84.

33. Presidential Press Conference, July 8, 1941, Reel 9.

34. Lindbergh, *Wartime Journals*, 515–16.

35. Keegan, *Second World War*, 106–7 and 538–39; Gannon, *Operation Drumbeat*, 82–96; Shirer, *Third Reich*, 1149–53.

36. Rosenman, *Public Papers and Addresses*, 10:272–77.

37. Wilson, *First Summit*, 94–238; Welles, *Time for Decision*, 174–77.

38. Freidel, *Rendezvous with Destiny*, 392–93.

39. Rosenman, *Public Papers and Addresses*, 10:384–92.

40. Ibid., 10:438–44; Presidential Press Conference, Oct. 28, 1941, Reel 9; Leahy diary, Oct. 29, 1941, Box 10, pp. 132–36.

41. Freidel, *Rendezvous with Destiny*, 393–95.

## CHAPTER 11: HULL LOSES CONTROL

1. Jonathan Utley, "The United States Entry into the Pacific War," 1–2, Gellman Papers.

2. *Orange County Register*, Aug. 4, 1994, 22, Gellman Papers; Rusbridger and Nave, *Betrayal at Pearl Harbor*, 154, 159–60, and 177–80.

3. Freidel, *Rendezvous with Destiny*, 377–78.

4. Utley, *Going to War*, 64–81; Dallek, *Franklin D. Roosevelt*, 236; Hull, *Memoirs*, 1:717–24; Cole, *Roosevelt and Isolationists*, 488–92.

5. Moffat diary, Oct. 6–10, 1940; Hooker, *Moffat Papers*, 330–32; "America Faces the War," Dec. 30, 1940, 740.0011 EW 1939/8035, Record Group 59, National Archives, Washington, D.C.; Utley, *Going to War*, 83–137; Dallek, *Franklin D. Roosevelt*, 236–43; Hull, *Memoirs*, 1:724–30 and 888–916; Freidel, *Rendezvous with Destiny*, 380.

6. King diary, Apr. 17, 1941.

7. Stimson diary, May 27, 1941, Vol. 34; Walker diary, Oct. 14, 1944.

8. Conversations with Welles, Feb. 11, Apr. 29, and June 28, 1941, Fisher Papers.

9. Utley, *Going to War,* 138–56; Dallek, *Franklin D. Roosevelt,* 271–75 and 300–2; Pickersgill, *MacKenzie King Record,* 1:190; Moffat diary, July 10–12, 1941.

10. Moffat diary, Sept. 19–23, 1941.

11. Ibid., Dec. 1–4, 1941; Woodward, *British Foreign Policy,* 2:170–75.

12. Clausen and Lee, *Pearl Harbor,* 169.

13. Biddle diary, Dec. 7, 1941; memorandum by Hull, June 9, 1942, Farley Papers, Box 45; 1941 Calendar, Hull Papers, Reel 39; Utley, *Going to War,* 157–75; Dallek, *Franklin D. Roosevelt,* 302–10.

14. Acheson, *Present at the Creation,* 35.

15. Dallek, *Franklin D. Roosevelt,* 317–23; Burns, *Roosevelt,* 163–201; Gallagher, *Splendid Deception,* 162–72; Toland, *Adolf Hitler,* 691–97.

16. Cordell Hull medical records, July 6, 1945, Gellman Papers; Hull to Messersmith, Aug. 11, 1945, Hull Papers, Folder 146; Hull, *Memoirs,* 2:1724.

17. Pearl Harbor Committee Report, 457, 541, 551, and 560; *New York Times,* Nov. 24, 1945, 1; Hull, *Memoirs,* 2:1724; Prange, *At Dawn We Slept,* 682–84; Clausen and Lee, *Pearl Harbor,* 249–50.

18. Hinton, *Cordell Hull,* viii.

19. Wallace statement, Dec. 27, 1941, Wallace Papers, Reel 23.

20. Ickes, *Secret Diary,* 3:339.

21. Acheson, *Present at the Creation,* 14–15; Berle and Jacobs, *Navigating the Rapids,* xxxii–xxxiii and 377.

22. Sherwood, *Roosevelt and Hopkins,* 134–35.

23. Leahy diary, Dec. 14, 1941, Box 10, pp. 169–71; Anglin, *St. Pierre,* 3–129; Hooker, *Moffat Papers,* 358–62; Aglion, *Roosevelt and de Gaulle,* 54 and 59–61.

24. Dallek, *Franklin D. Roosevelt,* 317–23; Churchill, *Second World War,* 558–70.

25. Ickes diary, Dec. 21–23, 1941, Box 8; Anglin, *St. Pierre,* 82–126; Hooker, *Moffat Papers,* 362–70; Pickersgill, *MacKenzie King Record,* 1:318 and 320–22; Berle and Jacobs, *Navigating the Rapids,* 388–91; Hull, *Memoirs,* 2:1127–37; Welles, *Seven Decisions,* 61–64 and 162–63; Aglion, *Roosevelt and de Gaulle,* 61–67.

26. Sherwood, *Roosevelt and Hopkins,* 483 and 488.

27. Berle and Jacobs, *Navigating the Rapids,* 393 and 395; Israel, *War Diary,* 239–41 and 247; Krock, *Memoirs,* 203–5; Kimball, *Churchill and Roosevelt,* 1:.326.

28. King diary, Dec. 27, 1941, and Dec. 4, 1942.

29. Cordell Hull medical records, Oct. 30, 1944, Gellman Papers; 1942 Calendar, Hull Papers, Reel 35.

30. Israel, *War Diary,* 242–43.

31. Hull to FDR, Jan. 16, 1942, Hull Papers, Folder 148.

32. Hull, *Memoirs,* 2:1137–38; Hooker, *Moffat Papers,* 378–79.

33. Welles to McGurk, Dec. 17, 1941, 710, consultation 3/55, Record Group 59, National Archives, Washington, D.C.; Gellman, *Good Neighbor Diplomacy,* 120–22.

34. Welles to Bowers, Jan. 7, 1942, Bowers Papers.

35. Israel, *War Diary,* 237.

36. Gellman, *Good Neighbor Diplomacy,* 122–24.

37. Welles to Hull, Jan. 13, 1942, Hull Papers, Box 50.

38. Hull to Welles, Jan 15, 1942, Hull Papers, Box 50.

39. Welles, *Seven Decisions,* 105–6.

40. Radio broadcast, Jan. 21, 1942, Sevareid Papers, Box D-1; *New York Times,* July 29, 1945, part IV, 3:7.

41. Stimson diary, Jan. 25, 1942, Vol. 37; "Washington Merry-Go-Round," Aug. 29, 1944; Berle and Jacobs, *Navigating the Rapids,* 398; Hull, *Memoirs,* 2:1146–50; Welles, *Seven Decisions,* xii–xv and 115–17; Gellman, *Good Neighbor Diplomacy,* 124–25.

42. Berle and Jacobs, *Navigating the Rapids,* 399.

43. Welles to Pearson, Apr. 10, 1944, Pearson Papers, F 33, 2 of 3; Gellman, *Good Neighbor Diplomacy,* 125–26.

44. Hooker, *Moffat Papers,* 379–80.

45. Ibid., 378–79; 1942 Calendar, Hull Papers, Reel 39; Hull, *Memoirs,* 2:1149–50; radio memorandum, Feb. 1942, Pearson Papers, F 155, 3 of 3, Hull, Cordell #3.

46. Berle and Jacobs, *Navigating the Rapids,* 400.

## CHAPTER 12: WORKING FOR VICTORY

1. Gannon, *Operation Drumbeat,* xvi, 71, 96–99, and 388–90; Keegan, *Second World War,* 107–10.

2. King diary, Dec. 5, 1942; Hooker, *Moffat Papers,* 388; Larrabee, *Commander in Chief,* 644.

3. McJimsey, *Harry Hopkins,* 210–57; Langer diss., "Formation of American Aid Policy," 1–114; DeSantis, *Diplomacy of Silence,* 11–100.

4. Schuker to author, Dec. 11, 1990, Gellman Papers; Feingold, *Politics of Rescue,* 300–7; Breitman and Kraut, *American Refugee Policy,* 244–45; Breit-

man, *Architect of Genocide;* Gilbert, *Holocaust,* 19–823; Wyman, *Abandonment of Jews,* 311–13; Kimball, *Churchill and Roosevelt,* 2:293; Yahil, *Holocaust,* 451–56; Dawidowicz, *War against Jews,* 349; Laquer, *Terrible Secret,* 196–204.

    5. Rosenman, *Public Papers and Addresses,* 11:193–95 and 250; Presidential Press Conference, July 17, 1942, Reel 10; Hassett, *Off the Record,* 132–33.

    6. Berle diary, Feb. 1, 1942, Box 213.

    7. 1942 Calendar, Hull Papers, Reel 39; Welles, *Seven Decisions,* 120.

    8. Stuart, *Department of State,* 371–73.

    9. Biddle diary, Mar. 6, 1942.

    10. Ibid., Feb. 6, 1942; Ickes diary, Feb. 1–7, 1942, Box 8; Corrigan to Welles, Feb. 19, 1942, Corrigan Papers, Box 10; Welles, *World of Four Freedoms,* 55–65; Gellman, *Good Neighbor Diplomacy,* 172–73.

    11. Welles, *World of Four Freedoms,* 88–94.

    12. Bowers diary, Oct. 9, 10, and 11, and Duggan to Bowers, Oct. 14, 1942, Bowers Papers; "Washington Merry-Go-Round," Oct. 21, 1942; Israel, *War Diary,* 286.

    13. Memorandums on Welles, Aug. 26 and Sept. 25, 1942, Fisher Papers; memorandum, Nov. 17, 1943, Pearson Papers, G 242, 2 of 3; Graff, *Strategy of Involvement,* 379–80.

    14. Hurstfield, *America and French Nation,* 156–61; Bullitt, *For the President,* 505–6; Aglion, *Roosevelt and de Gaulle,* 112–15; Graff, *Strategy of Involvement,* 363–66.

    15. Wyman, *Paper Walls,* 209–13; Feingold, *Politics of Rescue,* 295–300; Dawidowicz, *War against Jews,* 345–47; Welles to Lazaron, July 2, 1940, Lazaron Papers, Box 13; Wise to Welles, Jan. 14, 1941, Wise Papers; Wyman, *Abandonment of Jews,* 84; Breitman and Kraut, *American Refugee Policy,* 146–66.

    16. Welles to Lazaron, Mar. 31, 1942, Lazaron Papers, Box 9; Woodward, *British Foreign Policy,* 4:344–59; Welles, *We Need Not Fail,* 17–27; Yahil, *Holocaust,* 607.

    17. Wyman, *Abandonment of Jews,* 42–51; Yahil, *Holocaust,* 606–8; Urofsky, *Voice That Spoke,* 3–254; Voss, *Rabbi and Minister,* 313.

    18. Voss, *Rabbi and Minister,* 314.

    19. Berle and Jacobs, *Navigating the Rapids,* 280; Stuart, *Department of State,* 378–79; Graff, *Strategy of Involvement,* 382–84; Welles, *World of Four Freedoms,* 11–15.

    20. Welles, *World of Four Freedoms,* 28–33; memorandum by Gosnell, Feb. 2, 1948, Welles file; Stuart, *Department of State,* 379–81; Graff, *Strategy of Involvement,* 385–95.

21. Welles, *World of Four Freedoms,* 66–82.

22. Welles to MacLeish, Aug. 13, 1942, MacLeish Papers, Box 20.

23. Welles, *World of Four Freedoms,* 95–108.

24. Sweetser to Grady, Aug. 7, 1941, and memorandum by Sweetser, Aug. 6, 1942, Box 32, and Sweetser to Welles, Aug. 5, Welles to Sweetser, Aug. 7, 1941, and interview with Welles, Nov. 27, 1942, Box 40, Sweetser Papers; memorandum by Gosnell, Feb. 2, 1948, Welles file.

25. Hooker, *Moffat Papers,* 388; Welles to Pearson, Feb. 25, 1948, Pearson Papers, G 87, 3 of 3; Welles, *Seven Decisions,* 172–81.

26. Biddle diary, Nov. 20, 1942.

27. Davis to Burlingham, Feb. 11, 1942, Davis Papers, Box 3.

28. Davies diary, Apr. 9, 1942, Box 11.

29. Berle and Jacobs, *Navigating the Rapids,* 836; Rockefeller Papers (Columbia Oral History Collection), 310–11, Gellman Papers; memorandum, July 27, 1942, Pearson Papers, G 247, 1 of 2.

30. Presidential Press Conference, Feb. 24, 1942, Reel 10.

31. Berle diary, Mar. 28, 1942, Box 213; Berle and Jacobs, *Navigating the Rapids,* 406.

32. King diary, Dec. 4, 1942.

33. Gray to Davis, Feb. 26, 1942, Davis Papers, Box 27.

34. Frances Hull to Davis, late Feb. 1942, Davis Papers, Box 27.

35. Davis to Burlingham, Feb. 11, 1942, Davis Papers, Box 3; memorandum on Hull, Feb. 13, 1942, Farley Papers, Box 45; Wallace to Hull, Mar. 30, 1942, Wallace Papers, Reel 23.

36. Nicholas, *Washington Dispatches,* 62–63; Alsop, *"I've Seen the Best of It,"* 144–45.

37. 1942 Calendar, Hull Papers, Reel 39; Hull, *Memoirs,* 2:1181–82; Berle and Jacobs, *Navigating the Rapids,* 410; Israel, *War Diary,* 258–59; Biddle diary, Apr. 24, 1942; Hassett, *Off the Record,* 42; Wallace to FDR, Mar. 26, 1942, Wallace Papers, Reel 23; Blum, *Price of Vision,* 58.

38. Biddle diary, May 14 and 15, 1942; Berle diary, Apr. 14 and May 14, 1942, Box 214; Presidential Press Conference, May 1, 1942, Reel 10; Blum, *Price of Vision,* 67–68 and 79; Hull, *Memoirs,* 2:1154–57.

39. Farley, *James Farley Story,* 349.

40. *New York Times,* Dec. 27, 1942; Welles to Wallace, Dec. 30, 1942, Wallace Papers, Reel 24.

41. Hull, *Memoirs,* 2:1379.

42. Memorandum by Hull, May 14, 1942, Hull Papers, Box 50; memorandum of conversation, May 14, 1942, Morgenthau Papers, Box 5, presidential diaries.

43. Memorandum of conversation, May 15, 1942, Morgenthau Papers, Box 5, presidential diaries; Blum, *Price of Vision*, 80; Stimson diary, May 21, 1942, Vol. 39.

44. Berle diary, June 27, 1942, Box 214; Farley, *James Farley Story*, 349.

45. Berle diary, July 25, 1942, Box 214; Hull, *Memoirs*, 2:1177–79; Nicholas, *Washington Dispatches*, 62–63.

46. Ferrell, *Dear Bess*, 481.

47. Grollman diss., "Cordell Hull," 186.

48. Memorandum by Sweetser, Aug. 6, 1942, Sweetser Papers, Box 32.

49. Hooker, *Moffat Papers*, 388.

50. Memorandum on Hull, Aug. 27, 1942, Fisher Papers; King diary, Dec. 4, 1942; Biddle diary, Dec. 31, 1942.

51. Burns, *Roosevelt*, 315–16; Hurstfield, *America and French Nation*, 185–93; Aglion, *Roosevelt and De Gaulle*, 150–55.

52. King diary, Dec. 5, 1943; Dallek, *Franklin D. Roosevelt*, 373–75.

53. Hassett, *Off the Record*, 166–67; Kimball, *Churchill and Roosevelt*, 2:178; Woodward, *British Foreign Policy*, 5:34–35; Davis, "Roosevelt's World Blueprint."

54. Perlmutter, *FDR & Stalin*, 247–49 and 256–58.

55. Welles, *World of Four Freedoms*, 109–21; Welles to Inman, Mar. 1 and 18, 1943, Inman Papers, Box 15; Nicholas, *Washington Dispatches*, 158 and 165.

56. Woodward, *British Foreign Policy*, 5:39–41; Kimball, *Churchill and Roosevelt*, 2:223–26; Nicholas, *Washington Dispatches*, 201–2; Graff, *Strategy of Involvement*, 397–400; Perlmutter, *FDR & Stalin*, 248.

57. Memorandum on Welles, early 1943, Fisher Papers.

58. Nicholas, *Washington Dispatches*, 163–64; Perlmutter, *FDR & Stalin*, 249; memorandum of conversation, May 7, 1943, 711.61/891 1/2, Record Group 59, National Archives, Washington, D.C.

59. Perlmutter, *FDR & Stalin*, 231–49.

60. Gellman, *Good Neighbor Diplomacy*, 191.

61. Feingold, *Politics of Rescue*, 167–239.

62. Perlmutter, *FDR & Stalin*, 248 and 253–54.

## CHAPTER 13: RUINING WELLES

1. Israel, *War Diary*, 262.

2. Ibid., 273; Stimson diary, June 2, 1942, Vol. 39; memorandum on Hull, June 11, 1942, Farley Papers, Box 45; Hull, *Memoirs*, 2:1229.

3. Berle and Jacobs, *Navigating the Rapids*, 415.

4. Israel, *War Diary,* 277; also see Stimson diary, July 7, 1942, Vol. 39.

5. Ickes diary, Feb. 1–7 and 8–15, and Mar. 30, 1942, Box 8; Biddle diary, Feb. 6 and 7, and May 22, 1942.

6. Wallace diary, Mar. 31, 1942, Box 13.

7. Bullitt, *For the President,* 551–53.

8. Farnsworth, *William C. Bullitt,* 232; Murphy, *Diplomat among Warriors,* 27.

9. Wallace diary, May 20, 1942, Box 14.

10. Bullitt, *For the President,* 555.

11. Ibid., 557–62; Castle diary, Aug. 30 and Sept. 2, 1942; Farnsworth, *William C. Bullitt,* 233; Brownell and Billings, *So Close to Greatness,* 286–89.

12. Israel, *War Diary,* 281; Gentry, *J. Edgar Hoover,* 287; Wallace Papers (Columbia Oral History Collection), 2656; Biddle diary, May 22, 1942; Morgan, *FDR,* 684.

13. Israel, *War Diary,* 281 and 324–25.

14. Ibid., 286; 1942 Calendar, Hull Papers, Reel 39.

15. Memorandum by Hoover, Oct. 29, 1942, Sumner Welles Federal Bureau of Investigation O.C. File, Washington, D.C., Gellman Papers.

16. Reston, *Deadline,* 103; confirmed by author in telephone conversation with James Reston, Dec. 13, 1991, Gellman Papers.

17. Robert Ferrell to author, Sept. 6, 1979, Gellman Papers.

18. Rockefeller interview, Gellman Papers; Rockefeller Papers (Columbia Oral History Collection), 354–59, Gellman Papers.

19. Memorandum for Hoover, Nov. 13, 1942, Sumner Welles Federal Bureau of Investigation O.C. File, Washington, D.C., Gellman Papers; Billings to Pearson, Feb. 21, 1967, Pearson Papers, G 247, 1 of 2; Daniels, *White House Witness,* 174–75.

20. Berle diary, Oct. 27, 1942, Box 214; King diary, Dec. 4, 1942; Ickes diary, Dec. 27, 1942, Box 9; Sulzberger, *Low Row of Candles,* 200; Hooker, *Moffat Papers,* 387.

21. Welles to Sweetser, Dec. 9, 1942, Sweetser Papers, Box 35.

22. Blum, *Price of Vision,* 91 and 136; Reston, *Deadline,* 112; Johnson, *Selected Letters,* 439–40.

23. Berle and Jacobs, *Navigating the Rapids,* 431.

24. Leahy diary, Mar. 4, 1943, Box 11; memorandum by Davies, Mar. 12, 1943, Davies Papers, Box 12; Woodward, *British Foreign Policy,* 5:31–32; Nicholas, *Washington Dispatches,* 163–64 and 172; Lash, *Diaries of Felix Frankfurter,* 246–47; "Washington Merry-Go-Round," June 16, 1943; Stimson diary, June 16, 1943, Vol. 43.

25. Stimson diary, June 18, 1943, Vol. 43.

26. Memorandum on Hull, early 1943, Farley Papers, Box 45; Loewenheim et al., *Roosevelt and Churchill,* 60; Hull, *Memoirs,* 2:1367 and 1570.

27. Berle and Jacobs, *Navigating the Rapids,* 434; Blum, *Price of Vision,* 172; Bullitt, *For the President,* 589–90.

28. Bullitt, *For the President,* 589.

29. Ickes diary, Feb. 14, 1943, Box 10.

30. Ibid., Mar. 6, 1943; memorandum on Hull, early 1943, Farley Papers, Box 45; 1942 Calendar, Hull Papers, Reel 39; Hull, *Memoirs,* 2:1213 and 1493; Berle and Jacobs, *Navigating the Rapids,* 434.

31. Hull, *Memoirs,* 2:1213.

32. Eden, *The Reckoning,* 436.

33. Ibid., 440–41.

34. Ickes diary, Mar. 6 and Apr. 6, 1943, Box 10; Berle and Jacobs, *Navigating the Rapids,* 406 and 434; Hull, *Memoirs,* 2:1213; Berle diary, Mar. 28, 1942, Box 213; Lash, *Diaries of Felix Frankfurter,* 204–5.

35. "Washington Merry-Go-Round," Apr. 8, 1943.

36. Lash, *Diaries of Felix Frankfurter,* 204–5 and 250.

37. Ickes diary, Apr. 25, 1943, Box 10; Biddle, *In Brief Authority,* 179–80.

38. Wallace diary, Sept. 30, Box 23, and Oct. 12, 1943, Box 24; Biddle diary, Dec. 12, 1941; Blum, *Price of Vision,* 28, 78, 96–97, and 226; Nicholas, *Washington Dispatches,* 220, 248, and 255; Byrnes, *All in One Lifetime,* 152.

39. Biddle, *In Brief Authority,* 247.

40. Memorandum on Welles, 1943, and draft of *All in One Life Time,* Byrnes Papers.

41. Wallace Papers (Columbia Oral History Collection); *New York Times,* Dec. 26, 1961; Abell, *Drew Pearson Diary,* 33; Donovan, *Conflict and Crisis,* x and xii.

42. Memorandum by Hoover, May 3, 1943, Sumner Welles Federal Bureau of Investigation O.C. File, Washington, D.C., Gellman Papers; Wallace diary, May 23 and Sept. 30, 1943, Box 23.

43. Ickes diary, May 9, 1943, Box 10.

44. Bullitt, *For the President,* 514–16; Childs, *Witness to Power,* 15–17; Martin, *Cissy,* 446–47.

45. Biddle diary, May 6, 1943.

46. Memorandum on Hull, May 8, 1943, Farley Papers, Box 45; Wallace diary, Aug. 21, 1943, Box 23.

47. Castle diary, May 2, 1943; Israel, *War Diary,* 311; Graff, *Strategy of Involvement,* 401.

48. Berle and Jacobs, *Navigating the Rapids,* 438; memorandum on Welles, June 24, 1943, Farley Papers, Box 45; Farley, *James Farley Story,* 361.

49. Morgenthau diary, July 9, 1943, Vol. 647.

50. 1943 Calendar, Hull Papers, Reel 39; Welles to Early, July 12, 1943, Early Papers, Box 21; Nicholas, *Washington Dispatches*, 215–17; Israel, *War Diary*, 324.

51. Castle diary, July 19 and Aug. 1 and 5, 1943; Berle and Jacobs, *Navigating the Rapids*, 440; Hassett, *Off the Record*, 191.

52. Memorandum on Hull, Dec. 21, 1943, Krock Papers, Box 29; Wallace diary, Aug. 21, 1943, Box 23; presidential diary, Aug. 26, 1943, Morgenthau Papers, Box 5; Nicholas, *Washington Dispatches*, 231–32; Krock, *Memoirs*, 26, 35, and 63; Pearson to Welles, Feb. 15, 1945, Pearson Papers, F 33, 2 of 3; Krock, *Consent of the Governed*, 108–9.

53. Ickes diary, Aug. 15, 1943, Box 10; Pickersgill, *MacKenzie King Record*, 1:543; Kimball, *Churchill and Roosevelt*, 2:387–88.

54. Israel, *War Diary*, 322–23; Hull, *Memoirs*, 2:1230; Kimball, *Churchill and Roosevelt*, 2:429.

55. Memorandum, Folder: Hull, Cordell, Dec. 21, 1943, Krock Papers, Box 29; Hull, *Memoirs*, 2:1231; Krock, *Memoirs*, 205–7.

56. Memorandum on Hull, Aug. 16, 1943, Farley Papers, Box 45.

57. Hull, *Memoirs*, 2:1226; Berle and Jacobs, *Navigating the Rapids*, 443.

## CHAPTER 14: RESIGNATION

1. Welles to FDR, Aug. 16, 1943, President's Secretary File, Box 96; Berle and Jacobs, *Navigating the Rapids*, 836.

2. Wallace diary, Aug. 21, 1943, Box 23, and Aug. 21 and 23, 1943; Wallace Papers (Columbia Oral History Collection); Blum, *Price of Vision*, 237–41.

3. Berle and Jacobs, *Navigating the Rapids*, 443 and 445; Israel, *War Diary*, 323; Welles to Corrigan, Aug. 22, 1943, Corrigan Papers, Box 10; Welles to Lane, Aug. 22, 1943, Lane Papers, Box 21.

4. Wallace diary, Oct. 12, 1943, Box 24; Pearson to Welles, Aug. 24, 1943, Pearson Papers, F 33, 2 of 3.

5. *Maine Coast Sampler*, 13 and 19, Gellman Papers; *Bar Harbor*, 1, Gellman Papers; Street, *Mount Desert*, 164.

6. Berle and Jacobs, *Navigating the Rapids*, 444; *Washington Herald*, Aug. 24, 1943; *Washington Post*, Aug. 26, 1943; *New York Times*, Aug. 27, 1943; *Time*, Aug. 23, 1943, 17–18.

7. Wallace diary, Aug. 24, 1943, Box 23; Castle diary, Aug. 24, 1943; Pearson to Welles, Aug. 25, 1943, Pearson Papers, F 33, 2 of 3.

8. Berle and Jacobs, *Navigating the Rapids*, 444; Israel, *War Diary*, 323, 327; *New York Herald Tribune*, Aug. 26, 1943; Hull, *Memoirs*, 2:1242; *New York Times*, Aug. 29, 1943.

9. Ickes diary, May 24, 1942, Box 8, and Aug. 29, 1943, Box 10; Wallace diary, Aug. 24, 1943, Box 23; Castle diary, Aug. 27, 1943.

10. Brinkley, *Washington Goes to War,* 186–87.

11. Hull to McLaughlin, Sept. 17, 1942, Hull Papers, Box 50.

12. "Washington Merry-Go-Round," Aug. 26, 1943.

13. Ibid., Aug. 31, 1943.

14. Ickes diary, Sept. 5, 1943, Box 11; Pearson to Blagden, Sept. 9, 1943, Pearson Papers, G 210, 2 of 5.

15. Berle and Jacobs, *Navigating the Rapids,* 444; Kimball, *Churchill and Roosevelt,* 2:430–31; Pickersgill, *MacKenzie King Record,* 1:557.

16. Hull, *Memoirs,* 2:1254–55.

17. *Editor and Publisher,* Aug. 30, 1943, Pearson Papers, G 236, 1 of 3.

18. Presidential Press Conference, Aug. 31, 1943, Reel 11.

19. Pearson to Blagden, Sept. 9, 1943, G 210, 2 of 5, and Pearson to Filler, Sept. 13, 1943, F 104, 3 of 3, Pearson Papers; Klurfeld, *Behind the Lines,* 68–79; Pilat, *Drew Pearson,* 175–79.

20. Pearson to Welles, Aug. 30, 1943, Pearson Papers, F 33, 2 of 3.

21. Ibid.; memorandum for the president, Sept. 3, 1943, and Hull to Byrnes, Sept. 14 and Oct. 4, 1943, Byrnes Papers; memorandum, Folder: Hull, Cordell, Dec. 21, 1943, Krock Papers, Box 29.

22. Telemeter to Hoover, Sept. 2, and Hoover to Watson, and memorandum for the attorney general, Sept. 14, 1943, Sumner Welles Federal Bureau of Investigation O.C. File, Washington, D.C., Gellman Papers.

23. Memorandum for attorney general, Sept. 14, 1943, Sumner Welles Federal Bureau of Investigation O.C. file, Washington, D.C., Gellman Papers.

24. "Washington Merry-Go-Round," Sept. 10, 1943.

25. *St. Louis Post-Dispatch,* Sept. 5, 1943; *Time,* Sept. 6, 1943, 6.

26. Stimson diary, Sept. 7, 1943, Vol. 44; *New York Times,* Sept. 27, 1943, 18.

27. Blum, *Price of Vision,* 248.

28. Berle and Jacobs, *Navigating the Rapids,* 446; Israel, *War Diary,* 330.

29. Daniels to Robins, Sept. 9, 1943, Daniel Papers, Box 821.

30. Welles, *Seven Decisions,* 150; Berle and Jacobs, *Navigating the Rapids,* 836; Hassett, *Off the Record,* 150–204; Kimball, *Churchill and Roosevelt,* 2:454.

31. Welles to Hull, Sept. 21, 1943, President's Secretary File, Box 96; Wallace diary, Oct. 12, 1943, Box 24.

32. Welles to FDR, Sept. 21, 1943, President's Secretary File, Box 96.

33. Draft and Executive Order 9380, Sept. 25, 1943, Byrnes Papers.

34. Blum, *Price of Vision,* 260.

35. Bullitt, *For the President,* 517.

36. Welles to MacLeish, Oct. 2, 1943, MacLeish Papers, Box 20; Taussig to Welles, Oct. 3, 1943, Taussig Papers, Box 35; Morgenthau to Welles, Oct. 6, 1943, Morgenthau Papers, Box 670.

37. Frankfurter to Welles, late Sept. 1943, Frankfurter Papers, Box 111.

38. Castle diary, Sept. 10, 1943.

39. Israel, *War Diary,* 324.

40. Boswell diss., "Buddha Bill," 207–8.

41. Guffey to Bowers, Mar. 8, 1943, Bowers Papers.

42. Memorandum on Bullitt, Mar. 30, 1943, Farley Papers, Box 45.

43. Brownell and Billings, *So Close to Greatness,* 298–300; *New York Times,* Oct. 31, 1943, sec. IV, 7.

44. Berle and Jacobs, *Navigating the Rapids,* 448–49.

45. Memorandum to Hull, Aug. 26, 1943, Berle Papers, Box 215.

46. Wise to Welles, Oct. 3, 1943, Wise Papers, Box 66–3.

47. Lazaron to Welles, Nov. 4, 1943, Lazaron Papers, Box 9.

48. Israel, *War Diary,* 325.

## CHAPTER 15: HULL'S LAST YEAR

1. Israel, *War Diary,* 323; Stuart, *Department of State,* 383.

2. Memorandum for the president, Sept. 21, 1943, Byrnes Papers; Stuart, *Department of State,* 383.

3. Memorandum on Stettinius, Apr. 18, 1945, Farley Papers, Box 45; McJimsey, *Harry Hopkins,* 293; Krock, *Memoirs,* 180.

4. Executive Order 9380, Sept. 25, 1943, Byrnes Papers.

5. Walker, "E. R. Stettinius, Jr.," 1–10; Campbell, *Masquerade Peace,* 9.

6. Messersmith to Watson, Sept. 27, 1943, Watson Papers, Box 25; Stettinius to Welles, Sept. 28, 1943, Stettinius Papers, Box 716; *New York Times,* Sept. 26, 1943.

7. Welles, *Where Are We Heading?,* 53–54.

8. Hull, *Memoirs,* 2:1256.

9. Campbell, *Masquerade Peace,* 9 and 293.

10. Bowers, *My Life,* 318; Duggan, *The Americas,* 60 and 102–3.

11. Rockefeller Papers (Columbia Oral History Collection), 457–58, Gellman Papers.

12. Pearson to Welles, Dec. 27, 1943, Pearson Papers, F 33, 2 of 3.

13. Campbell and Herring, *Diaries,* 73–75.

14. 1943 Calendar, Hull Papers, Reel 39; Bowers diary, Sept. 2 and Nov. 7, 1943; Bowers, *My Life,* 301.

15. McJimsey, *Harry Hopkins,* 313–14.

16. Hull, *Memoirs,* 2:1254–55; Berle and Jacobs, *Navigating the Rapids,* 449; Woodward, *British Foreign Policy,* 2:579–80; Leahy diary, Sept. 17 and 23, 1943, Box 11, 28; Kimball, *Churchill and Roosevelt,* 2:462–64 and 490; Sulzberger, *Low Row of Candles,* 221; memorandum by Corrigan, Dec. 1, 1943, Corrigan Papers, Box 10; Wallace diary, Sept. 30, 1943, Box 23.

17. Farley, *James Farley Story,* 362.

18. Cordell Hull medical records, Oct. 20, 1944, Gellman Papers; memorandum on Hull, Dec. 10, 1943, Farley Papers, Box 45; Wallace diary, Oct. 12, 1943, Box 24; Leahy diary, Sept. 23, 1943, Box 11; Hull, *Memoirs,* 2:1253–55 and 1274–78; Sulzberger, *Low Row of Candles,* 221.

19. Ickes diary, Nov. 13, 1943, Box 11; *New York Times,* Nov. 10, 1943; "Washington Merry-Go-Round," Nov. 12, 1943.

20. Hull, *Memoirs,* 2:1277–1313; Woodward, *British Foreign Policy,* 2:581–94; James, *Anthony Eden,* 276–77; DeSantis, *Diplomacy of Silence,* 102–3.

21. Hull, *Memoirs,* 2:1279–1318; James, *Anthony Eden,* 276–77; Hassett, *Off the Record,* 216 and 218–19; Cordell Hull medical records, Oct. 20, 1944, Gellman Papers; memorandum by Corrigan, Dec. 1, 1943, Corrigan Papers, Box 10; Farley, *James Farley Story,* 362.

22. Freidel, *Rendezvous with Destiny,* 475–76; Dallek, *Franklin D. Roosevelt,* 419–20.

23. Hull, *Memoirs,* 2:1314–15.

24. Lash, *World of Love,* 90.

25. Memorandum by Corrigan, Dec. 1, 1943, Corrigan Papers, Box 10.

26. Ickes diary, Nov. 13, 1943, Box 11; Castle diary, Nov. 11, 1943; *New York Times,* Nov. 10, 1943; "Washington Merry-Go-Round," Nov. 12, 1943; memorandum on Welles, Nov. 22, 1943, Farley Papers, Box 45; memorandum, Nov. 17, 1943, Pearson Papers, G 242, 2 of 4; Divine, *Second Chance,* 154–55.

27. Welles to Pearson, Feb. 17, 1948, Pearson Papers, F 33, 2 of 3; Freidel, *Rendezvous with Destiny,* 477–79; McJimsey, *Harry Hopkins,* 301–4; Dallek, *Franklin D. Roosevelt,* 425–30; Burns, *Roosevelt,* 402–5.

28. Dallek, *Franklin D. Roosevelt,* 430–40; Burns, *Roosevelt,* 406–14; Freidel, *Rendezvous with Destiny,* 479–90.

29. Freidel, *Rendezvous with Destiny,* 492–93; Pearson to Welles, Dec. 14, 1943, Pearson Papers, F 33, 2 of 3; Biddle diary, Dec. 17, 1943.

30. King diary, Dec. 6, 1943; Pickersgill, *MacKenzie King Record,* 1:601.

31. Memorandum on Hull and the Moscow conference, Nov. 22, 1943, Farley Papers, Box 45.

32. Memorandums on Hull and Welles and Hull and the Moscow conference, Dec. 10, 1943, Farley Papers, Box 45.

33. Memorandum on Hull, Dec. 21, 1943, Krock Papers, Box 29; Krock, *Memoirs*, 205–7.

34. Berle and Jacobs, *Navigating the Rapids*, 450; Sherwood, *Roosevelt and Hopkins*, 757; Stuart, *Department of State*, 389–96.

35. Park, *Impact of Illness*, 225–33; Gallagher, *Splendid Deception*, 178–91.

36. Freidel, *Rendezvous with Destiny*, 508–15.

37. Bullitt, *For the President*, 602–3.

38. Ibid., 603–4.

39. Leahy diary, Mar. 11, 1944, Box 11; Ickes diary, July 2, 1944, Box 12; Blum, *Price of Vision*, 383.

40. Stimson diary, May 17, 1944, Vol. 47; Ickes diary, July 2, 1944, Box 12; memorandum of conversation, May 7, 1944, Morgenthau Papers, Box 5, presidential diaries; Blum, *Price of Vision*, 383.

41. Bullitt, *For the President*, 604–5; Farnsworth, *William C. Bullitt*, 176–77.

42. Memorandum on Hull, Jan. 19, 1944, Fisher Papers; 1944 Calendar, Hull Papers, Reel 40; Cordell Hull medical records, Oct. 20, 1944, Gellman Papers; Hull, *Memoirs*, 2:1493 and 1554.

43. Davies diary, Mar. 5, 1944, Box 14.

44. Blum, *Price of Vision*, 312.

45. Memorandum on Hull, Sept. 10, 1943, Wise Papers; Schuker to author, Dec. 11, 1990, Gellman Papers; Wyman, *Abandonment of Jews*, 190.

46. Morgenthau diary, Dec. 18, 1943, Vol. 688; Morgenthau, *Mostly Morgenthaus*, 324–25; Wyman, *Abandonment of Jews*, 184–85; Feingold, *Politics of Rescue*, 239–40.

47. Feingold, *Politics of Rescue*, 241–47; Morgenthau, *Mostly Morgenthaus*, 326–33; Breitman and Kraut, *American Refugee Policy*, 190–202.

48. Rockefeller Papers (Columbia Oral History Collection), 352–54, Gellman Papers.

49. Bowers to Duggan, Nov. 4, 1943, Bowers Papers.

50. Jonathan to Josephus Daniels, Dec. 4, 1943, Daniel Papers, Box 824; Wallace to Rockefeller, Dec. 15, 1943, Wallace Papers, Box 87.

51. Bowers diary, Nov. 7, 1944; Pearson to Welles, Nov. 29, 1943, Pearson Papers, F 33, 2 of 3; Duggan, *The Americas*, 103.

52. Gellman, *Good Neighbor Diplomacy*, 185–87.

53. Blum, *Price of Vision*, 309; Rockefeller interview, Aug. 11 and 12, 1976, Gellman Papers.

54. Morgenthau diary, Aug. 18, 1944, Box 763; Rockefeller Papers (Columbia Oral History Collection), 352–54, Gellman Papers; Dilks, *Diaries*, 654;

Woodward, *British Foreign Policy,* 4:73–79; Pearson to Welles, Nov. 29, 1943, Pearson Papers, F 33, 2 of 3; Gellman, *Good Neighbor Diplomacy,* 191–95.

55. Roosevelt, *F.D.R.,* 2:1495.

56. Ibid., 2:1511–12; Roosevelt to Bowers, Mar. 24 and Apr. 25, 1944, Bowers Papers; Long diary, Sept. 29, 1944, Box 5; Rockefeller Papers (Columbia Oral History Collection), 377–79, Gellman Papers; Presidential Press Conferences, July 9 and 11, and Oct. 13, 1944, Reel 12; Rosenman, *Public Papers and Addresses,* 13:298–300 and 419–20.

57. Duggan to Hull, July 19, 1944, Hull Papers, Box 53; also see memorandum by Morgenthau, Sept. 6, 1944, Morgenthau Papers, Box 770; Rockefeller Papers (Columbia Oral History Collection), 351 and 357–58, Gellman Papers; Duggan, *The Americas,* 101–7 and 199–201.

58. Divine, *Second Chance,* 184–85; Hilderbrand, *Dumbarton Oaks,* 30–66.

59 Divine, *Second Chance,* 190–203.

60. Wallace diary, Oct. 12, 1943, Box 24; *New York Times,* Oct. 16, 1943; Welles to Pearson, Nov. 23, 1943, Pearson Papers, F 33, 2 of 3; Welles to Wallace, May 15, 1944, Wallace Papers, Reel 50–1253; Welles, *Seven Decisions,* 154.

61. *New York Herald Tribune,* May 19 and 30, and June 25, 1944; Welles, *Where Are We Heading?,* 23; Welles, *Time for Decision,* 240–41 and 403–5; Welles, "Shaping of Our Future," 41–44; Gellman, *Good Neighbor Diplomacy,* 214–16.

62. *New York Herald Tribune,* Mar. 10, 1944, and also see Apr. 26 and Oct. 13, 1944.

63. Welles to Pearson, Dec. 20, 1943, Pearson Papers, F 33, 2 of 3; Welles to Corrigan, Dec. 6, 1943, Corrigan Papers, Box 10; Davies diary, Jan. 6, 1944, Box 14; Ickes diary, May 7, 1944, Box 11; Welles to Lazaron, Oct. 29, 1943, Lazaron Papers, Box 9; memorandum on Welles, May 16, 1944, Fisher Papers.

64. Berle and Jacobs, *Navigating the Rapids,* 456; Lash, *World of Love,* 139; Burns, *Roosevelt,* 515; James and Brown, *Book Review Digest 1944,* 795–96.

65. Stimson diary, Sept. 12, 1944, Vol. 48.

66. Stettinius diary, July 6, 1944, Box 241; Morgenthau diary, Aug. 18, 1944, Box 763; Welles, *Time for Decision,* 55.

67. "Washington Merry-Go-Round," Sept. 17, 1944.

68. *New York Times,* Oct. 16, 1943; Davies diary, Nov. 26, 1944, Box 14.

69. Reston, *Deadline,* 103; telephone conversation between author and James Reston, Dec. 13, 1991, Gellman Papers.

70. Dallek, *Franklin D. Roosevelt*, 454–65 and 485–98; Burns, *Roosevelt*, 441–42 and 473–83.

71. 1944 Calendar, Hull Papers, Reel 40; Hull, *Memoirs*, 2:1455; DeSantis, *Diplomacy of Silence*, 116–17.

72. Memorandum of conversation, May 7, 1944, Morgenthau Papers, Box 5, presidential diary; Israel, *War Diary*, 356.

73. Welles to Wallace, July 22, 1944, Wallace Papers, L 19–241; Hull, *Memoirs*, 2:1714; Freidel, *Rendezvous with Destiny*, 525–38; Divine, *Foreign Policy*, 91–125, and *Second Chance*, 205–11; Ferrell, *Choosing Truman*, 1–95.

74. Perlmutter, *FDR & Stalin*, 259–78.

75. Ibid., 267; Hilderbrand, *Dumbarton Oaks*, 67–244; Divine, *Second Chance*, 215–28.

76. Hull, *Memoirs*, 2:1602–22; Farley, *James Farley Story*, 369; Krock, *Memoirs*, 208; Morgenthau, *Mostly Morgenthau*, 350–90; Freidel, *Rendezvous with Destiny*, 550–53.

77. Divine, *Foreign Policy*, 91–164.

78. Pickersgill, *MacKenzie King Record*, 2:65 and 67.

79. Burns, *Roosevelt*, 503–6.

80. Park, *Impact of Illness*, 233–43.

81. Freidel, *Rendezvous with Destiny*, 562–67.

82. Hassett, *Off the Record*, 294.

83. 1944 Calendar, Hull Papers, Reel 40; Hull, *Memoirs*, 2:1455 and 1714; Blum, *Price of Vision*, 382.

84. Stimson diary, Sept. 25, 1944, Vol. 48; Israel, *War Diary*, 383.

85. Hull, *Memoirs*, 2:1622.

86. Pearson to Welles, Aug. 18, 1944, and Welles to Pearson, Aug. 30, 1944, and Sept. 14, 1944, Pearson Papers, F 33, 2 of 3; *Newsweek*, Aug. 21, 1944, 96, 98, 100, and 102; *New York Times*, Oct. 5 and 12, 1944.

87. Stimson diary, Sept. 20, 1944, Vol. 48.

88. Long diary, Sept. 29, 1944, Box 5; *New York Times*, Oct. 13, 1944; Abell, *Drew Pearson Diary*, 85; Campbell and Herring, *Diaries*, 160.

89. Welles to Corrigan, Oct. 6, 1944, Corrigan Papers, Box 10.

90. Morgenthau diary and memorandum of conversation, Aug. 18, 1944, Box 763, and Sept. 8, 1944, Box 770; Rockefeller Papers (Columbia Oral History Collection), 352–54, Gellman Papers.

91. Memorandum on Hull, Apr. 18, 1945, Farley Papers, Box 45; Blum, *Price of Vision*, 382.

92. Memorandum on Hull, Sept. 29, 1944, Farley Papers, Box 45; Farley, *James Farley Story*, 368.

93. Krock, *Memoirs*, 208.

94. Hull, *Memoirs*, 2:1622; McJimsey, *Harry Hopkins*, 342–46.

95. Cordell Hull medical records, Oct. 20, 1944, Gellman Papers; Israel, *War Diary*, 386; Stiller, *George S. Messersmith*, 208.

96. Walker diary, Oct. 14, 1944.

97. Nicholas, *Washington Dispatches*, 432.

98. Cordell Hull medical records, Oct. 21, 1944, Gellman Papers; Stettinius diary, Oct. 5, 1944, Notter file, Box 158, Record Group 59, National Archives, Washington, D.C.; Israel, *War Diary*, 386–87; Berle and Jacobs, *Navigating the Rapids*, 470; Krock, *Memoirs*, 209–10; Hull, *Memoirs*, 2:1714–19.

99. Acheson, *Present at the Creation*, 87; Nicholas, *Washington Dispatches*, 452 and 458; Hassett, *Off the Record*, 297; Hull, *Memoirs*, 2:1715–18.

100. Davies diary, Nov. 26, 1944, Box 15.

101. Hull to FDR, Nov. 21, 1944, Hull Papers.

102. FDR to Hull, Nov. 21, 1944, Hull Papers.

103. Presidential Press Conference, Nov. 27, 1944, Reel 12; Ickes diary, Dec. 2, 1944, Box 12; Stimson diary, Nov. 27 and Dec. 12, 1944, Vol. 49; Saavedra Lamas to Hull, Dec. 14, 1944, Hull Papers, Box 54; Sayre to Hull, Nov. 28, 1944, Sayre Papers, Box 4; memorandum on Hull, Apr. 18, 1945, Farley Papers, Box 45.

104. Nicholas, *Washington Dispatches*, 466.

105. Stuart, *Department of State*, 397.

106. Roosevelt, *My Parents*, 183–84; Murphy, *Diplomat among Warriors*, 447.

107. Acheson, *Present at the Creation*, 88.

108. Hull, *Memoirs*, 2:1109–11; Krock, *Memoirs*, 203.

## CHAPTER 16: ROOSEVELT'S LAST MONTHS

1. Cordell Hull medical records, Dec. 22, 1944, and Jan. 8 and 31, 1945, Gellman Papers; Krock, *Memoirs*, 211.

2. Memorandum on Hull, Apr. 18, 1945, Farley Papers, Box 45.

3. Bowers to Daniels, Dec, 2, 1944, and Daniels to Bowers, Dec. 9, 1944, Daniel Papers, Box 829.

4. Bowers diary, Nov. 7, 1944; memorandums on Nov. 25 and 29, 1944, and Jan. 27 and Feb. 3, 1945, Fisher Papers; Welles to MacLeish, Dec. 5, 1944, and Aug. 20, 1945, MacLeish Papers, Box 20; Welles to Wallace, Jan. 19, 1945, R-27, 837, and Wallace to Welles, Feb. 8, 1945, R-30, 754, Wallace Papers; Pearson to Welles, Feb. 15, 1945, Pearson Papers, F 33, 2 of 3.

5. McJimsey, *Harry Hopkins*, 347–49; Nicholas, *Washington Dispatches*, 458, 464, and 469; Stuart, *Department of State*, 397.

6. Nicholas, *Washington Dispatches,* 468.

7. Ibid., 470; Ickes diary, Dec. 2, 1944, Box 12; presidential diary, memorandum of conversation, Nov. 27, 1944, Morgenthau Papers, Box 6.

8. Stuart, *Department of State,* 414–16.

9. Davies diary, Nov. 26, 1944, Box 15.

10. Schwarz, *Liberal,* 248; Rockefeller Papers (Columbia Oral History Collection), 435–36, Gellman Papers; Hassett, *Off the Record,* 303–4; Nicholas, *Washington Dispatches,* 468, 475, 479, and 485; Stuart, *Department of State,* 397–99.

11. Heinrichs, *Amercian Ambassador,* 1–371.

12. Johnson, *Turbulent Era,* 2:1383–86.

13. Isaacson and Thomas, *Wise Men,* 221, 223–34, and 238–45.

14. Ibid., 225–26; Bohlen, *Transformation,* 11–80; DeSantis, *Diplomacy of Silence,* 126–31.

15. Freidel, *Rendezvous with Destiny,* 577–92; Dallek, *Franklin D. Roosevelt,* 507–19; Burns, *Roosevelt,* 573–82; McJimsey, *Harry Hopkins,* 360–69; Park, *Impact of Illness,* 250–82; DeSantis, *Diplomacy of Silence,* 132–37; Isaacson and Thomas, *Wise Men,* 244–46.

16. McJimsey, *Harry Hopkins,* 371–73; Freidel, *Rendezvous with Destiny,* 593–98.

17. Rockefeller Papers (Columbia Oral History Collection), 435–36, Gellman Papers; Campbell and Herring, *Diaries,* 158–60; Schwarz, *Liberal,* 248.

18. Rockefeller interview, Aug. 11 and 12, 1976, Gellman Papers.

19. Memorandum on Welles, Feb. 3, 1945, Fisher Papers; *New York Times,* Apr. 12, 1945.

20. Gellman, *Good Neighbor Diplomacy,* 148–50 and 196–203.

21. Ibid., 204–9.

22. Ibid., 204; Stiller, *George S. Messersmith,* 212–17.

23. Dallek, *Franklin D. Roosevelt,* 520–27.

24. Biddle diary, Mar. 2 and 16, 1945.

25. Pickersgill, *MacKenzie King Record,* 2:325–31 and 334; Ferrell, *Ill-Advised,* 28–48.

26. King diary, Mar. 13, 1945.

27. Shoumatoff, *Unfinished Portrait,* 80–90; Burns, *Roosevelt,* 198–99.

28. Hassett, *Off the Record,* 324–25.

29. DeSantis, *Diplomacy of Silence,* 138; Freidel, *Rendezvous with Destiny,* 601–2.

30. King diary, April 23 and 24, 1940; Bishop, *FDR's Last Year,* 633–720.

31. Shoumatoff, *Unfinished Portrait,* 98–119.

32. Ibid., 119–22; Lippman, *Squire of Warm Springs,* 237–40.

33. Leahy diary, Apr. 12, 1945, Box 12, 55; Berle and Jacobs, *Navigating the Rapids,* 526–28; Brinkley, *Washington Goes to War,* 273; Nicholas, *Washington Dispatches,* 539–40.

34. FDR's services, Apr. 18, 1945, Farley Papers, Box 45.

35. Hull, *Memoirs,* 2:1721.

36. *New York Times,* Apr. 17, 1945.

37. Davies diary, Apr. 12, 1945, Box 16.

38. Emerson to Israel, Feb. 7, 1977, Cohen Papers, Box 9.

## CHAPTER 17: THOSE WHO SURVIVED

1. Memorandum on Truman, Apr. 18, 1945, Farley Papers, Box 45; Donovan, *Conflict and Crisis,* xiii, xiv, and xvii; Kimball, *Churchill and Roosevelt,* 3:632–33.

2. Nicholas, *Washington Dispatches,* 546–47.

3. A. Vandenberg diary, Apr. 13, 1945, Box 6; Vandenberg, *Private Papers,* 167–68.

4. Stimson diary, Apr. 29, 1945, Vol. 51.

5. Rockefeller interview, Aug. 11 and 12, 1976, Gellman Papers; Rockefeller Papers (Columbia Oral History Collection), 457–58, Gellman Papers.

6. Isaacson and Thomas, *Wise Men,* 261–68.

7. Divine, *Second Chance,* 292–98; DeSantis, *Diplomacy of Silence,* 138–39.

8. Isaacson and Thomas, *Wise Men,* 276–87; DeSantis, *Diplomacy of Silence,* 142–54; McJimsey, *Harry Hopkins,* 374–91.

9. Walker, "E. R. Stettinius, Jr.," 77; Nicholas, *Washington Dispatches,* 584–85; Rockefeller Papers (Columbia Oral History Collection), 623–25, Gellman Papers.

10. McJimsey, *Harry Hopkins,* 392–97.

11. *Time,* Nov. 7, 1949, 21; Walker, "E. R. Stettinius, Jr.," 82.

12. Memorandum on Hull, Mar. 1, 1945, Farley Papers, Box 45; Cordell Hull medical records, Oct. 21, 1944, Gellman Papers; Caldwell, *Last Crusade,* 9–13.

13. King diary, Mar. 10, 1945; Pickersgill, *MacKenzie King Record,* 2:330–31.

14. Memorandum on Hull, Apr. 18, 1945, Farley Papers, Box 45; Blum, *Price of Vision,* 456.

15. Memorandum by Savage, May 3, 1945, Pasvolsky Papers, Box 5; San Francisco conference, Messersmith Papers, Vol. III, No. 14, Box 9; "Washington Merry-Go-Round," Feb. 20, 1945; Hull, *Memoirs,* 2:1722–23; Stiller, *George S. Messersmith,* 221.

16. Memorandums of conversations, May 10 and June 6, 1945, Pasvolsky Papers, Box 4; San Francisco conference, May 12, 1945, Austin Papers, Box 68;

Davies diary, May 22, 1945, Box 17; Stimson diary, June 4, 1945, Vol. 51; presidential diary, memorandum of conversation, June 20, 1945, Morgenthau Papers, Box 7; memorandum of Hull, Apr. 2, 1946, Hull Papers, Box 55; "Washington Merry-Go-Round," July 31, 1945; Krock, *Memoirs*, 209–11.

17. Memorandum of conversation, June 6, 1945, Pasvolsky Papers, Box 4.

18. Hull, *Memoirs*, 2:1719–28.

19. Frances Hull to Milton, May 14, 1937, Milton Papers, Box 21.

20. Hull, *Memoirs*, 2:1725; *Washington Star*, Dec. 5, 1945.

21. Hull, *Memoirs*, 2:1724–27; Cordell Hull medical records, Sept. 12, 1946–Jan. 2, 1949, Gellman Papers; *Washington Star*, Oct. 1 and Nov. 3, 1946, Oct. 1, 1947, and Oct. 1, 1948.

22. Pearson to Welles, Jan. 31, 1948, Pearson Papers, F 33, 2 of 3; Hull, *Memoirs*, 2:1725–26; *Washington Star*, Oct. 1, 1947.

23. Hull, *Memoirs*, 2:1721.

24. Ibid., 2:1540.

25. Acheson, *Present at the Creation*, 87–88.

26. Branscomb to Hull, Mar. 17, 1951, and Hull to Branscomb, Apr. 4, 1951, Austin Papers, Box 48.

27. Press release, May 9, 1951, Austin Papers; author to Cordell Hull Foundation for International Education, Oct. 6, 1989, and Brinker to author, Oct. 25, 1989, Gellman Papers; newspaper article, Mar. 8, 1954, Austin to Dustin, July 26, 1955, Austin Papers, Box 48.

28. Cordell Hull medical records, Apr. 12, 1951–Aug. 29, 1952, Gellman Papers; *New York Times*, July 24, 1955.

29. *Staunton Daily News Leader*, Apr. 16, 1940, and Mar. 26 and 27, 1954, Gellman Papers; *New York Herald Tribune*, Mar. 27, 1954; *New York Times*, July 27, 1955.

30. *New York Times*, July 24 and 25, 1955.

31. Ibid., July 24, 1955.

32. Ibid., July 27, 1955.

33. Welles to Lazaron, Feb. 16 and Oct. 5, 1946, Lazaron Papers, Box 9; Welles to Kohler, Dec. 26, 1945, and May 9, 1947, *Virginia Quarterly Review*, Box 63 (292-A).

34. Welles to Wallace, June 1, 1945, Wallace diary, Box 35; Welles to Pearson, Mar. 21, 1945, Pearson Papers, F 33, 2 of 3; memorandums on Welles, Feb. 3 and May 17, 1945, Fisher Papers; *New York Times*, Feb. 2, and 3, Mar. 24, and Apr. 18, 1945.

35. *Washington Post*, Dec. 7, 1948, 13; Vandenberg to Welles, Dec. 7, 1948, and Welles to Vandenberg, Dec. 9, 1948, A. Vandenberg Papers, Box 3; radio address by Welles, Dec. 17, 1947, Sweetser Papers, Box 40; Welles to

Wise, Aug. 15, 1946, Wise Papers, Box 85–9; *New York Times,* June 15, 1945, and Feb. 11, 16, and 18, Apr. 15, May 25, Aug. 15 and 18, and Oct. 2 and 3, 1946; Welles to Inman, Aug. 9, 1947, Inman Papers, Box 16; Welles, *Where Are We Heading?,* 224–41.

36. *New York Times,* Oct. 7 and 9, 1945, and Feb. 17, 1947.

37. Welles, *Where Are We Heading?,* 370.

38. Welles to Pell, Nov. 11, 1946, Pell Papers, Box 15; *New York Times,* May 27 and Dec. 2, 1946, and Jan. 6, 1947; Millis and Duffield, *Forrestal Diaries,* 172.

39. *New York Times,* Feb. 4, Apr. 17, and Dec. 24, 1945; Wise to Welles, Oct. 31, 1945, and Welles to Wise, Nov. 3, 1945, Wise Papers; Voss, *Rabbi and Minister,* 315.

40. Welles to Wise, May 23, 1946, and Wise to Welles, May 20, 1946, Wise Papers; Welles to Lazaron, Mar. 4 and Apr. 15, 1946, and Apr. 22, 1947, and Lazaron to Welles, Apr. 19, 1946, Lazaron Papers, Box 9; *New York Times,* May 15, 1946.

41. Welles to Wise, Jan. 14 and May 15, 1948, Wise Papers, Box 125–7; *New York Times,* Nov. 18, 1948; Welles, *We Need Not Fail;* Cohen, *Truman and Israel,* 276–81.

42. *New York Times,* Dec. 27 and 28, 1948, and Jan. 28, 1949; Welles to Austin, Jan. 10, 1949, Austin Papers, Box 65; confidential sources.

43. "Washington Merry-Go-Round," Jan. 1, 1949.

44. Clark to White, Mar. 31 and May 10, 1950, F. White Papers; D'Emilio and Freedman, *Intimate Matters,* 288–95; D'Emilio, *Sexual Politics,* 241–43.

45. Confidential sources who did not wish to be cited.

46. Welles to Inman, Feb. 21 and Apr. 8, 1949, Inman Papers, Box 16; Berle to Welles, June 24, 1949, and Welles to Berle, June 27, 1949, Berle Papers, Box 84.

47. Welles to Johnson, June 9, 1949, Johnson Papers, Box 110 (8476); Welles to Berle, June 27, 1949, Berle Papers, Box 84; Abell, *Drew Pearson Diary,* 61; Welles to Pearson, Oct. 20, 1948, Pearson Papers, G 87, 3 of 3; *Baltimore Sun,* Aug. 8, 9, and 15, 1949; *New York Times,* Aug. 9, Sept. 21, and Nov. 29, 1949.

48. Abell, *Drew Pearson Diary,* 76 and 85; Welles to Johnson, Aug. 21, 1949, Johnson Papers, Box 110 (8476).

49. Memorandum on Jackson, Jan. 27, 1945, Fisher Papers; Millis and Duffield, *Forrestal Diaries,* 173 and 283; Sulzberger, *Low Row of Candles,* 578.

50. Welles to Pearson, Feb. 7 and 17, 1948, Pearson Papers, F 33, 2 of 3.

51. Welles, *Seven Decisions,* ix.

52. Ibid., x–xi; Abell, *Drew Pearson Diary,* 136–37.

53. Welles to Wallace, Sept. 15, 1952, Wallace Papers, R-49, 55.

54. Welles to Rosenman, June 17, 1949, Rosenman Papers.

55. Abell, *Drew Pearson Diary*, 85.

56. Ibid., 136–37 and 180; Welles to Kohler, Sept. 5, 1950, and Sept. 3, 1951, *Virginia Quarterly Review*, Box 63 (292-A); Welles, *Seven Decisions*, 210–31.

57. Abell, *Drew Pearson Diary*, 180; *New York Times*, Jan. 9 and Feb. 20, 1952, and Sept. 25, 1961.

58. As quoted in Morgan, *FDR*, 685.

59. Abell, *Drew Pearson Diary*, 228; *New York Times*, July 1, 1952, and Feb. 1, 1953.

60. Abell, *Drew Pearson Diary*, 228, 281, and 442.

61. Capote, "Unspoiled Monsters," 122, and *Answered Prayers*, 59.

62. *New York Times*, Sept. 26 and 30, 1961; Berle and Jacobs, *Navigating the Rapids*, 754; "Washington Merry-Go-Round," Sept. 28, 1961; Grainger to Pearson, Oct. 31, 1961, Pearson Papers, F 33, 2 of 3.

63. *The Cosmos Club*, Gellman Papers.

64. *Oxon Hill Manor*, 1–14, Gellman Papers; Washington Post, Aug. 1, 1994, D3.

65. Interview with George Olmsted, Jr., owner of the manor, Sept. 2, 1976, Gellman Papers; confidential sources.

66. Interview with John B. Cochran, May 27, 1976, Gellman Papers; confidential sources.

67. "Walter Scott's Personality Parade."

68. Childs, *Witness to Power*, 17.

69. Bullitt, *For the President*, xiii and 611–14.

70. Brownell and Billings, *So Close to Greatness*, 306–10.

71. Bullitt, "How We Won the War."

72. Brownell and Billings, *So Close to Greatness*, 311–14.

73. Freud and Bullitt, *Thomas Woodrow Wilson*; *New York Times*, Jan. 29, 1967, 3, 12, and 44; Gay, *Freud*, 553–62.

74. *New York Times*, Feb. 8, 16, and 21, 1967.

75. Berle and Jacobs, *Navigating the Rapids*, 829.

76. "Washington Merry-Go-Round," Feb. 20, 1967.

77. Robert Murphy, *Diplomat among Warriors*, 35.

78. U.S. Department of the Interior, *Home*.

79. *Orange County Register*, Apr. 27, 1988, 1; *Los Angeles Times*, Apr. 28, 1988, pt. II, 1 and 8, and Dec. 11, 1988, pt. VI-A, 3; advertisements for the endowed chair, 1992, Gellman Papers.

80. *The Franklin Delano Roosevelt Memorial*, Gellman Papers; *Orange County Register*, Dec. 28, 1994, 5, Gellman Papers.

# BIBLIOGRAPHY

## BOOKS

Abell, Tyler, ed. *Drew Pearson Diary.* New York: Holt, Rinehart & Winston, 1974.

Abramson, Rudy. *Spanning the Century: The Life of W. Averell Harriman.* New York: Morrow, 1992.

Acheson, Dean. *Present at the Creation: My Years in the State Department.* New York: Norton, 1969.

Aglion, Raoul. *Roosevelt and de Gaulle: Allies in Conflict: A Personal Memoir.* New York: Free Press, 1988.

Alsop, Joseph. *"I've Seen the Best of It": Memoirs.* New York: Norton, 1992.

Alsop, Joseph, and Robert Kinter. *American White Paper.* New York: Simon & Schuster, 1940.

Anglin, Douglas. *The St. Pierre and Miquelon Affaire of 1941.* Toronto: Univ. of Toronto Press, 1966.

Bankhead, Tallulah. *Tallulah: My Autobiography.* New York: Harper & Bros., 1952.

Berle, Beatrice, and Travis Jacobs, eds. *Navigating the Rapids.* New York. Harcourt, Brace, Jovanovich, 1973.

Beschloss, Michael. *Kennedy and Roosevelt: An Uneasy Alliance.* New York: Norton, 1980.

Biddle, Francis. *In Brief Authority.* New York: Doubleday, 1962.

Bishop, James. *FDR's Last Year: April 1944–April 1945.* New York: Pocket Books, 1975.

Block, Maxime, ed. *Current Biography 1943.* New York: H. W. Wilson, 1944.

Blum, John, ed. *From the Morgenthau Diaries.* 3 vols. Boston: Houghton Mifflin, 1959–1967.

————, ed. *The Price of Vision.* Boston: Houghton Mifflin, 1973.

Bohlen, Charles. *The Transformation of American Foreign Policy.* New York: Norton, 1969.

Borg, Dorothy, and Shumpei Okamoto, eds. *Pearl Harbor as History.* New York: Columbia Univ. Press, 1973.

Bowers, Claude. *My Life.* New York: Simon & Schuster, 1962.

Breitman, Richard. *The Architect of Genocide: Himmler and the Final Solution.* New York: Knopf, 1991.

Breitman, Richard, and Alan Kraut. *American Refugee Policy and European Jewry, 1933–1945.* Bloomington: Indiana Univ. Press, 1987.

Brinkley, David. *Washington Goes to War.* New York: Knopf, 1988.

Brownell, Will, and Richard Billings. *So Close to Greatness: A Biography of William C. Bullitt.* New York: Macmillan, 1987.

Bullitt, Orville, ed. *For the President: Personal and Secret.* Boston: Houghton Mifflin, 1977.

Burke, Robert, ed. *The Diary Letters of Hiram Johnson, 1917–1945.* Vols. 5–7. New York: Garland, 1983.

Burns, James. *Roosevelt: The Soldier of Freedom.* New York: Harcourt, Brace, 1970.

Byrnes, James. *All in One Lifetime.* New York: Harper & Bros., 1958.

Caldwell, Mark. *The Last Crusade: The War on Consumption, 1862–1954.* New York: Atheneum, 1988.

Campbell, Thomas. *Masquerade Peace: America's UN Policy, 1944–1945.* Tallahassee: Florida State Univ. Press, 1973.

Campbell, Thomas, and George Herring, eds. *The Diaries of Edward R. Stettinius, Jr.* New York: New Viewpoints, 1975.

Capote, Truman. *Answered Prayers.* New York: Random House, 1987.

Chernow, Ron. *The Warburgs: The Twentieth-Century Odyssey.* New York: Random House, 1993.

Childs, Marquis. *Witness to Power.* New York: McGraw-Hill, 1975.

Churchill, Winston. *The Second World War,* Vol. 3: *The Grand Alliance.* New York: Bantam Books, 1962.

Clausen, Henry, and Bruce Lee. *Pearl Harbor: Final Judgment.* New York: Crown, 1992.

Clifford, J. Garry, and Samuel Spencer. *The First Peacetime Draft*. Lawrence: Univ. of Kansas Press, 1986.

Cohen, Michael. *Truman and Israel*. Berkeley: Univ. of California Press, 1990.

Cole, Wayne. *Roosevelt and the Isolationists, 1932–45*. Lincoln: Univ. of Nebraska Press, 1983.

Cook, Blanche. *Eleanor Roosevelt, 1884–1933*. Vol. 1. New York: Viking, 1992.

Crane, Katharine. *Mr. Carr of State*. New York: St. Martin's Press, 1960.

Dallek, Robert. *Democrat and Diplomat: The Life of William E. Dodd*. New York: Oxford Univ. Press, 1968.

———. *Franklin D. Roosevelt and American Foreign Policy, 1932–1945*. New York: Oxford Univ. Press, 1979.

Daniels, Jonathan. *White House Witness, 1942–1945*. New York: Doubleday, 1975.

Davids, Jules, ed. *Perspectives in American Diplomacy*. New York: Arno Press, 1976.

Davies, Joseph. *Mission to Moscow*. New York: Simon & Schuster, 1941.

Davis, Kenneth. *FDR: The Beckoning of Destiny, 1882–1928*. New York: Putnam, 1975.

———. *FDR: The New Deal Years, 1933–1937*. New York: Random House, 1986.

Dawidowicz, Lucy. *The War against the Jews, 1933–1945*. New York: Holt, Rinehart & Winston, 1975.

D'Emilio, John. *Sexual Politics, Sexual Communities: The Making of a Homosexual Minority in the United States, 1940–1970*. Chicago: Univ. of Chicago Press, 1983.

D'Emilio, John, and Estelle Freedman. *Intimate Matters: A History of Sexuality in America*. New York: Harper & Row, 1988.

DeSantis, Hugh. *The Diplomacy of Silence: The American Foreign Service, the Soviet Union, and the Cold War, 1933–1947*. Chicago: Univ. of Chicago Press, 1980.

Dilks, David, ed. *The Diaries of Sir Alexander Cadogan 1938–1945*. New York: Putnam, 1972.

Divine, Robert. *Second Chance: The Triumph of Internationalism in America during World War II*. New York: Atheneum, 1967.

———. *Foreign Policy and U.S. Presidential Elections 1940–1948*. New York: New Viewpoints, 1974.

Dodd, William, and Martha Dodd, eds. *Ambassador Dodd's Diary*. New York: Harcourt Brace, 1941.

Donovan, Robert. *Conflict and Crisis: The Presidency of Harry S. Truman*. New York: Norton, 1977.

Duggan, Laurence. *The Americas: The Search for Hemispheric Security.* New York: Henry Holt, 1949.

Eden, Anthony. *The Reckoning: Memoirs of Anthony Eden, Earl of Avon.* Boston: Houghton Mifflin, 1965.

Ellis, L. Ethan. *Republican Foreign Policy, 1921–1933.* New Brunswick, N.J.: Rutgers Univ. Press, 1968.

Farley, James. *Behind the Ballots.* New York: Harcourt Brace, 1938.

———. *James Farley Story.* New York: McGraw-Hill, 1948.

Farnsworth, Beatrice. *William C. Bullitt and the Soviet Union.* Bloomington: Indiana Univ. Press, 1967.

Fecher, Charles, ed. *The Diary of H.L. Mencken.* New York: Knopf, 1989.

Feingold, Henry. *The Politics of Rescue: The Roosevelt Administration and the Holocaust, 1938–1945.* New Brunswick, N.J.: Rutgers Univ. Press, 1970.

———. *A Time for Searching: Entering the Mainstream, 1920–1945.* Baltimore, Md.: Johns Hopkins Univ. Press, 1992.

Feis, Herbert. *1933: Characters in Crisis.* Boston: Little, Brown, 1966.

Ferrell, Robert, ed. *Dear Bess: The Letters from Harry to Bess Truman, 1910–1959.* New York: Norton, 1983.

———. *Ill-Advised: Presidential Health and Public Trust.* Columbia: University of Missouri Press, 1992.

———. *Choosing Truman: The Democratic Convention of 1944.* Columbia: University of Missouri Press, 1994.

Freedman, Max, ed. *Roosevelt and Frankfurter.* Boston: Little, Brown, 1967.

Freidel, Frank. *Franklin D. Roosevelt: The Apprenticeship.* Boston: Little, Brown, 1952.

———. *Franklin D. Roosevelt: The Ordeal.* Boston: Little, Brown, 1954.

———. *Franklin D. Roosevelt: The Triumph.* Boston: Little, Brown, 1956.

———. *Franklin D. Roosevelt: Launching the New Deal.* Boston: Little, Brown, 1973.

———. *Franklin D. Roosevelt: A Rendezvous with Destiny.* Boston: Little, Brown, 1990.

Freud, Sigmund, and William Bullitt. *Thomas Woodrow Wilson: Twenty-Eighth President of the United States: A Psychological Study.* Boston: Houghton Mifflin, 1967.

Gallagher, Hugh. *FDR's Splendid Deception.* New York: Dodd, Mead, 1985.

Gannon, Michael. *Operation Drumbeat: The Dramatic True Story of Germany's First U-Boat Attacks in World War II.* New York: Harper & Row, 1990.

Gay, Peter. *Freud: A Life for Our Times.* New York: Norton, 1988.

Gellman, Irwin. *Roosevelt and Batista: Good Neighbor Diplomacy in Cuba, 1933–1945.* Albuquerque: Univ. of New Mexico Press, 1973.

―――. "The New Deal's Use of Nazism in Latin America." In *Perspectives in American Diplomacy,* edited by Jules Davids, 178–200. New York: Arno Press, 1976.

―――. *Good Neighbor Diplomacy: United States Policies in Latin America, 1933–1945.* Baltimore, Md.: Johns Hopkins Univ. Press, 1979.

Gentry, Curt. *J. Edgar Hoover: The Man and His Secret.* New York: Norton, 1991.

Gibson, Hugh, ed. *The Ciano Diaries 1939–1943.* New York: Doubleday, 1946.

Gilbert, Martin. *The Holocaust: The History of the Jews.* New York: Holt, Rinehart & Winston, 1985.

Graebner, Norman, ed. *An Uncertain Tradition: American Secretaries of State in the Twentieth Century.* New York: McGraw-Hill, 1961.

Graff, Frank. *Strategy of Involvement: A Diplomatic Biography of Sumner Welles.* New York: Garland, 1988.

Gruening, Ernest. *Many Battles: The Autobiography of Ernest Gruening.* New York: Liveright, 1973.

Hand, Samuel. *Counsel and Advise: A Political Biography of Samuel I. Rosenman.* New York: Garland, 1979.

Hardeman, D.B., and Donald Baem. *Rayburn, A Biography.* Texas: Texas Monthly Press, 1987.

Hassett, William. *Off the Record with F.D.R. 1942–1945.* New Brunswick, N.J.: Rutgers Univ. Press, 1958.

Heinrichs, Waldo. *American Ambassador: Joseph C. Grew and the Development of the United States Diplomatic Tradition.* Boston: Little, Brown, 1966.

―――. *Threshold of War: Franklin D. Roosevelt and American Entry into World War II.* New York: Oxford Univ. Press, 1988.

Herzstein, Robert. *Roosevelt and Hitler.* New York: Paragon House, 1989.

Hilderbrand, Robert. *Dumbarton Oaks: The Origin of the United Nations and the Search for Postwar Security.* Chapel Hill: Univ. of North Carolina Press, 1990.

Hinton, Harold. *Cordell Hull: A Biography.* New York: Doubleday, Doran, 1942.

Hooker, Nancy, ed. *The Moffat Papers.* Cambridge, Mass.: Harvard Univ. Press, 1956.

Hull, Cordell. *The Memoirs of Cordell Hull.* 2 vols. New York: Macmillan, 1948.

Hurstfield, Julian. *America and the French Nation, 1939–1945.* Chapel Hill: Univ. of North Carolina Press, 1986.

Ickes, Harold. *The Secret Diary of Harold L. Ickes.* 3 vols. New York: Simon & Schuster, 1953–54.

Isaacson, Walter, and Evan Thomas. *The Wise Men: Six Friends and the World They Made: Acheson, Bohlen, Harriman, Kennan, Lovett, McCloy.* New York: Simon & Schuster, 1986.

Israel, Fred. *Nevada's Key Pittman.* Lincoln: Univ. of Nebraska Press, 1963.

———. *The War Diary of Breckinridge Long.* Lincoln: Univ. of Nebraska Press, 1966.

Israel, Lee. *Miss Tallulah Bankhead.* New York: G. P. Putnam's Sons, 1972.

James, Mertice, and Dorothy Brown, eds. *Book Review Digest 1944.* New York: H. W. Wilson, 1945.

James, Robert. *Anthony Eden.* New York: McGraw-Hill, 1987.

Johnson, Walter, ed. *Selected Letters of William Allen White.* New York: Henry Holt, 1947.

———, ed. *The Turbulent Era: A Diplomatic Record of Forty Years, 1904–1945.* Vol. 2. Boston: Houghton Mifflin, 1952.

Keegan, John. *The Second World War.* New York: Viking, 1990.

Kimball, Warren, ed. *Churchill and Roosevelt: The Complete Correspondence.* 3 vols. Princeton, N.J.: Princeton Univ. Press, 1984.

———. *The Juggler: Franklin Roosevelt as Wartime Statesman.* Princeton, N.J.: Princeton Univ. Press, 1991.

Klurfeld, Herman. *Behind the Lines: The World of Drew Pearson.* Englewood Cliffs, N.J.: Prentice Hall, 1968.

Krock, Arthur. *Memoirs.* New York: Funk and Wagnalls, 1968.

———. *Consent of the Governed.* Boston: Little, Brown, 1971.

Laqeur, Walter. *The Terrible Secret: Suppression of the Truth about Hitler's "Final Solution."* London: Weidenfeld & Nicolson, 1980.

Larrabee, Eric. *Commander in Chief: Franklin Delano Roosevelt, His Lieutenants, and Their War.* New York: Harper & Row, 1987.

Lash, Joseph. *Eleanor and Franklin: The Story of Their Relationship, Based on Eleanor Roosevelt's Private Papers.* New York: Norton, 1971.

———, assisted by Jonathan Lash. *From the Diaries of Felix Frankfurter.* New York: Norton, 1975.

———. *A World of Love: Eleanor Roosevelt and Her Friends 1943–1962.* New York: Doubleday, 1984.

———. *Dealers and Dreamers: A New Look at the New Deal.* New York: Doubleday, 1988.

Lindbergh, Charles. *The Wartime Journals of Charles A. Lindbergh.* New York: Harcourt Brace Jovanovich, 1970.

Link, Arthur. *Wilson the Diplomatist: A Look at His Major Foreign Policies.* Chicago: Quadrangle, 1963.

Loewenheim, Frances, Harold Langley, and Manfred Jones, eds. *Roosevelt and Churchill*. New York: Saturday Review Press, 1975.

Lippman, Theo, Jr. *The Squire of Warm Springs: F.D.R. in Georgia 1924–1945*. Chicago: Playboy Press, 1977.

Logan, John. *No Transfer: An American Security Principle*. New Haven, Conn.: Yale Univ. Press, 1961.

MacLean, Elizabeth. *Joseph E. Davies: Envoy to the Soviets*. Westport, Conn.: Praeger, 1992.

MacMaster, Richard. *Augusta County History*. Staunton, Va.: Augusta County Historical Society, 1987.

Marks, Frederick. *Wind over Sand: The Diplomacy of Franklin Roosevelt*. Athens: Univ. of Georgia Press, 1988.

Martin, Ralph. *Cissy*. New York: Simon & Schuster, 1979.

McJimsey, George. *Harry Hopkins: Ally of the Poor and Defender of Democracy*. Cambridge, Mass.: Harvard Univ. Press, 1987.

Millis, Walter, and Eugene Duffield, eds. *The Forrestal Diaries*. New York: Viking, 1951.

Morgan, Ted. *FDR: A Biography*. New York: Simon & Schuster, 1985.

Morgenthau, Henry, III. *Mostly Morgenthaus: A Family History*. New York: Ticknor & Fields, 1991.

Morison, Elting. *Turmoil and Tradition: A Study of the Life and Times of Henry L. Stimson*. New York: Atheneum, 1964.

Muggeridge, Malcolm, ed. *Ciano's Diplomatic Papers*. London: Odhams, 1948.

Murphy, Robert. *Diplomat among Warriors*. New York: Doubleday, 1964.

Nicholas, Herbert, ed. *Washington Dispatches, 1941–1945*. Chicago: Univ. of Chicago Press, 1981.

Nicolson, Nigel, ed. *Diaries and Letters of Harold Nicolson: The War Years, 1939–1945*. Vol. 2. New York: Atheneum, 1967.

Nixon, Edgar, ed. *Franklin D. Roosevelt and Foreign Affairs*. 3 vols. Cambridge: Belnap, 1969.

Park, Bert. *The Impact of Illness on World Leaders*. Philadelphia: Univ. of Pennsylvania Press, 1986.

Perlmutter, Amos. *FDR & Stalin: A Not So Grand Alliance*. Columbia: Univ. of Missouri Press, 1993.

Phillips, William. *Ventures in Diplomacy*. Boston: Houghton Mifflin, 1953.

Pickersgill, J. W., ed. *The MacKenzie King Record*. 2 vols. Canada: Univ. of Toronto Press, 1960 and 1968.

Pilat, Oliver. *Drew Pearson: An Unauthorized Biography*. New York: Harper's Magazine Press, 1973.

Prange, Gordon. *At Dawn We Slept: The Untold Story of Pearl Harbor.* New York: McGraw-Hill, 1981.

Pratt, Julius. "Cordell Hull, 1933–44." Vols. 12 and 13. In *The American Secretaries of State and Their Diplomacy,* edited by Robert Ferrell. New York: Cooper Square Publishers, 1964.

Reston, James. *Deadline.* New York: Random House, 1991.

Reuth, Ralf Georg. *Goebbels.* New York: Harcourt Brace, 1993.

Reynolds, David. *The Creation of the Anglo-American Alliance 1937–41.* Chapel Hill: Univ. of North Carolina Press, 1981.

Rock, William. *Chamberlain and Roosevelt: British Foreign Policy and the United States.* Columbus: Ohio State Univ. Press, 1988.

Rollins, Alfred, Jr. *Roosevelt and Howe.* New York: Knopf, 1962.

Roosevelt, Eleanor. *This I Remember.* New York: Harper & Bros., 1949.

Roosevelt, Elliott, ed. *F.D.R.: His Personal Letters.* 2 vols. New York: Duell, Sloan & Pearce, 1950.

Roosevelt, Elliott, and James Brough. *A Rendezvous with Destiny: The Roosevelts of the White House.* New York: Putnam, 1975.

Roosevelt, James. *My Parents: A Differing View.* Chicago: Playboy Press, 1976.

Roper, Daniel. *Fifty Years of Public Life.* Durham, N.C.: Duke Univ. Press, 1941.

Rosenman, Samuel, ed. *The Public Papers and Addresses of Franklin D. Roosevelt.* 13 vols. New York: Harper & Bros., Random House, and Macmillan, 1938–1950.

Rusbridger, James, and Eric Nave. *Betrayal at Pearl Harbor: How Churchill Lured Roosevelt into World War II.* New York: Summit Books, 1991.

Russell, Ruth, with Jeanette Muther. *A History of the United Nations Charter: The Role of the United States, 1940–1945.* Washington, D.C.: Brookings, Institution, 1958.

Schlesinger, Arthur, Jr. *The Age of Roosevelt.* 3 vols. Boston: Houghton Mifflin, 1957–1960.

Schwarz, Jordan. *Liberal: Adolf A. Berle and the Vision of an American Era.* New York: Free Press, 1987.

———. *The New Dealers: Power Politics in the Age of Roosevelt.* New York: Knopf, 1993.

Shapiro, David. *Neurotic Styles.* New York: Basic Books, 1965.

Sherwood, Robert. *Roosevelt and Hopkins: An Intimate Biography.* New York: Harper & Bros., 1950.

Shirer, William. *The Rise and Fall of the Third Reich: A History of Nazi Germany.* Greenwich, Conn.: Fawcett, 1959–1960.

———. *Twentieth Century Journey: The Nightmare Years, 1930–1940.* Boston: Little, Brown, 1984.

Shoumatoff, Elizabeth. *FDR's Unfinished Portrait: A Memoir.* Pittsburgh: Univ. of Pittsburgh Press, 1990.

Spaulding, E. Wilder. *Ambassadors Ordinary and Extraordinary.* Washington, D.C.: Public Affairs Press, 1961.

Stiller, Jesse. *George S. Messersmith: Diplomat of Democracy.* Chapel Hill: Univ. of North Carolina Press, 1987.

Stimson, Henry, and McGeorge Bundy. *On Active Service in Peace and War.* New York: Harper & Bros., 1947–48.

Street, George. *Mount Desert.* Cambridge: Riverside, 1965.

Stuart, Graham. *The Department of State: A History of Its Organization, Procedure, and Personnel.* New York: Macmillan, 1949.

Sulzberger, C.L. *A Low Row of Candles: Memoirs and Diaries, 1934–1954.* New York: Macmillan, 1969.

Thomson, James C., Jr. "The Role of the Department of State." In *Pearl Harbor as History,* edited by Dorothy Borg and Shumpei Okamoto, 82–91. New York: Columbia Univ. Press, 1973.

Timmons, Bascom. *Garner of Texas: A Personal History.* New York: Harper & Bros., 1948.

Toland, John. *Adolf Hitler.* New York: Doubleday, 1976.

Urofsky, Melvin. *A Voice That Spoke for Justice: The Life and Times of Stephen S. Wise.* Albany: State Univ. of New York Press, 1982.

Utley, Jonathan. *Going to War with Japan, 1937–1941.* Knoxville: Univ. of Tennessee, 1985.

Vandenberg, Arthur, Jr. *The Private Papers of Senator Vandenberg.* Boston: Houghton Mifflin, 1952.

Voss, Carl. *Rabbi and Minister: The Friendship of Stephen S. Wise and John Haynes Holmes.* New York: World Publishing, 1964.

Walker, J. Samuel. *Henry A. Wallace and American Foreign Policy.* Westport, Conn.: Greenwood, 1976.

Walker, Richard. *E. R. Stettinius, Jr.* Vol. 14 in *The American Secretaries of State and Their Diplomacy,* edited by Robert Ferrell. New York: Cooper Square Publishers, 1965.

Ward, Geoffrey. *Before the Trumpet: Young Franklin Roosevelt, 1882–1905.* New York: Harper & Row, 1985.

——— *A First Class Temperament: The Emergence of Franklin Roosevelt.* New York: Harper & Row, 1989.

Watkins, T.H. *Righteous Pilgrim: The Life and Times of Harold Ickes, 1874–1952.* New York: Henry Holt, 1990.

Watters, Mary. *The History of Mary Baldwin College.* Staunton, Va.: Mary Baldwin College, 1942.

Webster, Paul. *Pétain's Crime: The Full Story of French Collaboration in the Holocaust.* Chicago: Ivan R. Dee, 1991.

Wehle, Louis. *Hidden Threads of History: Wilson through Roosevelt.* New York: Macmillan, 1953.

Weil, Martin. *A Pretty Good Club: The Founding Fathers of the U.S. Foreign Service.* New York: Norton, 1978.

Weitz, John. *Hitler's Diplomat: The Life and Times of Joachim von Ribbentrop.* New York: Ticknor & Fields, 1992.

Welles, Sumner. *Naboth's Vineyard.* 2 vols. New York: Payson & Clarke, 1928.

———. *The World of the Four Freedoms.* New York: Columbia Univ. Press, 1943.

———. *The Time for Decision.* New York: Harper & Bro., 1944.

———. *Where Are We Heading?* New York: Harper & Bros., 1946.

———. *We Need Not Fail.* Boston: Houghton Mifflin, 1948.

———. *Seven Decisions That Shaped History.* New York: Harper & Bros., 1950.

Welles, Sumner, et al. *Laurence Duggan, 1905–1948: In Memoriam.* Stamford, Conn.: Overbrook Press, 1949.

White, John, Jr. *The American Railroad Passenger Car.* Part I. Baltimore, Md.: Johns Hopkins Univ. Press, 1978.

Wilson, Theodore. *The First Summit: Roosevelt and Churchill at Placentia Bay, 1941.* Boston: Houghton Mifflin, 1969.

Woodward, Ernest. *British Foreign Policy in the Second World War.* 5 vols. London: HMO, 1970–1976.

Wyman, David. *Paper Walls: America and the Refugee Crisis, 1938–1941.* Boston, Mass.: Univ. of Massachusetts Press, 1968.

———. *The Abandonment of the Jews: America and the Holocaust, 1941–1945.* New York: Pantheon, 1984.

Yahil, Leni. *The Holocaust: The Fate of European Jewry, 1932–1945.* New York: Oxford Univ. Press, 1990.

## GOVERNMENT PUBLICATIONS

Conn, Stetson, and Byron Fairchild. *The Framework of Hemispheric Defense.* Washington, D.C.: GPO, 1960.

General Service Administration, Historical Service No. 3. *Executive Office Building.* Washington, D.C.: GPO, 1970.

Notter, Harley. *Postwar Foreign Policy Preparation, 1939–1945.* Washington, D.C.: GPO, 1950.

U.S. Congress, *Hearings before the Joint Committee of the Pearl Harbor Attack.* GPO: 79th Cong., 1st Sess., 1946.

U.S. Department of the Interior, National Park Service. *Home of Franklin D. Roosevelt.* Washington, D.C.: GPO, 1982.

U.S. Department of State. *Foreign Relations of the United States, 1933–1945.* Washington, D.C.: GPO, 1950–1967.

## ARTICLES

Bullitt, William. "How We Won the War and Lost the Peace." *Life,* Aug. 30, 1948, 83, 84, 86–88, 92, 94, and 97, and Sept. 6, 1948, 86, 88, 90, and 103.

Capote, Truman. "Unspoiled Monsters." *Esquire,* May 1976, 122.

Clifford, J. Garry. "A Note on the Break between Senator Nye and President Roosevelt in 1939." *North Dakota History* (Summer 1982): 14–16.

Davis, Forrest. "Roosevelt's World Blueprint." *Saturday Evening Post,* April 10, 1943, 20, 21, 109, and 110.

"The Fortune Survey." *Fortune,* June 1940, supplement.

Hilton, Stanley. "The Welles Mission to Europe, February-March 1940: Illusion or Realism?" *Journal of American History* 58 (June 1971): 101–102.

Lerner, Max. "Behind Hull's Embargo." *The Nation* (May 28, 1938): 607–10.

——— "Roosevelt, Hitler, and the Search for a New Order in Europe." *Diplomatic History* 15 (Fall 1991): 611.

Offner, Arnold. "Appeasement Revisited: The United States, Great Britain and Germany, 1933–1940." *Journal of American History* 64 (Sept. 1977): 373–93.

Overaker, Louise. "Campaign Funds in a Depression Year." *American Political Science Review* 27 (Oct. 1933): 782.

Roosevelt, Franklin. "Our Foreign Policy: A Democratic View." *Foreign Affairs* 6 (July 1928): 573–86.

"Walter Scott's Personality Parade." *Parade,* Feb. 19, 1978.

Ward, Geoffrey. "The House at Hyde Park." *American Heritage* (April 1987): 41–50.

Welles, Sumner. "The Shaping of Our Future." *Reader's Digest* 44 (July 1944): 41–44.

## UNPUBLISHED THESES

Boswell, George. "Buddha Bill: The Roller-Coaster Career of William C. Bullitt, 1936–1940." Ph.D. diss., Texas Christian University, 1972.

Grollman, Catherine. "Cordell Hull and His Concept of a World Organization." Ph.D. diss., University of North Carolina, 1965.

Hanson, Gail. "Sumner Welles and the American System." Ph.D. diss., SUNY at Stony Brook, 1990.

Langer, John. "The Formation of American Aid Policy toward the Soviet Union, 1940–1943: The Hopkins Shop and the Department of State." Ph.D. diss., Yale University, 1975.

Milner, Cooper. "The Public Life of Cordell Hull: 1907–1924." Ph.D. diss., Vanderbilt University, 1960.

Mishler, Edward. "Francis White and the Shaping of United States-Latin American Policy, 1921–1933." Ph.D. diss., University of Maryland, 1975.

Wiebel, Michael. "A Strange Odyssey: The Sumner Welles Mission to Europe." M.A. thesis, University of Kansas, 1968 (Gellman Papers).

## MANUSCRIPT COLLECTIONS

Austin, Warren. Papers. Manuscript Division, Guy W. Bailey Memorial Library, University of Vermont, Burlingham, Vermont.

Berle, Adolf. Papers. Franklin D. Roosevelt Library, Hyde Park, New York.

Biddle, Frances. Papers. Franklin D. Roosevelt Library, Hyde Park, New York.

Bowers, Claude. Papers. Manuscript Division, Indiana University, Bloomington, Indiana.

Breckinridge, Sophonisba. Papers. Library of Congress, Manuscript Division, Washington, D.C.

Byrnes, James. Papers. Special Collections, Robert Muldrow Cooper Library, Clemson University, Clemson, South Carolina.

Carr, Wilbur. Papers. Library of Congress, Manuscript Division, Washington, D.C.

Castle, William. Papers. Harvard University, Houghton Library, Cambridge, Massachusetts.

Clapper, Raymond. Papers, Library of Congress, Manuscript Division, Washington, D.C.

Cohen, Benjamin. Papers. Franklin D. Roosevelt Library, Hyde Park, New York.

Columbia Oral History Collection. Columbia University, Butler Library, New York, New York.

Corrigan, Frank. Papers. Franklin D. Roosevelt Library, Hyde Park, New York.

Daniels, Josephus. Papers. Library of Congress, Manuscript Division, Washington, D.C.

Davies, Joseph. Papers. Library of Congress, Manuscript Division, Washington, D.C.

Davis, Norman. Papers. Library of Congress, Manuscript Division, Washington, D.C.

Dodd, William. Papers. Library of Congress, Manuscript Division, Washington, D.C.

Early, Stephen. Papers. Franklin D. Roosevelt Library, Hyde Park, New York.

Farley, James. Papers. Library of Congress, Manuscript Division, Washington, D.C.

Feis, Herbert. Papers. Library of Congress, Manuscript Division, Washington, D.C.

Fisher, Louis. Papers. Franklin D. Roosevelt Library, Hyde Park, New York.

Frankfurter, Felix. Papers. Library of Congress, Manuscript Division, Washington, D.C.

Gellman, Barbara L. Papers. Franklin D. Roosevelt Library, Hyde Park, New York.

Gibson, Hugh. Papers. Hoover Institution on War, Revolution and Peace, Stanford University, Stanford, California.

Henderson, Loy. Papers. Library of Congress, Manuscript Division, Washington, D.C.

Hornbeck, Stanley. Papers. Hoover Institution on War, Revolution and Peace, Stanford University, Stanford, California.

Hull, Cordell. Medical Records. Gellman Papers, Franklin D. Roosevelt Library, Hyde Park, New York.

Hull, Cordell. Papers. Library of Congress, Manuscript Division, Washington, D.C.

Ickes, Harold. Papers. Library of Congress, Manuscript Division, Washington, D.C.

Inman, Samuel. Papers. Library of Congress, Manuscript Division, Washington, D.C.

Johnson, Louis. Papers. University of Virginia, Manuscript Department, Alderman Library, Charlottesville, Virginia.

King, MacKenzie. Papers. University of Toronto, Toronto, Canada.

Knox, Frank. Papers. Library of Congress, Manuscript Division, Washington, D.C.

Krock, Arthur. Papers. Princeton University, Department of Rare Books and Special Collections, Princeton, New Jersey.

Lane, Arthur. Papers. Yale University Library, Manuscripts and Archives, New Haven, Connecticut.

Lazaron, Morris. Papers. Manuscript Collections, Hebrew Union College, Cincinnati, Ohio.

Leahy, William. Papers. Library of Congress, Manuscript Division, Washington, D.C.

Long, Breckinridge. Papers. Library of Congress, Manuscript Division, Washington, D.C.

MacLeish, Archibald. Papers. Library of Congress, Manuscript Division, Washington, D.C.

Messersmith, George. Papers. Special Collections, University of Delaware, Newark, Delaware.

Milton, George F. Papers. Library of Congress, Manuscript Division, Washington, D.C.

Moffat, J. Pierrepont. Papers. Harvard University, Houghton Library, Cambridge, Massachusetts.

Moore, John B. Papers. Library of Congress, Manuscript Division, Washington, D.C.

Moore, R. Walton. Papers. Franklin D. Roosevelt Library, Hyde Park, New York.

Morgenthau, Henry, Jr. Papers. Franklin D. Roosevelt Library, Hyde Park, New York.

Official File. Franklin D. Roosevelt Library, Hyde Park, New York.

Pasvolsky, Leo. Papers. Library of Congress, Manuscript Division, Washington, D.C.

Peabody, Endicott. Papers. Harvard University, Houghton Library, Cambridge, Massachusetts.

Pearson, Drew. Papers. Manuscript Collections, Lyndon Baines Johnson Library, Austin, Texas.

Pell, Herbert. Papers. Franklin D. Roosevelt Library, Hyde Park, New York.

Phillips, William. Papers. Harvard University, Houghton Library, Cambridge, Massachusetts.

Presidential Press Conferences of Franklin D. Roosevelt. Franklin D. Roosevelt Library, Hyde Park, New York.

President's Personal File. Franklin D. Roosevelt Library, Hyde Park, New York.

President's Secretary File. Franklin D. Roosevelt Library, Hyde Park, New York.

Rockefeller, Nelson. Papers. Columbia Oral History Collection, Columbia University, Butler Library, New York, and the Gellman Papers, Franklin D. Roosevelt Library, Hyde Park, New York.

Rosenman, Samuel. Papers. Franklin D. Roosevelt Library, Hyde Park, New York.

Sayre, Francis. Papers. Library of Congress, Manuscript Division, Washington, D.C.

Sevareid, Eric. Papers. Library of Congress, Manuscript Division, Washington, D.C.

Steinhardt, Laurence. Papers. Library of Congress, Manuscript Division, Washington, D.C.

Stettinius, Edward, Jr. Papers. University of Virginia, Manuscript Department, Alderman Library, Charlottesville, Virginia.

Stimson, Henry. Papers. Yale University Library, Manuscripts and Archives, New Haven, Connecticut.

Sweetser, Arthur. Papers. Library of Congress, Manuscript Division, Washington, D.C.

Taussig, Charles. Papers. Franklin D. Roosevelt Library, Hyde Park, New York.

Vandenberg, Arthur. Papers. Michigan Historical Collections, Bentley Historical Library, University of Michigan, Ann Arbor, Michigan.

Vandenberg, Helen. Papers. University of Michigan, Ann Arbor, Michigan.

Walker, Frank. Papers. Manuscript Collections, University of Notre Dame, South Bend, Indiana.

Wallace, Henry. Papers. Franklin D. Roosevelt Library, Hyde Park, New York; Library of Congress, Manuscript Division, Washington, D.C.; and The University of Iowa Libraries, Iowa City, Iowa.

Watson, Edward. Papers. University of Virginia, Manuscript Department, Alderman Library, Charlottesville, Virginia.

Welles, Sumner. File. War Branch History, Record Group 59, National Archives, Washington, D.C.

White, Francis. Papers. John Work Garrett Library, The Johns Hopkins University, Baltimore, Maryland.

White, Harry. Papers. Princeton University, Department of Rare Books and Special Collections, Princeton, New Jersey.

White, William. Papers. Library of Congress, Manuscript Division, Washington, D.C.

Wilson, Hugh R. Papers. Herbert Hoover Presidential Library, West Branch, Iowa.

Wise, Stephen. Papers. Jewish Historical Archives, Waltham, Massachusetts.

# ACKNOWLEDGMENTS

As I WAS FINISHING THIS BOOK, a friend told me that I had been destined to write it. That might be the case, but without the assistance of many others I probably would never have finished it, and these acknowledgments are but small thanks for all the help I received.

For many years, Pat Dowling and Milton Gustafson at the National Archives led me through the vast maze of State Department records. Carolyn Sung and Charles Cooney at the Manuscript Division of the Library of Congress made certain to show me any collection of papers that touched even remotely on my chosen topic. At the Franklin D. Roosevelt Library, William Emerson and later Verne Newton were extremely helpful; Raymond Teichman assisted in the establishment of the Barbara Gellman collection; and Mark Renovitch handled my request for photographs with speed, kindness, and professionalism. John Sears of the Franklin and Eleanor Roosevelt Institute supplied me with information on the Franklin Delano Roosevelt Memorial. Mary Knill of the Lyndon Baines Johnson Library granted me access to previously closed files from the Drew Pearson papers and then assisted me with the photographic collection. Michael Kohl, head of special collections at Clemson University, assisted with the material in the James Byrnes collection. The reference staff at the Newport Beach Public Library—particularly Susan Warren, Susan Lamb, Jan Ferry, and Linda Mc-Sweeney—has been wonderful in handling my countless requests for interlibrary loans and in meeting other research needs.

I have been able to fill in wide gaps in the historical record because several individuals shared their knowledge with me. James Roosevelt spent hours with me explaining his father's motives. Orville Bullitt graciously answered questions about his brother. Nelson Rockefeller granted me access to his oral history and several long interviews. James Reston and Marquis Childs confirmed and elaborated on their writings. Jack Anderson allowed me use of the "Washington Merry-Go-Round" archives, which are conveniently catalogued by topic and individual as an aid to researchers.

Virtually nothing has been written about R. Walton Moore. Mary Walton Livingston provided me with some of her correspondence and her great uncle's unpublished autobiography. These documents are historical treasures, and I shall be forever grateful for Mrs. Livingston's willingness to share them. Frances Hull is also a somewhat shadowy figure. William Pollard, archivist at Mary Baldwin College, supplied material on her background. Edward and Tae Bonfoey (Frances Hull's niece) answered questions about her. Evarts Opie, Jr., publisher of the Staunton *Daily News Leader,* granted access to his newspaper's archives. Richard Young, president of the Temple House of Israel in Staunton, searched the minutes of his congregation's meetings for information on Frances's Jewish heritage. Monique Bleier introduced me to Philip Heller Sachs and his wife Beverly, who shared their knowledge about Frances's brother Henry.

Various scholars freely talked about their areas of specialization and provided clues to new sources. Robert Dallek spent hours discussing the role of Franklin Roosevelt in foreign affairs. Robert Ferrell passed on important material from several collections. Ted Wilson supplied me with a valuable thesis on the Welles mission. Richard Harrison explained the role of the British during the 1930s. Jesse Stiller discussed the role of George Messersmith; Ed Mishler, the importance of Francis White; Sam

Walker, the significance of Henry Wallace; Arnold Offner, the role of the Nazis; Mark Stoler, military affairs; and Warren Cohen, East Asian affairs.

Without question, America's response to the destruction of European Jewry is the most divisive issue touched on in this narrative. In this area I profited from the opinions of David Wyman, Stephen Schuker, and Richard Breitman; Colonel Alan Winner, who fought in World War II, provided his firsthand observations, and my sister Marianne also offered her viewpoint.

As tempted as I was to write psychohistory, I avoided this approach. Barton Blinder, M.D., Ph.D., a gifted psychiatrist, provided some guidelines regarding the emotional and physical problems that might have affected my principal figures; Robert Postman, Ph.D., a well-respected psychologist, also interpreted some of my characters' behavior. However much I would have liked to use their opinions in the text proper, I refrained from doing so and instead relied on the information solely for background. As for Hull's medical records, I depended on Lawrence Klein, M.D., to interpret them.

Some individuals deserve special mention for their support. Donald Giffin started me on my quest to do original research. I was then fortunate to study with David Pletcher, arguably the finest scholar of American diplomatic relations in the nineteenth century. Martin Ridge added a note of caution and further reflection. Arthur Schlesinger, Jr., encouraged me throughout this project with his kindness and his faith in the subject. Waldo Heinrichs has answered questions in his area of specialization and commented on an early version of the manuscript. Thomas Keneally also read the completed manuscript and commented on its value. My aunt, Lenora Seigelman, also deserves special mention for all her assistance and her many kindnesses.

The Johns Hopkins University Press could not have been more supportive. Jack Holmes, Michael Donatelli, and Gregg Wilhelm accommodated my needs with grace. Douglas Armato has shown his enthusiasm, and Inger Forland has gone beyond the call of duty in her high expectations for the success of my work. Finally, Henry Tom, my executive editor, has abundantly demonstrated his quiet patience and endless faith in my project; he kept pushing me to meet his exacting standards, never allowing me to accept good when I could achieve better.

At Princeton Editorial Associates, Peter Strupp directed Donna Regen, who did a fine job editing my bibliography and footnotes. Peter himself edited the text; if an author can accept penetrating criticism, Peter is an editor in a class by himself.

Six families require special mention. Wayne Cole commented on my manuscript, set me straight on a number of occasions, and saved me from errors of fact and interpretation. His wife, Virginia, kindly allowed me to monopolize her husband's time. J. Garry Clifford and his wife Carol opened their home to me. Garry read an early draft, answered innumerable inquiries, and sent me crucial documents from manuscript collections that I never knew existed. Jonathan Utley, an expert on East Asian affairs and Cordell Hull, commented on the manuscript and answered my questions. His wife, Carol Marin, accepted these long, involved, and occasionally esoteric discussions with her usual forebearance. I have known William and Marilyn Brinker since our days in graduate school. Bill provided me with the photographs of Cordell Hull's birthplace, found additional material on the Cordell Hull Foundation, and interviewed local dentists about the typical treatment likely to have been given to patients with Hull's dental problems in the 1930s and 1940s. Manny and Martha Gochin also assisted me by taking photographs of R. Walton Moore's church and final resting place; in addition, Manny took photographs of the Carlton and Wardman Park hotels. Finally, Frank Freidel read every chapter and provided detailed comments. His wife, Madeline, was extremely considerate. When I questioned my ability to continue, Frank supplied the gentle encouragement to keep me going. I will never forget his kindnesses; he was a class act.

During the course of writing and research, Barbara Gellman, my wife of almost twenty-three years, passed away. In her memory, I have given the Franklin D. Roosevelt Library my papers. I have dedicated this book to our children in the hope that they will leave a legacy beyond mine and their mother's.

I have been fortunate to have remarried. Gloria Gae is a scholar in her own right, and she has wholeheartedly supported this project. Her mother, Gloria, has cheerfully listened to me read the draft chapters aloud and has made cogent suggestions. My father-in-law, Robert F. Seeburger, a giant in his own field of lumber and furniture, read an early version of the manuscript and offered his advice. He recently passed away, but his memory survives through his many good works.

All of the above have given their time, energy, and best wishes in measure far beyond what I deserve. Errors in fact and interpretation are mine alone. I hope that the finished product justifies their faith in me; in many ways that was my driving force.

# INDEX

Library of Congress Cataloging-in-Publication Data

Gellman, Irwin F.
    Secret affairs : Franklin Roosevelt, Cordell Hull, and Sumner Welles /
Irwin F. Gellman.
        p.    cm.
    Includes bibliographical references and index.
    ISBN 0-8018-5083-5
    1. Roosevelt, Franklin D. (Franklin Delano), 1882–1945—Friends and
associates. 2. Hull, Cordell, 1871–1955. 3. Welles, Sumner, 1892–  .
4. United States—Foreign relations—1933–1945. 5. World War,
1939–1945—Diplomatic history. I. Title.
E807.G44   1995
973.917′092′2—dc20
    [B]                                                            94-46558
                                                                        CIP